Learn

Microsoft®
Visual
C++®6.0
Now

Chuck Sphar

PUBLISHED BY
Microsoft Press
A Division of Microsoft Corporation
One Microsoft Way
Redmond, Washington 98052-6399

Library of Congress Cataloging-in-Publication Data.
Sphar, Chuck, 1947-
    Learn Microsoft Visual C++ 6.0 Now / Chuck Sphar.
       p. cm.
    Includes index.
    ISBN 1-57231-965-8
    1. C++ (Computer program language) 2. Microsoft Visual C++.
    I. Title.
    QA76.73.C153S694 1999
    005.13'3--dc21
                                    98-52133
                                        CIP

Printed and bound in the United States of America.

1 2 3 4 5 6 7 8 9 QMQM   4 3 2 1 0 9

Distributed in Canada by ITP Nelson, a division of Thomson Canada Limited.

A CIP catalogue record for this book is available from the British Library.

Microsoft Press books are available through booksellers and distributors worldwide. For further information about international editions, contact your local Microsoft Corporation office or contact Microsoft Press International directly at fax (425) 936-7329. Visit our Web site at mspress.microsoft.com.

Acquisitions Editor: Eric Stroo
Project Editor: Holly Thomas
Technical Editor: Michael Hochberg

For Pam, always.

CONTENTS *at a glance*

TABLE OF CONTENTS

PART **3**   Rounding Out Your MFC Skills

Acknowledgments

This book has been fun to write, but I couldn't have done it alone. The greatest thanks of all go to my wife, Pam, who backs me all the way. I also had quite a bit of help from Buji-san, Striper, Tippy, and Sydney, keyboard walkers extraordinaire who probably sneaked in a meow here and there.

I want to thank some great folks at Microsoft Press: Eric Stroo, acquisitions editor; John Pierce, managing editor; Holly Thomas, project editor and principal manuscript editor; Michael Hochberg, principal technical editor; Linda Ebenstein, technical editor; Ina Chang, manuscript editor; Cheryl Penner, principal proofreader; Karen Lenburg, proofreader, and the whole host of proofreaders who worked on this project; Rob Nance, interior graphic artist; Elizabeth Hansford, principal desktop publisher; desktop publishers Dan Latimer, Dick Carter, Elizabeth Sanders, Gina Cassill, and Stuart Greenman; Bill Teel, computer wizard; and Julie Kawabata, indexer. Thanks also to many others I can't name here.

Thanks as well to my agent Claudette Moore, at Moore Literary Agency, and her assistant, Debbie McKenna.

Although I spent six years documenting Visual C++ and MFC at Microsoft, I needed someone looking over my shoulder to catch the worst mistakes. My gratitude to Gonzalo Isaza, the MFC quality assurance lead, who carefully read the entire manuscript in his spare time, and to Mike Blaszczak, the MFC development lead, who answered many questions. Thanks also to Walter Sullivan, Kathleen Thompson, Jocelyn Garner, and the members of the Visual C++ documentation team. Any mistakes that remain are mine.

A final thanks to the designers of Visual C++ and MFC, especially Mark Walsen, Scott Randell, and Dean McCrory, who spent a lot of time teaching me over the years. I hope I caught what they were pitching.

Introduction

Welcome to *Learn Microsoft Visual C++ 6.0 Now*. You're about to begin learning the most powerful, flexible way to program for Microsoft Windows. This book is designed to help you climb three challenging learning curves at once: Windows programming, the C++ programming language, and the Microsoft Foundation Class Library.

Microsoft Press publishes an impressive line of books about Microsoft Visual C++. However, most of them are aimed at experienced C++ programmers who may already understand programming for Windows, and there is a need for a book that begins with fewer assumptions about what you already know. Consider *Learn Microsoft Visual C++ 6.0 Now* that book—your on-ramp to Visual C++ 6.0 and the Microsoft Foundation Class Library 6.0 (hereafter simply MFC or the MFC library), as well as to more advanced books about them. The bonus is that this book includes a full working copy of Visual C++ 6.0.

What Visual C++ and MFC Are

Visual C++ is a visually oriented software development environment, geared specifically to writing programs for the Windows operating system in C++. With Visual C++, you can write any kind of program that it's possible to write in either the C++ language or the C language. C++ is a superset of C. MFC is the preferred way to write Windows applications in Visual C++. MFC is a set of C++ classes that comprise a functioning generic Windows application that's ready for you to customize. You begin with the MFC AppWizard, which generates a set of starter files. Then you add code to implement the features that make your application unique. This book teaches the MFC fundamentals that help make Visual C++ so versatile.

Who This Book Is For

Learn Microsoft Visual C++ 6.0 Now makes the following assumptions about your skill and knowledge levels:

■ First of all, you know how to program in some language. Perhaps it's C or even C++, but it might be Basic or Pascal or some other programming language. By "know how to program," I mean that you understand basic program flow, looping, branching, function or subroutine calls, parameter passing, and compiling a program. If you don't fit this description, I recommend that you find a good course or book on programming fundamentals before you attempt C++, Windows, or this book.

■ Second, you want to program for Windows, and you want to do so with C++, but you might have little or no Windows programming experience.

■ And third, even if you do have some Windows or C++ programming experience, you haven't programmed with Visual C++.

Charting Your Course

The following list suggests where and how you might concentrate within this book, depending on your expertise and priorities.

■ If you already know some Windows programming—perhaps you've programmed in Microsoft Visual Basic or C—you'll most likely read Chapter 1, carefully study Chapters 2 through 5 to learn C++

fundamentals, skim Chapter 6, and then read the rest of the book, which puts C++ to practical use for programming Windows. There isn't room to cover the entire language in detail, but this will be a good introduction.

- If you've heard about the MFC library and object-oriented programming (usually abbreviated OOP), consider skimming Chapters 1 through 4, and then read Chapter 5, skim Chapter 6, and read the rest of the book closely. You'll learn the basics of OOP and quite a bit of MFC.

- If you know only basic programming techniques but want to grow into a versatile modern language such as C++ and want to begin learning Windows programming, take this book a step at a time and pay particular attention to all the hands-on examples. The online documentation for Visual C++ is a good supplement for C++ language and Windows details. I'll point out useful Help topics as we go. Exercises with solutions will let you test your skills.

- If you have used some other C++ programming product and now want to learn Visual C++, read Chapter 1, skim Chapters 2 through 5, and dig into the remaining chapters.

Learning By Doing

Nearly all readers will find it valuable to work through the book's many hands-on examples. Most of the examples are small enough that you can painlessly type in the code and try them out. If you're a beginner you'll discover that doing is learning, and more advanced readers will find that fluency grows out of the fingers. The more you actually work with the code, the more you'll carry away from this book.

You'll encounter the code for the examples in "Try it now" sections. These detail the steps you should take if you're working through the examples. It's important to do all of the "Try it now" sections in a chapter if you do any of them. Occasionally, I'll also mention a technique in passing and suggest that you go to Visual C++ on the spot and "try it." Then, at the end of each chapter, you'll find several exercises in a "Try It Your-self" section. Work through them. Answers are supplied either with the exercises or as implementations in the companion code. I'll tell you where to find this code for each exercise.

> **NOTE** In some cases, I'll show you code examples with the less pertinent comments and code omitted in order to clarify a point I'm trying to make.

The book's principal example is MyDraw, a simple vector drawing program with many interesting features. Along with many smaller examples, we'll develop MyDraw step by step throughout most of the book. Table 10-2 in Chapter 10 describes the 11 steps in MyDraw's development.

> **NOTE** If you decide to skip some steps in the MyDraw example and then jump in, you can begin with my code for the appropriate step. For each of the 11 steps of MyDraw, you'll find a numbered version of the source code, complete up to that point, in the companion code. For example, the code for step 0 is in the MyDraw0 directory (C++ programmers start counting from 0, not 1), and code for step 1 is in the MyDraw1 directory. Each chapter announces which step it's for. The section "Installing the Samples on Your Computer" later in this introduction will show you how to install the sample programs onto your hard drive. To start with a particular step, look in the appropriate directory for that step on your hard drive. Then follow directions to add new code.

What This Book Covers

Although Visual C++ lets you write any code that can be written in C or C++, *Learn Microsoft Visual C++ 6.0 Now* focuses on the central purpose of Visual C++: programming Windows in C++, using MFC. In the book's three parts—"Getting to Know Visual C++," "Fundamental MFC Skills," and "Rounding Out Your MFC Skills"—I'll teach you how to do each of the following:

■ Work within the Visual C++ programming environment, using its wizards to generate a set of starter files that get you going quickly, its source code and resource editors to write your code, its build system to compile and link your code, and its Help system to answer your questions. Chapter 1 walks you through the Visual C++ environment and gets you started with your first Visual C++ program.

- Use the most common elements of the C++ language, including classes and object-oriented programming techniques. Chapters 2 through 5 cover C++ syntax, pointers and references, classes, and object-oriented programming.

- Understand the Win32 Application Programming Interface (API) and the fundamental concepts of Windows programming, including windows, device contexts, coordinate systems, drawing with the Windows Graphical Device Interface (GDI), scrolling, printing, dialog boxes, and controls. Chapter 6 introduces the Win32 API and Windows from a programmer's perspective.

- Build your program atop MFC, which provides the framework of a working Windows application. You'll see in Chapter 7 that you can run the MFC AppWizard to generate code for the foundation of your program, compile that code, and immediately have a rather impressive generic Windows program—although still with many blanks to fill in before it becomes *your* program. This is where we will begin the evolution of the MyDraw application. In Chapter 8, we'll examine the AppWizard-generated code, relating it to the fundamental Windows concepts from Chapter 6 and to the structure and functionality of MFC. Then, following Chapter 8, we'll write several MFC Windows applications and continue with MyDraw.

- Take advantage of additional AppWizard and MFC components that help you develop sophisticated features in your program that you might otherwise never even attempt. For example, Chapters 16 through 20 show you how to save your program's data to a file, print the data on multiple pages with headers and footers, add toolbars that can dock to a window edge or float free, add dialog boxes full of powerful controls, and give the program a split personality by supplying two ways to view your data in a splitter window—such as viewing spreadsheet cells or a chart in Microsoft Excel. Without MFC, a good number of these features are so difficult that many small applications simply don't implement them. MFC makes adding these features easy.

- Use a variety of Windows graphics techniques. Chapter 11 shows how to let your users draw with the mouse. Chapter 12 introduces drawing in color. Chapter 15 explains scrolling. Chapter 17 shows you how to print a multipage document with headers and footers. Chapter 18 teaches you to manage user selection of objects in a window, including providing visual feedback by drawing selection handles on the object. And Chapter 20 shows how to split your program's window into multiple panes, each of which displays a different view of your data.

Visual C++ is a large, complex product. In addition to writing Windows applications with MFC, you can use Visual C++ for many other purposes. Most of those purposes require advanced programming skills and knowledge of advanced technologies such as Object Linking and Embedding (OLE), Microsoft ActiveX controls, database programming, and the Internet. This is an introductory book aimed at a less seasoned audience, so I leave advanced topics to other books. I'll describe some of those advanced topics and tell you where to go to learn them in Chapter 21.

A Few Conventions

I use a few housekeeping conventions that will help you understand what to do as you move through the book. Code lines that you are to type in or modify appear in **boldface** type. In some cases, I'll show you code examples with the less pertinent comments and code omitted in order to clarify a point I'm trying to make. I'll also use the ellipsis character (...) when I leave out part of a line of code, and the vertical ellipsis character (⋮) when I leave out several lines of code. New terms appear in *italics* the first time I use and define them. Many technical elements (class names, functions, and so on) are italicized throughout. References to the sample code take the form "...can be found in the \learnvcn\ChapXX folder in the companion code." When you see this, look in the appropriate folder on your hard drive, assuming you have already installed the files. (See the section "Installing the Samples on Your Computer" later in this introduction.) Boxed tips, warnings, notes, and sidebars set off information that you might want to bookmark for future reference. And, as I've noted, the "Try it now" sections take you through every step. Don't skip over them if you really want to understand this material.

Each of the books I mention in the book is cited again in Chapter 21. And finally, in the Appendix, you'll find valuable background material on understanding the MFC source code files that accompany Visual C++ and how to find classes and functions in them. The files can teach you a great deal about how MFC works and, sometimes, about why your own code fails to work.

Using the Companion CD-ROM

A CD-ROM is included in the back of this book. It includes all of the sample code found in this book. The executable program files are not provided, so you have to build them in order to run a project. You can use the sample projects to help you learn about Visual C++. As you work through the Try It Yourself exercises in the book, follow along in the provided code.

Installing the Samples on Your Computer

The install program copies the sample project folders and files to a folder named learnvcn on your hard disk. To install the samples, follow these four steps (these steps are also in the file readme.txt on the companion CD):

1. Close any currently running programs.

2. With the *Learn Microsoft Visual C++ 6.0 Now* compact disc in your CD-ROM drive, click Start on the Windows taskbar and then click Run. The Run dialog box appears.

3. In the Open box, type *D:\Examples\setup.exe.* (If your CD-ROM drive is associated with a different drive letter, such as *E*, type it instead.)

4. Click OK and then follow the directions on the screen.

> **NOTE** The examples in the book are geared to Windows 95 or 98, but because they don't do anything exotic, they should work as well on Windows NT. If you have Windows 3.1 or 3.11, you must upgrade to at least Windows 95 before attempting to use this book.

Installing Visual C++ on Your Computer

The *Learn Microsoft Visual C++ 6.0 Now* CD also includes the Introductory Edition of Microsoft Visual C++ 6.0. You can create, build, run, debug, and edit your C++ programs with the included version of Visual C++.

> **WARNING** If you already have any of the Microsoft Visual Studio programming products—such as Visual Basic, Visual J++, or an earlier version of Visual C++ than version 6.0—Setup warns you of possible conflicts. Proceed with installation unless you have a version of Visual C++ already installed on your system. I recommend you uninstall any earlier version of Visual C++ before installing the Introductory Edition. If you already have another version of Visual C++ 6.0 installed, you do not need to install the Introductory Edition.

> **TIP** One limitation of the Introductory Edition of Visual C++ 6.0 is that each time you run your program inside Visual C++ you must respond to a dialog box that reminds you of the terms of your Visual C++ license agreement. After you read the license agreement, just click OK in the dialog box and proceed.

Visual C++ requires Microsoft Internet Explorer 4.01 Service Pack 1a (supplied on the companion CD). Microsoft Visual Studio 6.0 Service Pack 1 is optional, and can be obtained at the following website: *http://msdn/microsoft.com/vstudio/sp/*. Or you can contact Microsoft at the address in the section "Support," at the end of the introduction.

Install Visual C++ (this will also install Internet Explorer if you do not have the correct version on your system already, as well as a pile of Visual C++ documentation and some development tools). Then install Visual Studio 6.0 Service Pack 1.

To install Visual C++ 6.0, follow these steps (also in the readme.txt file on the companion CD):

1. Close any currently running programs.

2. Insert the *Learn Microsoft Visual C++ 6.0 Now* compact disc into your CD-ROM drive.

3. On the taskbar, click the Start button and then click Run. The Run dialog box appears.

4. In the Open box, type *D:\VCIntEd\Disk1\setup.exe.* (If your CD-ROM drive is associated with a different drive letter, such as *E*, type it instead.)

5. Click OK, and then follow the directions on the screen.

Viewing Documents in the Companion Code

Sometimes I will refer you to a text document in the companion code. These documents are in Microsoft Word format, but if you do not have Microsoft Word, they can be opened in the WordPad accessory supplied with Windows. WordPad can be found in the Accessories subfolder of the Programs folder on the Start menu.

What You'll Need to Use This Book

Learn Microsoft Visual C++ 6.0 Now includes a complete copy of Microsoft Visual C++ version 6.0, Introductory Edition, released in 1998. You can install this version or buy the Standard Professional or Enterprise Edition. The Standard Edition is similar to the Intoductory Edition, but does not have the same license restrictions. The Professional Edition includes everything in the Introductory Edition and more. The Enterprise Edition is geared to advanced database programming in large corporations.

IMPORTANT The license agreement for Visual C++ 6.0 Introductory Edition doesn't allow you to redistribute programs that you write with Visual C++.

Visual C++ 6.0 Introductory Edition requires the following hardware and software:

Computer/Processor	PC with a Pentium-class processor Pentium 90 or higher recommended
Memory (RAM)	24 MB for Windows 95 or later 32 MB for Windows NT 4.0 or later 48 MB recommended on all platforms

Hard disk	Typical installation: 225 MB
	Maximum installation: 305 MB
	IE 4.01 Service Pack 1a: 43 MB (typical)
	These installation figures include documentation
Drive	CD-ROM drive
Display	VGA or higher resolution
	Super VGA recommended
Operating system	Windows 95 or later, or Windows NT 4.0 with NT Service Pack 3 or later
Peripheral/Miscellaneous	Microsoft Mouse or compatible pointing device

Support

Every effort has been made to ensure the accuracy of this book and the contents of the companion disc. Microsoft Press provides corrections for books through the World Wide Web at:

http://mspress.microsoft.com/mspress/support/

If you have comments, questions, or ideas regarding this book or the companion disc, please send them to Microsoft Press using postal mail or e-mail to:

Microsoft Press
Attn: *Learn Microsoft Visual C++ 6.0 Now* Editor
One Microsoft Way
Redmond, WA 98052-6399
msinput@microsoft.com

PART

1

Getting to
Know Visual C++

Chapter

The Visual C++ Environment

You can use Microsoft Visual C++ 6.0 to write any sort of program that can be written in either C or C++. The chances are, however, that you bought Visual C++ to program Microsoft Windows applications in C++. If so, you have the right tools: the C++ language, which is an object-oriented superset of C; the Microsoft Foundation Class Library 6.0 (MFC, or the MFC library, for short), which greatly amplifies your ability to write for Windows and the Visual C++ development environment; and last but by no means least, this book.

The Visual C++ integrated development environment (IDE) provides facilities for managing every stage of your program, from creating source code, to building (compiling and linking) the code, to testing, debugging, and optimizing the code. In this chapter, I'll prepare you for the hands-on work that comes in later chapters with a tour of the Visual C++ development environment, emphasizing practical techniques that make your programming easier.

This chapter focuses on the following components of the Visual C++ IDE:

- The online Help system, which you use to find information about the IDE, the C and C++ languages, and the classes and functions available in code libraries, such as the MFC library

- Projects and workspaces, which help you manage large programs that have multiple source code files

- The build system, with which you compile and link the appropriate files to create your executable program

- Wizards and other tools that simplify creating and editing your source code files and resources

We'll cover a lot of ground quickly in this chapter, so keep two things in mind: First, you'll see most of these topics again, in more detail. Second, this is a hands-on book. I strongly urge you to try things out for yourself as you read. Just as the best way to learn French is to live in France, the best way to learn Visual C++ is to use it.

Running Visual C++

Once you've installed Visual C++ by following the instructions in the Introduction of this book, you can run it from the Windows Start menu.

 Try it now

Follow these steps to run Visual C++:

1. Click Start on the Windows taskbar.

2. On the Start menu, click Programs.

3. Click Microsoft Visual C++ 6.0. (If you install Visual C++ as a standalone product, it will appear as Microsoft Visual C++ 6.0 on the Programs menu. If you install it as part of Microsoft Visual Studio, Visual C++ will be listed under Visual Studio 6.0 in the Programs menu.)

4. Figure 1-1 shows the Visual C++ window open with a program being displayed. Your window will not have a program in it yet, because we have not specified a program, but I thought I'd show you the Visual C++ window in all its glory.

TIP When Visual C++ opens, a Tip Of The Day window displays a handy tip. You can use the Next Tip button to view more tips, or you can click Close and go to work. If you don't want to see the tips each time you start Visual C++, clear the Show Tips At Startup check box before you close the Tip Of The Day window. You can always view tips again by selecting Tip Of The Day on the Visual C++ Help menu. It's useful to leave Tip Of The Day on autopilot while you're new to Visual C++.

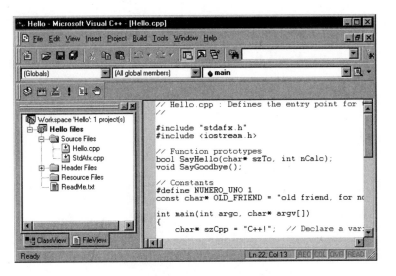

Figure 1-1. *The Visual C++ environment with a program displayed.*

Once you've run Visual C++, you either need to create a new project or load an existing one. I'll discuss projects after a brief tour of the online Help system.

Getting Help in Visual C++

It's customary to tack this section on at the end of a book's first chapter—or even to exile it to an appendix. But Visual C++ is a big product, and its Help system is positively huge—orders of magnitude larger than the Windows 95 Help system, for example. You will use Help all the time, so it is paramount that you learn how to narrow your searches, and how to leave a trail of breadcrumbs and locate your place on the map. (See "Lost in the Woods" later in this chapter.)

First, let's see how to control which components of Help are installed on your hard disk and briefly look at how the Help system is organized. Then we'll zero in on how to use it effectively.

Big Help, Little Help

If you're using the Introductory Edition of Visual C++ that comes with this book, Help consists only of Visual C++ topics—as you would expect. But if you're using another version of Visual C++ (the version included in the Microsoft Visual Studio products, or the stand-alone Standard, Professional, or Enterprise editions), the Help system contains topics for all of the Visual Studio products, including Visual Basic, Visual InterDev, Visual J++, Visual FoxPro, Visual SourceSafe, the Windows Application Programming Interface (API), and more. All of this Help is tied together with one table of contents, one index, and one search system. This means that any given attempt to find information specific to Visual C++ can turn up topics that have nothing whatsoever to do with Visual C++. So, if you're using one of these other versions of Visual C++, you'll need some Help strategies that go beyond what works for the Introductory Edition.

First, when you install Visual C++, you can specify which Help components you want loaded onto your hard disk, for fastest access, and which ones you want left on the CD, for slower access but less consumption of precious hard disk space. For the Introductory Edition that accompanies this book, Help simply installs when you install Visual C++, but for other editions you have a choice:

- The Typical option in Visual C++ Setup installs a minimal number of files on your hard disk, leaving the Microsoft Developer Network (MSDN) library on the CD. You'll need to keep the CD in your drive while you're programming.

- The Custom option in Setup lets you specify which portions of MSDN Help to install on your hard disk. You'll still see the full table of contents, and if you select a topic still on the CD, you'll be prompted to insert the CD.

Second, you'll need to be able to spot an inapplicable topic, such as one for Visual Basic instead of Visual C++. You can usually tell the difference, but not always. Examine Help topics carefully for references to specific products, or for topic presentation styles that you've come to recognize. It's worth exploring Help just to get a feeling for this problem.

Third, you'll want to weed out the parts of Help that won't help. You can focus your Help searches with documentation *subsets*. In the advanced versions of Visual C++, you can define a subset to contain designated portions of the documentation. When you select a subset, subsequent searches are confined to the documents in the subset. The subset applies to the Contents, Index, and Search tabs. To learn more about subsets, search Help (in the Professional or Enterprise Editions of Visual C++) for *subset*. Select the first topic in the list: "Creating and Using Subsets."

Help Fundamentals

There are four ways to get help while you're programming with Visual C++. Each of the following approaches (except F1 Help) is represented in the Help window as a tab that you can click.

- **F1 Help.** This is the quickest way is to obtain help. Simply click a word, highlight a phrase, or click an error message, and press F1. If the keyword or phrase is in the Help index, this will open a topic for it in most cases. You can use F1 Help in a Source Code editor window, a Help window, or the Output window.

- **The Help index.** Like a good book, Help has a large index. It's not perfect. Not everything you might look for is there, but a lot is. Use the Index tab in the Visual C++ Introductory Edition window (hereafter known as the Help window) before you try other search approaches—except for F1 Help.

- **The full-text search mechanism.** Help is online, so you can search every nook and cranny of the text in the Help system. Whereas the index allows you to take careful aim, search is more like a shotgun.

It may turn up 1000 irrelevant topics as well as the ones you need, but sometimes it's the only method that works, especially if the index fails you. Fortunately, you can fine-tune your search in a variety of ways, as we'll see later in the chapter.

- **The table of contents.** Again like a book, Help has an elaborate table of contents. Use the Contents tab in the Help window when you want to read everything about a subject. It's like reading or skimming a book when the subject is new to you or you're really rusty. Finding where to start in the table of contents can be tricky, so sometimes you need a combination of the index, search, and contents mechanisms to get going.

Opening the Help window

Click Contents, Search, or Index on the Visual C++ Help menu. This opens the Help window with the selected tab open.

NOTE The Help window is no longer an integral window within the main Visual C++ window for version 6.0, as it was for the past several versions. Now Help runs as a separate program and uses its own window.

Navigating in the Help window

Microsoft uses Internet Explorer Web-browsing technology to display Help topics as Hypertext Markup Language (HTML) documents—giving Help the look of the World Wide Web.

- Use the Contents, Index, and Search tabs in the navigation pane on the left side of the window to locate topics.

- Click the hypertext links (also called hyperlinks, blue and underlined by default) in the topic display pane on the right to explore related topics. Links you've followed turn purple (by default).

- Use the row of hyperlinks that appears below the title in many topics: links to overviews, how-to topics, frequently asked questions, a local home page for the subject area, and, possibly, code samples and other useful topics.

- Use the Back and Forward arrows on the Help toolbar to retrace your path through a series of topics.

- If you get lost, use the Home button on the toolbar to get to a known starting place: the home page for the Help system. From there you can get to various places within the Visual C++ documentation.

- Click the Home button, then other links to trace the chain of documentation down through Visual C++ Help.

To connect to a site on the Web, do one of the following:

- Click a URL (Web address).

- Select URL on the Go menu, and type a URL in the URL dialog box that appears.

- Go back to the Visual C++ window, select Microsoft On The Web on the Help menu, and select one of the options that appears on the submenu. Web topics are displayed in Internet Explorer.

Try it now

Explore Help. Click the Index, Search, and Contents tabs. Examine a few subjects by using these tabs. Follow some links. Go home. Climb down the hierarchy of start pages. Go online.

TIP Visual C++ includes both the MFC and Active Template Library (ATL) code libraries. You'll often get topics on one when you look for topics on the other. That's unfortunate, because the two libraries have many similarly named elements, and you normally don't use them together. Caution is required. ATL class names don't begin with the letter C as MFC class names do. Don't worry if this does not make sense to you right now. It will.

Narrowing Your Searches

It's easy to be too general in Visual C++ Help, on both the Index tab and the Search tab. With a little patience, you can significantly narrow your search.

Zeroing in with the index

The Index tab is like the index in a book, and you search it the same way, using keywords and phrases. As with any book index, you can just scroll through the Index tab and hope to stumble over something useful. But the Visual C++ index is huge, with many thousands of entries, so you normally check the Help index by guessing keywords, typing them into the Type In The Keyword To Find box, and exploring the results. If your keyword is in the index, it appears at the top of the lower pane on the Index tab. The topic or topics it leads to may be relevant and useful, or not. Here are several ways to improve your chances of zeroing in on the relevant topics:

- Use more specific keywords or phrases, for example, "creating ActiveX controls" (five topics found) instead of "ActiveX controls" (seven topics, two of them irrelevant). There's a movement in the Visual C++ documentation team toward indexing general topics with general keywords and more specific topics with specific keywords or longer phrases. This trend is gradually improving the index, and you can take advantage of it by tailoring your keywords appropriately.

- If you're after more general information, think accordingly. Just as highly specific information isn't likely to reside in a general topic, specific topics don't offer the larger picture. For example, the topic "Using database classes in ActiveX Controls" does not give an overview of database classes. (Check the Help index for *activex controls*, scroll down, and double-click "database classes in.") You would have to look in the topic "Databases: Overview" for the more general information. (On the Contents tab, look up Overviews by double-clicking Visual C++ 6.0 Introductory Edition, and then Welcome To The Visual C++ 6.0 Introductory Edition, and then Using Visual C++. Then double-click Visual C++ Programmer's Guide, and then Adding Program Functionality, and then Overviews, and finally, Databases: Overview.)

NOTE Hereafter, if I instruct you to search the Help index for something, and *something* is in italics, that's what you should enter in the Type In The Keyword To Find box. I put quotation marks around the titles of Help topics the keywords lead you to. Note that keywords in the topics index are case-sensitive. This means that topic keywords with identical wording but different capitalization may take you to two very different places in Help. Be sure to follow my wording and carefully check the way topics appear. If I say "check the Help index for *x*," use the Index tab in Help. If I say "search Help for *x*," use the Search tab.

■ When you get to the right neighborhood in the index, look around. There might be a dozen entries related to files, for example, some more relevant than others. It's no accident that the Index tab lets you see twenty or so entries at a time with the default Help window size. You can also maximize the Help window to see even more listings at once.

■ Try synonyms or other closely related words: *serialization*, *files*, *storing data*, *storing objects*, *writing to a file*, *persistence*. If one doesn't work, another might. Good indexers try to think of all the possible words you might use to find a topic, so most topics are indexed to five or ten different keywords.

■ Try variations of your search words: *use*, *using*, *working with*, *work*, *creating*, *create*.

Nobody can create the perfect index, but with a little thought you can make better use of what's available.

TIP The Index tab is your best bet for narrowing your search, so make it your first search strategy, before you resort to the Search tab or the Contents tab.

Narrowing with the Search tab

The Search tab in Help is designed to find, anywhere in the documentation, every occurrence of the word or words you enter in the box labeled Type In The Words To Search For. Thus it's called a full-text search. Usually, the Search tab returns a large number of topics—often hundreds or thousands of topics—unless you work at narrowing your search.

TIP The best way to narrow a search is to use the Search tab only after you've tried the Index tab.

When you do resort to the Search tab, try some of the following techniques to zero in on the desired topic:

■ **Search the results of a previous search.** To do this, you search once, then set the Search Previous Results option to limit the next search to those topics already found. You can continue narrowing the search this way for several rounds.

- **Search topic titles only.** Instead of searching the entire text of all available topics, you search only within their titles by setting the Search Titles Only option. This approach tends to turn up more pertinent topics.

- **Formulate your search queries carefully.** Use quotation marks to search for an exact phrase. A search for *double quotes* uncovers any topic that contains either word—*double* or *quotes*—whereas a search for *"double quotes"* (including the quotation marks) finds topics that contain those two words together in that order. Enclosing the phrase in quotation marks reduces the number of topics found from 59 to 39. (In this search, I did not have any of the three options at the bottom of the Search tab selected.) Try it.

- **Use wildcards.** * matches any characters and ? matches a single character, just as in MS-DOS.

- **Use the Boolean operators AND, OR, NOT, and NEAR.** The query *CFile NEAR close* searches for the word *CFile* within eight words of the word *close*. Boolean operators let you construct very precise search criteria. The query *CFile AND (close OR open) NOT serialization*, for example, looks for *CFile* in the same topic with either *close* or *open* as long as the topic doesn't include the word *serialization*. This query finds 42 topics. In this case, parentheses around the OR clause make your intentions absolutely clear.

- **Use a subset if you're using Help for Visual C++ 6.0 Professional or Enterprise Edition.** Subsets aren't available in the Introductory edition. Subsets limit the search to a portion of the documentation. (See the earlier sidebar "Big Help, Little Help" for more information.)

You can combine many of these techniques. Detailed information on refining queries is available on the Contents tab in Help, under Welcome To The MSDN Viewer Help. Look under MSDN Library Help.

Try it now

Try the following full-text search, using the Search tab. Type *CFile AND (close OR open) NOT serialization.* Then narrow the search further by checking the Search Previous Results box on the Search tab and searching for *"close member function"* (with the quotation marks).

How many topics turn up? Start over with the first search and turn off Search Previous Results. From the initial search results, search for *close member function* again with Search Previous Results turned on, but without the quotation marks. How many topics show up this time?

Lost in the Woods

Because Help is so vast, covering thousands of pages of documentation (and many more if you have a version other than the Visual C++ 6.0 Introductory Edition), you can get lost. Furthermore, you might find just the right topic today, yet be unable to find your way back to that topic tomorrow. Here are some strategies for coping with these problems.

You are here: the Locate button

Lost? Click the Locate button on the Help toolbar. This opens the Contents tab in the Help window and shows you where the currently displayed topic is located within the whole documentation set. This is like seeing the phrase "You Are Here" on a shopping mall map.

Going home

I've already described the Home button on the toolbar and the page full of links it takes you to. You can use those links as another way to navigate the documentation set. Try it.

Leaving a trail of bread crumbs: the Favorites tab

When you've found a topic that you know you'll want to revisit, save it as a favorite—just as you would on the Web. When it's no longer a favorite, you can delete it from the Favorites tab in the Help window.

■ To add the current topic to the Favorites tab, click Add on the Favorites tab.

TIP You can give the topic a more useful title before you click Add to add it to your favorites. Just edit the title in the Current Topic box. You can use your own words to give the topic a handy title on the Favorites tab without altering its original title in the Help system.

■ To go to a favorite topic, click the Favorites tab and double-click the topic you want.

Additional information about the Favorites tab is available on the Contents tab in Help, under Welcome To The MSDN Viewer Help. Look under MSDN Library Help.

Studying the terrain

The more you know about how Help is organized, the easier and more fruitful your searches will be. Spend time browsing through the Contents tab to see what's there and how it's arranged.

The Visual C++ documentation is divided into the major sections and subsections shown in Figure 1-2.

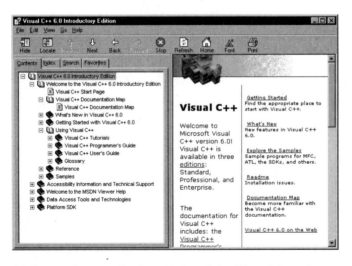

Figure 1-2.   *Major sections and subsections of the Visual C++ documentation.*

Here's a brief description of the main items:

■ The Visual C++ Tutorials teach key MFC programming techniques. The main tutorial, called Scribble, is like a shorter version of this book and doesn't cover nearly as many topics. It does, however, cover some advanced subjects that I don't, including Object Linking and Embedding (OLE) and databases.

■ The Visual C++ Programmer's Guide covers programming topics—primarily using MFC. It is mainly organized around the general phases of developing an application, so think about where you are in the development process as a guide to where to look for relevant information. Among the headings under the Visual C++ Programmer's Guide, you'll see things like Porting And Upgrading, Beginning Your Program, Compiling And Linking, and Debugging. Two sections of the Programmer's Guide entitled "Adding User Interface Features" and "Adding Program Functionality" divide up the bulk of your programming tasks into those that implement visible user-interface features such as toolbars, windows, and controls, and those that involve programming the engine of your application under the hood.

■ The Visual C++ User's Guide covers topics on using the development environment's editors, wizards, and other tools.

■ The Glossary defines hundreds of terms to help you understand all the jargon and special lingo of programming with Visual C++.

■ The Reference is really a collection of several separate references for MFC, ATL, the C and C++ languages, the *iostream* input/output facilities, and the Standard C++ Library. Each reference documents all of the classes, functions, macros, and other elements that make up the code libraries available with Visual C++. References for the C/C++ run-time library, the C/C++ preprocessor, and the Build Errors (error message reference) are all part of the Visual C++ Programmer's Guide rather than the Reference.

■ The Samples are a collection of programs that you can build and run. They illustrate a variety of basic and advanced programming techniques. You can locate an appropriate sample and load it onto your hard disk via Help. See the topic Retrieving Samples under MSDN Library Help, found under Welcome To The MSDN Library on the Contents tab.

Loose Ends

Additional information about using Visual C++ Help is available on the Contents tab in Help, under Welcome To The MSDN Viewer Help. Look under MSDN Library Help. Besides the topics we've already touched on, you'll also find guidance on:

- Copying or printing Help topics
- Customizing the Help viewer (the MSDN Library window)

Projects and Workspaces

At the heart of every Visual C++ program under development is a *project*, which is housed in a *workspace*. It's possible in Visual C++ to house multiple projects in one workspace. For example, if you're writing a dynamic-link library (DLL), you might have a workspace with one project for the DLL and another project for the small program you write to test the DLL. We won't use multiple-project workspaces in this book, but if you'd like to know more about them, you can check the Help index for *projects*. Double click the first appearance of "projects" in the list of topics. In the Topics Found window that appears, double-click "Overview: Working with Projects."

Projects

When you begin a new program, the first thing you do is create a project for it by selecting the New command on the File menu. For example, a project might be for a game program you're writing, or a small utility program you have in mind. The name you specify for your project is used as the basis for naming a variety of other files in the project, starting with the project file, projname.dsp. (The .dsp extension means Developer Studio project. Developer Studio is an old name for the integrated development environment, or IDE, used by Microsoft Visual Studio applications, including Visual C++.)

The project file maintains information about which source code files and resource files your program uses and about any settings you have specified for controlling how Visual C++ builds your program. The Visual C++ build system uses this information when it compiles and links your files to create an executable program.

Throughout this book, you'll create just two kinds of projects, both using wizards available through the New dialog box. In Chapters 2 through 5, you'll use the wizard for Win32 Console Application projects. In later chapters, you'll use the MFC AppWizard (for .exe files). However, there are many other kinds of projects available through the New dialog box. As you gain some fluency with Visual C++, you may want to investigate these other options further.

Workspaces

When you create a project, you also by default create a workspace. Your workspace file, projname.dsw (*dsw* for Developer Studio workspace), maintains information about which Visual C++ windows are open and where they are located, as well as any settings you have specified for your workspace.

When you create a project, Visual C++ uses default settings for the project and the workspace, but you can alter these as you work:

- To change build settings for the project, select Settings on the Project menu.

- To change workspace settings, select either Options or Customize on the Tools menu.

The Workspace tab in the Options dialog box lets you specify various options for your windows, status bar, and other components of the workspace. The Editor tab in the Options dialog box lets you specify settings for the Source Code editor. The Customize dialog box lets you rearrange, add, or delete toolbar buttons, menu commands, keyboard shortcuts, and the tools on the Visual C++ Tools menu. For more information, check the Help index for *customizing*.

Working with Your Project

You will usually work through the following stages to develop your applications. This section describes each stage in turn.

- Create a project. This creates the initial files on which your work will be based.

- Use the Workspace window and its ClassView, FileView, and ResourceView tabs to work with the C++ classes, files, and resources in your project.

- Add files to the project, or remove files from the project.

- Edit source code and resources in the project.

- Specify a build configuration for the project (Debug or Release build).

- Build the project (compile and link its code).

- Correct any compiler or linker errors.

- Execute and test the resulting executable file.

- Debug the project.

- Profile and optimize the code (optional).

Creating a Project

Projects come in some 16 varieties. I'll show you how to create a Win32 Console Application, the simplest project type, which we'll be using in Chapters 2 through 5. After Chapter 5, we'll use another other project type, an MFC application. The sequence of steps involved in creating each of the 16 types is generally similar, although the wizards used to create some project types are more detailed than others. For some project types, Visual C++ creates many files to help you get started. For other project types, Visual C++ creates no starter files. For more information about each variety, check the Help index for *project types*.

A console application uses a set of Console API functions to display its output in a character-mode window, like an MS-DOS window. Because writing console applications requires no more overhead than writing a *main* function, we'll use them to test simple C++ programs. To create a Win32 Console Application project, follow these steps, and refer to Figure 1-3 as needed:

1. Click New on the File menu.

2. In the New dialog box click the Projects tab.

3. Click Win32 Console Application.

4. In the Project Name box, type the project name. We'll name this first project First.

5. Use the Location box to specify a location for the project's files. You can browse for the right directory by clicking the Browse button next to the Location box.

6. Select the Create New Workspace option.

7. Make sure Win32 is checked in the Platforms box.

8. Click OK.

That's just the first step in creating project First. Stay tuned.

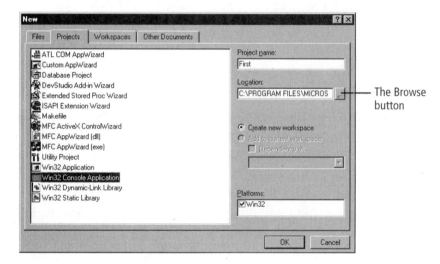

Figure 1-3. *The Projects tab in the New dialog box.*

Next, follow the instructions in the wizard dialog boxes that follow the New dialog box. For a Win32 Console Application there's only one such box:

1. In the Step 1 Of 1 dialog box (see Figure 1-4 on the next page), select A "Hello, World!" Application.

2. Click Finish.

3. In the New Project Information dialog box, examine the information presented to make sure it's what you wanted. Then click OK.

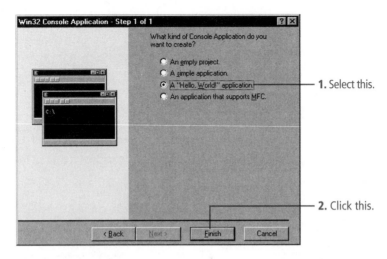

1. Select this.

2. Click this.

Figure 1-4. *The AppWizard dialog box for a Win32 Console Application.*

The directories and files created

Visual C++ creates a project directory in the location you specified in the Location Edit box of the New dialog box. The directory contains one or more files. For a Win32 Console Application, the directory will contain three source code files (two .cpp files and one .h file), a project file (.dsp), a workspace file (.dsw), and a ReadMe file (.txt). Visual C++ also creates a few support files that it uses, but we don't need to worry about those. The ReadMe file explains the purposes of the other files in the directory. Other project types result in additional files.

In addition to these files, your project directory contains one subdirectory—Debug. For projects that have Windows resources, there's also a Res subdirectory that contains resource-related files (see "Using ResourceView" later in this chapter). The Debug subdirectory contains intermediate files created by building your project. Later, when you create a Release build (see "Specifying the Project Configuration"), Visual C++ also creates a Release subdirectory for use in that build.

This scheme neatly manages the two kinds of project builds (Debug and Release). The project's source code files are stored in the project directory. Intermediate files created by the builds are stored in subdirectories.

Try it now

Follow the directions just presented to create a new Win32 Console Application project called First. We'll build the program shortly.

Using the Workspace Window

When you create a new project, it becomes the current project in Visual C++. You'll see the Workspace window (not titled) on the left side of the Visual C++ main window unless you have rearranged your windows. Figure 1-5 shows the ClassView tab of the Workspace window with our application project First open. The Workspace window has several downward-facing tabs. For our console application, the tabs are labeled ClassView and FileView. For an application that has Windows resources, there's also a ResourceView tab.

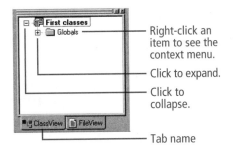

Figure 1-5.   *The ClassView tab of the Workspace window.*

Here's how you can control the Workspace window:

- To open the Workspace window if it is not visible, click Workspace on the View menu.

- To close the Workspace window and gain a little more space in the Visual C++ main window, click the close button (marked by an *X*) on the Workspace window.

- There's also a Workspace button on the Visual C++ Standard toolbar—it shows a folder over a window. Use this button to toggle the visibility of the Workspace window.

Try it now

Get used to working with the Workspace window by hiding it, then displaying it. Use both the Workspace command on the View menu and the Workspace button on the toolbar.

Using ClassView

Click the ClassView tab in the Workspace window to see a list of any C++ classes in your project. I'll discuss classes in Chapters 4 and 5. The project we just created lists only a Globals folder, for global variables and functions; it has no classes yet.

Although I'll explain many of the terms mentioned in the following guidelines in subsequent chapters, it's worth taking a few moments now just to learn your way around.

■ To view the members of a class in ClassView, click the plus sign in front of the class name. This expands the members listed under the class name, much as you expand a title in Help.

■ To open the header file (.h) for a class, double-click the class name. I'll talk about header and implementation files in Chapter 3.

■ To open the implementation file and scroll it to the definition of a class member function, expand the list of members for the class in ClassView, then double-click the member function name.

■ To add a new class via ClassView, right-click the topmost heading (click it with the right mouse button) in ClassView. On the context menu that appears, select New Class. In the New Class dialog box, specify a class type and fill in the class information. Click OK. For more information, check the Help index for *New Classes*. If you need to delete a class, open the source code files that define it, then select and delete the code.

■ To add a new member to a class, right-click the class name and choose one of the Add commands on the context menu that pops up. I'll give examples of all of these operations later in this chapter.

- To delete a class member, right-click it in ClassView. On the context menu that appears, click Delete. ClassView deletes the member's prototype but it only comments out the member's definition. (I'll make these terms clear in Chapters 2 through 5.)

For more information, check the Help index for *ClassView*. We'll practice these techniques in Chapters 2 through 5.

✎ **IP** Throughout Visual C++, it's worth right-clicking windows, toolbars, and other objects, such as filenames or class names. Many of them have context menus with useful commands. Try it.

Using FileView

Click the FileView tab (see Figure 1-6) in the Workspace window to see a set of folders containing source files (with the .cpp extension), header files (with the .h extension), and resource files (with the .rc extension). In the MFC programming you'll do while reading this book, ClassView will be a more natural and useful way to view and access your files. But while classes are the more natural entity for working in Visual C++, FileView has its uses too. Here are some common FileView tasks:

- To open a file from FileView, double-click the filename.

- For other actions you can take on a file in FileView, right-click on a filename and choose from the context menu that pops up.

For more information, check the Help index for *FileView*.

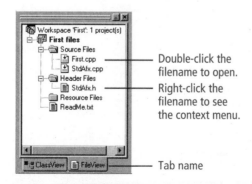

Figure 1-6. *The FileView tab of the Workspace window.*

Try it now

In your project First, open a file from the FileView tab. To close the file, click its close button (the *X*) or click Close on the Visual C++ File menu.

Using ResourceView

At this point you will not see a ResourceView tab (we'll talk about that in a moment), but if you did, it would look like Figure 1-7. The ResourceView tab in the Workspace window shows a set of folders containing *resources* of various types. Windows uses compiled resources to store the text and images that make up the Windows user interface: menus, dialog boxes, toolbars, icons, and others. A resource specifies the appearance of such an object. Using Windows resources saves you from having to draw menus, buttons, and other visual objects yourself—the prefabricated images available through Visual C++ save time and promote consistency among Windows programs. Since the wizard for a Win32 Console Application doesn't generate a resource file, you won't see a ResourceView tab in the Workspace window for the First project. (But you could add a resource file to the First project. Win32 Console Applications can use Windows resources, such as dialog boxes, and they can also use MFC classes.) Because program First doesn't use resources, Figure 1-7 shows the ResourceView tab for a generic MFC application.

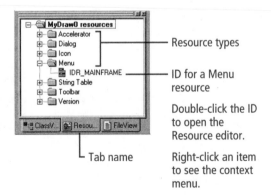

Figure 1-7.   *The ResourceView tab of the Workspace window.*

You can use ResourceView not only to view existing resources but also to edit them. Use the Resource command on the Insert menu to create new ones.

- To edit an existing resource, open the appropriate folder in ResourceView, for example, Menus. Double-click the ID of the resource you want to edit, such as *IDR_MAINFRAME*. In the Resource editor that opens up, edit the resource. For information on editing resources, check the Help index for *resource editors* and double-click "overview."

- To create a new resource (in an application that uses resources), select Resource on the Insert menu. In the Insert Resource dialog box, double-click the type of resource you want to create, such as a menu resource. Edit the new resource in the Resource editor window that opens. If the application already uses resources, our newly added resource will be saved to the existing resource (.rc) file. If the application doesn't already have a resource file (meaning it does not use resources), you're prompted to save newly created resources in an .rc file. You need to supply a name for the .rc file, and then you need to add the .rc file to your project; at that point, the ResourceView tab appears. For more information, check the Help index for *resource editors*, and double-click "creating new resources." I'll introduce you to most of the resource editors as we proceed.

- To delete a resource, select it in ResourceView. Press the Delete key.

For information on copying resources, check the Help index for *Resources* and double-click "copying." I'll cover more resource topics in later chapters. I'll also give you some practice with resource creation and deletion in the next section.

Adding and Removing Project Files

Projects typically contain the following kinds of source files:

- **Header files,** also known as include files, with the .h file extension
- **Implementation, or source, files,** with the .cpp extension for C++, or the .c extension for C

- **Resource files,** with the .rc extension; also files with the extensions .bmp and .ico and other files that contain graphical elements such as toolbar button images or icons

These are the files that the build system compiles for binary resources such as menus, toolbars, dialog boxes, and icons, and for C or C++ code.

From time to time, you'll need to add new header and implementation files to your project:

- To create new .h, .cpp, or .c files and add them to your project, select New on the File menu. In the New dialog box, click the Files tab. Click C/C++ Header File or C++ Source File. Make sure the Add To Project option is selected. Type a filename (using a .cpp extension for C++, a .c extension for C, or a .h extension for a header file). Specify the location for the new file if it's different from the current project directory, and click OK.

- To add an existing .cpp, .c, or .rc file, select Add To Project on the Project menu. On the submenu, click Files. In the Insert Files Into Project dialog box, click any files you want to add, then click OK. (To select multiple files, hold down the Shift or Ctrl key while selecting.)

- To add an existing .h file to your project, just refer to the header filename in an *#include* statement in a .cpp or .h file that is already in the project. You don't need to manually add the file to the project.

- To delete a file from the project, open FileView, select the filename, and press the Delete key. This removes the file from the project but does not delete the file from your hard disk.

 Try it now

Create a new .h file and a new .cpp file in the First project. Then delete them from the project. (You can even delete these particular files, if you like, in Windows Explorer—we don't need them any more.)

Try it now

Let's practice creating a resource. We'll delete it from program First afterward. With the First project open in Visual C++, use the Insert menu to create a new dialog resource. Save the dialog resource in a file called First.rc by clicking Save As on the File menu. Close the Dialog editor window by clicking Close on the File menu. Add the file First.rc to the project. To remove the practice resource from the project, click the new dialog resource (called *IDD_DIALOG1* by default) in ResourceView (which is now available), and press the Delete key. Now we're back where we started.

Editing Source Code and Resources

Now that you know how to create a Visual C++ project and manage its files, classes, and resources, let's turn to writing and editing the source code and resources that constitute your program. We'll look at the Source Code editor and the Resource editors, and then move on to compiling and linking what you've created.

Editing C/C++ source code

You'll use the Visual C++ Source Code editor, shown in Figure 1-8, to write and edit your code. To start the Source Code editor, either create a new .h or .cpp file or open an existing file.

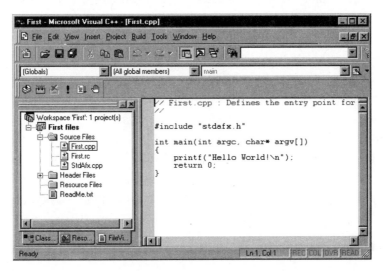

Figure 1-8. *The Visual C++ Source Code editor with the file First.cpp open.*

The Source Code editor automatically color codes various syntax elements in the program, which makes the source files easier to read. Check the Help index for *syntax coloring*. The editor can also emulate two popular source code editors: Brief and Epsilon. Check the Help index for *editor emulation*. Visual C++ provides various ways to locate classes, functions, and other items in your source code files, including ClassView. We'll meet others, including WizardBar and the Find commands, later. I'll get you started with the Source Code editor in Chapter 2, but this is a good place to talk briefly about indenting, or *pretty-printing*, your source code files.

Most of us have our own preferences for the appearance of our source code—what's indented, how much it's indented, and where the curly braces go. For example, here are two commonly used ways to declare a function:

```
void functionA() {          // Opening brace here
    // Lines of code
}

void functionB()
{                           // Opening brace here
    // Lines of code
}
```

Both of these coding styles are popular, and programmers sometimes defend their favorite with religious zeal. You can control the style of your code in the Options dialog box (select Options on the Tools menu). Use the Tabs tab in the dialog box to specify settings for different types of files, such as C/C++ source code files, Visual Basic Scripting (VBScript) macros, and so on. Select the file type in the drop-down list. Specify the number of spaces each press of the Tab key represents, how much to indent, and whether to insert actual tab characters or spaces. You can also specify several options for the behavior of indents, including whether to indent the curly braces around a function body or not. If you use the Smart Indent option, you can have Visual C++ imitate the style used in the previous *n* lines of code (default is 100 lines). Check the Help index for *pretty-print code*.

Editing resources

Edit the menus, dialog boxes, and other resources in your program using the Visual C++ resource editors. There's a different editor for each resource type. I'll illustrate the use of most of these during the course of the book. Go back to the section "Using ResourceView" for introductory information about opening, editing, and creating resources.

Specifying the Project Configuration

While you're developing your program, you'll usually work in a *Debug build* configuration. In a Debug build, the compiler includes debugging information that the Visual C++ debugger can use if you encounter logic errors. When you're ready to release the program for general use (and occasionally during development for testing), you switch to a *Release build*. Debug and release are the two main types of project configurations. Advanced programmers can add specialized configurations of their own.

In order to switch between Debug and Release builds, you'll need to change the active configuration for your project. To do so, click Set Active Configuration on the Build menu. In the Set Active Project Configuration dialog box, click either Win32 Debug (the default) or Win32 Release. Then click OK.

Since developing a program always requires debugging, the default configuration is a Debug build. This is set for you initially, so you only have to change the active configuration when you're ready to do a Release build, or when you've finished a Release build and need to revert to Debug build again.

Building Your Project

After you have edited the code and resources for your project, it's time to build it. Visual C++ includes a build system that lets you compile and link your program with a single command.

> **NOTE** To build the project, click Build projname.exe on the Build menu, or press F7.

The build process invokes the appropriate resource and language compilers, the linker, and other tools. It produces intermediate files in the appropriate subdirectory (based on the active configuration) and, if there are no build errors (compiler or linker errors), generates the final executable (.exe) file.

During the build, you'll see messages in the Visual C++ Output window marking the build's progress and listing any errors or problems found. The Output window opens during a build if it wasn't open before. The Output window has several tabs. Build output appears on the Build tab. Figure 1-9 shows the Output window and the messages generated during an error-free build.

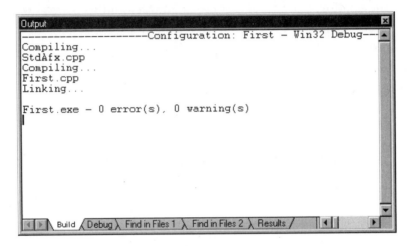

Figure 1-9. *The Visual C++ Output window during an error-free build.*

 ## Try it now

Build the First program that we created earlier by following the steps I just described. Take a look at the output in the Output window. What do you see when the build finishes?

 IP The build system creates a Build Log that you can examine later. The Build Log is a handy record of past builds and the errors you made and corrected. The log is stored in your project directory in an HTML file named Projname.plg, which you can examine in your Web browser. The file is not visible in FileView, so open it outside Visual C++.

Correcting Build Errors

Build errors are errors of syntax, file problems, and the like, as opposed to logic errors. To correct logic errors, use the debugger (see Chapter 13). To correct build errors, follow these steps:

1. Double-click an error message in the Visual C++ Output window. This opens the source code to where the error occurred and points to the line that contains the error. (Sometimes the error has occurred somewhat before this line, so if you do not see the error in the line being pointed to, examine the preceding few lines.) Figure 1-10 shows the Output window and the messages generated during a build in which errors have occurred.

2. Click on the error message number in the error message line in the Output window and press the F1 key to get information about the error.

3. Correct the code and rebuild.

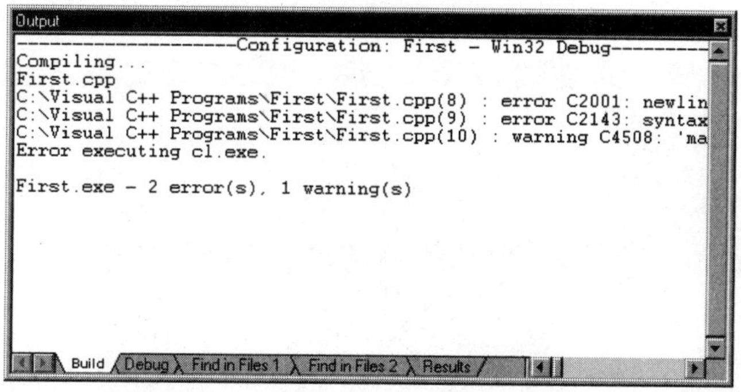

```
Output                                                                    ×
---------------------Configuration: First - Win32 Debug----------
Compiling...
First.cpp
C:\Visual C++ Programs\First\First.cpp(8) : error C2001: newlin
C:\Visual C++ Programs\First\First.cpp(9) : error C2143: syntax
C:\Visual C++ Programs\First\First.cpp(10) : warning C4508: 'ma
Error executing cl.exe.

First.exe - 2 error(s), 1 warning(s)




  Build / Debug \ Find in Files 1 \ Find in Files 2 \ Results /
```

Figure 1-10.   *The Visual C++ Output window during a build in which errors occurred.*

Errors often occur in cascades—one or two legitimate errors result in additional (sometimes several) error messages in successive lines of code. It's usually a good strategy to correct the first few errors listed, then build again without examining the later errors. If there was an error cascade in the first build, it often disappears in subsequent builds. For relatively small programs, it's practical to fix a few errors, build again, fix more, build again, and so on.

Correcting errors often requires a good bit of detective work and lots of reading in the documentation. You can find the error message documentation by checking the Help index for *build errors*. Double-click "fixing." I'll supply an exercise to try the error mechanism after the next section.

Running Your Program

After a successful build with no build errors, you can run your program within the Visual C++ environment.

 OTE To run the program, select Execute projname.exe on the Build menu, or press Ctrl+F5.

 ### Try it now

Run the First program. Note that after it prints "Hello, World!" in the window, Visual C++ prints the sentence "Press any key to continue." Only the first line is part of program First's output. Figure 1-11 shows the output of the First program.

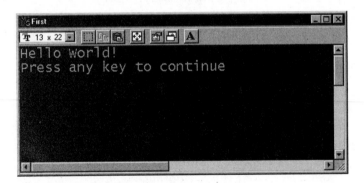

Figure 1-11. *The First program's output.*

 ### Try it now

In program First, use FileView to open the file First.cpp. In that file, introduce an intentional error: in the *printf* line, delete the concluding double quotation mark. The line should now look like this:

```
printf("Hello World!\n);
```

Build the program. You'll get two errors and one warning. Double-click the first error message in the Output window, the one that says "newline in constant." A small blue arrow points to the offending line of code in the Source Code editor window. In the Output window, click directly on the error number, 2001, then press the F1 key. Visual C++ Help opens the topic for that error number. The compiler apparently takes the erroneous line to be an improperly formed constant. We know it's caused by a missing double quotation mark. The second error and the warning apparently occur as a cascade from the first error.

The warning shows up because the warning level is set to 3 (by default) in the Project Settings dialog box. Select Settings on the Project menu, click the C/C++ tab, make sure the Category drop-down list says "General," and examine the Warning Level box. A warning level set this high causes the compiler to be picky in the potential problems it points out as warnings. This can be valuable, so it's good to leave the level set fairly high.

Try it now

The trick to diagnosing the real problem with program First is to recognize that a character string was intended, which should lead you to note the missing double quotation mark. Restore the double quotation mark and build again. This time there should be no errors or warnings.

Debugging Your Program

If you encounter logic errors while the program is running, use the debugger to find and fix them. Chapter 13 includes a tour of the debugger.

Profiling and Optimizing Programs

Profiling uses the profiler tool to help locate bottlenecks and inefficiencies in your code. Optimizing increases the speed of your code or reduces the amount of space the program requires. Since these relatively advanced abilities are not supported in the Introductory Edition of Visual C++, I won't cover them, but you can check the Help index for *profiling* and *optimizing* (double-click "code") to learn more about them.

Using Wizards and Other Visual C++ Tools

Visual C++ gives you lots of help with your programming, primarily through its extensive set of wizards. A wizard is a tool that looks like a sequence of dialog boxes. It guides you through a complicated process of making choices. I'll very briefly summarize the key wizards and tools here, but you'll meet them in more detail later in the book:

■ Use AppWizard to create a set of starter files at the beginning of a project. Most of the project types listed in the New dialog box invoke AppWizard to create the projects and their files. You already encountered AppWizard when you created the project for program First.

■ Use ClassWizard as you program to add C++ classes and class members, manipulate MFC message maps, work with automation properties and methods, operate on ActiveX events, and perform many other tasks.

■ Use WizardBar as a shortcut to ClassWizard's functionality and as a navigation tool for finding classes and functions in your source code files. WizardBar is a toolbar. We'll use WizardBar extensively.

Besides the wizards, you can use the commands on the Tools menu. For example:

■ Use the Source Browser command to invoke the Visual C++ source browser. (See the Appendix for information about the source browser.)

■ The Error Lookup command helps you look up an error message when you know the error number.

■ The Spy++ tool lets you spy on Windows messages in real time.

■ The MFC Tracer tool enables MFC's *TRACE* macro for printing diagnostic output strings.

You can also add your own tools to the Tools menu: Select Customize. In the Customize dialog box, click the Tools tab. For more information, check the Help index for *customizing,* and double-click " Tools menu."

Working with Your Workspace Windows

As you develop your program, you'll use a variety of different windows in Visual C++: Source Code and Resource editor windows, the Workspace and Output windows, and various debugger windows. You'll need a few basic window-handling techniques. In the next two sections, I'll discuss the two kinds of windows found in Visual C++, *document windows* and *docking windows*. I'll offer practical guidelines that make your programming with Visual C++ easier and more productive, and that make the most of the available work area.

> **IMPORTANT**   Keeping all of Visual C++'s windows where you want them as you move from task to task can be difficult. Sometimes the windows will seem to misbehave, and you can have a frustrating time straightening them out. It's worth the time it takes to read the next few pages and try the techniques I describe.

To see the distinction between document windows and dockable windows, try the following experiment.

Try it now

With the First project open, and the First.cpp file displayed in the code editor window, close the Workspace window and the Output window. You can close each of them by clicking the Close button. Any windows left open—besides the menu bar and several toolbars—are document windows. In this case, there's one document window, titled First.cpp. The Workspace and Output windows (and the menu bar and toolbars) are dockable windows.

Document windows contain and are used to edit your code and resources. Dockable windows are part of the machinery of Visual C++. They display, and often allow you to manipulate, information about your project and its files and classes. Dockable windows also display output during builds, searches, and debugging sessions, and information about the current state of your computer's memory and the code you're running or debugging in Visual C++.

Document Windows

Document windows are normal framed windows that contain documents, such as Source Code editor documents (.h and .cpp files) or Resource editor documents (for example, dialog editor and menu editor documents). These windows have frames with Minimize, Maximize, and Close buttons, system menus, and borders you can drag to resize the windows—just like the windows you've used in other Windows applications.

Managing document windows

Manage your document windows with the File and Window menus. File menu commands open, close, save, and print document window contents. Window menu commands let you switch back and forth among open document windows as well as arrange them. You can cascade, tile, and split them.

To open recently-used source code files or workspaces, click a filename in the list of most recently used files on the File menu. To expose open document windows that are buried, use the list of open documents on the Window menu.

Getting the most available work space

Use one or more of the following methods to gain maximum work space in the Visual C++ main window:

- Close unneeded windows, especially docking windows, such as the Output window. You might also close the Workspace window while you're really writing code—you can always reopen the Workspace or Output windows by clicking their toggle buttons on the Standard toolbar. You can also pop open a list of all open windows from that toolbar. See Figure 1-13 for the button locations.

- Maximize the document window you're currently working in. This hides all other document windows, but they remain available from the Window menu. The Minimize, Maximize, and Close buttons for a maximized document window appear just under those for Visual C++ itself. See Figure 1-8 for the button locations.

- Use the Split command on the Window menu to work in more than one part of the document at the same time.

■ Consider using the Full Screen command on the View menu. This removes menus, toolbars, and everything else but your current document window and a tiny toolbar that lets you end the full screen mode. (If the toolbar isn't there, press the Escape key.)

Using a document window's context menu

Right-click a document window to pop up a context menu (also known as a shortcut menu). For document windows, the context menu includes such commands as Cut, Copy, Paste, and Insert/Remove Breakpoint, as well as commands for obtaining information about the C++ class or function under the cursor. If the document is a Resource editor document, the commands change to those appropriate for the resource type you're editing.

Docking Windows

A docking window can be attached to any edge of the main window in Visual C++. This feature lets you position such windows most usefully for the way you work. Docking windows can also be floated in the middle of the main window rather than docked. Figure 1-12 shows one docked window (Workspace) and one floating window (Output). Docking windows always stay on top of other windows, so Visual C++ adjusts document windows to make room for newly opened docking windows.

> **TIP** If your main Visual C++ window becomes too crowded, try closing some windows and adjusting others with the Cascade and Tile commands as well as the Minimize, Restore, and Maximize commands.

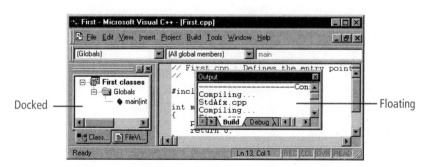

Figure 1-12. *A docked docking window and a floating docking window (with toolbars hidden).*

Manipulating docking windows

To manipulate a docking window, click on the raised *knurls* (knobs) along one edge of the window (Figure 1-12 shows these knurls). Drag the window by its knurls to redock it to a different side of the main window. Double-click the knurls to turn off docking and float the window. (Double-click the title bar of a floating window to redock it to the last docking position it occupied. Double-click a docked window to float it.)

Try it now

Redock the Workspace window in turn to the top, right, and bottom edges of the main window. Double-click the knurls on the window to float it. Double-click the title bar to redock it. I prefer to keep the Workspace window docked on the left and the Output window, when open, docked on the bottom. Your preferences might differ from mine, so experiment.

Docking windows outside the debugger

Unless you count the menu bar and any open toolbars, which are also docking windows, most of the time you'll see only two docking windows in Visual C++: the Workspace and Output windows. I usually like to keep the Workspace window open, but I sometimes close it to free up more space. I prefer to hide the Output window most of the time. It reappears automatically if you start a build, search, or some other action that sends its output to that window. The Workspace and Output buttons on the Standard toolbar (Figure 1-13) are handy for managing both windows.

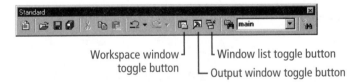

Figure 1-13. *The Workspace, Output, and Window list buttons on the Standard toolbar.*

Docking windows in the debugger

If you run your program in the debugger, you'll encounter several other docking windows: Watch, Call Stack, Memory, Variables, Registers, and Disassembly. I'll cover the use of those windows in Chapter 13. For now, just be aware that manipulating the windows themselves is very much like manipulating the nondebug docking windows.

Context menus in docking windows

The context or shortcut menus you get by right-clicking in a window vary widely from one docking window to another. The menus also vary based on which object you click inside the window. For example, on the ClassView tab in the Workspace window the menu changes as you click a class name, a class member name, the topmost title of the class list, or empty space within the window. Try it. You'll see differences in the other windows too, so experiment.

Managing docking windows

Unlike document windows, you don't manage docking windows from the Window menu or the File menu. Instead, you use the View menu's commands to open the Workspace or Output window or any of the docking windows in the debugger. The debugger windows open from the Debug Windows command on the View menu. Click a docking window's Close button to close the window.

You can also open and close any of the docking windows from toolbars. The Standard toolbar contains Workspace and Output buttons. The Debug toolbar contains buttons for the debug windows.

Toolbars and Menus

Visual C++ also uses menus and toolbars extensively. Instead of describing the menus or toolbars in detail here, I'll introduce them as they come up in the chapters ahead. The following general comments will suffice for now.

- To display a Visual C++ toolbar, right-click anywhere in the toolbar area below the menu bar—but not in a toolbar that's already open. On the context menu that pops up, click the toolbar whose visibility you want to toggle on. Close toolbars in the same way. You'll probably always want the Standard toolbar on display, along with WizardBar. The Build toolbar is also handy. Many of the other toolbars, such as the Debug toolbar, come and go as needed.

■ You can customize toolbars and menus by adding, removing, and moving command buttons. Click Customize on the Tools menu, then click the Commands tab for menu commands, or the Toolbars tab for toolbars. Try it. Check the Help index for *customizing* and double-click "toolbar buttons" and "toolbars." You can also create new toolbars of your own; these can contain existing commands or buttons for commands that you create yourself by writing VBScript macros or by recording sequences of actions in Visual C++. I'll say just a bit more about macros near the end of the chapter, under "Tips and Tricks."

■ The menu bar and the toolbars are dockable windows, so you can dock them to any side of the main Visual C++ window or float them in the center. Try it.

Searching in Visual C++

Visual C++ provides versatile search tools, both for searching the contents of open files and for searching files on disk. In addition to commands on the Edit menu, Visual C++ puts the following search-related controls on the Standard toolbar (Figure 1-14):

■ A Search button (binoculars with a question mark). This button opens the Search tab in Visual C++ Help. It's for finding information rather than text strings in your files.

■ A Find drop-down list. This is a shortcut for the Find command on the Edit menu.

■ A Find In Files button (binoculars and a folder). This is a powerful disk-file search tool. See the Appendix for a description and an example.

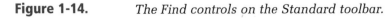

Figure 1-14.   *The Find controls on the Standard toolbar.*

Search and Replace

To do a standard search or replace operation in the current source code file, select Find or Replace on the Edit menu. Use Find to search the file for a particular text string. Use Replace to find occurrences of a string and replace them with another string.

Both Find and Replace allow you to customize the search in various ways:

- You can match only whole words—*thin* matches *thin* but not *think*.

- You can require that cases match—*back* matches *back* and *backed* but not *Back* or *BACK*. Otherwise, *back* matches both *Back* and *BACK*.

- You can use regular expressions like those used with Unix-style Grep command. The Find and Replace dialog boxes give extensive assistance in formulating regular expressions.

- You can limit searches to the selected text or search the whole file.

- You can use the Find command option, Mark All, to put a bookmark on each found instance in the file. This lets you examine each find later by stepping through the bookmarks. I'll discuss bookmarks shortly.

TIP Before you give either a Find or Replace command, you can click in a text string in your source code file. The string appears in the Find What box when you open either the Find or Replace dialog box.

The Find Drop-Down List Control

The Find drop-down list on the Standard toolbar is a handy shortcut to search the current file. Just click the control, type the string you'd like to find in the drop-down box, and press the Enter key. Try it. Like the Find What and Replace With boxes in the Find and Replace dialog boxes, the drop-down list in the Find control stores all recent searches, even across Visual C++ sessions. To search for a string you recently searched for, open the drop-down list box and click the desired string.

The Find In Files Command

The Find In Files command, found either on the Standard toolbar or on the Edit menu, is a powerful search facility that can search files on disk as well as files that are currently open. This command is like the well-known Grep command available on Unix and MS-DOS-based systems. I cover the Find In Files command in some detail in the Appendix.

Bookmarking in Source Code Files

Especially in large programs, you'll often find yourself working with code in several files and in several locations within a file. It's sometimes handy to *bookmark* these locations so you can find them later.

- To bookmark a spot in a source code file, click the spot you want to bookmark. Click Bookmarks on the Edit menu. In the Bookmark dialog box, type a name for the bookmark—make it something you'll remember later. Then click Add and close the dialog.

- To find a bookmark later, click Go To on the Edit menu. In the Go To dialog box, click Bookmark in the Go To What box. Then either type a bookmark name in the Enter Bookmark Name box, or click the drop-down list arrow to display all of the bookmarks. Click the one you want, and then click Go To.

- To remove a bookmark, select it and click Delete in the Bookmark dialog box.

Bookmarks in code files are similar to Favorites in Help, but the two are completely separate systems.

Microsoft on the Web and MSDN Online

Visual C++ comes to you on a set of compact discs. However, in addition to what's on those discs, you can use the *Internet* to access a wealth of information, product news, answers to frequently asked questions (FAQs), online support, Web information, and free downloads. In addition to the MSDN library and Visual C++'s Help system, there's more at Microsoft's Web site, reached by way of MSDN Online. Some of it is free, and some requires a subscription fee. I'll discuss these online services more in Chapter 21, but here are your routes to them:

- In Visual C++, click the Microsoft On The Web command on the Help menu.

- You can access Internet addresses from the URL command on the Visual C++ Introductory Edition Go menu.

Microsoft On The Web lets you access additional extensive documentation, including numerous technical articles and a number of books, such as *The Windows Interface Guidelines for Software Design* and *Inside OLE*. On the Visual C++ Help menu, select Microsoft On The Web and then MSDN Online. After your browser connects to the MSDN Online website, follow the link in the left-hand pane to MSDN Library Online. On that web page, you can explore the MSDN Library contents by expanding topic headings, or you can search for specific text strings. Also note the Advanced search button.

Tips and Tricks

To close out this chapter, I'll pass along a few tips for using Visual C++ that you should know about before we really get to work.

- Use the Advanced command on the Edit menu. This command opens a hierarchical menu with several useful commands. To learn more about these commands, check the Help index for *untabify command*, which opens the topic "How Do I Replace Tabs With Spaces?" Near the top of that topic, click the link to FAQ. Explore the links in the topic "Frequently Asked Questions: Text Editor."

- Use the new *IntelliSense* options. As in applications like Microsoft Word and Microsoft Excel, Visual C++ includes IntelliSense, or autocomplete, technology that completes parameter lists, provides type information, helps you select the right class member to invoke, and more. You can either use IntelliSense in automatic mode— IntelliSense tries to anticipate where you're going as you type—or you can control how IntelliSense works for you via the Editor tab in the Options dialog box (Tools menu). If you choose to turn off the automatic functioning of IntelliSense, you can still get its functionality via the following commands on the Edit menu: List Members, Type Info, Parameter Info, and Complete Word. Check the Help index for *IntelliSense* and choose the "About Automatic Statement Completion" topic.

■ Use the *Gallery* to insert prefabricated *components* into your program. You can add Microsoft ActiveX controls (provided you've selected the right option in the AppWizard tool) or other Visual C++ components. For example, you can add the Microsoft FlexGrid (MSFlexGrid) ActiveX control and use it in one of your windows or dialog boxes to manage tabular data. Or you can add system information to your program's About dialog box—this option lets your users examine information about their systems from the About dialog box, all with minimal coding on your part. I'll illustrate this using the Gallery later in the book. Meanwhile, you can check the Help index for *gallery*, double-click "Gallery" (capitalized), and choose the topic "Reusing Code: Overview."

■ Customize your working environment in Visual C++ with your own macros written in the VBScript macro language. Macros are small routines that do useful things in the environment, such as automating complex or repetitive sequences of commands. There are two ways to create them. First, you can simply record a sequence of commands. The recorded commands form a named macro that you can then associate with a menu command, toolbar button, or key combination. When you give the command, you run the macro. Second, you can create a macro file (via the New dialog box on the File menu) and write your own code in the VBScript macro language. For information about macros, including recorded macros, check the Help index for *macro*, double-click it, and choose the topic "Overview: Macros." Several books are available about the VBScript, or Visual Basic, Scripting Edition, language.

Try It Yourself

Here are your first extra-credit exercises. See what you can do.

1. Spend some time trying things in the Visual C++ menus.

I haven't covered all of the menus, so it's well worth your while to see what they do. Of course, some will require that special conditions exist before they can be used. By the end of the book, we'll have used and discussed nearly all of the menu commands.

2. Take the time to browse the Visual C++ documentation.

Use the Contents tab in the Help window to become familiar with the overall layout and contents of the Visual C++ documentation. The more familiar it is, the easier it will be to locate the answers to your questions. In particular, on the Contents tab, go to Welcome To The Visual C++ 6.0 Introductory Edition and check out the topics under Visual C++ Documentation Map.

What's Next?

Now that you have a pretty good idea about using the features of the Visual C++ environment, or IDE, it's time to start programming.

- If you don't know the C++ language yet, read Chapters 2 through 5. Those chapters contain numerous C++ programming exercises.

- If you do know C++, you might want to skim Chapters 2 through 5, then dig into Chapter 6 on Windows programming and Chapters 7 and 8 on programming with the MFC library. If you're already a Windows veteran, you can skim Chapter 6. Chapter 7 starts the MFC sequence, which spans the rest of the book.

C++ Basics

This chapter covers the most commonly used elements of the C++ programming language. Chapter 3 continues the story by covering C++ pointers, references, header files, and scope. In Chapters 4 and 5, we get into C++ classes and object-oriented programming. You'll need all of this when you move on to programming for Microsoft Windows with the Microsoft Foundation Class Library 6.0 (MFC) in Part 2.

I make an important assumption here: that you have done at least some programming—preferably in C, but possibly in Basic, Pascal, or some other procedural programming language. I don't expect a great deal—just that you understand a few essential concepts, including the basic flow of control in a program, looping and branching structures, functions (also known as procedures or subroutines), parameters, basic data types, input and output, and compiling a program. If you're puzzled by any of those terms, I strongly recommend that you take a beginning programming course or study a beginning programming text before you jump into C++, Windows, MFC, and this book. The water really is too deep for non-swimmers.

C++ is a complex programming language, many of whose elements are arcane and abstract. It's also a big language, designed and intended for professional use, and that means I can't possibly present more than the basics here. The emphasis in this book is on using Visual C++ for its primary purpose, which is programming Windows, using MFC. I'll be as clear and practical as possible, but I'm sure you'll want to supplement this introductory course with deeper study of C++.

MFC is an *application framework* constructed out of the raw materials of C++, primarily classes. MFC provides, in essence, a working Windows application—a framework into which you can fit your own code to define what this application does. The framework supplies much of the look of Windows—things such as menus, toolbars, dialog boxes, controls, and scroll bars. It also supplies mechanisms that make things like saving your data to a file or printing it relatively easy. The framework's parts are C++ classes that represent application components, such as the application's main window, its dialog boxes, character strings, graphical objects like rectangles and points, and even the application itself, as objects. So, in order to use Visual C++ for its primary purpose, you need to know enough C++ to work within MFC.

We're fortunate that the developers of MFC stuck with a solid core of C++ fundamentals—features that aren't prone to problems. For the good of all, they have avoided some of the more challenging C++ features and techniques, such as multiple inheritance. Still, you need a good grasp of the fundamentals if you're to understand how MFC is written and how it works, and especially if you're going to program with MFC. One resource that many of the MFC developers rely on is the *C++ Primer,* 3rd edition, by Stanley B. Lippman and Josee Lajoie, (Addison-Wesley 1998), but there are many other suitable books. If you become really serious about C++, you'll also want *The Annotated C++ Reference Manual* (affectionately known as the "ARM") by Margaret A. Ellis and Bjarne Stroustrup (Addison-Wesley 1990). Stroustrup is the original architect of C++ and chairs the American National Standards Institute (ANSI) committee on C++ language extensions.

The most important thing you'll get from this book is a good grasp of C++ classes, along with the object-oriented design and programming concepts that underlie classes. Along the way, though, we'll look at a good many elements of C++ syntax and usage. Where there's more to the story than I have room to tell, I'll point you to appropriate topics in the Visual C++ documentation. And at the end of Chapter 5, I'll tell you which elements I'm intentionally excluding. You can do your postgraduate work on them later.

Hello in C++

Let's begin traditionally and practically, by writing a small C++ program—a slightly souped-up version of the infamous "Hello, World!" program that kicks off most efforts to learn a new programming language. This will be a bit more complicated than the program First, which we created in Chapter 1, because Hello is designed to illustrate a number of C++ fundamentals.

Creating the Program

Follow along as I take you on a tour through the basics of C++.

Try it now

First, in Visual C++, take the steps described in the next five sections to write and save your code.

Creating a new project

Create a new Win32 Console Application named Hello. (The process is much like the one you followed in Chapter 1.) On the File menu, open the New dialog box. On the Projects tab, specify the options shown in Table 2-1. Use the location box to choose a directory to place your application in. Then click OK, which opens AppWizard. The AppWizard dialog title will be Win32 Console Application, because that is the type of application we are developing.

Option	Setting
Project Type	Win32 Console Application
Project Name	Hello
Create New Workspace	Selected
Platforms	Win32 checkmarked

Table 2-1. *Options to set on the Projects tab of the New dialog box.*

Using AppWizard to specify project options and generate files

1. In AppWizard, click the option A Simple Application. (Refer to Figure 1-5.)

2. Click Finish to open the New Project Information dialog box. Examine what the wizard is creating for you, then click OK.

The program's *main* function is in the file Hello.cpp. The project is also set up for *precompiled headers* in the files Stdafx.h and Stdafx.cpp. (I'll describe precompiled headers in Chapter 3.)

Opening the Hello.cpp file for editing

1. In the Workspace window, click the FileView tab. Figure 2-1 shows Visual C++ with the Workspace window open and the next three steps already completed.

2. Click the plus sign (+) in front of Hello Files.

3. Click the plus sign in front of the Source Files folder.

4. Double-click the Hello.cpp file icon to open the file. Figure 2-1 shows Hello.cpp open for editing in the Source Code editor window at the right of the Workspace window.

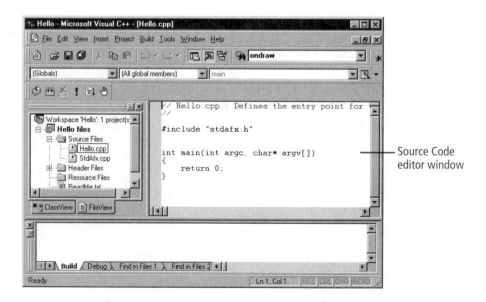

Figure 2-1.   *The file Hello.cpp open for editing.*

Adding code to the Hello.cpp file

Type the boldface lines shown in the following program listing into the Hello.cpp code—and don't forget the semicolon (;) at the end of most lines:

```cpp
// Hello.cpp : Defines the entry point for the console application.
//

#include "stdafx.h"
#include <iostream.h>

// Function prototypes
bool SayHello(char* szTo, int nCalc);
void SayGoodbye();

// Constants
#define NUMERO_UNO 1
const char* OLD_FRIEND = "old friend, for now. ";

int main(int argc, char* argv[])
{
    char* szCpp = "C++!";  // Declare a variable

    // Call a function with a Boolean result.
    if(SayHello(szCpp, 2))
    {
        // Call a function with no result.
        SayGoodbye();
    }
    return 0;
}


/////////////////////////////////////
// Global function definitions

// SayHello takes two parameters and returns a result.
bool SayHello(char* szTo, int nCalc)
{
    // Use an iostream object for output.
    cout << "Hello, " << szTo << " You're Number " << NUMERO_UNO
        << ".\n";
    return (nCalc + (nCalc * 2)) < (24/nCalc);
}

// SayGoodbye takes no parameters and returns no result.
void SayGoodbye()
{
    cout << "Bye, " << OLD_FRIEND << endl;
}
```

Saving your work

Click the Save command on the File menu to save your work.

TIP When you build your program, Visual C++ automatically saves any un-
saved files.

Building and Running the Program

Next you need to compile or build the program, and run it. I described
compiling and building in Chapter 1. Correct any build errors you encounter. Figure 2-2 shows the output of the Hello program just after it
has run.

Figure 2-2. *Output of the Hello application.*

The C++ in Hello

The Hello application is very simple, but it introduces the following elements of C++:

■ C++ comments

■ Preprocessor directives used to include header files and libraries

■ C++ constants

■ C++ keywords

- Literals

- Statements

- Variables and data types

- Strings

- Allocating memory for variables

- Functions and parameters

- Function prototypes

- Returning a result from a function

- The C/C++ run-time library

- The *main* function

- Expressions and operators

- C++ control statements

- C++ input/output via iostreams

That's quite a bit of territory to describe, so let's get started.

C++ Comments

The Hello program contains several *comments.* C++ uses two forward slashes (//) to begin a comment line:

```
// This is a comment in C++
```

Everything on the same line after the two slashes is part of the comment. If you want to extend a comment to more than one line, each line should begin with the comment slashes. You can also start a comment after a C++ statement, like this:

```
char* szCpp = "C++!";   // Declare a variable
```

You can also use C-style comment delimiters:

```
/* comment
   on two lines */
```

Unlike the C++-style comments, these can extend over multiple lines. For an excellent guide to commenting styles and thousands of other things any programmer should know, I recommend Steve McConnell, *Code Complete: A Practical Handbook of Software Construction* (Microsoft Press, 1993).

Preprocessor Directives

Following the comment at the beginning of program Hello is an *#include* directive. Like the C language, C++ uses a *preprocessor*. The preprocessor is a program that runs before the compiler. It looks for *preprocessor directives* such as

```
#include <iostream.h>
#define NUMERO_UNO 1
```

The preprocessor replaces an *#include* directive with the entire contents of the file named after the directive. In Hello, two files are included, Stdafx.h and iostream.h. I'll say more about the contents of iostream.h shortly. The purpose of including a file is to allow you to use the functions, classes, variables, and other code elements defined there. The wizard adds an *#include* directive for Stdafx.h as a convenience—there is nothing of any importance in that file. It's provided in case you want to include any of the MFC code.

> **TIP** I recommend that if you're going to use MFC you use the MFC AppWizard (.exe) option in the New dialog box rather than create a console application, which runs in an MS-DOS window. Some applications do make sense as console applications, even with MFC, but MFC is primarily for writing Windows applications, and that's the focus of this book. Leaving the *#include* in place for Stdafx.h hurts nothing, though, so we'll simply ignore it.

The angle brackets around the filename iostream.h indicate that it's a file that comes with your Visual C++ system. The preprocessor knows where to look for such files. Hello also shows an *#include* directive that encloses a filename with double quotes. They tell the preprocessor that the file is part of your program. The preprocessor looks first in the current directory, and then it looks in a path that you can define in Visual C++ using the Directories tab in the Options dialog box. You open the Options dialog box with the Options command on the Tools menu.

Each preprocessor directive always appears on a line by itself, starting at the far left margin, and unlike a C++ statements, it doesn't end with a semicolon. I'll explain *#define* directives in the next section.

C++ Constants

A *#define* directive tells the preprocessor to replace a symbol with its value everywhere in the program file. Here, the symbol is *NUMERO_UNO*, and the value is 1:

```
#define NUMERO_UNO 1        //#define symbol value
```

A *#define* directive lets you define a meaningful name so that your code isn't full of cryptic numbers. This makes your code more readable. You can also define a constant in one place, so that if you must change it later, you don't have to search the whole program for multiple instances of that constant.

But C++ also provides a better way to declare constants, the *const* declaration. Here are some examples:

```
const int NUMERO_UNO = 1;
const char* OLD_FRIEND = "old friend, for now.";
```

The *const* approach is usually better than *#define* because it is *type-safe*. C++ checks to ensure that the data with which the symbol is initialized is consistent with the type declared after the *const* keyword. You should normally use *const* rather than *#define* unless you're creating a C++ *preprocessor macro*, an advanced topic that this book doesn't cover. (For an introduction to macros, check the Help index for *preprocessor,* and choose the subtopic "macros.") C/C++ language macros are not to be confused with the VBScript macros that you can write in Visual C++ to automate common tasks. (Check the Help index for *macro.*)

The *const* keyword has many uses in C++. Besides declaring constants with it, you can cause function parameters and function results to be read-only values, thereby protecting them from unwanted alteration. I'll give you a few pointers about the *const* keyword in "Passing a *const* Pointer," in Chapter 3. You can also check the Help index for *const* and choose the topic "const" in the Visual C++ Programmer's Guide.

You'll encounter other preprocessor directives later in the book. Meanwhile, to learn more about the preprocessor, check the Help index for *preprocessor,* and choose the subtopic "overview" and also the subtopic "directives."

OTE   C++ is *case sensitive*—in other words, the identifier BIG is *not* the same as Big or big. Capitalizing constant names is just a convention that many programmers use.

C++ Keywords

C++ reserves a number of identifiers for its own use. For example, *for*, *if*, and *int* are *keywords*. You can't use the keywords as names for variables, functions, and so on. For a list of standard C++ keywords and a list of Microsoft-specific additional keywords, check the Help index for *keywords* and choose the subtopic "C and C++ list."

Literals

Literals are values in a program, some examples of which are shown in Table 2-2. Literals are constants, and although they're stored in memory, you can't access their addresses. Every literal is of some type, such as *int*, *double*, or *char**. (The asterisk means "pointer to," so *char** means "pointer to char.") Integer literals are treated as signed *int* values. You can specify literals of particular integer types using notations like the following (see the section "Variables and Data Types" for more about C++ *types*):

- **1L or 1l**   a long integer (read as "one-ell")
- **1U or 1u**   an unsigned integer
- **1UL or 1ul**   an unsigned long integer
- **c**   where *c* is any literal character of type *char*

You can also represent nonprintable characters in C++:

- **\n**   newline
- **\t**   horizontal tab

- **\v**   vertical tab
- **\b**   backspace
- **\r**   carriage return
- ****   backslash
- **\'**   single quote
- **\"**   double quote

Literal	Description
1	Decimal number
3.1415	Decimal floating point number
5E2 or 5e2	Decimal number in scientific notation
0x14	Hexadecimal number, base 16 (= 20 decimal)
077	Octal number, base 8 (= 63 decimal)
"Windows! Windows! Windows!"	String literal

Table 2-2.   *Common literal constants in C++.*

Statements

A C++ *statement* is a single declaration, command, or computation ending with a semicolon. Preprocessor directives are not statements as such. Here are three examples of statements, all taken from the Hello application:

```
const char* OLD_FRIEND = "old friend, for now. ";

char* szCpp = "C++!";

if(SayHello(szCpp, 2))
{
    SayGoodbye();
}
```

The first statement declares and initializes a constant called *OLD_FRIEND*. The second statement declares and initializes a variable called *szCpp*. The final statement is an *if* statement, one of several C++

statements that control program flow; if the condition in parentheses evaluates to true, the next statement, a function call, is executed.

A *compound* statement is a group of two or more statements combined in one larger statement. For example, the three statements contained within curly braces after the *while* statement here:

```
while(bCond)
{
    x = GetRecords();
    y = ProcessData();
    bCond = x < y;
}
```

Variables and Data Types

A *variable* is a named location in memory, a place for a program to store information. Given effective symbolic names, variables help you model the problem you're solving. Variable names—like any *identifiers* (names) in C++—can be of any length and can include any alphabetic or numeric character and the underscore.

> **NOTE** Global variables and local variables declared *static* are guaranteed to be initialized to 0 (zero). Other C++ variables, including nonstatic local variables and class data members, aren't automatically initialized. Until you initialize such variables, their content is undefined (read "garbage").

Hello uses one variable, called *szCpp*. We declare and initialize *szCpp* at the same time, like this:

```
char* szCpp = "C++!";
```

The most important thing about a variable is its *type*. The type of *szCpp* is *char** (character string). In addition to the standard types described in Table 2-3, C++ gives you several ways to create types of your own, as shown in Table 2-4. This is a very powerful capability, and C++ takes it about as far as it can go.

Check the Help index for *integral types,* and choose the subtopic "table of." Table 2-4 in that Help topic describes the sizes of these types as implemented in Visual C++. (You can also build and run the Sizes program in the \learnvcn\Chap02 folder in the companion code. The Sizes program lists common variable sizes using the *sizeof* operator.)

Type	Description
int, long, short *int n;* *long l;* *short s;*	Integer data types. In Visual C++, *int* and *long* variables are 4 bytes, and *short* variables are 2 bytes.
char *char c;* *char* string;*	Technically also a 1-byte integer type, *char* holds character data. The contents of a *char* variable is a numeric ASCII code for the character it represents. A *char* variable can hold negative and positive values ranging from −128 to +127. Check the Help index for *ASCII character codes*.
bool *bool b;*	Also an integer type, but acts as a Boolean value. Possible values: *true* or a nonzero value, *false* or 0 (zero). In MFC, you can also use *TRUE* and *FALSE*.
float, double, long double *float f;* *double d;* *long double ld;*	Floating-point numbers—numbers with a fractional part. The floating-point variations have different precisions (numbers of significant digits after the decimal point). In Visual C++, *float* is 4 bytes, and *double* and *long double* are 8 bytes.

Table 2-3.   *Fundamental C++ data types.*

The size of a type is measured in bytes and tells you the range of numbers or characters the type can hold. Types marked with the *unsigned* qualifier hold only 0 or positive values:

```
unsigned int n;    // Range: 0 through INT_MAX
```

Types marked with the *signed* qualifier can hold negative numbers, 0, or positive numbers. (Because they represent negative as well as positive numbers, signed types represent a smaller range of positive numbers.) The integer types, including *char*, are signed by default and aren't necessarily marked by the *signed* qualifier.

> **TIP** A *portable* program is one that can be adjusted or translated so it can run in another environment, such as a different operating system or machine. If you want your code to be portable, it shouldn't rely on the size of these types. Instead, treat an *int* as an *int*, without basing anything in your code on whether *int* is 2 bytes, 4 bytes, or something else.

Type	Description

enum
 	
``
enum Color
{
    Red   // 0 by default
    White   // 1, etc.
    Blue = 25 // Can specify
};
``
	Enumerated type. In C++, *enums* are real type specifiers. An *enum* such as *Color*, in the left column, gives you a way to specify sets of related constants, such as colors, days of the week, etc. In your code, you can use the *enum's* members by name:
	``
	Color MyColor=Blue;
	SetColor(Red);
	if(MyColor == Blue)...
	``

struct
 	
``
struct Student
{
    char* szName;
    char* arcCourses[];
    int nAge;
};
``
	In C++, a *struct*, or structure, is a full-fledged data type. Structures in C++ have much in common with *classes*—see the discussion in Chapter 4 under classes. Use type *Student* like this:
	``
	Student currStudent;
	Student* GetStudent(int nIndex);
	int age = currStudent.nAge;
	``

typedef
 	
``
typedef double salary;
typedef char* string;
salary mySalary; // Salary variable
string szName;   // String variable
``
	Create your own names for existing types—a *typedef* declaration creates a synonym for an existing type. *Typedefs* make your code more readable.

pointer	See "Pointers" in Chapter 3.
reference	See "References" in Chapter 3.
class	See "The C++ in Program Shape2" in Chapter 4.
array	See "Arrays" later in this chapter.
character string	See "Strings" in this chapter and "Pointers and Strings" in Chapter 3.

Table 2-4.   *Additional types and type creation mechanisms in C++.*

Variable naming conventions

Windows programmers have largely adopted the practice of naming variables using *Hungarian notation* (so named because its originator, Microsoft developer Charles Simonyi, is Hungarian). The idea behind Hungarian notation is to make the variable's data type part of its name, as you can see from the following examples:

- **pInt**, a pointer to *int*
- **bDone**, a Boolean value
- **nCount**, an integer value

Prefixing an abbreviated code for the data type might be a bit distracting at first, but it pays off in fewer errors and greater clarity, both for readers of the code and for the programmer. Table 2-5 shows some of the most common Hungarian prefixes.

Hungarian Prefix	Data Type
b	*bool* or *BOOL* (Boolean)
by	*BYTE* (unsigned char)
c or *ch*	*char*
d or *dbl*	*double*
f or *fl*	*float*
fn	*function*
L or *l*	*long*
n or *i*	*int*
p	pointer
sz	zero-delimited string (C or C++-style string with a Null character at the end)
str	MFC *CString* object
ar	array
pt	point (used in geometry)
rect	rectangle
wnd	window

Table 2-5. *Common Hungarian prefixes for naming variables.*

Arrays

You should already be familiar with the concept of an *array*, a variable that can contain multiple elements of a stated type. Although C++ arrays are like those in C, with which you may be familiar, I'll briefly cover the rules and syntax of arrays here.

Declare an array with this notation:

```
int arInts[10];    // Basetype Arrayname[dimension];
```

The type specified here is the *base type* of the array—the type of each of its elements. The array's name is *arInts* (note the Hungarian name I've used), and it is *dimensioned* to contain 10 *int* elements. Note that C++ array indexes always start at 0 (zero). It's a common error to index an array in a *for* loop starting at 1. The result is that you begin with the second element in the array and then try to access a nonexistent array element beyond the end of the array. This usually leads to erroneous performance; it's the programmer's responsibility to avoid this error.

You can initialize an array like this:

```
int arInts[5] = {0, 1, 2, 3, 4};
```

Or like this:

```
int arInts[5];
for(int i = 0; i < 5; i++)
{
    arInts[i] = i;
}
```

You can set or get individual elements of an array by using the array subscript operator []. The *for*-loop example just above shows how to set an element. Here's an example of getting an element:

```
int arInts[5];
int count = 3;
int n = arInts[count];    // Or int n = arInts[3];
```

You can declare an array to contain any C++ data type except references. Thus you could have an array of *char*, an array of *double*, an array of *float*, an array of *long*, an array of *struct*, an array of some user-defined class type, an array of pointers, and so on. An array of *char* is also known as a character string. (See the next section.) As you'll see later, array notation and pointer notation are equivalent.

You can create arrays of one or multiple dimensions to contain any data type (except a reference). Here are several illustrations of one and two-dimensional array declarations and array accesses:

```
char arcGrades[25];
int ariChessBoard[8][8]
arcGrades[3] = 'A';
ariChessBoard[3][4] = currPiece;
currPiece = ariChessBoard[7][7];
```

The first two lines declare arrays of one and two dimensions, respectively. The first line represents a column of student grades. The second line represents the squares on a chessboard. To specify the dimensions of a two-dimensional array—such as the chessboard—enclose each dimension in square brackets. Similarly, to access a given array element, specify both dimensions, each in a separate set of square brackets, as shown in the last two lines of code above.

Strings

In C++, as in C, a *string* is a variable of type *char**—a pointer to *char*. But there are really two ways to look at strings:

■ As a pointer to *char*:

```
char* sz = " Strings ";
```

■ As an array of *char*:

```
char sz[] = " Strings ";
// or
char sz[] = {'S', 't', 'r', 'i', 'n', 'g', 's'};
```

Happily, the two views of a string, and the two notations—pointer and array—are entirely equivalent. You can declare a string either way. And you can use either notation to access characters in the string, regardless of how the string was declared. I'll illustrate this with examples in the section "Pointers and Strings" in Chapter 3.

C++ strings, like C strings, are called *zero-terminated*, or *null-terminated*, strings. That is, if we declare the string

```
char* szCpp = "C++!";
```

the string *sz* has four characters, and the *strlen* function (from the C/C++ run-time library—check the Help index for *strlen*) will return 4 for the string's length. But when storage for the string is allocated, not four but five characters are allocated. The last one is a marker for the end of the string, and is filled with the ASCII Null character, ASCII zero, symbolized in C++ by \0. Figure 2-3 shows this configuration.

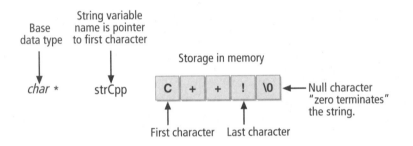

Figure 2-3.   *Structure of a C++ string.*

Zero termination makes C++ strings a little easier to work with than they might otherwise be, but they're still pretty cumbersome. So when we get to MFC, you'll be happy to find class *CString*. (Most C++ class libraries, like MFC, contain a string class.) *CString* defines a *string* object, and using *CString* is about as easy as handling strings in Basic. The *CString* object does lots of the extra work for you, so you can do things like this (and much more):

```
CString str1 = "Strings";
CString str2 = " are easy in ";
CString str3 = "MFC.";
CString str4 = str1 + str2 + str3; // String concatenation
cout << str4 << endl;

// Prints "Strings are easy in MFC."
```

You won't be able to use *CString* outside of MFC, however. It's too tightly interwoven with the rest of the MFC library.

Type conversion and casting

The Hello application doesn't illustrate type conversion, but the topic is related to types and variables, so this is a good place to describe it.

C++ is a strongly typed language. The compiler does extensive type checking to ensure that correct types and numbers of parameters are passed to functions and that dangerous errors are avoided. If possible, the compiler automatically converts the value passed to the type expected. If that's not possible, the compiler reports a compile error. In this regard, C++ is much stricter than C, but this strictness helps you write more reliable code.

Sometimes a statement mixes values of more than one type, perhaps *int* and *long*, or *int* and *char*, as in the third statement below:

```
int n = 3;
char c = 'b';      // ASCII code 66
int n2 = n + c;    // Mixed arithmetic
```

Or a function might require a parameter or return a result of a type other than what you need. Two things can occur in these situations:

- Like C, C++ makes some type conversions for you automatically—but usually not without telling you.

- You can also make type conversions explicitly, using a technique called *casting*.

When C++ makes automatic type conversions, it converts the narrower type (in bytes), such as a 1-byte *char*, to match the wider type, such as a 4-byte *int*. Then it carries out the operation using the widened type. (The conversion doesn't change the actual variable in memory.) Note that automatic type conversions are always *promotions* from a narrower type to a wider type. These result in no data loss. Converting from a wider type to a narrower type can cause loss of data or precision.

There are two notations for making an explicit type conversion, or cast:

- *(int)value* Changes value to an *int*.

- *int(value)* Also changes value to an *int*.

The first notation here is the older, C-style cast. In its effect it's equivalent to the second notation, the newer C++-style cast, but C++ can only type check the newer version, not the older. When you make an older C-style cast, you're overriding the automatic conversion mechanism. The ability to check types, therefore, makes the newer notation preferable. You're likely to see both notations in the MFC source code files and other C++ code you read. I'll use both as well.

 OTE   Technically, the notation *int(value)* constructs an *int* object whose value is set to *value*. This isn't really a cast, but it has the same effect as a cast.

ARNING   In making your own explicit type casts with either notation, there's a real danger of trying to perform a narrowing conversion—from a wider type to a narrower type. This kind of conversion can cause data loss. See the following discussion.

Explicit type casts can be dangerous, so be careful.

Here's an example of passing to a function an actual parameter that's wider than the what the formal parameter calls for:

```
void func(float f)
{
    cout "f = " << f << endl;  // Prints f = 1.98765 in call below
}
// Call func:
double d = 1.98765432
func(d);    // Pass a double value to a float parameter
```

The function prints *f = 1.98765*. Several digits of the fractional part are lost in converting from the wider *double* type to the narrower *float* type. Unless this is what you intend, it's a problem.

 OTE   C++ assumes all floating point numbers are of type *double* unless you specify otherwise. So 3., 3.95, and 3.0 are all *double*. You can force them to be *float* instead with notation like this: 3.f, 3.95f, and 3.0f.

You can at least be alerted to such conversion problems by setting the *warning level* for your build to Level 2 or higher. On the Visual C++

Project menu, select Settings. In the Settings dialog box, click the C/C++ tab. In the Category box, select General. In the Warning Level box, select Level 2, Level 3, or Level 4. When you build again, dangerous conversions will generate warning messages. The higher the warning level, the stricter the results—Level 4 is downright annoying.

There will be times when you must use an explicit cast. Be cautious when you do, apply the newer C++ style of cast notation, and use the warning level mechanism to check yourself.

C++ also provides four special cast operators: *dynamic_cast*, *static_cast*, *const_cast*, and *reinterpret_cast*. Although these are now the recommended way to cast, their usage is somewhat advanced, so I won't discuss them here. Check the Help index for *casting operators* (some of the operators will make more sense by the time you've read Chapter 5). MFC defines additional casting operators; check the Help index for *casting types*.

Allocating Memory for Variables

Although Hello involves only a little memory allocation, I should say a bit about the two main ways to allocate memory for your variables in C++.

Hello allocates memory for the string variable *szCpp*. To be specific, it allocates 5 bytes—one for each character in the string "C++!" and 1 additional byte for the terminating null character. Where is this chunk of storage? Each running program has two pools of memory available for any storage it needs: the *stack* and the *heap*.

On the stack

The stack is a temporary storage area that the system uses—a scratch pad or short-term memory, really. The stack is like a stack of cafeteria trays. Each new tray you add (or push) goes on top, and if you take a tray off the stack (otherwise known as *popping*), you take it from the top. Stacks are last in, first out (LIFO) data structures. The last item pushed is the first item popped.

C++ uses the stack mainly for function calls. As a function is called, various items are pushed onto the top of the stack: a return address for when the function ends, any parameters that were passed to the function, the result returned by the function—even local variables declared in the function go on the stack. So as function *A* calls function *B*, which calls function *C*, the stack grows. As each of the functions returns—*C*, and then *B*, and then *A*—the items on the stack belonging to that function are removed. The stack shrinks.

To allocate memory on the stack, declare local variables as in these examples:

```
void MyFunction()
{
    char* szCpp = "C++!";        // String
    int nInt;                    // Integer
    double dSalary = 80000.0;    // Double
    MyClass arMyC[10];           // Array of objects
    MyClass* arMyC2[10];         // Array of pointers
    }
```

Local variables are automatically cleared from the stack (in ancient C lingo, these are called *automatic*, or *auto*, variables). That is, when the function returns, these variables are said to *go out of scope*, meaning they no longer exist.

The variable *szCpp* is a special case. It's a *pointer* variable (I'll cover pointers in detail in Chapter 3. For now, just be aware that a pointer is a variable that contains the *memory address* of another variable—it *points* to another location in memory, and you can use the pointer variable to examine or change the value it points to.) The pointer variable *szCpp* is indeed stored on the stack, but the data it points to—the characters of the literal string—are stored elsewhere, in a data segment of the program The variables *arMyC* and *arMyC2* are arrays on the stack. The first, *arMyC*, contains objects created from the C++ class *MyClass*. (We'll cover classes in Chapter 4.) The second, *arMyC2*, contains pointers to *MyClass* objects. The array itself is on the stack, but the objects that the pointers stored in the array actually point to are on the heap.

N | **OTE**   The stack is often called the *stack frame* or just the *frame* in Visual C++ documentation.

On the heap

The heap is a more permanent storage area—sort of a long-term memory. The program allocates heap storage with the C++ *new* operator. A call to *new* allocates the storage requested and returns a pointer to it. You can keep the pointer around in a variable for as long as you need it.

Unlike stack memory, you allocate heap memory explicitly—this means that you have to call *new*. You also have to delete the memory explicitly, with a call to the C++ *delete* operator. Every call to *new* must be balanced by a call to *delete*, because unlike the stack, the heap isn't automatically cleaned up. C++ has no *garbage collection* system—the process of automatically removing objects that are no longer in use. You must explicitly delete the heap objects you create.

To allocate memory on the heap, call *new*, as in these examples:

```
int* pInt = new int;         // Single integer on heap
int* arInt = new int[10];    // Array of integers on heap
int** arpInt = new int*[10]; // Array of pointers to ints
```

The *new* operator allocates enough memory for an object of the specified type and returns a pointer to the allocated memory. In the second example, *new* allocates space for 10 integers on the heap—unlike the array example in the previous section on the stack, here the array itself is an object on the heap. In Chapter 4, I'll introduce C++ classes. We'll see there that *new* is also used to allocate memory for class objects. The third example uses fairly exotic syntax to allocate not an array of *ints*, but an array of pointers to *ints*. The array stores pointers. The program arPtrs, on the next page, illustrates deallocating such an array of pointers. You might want to dog-ear the page so you can return to it after you've read more about pointers in Chapter 3.

> ![NOTE icon] OTE Besides using *new* to allocate heap memory, you can still use C/C++ run-time library functions (described later in this chapter) like *malloc*. Using *new* is preferable in C++ programs, however, and it's a bad idea to mix *new* and *malloc* calls.

Memory leaks

What happens if you fail to call *delete* for a pointer to some heap memory? You have a *memory leak*. The chunk of storage you didn't free up is like an island in the heap, taking up space after its usefulness has ended—space that you could happily reuse. If a program has enough memory leaks, it can even run out of heap memory. Check the Help index for *memory leaks*, then choose the subtopic "detecting."

To delete an array on the heap, such as the array example in the previous section, call *delete* with this notation:

```
delete [] arInt;    // Deletes space the size of 10 integers
                    // (the array itself)
```

If the array contains pointers, you first need to loop through the array, calling *delete* on each element. Only then can you call *delete* with the array notation shown above, as the program arPtrs illustrates.

Try it now

Create and build program arPtrs, using the same techniques you employed for program Hello (See Hello in C++ , earlier in this chapter):

```
// arPtrs.cpp : Defines the entry point for the console application.
//

#include "stdafx.h"
#include <iostream.h>

int main(int argc, char* argv[])
{
    int** arInt = new int*[10];        // Allocate array of pointers.
    // Fill it with pointers.
    for(int i = 0; i < 10; i++)
    {
        arInt[i] = new int;            // Allocate pointer element.
        *arInt[i] = i;                 // Initialize value pointed to.
    }

    // Print out the values of the pointers.
    //  Syntax shown prints the values.
    //  Remove the * to print the addresses stored in the array.
    for(int j = 0; j < 10; j++).
```

```
    {
        cout << *arInt[j] << ", ";
    }
    cout << endl;

    // Delete all pointers stored in array
    for(int k = 0; k < 10; k++).
    {
        delete arInt[k];      //
Delete each pointer element individually.
    }
    delete [] arInt;          // Delete array itself.

    return 0;
}
```

The first line allocates—on the heap—a pointer to an array, which contains pointers to *ints*. The first *for* loop allocates a pointer to enough memory for an *int*. The loop then assigns an integer value to each of the *ints* pointed to. The loop repeats for each element in the array. After writing out the array's contents by way of the second *for* loop, the code uses a third *for* loop to loop through the array, destroying each pointer individually. Following that loop, the program deletes the array itself: 40 bytes allocated at the beginning to hold 10 pointers.

IP If you run a program in the Visual C++ debugger, you can arrange for Visual C++ to write messages about any memory leaks in the Debug tab of the Output window when the application ends. It's good to check the Output window for messages fairly often, so you an catch memory leaks early.

Functions and Parameters

You should already be generally familiar with *functions* (or procedures or subroutines, as some languages call them). In C++ as in most languages, a function encapsulates some important action that the program takes. Functions are modular, independent chunks of code that you can call more than once from different places in the program. You can sometimes even reuse a function in other programs. The C/C++ run-time library, for example, is a collection of reusable functions, which we'll get to shortly.

Functions come in several flavors:

■ Some functions take *parameters*, and some don't. Parameters are values that you pass to the function, on which it bases its work. They make a function more general purpose by enabling it to act on a variety of input data.

■ Some functions return a *result*, and some don't. In C++ they're all called functions regardless of whether they return a result.

There are three functions in the Hello application: *SayHello*, *SayGoodbye*, and *main*. *SayHello* takes two parameters and returns a result. *SayGoodbye* does not take any parameters or return a result. *SayHello* and *SayGoodbye* are *global functions*—declared at the global level rather than, say, inside a C++ class. I'll say more about this in the section on scope in Chapter 3.

SayHello's parameter list contains two *formal parameters*. Formal parameters are placeholders, specifying for function callers the types of data to pass to the function. Each formal parameter has two parts: the parameter's *type* and its *name*—just like variable declarations:

```
bool SayHello(char* szTo, int nCalc);
```

The first parameter in *SayHello* is of type *char** (or "pointer to *char*"), and is called *szTo*. The second parameter to *SayHello* is of type *int*, and is called *nCalc*. When we call *SayHello*, we pass it the following *actual parameters* (often called the function's *arguments*): the value in *szCpp*, a *char**, for the first parameter and the integer literal 2 for the second. The call looks like this:

```
SayHello(szCpp, 2)
```

There'll be a good deal more to say about parameters after we cover pointers and references in Chapter 3. Notice that the function *main* takes two parameters. I'll say more about *main* later in this chapter.

Function prototypes

The *SayHello* and *SayGoodbye* functions appear twice in Hello. The first appearance just specifies the functions' types, names, and parameter lists—this first appearance is called a *function prototype*. Here again are the function prototypes in Hello:

```
bool SayHello(char* szTo, int nCalc);
void SayGoodbye();
```

The second time these functions are used is in the *main* function. In this case, the function names have to be declared before *main* so that the compiler can check actual parameter types against formal parameter types. The functions' bodies, or *definitions*, come after *main*. There's no requirement to arrange declarations and definitions this way, however—we could just as easily put the full function definitions before *main* and skip the prototypes. I like to put *main* up front, so I use the prototypes. More typically, the prototypes would be in a header (include, or .h) file, and the function definitions would be in an implementation (.cpp) file. I'll illustrate that kind of arrangement later under "Header and Implementation Files" in Chapter 3.

OTE *Declare* and *define* are important terms. A *declaration* publicly declares a function's return type, name, and parameter list, or a variable's type, but it doesn't cause any memory to be allocated. A *definition* (or *implementation*) fills in the body of the functions and causes memory to be allocated. A statement is a definition if it causes any storage to be allocated. For example, the statement *int i;* allocates storage, so that's a definition. A function prototype doesn't allocate storage, so that's a declaration. Actually, a definition can also be a declaration if it introduces a name for the first time in a particular scope. Check the Help index for *declaration statements*.

Returning a Result from a Function

SayHello's prototype shows it returning a result of type *bool*, or Boolean, whose possible values are *true* and *false* (or nonzero and 0). Boolean functions usually return one of these values, depending on some condition in the function. In *SayHello*, the result is determined by the evaluation of an expression involving the input parameter *nCalc*. In general, a function can return a result of any data type. It can also return a *pointer* or a *reference*. I'll discuss those later in Chapter 3. I'll also discuss some cautions in returning these types.

You return the result with the *return* keyword. In a function that returns a result, you must call *return* and specify a value of the right type as its result.

```
int MyFunction()
{
    return 3;     // Often this is a variable or expression.
}
```

You can also use *return* in functions that don't return results (functions with a *void* return type). In that case, you don't specify a return value. The purpose of this usage of *return* is to return early when something is wrong, or when you determine that the remainder of the function doesn't need to be executed. Here's an example that returns early when conditions aren't right:

```
void MyFunction(int nParam)
{
    if(nParam < 21)
        return;    // Return now if conditions are not right.

    // Otherwise, do something useful and return after
    // completing the function.
}
```

You probably noticed that the function *main* also returns a result—an *int*. I'll say more about that when I discuss *main* later in this chapter.

The C/C++ Run-Time Library

When you need to accomplish a specific task, you may not have to reinvent the wheel. Every C or C++ compiler supplies a library of useful functions, constants, variables, and types, called the *run-time library*. Technically, this library is not part of the language, but it is a standard requirement for any implementation of the language. In Visual C++, C and C++ use the same run-time library. Its items fall into the following categories:

- Argument access (for functions with variable numbers of arguments).

- Buffer manipulation. A buffer is a block of memory that you can examine and manipulate through a pointer to the block. It's common, for example, to read a file into a large buffer in memory and work with the buffer rather than directly with the file.

- Items used to work with multibyte character systems (such as Unicode). Multibyte character systems are used for languages such as Chinese and Japanese that have large numbers of characters and require more than 1 byte of storage to represent every possible character.

■ Data conversion.

■ Debugging functions used with the debug version of the run-time library.

■ Directory control.

■ Error and exception handling. Exceptions provide a formal mechanism for responding to unexpected conditions, such as running out of heap memory or not finding a file.

■ File handling.

■ Floating-point support.

■ Input and output.

■ Functions used in making international versions of your program.

■ Memory allocation.

■ Environment control.

■ Searching and sorting.

■ String manipulation.

■ System calls.

■ Time management.

To find a useful function in the run-time library when you aren't sure what functions are available for what you want to do, check the Help index for *FUNCTIONS* (with the capitalization), then choose the subtopic "run-time by category." If you know the function name, check the Help index for the name.

In addition to the run-time library, Visual C++ includes the Standard C++ library, a library of functions and classes based on C++ templates. You can use the library with MFC, but this book doesn't cover templates, so I won't discuss the Standard C++ library further. Check the Help index for *standard C++ library overview.*

You might also find the *C*++ language reference in Visual C++ Help useful. Check the Help index for *C*++ *language reference*. There's also a C language reference.

The *main* Function

Following Hello's #*include* directive, the function prototypes, and the constant definitions, you see the body of the program. Every C++ program begins by executing a function called *main*. The *main* function in a C++ program is a special function that always has the name "main," but you write it. Here's *main* from Hello:

```
int main(int argc, char* argv[])
{
    char* szCpp = "C++!";    // Declare a variable.

    // Call a function with a Boolean result.
    if(SayHello(szCpp, 2))
    {
        // Call a function with no result.
        SayGoodbye();
    }
    return 0;
}
```

To illustrate *main's* role as the program's "ringmaster," the sequence of events in Hello's execution goes like this:

1. C++ does some preparatory set-up.

2. *main* begins to execute.

3. *main* declares and initializes the variable *szCpp*. This allocates storage for *szCpp* on the program's stack. The total amount of storage is determined by the length of the initialization string. See "Strings," earlier in this chapter.

4. *main* calls the function *SayHello*. *SayHello's* parameters are placed on the stack, along with space for *SayHello's* returned result (a *bool*).

5. *SayHello* executes, first printing a message (the statement involving *cout*, which I'll explain a bit later), then evaluating an expression involving *nCalc*, and finally returning the result of that evaluation to *main*.

6. Back in *main*, *SayHello's* result, a Boolean value, is used as the condition for an *if* statement. If *SayHello* returns *true* (it does, given these actual parameters), the statement inside the *if* statement's block executes a call to function *SayGoodbye*. If *SayHello* returns false, the body of the *if* statement is skipped.

7. In this case, *SayGoodbye* executes, printing a message. There are no parameters, local variables, or function results to place on the stack, but a return address is stored there so execution can jump back to *main* at a point just after *SayGoodbye* is called.

8. Back in *main*, the *if* statement completes when *SayGoodbye* returns and the *if* statement's closing curly brace is encountered.

9. When the *main* function reaches the statement *return 0*, the function returns the value *0*, indicating that all went well, and the program ends. The *main* function could return some other value if it encountered problems.

Like other functions, *main* can have a result type (or it can specify *void*). If it does declare a result type, you must have a *return* statement in the function as follows:

```
void main()
{
  // No return statement
}
```

– or –

```
int main()
{
    return 0;    // Return some meaningful int value
}
```

The *main* function can also take parameters, as shown here:

```
int main(int argc, char* argv[])...
```

The parameters passed to *main* allow you to access any arguments specified on the command line when the program is run in an MS-DOS box. The *argc* parameter tells how many arguments were specified in running the program (plus one). The *argv* parameter is an array of C/C++ null-terminated strings containing the arguments. Given a command line like this:

```
c:\>Testprogram arg1 arg2 arg3
```

the *argc* parameter to Testprogram's *main* function has the value 4. The name of the program is the first parameter, along with its full path. If Testprogram is stored in C:\Programs, the values stored in argv[0] through argv[3] are:

```
argv[0] - C:\PROGRAMS\TESTPROGRAM.EXE
argv[1] - arg1
argv[2] - arg2
argv[3] - arg3
```

I won't use command-line arguments in this book, but because AppWizard writes *main* that way, that's the way I'll leave it.

Expressions and Operators

A statement whose components evaluate to a single value is called an *expression*. For example, the following is an arithmetic expression:

```
x + 1 - y / sin(theta)
```

and the following is a Boolean (logical) expression:

```
x < y
```

An *operator* defines a relationship between two *operands*. For example, the < operator, signifying less than, relates its operands, x and y, in the Boolean expression above. C++ has arithmetic, logic, and other operators, described in the following section.

Expressions

The result returned by *SayHello* is determined by the following expression:

```
(nCalc + (nCalc * 2)) < (24/nCalc);
```

This particular expression is a relational expression. It evaluates to either *true* or *false*, depending on whether the evaluation of the first subexpression,

```
(nCalc + (nCalc * 2))
```

is less than the evaluation of the second subexpression,

```
(24/nCalc)
```

Here's the comparison:

```
(nCalc + (nCalc * 2)) < (24/nCalc)
// subexpression1     < subexpression2
```

Each of the two subexpressions is an arithmetic expression that evaluates to a number.

Operators

The overall expression above illustrates several C++ *operators*: + (addition), * (multiplication), < (less than), and / (division). Besides these relational and arithmetic operators, C++ includes a good many others, as shown in Table 2-6. The items on either side of most operators are the operands. For additional information about operators in C++, check the Help index for *operators* and choose the topic "C++ Operators"

Operator Category	Operators		Examples	Comments
Arithmetic	+	Addition	2 + 3	*Modulus* gives the remainder of dividing its operands. The example here reports a remainder of 1.
	−	Subtraction	3 - 2	
	*	Multiplication	3 * 4	
	/	Division	12 / 6	
	%	Modulus	7 % 2	
Logical and relational	<	Less than	i < 10	*Logical* operators such as && and | | compare two conditions for truth— both true (&&), and either or both true (| |). Once the condition being tested for is satisfied, further operators are not evaluated. For example, if the first operand of the | | operator is *true*, the operator returns *true* without evaluating the second operand. Note that !true = false and !false = true. (The & and | symbols are also used for the *bitwise* operators.)
	>	Greater than	i > 10	
	<=	Less or equal	i <= 10	
	>=	Greater or equal	i >= 10	
	==	Equal	i == 10	
	!=	Not equal	i != 10	
	&&	Logical AND	cond1 && cond2	
	||	Logical OR	cond1 || cond2	
	!	Logical NOT	!bCondition	
Increment and decrement	i++	Postfix increment		The prefix form increments or decrements the variable before evaluating it. Postfix evaluates, then applies the operator.
	++i	Prefix increment		
	i--	Postfix decrement		
	--i	Prefix decrement		

Table 2-6. *C++ operators.* *(continued)*

Table 2-6 *continued*

Operator Category	Operators		Examples	Comments
Bitwise	~	Bitwise not	~myInt	These allow you to test, set, and otherwise manipulate individual bits in an integer-type value. *FLAG* would contain coded information in several bit flags.
	<<	Left bit shift	myInt << 2	
	>>	Right bit shift	myInt >> 2	
	&	Bitwise and	myInt & FLAG	
	|	Bitwise or	myInt | FLAG	
	^	Bitwise xor	myInt ^ FLAG	
Assignment	=	Assignment	x = 24;	If x is 3, x += 1 is 4.
	=	Compound assign	x = y = 17;	
	+=	Add, then assign	x += 1;	
	-=	Subtract, assign	x -= 2;	
	*=	Multiply, assign	x *= 3;	
	/=	Divide, assign	etc.	
	%=	Modulus, assign		
	<<=	Shift left, assign		
	>>=	Shift right, assign		
	&=	Bitwise &, assign		
	|=	Bitwise |, assign		
	^=	Bitwise xor, assign		
sizeof			sizeof(float)	*sizeof* returns the number of bytes in a data type.
Arithmetic *if*	?:		i > j ? i : j	Arithmetic *if* chooses an alternative based on a condition—compactly, inside an expression, without using the keyword *if*.
Others	::	Scope resolution	::GlobalFunc();	Call outside scope.
	[]	Array subscript	myArray[3]	Access array element.
	()	Function call	SayGoodbye();	Call function.
	.	Member selection	myObj.m_nHeight	*myObj* is non-pointer.
	->	Member selection	pMyObj->m_nHeight	*pMyObj* is a pointer.
	new	Allocate memory	pMyObj = new Obj;	Allocate a pointer.
	delete	Deallocate	delete pMyObj;	Deallocate a pointer.
	*	Indirection	int* pInt;	Declare a pointer to *int*.
	*	Dereference	obj = *pMyObj:	Get value at address.
	&	Address	pMyObj = &myObj;	Get address of variable.
	-	Unary negation	-2	
	+	Unary positive	+3	
		(type)target cast	int i = (int)y;	Convert y to *int*, C style.
		type(target) cast	int i = int(y);	Convert y to *int*, C++ style.

Operator Category	Operators	Examples	Comments

Comma	,	`for(int i = 0;`
		`i < 10;`
		`i++, j++)...`
			You can separate a series of expressions with commas, as in the third expression in the *for* statement. The expressions are evaluated left to right.

Precedence

Some C++ operators have precedence over others during expression evaluation. For example, multiplication and division are evaluated before addition and subtraction in an expression like this:

```
6 + 3 * 4 / 2 + 5
```

With the precedence specified above—evaluating the multiplication, then the division, then the first and second additions—the expression evaluates to 17, as if it contained parentheses:

```
6 + ((3 * 4) / 2) + 5
```

Evaluating the innermost parentheses first, we arrive at 6 + (12/ 2) + 5. And then, evaluating the remaining parentheses, we get 6 + 6 + 5 = 17. Without the precedence rules (or the parentheses), working strictly from left to right, the original expression would evaluate to 23. Adopting some other evaluation ordering convention might lead to other answers. Operators with the same precedence, such as + and -, are evaluated from left to right. The C++ precedence rules prevent ambiguity, but you can make your expressions much more readable and less error prone by liberally using parentheses.

For more details on precedence and associativity—the order in which particular operands are evaluated, left to right or right to left—check the Help index for *operator precedence*.

The most common operator error

The most common error with operators is that of using the assignment operator (=) when you intend the equality operator (==).

For example:

```
if(c = 'a') ...
```

Instead of comparing the variable *c* and the character *a* for equality, this expression *assigns* the value *a* to the variable *c* (and in this example, the *if* condition is always true, which probably isn't what's intended). One way to avoid this all-too-common error is to reverse such expressions as a matter of standard practice:

```
if('a' = c) ...
```

This yields a compiler error because the assignment won't work in this direction. The error instructs you to write the expression as:

```
if(c == 'a')...   or   if('a' == c)...
```

which is what we meant in the first place.

C++ Control Statements

Because *SayHello* returns a *bool*, I call the function right in the *if* statement in Hello's *main* function, like this:

```
if(SayHello(szCpp, 2))
{
    // Call a function with no result.
    SayGoodbye();
}
```

I could instead do it in a wordier way, using an extra variable:

```
bool bResult = SayHello(szCpp, 2);
if(bResult)
{
    // Call a function with no result.
    SayGoodbye();
}
```

The result of *SayHello* is the condition on which the *if* statement hinges. If *SayHello* returns *true*, the *if* statement's body is executed—in this case, the call to *SayGoodbye*. If *SayHello* returned *false*, *SayGoodbye* would not be executed. You should be familiar with *if* statements, although you might think the C++ syntax seems strange. Table 2-7 shows a more complete *if* statement, along with other C++ control structures.

You can *nest* control structures, one inside the other. The example for the *continue* statement in Table 2-7 shows an *if* statement nested inside a *while* loop. You can nest any of the structures within any of the others, and there is no limit to the level of nesting.

By the way, I used curly braces for the body of *main*'s *if* statement in Hello. With only one statement to execute when the *if* condition is true, the braces are not actually required:

```
if(SayHello(szCpp, 2))
    SayGoodbye();
```

But using them consistently helps prevent many errors.

Control Structure	Example	Comments

`if(condition1)`
`{`
    `// Statements if`
    `// condition1 true`
`}`
`else if(condition2)`
`{`
    `// Statements if`
    `// condition2 true`
`}`
`else`
`{`
    `// Statements if`
    `// both 1 & 2 false`
`}`
	`if(i != 0)`
	`{`
	    `DoFunction();`
	    `AddNumbers();`
	`}`
	`else`
	`{`
	    `DoOtherFunction();`
	`}`
		Branching control. Lets you do different things under different conditions. *else if* and *else* are optional.

`while(condition)`
`{`
    `// Statements`
`}`
	`i = 0;`
	`while(i <= 100)`
	`{`
	    `i = DoFunction();`
	    `AddNumbers();`
	`}`
		Looping control. Evaluates condition before entering loop, so might never execute if condition is initially false. The counter, *i*, is only one way to set a terminating condition for the loop. Any Boolean expression will do.

Table 2-7.   *C++ control structures.*   *(continued)*

Table 2-7 *continued*

Control Structure	Example	Comments
| ```
do
{
    // Statements
} while(condition);
``` | ```
do
{
    b = DoFunction();
    AddNumbers();
} while(b);
``` | Looping control. Always executes statements at least once, then evaluates condition. Uses a Boolean variable for the condition. |
| ```
for(init; term; inc)
{
    // Statements
    ⋮
}
``` | ```
for(int i = 0; i < n; i++)
{
    DoFunction(i);
    AddNumbers(myArray);
}
``` | Looping control. Executes statements as long as the term condition is met. The loop index is initialized through the init condition, and is incremented (or decremented) by the inc condition. |
| | ```
for(int i;...
    ⋮
for(int i;...    // Illegal
    ⋮
``` | Note: You can't use *i* again in a following *for* loop unless the first *for* loop has ended. |
| | ```
int i;
for(i = 0; ...
``` | It's as if *i* were declared like this. |
| ```
Switch(value)
{
    case C1: Action;
        break;
    case C2:
    {
        Action;
        Action;
    }
        break;
    default: Action;
        break;
}
``` | ```
switch(ch)
{
    case 'a':
    {
            DoA();
            CallHome();
    }
        break;
    case 'b': DoB();
        break;
    case 'c': DoC();
        break;
    default: DoDefault();
        break;
}
``` | Multi-way branching control. Useful when the alternative is a deeply nested *if* statement. Note the use of curly braces to contain multiple instructions for a case. |
| ```
break
``` | See switch example above. | Terminates the smallest enclosing of *while*, *do*, *for*, or *switch* statement. |
```

Control Structure	Example	Comments

continue	```while(x < 100)```
	```{```
	``` if(bTest)```
	``` continue;```
	``` // Other statements```
	```}```
		Jumps out of current iteration; starts on next iteration of *while*, *do*, or *for* loop.

goto	```goto label;```
	``` // Statements```
	```label:```
	``` // Label can't immediately```
	``` // precede a closing right```
	``` // brace, unless you use a```
	``` // null statement:```
	```label: ;```
	```}```
		Unconditional transfer of control to some other place. Advice: Don't use goto.

C++ Input/Output via Iostreams

The iostream.h file in Hello defines the C++ way to do input and output. An *iostream* is an object that treats input or output as a stream of data. You send output by inserting it into an output stream, and you obtain input by extracting it from an input stream.

In Hello, I use *iostream* in *SayHello* and *SayGoodbye*. Here's the example from *SayHello*:

```
cout << "Hello, " << szTo << " You're Number " << NUMERO_UNO << ".\n";
```

This line inserts the string "Hello, C++! You're Number 1." into an output stream object called *cout*. The *cout* object (pronounced "see-out") is a standard C++ *iostream* object that refers to the *standard output* (like *stdout* in C), which usually corresponds to your screen, or to a window on the screen. There's a corresponding *input stream* object called *cin* that refers to the *standard input* (like *stdin* in C), which usually corresponds to the keyboard. In Visual C++, inserting the string into *cout* using the insertion operator (<<) causes the inserted string to be displayed in an MS-DOS window, as in Figure 2-2.

The first insertion operator in *SayHello* inserts "Hello, " the literal string. The additional insertion operators continue the stream by inserting, successively, the value of *SayHello*'s *szTo* parameter, another literal string; the value of the constant *NUMERO_UNO*; a period; and finally, the special character called a *newline*, symbolized by a \n. This character is part of the string output, so it's placed within quotation marks. The newline character tells *cout* to end the present line and begin a new line. If there were any more output in Hello, it would go on the next line. (The output, as seen in Figure 2-2, is followed by the text "Press any key to continue." This text is not part of Hello's output—Visual C++ adds it to tell you how to close the MS-DOS window when you are finished.)

In the output stream in the *SayGoodbye* function, there's one difference. Instead of using \n to terminate one line of output and start another, I use an *iostream manipulator, endl* (end line). The *endl* manipulator serves the same purpose as \n. It's only one of many manipulators available for various purposes in input and output streams. Check the Help index for *output streams* and choose the subtopic "Output." Click Location and then click Using Insertion Operators And Controlling Format.

Notice that the insertion operator for *cout* works for a variety of data types, including both character and numeric data. This is because of a C++ technique called *operator overloading*. I'll say more about overloading later when I discuss C++ classes. Check the Help index for << *operator* and choose the second topic in the Topics Found dialog box.

For completeness, here's a brief example of C++ input, using the *iostream* object *cin*:

```
int n;
cout << "Please enter an integer: \n";
cin >> n;
```

The *cout* object is used to display a prompt on the screen. Then the *cin* object waits for the user to type a number and press the Enter key. The value typed is extracted from the input stream into the variable *n*. Here's a simple loop that reads data via *cin*:

```
char c;
while(cin >> c)
    // Do something with the latest character.
```

C++ also supplies a stream for error-message output, called *cerr*.

The *iostream* facility includes a mechanism for connecting an input or output stream to a file. For more information about connecting to files and other aspects of using *iostream* in your C++ programs, check the Help index for *iostream* and choose the topic "iostream Programming."

In C++, *iostream* objects take the place of functions like *Print* in Basic, *WriteLn* in Pascal, and *printf* in C. (C run-time library functions like *printf* are still available in C++ because C++ is a superset of C.) Using the *iostream* objects is the normal way to perform input/output in C++. However, the only places you'll use them in this book are in Chapters 3 through 5, where we write raw C++ code. Starting in Chapter 6, we'll manage input and output very differently, using the facilities in MFC and Windows.

And there you have Hello, although we're far from finished with C++. I'll see you in Chapter 3, after you've experimented for a while.

Try It Yourself

The best way to learn C++ is to write code and see what happens. I do recommend that you buy a good C++ book, but this chapter, the next three chapters, and the Visual C++ documentation will provide most of what you need.

If you haven't been working along with me through this chapter, I recommend that you go back now and type in each of the examples and build them. They're short, and they'll give you a better feeling for the structure and syntax of C++ programs and how to build them with Visual C++. You can't accomplish that nearly as well just by reading.

If you have problems building the examples, you might want to look ahead to Chapter 13 on debugging.

After you build an example, experiment with it. Remove, add, and rearrange things. Comment out lines of code by preceding them with double slashes (//). Write your own variants and see what happens. You'll trip up now and then, but you'll also learn quite a bit.

What's Next

In Chapter 3, I'll introduce you to C++ pointers and references. These are powerful tools, but not without their dangers. Among other topics, I'll cover:

- The pitfalls of using pointers and references, and how to avoid them
- Using C++ header files (also called *include* files) and implementation files
- Understanding the scope (visibility) of a variable or function

When you finish, you'll be able to point and refer with the best of them, and you'll know a lot more about the mechanics of managing programs with multiple files and complicated scopes.

C++ Scope, Pointers, and References

This chapter continues where Chapter 2 left off—with more C++ fundamentals. We'll cover the following topics:

- Scope: what's visible *where* in your program
- The pointer, a versatile but dangerous programming tool
- The reference, an alternative to the pointer
- Header and implementation files

Scope, Part 1

What parts of a C++ program have access to a given variable, type, constant, or function? This varies depending on what *scope* the item is declared in and used in. Consider the Scope1 program.

Try it now

Create the Scope1 program as a Win32 Console Application. Follow the same directions as in the "Hello in C++" section in Chapter 2, but name the project Scope1. Edit the Scope1.cpp file, and make your file look like the one on the next page by entering the boldface code.

```cpp
// Scope1.cpp : Defines the entry point for the console application.
//

#include "stdafx.h"
#include <iostream.h>

int n1;    // Global n1

// Two function prototypes (global functions)
void f1(int n);
void f2(int n);

int main(int argc, char* argv[])
{
    // n2 not visible here; not declared yet
    // Error if next line not commented
    // cout << "n2 = " << n2 << "    Error: n2 not visible here\n";
    int n2 = 9;
    cout << "In main, n2 = " << n2 << endl;

    n1 = 1;    // Initialize global n1
    cout << "In main, n1 = "  << n1 << endl;

    // Call the functions.
    f1(2);
    f2(3);

    return 0;
}

void f1(int n)
{
    int n1 = 10;    // Local n1, hides global n1
    cout << "In f1, n1 = " << n1 << ", n = " << n << endl;
}

void f2(int n)
{
    // In f2, n1 is the global n1.
    cout << "In f2, n1 = " << n1 << ", n = " << n << endl;
    for(int i = 0; i < 10; i++)
    {
        // In the for loop, n1 is the global n1.
        if(i == 0)
            cout << "In f2's for loop, n1 = " << n1 <<
                ", n = " << n << ", i = " << i << endl;
    }
```

```
        cout << "After the for loop, i = " << i << endl;

        {   // Local block in f2 establishes a subordinate local scope.
            // Inside this block, n1 is the global n1.
            cout << "In f2's local block, n1 = " << n1 <<
                ", n = " << n << endl;
            int x = 7;     // x is local to this block
        }
        // Error if next line is uncommented.
        // cout << "Outside local block, x = " << x << endl;
}
```

Scope1 demonstrates the following kinds of scope:

- **Global scope (now often called namespace scope).** Items declared at global scope are visible throughout the file they're declared in and can be made visible in other parts of the program as well. (I'll say more about this in a moment.) The variable *n1* declared outside *main* is global, so we can access it in *main* to examine or change its contents. This *n1* is visible inside the *main*, *f1*, and *f2* functions. In particular, it's visible anywhere in the Scope1.cpp file following its declaration. (We can't access it preceding its declaration in the file.) The variable *n2* declared in *main* illustrates the same concept. Above the declaration, *n2* is unknown. Below it, *n2* is visible. Functions *main*, *f1*, and *f2* are also global.

- **Local scope.** Each function or other *block* (code surrounded by curly braces) defines its own local scope. A variable declared inside *main*, *f1*, or *f2* is not visible outside its function, so declaring a new local variable *n1* inside function *f1* is fine. The name *n1* can be re-used inside the function. However, function *f1*'s variable *n1* is said to *hide* the global variable *n1* because both have the same name. The output statement in *f1* demonstrates this: the *n1* that it outputs is its own local *n1* (value *10*). In *f2*, however, there's no local *n1* variable, so the output statement there outputs the global *n1* (value *1*). You can prefix the *scope resolution operator* (::) to *n1* inside *f1* to cause it to refer to the global *n1* instead of the local *n1* (try it in Scope1):

```
cout << "In f1, n1 = " << ::n1 << " and n = " << n << endl;
```

Also note that function parameters, such as *n*, are considered to be within the function's local scope. In other words, they're visible inside the function. And finally, just as *main* can't see items declared in *f1*, *f1* can't see items in *main*, although you might have expected otherwise. The global scope is outside of *main* and all functions.

■ **Subordinate local scope (shown as a pair of curly braces inside a function).** Inside function *f2*, there are two subordinate local scopes. The body of the *for* loop is one:

```
for(...)
{
    // A local scope
}
```

and the freestanding pair of curly braces below it define the other:

```
{
    // A second local scope
}
```

Let's look more closely at those two subordinate local scopes. Here's how the scope rules work for the *for* loop and the freestanding pair of braces in the Scope1 program:

■ Inside *f2*'s *for* loop, the *n1* printed out is the global *n1*, visible so deep within the nested scopes because no local *n1* hides it. We could declare a new *n1* inside the *for* loop, and it would hide the global *n1*. Try it.

■ The *for* loop's loop-control variable, *i*, is declared within the head of the *for* statement, but it is not local to the loop, as it is in some languages. You can still access *i*'s value after the loop ends. The *cout* statement following the loop demonstrates this: it outputs "After the *for* loop, i = 10." It's as if the variable *i* were declared before the *for* statement, like this:

```
int i;
for(i = 0;...
```

■ The other local scope, delineated by two curly braces after the body of the *for* loop, is another block. If we declared an *n1* within *f2* but outside this block, and then declared another *n1* inside the block, the inner *n1* would hide the outer one. (Such a block is sometimes used to localize a variable's scope as much as possible, destroying the variable immediately after its use rather than keeping it around for the duration of a long function, as the variable *x* shows.)

> **WARNING** Suppose *f1* or *f2* changed the global *n1*—just reset its value. This is called a *side effect*. The caller of the function might not be aware of the side effect, with potentially dangerous consequences. To avoid side effects, use parameters and function results to change variables in the environment outside your function. Doing so makes it clear that the change is intended. If you pass a global variable as the actual value of a function parameter, any change to the variable is more explicit. Similarly, if you assign a function's return value to a global variable, the change is explicit and obvious. The trouble with side effects is that they're subtle. Even if a side effect is intentional, forgetfulness can later turn it into a mystery. So sometime in the future, you'll find yourself wondering why your program isn't working properly, and you'll have to spend hours debugging it. You might as well do it right the first time.

There is one more kind of scope in C++, called *class scope,* which I'll describe when we talk about classes in Chapter 5. The output of Scope1 is shown below. By looking at this output and referring to the program code, you can see where the various *n1* variables are visible and where they aren't.

```
In main, n2 = 9
In main, n1 = 1
In f1, n1 = 10, n = 2
In f2, n1 = 1, n = 3
In f2's for loop, n1 = 1, n = 3, i = 0
After the for loop, i = 10
In f2's local block, n1 = 1, n = 3
```

Here are two more special scope situations worth knowing about. They deal with the visibility of global variables defined in different files.

■ In the first situation, a global variable *x* is defined in file A.cpp (that is, the storage for *x* is allocated in file A.cpp). Let's say you also want to use *x* in file B.cpp. You can make the *x* in file A.cpp visible in file B.cpp by declaring *x* in B.cpp with the keyword *extern*. (Check the Help index for *extern*.) The Scope2 program, in the \learnvcn\Chap03 folder in the companion code, illustrates using *extern* this way.

■ In the second situation, files A.cpp and B.cpp each define a global variable *myInt*, but they are not intended to be the same *myInt*. Without further coding on your part, you'll get a linker error because you've defined two global variables with the same name (even though they're in different files). However, you can make the two variables distinct without having to change the name of either of them. Define either variable or both variables as *static*, which makes a variable (or other item) invisible outside its file. (Check the Help index for *static*. I'll also discuss other uses of the *static* keyword later in the book.) The Scope3 program, in the \learnvcn-\Chap03 folder in the companion code, illustrates using *static* as described here.

One more thing about scope: local variables go out of scope at the end of their function (unless they're defined as *static*). When a variable goes out of scope, any pointer or reference to it has an undefined value. (We'll get to pointers and references shortly.) The reason that local variables go out of scope is that they are allocated on the stack, and when the function returns, all of the storage on the stack that was associated with the function becomes undefined. Allocating a variable on the stack is like putting a cafeteria tray on top of a stack of trays. When the function returns, it's as if the tray is removed from the stack of trays—it's gone.

Pointers

One of the most widely used features in C and C++ is the *pointer*. As we saw in Chapter 2, a pointer is a variable that contains the address of some location in memory. In most cases, it's the address of another variable. Figure 3-1 shows the relationship between a pointer and the thing it points to—its *target*. Pointers in C++ work the same way as in C.

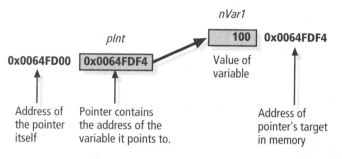

Figure 3-1.   *A pointer and its target.*

This tour of pointers will necessarily be brief, but thorough enough to show you that there's quite a bit to learn about them. I'll use a number of small C++ programs to demonstrate the following:

- Declaring and initializing a pointer

- Accessing or changing the value of the object pointed to

- Naming pointers most effectively

- Manipulating arrays and strings through pointers, using *pointer arithmetic*

- Using pointers in function parameters and function results

- Understanding that a pointer can point to a variety of things: variables, arrays, strings, structs, classes, struct or class members, *Null*, *void**, functions, and other pointers

- Exercising caution in using pointers

Pointer Basics

The brief C++ program on the following page, named Pointer, shows how to declare and initialize a pointer and how to access or change the value of the object it points to.

Try it now

Create another Win32 Console Application called Pointer. You should be getting pretty good at this by now.

```
// Pointer.cpp : Defines the entry point for the console application.
//

#include "stdafx.h"
#include <iostream.h>

int main(int argc, char* argv[])
{
    // Declare and initialize an ordinary integer variable.
    int nVar1 = 100;
    // Declare a pointer to nVar1.
    int* pInt = &nVar1;

    // Show that the pointer does point to nVar1.
    cout << "nVar1 = " << nVar1 << "      *pInt = " << *pInt << endl;
    // Show that the address of nVar1 == the value stored in pInt.
    cout << "&nVar1 = " << &nVar1 << "      pInt = " << pInt << endl;

    // Get the value of nVar1 via the pointer.
    int nVar2 = *pInt;
    // Change the value of nVar1 via the pointer.
    *pInt = 200;

    // Show the value retrieved via the pointer.
    cout << "nVar2 = "<< nVar2 <<
    // Also show nVar1's new value.
       "      nVar1 now = "<< nVar1 << endl;

    return 0;
}
```

The Pointer program declares an *int* variable, *nVar1*. The following statement then creates a pointer that contains the memory address of *nVar1*—this is how *pInt* points to the variable:

```
int* pInt = &nVar1;
```

On the left side of the assignment operator, the variable *pInt* is declared as a pointer to *int*. The *indirection* operator (*) tells us that *pInt* is a pointer to an *int*. On the right side of the assignment, the *address* operator (&, the ampersand), obtains the address of variable *nVar1*. The address is assigned to the pointer to initialize its value. That's what a pointer is: the address of some memory location.

WARNING   It's a convention of Microsoft Foundation Class Library programmers to write pointers with the notation shown above: *int* pInt*, with the * adjacent to the data type rather than the variable name. However, there's a danger in this practice if you aren't careful. Consider these declarations:

```
int* pInt, pInt2;
```

Only the first variable is a pointer here. Although *pInt2* is named like a pointer, the * applies only to the first variable when several variables are declared on the same line. Both of the following forms are correct, but with different meanings:

```
int *pInt, *pInt2;    // Both pInt and pInt2 are pointers.
int *pInt, pInt2;     // pInt is a pointer, but not pInt2.
```

The MFC way is clearer in that the * is really part of the type name. But be careful when declaring multiple pointers of the same type on one line.

Two output statements follow the pointer assignment *int* pInt = &nVar1*:

```
cout << "nVar1 = " << nVar1 << "     *pInt = " << *pInt << endl;
cout << "&nVar1 = " << &nVar1 << "     pInt = " << pInt << endl;
```

They show two facts about pointers:

- *nVar1* and the object *pInt* points to have the same value: *pInt* really does point to *nVar1*.

- The address of *nVar1* is the same as the value stored in *pInt*: it's this address that makes *pInt* a pointer to *nVar1*.

Next, the Pointer program shows the syntax for accessing the value of *nVar1* through the pointer to *nVar1*:

```
int nVar2 = *pInt;
```

Here, the * is serving as the *pointer-dereference* operator. You can read this line as "*nVar2* is assigned the value stored at the address that *pInt* points to." The * operator in this case means "value of." You're said to be *dereferencing* the pointer—following it to its target so you can see what's there. You can distinguish the dereference operator from the indirection operator by position, even though both are represented by the * character.

The dereference operator precedes a pointer's name but is not part of a variable declaration, as is the indirection operator. Here are the two operators on separate lines:

```
int* pInt = &nVar1;    // Indirection operator *
int nVar2 = *pInt;     // Dereference operator *
```

> **NOTE** Many programmers use the following convention in naming pointers: prefix the variable name with the letter *p*, as in *pInt*. Where possible, I also try to indicate the data type the pointer is for. This helps keep me from mistaking a pointer for the object being pointed to. Here are more examples: *pWindow* (pointer to a window), *pPerson* (pointer to a person object), *pDblSalary* (pointer to a *double* variable representing a salary). How would you name a pointer to another pointer? *ppInt*.

Besides being able to access the value in *nVar1* through the pointer, you can also change that value through the pointer:

```
*pInt = 200;
```

This time the dereference operator appears on the left side of the assignment statement. The meaning here is "store the value 200 at the address pointed to by *pInt*."

The final output statement in the Pointer program shows the newly assigned value of *nVar2* and the new value of *nVar1*; *nVar1* began at 100 and has now been set to 200.

Under Microsoft Windows 95, Microsoft Windows 98, and Microsoft Windows NT, a pointer is stored as a 32-bit integer value. When run on my computer, the second *cout* statement in the Pointer program results in this output:

```
&nVar1 = 0x0064FDF4     pInt = 0x0064FDF4
```

The memory address of *nVar1* and the address stored in *pInt* are shown here in *hexadecimal* notation. (See the sidebar "Numerical Notation in C++.") The actual addresses printed out might differ when you run the Pointer program on your system, depending on such considerations as which other programs are running and how much RAM you have. Notice that the two addresses are the same—proof that what's stored in a pointer is indeed an address.

Numerical Notation in C++

You can use three different numerical notations in C++: hexadecimal, octal, and decimal. Hexadecimal and decimal are the most common.

■ Hexadecimal, or "hex," values are marked by the prefix "0x" and contain numbers in the base 16 system, whose digits are 0–9, and then A, B, C, D, E, F—where A = 10, B = 11, ... F = 15. For example, 0xE = 14 decimal; 0x10 = 16 decimal: 1×16 + 0×1. You can use uppercase or lowercase for the alphabetic digits—B is the same as b.

■ Octal values (base 8), whose digits are 0–7, are prefixed with a zero. For example, 077 = 63 decimal: 7×8 + 7×1.

■ Decimal values have no prefix. For example, 9; 300; –4400.34.

You can use the Windows Calculator accessory to convert bases. Click Scientific on Calculator's View menu. Select a base: Hex, Dec, Oct, or Bin. (Bin is binary.) Enter a number using the appropriate notation for its base, and select the base you want to convert the number to (the target base, or *radix*).

You can also use *scientific notation* to express *float*, *double*, or *long double* numbers—all are decimal numbers followed by the letter *e* or *E* (for *exponent*, not Hex E), followed by a decimal power of 10. For example, 2.0E4 = $2×10^4$, or 20,000; –3.334e–2 = $–3.334×10^{-2}$, or –0.0334.

Pointers and Arrays

You've encountered arrays before. Arrays in C and C++ have an interesting and useful relationship with pointers. In both languages, an *array name* is a pointer to the first element of the array. This means that pointers provide an alternative way to "walk" (loop, iterate, traverse) through the elements of an array. The program Array, shown on the following page, demonstrates using *pointer arithmetic* to walk through an array.

Try it now

Create the Array program as you created the Pointer program.

```cpp
// Array.cpp : Defines the entry point for the console application.
//

#include "stdafx.h"
#include <iostream.h>

int main(int argc, char* argv[])
{
    cout << "-------1. Using Array Notation---------\n";
    int arInt[] = {6, 5, 4, 3, 2};
    for(int i = 0; i < 5; i++)
        cout << "arInt[" << i << "] = " << arInt[i] << endl;

    cout << "-------2. Using Pointer Arithmetic-------\n";
    int* pArray = arInt;
    for(int j = 0; j < 5; j++)
    {
        cout << "arInt[" << j << "] = " << *pArray++ << endl;
    }

    return 0;
}
```

The Array program has two sections. The first section uses ordinary array notation in a *for* loop to walk the array's elements. The key piece of C++ is this array-access notation in the middle of the output stream:

```cpp
arInt[i]
```

That code applies the *array subscript* operator ([]) to the array to retrieve the value stored at the *i*th element of the array. Here, the value is inserted into the output stream.

The second section of the Array program introduces two changes. First, a pointer to *int* is declared, named *pArray*, and initialized with only the array name:

```cpp
int* pArray = arInt;
```

Remember that an array name is a pointer. After the initialization, *pArray* points to the first element of the array. Then, in the output stream, the array-access notation is replaced by a curious-looking bit of code:

```
*pArray++
```

What's going on? Two C++ operators are being applied to *pArray*. The dereference operator precedes the pointer name, so part of what we're doing is retrieving the value stored at the current location of *pArray*'s first element. Following the pointer name is the postfix increment operator (++). The other thing we're doing, then, is incrementing the pointer. That's commonly called pointer arithmetic. By adding 1 to the address stored in the pointer, we're moving the pointer so that it points to the next element of the array.

Questions might occur to you here: Which operator is applied first? And isn't an *int* more than 1 byte wide? So how does incrementing by 1 move the pointer to the next element? Let's take these questions one at a time.

For the first question, the dereference operator is applied first. It obtains the value that is stored at the pointer's current location, for immediate use. Then the increment operator moves the pointer to the next element, which leads to the second question. It's true, an *int* is wider than 1 byte, but the compiler is smart enough not to increment byte by byte. Instead, it increments by the size of the array's *base type,* so the pointer moves element by element. Since 32-bit *ints*—the base type here—are 4 bytes wide, each increment of 1 actually moves the pointer 4 bytes.

 ARNING Neither C nor C++ checks for the end of the array. That's your responsibility. In the Array program, running either *for* loop from 1 through 5 rather than from 0 through 4 would let the pointer "run off the end" of the array, because array indexes start at 0. The pointer would end up pointing to memory outside the array. If you used the array index or the pointer to change what you thought was the last array element, you might clobber memory that had been allocated to some other variable. This could lead to disaster—or at least to a tricky bug.

Pointers and Strings

Like a string in C, a C++ string is an array of characters. The name of a string variable is a pointer, like the name of any other array. The String program demonstrates using pointer arithmetic on a *char** variable.

Try it now

Create the String program as you've created other C++ programs:

```
// string.cpp
//

#include <stdafx.h>
#include <iostream.h>

int main(int argc, char* argv[])
{
    cout << "---Using Pointer Notation on an Array---\n";
    char arStr1[] = "Programming";
    char* pStr1 = arStr1;
    cout << arStr1 << endl;    // Show the full string first.
    while(*pStr1)
    {
        cout << "*pStr1 =" << *pStr1++ << endl;
    }

    return 0;
}
```

Program String uses a pointer to scan a string and print each character in turn. Remember that the name of the array, *arStr1*, is simply a pointer to the first character of the array. To walk the string, we declare a second pointer, this one to *char**, and initialize it with the string name. Using this second pointer to walk leaves the string name still pointing to the first character. The alternative, moving the original string pointer itself, *arStr1*, leaves the string name out of position at the end of the walk, so it's much safer to walk the string with an auxiliary pointer.

Try it now

Let's try a little experiment with pointer notation and strings in Microsoft Visual C++. Add these two lines to String.cpp just before the return statement:

```
char* sz = "Windows";
*sz = 'V';
```

The pointer *sz* points to the beginning of the string, so this should replace the "W" in "Windows" with "V." Build and run it. The program fails with an access violation. Why? There's an apparent bug in Visual C++ 6.0 when you dereference a string pointer this way while the /ZI compiler option is set (which it is by default, to support the "edit and go" feature in the debugger). To work around it, select Settings on the Project menu. In the Settings dialog box, click the C/C++ tab and make sure the General option is set in the Category box. In the Project Options box, edit the /ZI option to /Zi (lowercase *i*). Click OK, rebuild, and run again. This workaround takes care of the access violation problem, a minor inconvenience I thought you should know about.

Pointers as Function Parameters and Function Results

Recall the earlier discussion about formal and actual parameters. In the Hello program's *SayHello* function, the first formal parameter was of type *char*—a pointer. What does it mean to pass a pointer to a function? And what would it mean to return a pointer as the function's result?

Pass by value

The default way to pass a parameter to a function is called *passing by value*. When you pass by value, the function doesn't get the actual piece of data that you supply in the function call. Instead, a copy of that data is made, and it's the copy that the function operates on. The function can alter the copy all it wants, and the original piece of data remains unchanged. Just remember that passing by value *passes a copy*.

The default way to return a function result is to return it by value. Again, a copy is made, and it is the copy that leaves the function and enters the outside world.

Pass by address

Suppose you have a large piece of data that you want a function to work on. In this case, let's say that you deliberately want the function to alter the data you pass to it, but the default is pass by value, which lets the function work only on a copy. (Not only that, but if you pass by value, copying that very large piece of data could be costly in time and memory.)

The solution, of course, is to pass a pointer to the data—using *pass by address*. This way, no copy of the data is used. The function can use the pointer to alter the original data regardless of where it actually is. (Technically, a copy *is* made, but it's of the pointer itself, so the copy points to the same place the original pointer does.)

Pass by address works just as well for returning a function result, only here the main motive is efficiency—there's no large data copy to return. Here's what the code for returning a pointer might look like:

```
Thing* MyFunction()
{
    // Do something to create a Thing
    return &Thing;
}
```

One other advantage of passing and returning pointers is that they enable you to return more than one result. You can use pointer-type parameters to return additional results. Figure 3-2 shows multiple returns schematically.

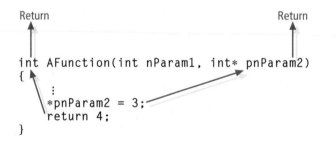

Figure 3-2.   *Using both the function return value and a function parameter to return results.*

In an upcoming section, I'll caution you about unsafe things you could do with returned pointers. The cautions won't usually apply to pointer-type parameters, just to function return values.

I'll also soon show you a third parameter-passing strategy, known as *pass by reference,* that is not available in C.

Passing a *const* pointer

Note one other thing about pointers. Suppose your main reason for passing by address rather than passing by value is to avoid the copying overhead, and you don't want the data itself to be modified in the function. In that case, you can declare the parameter with a *const* modifier, like this:

```
void MyFunction(const Thing* pThing)
```

Using *const* this way causes the compiler to enforce your wishes. The *Thing* pointed to by *pThing* can't be modified in the function. Passing *const* parameters is a good practice when you really don't intend to have the function modify the data.

What pointers can point to

Besides pointing to ordinary variables and to arrays and strings, pointers can point to a variety of other things. Table 3-1 summarizes what else a pointer can point to.

Pointer Target	Remarks
Null	A pointer can point to nothing. My advice is to set any pointer not pointing to a particular object to *Null* (a *null* pointer is like a pointer to 0). If you inadvertently try to dereference such a pointer, your application will perform an access violation and crash, but that's probably better than having it point to who knows where.

struct	A *struct*, covered in more detail in Chapter 4, is a named collection of variables, such as this:
	
	```struct MyStruct```
	```{```
	``` int nInt;```
	``` char ch;```
	```};```
	
	We can declare a *struct*-type variable and treat it as we do other variables, including the use of pointers:
	
	```MyStruct aStruct;```
	```MyStruct* pStruct = &aStruct;```

Table 3-1. *Some pointer targets.* *(continued)*

Table 3-1 *continued*

Pointer Target	Remarks
Class objects	A *class*, also covered in Chapter 4, is a *struct* with greater powers, such as: ```class MyClass\n{\n int nInt\n void MemberFunction();\n};\n\nMyClass aClass;\nMyClass* pclass = &aClass;```
Functions	A *function pointer* is handy when you need to pass a function as a parameter. Doing so lets function *A* call an arbitrary function *B* whose address is passed to *A*. (Advanced topic)
Class member function	You can obtain the address of a class member function (member functions are covered in Chapter 4) and use it somewhat as you would a pointer to a global function. (Advanced topic)
void	A pointer to *void* can be assigned the value of any other pointer that was not declared *const*. For example, a variable of type *void*∗ can be assigned the value of a variable of type *char*∗ or *int*∗. A pointer to *void* is useful when the object's type isn't known or might vary. You can't dereference this kind of pointer without first converting it to another pointer type. (Advanced topic) Hierarchies of class objects are a better mechanism to use than pointers to *void* (see Chapter 5).
Another pointer	Because you can define a pointer to any variable, you can define a pointer to a pointer. This is called *double indirection,* and it has its uses. (Advanced topic, but see the discussion of an array of pointers below.)

Like any other variable type, pointers can be stored in an array. What good is an array of pointers? Consider an array of strings:

```
char* arSzs[] = { "alpha", "beta", "gamma", "delta" };
for(int i = 0; i < 4; i++)
{
    cout << "string " << i << ": " << arSzs[i] << endl;
}
```

Since a *char** is a pointer, an array of strings is really an array of pointers. You can see this in Figure 3-3. The array name in this case is also an example of a pointer to a pointer. The array name is a pointer to the first element in the array—which in this case is another pointer. The array name, then, is a pointer to a pointer to *char*. (Try it. Create a small program that incorporates the code shown on the preceding page.)

N̵OTE C++ doesn't allow you to create an array of references. I'll cover references later in the chapter.

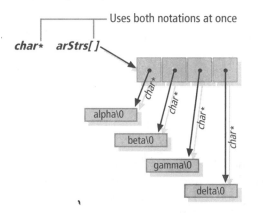

Figure 3-3.   *An array of strings is an array of pointers.*

An array of pointers can be useful for all kinds of tasks. For example, if you need to sort an array of large data objects, a good strategy is to use a second array containing pointers to the objects. Then, instead of moving the objects themselves around as you work through your sort algorithm, you can move the smaller-sized pointers—a considerable gain in efficiency. By the way, storage allocated on the heap for an array has to be deallocated properly. (It's more common to allocate arrays on the stack, but sometimes you need a heap allocation.) You can allocate the array storage on the heap by using *new*, like this:

```
int *arInts = new int[4];
```

This allocates space for four *int* variables, which we can then access with array notation, as shown in the code snippet on the next page.

```
arInts[0] = 0;
    ⋮
cout << arInts[0] << endl;
```

Because the array above was allocated with *new*, it must be deallocated with *delete*. But it's not sufficient to do this:

```
delete arInts;
```

Recall that an array's name is a pointer to its first element. So, the preceding *delete* statement deallocates only the first element of *arInts*. What we really need to do is deallocate the whole array. The following notation does that correctly, then sets the pointer to *Null*, signifying that it's not currently in use:

```
delete [] arInts;
arInts = NULL;
```

We briefly discussed allocating and deallocating arrays on the heap—including arrays of pointers—in Chapter 2. I strongly recommend that you now return to that discussion to help round out what you've seen here.

 OTE Calling *delete* for a pointer set to *Null* is harmless. But calling *delete* for a pointer whose value is undefined (neither *Null* nor the address of a legitimate object) causes problems. Trying to delete an undefined pointer is much like trying to dereference one. Such "stray pointers" are often hard to debug because the symptoms can be far removed from the action that caused them, like a car hitting a tree a mile from where the tie rod broke.

References

C++ introduces a new kind of variable: a *reference* variable. The Refer1 program gives a simple example.

 Try it now

Create the Refer1 program as you have created other C++ programs:

```
// Refer1.cpp : Defines the entry point for the console application.
//

#include "stdafx.h"
#include <iostream.h>
```

```
int main(int argc, char* argv[])
{
    // Declare an int variable and a reference to it.
    int myInt = 3;
    int& rMyRef = myInt;

    // Show that rMyRef does refer to myInt.
    cout << rMyRef << endl;     // Outputs 3

    // Change rMyRef by changing myInt.
    myInt += 1;                 // Now equals 4
    cout << rMyRef << endl;     // Outputs 4

    // Change myInt through rMyRef.
    rMyRef += 1;
    // Next line outputs "rMyRef = 5    myInt = 5".
    cout << "rMyRef = " << rMyRef << "    myInt = " << myInt << endl;

    return 0;
}
```

A reference is an *alias* for another variable—another name for the same object. The reference is not a separate object by itself, the way a pointer is. It's just a name. In the example above, *rMyRef* is said to *refer* to *myInt*—it's an alias for *myInt*. Anything you can do to *myInt* directly, you can also do by way of the reference *rMyRef*.

While it looks and acts somewhat like a pointer, a reference must be initialized to refer to a particular variable, and after that it can't be assigned a different variable to refer to. *Remember: a reference must refer to an existing object*—one that stays in existence for the life of the reference. Pointer variables are more, well, variable.

You can use references as shown in the Refer1 program, but their best use is as function parameters and results. They can really boost your efficiency as long as you abide by the few rules we've just covered.

> **NOTE**   Because references are just names, not real objects, it's an especially good idea to give them distinctive names. In Refer1, I prefixed the name *MyRef* with 'r' for reference: *rMyRef*. A more thoroughly Hungarian name, adding the data type of the object referred to, would be something like *rIntMyRef*.

Pass by Reference

We've covered two other parameter-passing mechanisms:

- **Pass by value,** in which a copy is passed and the original can't be modified through the copy

- **Pass by address,** in which a pointer is passed and the original can be modified through that pointer (unless the pointer parameter is *const*)

The third and final parameter-passing mechanism in C++ is called *pass by reference*. The formal parameter specifies a reference type—*BigObject&* in this example:

```
void MyFunction(BigObject& rBo);
```

and the actual parameter that you pass—a nonreference variable (a real object, not a pointer to one)—initializes the reference parameter:

```
BigObject myBo;      // myBo really exists as an object on stack
MyFunction(myBo);    // myBo used to initialize a reference parameter
```

MyFunction can modify *myBo*, the original object, through the reference to it (unless we precede the parameter declaration with the *const* keyword). The following program, Refer2, illustrates how the object that a reference parameter refers to can be changed.

Try it now

Create the Refer2 program as you have created other C++ programs:

```
// Refer2.cpp : Defines the entry point for the console application.
//

#include "stdafx.h"
#include <iostream.h>

struct BigObject
{
    int Var1;
    double arDbl[2000];      // Allocates space for 2,000 doubles
};
```

```
void MyFunction(BigObject& bo);

int main(int argc, char* argv[])
{
    BigObject myBo;
    myBo.Var1 = 0;
    cout << "Before MyFunction call, myBo.Var1 = " <<
        myBo.Var1 << endl;

    MyFunction(myBo);
    cout << "After MyFunction call, myBo.Var1 now = " <<
        myBo.Var1 << endl;

    return 0;
}

void MyFunction(BigObject& bo)
{
    cout << "Entering MyFunction, bo.Var1 = " << bo.Var1 << endl;
    bo.Var1 = 100;
}
```

The Refer2 program declares a *struct* type called *BigObject*. *BigObject* contains two *member variables:* an *int* and a large array of *doubles*. In *main*, Refer2 creates a *BigObject* named *myBo* on the stack and initializes its *int* member variable, *Var1*. (In real life, we'd also initialize the array member variable, but just having the space allocated for 2,000 doubles is all we need here to make the point that *myBo* is big.) Then *main* calls *MyFunction*, passing it the *BigObject* by reference. Notice that in the function call we just pass the object's name, with no *&* or other decorations— we're passing a real object as follows:

```
MyFunction(myBo);
```

MyFunction reaches out through the reference parameter to alter one of *myBo's* member variables. The three output statements track the variable's value before, during, and after the function call and demonstrate how the reference works.

What good did the reference do us? Because we passed by reference rather than by value, we eliminated the need to copy the *BigObject* as it was being passed. With small objects like *ints* or *chars*—or anything less than or equal to 32 bits—passing by value may be the better way to go, unless you need to modify the original object from your function. But with large data objects, passing by reference (or pointer) can be much more efficient. I'll further discuss the pros and cons of references in the next section.

The other side of passing by reference involves returning a function result via a reference. This works much like returning a result via a pointer. However, both of these methods of returning results demand caution, as I'll explain in the next section.

Pointer and Reference Guidelines and Cautions

We've covered all three methods of passing parameters and returning function results in C++: pass by value, pass by address (pointer), and pass by reference. Which should you use in a given situation? Here are some guidelines.

Guidelines for Passing Parameters and Returning Results

■ For small data objects (those smaller than or equal to 32 bits), pass by value.

■ For large data objects, pass by address or by reference. If you need to access individual elements of a long stretch of memory, for example, a pointer works well to walk the data. But, because of all the pointer dereferencing needed to access the elements via pointer notation, it might be more efficient to pass a reference to an array and use array notation. By the way, remember that arrays are always passed by address—unless you specify pass by reference. That's because an array name is a pointer.

■ If you need to *modify* an original data object of any size, pass by address or by reference. The copy you get if you pass by value prevents such modifications.

■ The guidelines given above also apply to returning function results, but there are some special cautions that complicate the picture. I'll get to those shortly.

- If you must return a value that is created as a *local variable* in a function, always return it by value, regardless of size. I'll explain why in a moment.

- A reference must refer to an existing object. The easiest way to guarantee that an object exists is to pass the original object yourself, by reference. If the object exists outside a function, it's safe to create a reference to it from inside the function.

- If you don't need to alter a large object that is passed to a function or returned from one, declare a *const* parameter (reference or pointer) or a *const* return type. This function prototype shows both:

  ```
  const BigObject& MyFunction(const BigObject& bo);
  ```

  MyFunction can't alter a *BigObject* passed to it via the *const* parameter *bo*. Likewise, *MyFunction* returns an unalterable *const* object via the return mechanism.

Use *const* liberally. It makes for more reliable programs. You can declare a non-*const* pointer to non-*const* data, a *const* pointer to non-*const* data, a non-*const* pointer to *const* data, or a *const* pointer to *const* data:

```
int* pInt = 10;               // non-const pointer to non-const data
int* const pInt = 10;         // const pointer to non-const data
const int* pInt = 10;         // non-const pointer to const data
const int* const pInt = 10;   // const pointer to const data
```

TIP How to tell what's what: If the *const* keyword precedes the data type name, the data is *const*. If *const* precedes the pointer name, the pointer is *const*.

These variations let you control precisely what can and can't be changed: it's the non-*const* part, if there is one, that can change—the pointer itself, the data it points to, or both. You can and should use *const* in the same way for references. And you can also use these variations in function parameters and function return types.

Returning Results: Caution Required

I promised earlier to explain the pitfalls of some ways of returning a function result. We'll consider returning local objects from a function, returning a pointer or reference to an object that exists outside the function, and making sure a returned pointer is properly deleted after use.

Returning a local object

Be careful how you return a local object. A local object is a local variable (of any type) in a function. Always return such an object by value, regardless of its size. Local variables are destroyed when they go out of scope at the end of the function. Consequently, if you return a pointer or reference to a local object, the pointer or reference has an undefined value after the function returns. If you then use the pointer or reference to change what you thought was the returned object, you instead write over memory in another part of your program or get an access violation. As with "running off the end" of an array, this mistake could make your program crash and provide hours of debugging practice. The following function illustrates the problem:

```
BigObject& MyFunction()
{
    BigObject bo;      // Local variable, created on stack
    return bo;         // By reference
}   // bo goes out of scope when MyFunction returns
```

Using a reference as the return type here is bad news. Returning a pointer to *bo* would be equally likely to result in a program failure.

The next function returns a local object correctly, by value, so that what is returned is a copy of the object. The copy continues to exist even though the original goes out of scope.

```
BigObject MyFunction()
{
    BigObject bo;
    return bo;          // Return a copy
}
```

Returning a *BigObject* by value requires a costly copy, so here's an alternative way to get a *BigObject* from *MyFunction* without a copy:

```
BigObject myBo;
:
```

```
MyFunction (myBo);
    ⋮
void MyFunction(BigObject& bo)
{
    // Alter bo in some useful way
}
```

In this case, you'd create the *BigObject* outside of *MyFunction*, pass it in by reference, and let the function operate on the original via the reference parameter. There's less overhead and no danger of trying to return a local object the wrong way.

References and existing objects

References need to refer to an existing object. This is an absolute requirement, because a reference is just an alias, another name for that object. The simplest way to ensure that a reference refers to an existing object is to create that object yourself and use a reference parameter to pass it to functions. The last example in the previous section shows how to do this.

What kind of object can you return a reference to with the *return* keyword? It must be an object that you created yourself, or that some other agency created outside of the function. You can safely return a reference to an object that is global to the function, or to an object that, say, Windows created. In the first case, involving an object that is global, it's usually better just to pass the object in and out via a reference parameter than to use *return*. In the second case, if Windows or MFC is responsible for both creating and destroying the object, a reference to it is fine, as long as the object continues to exist for the life of your reference variable. For example, Windows allocates storage for a device context object (you'll learn about those in Chapter 6) and you obtain a *handle* to the object. The handle is really a pointer under the hood, but the object is on loan to you. Windows created it and Windows will destroy it. You're free to use it in the meantime, as long as you give it back to Windows when you're done.

What if you create the object inside the function with the C++ *new* operator? Can you return a reference to that object? Well, the object is created on the heap instead of the stack, so it continues to exist after the function returns. Therefore, the answer is yes, you can return a reference to this object. The Refer3 program on the next page illustrates how this is done.

Try it now

Create the Refer3 program as you have created other C++ programs:

```cpp
// Refer3.cpp : Defines the entry point for the console application.
//

#include "stdafx.h"
#include <iostream.h>

struct Object
{
    int a;
    int b;
};

Object& MyFunction();

int main(int argc, char* argv[])
{
    Object& rMyObj = MyFunction();
    cout << "rMyObj.a = " << rMyObj.a << endl;

    delete &rMyObj;     // Delete object referred to
    return 0;
}

Object& MyFunction()
{
    Object* o = new Object;     // Create object on heap
    o->a = 20;                  // Set its value
    o->b = 25;
    return *o;                  // Return the object itself
}
```

The technique in the Refer3 program works—the reference variable *rMyObj* in *main* is initialized to the value returned by *MyFunction*. Yet a problem remains. Someone, sometime must delete the memory block sitting out there in the heap. How? We lost the pointer to that memory when *MyFunction* returned. (The variable was a local variable that went out of scope.) But we still have a reference to the object, *rMyObj*, and we can take the address of that reference—it's the same as the address of the memory in the heap, after all—and call *delete* on the resulting pointer:

```cpp
delete &rMyObj;
```

That takes care of that—the memory block is gone, although there's still an issue of how we can count on whoever calls *MyFunction* to perform this essential bit of cleanup. I'll soon say more about this under "Who deletes the pointer?"

Pointers and existing objects

A pointer should either point to *Null* or to a legitimate existing object. If it does neither—in other words, if the pointer is undefined—trying to dereference it will yield unpredictable results and create an elusive bug. Dereference a *null* pointer instead and you'll still get an access violation, but you'll have a somewhat easier time determining where the problem occurred. This is why I recommend always setting a pointer to *Null* as soon as you delete what it points to.

What about returning a pointer from a function that used *new* to create the object pointed to? The story is much the same as it was for references to such objects. You can do it, but there's a risk because you have to rely on someone, sometime, deleting the pointer. If it's not deleted, there'll be a memory leak.

Who deletes the pointer?

I've raised an issue for both pointers and references: when your function returns a pointer or reference to an object created on the heap with *new*, who is responsible for calling *delete* for that pointer?

The function that created the pointer or reference can't be responsible—when the pointer or reference is returned, the function has finished running. So it's the caller's responsibility to call *delete*. The awkwardness here is that *the function* called *new*, but you (or someone else) have to remember to call *delete*. Sometimes the caller will be someone else's program, and at other times it might be yours—maybe six months or a year from now.

We're all human. We tend to overlook little loose ends like this, and an undeleted pointer or reference is almost certain to result in memory leaks sooner or later. This is why it's generally considered poor programming practice to return a pointer that the caller must then delete. You can document that it's the caller's job to call *delete* for the pointer or reference, but who reads documentation? (Ask me—I write the stuff.) Sometimes you'll take the risk, but the stakes can be high. It's usually better to return an actual object by value or to work with a preexisting object that you pass to your function by address or by reference. Consider yourself warned.

Header and Implementation Files

So far, for the most part, we've put everything that's in the example programs (both declarations and definitions) into a single .cpp file—a C++ *implementation* file. But the more usual way to program in C++ is to put the declarations in a *header* file (with the .h extension) and the definitions in a .cpp file. Then the .cpp file *includes* the .h file, like this:

```
#include "myHdr.h"
```

Header and implementation files in C++ are just like the ones in C. Let's create Refer4, a version of the Refer3 program that divides the code into a header file and an implementation file. The implementation (.cpp) file must *include* the header. Create these files with the wizard as usual, naming the project Refer4:

Try it now

Create two programs: Refer4.cpp and Refer4.h.

1. Create the Refer4.cpp program as you have created other C++ programs. Edit Refer4.cpp to look like this:

```
// Refer4.cpp : Defines the entry point for the console...
//

#include "stdafx.h"
#include <iostream.h>
#include "Refer4.h"

int main(int argc, char* argv[])
{
    Object& rMyObj = MyFunction();
    cout << "rMyObj.a = " << rMyObj.a << endl;
```

```
        delete &rMyObj;      // Delete object referred to
        return 0;
}

Object& MyFunction()
{
    Object* o = new Object;    // Create object on heap
    o->a = 20;                 // Set its value
    o->b = 25;
    return *o;                 // Return the object itself
}
```

2. Create Refer4.h, a header file, add the following code, and add it to the project. To create the header file, use the New command on the File menu. In the New dialog box, click the Files tab. Click C/C++ Header File and give the file a name—Refer4.h—in the File Name box. Confirm that the Add To Project option is checked and that the project name is Refer4. Click OK to create the header file as part of the Refer4 project.

```
// Refer4.h
// Declares a type and a function prototype.

struct Object
{
    int a;
    int b;
};

Object& MyFunction();
```

Why divide things up this way? Suppose I develop a really useful data type, such as the *Object* struct in Refer4.h. I might want to use that same type again and again in other programs. If the type declaration is embedded in a .cpp file for program A, I have to make a copy of it and paste the copy into program B's .cpp file to use the type there. But if the type declarations, function declarations, constants, and other reusable items are in one or more header files, any program can reuse them simply by including the header files. Furthermore, many C++ programs are large enough to divide their code into multiple .cpp files. Several of those .cpp files might need to include the same declarations; so, again, separating those elements into header files can be helpful.

> **N** | **OTE** The header doesn't have to be called Refer4.h. Object.h might be a more meaningful name because it contains a declaration of the *Object* type.

Follow this rule: Put all executable code—function body definitions and anything else that allocates storage—in the .cpp files. Put only declarations in the .h files. This simple step will avoid linker errors due to multiple definitions of the same object. These linker errors would occur if several implementation files included the same header file.

Preventing Multiple Inclusion

A problem sometimes crops up in using header files. You can inadvertently include the same header file more than once in the same .cpp file. This happens when header file B includes header file A (yes, a header can include other headers), and implementation file C includes both A and B. C gets two copies of A, and you get really scary error messages. To prevent that, don't include A in C; include only B. Figure 3-4 illustrates the problem and the solution. Drawing a diagram like this can be a big help in keeping your headers straight.

You can also take formal coding steps to prevent multiple inclusion, using conditional preprocessor directives. For more information and an MFC example, see "Reading the AppWizard Files" in the Appendix.

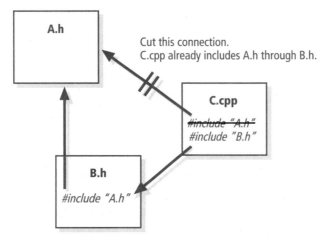

Figure 3-4.   *Correctly and incorrectly including header files.*

Precompiled Headers

I offer one last comment about using headers. In Visual C++, you can *precompile* any code that is quite stable—that is, any code that you aren't making frequent changes in. By precompiling, you cut down on the amount of code that has to be recompiled each time you make a change and build your program.

Header files are one kind of code that you can usefully precompile. Especially when you're using a large code library like MFC, precompiling headers can greatly reduce build time—a savings that gives you faster turnaround and improves your productivity. In MFC projects, headers are precompiled by default. For more information about how this happens, search Help for *precompiled headers* and choose the subtopic "creating." In MFC programs, the StdAfx.h file is the heart of the precompiled header mechanism—although, in the simple console applications we're creating in the book, StdAfx.h doesn't play much of a role. To set up a console application that does use MFC and, therefore, does use the precompiled header mechanism extensively, create your console application as usual, but do not select "A Simple Application" in AppWizard. Instead, select the fourth option, "An Application That Supports MFC." If you followed the steps in Chapter 1 to create a new Win32 Console Application, you've seen the four options I refer to.

Try It Yourself

Test yourself with the following extra-credit work.

1. Practice with pointers

Write a small program in which you do the following:

- Create an array of 26 *char* elements (not *char**).
- Initialize the array with the 26 letters of the English alphabet.
- Walk the array backward with a pointer (not the array name itself but a separate pointer), outputting the letters in reverse alphabetical order.

See program Ch3ex1 in the \learnvcn\Chap03 folder in the companion code for one solution.

2. More practice with pointers

Write another small program in which you try these exercises:

- Create a stack data structure using an array of 20 pointers to *char* (not pointers to *char**). You'll need a second pointer to *char* to represent the top of the stack—the "stack pointer." As you add elements to the stack (*push* them), always do so at the top, then advance the pointer (watching for the end of the array). As you remove elements from the stack (*pop* them), always move the pointer back toward the beginning of the array, then get the element there. Watch for element 0.

- Push the string "purtsuorts" onto the stack.

- Pop the stack's complete contents, printing elements as you go. You should end up with the word "purtsuorts" spelled backward—stroustrup.

See program Ch3ex2 in the \learnvcn\Chap03 folder in the companion code for one solution.

What's Next?

In Chapter 4, we explore the central feature of C++, the C++ class. Classes are essential for creating your own complex data types and for doing object-oriented programming. The following are among the topics we'll cover:

- Classes and objects

- Class member variables and functions

- Controlling outside access to class data

C++ Classes

This chapter and the next round out our coverage of the C++ language with a series of programs that illustrate the use of C++ *classes*. Classes are the principal way in C++ to create new *programmer-defined data types*. They're also the basis for *object-oriented programming* (commonly known as OOP). I'll approach the subject of OOP by stages in this chapter and Chapter 5 by taking you through the following programs:

- The Shape1 program introduces three new data types designed for use in software that draws and manipulates geometric shapes such as rectangles and ellipses. In Shape1, the C++ is much like C—not a bad place to begin when classes and OOP are new to you.

- The Shape2 program gets serious about objects. This code asks, "Why shouldn't an object be responsible for its own behaviors?" It answers by introducing classes. Shape2 uses classes as the basis for new versions of the three data types used in Shape1. The classes contain functions as well as data, making them very powerful and versatile programming constructs.

- The Shape3 program in Chapter 5 finally approaches the goal of fully using the characteristics of OOP. By introducing the ability of C++ to derive a new class from an existing one, it brings us to those characteristics that most define OOP: *encapsulation, inheritance,* and *polymorphism*. In Chapter 5, we'll first look at encapsulation—the ability of a class object to contain, and even hide, data. We'll look at how you can derive one class from another and how the *derived class* inherits the characteristics of its *base class*. We'll see what the resulting *class hierarchies* are like. We'll look at how to *override* the characteristics of a base class in a class derived from the base. And we'll take polymorphism—which translates roughly as "many shapes"—pretty literally.

■ Several other small programs in this chapter and the next will demonstrate other aspects of C++, including access specifiers, constructors and destructors, and static class members. In Chapter 5, I'll also discuss class scope and briefly cover operator overloading.

Among the additional C++ topics this chapter covers are the following:

■ Function overloading

■ Class member functions

■ The *this* pointer

■ Information hiding and control of outside access to class members

■ Microsoft Foundation Class Library 6.0 (MFC) source code conventions

■ Static variables

■ Friend functions and classes

Objects and Classes

In the programming world, there are (at least) two definitions of the word *object.* The most basic definition is "a region of storage that has a specific data type." *Strings, ints,* and *floats,* for example, are considered objects. The C++ and OOP definition of an object, however, is "a region of storage plus a set of operations that can manipulate that storage." In this case, an object is also referred to as a *class object.*

So what is a *class* and what's its relationship to an object? One way of looking at it is to say that a class is like a cookie cutter and objects are like cookies. In essence, a class is a data type, like *int* or *float*, but programmer-defined rather than built in. Another way to say it is that a class is a plan, like a blueprint, that you use to create real objects in your program. A class defines the structure and behaviors of its objects by defining *data members* and *member functions*. Within the class declaration, data members (also called member variables) look much like one or more ordinary variable declarations, while member functions look much like function prototypes.

Here's a very simple C++ class, in the form of a C-like *struct*:

```
struct Employee
{
    // Member variables (data members)
    string m_strName;
    string m_strSocialSecurityNumber;
    double m_dSalary;

    // Member functions
    void SetName(string name);
    void SetSSN(string SSN);
    void SetSalary(double salary);
    string GetName();
    string GetSSN();
    double GetSalary();
    void ComputeMonthlyPay();
};
```

If you have a background in C, this might look like a very strange *struct* to you. If you're a Pascal programmer, it also looks strange—like a Pascal record with function declarations thrown in. But in C++, this is both a legitimate *struct* and a class. In fact, there are three kinds of classes in C++:

■ Classes declared with the *struct* keyword

■ Classes declared with the *union* keyword

■ Classes declared with the *class* keyword

I'll cover the *struct* and *class* variations later in this chapter. *Unions* are somewhat advanced (and, frankly, somewhat archaic), so I won't explain them further. Check the Help index for *union* and read the first two topics listed in the Topics Found dialog box.

Using the class *Employee*, you can write code like the following:

```
Employee empCurrent;
empCurrent.SetName("Smith, John");
empCurrent.m_strSocialSecurityNumber = "555-55-5555";

    ⋮
cout << empCurrent.GetName() << endl;
```

The first line declares a variable of type *Employee*, named *empCurrent*—*empCurrent* is a class object. It contains the *members* (data members and member functions) listed in the *struct* declaration. The second line shows how to call a member function of the object. The third line demonstrates accessing a data member directly. And the final line shows another member function call.

Notice how we declared the *empCurrent* variable—its data type, then the variable name:

```
Employee empCurrent;
```

Creating a Class from Scratch

A class usually represents an abstraction, such as a point, a geometric shape, a document, or an employee. MFC, for example, has classes to represent documents, dialog boxes, and even the application as a whole. Later in the book, we'll write a drawing program that lets you draw rectangles and ellipses. Rectangles and ellipses have features in common, such as location, size, color, and so on. Abstractly, each is a geometric shape. So, we'll develop a shape class that can represent a rectangle, an ellipse, or whatever other shape we care to specify. Working out the shape class includes listing things you can do with a shape: create it, draw it, move it, color it, rotate it, inflate it, destroy it. Notice how this begins to treat a shape as a *thing*—an object—that we can manipulate.

As we move toward implementation, we'll concern ourselves with two attributes that each two-dimensional shape has: a bounding rectangle, within which the entire shape lies, and an ID of some sort to identify the shape's type (rectangle, ellipse, and so on). (A more complete design might include a color, an orientation, and other attributes.) Figure 4-1 shows the bounding rectangle of an ellipse.

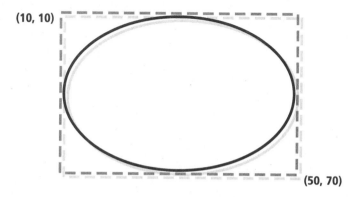

(10, 10)

(50, 70)

Figure 4-1.   *A shape's bounding rectangle.*

Here's a simple shape class:

```
struct Shape
{
    Rect    m_rectShape;    // Bounding rectangle
    ShpType m_typeShape;    // Shape: rectangle, ellipse...
};
```

We're aiming toward a real drawing program, but since we are working in a character-mode environment for the time being, we'll simply display a string for each shape we'd draw if we could. The string will contain the shape's type and the coordinates of its bounding rectangle. The *x* and *y* coordinates of the top left corner will come first, followed by the *x* and *y* coordinates of the bottom right corner. Examples of such strings are *rectangle at (0, 0, 20, 20)* and *ellipse at (30, 35, 127, 140)*.

Later in the book, we'll replace the above implementation of the drawing operation with a Microsoft Win32 API function call that really draws a rectangle or ellipse within the specified bounding rectangle.

The Shape1 program begins to demonstrate how classes work.

The Shape1 Program

Shape1 is a rather C-like program, but it illustrates the following aspects of C++, among others:

- Using the *struct* keyword to define a class

- *structs* with member functions

- Declaring, initializing, using, and destroying objects on the stack and the heap

- Creating and using an array of Shape objects

- A C-like approach to implementing what can be done with a shape

- Inline member function definitions

 Try it now

Create the Shape1 project as a Win32 Console Application. Create the four code files listed below. You'll create the Shape1.cpp file when you create the Shape1 project. Then add the three .h files with the New command. To add a .h file select C/C++ Header File on the Files tab in the New dialog box.

- **CPoint.h,** a header file declaring the *Point* class. A rectangle is defined by points at two corners, top left and bottom right.

- **CRect.h,** a header file declaring the *Rect* class. Each shape is contained within a bounding rectangle.

- **Shape.h,** a header file declaring the *Shape* class.

- **Shape1.cpp,** the main file. This file contains the *main* function and implementations for all three of the header files.

CPoint.h

```
// CPoint.h

struct Point
{
// Constructors
    Point(){ x = 0; y = 0; };
    Point(int ix, int iy){ x = ix; y = iy; };

// Attributes
    int x;
    int y;
};
```

CRect.h

```
// CRect.h

#include "CPoint.h"

struct Rect
{
// Constructors
    Rect() { m_ptTopLeft = Point(); m_ptBotRight = Point(10,10); };
    Rect(Point tl, Point br) { m_ptTopLeft = tl; m_ptBotRight = br; };

// Attributes
    Point m_ptTopLeft;
    Point m_ptBotRight;

    void SetRect(Point tl, Point br)
                { m_ptTopLeft = tl; m_ptBotRight = br; };
    void SetRect(int x1, int y1, int x2, int y2)
                { m_ptTopLeft.x = x1; m_ptTopLeft.y = y1;
                  m_ptBotRight.x = x2; m_ptBotRight.y = y2; };
};
```

Shape.h

```
// Shape.h

#include "CRect.h"

// Constant for use in generating random shape types
const int NUM_TYPES = 2;

// Possible shape types
enum ShpType
{
    shpRectangle,
    shpEllipse
    // Could add others here
};

// The Shape class
struct Shape
{
    Rect m_rectShape;       // Bounding rectangle of shape
    ShpType m_typeShape;    // Rectangle, ellipse, and so on
};
```

(continued)

Shape1.cpp

```cpp
// Shape1.cpp : Defines the entry point for the console application.
//

#include "Stdafx.h"
#include "Shape.h"
#include <Stdio.h>     // For printf, sprintf
#include <Assert.h>    // For assert
#include <Stdlib.h>    // For rand, srand, abs
#include <Time.h>      // For time
#include <String.h>    // For strcpy

// Global function prototypes
void DrawShape(Shape* pS);
void MoveShape(Shape* pS, Point p);
int RandomCoord();
ShpType RandomType();

const int COORD_MAX = 1000;

/////////////////////////////////////
// main
int main(int argc, char* argv[])
{
    // Create a shape on the stack.
    Shape shp1;
    shp1.m_rectShape = Rect(Point(20, 20), Point(50, 50));
    shp1.m_typeShape = shpRectangle;
    DrawShape(&shp1);

    // Move a shape in coordinate space.
    MoveShape(&shp1, Point(25, 25));
    DrawShape(&shp1);

    // Create a shape on the heap.
    Shape* pShp2 = new Shape;
    assert(pShp2 != NULL);
    pShp2->m_rectShape = Rect(Point(100, 100), Point(150, 150));
    pShp2->m_typeShape = shpEllipse;
    DrawShape(pShp2);

    delete pShp2;

    // Create 20 random shapes in an array.
    Point pt1, pt2;
```

```
Shape* arShps[20];
srand((unsigned)time(NULL));      // Seed random number generator
for(int i = 0; i < 20; i++)
{
    // Create next shape.
    Shape* pShp = new Shape;
    assert(pShp != NULL);
    // Give it some coordinates.
    pt1 = Point(RandomCoord(), RandomCoord());
    pt2 = Point(RandomCoord(), RandomCoord());
    pShp->m_rectShape = Rect(pt1, pt2);
    // Specify whether it's a rectangle or an ellipse.
    pShp->m_typeShape = RandomType();
    // Add it to the array.
    arShps[i] = pShp;
    // "Draw" the shape (as a string).
    DrawShape(arShps[i]);
}

// Move a shape.
MoveShape(arShps[0], Point(20,20));
DrawShape(arShps[0]);

// Delete all shapes.
for(int j = 0; j < 20; j++)
{
    delete arShps[j];
}

return 0;
}


/////////////////////////////////////
// Global function definitions

// "Draw" the shape.
void DrawShape(Shape* pS)
{
    Rect rect = pS->m_rectShape;
    int x1 = rect.m_ptTopLeft.x;
    int y1 = rect.m_ptTopLeft.y;
    int x2 = rect.m_ptBotRight.x;
    int y2 = rect.m_ptBotRight.y;
```

(continued)

```
// Determine shape type, represented as a string.
char szType[20];
switch(pS->m_typeShape)
{
case shpRectangle: strcpy(szType, "rectangle");
    break;
case shpEllipse: sprintf(szType, "%s", "ellipse");
    break;
default: strcpy(szType, "errorShapeType");
};

// "Draw" shape as a string.
//  Example: "rectangle at (34, 76, 987, 800)"
printf("%s at (%d,%d,%d,%d)\n", szType, x1, y1, x2, y2);
}

// Shift shape to new position p.
void MoveShape(Shape* pS, Point p /* New m_ptTopLeft */)
{
    Rect rect = pS->m_rectShape;
    int width = abs(rect.m_ptBotRight.x - rect.m_ptTopLeft.x);
    int height = abs(rect.m_ptBotRight.y - rect.m_ptTopLeft.y);

    // New m_ptTopLeft corner is p.
    pS->m_rectShape.m_ptTopLeft = p;
    // New m_ptBotRight corner calculated from p using size of shape.
    pS->m_rectShape.m_ptBotRight = Point(p.x + width, p.y + height);
}

//////////////////////////////////////
// Global Helper functions

// Generate a random positive coordinate
//  within a COORD_MAX by COORD_MAX drawing area.
int RandomCoord()
{
    // Base new coordinate loosely on last coordinate.
    static int nLastCoord;   // Automatically initialized to 0,
                             //  then altered on each call.

    // Get a pseudorandom number between 0 and RAND_MAX (32,767).
    int nNextCoord = rand();
```

```
    int nFudge = rand() % 100;   // Generate a fudge factor: 0 to 99
    // Use (larger of new number and old number) + fudge factor.
    nLastCoord = (nNextCoord > nLastCoord ? nNextCoord :
                                             nLastCoord);
    // Restrict the number to a value between
    //  0 and COORD_MAX - 1 (inclusive).
    nLastCoord = (nLastCoord + nFudge) % COORD_MAX;
    return nLastCoord;
}


// Pseudorandomly generate a rectangle or ellipse shape type.
ShpType RandomType()
{
    // 0 to 1 (= shpRectangle to shpEllipse)
    return (ShpType)(rand() % NUM_TYPES);
}
```

The C++ in the Shape1 Program

The *main* function in the Shape1 program is in the file Shape1.cpp.
Shape1.cpp uses the #*include* directive to include:

■ The file Shape.h, a header file that declares *Shape* as a *struct*, along
  with an enumeration (named *ShpType*) of the allowed shape types
  (rectangles and ellipses)

■ Several headers from the C/C++ run-time library that enable program Shape1 to use a number of run-time functions

The file Shape1.cpp includes several other headers indirectly—the
header Shape.h includes CRect.h, and CRect.h includes CPoint.h. In
other words, by including Shape.h, we include the headers it includes
and the headers that each of those included files includes. By this indirect method, Shape1.cpp also includes CRect.h and CPoint.h, as illustrated in Figure 4-2.

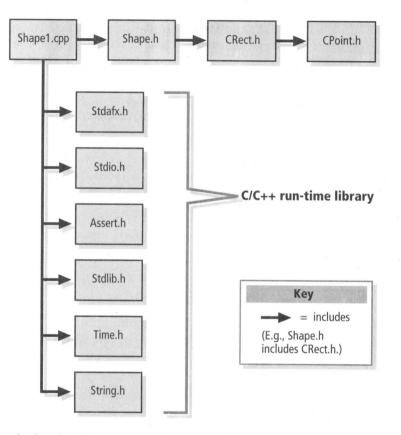

Figure 4-2. *The header file structure of program Shape1.*

CPoint.h and CRect.h declare two other *structs*: *Point* and *Rect*. *Point* defines a geometric point—an object with an *x* coordinate and a *y* coordinate—in a simple coordinate system, shown in Figure 4-3. *Rect* defines a rectangle in that same space. *Rect* is defined by the coordinates (points) of its top left and bottom right corners. These coordinates are specified in *Rect* as data members of type *Point*.

Struct *Shape*, in turn, defines in coordinate space the rectangle that *bounds* the shape—a box within which the shape is drawn. *Shape* also contains a *ShpType* data member set to the type of shape that the *Shape* object represents: a rectangle or an ellipse.

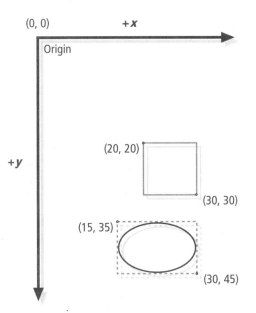

Figure 4-3. *The coordinate system for program Shape1.*

NOTE There's a reason for putting the coordinate system's origin at the top left and extending positive *y* values downward. You'll see why when we get to Microsoft Windows coordinate systems in Chapter 6.

The *structs* in the Shape1 Program

All three classes in program Shape1 are declared using the *struct* keyword. The *Shape* class is a simple C++ *struct* with two data members. The other classes, *Point* and *Rect*, contain member functions as well as data members. The ability of the C++ *struct* to contain functions is further evidence that a *struct* is really a class.

Constructors

The *Point* class declares two special functions known as *constructors*. A constructor always has the same name as its class, and its purpose is to initialize that class. A constructor can take parameters, but it can't return a result.

The following constructor, from the *Rect* class, shows one other useful thing about constructors:

```
Rect() { m_ptTopLeft = Point(); m_ptBotRight = Point(10,10); };
```

Notice that the *m_ptTopLeft* and *m_ptBotRight* data members are set to the following expressions:

```
Point()          // Equivalent to Point(0,0)
Point(10,10)
```

The above expressions are explicit calls to the *Point* class constructors—the first one takes no parameters and the second one takes two parameters. Each call constructs (creates) and initializes a *Point* object that we then assign to one of the *Rect* data members. Without the *Point* constructor, we'd have to write the *Rect* constructor's code more like this:

```
Rect()
{
    Point pt1, pt2;
    pt1.x = 0; pt1.y = 0;
    pt2.x = 10; pt2.y = 10;
    m_ptTopLeft = pt1;
    m_ptBotRight = pt2;
};
```

Having the *Point* constructor greatly simplifies the code.

You won't always call constructors explicitly. They're more likely to be called implicitly by way of variable declarations and initializations. But in the example above, calling the constructor explicitly is very handy. I'll have more to say about constructors later, in Chapter 5.

Function overloading

Like the *Point* class, the *Rect* class has two constructors. *Rect* also has two ordinary member functions that are both named *SetRect*. You might already have noticed that the *Point* class has two member functions with the same name and that the *Rect* class has two *pairs* of member functions with the same name. In C++, using the same function name with a different set of parameters is called *function overloading*.

It's often useful to have multiple versions of a function that take different parameters; you'll see that a lot in MFC. Both class member functions and global functions can be overloaded. The parameter lists must be different. (It's not enough for just the return type to be different.) You can overload a function as many times as you like, either in its class or in a subclass.

Defining member functions inline

Take a closer look at the member functions of classes *Point* and *Rect*. Following the function prototype—the function's return type, name, and parameter list—is additional code enclosed by curly braces { }. When a member function is very short and simple, as these member functions are, we often define the functions *inline*. This means that the compiler can, if it chooses, replace each call to such a function, wherever and however often such calls occur, with the code between the curly braces. This eliminates the time it takes to make a function call during execution of the program. However, an increase in the amount of memory needed usually offsets that gain if the function is more than a couple of lines long.

Also, programs that use a class containing an inline member function have to be recompiled if the inline function changes. That's normally not the case with noninline functions. Use inline member functions only when they're small and rather stable, but do use them. Keep in mind, though, that inline functions are really just a hint to the compiler, which it might ignore. It's a chance to optimize your code, but not a guarantee that it will be optimized.

You can also use the *inline* keyword to declare global functions:

```
inline void MyGlobalFunction()
{
   ⋮
}
```

Check the Help Index for *inline*.

Run-Time Functions in the Shape1 Program

Program Shape1 employs several functions from the C/C++ run-time library, so it needs to include the appropriate header file for each. Among the run-time functions it uses are these:

- ■ *printf* **and** *sprintf*, from the file Stdio.h. Notice that I didn't include Iostream.h for this program. Instead, I chose to use *printf*, familiar to generations of C programmers, and its relative *sprintf*. The *printf* function prints formatted output to the standard output device (usually the console). Sometimes *printf* is easier to use than *cout*. The *sprintf* function formats a string just as *printf* does, but the result is placed in a character buffer (string) that you supply. It's a nice way to build up complex output strings, especially when you need them for uses other than printing—such as displaying a formatted string in a dialog box. For format specifications that these functions use, such as %s and %d, check the Help index for *format specification fields* and double-click the subtopic *printf*.

- **assert,** from the file Assert.h. This is a brief introduction to *assertions*, useful for error checking and debugging. Each time I call *new* to create an object on the heap—a call that could fail if there isn't enough memory available for the allocation—I check the pointer that *new* returns, using the *assert* function, like this:

```
assert(pShp != NULL);
```

I *assert*, or claim, that the expression in parentheses is true. If it isn't, *assert* aborts the program with an error message. In the Shape1 program, the assertion is false (it "fails") if *new* fails and returns a *Null* pointer.

- **rand** and **srand,** from the file Stdlib.h. I use these functions to generate some random data in *main*. In the helper functions *RandomCoord* and *RandomType*, I call the *rand* function to generate a random (actually pseudorandom, or "sort of" random) integer that I then convert to a random coordinate or a random shape type. Before calling *rand* for the first time, I call *srand* to seed, or initialize, the random number generator.

- **time,** from the file Time.h. A good way to seed the random number generator is to base the seed on the current time, obtained through the run-time function *time*. Suitably cast to an *unsigned int*, the result of *time* makes a fine parameter for the *srand* call. Each time we seed the generator this way and then repeatedly call *rand,* we get a different sequence of pseudorandom numbers. Since the seed is dependent on the time, the chances of getting the same seed, and thus the same pseudorandom sequence are extremely low.

- ***strcpy,*** from the file String.h. In the *DrawShape* function, I show two ways to prepare strings for output. The first is a call to *sprintf,* discussed earlier. The second uses the *strcpy* (string copy) function to copy the characters of one string into another string.

- ***abs,*** from the file Stdlib.h. (It's also in Math.h.) The absolute value function returns a positive value, given either a positive or a negative value. I use it to cancel out negative numbers because I want only positive drawing coordinates.

Restricting random numbers to a range by using the modulus operator

The two randomizing functions I wrote for the Shape1 program also illustrate how to restrict the random numbers you get so they fall into a range you want. The *rand* function generates a pseudorandom integer in the range *0* to *RAND_MAX* (32,767). But suppose I want only random 0s and 1s—random *shpRectangles* and *shpEllipses.* That's what I want, for example, in the *RandomType* function. To obtain only these two small numbers, I use the *modulus* operator (%) like this:

```
rand() % NUM_TYPES     // NUM_TYPES = 2
```

The modulus operator yields the *remainder* after dividing the first operand by the second. The expression above equals either 0 or 1, every time. For instance, if the *rand* call generates the number 1001, dividing 1001 by 2 results in 500 with a remainder of 1. The modulus operator returns that 1, which is the value defined for *shpEllipse* in the *ShpType* enumeration.

The *main* Function in the Shape1 Program

In *main,* the Shape1 program creates, uses, and destroys a number of *Shape* objects. It also fills an array with pointers to *Shape* objects. The *main* function demonstrates constructing *Shape* objects on the stack (the *shp1* object) and on the heap (the object pointed to by *pShp2* and the 20 objects pointed to by the elements of the array *arShps*). Note that I'm careful to call *delete* for all of those pointers to heap objects when I finish with them (but I don't use the *delete [] arShps* call because *arShps* itself is declared on the stack as a local variable). Also notice the use of *Rect* and *Point* constructors.

The most interesting code in *main* is the *for* loop in which I fill an array with 20 pointers to *Shape* objects:

```
// Create 20 random shapes in an array.
    Point pt1, pt2;
    Shape* arShps[20];                   // Declare array of Shape pointers
    srand((unsigned)time(NULL));         // Seed random number generator
    for(int i = 0; i < 20; i++)
    {
        // Create next shape.
        Shape* pShp = new Shape;         // Create Shape, get pointer to it
        assert(pShp != NULL);
        // Give it some coordinates.
        pt1 = Point(RandomCoord(), RandomCoord());
        pt2 = Point(RandomCoord(), RandomCoord());
        pShp->m_rectShape = Rect(pt1, pt2);
        // Specify whether it's a rectangle or an ellipse.
        PShp->m_typeShape = RandomType();
        // Add it to the array.
        arShps[i] = pShp;                // Assign pointer to array element
        // "Draw" the shape (as a string).
        DrawShape(arShps[i]);
    }
```

The key points in this code are the array declaration, the creation of each *Shape*, and the addition to the array of the pointer to each new *Shape*:

```
Shape* arShps[20];           // Declare array of Shape pointers
```

```
Shape* pShp = new Shape;     // Create Shape, get pointer to it
arShps[i] = pShp;            // Assign pointer to array element
```

A new pointer value is assigned to *pShp* on each pass through the *for* loop. But the loop stores a copy of the pointer in the array beforehand, so all of the pointers remain valid and we don't lose any of the heap objects.

What's Wrong with the Shape1 Program?

What's wrong with program Shape1? It's not nearly object-oriented enough! Our first inclination was to *do* things with *Shape* objects. Still thinking like C or Pascal programmers, we wrote global functions that draw a shape and move a shape. In fact, most of the code in the Shape1 program is in those global functions. The *Shape* class itself is just a little *struct* with two data members.

What we really want is to make the *Shape* object do the work. To do that, the functions need to be inside the *Shape* object. They need to become the *Shape's* behavior—what it does (on command) rather than what we do to it with some global function. So that's the plan for the next version, program Shape2. We'll move as much functionality as we can *inside* the *Shape* class.

While we're at it, we'll start using the *class* keyword. Although a *struct* is a *class,* my preference is to use the *struct* keyword, without member functions, for things that are still C-like, and the *class* keyword for objects that have behavior.

The Shape2 Program

Program Shape2 is more object-oriented than program Shape1. The biggest change is to convert the two global functions, *DrawShape* and *MoveShape*, to member functions of the *Shape* class. These are the two global functions in Shape1 that require a parameter that is a pointer to *Shape*. Their names are now *Draw* and *Move*—because they're inside the *Shape* object, the "Shape" portion of their names is no longer needed.

The class now uses the *class* keyword instead of *struct* and has a new name, *CShape*, based on an MFC class-naming convention. The *C* prefix means "class." All MFC classes (including a few MFC *structs*) follow this convention. A related convention governs naming class data members, such as *CShape's* member *m_rectShape*. Class data members' names begin with *m_* (for "member variable"). The one place I haven't used the *m* convention is in the names of the *x* and *y* members of the *Point* class. It seems handier to keep them very simple. In the same vein, I've renamed classes *Point* and *Rect* to *CPoint* and *CRect*.

Program Shape2 shows the following C++ features:

■ Full-fledged class member functions

■ Member functions not defined inline

■ Member function access to other class members

- The *this* pointer, used to point to an object from inside the object's own code

- The *static* keyword, used here inside a function

- Access specifiers, for controlling user access to certain class members

Try it now

Here's the code for program Shape2. As you did in Shape1, create the Shape2 project, and add the following code files:

- **CPoint.h,** a header file declaring the *CPoint* class.

- **CRect.h,** a header file declaring the *CRect* class.

- **Shape.h,** a header file declaring the *CShape* class.

- **Shape2.cpp.** This file contains the *main* function and implementations for all three of the header files.

CPoint.h

```
// CPoint.h

class CPoint
{
public:
// Constructors
    CPoint(){ x = 0; y = 0; };
    CPoint(int ix, int iy){ x = ix; y = iy; };

// Attributes
    int x;
    int y;
};
```

CRect.h

```
// CRect.h

#include "CPoint.h"
```

```
class CRect
{
public:
// Constructors
    CRect()
        { m_ptTopLeft = CPoint(); m_ptBotRight = CPoint(10,10); };
    CRect(CPoint tl, CPoint br)
        { m_ptTopLeft = tl; m_ptBotRight = br; };

// Attributes
    CPoint m_ptTopLeft;
    CPoint m_ptBotRight;

    void SetRect(CPoint tl, CPoint br)
                { m_ptTopLeft = tl; m_ptBotRight = br; };
    void SetRect(int x1, int y1, int x2, int y2)
                { m_ptTopLeft.x = x1; m_ptTopLeft.y = y1;
                  m_ptBotRight.x = x2; m_ptBotRight.y = y2; };
};
```

Shape.h

```
// Shape.h

#include "CRect.h"

// Constant for use in generating random types
const int NUM_TYPES = 2;

class CShape
{
public:
    // Possible shape types
    enum ShpType     // Nested enum
    {
        shpRectangle,
        shpEllipse
    };

// Constructors
    CShape() { m_rectShape = CRect(CPoint(), CPoint(10,10));
                m_typeShape = shpRectangle; };
```

(continued)

```
        CShape(CRect r, ShpType t) { m_rectShape = r; m_typeShape = t; };

// Attributes
    void SetRect(CRect r) { m_rectShape = r; };
    void SetType(ShpType t) { m_typeShape = t; };

    CRect GetRect() const { return m_rectShape; };
    ShpType GetType() const { return m_typeShape; };

// Operations
    void Draw();
    void Move(CPoint p);

// Implementation
private:
    CRect m_rectShape;      // Bounding rectangle of shape
    ShpType m_typeShape;    // Rectangle, ellipse, and so on
};
```

Shape2.cpp

```
// Shape2.cpp : Defines the entry point for the console application.
//

#include "Stdafx.h"
#include "Shape.h"
#include <Stdio.h>      // For printf, sprintf
#include <Assert.h>     // For assert
#include <Stdlib.h>     // For rand, srand, abs
#include <Time.h>       // For time
#include <String.h>     // For strcpy

// Global function prototypes
int RandomCoord();
CShape::ShpType RandomType();

const int COORD_MAX = 1000;

//////////////////////////////////////
// main
int main(int argc, char* argv[])
```

```
{
    // Create a shape on the stack.
    CShape shp1;
    shp1.SetRect(CRect(CPoint(20, 20), CPoint(50, 50)));
    shp1.SetType(CShape::shpRectangle);
    shp1.Draw();

    // Move a shape in coordinate space.
    shp1.Move(CPoint(25, 25));
    shp1.Draw();

    // Create a shape on the heap.
    CShape* pShp2 = new CShape
                        (CRect(CPoint(100, 100), CPoint(150, 150)),
                         CShape::shpEllipse);
    assert(pShp2 != NULL);
    pShp2->Draw();

    delete pShp2;

    // Create 20 random shapes in an array
    CPoint pt1, pt2;
    CRect rect;
    CShape* arShps[20];
    srand((unsigned)time(NULL));
    for(int i = 0; i < 20; i++)
    {
        CShape* pShp = new CShape();
        assert(pShp != NULL);
        pt1 = CPoint(RandomCoord(), RandomCoord());
        pt2 = CPoint(RandomCoord(), RandomCoord());
        rect = CRect(pt1, pt2);
        pShp->SetRect(rect);
        pShp->SetType(RandomType());
        arShps[i] = pShp;
        arShps[i]->Draw();
    }

    // Move a shape.
    arShps[0]->Move(CPoint(20,20));
    arShps[0]->Draw();

    // Delete all shapes.
    for(int j = 0; j < 20; j++)
```

(continued)

145

```
        {
            delete arShps[j];
        }


    return 0;
    }


    ///////////////////////////////////
    // CShape definitions

    void CShape::Draw()
    {
        int x1 = m_rectShape.m_ptTopLeft.x;
        int y1 = m_rectShape.m_ptTopLeft.y;
        int x2 = m_rectShape.m_ptBotRight.x;
        int y2 = m_rectShape.m_ptBotRight.y;

        // Determine shape type, represented as a string
        char szType[20];
        switch(m_typeShape)
        {
        case shpRectangle: strcpy(szType, "rectangle");
            break;
        case shpEllipse: sprintf(szType, "%s", "ellipse");
            break;
        default: strcpy(szType, "errorShapeType");
        };

        // "Draw" shape as a string.
        //   Example: "rectangle at (34, 76, 987, 800)"
        printf("%s at (%d,%d,%d,%d)\n", szType, x1, y1, x2, y2);
    }

    // Shift shape to new position p.
    void CShape::Move(CPoint p /* New m_ptTopLeft */)
    {
        int width = abs(m_rectShape.m_ptBotRight.x -
                        m_rectShape.m_ptTopLeft.x);
        int height = abs(m_rectShape.m_ptBotRight.y -
                        m_rectShape.m_ptTopLeft.y);

        m_rectShape.m_ptTopLeft = p;
        m_rectShape.m_ptBotRight = CPoint(p.x + width, p.y + height);
    }
```

```
/////////////////////////////////////
// Global Helper functions

// Generate a random positive coordinate
//   within a COORD_MAX by COORD_MAX drawing area.
int RandomCoord()
{
    // Base new coordinate loosely on last coordinate.
    static int nLastCoord;    // Automatically initialized to 0,
                              //   then altered on each call.

    // Get a pseudorandom number between 0 and RAND_MAX (32,767).
    int nNextCoord = rand();
    int nFudge = rand() % 100;  // Generate a fudge factor: 0 to 99.
    // Use (larger of new number and old number) + fudge factor.
    // Restrict the number to a value between
    //   0 and COORD_MAX - 1 (inclusive).
    nLastCoord = abs((nNextCoord > nLastCoord ? nNextCoord :
                     (nLastCoord + nFudge)) % COORD_MAX);
    return nLastCoord;
}

// Pseudorandomly generate a rectangle or ellipse shape type
CShape::ShpType RandomType()
{
    // 0 to 1 (= shpRectangle to shpEllipse)
    return (CShape::ShpType)(rand() % NUM_TYPES);
}
```

The C++ in the Shape2 Program

Program Shape2 adds several more serious class member functions. These do more than just set or get the value of a data member. I'll cover the essentials of member functions, introduce the mysterious *this* pointer, and explain access specifiers—how to control access to class members using the *public* and *private* keywords. This still isn't the definitive Shape program, but it's a big step closer.

Member functions

Class member functions can be defined inline or not. Program Shape2 includes examples of both. To call a member function, use member selection syntax, either a dot for an object allocated on the stack or the pointer member access operator (->) for an object allocated on the heap. This code, from the *main* function, illustrates the member selection syntax:

```
// Create a shape on the stack.
CShape shp1;
shp1.SetRect(CRect(CPoint(20, 20), CPoint(50, 50)));
shp1.SetType(CShape::shpRectangle);
shp1.Draw();
  ⋮
// Create a shape on the heap.
CShape* pShp2 = new CShape
                    (CRect(CPoint(100, 100), CPoint(150, 150)),
                     CShape::shpEllipse);
assert(pShp2 != NULL);
pShp2->Draw();
```

You can also use the pointer member access operator to access an object on the stack through a pointer to the stack object:

```
// Create a shape on the stack
CShape shp3;                         // Shape on stack
CShape* pShp4 = &shp3;               // Pointer to shape
pShp4->SetType(CShape::shpEllipse);  // Use -> to access shape
```

A member function is *inside* its class. As such, it has full access to all data members inside that class. This is true even if some of those members are declared as *private* or *protected*—we'll get to access specifiers shortly. (The only time a member function doesn't have this access is when the function is declared *static*. I'll say more about the *static* keyword later.) If you look in Shape2.cpp at the definitions for *CShape::Draw* and *CShape::Move*, you'll see the following:

■ The function name is *qualified,* or preceded by the class scope resolution operator, as in *CShape::*. Because the function definition is textually separate from its prototype within the *CShape* class declaration (in Shape.h), you must qualify the function name to tie the definition to the prototype. Even though the definition and prototype are textually separate, the definition lies within the class's scope. (I'll say more about class scope in Chapter 5, but for now, all you need to know is that more than one class can include a member function named *Draw,* for example.) Forgetting to qualify member function definitions is a common error to watch out for. Here's how the member function declarations from Shape.h, are laid out:

```
class CShape
{
    ⋮
    void Draw();
    void Move(CPoint p);
    ⋮
};
```

And here's how a member function definition, from Shape2.cpp, is laid out:

```
void CShape::Draw()
{
⋮
}
```

- Because the member function definitions are within the scope of the *CShape* class, they can use the class's data member and member function names freely without any qualification.

- Because the *ShpType enum* is declared within the *CShape* class, *CShape::Draw* and *CShape::Move* can also use *ShpType* member names, such as *shpRectangle* and *shpEllipse*, without having to qualify them. By comparison, a *global* helper function, such as *RandomType*, would have to qualify *ShpType* member names with the class scope resolution operator in order to access them.

The *this* pointer

Although program Shape2 doesn't explicitly use it, now is a good time to explain the *this* keyword. Inside a class member function (that isn't declared *static*), you can use the keyword *this* as a pointer to the function's own object. For example, if you call *CShape::Draw* for a *CShape* object named *shp1*, inside the *Draw* function *this* would point to the *shp1* object. Within *Draw*, you could access a *CShape* data member through the *this* pointer, like this:

```
this->m_rectShape = rect;
```

However, it's unnecessary (and unconventional) to use this notation. All you need is:

```
m_rectShape = rect;      // Implies this->m_rectShape = rect;
```

The *this* pointer does have its explicit uses, though. It is useful any time you need the address of the current object.

When might you need that address? Here's an example. You can use *this* to facilitate communication between two objects. Suppose object *Client* needs to allow object *Accountant* to access *Client*'s class members. One way to do this (but not the easiest—see the *friend* keyword, described in "The Friend Program" later in this chapter) is for *Accountant* to maintain a pointer to *Client*. But how does *Accountant* get a pointer to *Client*? Object *Client* initially calls a member function of object *Accountant* in order to authorize access by passing *Accountant* a pointer that points back to *Client*. Then *Accountant* can use that pointer to access members of *Client*, thus setting up two-way communication between the objects. Figure 4-4 shows the results.

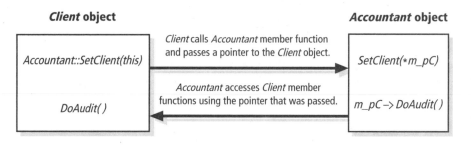

Figure 4-4.   *Objects that point to each other.*

Here's how we might do this. *Accountant*'s *SetClient* member function might look like this:

```
void Accountant::SetClient(Client* pC)
{
    m_pC = pC;     // Assign Client pointer to Accountant data member.
    :
}
```

In our example, the *Client* object creates the *Accountant* object, and as it does so, stores a pointer to the *Accountant* in a *Client* data member (name it *m_pA*). Next, the *Client* object uses that pointer to initialize the new *Accountant* object by calling *Accountant*'s *SetClient* member function:

```
m_pA->SetClient(this);    // Pass Client pointer to Accountant object.
```

Then, in a member function of *Accountant*, you might see code like the following, which uses *Accountant*'s pointer to *Client* (name it *m_pC*) to call *Client*'s *DoAudit* member function:

```
m_pC->DoAudit();          // Call Client member function
                          //  through Client pointer.
```

To summarize: First, *Client* calls *Accountant::SetClient*, passing a pointer to the *Client* object itself in the form of the *this* keyword. Then, within *SetClient*, *Accountant* stores the pointer. The *Accountant* object now contains a pointer to the *Client* object, and can use this pointer to access *Client*'s *public* member functions.

The *this* keyword isn't available outside class member functions, and it's not available inside a *static* member function.

Access specifiers

Take a look at the *CShape* class, in the Shape.h file. Near the beginning of the class declaration you see the keyword *public*. Later, just before the data members are declared, you see the keyword *private*. The basic structure of the class looks like this:

```
class CShape
{
public:
    // Public members


private:
    // Private members
};
```

The *public* and *private* keywords are *access specifiers*. The *public* specifier near the beginning tells us "the next members are public." Users of the class can freely access the public members, as if they have the same access privileges that one would have from inside the class member functions. All members of the class continue to be public until the next access specifier—the *private* specifier here. That keyword means "the following members are private." Users of the class have no access to these members, although one would still have access from inside the class member functions. The private declaration remains in effect until either another access specifier is encountered or the end of the class declaration is reached.

You can change access specifiers as many times as you like. For example, you might want two private sections, one up front and one near the end:

```
class CMyClass
{
    private:
    ⋮
    public:
    ⋮
    private:
    ⋮
};
```

Default access specifiers

By default, the members of a class declared with the *class* keyword are private. Even if there's no explicit *private* keyword at the beginning of the class declaration, the declaration behaves as if there were.

```
// What you see.
class Name
{
    // No access specifier here.
    // member functions
};
```

```
// What you actually get.
class Name
{
private:    // It's as if this were here.
    // member functions
};
```

That's why you'll so often see the *public* specifier at the beginning of a class declaration. You have to be explicit if you want to make members public. In effect, when you add the *public* keyword, you're revealing class members that would otherwise be hidden away in private.

The story is different if you declare your class with the *struct* keyword. In that case, the class members are public by default. If you want to hide any of them, you must explicitly supply the *private* keyword. One reason for using the *class* keyword when we want a class to really act as a class and not as "just a *struct*," is that the *class* keyword comes with the assumption that you'll want at least some members to be private. That's not a bad default assumption.

Information hiding

Why would we declare the *CShape* data members private? Why limit outside access? There's a valuable principle of software engineering that says: *Anything that outsiders don't have to know about should be hidden.* The idea is to make the class a black box, giving class users a specific public interface through which they are to conduct all of their interactions with objects of the class. Implementation details are to be hidden—declared private. Of course, people with access to the source code can simply look at the class and see what's being hidden, so what exactly do we mean? Hidden means "access restricted." The *private* specifier enforces our desire that the members it shields not be accessible to class users. The compiler will not let users access them directly. However, if users need some sort of indirect access, and they often do, it's up to the class designer to provide public *access functions*. These are functions like the ones in *CShape* that begin with "Set" or "Get." They let you access the hidden implementation in a controlled way.

There are at least two good reasons for such strict control:

1. Suppose I need to do more than just assign a parameter to a private data member. Let's say you call a member function, passing an *int* value to be stored in the class. But under the hood, I need to create an object of some sort and pass your *int* value to the new object. In other words, there can be extra operations to perform behind the scenes when you call a simple member function. As another example, I might need to increment or decrement a counter when you call a member function. Performing these kinds of extra operations by using private data members within the class ensures that those

things will happen. I probably can't count on users to remember to do the extras, or to do them in the right sequence, but with defensive coding, I can enforce my wishes.

2. If my class implementation is hidden, I can freely change it to some other implementation later, with as little impact on your program (that uses my class) as possible. As long as I don't change the public interface to the class—the access functions—the most you'll have to do is rebuild your code with my revised class. And you'll only have to do that if you want to take advantage of my new and improved implementation. For example, in its first version, my class might store data in an ordinary file. Later, I might decide to implement the class to store the data in a database instead. If I've hidden my implementation, that change will be transparent to you and other users of my class.

Should the data members always be private?

Hiding data members and some member functions makes sense in certain situations, but it isn't an absolute rule. If you look at the *CPoint* and *CRect* classes, you'll see that I haven't used the *private* specifier in them. Little utility classes like those should probably be as open and simple as possible. But some classes should hide their data. For example, a *handle* is an object through which you can access a chunk of private data indirectly—to access the data at all, you must obtain the handle and then use public access functions to work with the data the handle is for. If you don't want anyone to be able to change or use the value of the handle, you declare it as private. (The handle itself, as well as the object it connects you to, is private.) This is a common scenario, particularly in Windows programming.

Most classes in the MFC library are also quite open, with no private sections. The library's designers were wise enough to know they couldn't predict all possible ways programmers might use their classes, so the designers avoided things that might hinder future innovative users. If you eventually write classes that extend the MFC library, you'll want to adopt a similar attitude.

MFC source code commenting conventions

You might have noticed special comments in the classes we've looked at so far—comments like these:

```
// Constructors
// Attributes
// Operations
// Implementation
```

The comments follow an MFC convention that makes MFC source code files easier to read and understand. Most of the comments are used to group similar class members, such as constructors, in one easy-to-find place. The *Implementation* comment is the most interesting. It tells readers that "everything from here to the end of the class is part of the implementation, it isn't publicly documented, and you can't count on it remaining the same in the next version of the class." Typically, MFC leaves many of its class implementations open in the sense that they are public rather than private. So you can use members declared after the // *Implementation* line. But you do so at your own risk—your code may break if you rebuild with the next version of the class. For more information about MFC source code conventions, and about using the MFC source code files, see the Appendix, "The MFC Source Code." I'll be using MFC commenting and other MFC conventions throughout the book.

I'll have more to say about access specifiers, including a third specifier, *protected*, after we run through the Shape3 program in Chapter 5.

Static Variables

The *static* keyword reduces the need for global variables. Using *static*, you can declare a class data member that has the effect of a global variable (it retains its value) but is still local to the class. I'll illustrate this use of static in the Shape3 program in Chapter 5. You can also declare a local variable inside a function as static. The Shape2 program illustrates this in its global helper function *RandomCoord* (in the section "Shape2.cpp" earlier in this chapter), which generates the coordinates that define the *CPoints* and *CRects*.

Let's take a closer look at the problem I was trying to solve in the *RandomCoord* function. I wanted to base the next random coordinate on the previous random coordinate (if any). Thus I had to store the previous coordinate in a place where *RandomCoord* could access it. If *RandomCoord* were a class member function, I could store the previous coordinate in a class data member. But since *RandomCoord* is a global function, the best solution might appear to be a global variable (with file scope).

An even better solution is to use a static local variable inside *Random-Coord*. The first time *RandomCoord* is called, it finds the variable, *nLastCoord*, already initialized to zero—just what we want. (C++ automatically initializes static local variables, but not their nonstatic counterparts, to the appropriate form of zero: 0 for an *int*, say, or 0.0 for a *double*, or *Null* for a pointer variable.)

During the first call to *RandomCoord*, the function generates a new random coordinate and uses the larger of *nLastCoord* and *nNextCoord*. (I wanted next coordinates to be larger than previous ones.) The function then stores the resulting value in *nLastCoord*, ready to be used the next time the function is called.

Because *nLastCoord* is declared static, its value is retained between function calls. That's what makes the variable similar to a global variable. This property of static local variables is valuable any time you need this kind of permanence.

What's Still Wrong with the Shape2 Program?

We've made some progress in our shape class design. The operations we can perform on a *CShape* object are now part of the class itself. We have eliminated the global functions.

But *CShape* is still a bit awkward. In particular, the *Draw* member function still doesn't know what kind of object it's supposed to draw. It has to use a *switch* statement to find out what shape to draw. Ideally, we'd like *CShape* objects to contain that knowledge without the *switch* statement. They should know what they are without having to test their own identity.

In Chapter 5, the Shape3 program will take the next step—and, in the process, introduce class derivation, class hierarchies, inheritance, overriding, and polymorphism: all the ingredients of real OOP.

The Friend Program

Sometimes you'll want to skirt C++ access specifiers and get at hidden information from outside a class object. Any time two classes, or a class and a global function, are highly interdependent, you can use the *friend* specifier to give an outsider complete access to the innards of a class, including its private members. Think of it this way: you can use access specifiers to restrict outside access to your class's members, but you can use the friend mechanism to loosen the restrictions for selected outsiders. C++ taketh away, but it also giveth back. The keyword *friend* should not be overused—it's poor programming practice and sometimes dangerous to open up your class to too many outsiders—but, used judiciously, it can make life simpler.

The following are among the items that can be friends of a class (call it class *A*):

- A global function.

- A member function of another class (call it class *B*). Just the one member function has access to all of *A*.

- A whole class (*B*). All of class *B* has access to all of class *A*.

A friend is granted access to even the private members of the class that declares it a friend. Note that it's the class that *bestows* friendship; an outside function or class can't *seize* friendship.

Here is a brief, albeit not very realistic, example of a class containing friend declarations:

```
class A
{
    int a;
    friend void AGlobalFunction(int b, int c);
    friend char* B::AMemberFunction(int d);
```

(continued)

```
    friend class C;
    ⋮

};
```

The example shows how class *A* can declare each kind of item as a friend. Each function or class that class *A* singles out as a friend is granted the "key to the city." The Friend program in the next section provides a simple example in which a class is declared a friend of another class.

Try it now

Create the Friend program:

```cpp
// Friend.cpp : Defines the entry point for the console application.
//

#include "Stdafx.h"
#include <iostream.h>

class A
{
    friend class B;      // Can declare friends under any
                         //   access specifier; here it
                         //   happens to be private

public:
    // Constructor
    A(int n, char* psz) { m_int = n; m_psz = psz; };

private:
    int m_int;
    char* m_psz;
};

class B      // friend of A
{
public:
    // Constructor
    B(A* pA) { m_pA = pA; };

    // Functions allowed to access A's private members
    int GetAInt() { return m_pA->m_int; };
    char* GetAStr() { return m_pA->m_psz; };

private:
```

```
        // Pointer to A, declared private so users of B
        //  must use GetAInt or GetAStr to access A
        A* m_pA;
};

int main(int argc, char* argv[])
{
        // Construct an A object
        A a(4, "This is an A object.");

        // Construct a B object initialized
        //  with a pointer to the A object
        B b(&a);

        // Demonstrate access to private member of A via a B object
        cout << b.GetAInt() << "   " << b.GetAStr() << endl;

        return 0;
}
```

In *main*, we create an *A* object and a *B* object. In constructing the *B* object, we pass it a pointer to the *A* object so it can communicate with the *A* object. Then we show that the member functions of *B*, *GetAInt*, and *GetAStr* can access the private members of *A*. That's only possible because of the friend declaration.

N OTE   Friendship is one-way. *B* is a friend of *A* and has access to all of *A*, including its private members, but *A* is not a friend of *B* and has access to only its public members.

Try It Yourself

As in previous chapters, I urge you to make the following effort. Type the example programs we've just walked through, and then build and run them. There is no substitute for hands-on experience.

Here are a few more things to try.

1. Add a constructor to the *CRect* class.

In the Shape2 program, *CRect* has two constructors, one that takes no parameters, and one that takes two *CPoint* parameters. Add a third constructor that takes four *int* parameters. The first two *ints* specify the top left corner, and the last two specify the bottom right corner. Test your new constructor. Although no solution is provided, there are several examples of code with multiple constructors in the companion code.

2. Study the C/C++ run-time library.

Review the introduction to the run-time library in Chapter 2. That description covers how to locate topics in the run-time library. The more familiar you become with the library's contents, the less you'll need to "reinvent the wheel."

What's Next?

In Chapter 5, we'll finish up with C++ and object-oriented programming by covering class derivation, class hierarchies, inheritance, and a few topics we haven't found a place for yet.

Object-Oriented Programming

We got a good start on C++ classes in the previous chapter with Shape1 and Shape2, but there's more to say. This chapter presents several programs, including Shape3, that finish up our exploration of classes. Then we move to higher ground for an overview of object-oriented programming concepts and terminology.

Program Shape3 introduces the following C++ features:

- Deriving one class from another

- Inheritance

- Overriding and virtual functions

- Polymorphism—the ability to treat a base class and its derived classes as one

- Abstract classes and class hierarchies

- The rest of the story on access specifiers

- Class destructors and static class members

- More about constructors and destructors, including default constructors, copy constructors, member initialization lists, and operator overloading

- Class scope

The Shape3 Program

What if each kind of shape had its own class? Then we could code that class to "just know" what kind of shape it was. Shape3 shows you how that's done. We revisit the *CShape* design and turn the class into a base class, from which we derive two subclasses, *CShpRectangle* and *CShpEllipse*.

This strategy—using a separate class for each shape type—works well as long as there aren't too many types, and for our purposes it illustrates a lot of C++. If there were 100 shape types, or even 30, however, you'd probably prefer an approach more like that in program Shape2, in which one class represents all shapes, and the class contains a data member that indicates the shape type.

Here's program Shape3. I don't show the *CPoint* and *CRect* classes, which haven't changed since program Shape2. You'll find their code listings in Chapter 4 if you need to refer back to them.

Try it now

Create a Win32 Console Application called Shape3, containing the following three files (and don't forget to go get *CRect* and *CPoint*). This exercise is long, but persevere—C++ is just starting to get good!

- **Shape.h,** a header file declaring the *CShape* classes.

- **Shape.cpp,** an implementation file for the *CShape* classes.

- **Shape3.cpp,** the file that contains the *main* function.

Shape.h

```
/////////////////////////////////////
// Shape.h

#include "crect.h"

// Constant for use in generating random types
const int NUM_TYPES = 3;

// Abstract base class: can't construct CShape objects,
//   only objects of its derived classes
```

```
class CShape
{
public:
    // Possible shape types
    enum ShpType            // Nested enum: qualify outside
                            //   mentions with CShape::
    {
        shpRectangle,
        shpEllipse
    };

// Constructors
    CShape() { m_rectShape = CRect(CPoint(0,0), CPoint(10,10));
               m_typeShape = shpRectangle; };

// Attributes
    void SetRect(CRect r) { m_rectShape = r; };

    CRect GetRect() const { return m_rectShape; };
    ShpType GetType() const { return m_typeShape; };
    // No SetType: type now determined by subclass

    virtual void Draw() = 0;    // Class is abstract; must override
    void Move(CPoint p);

// Implementation
protected:
    CRect m_rectShape;          // Bounding rectangle of shape
    ShpType m_typeShape;        // Rectangle, ellipse,...

public:
    virtual ~CShape();
};

// Concrete subclass of abstract base class CShape
class CShpRectangle : public CShape
{
public:
// Constructors: initialize class, including instance counter
    CShpRectangle() { m_rectShape = CRect(CPoint(0,0), CPoint(10,10));
                      m_typeShape = shpRectangle; nCountShpRects++; };

    CShpRectangle(CRect r)
                  { m_rectShape = r; m_typeShape = shpRectangle;
                    nCountShpRects++; };
```

(continued)

163

```
// Attributes inherited (SetType, GetRect, GetType)


// Operations (Move is inherited)

    void Draw();          // Overrides CShape::Draw

// Implementation
public:
    // The static data member must be public so we can access
    //  it from outside objects of the class. The destructor
    //  must be public so we can explicitly call delete on objects
    //  of the class from outside objects of the class.

    // Data members inherited
    // Add
    static int nCountShpRects;    // Initialized at file scope
                                  //  in shape3.cpp

    ~CShpRectangle();    // Destructor: virtual because base
                         //  class destructor is
};

// Concrete subclass of abstract base class CShape
class CShpEllipse : public CShape
{
public:
// Constructors
    CShpEllipse() { m_rectShape = CRect(CPoint(0,0), CPoint(10,10));
                m_typeShape = shpEllipse; nCountShpElls++; };

    CShpEllipse(CRect r)
                { m_rectShape = r; m_typeShape = shpEllipse; nCountShpElls++; };

// Attributes inherited

// Operations (Move is inherited)

    void Draw();                 // Overrides CShape::Draw

// Implementation
public:
    // Data members inherited
    // Add
    static int nCountShpElls;  // Initialized to zero automatically

    ~CShpEllipse();              // Destructor: virtual because base
                                 //  class destructor is
};
```

Shape.cpp

```cpp
// Shape.cpp

#include <stdafx.h>
#include "Shape.h"
#include <stdio.h>          // For printf
#include <stdlib.h>         // For abs

////////////////////////////////////
// CShape definitions

// Shift shape to new position.
void CShape::Move(CPoint p /* New topLeft */)
{
    // Get shape's size.
    int width = abs(m_rectShape.botRight.x - m_rectShape.topLeft.x);
    int height = abs(m_rectShape.botRight.y - m_rectShape.topLeft.y);

    // Set its new coordinates (move it).
    m_rectShape.topLeft = p;
    m_rectShape.botRight = CPoint(p.x + width, p.y + height);
}


// Empty destructor
CShape::~CShape()
{
}


////////////////////////////////////
// CShpRectangle definitions

// Draw overrides base class version.
void CShpRectangle::Draw()
{
    // Get coordinates in shortened forms for ease of use in printf.
    int x1 = m_rectShape.topLeft.x;
    int y1 = m_rectShape.topLeft.y;
    int x2 = m_rectShape.botRight.x;
    int y2 = m_rectShape.botRight.y;

    // "Draw" the shape as a string like
    //    "rectangle at (34, 76, 987, 800)".
    printf("rectangle at (%d,%d,%d,%d)\n", x1, y1, x2, y2);
}
```

(continued)

```
// Virtual destructor: removes current rectangle object
//   from total of such objects.
CShpRectangle::~CShpRectangle()
{
    nCountShpRects--;    // Decrement: we're destroying one.
}


/////////////////////////////////
// CShpEllipse definitions
void CShpEllipse::Draw()
{
    int x1 = m_rectShape.topLeft.x;
    int y1 = m_rectShape.topLeft.y;
    int x2 = m_rectShape.botRight.x;
    int y2 = m_rectShape.botRight.y;

    // "Draw" the shape as a string like
    //   "ellipse at (34, 76, 987, 800)"
    printf("ellipse at (%d,%d,%d,%d)\n", x1, y1, x2, y2);
}

// Virtual destructor: removes current ellipse object from
//   total of such objects.
CShpEllipse::~CShpEllipse()
{
    nCountShpElls--;    // Decrement: we're destroying one.
}
```

Shape3.cpp

```
// Shape3.cpp : Defines the entry point for the console application.
//


#include <stdafx.h>
#include "Shape.h"
#include <stdio.h>        // For printf
#include <assert.h>       // For assert
#include <stdlib.h>       // For rand, srand, abs
#include <time.h>         // For time

// Global function prototypes

int RandomCoord();
CShape::ShpType RandomType();
```

```
// Initialize static class members at file scope.
int CShpRectangle::nCountShpRects = 0;
int CShpEllipse::nCountShpElls = 0;

////////////////////////////////////
// main
int main(int argc, char* argv[])
{
    // Create a rectangle shape on the stack.
    CShpRectangle shp1;
    shp1.SetRect(CRect(CPoint(20, 20), CPoint(50, 50)));
    shp1.Draw();

    // Move a shape in coordinate space.
    shp1.Move(CPoint(25, 25));
    shp1.Draw();

    // Create an ellipse shape on the heap.
    CShape* pShp2 = new CShpEllipse(CRect(CPoint(100, 100),
        CPoint(150, 150)));
    assert(pShp2 != NULL);
    pShp2->Draw();

    delete pShp2;

    // Create 10 random shapes in an array.
    CPoint pt1, pt2;            // Declare these outside
                               //   the for loop!
    CRect rect;
    CShape* arShps[10];        // Array of CShape pointers
    srand((unsigned)time(NULL));
    for(int i = 0; i < 10; i++)
    {
        // Prepare a randomly located bounding rectangle.
        pt1 = CPoint(RandomCoord(), RandomCoord());
        pt2 = CPoint(RandomCoord(), RandomCoord());
        rect = CRect(pt1, pt2);

        // Generate a random shape type.
        if(CShape::shpRectangle == RandomType())
        {
            // Construct a rectangle shape and add to array.
            CShpRectangle* pShp = new CShpRectangle(rect);
            assert(pShp != NULL);   // Must check when
                                    //   pShp is in scope.
            arShps[i] = pShp;       // Must add to array when pShp is
                                    //   in scope.
```

(continued)

```
                    // Print new total of objects of this type.
                    printf("Number of rectangles: %d\n",
                        CShpRectangle::nCountShpRects);
            }
            else
            {
                // Construct an ellipse shape and add to array.
                CShpEllipse* pShp = new CShpEllipse(rect);
                assert(pShp != NULL);
                arShps[i] = pShp;
                // Print new total of objects of this type.
                printf("Number of ellipses: %d\n",
                    CShpEllipse::nCountShpElls);
            }
            arShps[i]->Draw();                  // Polymorphic function call
        }

        // Move a shape.
        arShps[0]->Move(CPoint(20,20));     // Call inherited function.
        arShps[0]->Draw();                  // Polymorphic function call

        // Delete all shapes.
        for(int j = 0; j < 10; j++)
        {
            delete arShps[j];       // Invoke virtual destructors.
        }

        return 0;
    }


    /////////////////////////////////////
    // Global Helper functions

    // Generate a random positive coordinate within a 1000-by-
    // 1000-unit drawing area.
    int RandomCoord()
    {
        // Base new coordinate loosely on last coordinate.
        static int nLastCoord;      // Automatically initialized to 0,
                                    //   then altered on each call

        // Get a pseudorandom number between 0 and RAND_MAX (=32,767).
        int nNextCoord = rand();
        int nFudge = rand() % 100;  // Generate a fudge factor between
                                    //   0 and 99.
        // Use the larger of new number and old number (+ fudge factor).
        // Constrain the number to a value between 0 and 999 (inclusive).
```

```
    nLastCoord = abs((nNextCoord > nLastCoord ? nNextCoord :
        (nLastCoord + nFudge)) % 1000);
    return nLastCoord;
}

// Pseudorandomly generate a rectangle or ellipse shape type.
CShape::ShpType RandomType()
{
    // 0 to 1 (= shpRectangle to shpEllipse)
    return (CShape::ShpType)(rand() % NUM_TYPES);
}
```

The C++ in the Shape3 Program

The most important element of program Shape3 is the derivation of two new subclasses from class *CShape*. This program introduces most of the essential concepts of object-oriented programming (OOP). I'll also show you how to use class destructors as well as the constructors you saw in Chapter 4, and I'll introduce a *static* class data member.

> **NOTE** In program Shape3, I've separated the function definitions for *CShape* and its derived classes (in the file Shape.cpp) from the *main* function (in the file Shape3.cpp). This will make it easier to reuse the classes in other *CShape*-based programs.

Deriving One Class from Another

In C++, you can create a new class based on an existing one. This is called *deriving* a class, or *subclassing*. (See the sidebar titled "OOP Terminology" on page 202.) The original class is called the *base class,* or *ancestor*. The new class is called the *derived class,* or *subclass*.

A class can actually be derived from multiple base classes. However, this concept introduces the thorny subject of *multiple inheritance*, which is material too advanced to cover in this book. Check the Help index for *multiple inheritance* for more information.

Inheritance

When you derive class *B* from class *A*, *B* is said to *inherit* the characteristics of *A*. Here's what that means, given the schematic code on the following page, which also illustrates how to derive one class from another.

```
class A
{
public:
    int m_nMember1;
    void MemberFunction1();
};

class B : public A
{
public:
    int m_nMember2;
    void MemberFunction2();
};
```

Even though it doesn't name them, class *B* also has an *int* data member called *m_nMember1* and a member function called *MemberFunction1*, in addition to the new data member and member function that *B* does name. *B* inherits these from *A*, and you can use them freely with *B* objects. Does *A* have a data member *m_nMember2* or a member function *MemberFunction2*? No. The inheritance goes only one way, from the base class to the derived class.

The derived class can add new data members and member functions, as class *B* does. In this way, class *B* is said to *extend* class *A*. Can a derived class like *B* get rid of members it inherits but doesn't want? No. It's stuck with them. (In some cases you might be able to override unwanted member functions and leave them empty, or have them issue a warning or generate a guaranteed run-time error if called. Also see the discussion of the *is-a* and *has-a* relationships later in this chapter, "*Is-a* vs. *Has-a*.")

When you're working with a derived class, remember that it inherits from its base class, from the base class of the base class (if any), and so on, all the way to the root of the class hierarchy. When you look at a list of a class's members, you often need to follow the chain of ancestors back up the hierarchy to see everything that "belongs" to the class you started with. In the Microsoft Foundation Class Library 6.0 (MFC), for example, the documentation for a class doesn't list inherited members. But it does list the base class, with a hyperlink that you can follow to the documentation for that class. Always remember to look up the hierarchy.

What good are derivation and inheritance?

What's the value of derivation and inheritance? First, they allow you to customize a data type. With class derivation you can extend such a type, for example, to make it more versatile, and still get plenty of mileage from the base class through inheritance of its members.

Second, the derivation and inheritance mechanism is what drives class libraries like MFC. To create a new MFC application, as you'll see in Chapters 7 and 8, you derive new classes from several of MFC's library classes. Your derived version of MFC's *CWinApp* class, for instance, customizes that class's basic functionality to suit the needs of your particular application.

Beyond extending a base class by adding new members to a derived class, you can also modify what the base class does by overriding some of its member functions.

Overriding member functions

A derived class can *override* member functions (but not data or other members) of its base class. The derived class provides a new implementation of a function with the same prototype. Consider this schematic code:

```
class A
{
    virtual void MemFunc1(int i, float f);    // B overrides this.
    void MemFunc2();                          // B inherits this.
};

class B : public A
{
    void MemFunc1(int i, float f);    // Override
};
```

If class *B* supplies a prototype that duplicates one from its base class *A* (except for the *virtual* keyword, which is optional in *B*), the derived version overrides the base class version—at least when you're using an object of type *B*. If you're using an object of type *A* and call *MemFunc1*, the *A* version executes.

How is this different from function overloading? An overloaded function must have a different prototype. An overridden member function must have the same prototype. Overloaded member functions let you have several functions of the same name that take different parameters, for convenience. Overridden member functions in a derived class substitute different behavior for that defined in the base class versions of the functions. Thus an ellipse object draws itself differently from a rectangle object.

Virtual functions

You can override any member function, but the behavior of overridden nonvirtual functions and overridden virtual functions is different—and can lead to confusion and errors if you aren't careful. The Virtual program shown here illustrates the difference.

Try it now

Create the Virtual program.

```
// Virtual.cpp: Defines the entry point for the console application.
//

#include "stdafx.h"
#include <iostream.h>

class Base
{
public:
    void Do1() { cout << "Base::Do1\n"; };
    virtual void Do2() { cout << "Base::Do2\n"; };
};

class Derived : public Base
{
public:
    // Override nonvirtual function from Base.
    //  Call is resolved at compile time.
    void Do1() { cout << "Derived::Do2\n"; };

    // Override virtual function from Base.
    //  Call is resolved at run time.
    void Do2() { cout << "Derived::Do2\n"; };
};
```

```
int main(int argc, char* argv[])
{
    Derived d;
    Base* pBase;

    // Point to a Derived object through a Base pointer.
    pBase = &d;

    cout << "Use derived object to call Do1 and Do2"
         << "through a pointer to Base.\n";
    pBase->Do1();    // Calls Base::Do1, no polymorphism.
                     //  Call based on pointer type.
    pBase->Do2();    // Calls Derived::Do2 polymorphically.
                     //  Call based on underlying type.
    cout << endl;

    cout << "Call Do1 and Do2 through a Derived object.\n";
    d.Do1();            // Calls Derived::Do1, no polymorphism.
                        //  Call based on pointer type.
    d.Do2();            // Calls Derived::Do2 polymorphically.
                        //  Call based on underlying type.

    return 0;
}
```

The Virtual program shows that you can override nonvirtual functions as well as virtual ones, but the results might not be what you expect. The call to a virtual override is resolved at run time, so the actual type of the object determines which version of the function is called—the base class version or the derived class version. The call to a nonvirtual override is instead resolved at compile time, so the type of the pointer, not the type of the underlying object, determines which version is called. In Program Virtual, calling *Do1* through a pointer to *Base* calls *Base::Do1*, but calling *Do1* through a *Derived* object calls *Derived::Do1*.

You'll usually declare base class functions with the *virtual* keyword if you think derived classes are likely to override them. Whether to set up the class for overriding is really a design decision. Derived classes that override a virtual function provide the identical function prototype—with or without the *virtual* keyword. (The *virtual* keyword appears only in the class declaration, not in the function definition.) If class *A* declares function *F*, derived class *B* can choose not to override *F*—but class *C*, derived from *B*, can choose to override it. Class *B* simply inherits *A*'s version, while class *C* supplies its own version. In the example in the previous section, *B* inherits *MemFunc2* and doesn't override it.

For a more concrete example of overriding, consider classes *CShape* and *CShpRectangle*. *CShape* declares a virtual member function called *Draw*. *CShpRectangle* also supplies a *Draw* member function with the same prototype (minus the *virtual* keyword, and the *= 0* notation at the end). *CShpRectangle::Draw* overrides *CShape::Draw*. Examine this code from program Shape3:

```
CShape* arShps[10];          // Array of CShape pointers
  :
// Construct a rectangle shape and add to array.
CShpRectangle* pShp = new CShpRectangle(rect);
assert(pShp != NULL);        // Must check if pShp in scope.
arShps[i] = pShp;            // Add to array if pShp in scope.
  :
arShps[i]->Draw();           // Polymorphic function call
```

Even though the type of *arShps[i]* is *CShape**, C++ ensures that *CShpRectangle::Draw* is what gets called. This is due to the *virtual* function mechanism, which we'll take up in the next section.

Should you declare all or most member functions as virtual? No. Be sparing with virtual functions, because the underlying mechanism that makes them work takes up quite a bit of storage. The designers of MFC faced this overhead problem when they were creating class member functions to handle Microsoft Windows messages. If they had made hundreds of these functions virtual, the overhead would have been tremendous. So they found an alternative mechanism for implementing message-handler functions that avoids the use of too many virtual member functions—the message map. The lesson is to use virtual functions judiciously. Have good reasons for each one. And, unless you're writing a class library for others to use, feel free in your own code to override nonvirtual functions—just make sure you understand how they would behave in situations that would be polymorphic if you were using virtuals. If you want polymorphism, go virtual. (I'll explain polymorphism shortly.)

Some member functions are intended to be overridden. Others probably will never be, and still others might be overridden only rarely.

The virtual function mechanism

You've already observed that the array *arShps* holds pointers to *CShape*—the base class of *CShpRectangle*. But you create a new *CShpRectangle* (not a *CShape*) and store a pointer to it in one of the *CShape** elements of the array. This point is crucial: you can store a pointer of a derived type in a variable of its base type—here, a *CShpRectangle* pointer in the place of a *CShape* pointer. That's very useful, because now you can store a pointer to any type of shape derived from *CShape* in the array, all at once—ellipses and rectangles mixed.

Next, notice that after storing a *CShpRectangle* pointer in element *i* of the array, we call that element's *Draw* member function:

```
arShps[i]->Draw();     // Polymorphic function call
```

As you've already seen, the version of *Draw* called is *CShpRectangle*'s. How does this happen? Although *arShps[i]* has the type *CShape**, it's the type of the actual object stored in the array element that determines which version of *Draw* is called. This is determined not at compile time but at run time and is known as *dynamic binding,* or *run-time binding.* The compiler manages dynamic binding in a way that's transparent to the programmer.

Under the hood, dynamic binding is managed by the use of *virtual function tables.* Each class in a derivation hierarchy (the base class and each of its derived classes) has its own virtual function table in memory, created by the compiler. A virtual function table is an array that contains a function pointer for each virtual function in the class. At run time, code that the compiler created accesses the virtual function table for the class of the actual object whose member function is being called. (A class object contains a pointer to the virtual function table for its class.) Then, the correct virtual function is called through its pointer in the virtual function table. The compiler just follows these pointers as it sets up the function calls.

Polymorphism

Here is a powerful idea: that a pointer of type *CShape** can point to either a *CShpRectangle* or *CShpEllipse* object and that you can call the correct member function *Draw* through the base-class pointer without knowing which actual object type it points to. As I noted in Chapter 4, this concept is called *polymorphism*, derived from the Greek for "many forms."

Polymorphism is powerful for another reason as well. Later, when you want to expand the program's capabilities, you can derive a new *CShpTriangle* class from *CShape* and start storing *CShpTriangle* pointers in the *arShps* array—and the same call to the *Draw* member function of *arShps[i]* will work just as well for the new objects.

Is-a vs. has-a

If class *B* is derived from class *A*, we can say "*B* is an *A*" because of inheritance. The term *is-a* has a special meaning in OOP, signifying the relationship between a derived class and its base class.

There's another OOP relationship, called *has-a*. Suppose *D* is a class and class *C* contains a complete embedded *D* object (or a pointer to a *D* object) so that class *C* has a *D* inside it. An example of this is:

```
class C
{
    D d;     // d is a member of C
    D* pD;   // pD is a member of C
    :
};
```

Sometimes using a *has-a* relationship makes more sense than using *is-a*. For example, suppose we write class *CArray*, which contains a C++ array to hold its data and member functions, such as *GetAt*, *SetAt*, and *Length* with which to manage the data in the array.

Would *CArray* make a good base class for deriving a simple *CStack* class? Stacks are often based on arrays, so this might seem like a good idea, but what are the consequences? If you use *is-a*, *CStack* will inherit *CArray*'s data and member functions. Remember that to add an item to a stack, you *push* it; to remove an item from a stack, you *pop* it. Both operations are allowed only on the top item of the stack—you can't reach down into the middle. (Generations of programmers are familiar with this stack abstraction and its terminology.) Even if we add member functions *Push* and *Pop* to *CStack*, using an *is-a* relationship causes a problem. Inherited *CArray* members such as *SetAt* and *GetAt* allow careless programmers to access the middle of the stack, violating the stack abstraction.

It makes more sense in this case to use a *has-a* relationship, embedding a *CArray* object inside a *CStack* object, probably as a private member after the *//Implementation* line:

```
class CStack
{
public:
    void Push(int value);
    int Pop() const;

// Implementation
private:
    CArray arStack;
    int top;
};
```

You'd implement the *Push* and *Pop* member functions with calls to *CArray* members.

Designing Your Class Hierarchy

Without polymorphism, programmers would have to write (and rewrite) lots of *switch* statements to discriminate among the various types that might be present. With polymorphism, you simply need to follow a few rules when you design your *class hierarchy*. Here's an introduction to class hierarchies, followed by several guidelines for designing them. Figure 5-1 illustrates the usual way to represent a class hierarchy, using *CShape* as a model.

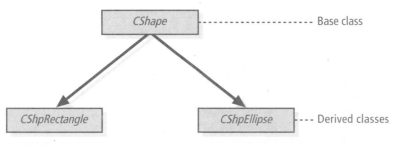

Figure 5-1. *The* CShape *class hierarchy.*

Abstract classes

One tool for creating class hierarchies is the abstract class. Some classes aren't meant to be used to create actual objects. Many base classes are incomplete in some way, so you must write derived classes to fill in the missing details. Such incomplete base classes are called *abstract classes*.

Class *CShape* is abstract. Notice how the *Draw* member function is declared in that class:

```
virtual void Draw() = 0;    // Class is abstract; must override.
```

This strange notation tells us and the compiler that "this function will not be implemented in this class—derived classes must implement it." The function prototype is called a *pure virtual function*. Notice that nowhere in program Shape3 is *CShape::Draw* further defined. The compiler and linker accept this because of the pure virtual prototype.

Any class that has one or more pure virtual functions is automatically an abstract class. There's no way a hypothetical *CShape* object, for example, could draw itself, because *Draw* is not defined.

A class might be incomplete in other, more conceptual ways, too, as we'll see when we later adapt the *CShape* class we're developing in this chapter to work within the MFC class hierarchy. In that case, it would be the responsibility of any programmer who uses the class to avoid creating objects of that class and to ensure that what's missing is filled in by any derived classes. When possible, use the pure virtual function notation to enforce your wishes in this regard.

Abstract classes are often used as base classes in class hierarchies. Usually an abstract class in a hierarchy represents a general concept, such as shape, and the derived classes implement the specific details of concrete shapes such as rectangles and ellipses. You'd never create an actual "shape" object; instead, you'd only create specific kinds of shapes, such as rectangles.

Anatomy of a class hierarchy

The overall class hierarchy has these features:

- At the top of the class hierarchy is a base class. It provides the functionality common to all classes in the hierarchy (such as common data members and member functions). The base class might or might not be an abstract class.

- Each derived class inherits all members from the base class (although a derived class doesn't have access to private members of the base class). Derived classes can also extend the base class by adding new data members and member functions as needed.

- Each derived class can also override any or all of the base class's member functions, especially virtual functions, to provide new behavior at the derived class level.

- The hierarchy can have more than one level: the topmost base class, one or more intermediate classes, and those classes at the bottom of the hierarchy. If we view the hierarchy as an upside-down tree, the topmost base class is the tree's *root* or trunk. The intermediate classes are *branches* (sometimes called *interior nodes*). And the classes at the bottom of the hierarchy, most distant from the root base class, are the *leaves*. In fact, this sort of tree analogy is often used to describe class hierarchies: *root classes, branch classes,* and *leaf classes*. Figure 5-2 on the following page illustrates class hierarchy structure.

- If there are intermediate classes in the hierarchy, they are derived from their own base classes and act as base classes themselves for classes derived from them. Such intermediate classes might have some characteristics of base classes and some characteristics of derived classes. For example, an intermediate class might be an abstract class, yet it might also override and extend members of its own base class.

- Classes at the same level in the hierarchy (derived from a common base class but not from each other) are siblings. Or, if the base class they have in common is more distant—further up the hierarchy, they're considered cousins.

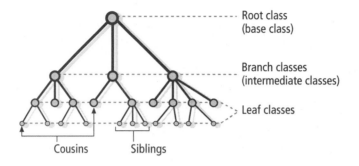

Figure 5-2.   *The structure and terminology of class hierarchies.*

Hierarchy design guidelines

When you design a class hierarchy, try to design it all at once. Think through questions like these:

- **Should the base class (and possibly some intermediate classes) be abstract?** In the *CShape* class hierarchy, it makes no sense to provide an implementation for *Draw* at the *CShape* level, so we declare *Draw* there as a pure virtual function. That makes *CShape* abstract, which makes sense conceptually—there's no such thing as a generic shape. All real shapes have a particular type and shape. Yet all actual shapes must draw themselves, so it's useful, for polymorphism, to declare *Draw* at the *CShape* level, even if you don't implement it there.

- **Which functions should be virtual?** It's clear that every shape type draws itself differently, so in the *CShape* class hierarchy, *Draw* is virtual. On the other hand, moving any shape is like moving any other, so *Move* can simply be inherited by derived classes. It doesn't need to be virtual.

- **How far is the hierarchy likely to be extended?** Some hierarchies never extend beyond two levels—for example, it's fairly unlikely (though not impossible) that anyone would derive a class from MFC's application class, *CWinApp*, and then derive another class from that. Normally, you can contain all you need in one *CWinApp* subclass, with no need to split the new members between two classes. On the other hand, some hierarchies can be extended a good deal more.

■ **What functionality should reside in the base class?** If there is functionality common to all classes in the hierarchy, it should go in the base class, where as many derived classes as possible can inherit it. Any functionality that is common to only some classes should be placed somewhat lower in the hierarchy, so it governs only a part of the tree. In the *CShape* hierarchy, all shape types have at least a type ID and a bounding rectangle in common. All of them can set or get certain data members. So those features should reside in the base class, *CShape*. On the other hand, each derived class draws itself in a different way, so each overrides *CShape::Draw*.

Access Specifiers in Class Hierarchies

Chapter 4 introduced the access specifiers *public* and *private*. The new class *CShape* introduces our third access specifier: *protected*. Here's that part of the class declaration:

```
// Implementation
protected:
    CRect m_rectShape;       // Bounding rectangle of shape
    ShpType m_typeShape;     // Rectangle, ellipse,...
```

The *protected* access specifier

Protected access is a mixture of public and private—public to some and private to others. Here are guidelines for interpreting access specifiers:

■ Members declared under the *public* access specifier in class *A* are publicly accessible. Outside users of the class can access them. Member functions in derived classes *B*, *C*, and so on can also access them. And, of course, member functions in class *A* can access them. They're really public.

■ Members declared under the *private* access specifier in class *A* are not accessible except to *A*'s own member functions. They are not accessible at all to outside users of the class. And they are not accessible to members of derived classes *B*, *C*, and so on. They're really private.

- Members declared under the *protected* access specifier in class *A* are private to outside users of the class but public to class *A* itself and to members of derived classes *B*, *C*, and so on. These members are private to some and public to others.

Access specifiers that apply to a whole class

Access specifiers can also be used in the heading of a class declaration, as shown in Table 5-1. These access specifiers apply to the class as a whole.

Specifier	Example	Remarks

public	class B : public A
	{
	   ⋮
	}
		Public members of *A* are public to *B*. Protected members of *A* are accessible to *B*, and they remain protected in *B*. Private members of *A* are not accessible to *B*. See the discussion after this table.

private	class B : private A
	{
	   ⋮
	}
		Public and protected members of *A* are accessible to *B*, and they remain private in *B*. Private members of *A* are not accessible to *B*.

protected	class B : protected A
	{
	   ⋮
	}
		Public and protected members of *A* are accessible to *B*, and they remain protected in *B*. Private members of *A* are not accessible to *B*.

Table 5-1.   *Access specifiers in class headings.*

Using the *protected* keyword to label a base class locks out outsiders but leaves access open to derived classes. The only alternatives, *public* and *private*, can in some situations either open the base class up too much (exposing hidden implementation details to the public) or close it too much (hiding things even from derived classes—which is the effect of using *private* in the base class). The *protected* keyword stakes out the middle ground, with just the right levels of exposure—open to derived classes but closed to the outside.

I've given you only the rudiments of access control, so keep in mind that there is more to the story. My advice for starting out is to keep everything public, then gradually experiment with the other variations. Check the Help index for *access specifiers*.

Destructors

A class *destructor* is the opposite of a class constructor. While the constructor is a function that initializes the class, the destructor is for "uninitializing" the class. One major use for a destructor is to deallocate heap memory that was allocated by the class. Destructors are cleanup functions. For example, a class with a data member that is a pointer might allocate memory for the object pointed to, perhaps in the constructor, perhaps elsewhere. While it's possible that you'd want to deallocate the memory earlier, your last chance to do so is in the class destructor. That's because a destructor is the last function called for a class before the class object is destroyed. (Similarly, a constructor is the first function called when the class object has just been created.)

The Shape3 program illustrates a second use for the destructor. I've set up a mechanism in the *CShape* derived classes that counts how many objects of each type currently exist. At the beginning of the program, there are no *CShpRectangles* and no *CShpEllipses*. As the program progresses and creates objects, the objects' constructors increment the counter. As the program deletes objects, their destructors decrement the counter. By the end of the program, when all objects have been destroyed, the counters are back to 0. To illustrate the counting, I have the object display a message with the latest count. You could experiment and display the count in the destructor and see it go to 0 as the objects are destroyed.

The counting is managed in the *CShpRectangle* and *CShpEllipse* constructors and destructors. Each constructor increments the count for its type of object. Each destructor decrements the count for its object type. For example, here are the two *CShpRectangle* constructors and the destructor. The boldface text shows the counting mechanism:

```
CShpRectangle() { m_rectShape = CRect(CPoint(0,0), CPoint(10,10));
                  m_typeShape = shpRectangle; nCountShpRects++; };

CShpRectangle(CRect r)
                { m_rectShape = r; m_typeShape = shpRectangle;
                  nCountShpRects++; };
  ⋮
CShpRectangle::~CShpRectangle()
{
    nCountShpRects--;      // Decrement: we're destroying one.
}
```

I'll explain the rest of the counting mechanism shortly, when I discuss static data members. Meanwhile, here are a few things you need to know about destructors:

■ A destructor, like a constructor, has the same name as its class. In the case of the destructor, however, the name is preceded by a tilde (~), so the full name of the destructor for *CShpRectangle* is *CShpRectangle::~CShpRectangle*.

■ A class's destructor is called automatically when a class object (on the stack) goes out of scope or when the C++ *delete* operator is called for a class object on the heap.

■ If a class has virtual functions, it should also have a virtual destructor. A virtual destructor declaration, within a class declaration, looks like this:

```
virtual ~CShape();
```

Unlike constructors, destructors can be virtual. Defining a virtual destructor ensures that the destructor for the proper object is called in a polymorphic situation. If the base class has a virtual destructor, so do its derived classes, even though the destructors have different names. You don't need to use the *virtual* keyword for a derived class destructor.

■ Like constructors, destructors can be defined inline.

■ When a reference to a class object goes out of scope, no destructor is called. A reference, remember, is only an alias for an already existing object.

■ Like a constructor, a destructor can't return a result. Unlike a constructor, a destructor can't take any parameters. You can do almost anything you like in a destructor. It's common to print debugging information in destructors, for example. You can also call another cleanup function from your destructor.

Static Class Members

In the previous section, I showed the roles of class *CShpRectangle*'s constructor and destructor in counting rectangle objects. Here's the rest of the story.

Using a static class data member

The problem I'm trying to solve is how to maintain ongoing information, such as a count of the *CShpRectangle* objects in existence. The solution is to declare a *static* data member in class *CShpRectangle* (and a similar one in class *CShpEllipse*). Using the *static* keyword on a class data member makes for a special data member. Instead of each *CShpRectangle* object containing its own copy of the data member, there is only one copy and all *CShpRectangle* objects use it. That's perfect for the kind of persistence I'm seeking. After the static data member has been declared, we still need a few more things:

- A way to initialize it. Unlike a static local variable declared in a function (which C++ automatically initializes to 0), a static class data member has to be initialized outside the class scope, at file scope, using the class scope resolution operator, like this:

  ```
  int CShpRectangle::nCountShpRects = 0;
  ```

- A way to increment and decrement the static class data member as objects are created and destroyed. I showed earlier, in "Destructors," how to do this with the classes' constructors and destructors.

- A way to output the static class data member's value from time to time. I do this in the *main* function of program Shape3:

  ```
  printf("Number of rectangles: %d\n", CShpRectangle::nCountShpRects);
  ```

This code shows an interesting property of static class data members. Normally, to access a data member of a class, you must have an object of the class to work through:

```
Object o;
o.m_member = 3;
```

But you can access a static class data member without an object—one doesn't even have to exist—by using the class scope resolution operator, as in the *printf* statement on the preceeding page.

Your static class data members can be hidden in a private section to enforce information hiding, but they still behave like global variables with respect to the class. This can be very handy. You can also use a static data member as a default argument to a class member function. That's not allowed with ordinary data members.

Static class member functions

A class member function can also be declared static. Within the class, such a function can access only other class members that are declared static, and it doesn't have access to the *this* pointer for its object. As with static data members, you can call a static member function without having an object. You do so outside of the class scope, using the class scope resolution operator. It's even possible to create a class with nothing but static members. The members are then available via the class scope resolution operator, as a sort of function library encapsulated in a class.

More About Constructors and Destructors

We're still not finished with even the rudiments of constructors and destructors. The following sections will take you through constructor and destructor overhead, sequence of constructor and destructor calls, member initialization lists, default constructors, copy constructors, and assignment operators. In the process of covering assignment operators, I'll also say a bit about writing overloaded operators for a class.

Constructor and destructor overhead

One thing to keep in mind about both constructors and destructors is that invoking one of them leads to a function call, and function calls take time and resources—that is, they have a cost. Constructors and destructors might be called in situations where you might not have expected them. For example:

- If you don't define a constructor or a destructor for your class, C++ automatically supplies one. These constructors and destructors are do-nothing functions, but they are still called at the appropriate times. You can't circumvent this.

■ When you use pass by value to pass a class object to a function or to return a class object from a function, a copy of the object is made. When the copy is created, its constructor is called. When the copy is later deleted, its destructor is called.

■ In some situations, the C++ compiler creates temporary objects in order to get its work done, and when it does, their constructors and destructors are called. (Try using printed messages in constructors and destructors to observe these objects.)

My point is that you need to be aware of these sources of overhead. Two books by Scott Meyers address this issue in detail and describe ways to reduce constructor and destructor overhead:

■ Scott Meyers, *Effective C++: 50 Specific Ways to Improve Your Programs and Designs*, 2nd edition (Addison-Wesley, 1997).

■ Scott Meyers, *More Effective C++: 35 New Ways to Improve Your Programs and Designs* (Addison-Wesley, 1995).

Sequence of constructor and destructor calls

The sequence in which constructors and destructors are called can be important. The most common of these situations involves a class that contains an embedded class object, such as the *Inner* object *ic*, embedded in class *Outer*, in program InitList.

Try it now

Create program InitList:

```
// InitList.cpp : Defines the entry point for the console application.
//

#include "stdafx.h"
#include <iostream.h>

// An Inner object will be embedded in an Outer object.
class Inner
```

(continued)

```
{
public:
    // Default constructor
    Inner() { i = 0; j = 0; cout << "Default Inner\n"; };

    // Constructor
    Inner(int n, int o);

    // Data members
    int i;
    int j;
};

// An Outer object will contain an Inner object.
class Outer
{
public:
    // Constructor with parameters
    Outer(int j, int o, int k, int& m, char chr);

    // Embedded object
    Inner ic;

    // Const member
    const int c;

    // Reference member
    int& ri;

    // Ordinary member
    char ch;
};

int main(int argc, char* argv[])
{
    // Create existing object to pass as reference parameter.
    int nInt = 5;
    // Construct Outer object with embedded Inner object.
    //   Initialize everything.
    Outer out(3, 9, 4, nInt, 'a');

    // Show that embedded Inner object as well as
    //   const, reference, and ordinary members were initialized.
    cout << "out.ic.i = " << out.ic.i << "   out.ic.j = " << out.ic.j
        << endl;
    cout << "out.c = " << out.c << "   out.ri = " << out.ri << endl;
    cout << "out.ch = " << out.ch << endl;

    return 0;
}
```

```
// Outer constructor with member initialization list
Outer::Outer(int j, int o, int k, int& m, char chr)
: ic(j, o), c(k), ri(m), ch(chr)    // Member initialization list
{
    cout << "Outer constructor with parameters\n";
}

// Inner constructor, which initializes Inner::i and Inner::j
Inner::Inner(int n, int o)
{
    i = n;
    j = o;
    cout << "Inner constructor with parameters\n";
}
```

In this example, a complete object of class *Inner* is constructed within the structure of a class *Outer* object. Which constructor is called first? It's as if the constructor for the member object *ic* is called before the constructor for the containing object. The compiler does some things behind the scenes, but this is the effect. If there are multiple embedded objects like *ic*, their constructors are called in the order of their appearance inside the containing class. The destructors are called in the reverse order.

Member initialization lists

A related issue sometimes arises: suppose you need to pass parameters to the constructor of the embedded object? The technique to use is to append a *member initialization list* to the constructor call for the containing class. The InitList program shows you how to use a member initialization list to initialize each of the following parameters:

■ The data members of an embedded object, such as object *ic*, of class *Inner.*

■ A *const* data member, *c,* which must already be initialized before the body of class *Outer*'s constructor begins to execute. (Yes, you can have *const* members.)

■ A data member of reference type, *ri*, which also must be initialized before the *Outer* constructor begins to execute. (Yes—you can have reference members, too.)

■ An ordinary data member, *ch*. The InitList program shows that you can use the initializer list mechanism to initialize ordinary data members instead of assigning values to them in the constructor body, in the usual way shown here:

```
Outer::Outer(int j, int o, int k, int& m, char chr)
: ic(j, o), c(k), ri(m)     // Member initialization list
{
    ch = chr;     //
  Initialize ordinary data member by assignment.
}
```

The member initialization list for the *Outer* constructor begins with a colon after *Outer*'s parameter list. Following the colon is a comma-delimited list of parameter associations like *ic(j, o)*, where *j* and *o* are being passed to the *n* and *o* parameters of *Inner*'s constructor. These items are called initializers. The whole member initialization list precedes the body of *Outer*'s constructor—because some members, such as the embedded *Inner*, the *const* member, and the reference member must be initialized before *Outer*'s constructor body begins to execute. Notice how the initializer for *Inner*

```
: ic(j, o)...// Inner initializer in Outer constructor call.
```

has the same form as *Inner*'s constructor, with two *int* parameters, *j* and *o*.

Because member initialization lists incur less overhead than assignments inside the constructor, they can be more efficient. A more important point is that member initialization lists are the only way to initialize class data members that are declared *const* or that are reference types. They cannot be given values by assignment.

Default constructors

A default constructor is one that has either no parameters or parameters with default values only. The default constructor allows you to create an object like this:

```
Object myObj;
```

Using this syntax results in a call to the default constructor, if one is supplied. (Inside the body of the default constructor, you can do anything you like, including initializing the object.) If you don't supply any constructors at all, C++ creates a default constructor behind the scenes and calls it. (Of course, it does no work when called.) If you do supply constructors but not a default constructor, the *myObj* syntax shown on the preceeding page results in an error. In this case, you would need to create the object with a parameter list that matches that of one of your constructors.

You should almost always supply a default constructor. Here's one for class *CShpRectangle*, for example (defined inline):

```
class CShpRectangle : public CShape
{
    ⋮

    CShpRectangle() { m_rectShape = CRect(CPoint(0,0), CPoint(10,10));
                      m_typeShape = shpRectangle; nCountShpRects++; };
    ⋮
}
```

Classes *CShpRectangle* and *CShpEllipse* have default constructors, but if it weren't for the object counts we increment in the constructors, these classes could simply inherit *CShape's* constructors and not implement any of their own. A derived class needs its own constructors if it adds data members not supplied by its base class, or if the constructors are needed for some special purpose such as our object counting. The versions of *CShpRectangle* and *CShpEllipse* that we develop in Chapter 14 don't define any constructors of their own. By the way, you might encounter the shorthand terms *ctor* and *dtor* for "constructor" and "destructor" in the MFC source code files.

Copy constructors

A *copy constructor* is called to make a correct copy of its object. The heading for a copy constructor looks like this:

```
Object(const Object& o)...
```

If you supply one for your class, a copy constructor is useful when an object must be copied but you can't accept the default way of copying. This usually happens in one of the two following situations:

■ When you initialize object *A* by assigning object *B* to it. *B*'s contents are copied *memberwise* into *A*'s storage. Memberwise copying means copying exactly what is in the data members. This can be a problem, as we'll see.

■ When you pass an object to a function by value, or return an object by value. In both cases, a copy is made of the object, and in both cases, memberwise copying is used by default.

So when is memberwise copying a problem? When the copied object contains a data member that is a pointer. Memberwise copying involves copying the contents of the pointer variable itself, but not the object it points to. You end up with object *A* and object *B* both containing pointers to the same object—call it *C*. The result we'd usually prefer in this situation is *A*'s pointer member pointing to a *copy* of object *C*—call it *D*. Figure 5-3 illustrates this situation.

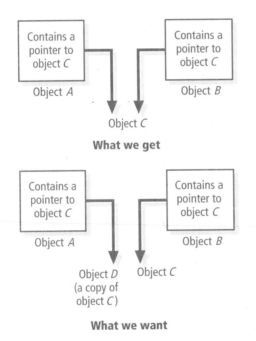

Figure 5-3.   *Imperfect results from a memberwise copy.*

The solution in such a case is to supply a copy constructor for your class. If one exists, it will be called whenever an object of the class is copied, doing the copying your way rather than the memberwise way.

What does a copy constructor look like, and how does it work? Program CopyProb illustrates the difference between memberwise copying and copying with a copy constructor.

Try it now

Create program CopyProb to see what a copy constructor does:

```cpp
// CopyProb.cpp : Defines the entry point for the console application.
//

#include "Stdafx.h"
#include <iostream.h>

// Two classes, HasPtr1 and HasPtr2, with identical data members.

// Class HasPtr1 has no copy constructor;
//   objects of the class will be copied memberwise.
class HasPtr1
{
public:
    // Default constructor
    HasPtr1() { cout << "In default constructor for HasPtr1.\n"; };
    char m_c;        // Non-pointer member
    int* m_pInt;     // Pointer member
};

// Class HasPtr2 has a copy constructor
//   that will be called for copying.
class HasPtr2
{
public:
    // Default constructor
    HasPtr2() { cout << "In default constructor for HasPtr2.\n"; };
    // Copy constructor
    HasPtr2(const HasPtr2&);
    char m_c;        // Non-pointer member
    int* m_pInt;     // Pointer member
};

// Global function
void Function(HasPtr2 HP2);

int main(int argc, char* argv[])
{
    // Memberwise copy.
    HasPtr1 hp1;
    hp1.m_pInt = new int;
    *hp1.m_pInt = 0;
    hp1.m_c = '0';
    cout << "\n1. Now memberwise copy hp1 into copy1.\n";
    HasPtr1 copy1 = hp1;     // Memberwise copy.
```

(continued)

```
cout << "*copy1.m_pInt = " << *copy1.m_pInt
    << "   *hp1.m_pInt = " << *hp1.m_pInt << endl;
cout << "copy1.m_pInt = " << copy1.m_pInt
    << "   hp1.m_pInt = " << hp1.m_pInt << endl << endl;
// The two addresses are the same due to memberwise copy.

// Copy with copy constructor.
HasPtr2 hp2;                    // Invokes default constructor.
hp2.m_pInt = new int;
*hp2.m_pInt = 1;
hp2.m_c = '1';
cout << "\n2. Now copy hp2 into copy2 with copy constructor.\n";
HasPtr2 copy2 = hp2;      // Invokes copy constructor.
cout << "*copy2.m_pInt = " << *copy2.m_pInt
    << "   *hp2.m_pInt = " << *hp2.m_pInt << endl;
cout << "copy2.m_pInt = " << copy2.m_pInt
    << "   hp2.m_pInt = " << hp2.m_pInt << endl;
// The two addresses are different; didn't memberwise copy.

cout << "\n3. Now show the difference between "
    << "initialization and assignment.\n";
// Initialize a new HasPtr2 object; invokes copy constructor.
cout << "Initialization: HasPtr2 copy3 = copy2. ";
HasPtr2 copy3 = copy2;
// Use assignment; do not invoke copy constructor.
cout << "Assignment: copy4 = copy2. ";
HasPtr2 copy4;
copy4 = copy2;

// Copy during pass by value.
cout << "\n4. Now pass a HasPtr2 object by value.\n";
Function(hp2);

return 0;
}

HasPtr2::HasPtr2(const HasPtr2& HP2)
{
    cout << "In copy constructor for HasPtr2.\n";
    m_pInt = new int;
    *m_pInt = *HP2.m_pInt;
    m_c = HP2.m_c;
}

void Function(HasPtr2 HP2)
{
    cout << "In Function, HP2.m_pInt = " << HP2.m_pInt << endl;
}
```

Program CopyProb demonstrates what happens when a class member that is a pointer is copied memberwise, as well as what happens if the class has a copy constructor. CopyProb contains two almost identical classes, *HasPtr1* and *HasPtr2*. Each has two data members: a *char* and a pointer to *int*.

In the first part of *main*, we construct a *HasPtr1* object and initialize its members. This involves using *new* to allocate space for the pointer to *int*, then setting the value of the object pointed to. When we then assign the *HasPtr1* object, *hp1*, to another *HasPtr1* variable, the contents of *hp1* are copied memberwise into the new object, *copy1*. When the pointer member is copied, the pointer variable itself is copied but the object it points to is not. You can see in the second *cout* statement that *hp1.m_pInt* and *copy1.m_pInt* have the same value—on my machine, both are 0x00770810, but it might be different on your machine. This tells us that *copy1* and *hp1* now point to the same *int* object. That's a problem.

The second part of *main* shows how class *HasPtr2*'s copy constructor is invoked to do the copying correctly. Here's the copy constructor:

```
HasPtr2::HasPtr2(const HasPtr2& HP2)
{
    cout << "In copy constructor for HasPtr2.\n";
    m_pInt = new int;
    *m_pInt = *HP2.m_pInt;
    m_c = HP2.m_c;
}
```

Memberwise copying gives incorrect results when there's a pointer member, so the copy constructor allocates space for a new *int* object and copies the *int* pointed to from within *hp2* into the *int* pointed to from within *copy2*. This time the *cout* statement shows that the two pointer addresses are different—they point to different *int* objects.

The third part of *main* makes an important distinction that affects copy constructors: in C++, the act of initialization is distinct from the act of assignment. Initialization occurs when you see syntax like this:

```
HasPtr2 copy3 = copy2;
```

The newly declared object *copy3* is initialized with the contents of *copy2*, an existing *HasPtr2* object, in one statement. This invokes the copy constructor. But the following code shows mere assignment instead:

```
HasPtr2 copy4;
copy4 = copy2;
```

The assignment invokes the default constructor, not the copy constructor. If we had written those lines as one line,

```
HasPtr2 copy4 = copy2;
```

the line would be an initialization instead of an assignment. This is subtle, but important. Because the copy constructor isn't called during assignment, overcoming the limitations of memberwise copying requires writing both an overloaded assignment operator, discussed in the next section, and a copy constructor for classes whose objects are likely to be assigned. *CShape* is certainly in that category.

> **TIP** If you define a copy constructor, always define an overloaded assignment operator as well—and vice versa.

The fourth part of *main* shows that the copy constructor is also invoked when we pass a *HasPtr2* object by value to a function. The *int* pointer inside the function named *Function* has a different value than *hp2*'s *m_pInt* member has. The copy constructor has made a copy of the *int* data member, as the output from program CopyProb shows.

What is the upshot of all of this? Write a copy constructor any time your class contains one or more pointer members.

> **TIP** You can use run-time functions such as *memcpy* and *memmove* to copy nonstandard objects, such as *CShapes*. And the *sizeof* operator tells you how many bytes to copy. Check the Help index for these functions.

Operator Overloading

One of the most powerful (although often misunderstood and misapplied) features of C++ is the ability to *overload* not only function names but C++'s own operators. The typical example is in a string class—a class that encapsulates a C/C++ null-terminated string in a class object, usually allowing the string to grow and shrink dynamically and making it much simpler to manipulate. A standard operation on strings is concatenation. Here's an example of concatenation that uses the MFC class *CString*:

```
CString str1 = "Learn Microsoft Visual C++ 6.0";
CString str2 = " Now";
CString strResult = str1 + str2;
cout << strResult << endl;

// This code will output "Learn Microsoft Visual C++ 6.0 Now"
```

In the example, the plus sign operator (+) has been overloaded by the *CString* class. It still has its old meaning in the old context: arithmetic addition. But in the new context, with string-type operands, it means string concatenation.

In Chapter 14, we'll use *CShape* and its derived classes in an MFC program (with suitable modifications). At that point, we'll derive class *CShape* itself from the MFC class *CObject*, in order to use some of *CObject*'s handy facilities. When you derive a class from *CObject*, you need to write a copy constructor and an overloaded assignment operator (=). Otherwise, you can't assign a *CShpRectangle* object to another *CShpRectangle* object. (For the rationale, check the Help index for *compiler errors with CObject-derived classes*.) Here's an overloaded assignment operator, named *operator=*, for our future version of *CShape*:

```
CShape& operator=(const CShape& s)
{
    // Handle the special case of assignment to self (shp1 = shp1)
    if(this == &s)
        return *this;
    // Otherwise, assign the members of s to the members of this.
    m_boxShape = s.m_boxShape;
    m_typeShape = s.m_typeShape;
    m_nColorShape = s.m_nColorShape;
    return *this;
}
```

Notice that the *operator=* function returns a reference to a *CShape* and takes a *const* reference to a *CShape* as parameter. That's standard syntax for an overloaded assignment operator. Inside the function, we assign the data members of the parameter *s* to those of *this CShape* object. Then we return (by reference) the value denoted by the dereferenced *this* pointer. If *CShape* contained any pointer data members, we'd have to take steps similar to those in the copy constructor described in the previous section. We'd want a duplicate of the object pointed to rather than a duplicate of the pointer itself.

Also notice the special-case code for assignment of an object to itself. To handle that gracefully, we return without doing any internal assignments if the address of *s* is the same as the value of the *this* pointer.

Keep in mind that although we've just written a function named *operator=*, we're really writing a special definition of the assignment operator (=) for *CShape* objects, so we can write things like:

```
CShape shp1;
CShape shp2;
  ⋮
// Code to set shp2 members goes here.
  ⋮
shp1 = shp2;    // Using the assignment operator
                //  invokes our function.
```

Note that if *CShape* defines an overloaded assignment operator, a derived class *CShpRectangle* must define its own version of the operator. That version of the operator is needed if *CShpRectangle* members that aren't defined in *CShape* are to be copied properly.

C++ lets you overload all but a tiny handful of its operators, with a few restrictions. Operator overloading is an advanced topic that I won't cover further in this book. Every C++ text warns of the semantic pitfalls of operator overloading. Assignment to self is just one of them. For more information, check the Help index for *operator overloading* and select the subtopic "general rules." But I would also consult a good C++ textbook. See Chapter 21 for a recommendation.

Scope, Part 2

In Chapter 3 and Chapter 4, I said I'd say more about class scope in Chapter 5, and here we are. A quick review of global scope and local scope will help you understand how class scope works. (See "Scope, Part 1" in Chapter 3 if your memory needs more of a jog.)

The outermost scope in a program is called *global scope,* or *file scope.* Things declared at this scope—global variables and functions, classes, the *main* function, constants, and various types—are visible (accessible) throughout the file, including inside *main* and other global functions and inside classes.

Local scope is separate. Local scope prevails within a function, or within a block (a pair of curly braces) inside a function, such as a *for*, *while*, or *if* statement, or a freestanding block. Things declared at this scope—local variables, constants, nested classes, and types—are visible only within their block or in subordinate blocks. You can use the *extern* and *static* keywords at file scope to make things visible or invisible in other files, as described in "Scope, Part 1" in Chapter 3.

The remaining scope is *class scope.* Class scope prevails within a class declaration and extends to class member function definitions. Things declared within a class—such as member functions, data members, types, and nested classes—are visible within the class. They are also visible within the bodies of the class's member function definitions. Unless declared public, they are invisible outside of the class. (Some items, such as static members, types, and nested classes, can be made visible outside of the class through the class scope resolution operator.)

Inline member function definitions declared outside the class body with the *inline* keyword are also within the class scope. Each member function (inline or not) also constitutes its own local scope, which is a subset of the entire class scope. And finally, class scope extends to derived classes. If class *B* is derived from class *A*, *B*'s member functions can access non-private members declared in *A*.

NOTE Items declared toward the end of a class declaration are visible at the beginning of the class declaration. Contrast that with local variables inside a function, which are not visible before the variable declaration.

Users of a class have access to its public interface: members that are declared under the *public* access specifier. They do not have access to members declared under the *protected* or *private* access specifiers (unless they're friends of the class). Derived classes' access to base class members is also controlled both by the use of access specifiers within the base class and by the use of access specifiers in the heading of the derived class. For details, see "Access Specifiers in Class Hierarchies," earlier in this chapter.

A class itself can be declared at global, class, or local scope. That is, you can declare a class at global scope or nest it within another class or within a function. Classes declared at class or local scope are not visible outside the containing scope. For more information, check the Help index for the following three items: *scope*, *nested classes*, and *nested class declarations*.

Object-Oriented Programming

Object-oriented programming (OOP) can be thought of as an extension of standard structured programming techniques. The *class* is a new element of modularity, added to the file and the function. OOP is a style of programming in which you model real-world objects—shapes, stereos, windows, documents—with software objects. It's possible to do OOP even in conventional programming languages like C, but C++ provides direct support for OOP and makes it easier and much more natural to think and code in terms of objects.

OOP languages like C++ are also highly extensible. In addition to the built-in data types—*ints*, *floats*, *chars*—C++ makes it possible to extend the type system indefinitely, especially when you consider the ability to overload C++ operators. Each new class you create, whether it is a base class or a derived class, is a new data type. A derived class inherits the data and behaviors of its base class, yet it can override and extend the functionality of its base class as well. This amounts to extending data types by deriving new types from them.

The ability to store a pointer to class *B* in a variable of type *A* ∗ (where *A* is a base class of *B*) greatly simplifies working with collections of objects in the same class hierarchy. You can, as we saw, store *CShpRectangles* and *CShpEllipses*—and later *CShpTriangles*—in an array of *CShapes*. And, using the virtual function mechanism, you can call the *Draw* member function of a *CShape* ∗ array element and expect the *Draw* member function of the actual object stored there to be called. This polymorphism lets objects work together while each behaves in its own way.

You can use OOP to a greater or lesser extent. For example, you might use it just to provide a single new data type in a program that otherwise greatly resembles a C program. Or, you might use an object-oriented design to model the entire problem you're trying to solve. MFC, for instance, models a Windows application and uses class objects extensively to represent windows, documents, dialog boxes, buttons, and even the application as a whole.

The object-oriented design process generally begins with careful specification of the problem. The next step is to study the problem for elements that might make good objects. As design goes on, you gradually develop the structure and behaviors of these objects. Eventually, you implement the objects, often as C++ classes in a hierarchy.

How Much OOP?

When the Application Frameworks (AFX) team at Microsoft began its work on an object-oriented application framework (a set of classes that provide the framework of a program using OOP techniques), it was highly object-oriented. Even simple data elements like *ints* and *chars* were housed in objects.

The AFX developers soon realized, however, that they had gone overboard. Their second application framework—developed after they scrapped a year's work on the first—became the MFC library. One of the hallmarks of MFC was that it was just object-oriented enough, and not a bit more. The AFX team could have written a completely new version of Microsoft Windows in C++, using an object-oriented approach in which every element of Windows would be represented by an object. They chose instead—wisely—not to rewrite Windows from scratch, nor to overdo the OOP. The MFC library that resulted represents a few primary Windows concepts—windows, device contexts, and a few others—as objects, but calls the original Windows API functions from within those objects. For example, class *CWnd* represents a window. Its *CWnd::ShowWindow* member function, for instance, calls the *ShowWindow* API function in the

Windows operating system. I'll have more to say about Windows and its relationship to MFC in "MFC and Windows" in Chapter 8.

Meanwhile, the AFX developers took to calling themselves "reformed OOPaholics." They had come back from excessive OOP to embrace a philosophy that puts object-oriented programming in its place as one of many software tools.

This is a philosophy worth heeding. New OOP enthusiasts always go overboard. But the smart ones end up like the AFX team, using OOP only when it's the right tool for the task.

OOP Terminology

You'll encounter two sets of OOP terms in the literature. Outside C++, much of the terminology is based on the Smalltalk language, which pioneered OOP concepts in the 1970s. Table 5-2 compares the two terminology systems.

Smalltalk Term	Equivalent C++ Term
Instance (noun); instantiate (verb) an object	Object (noun); create (verb) an object
Subclass (verb)	Derive (verb)
Subclass, descendant, child class (nouns)	Derived class
Superclass, ancestor, parent class	Base class
Property, instance variable	Member variable, data member
Class variable (one copy for all instances of the class)	Static data member
Method	Member function
Sending a message	Calling a member function

Table 5-2. *Competing systems of OOP terminology.*

I'll generally use the C++ terms because C++ programmers tend to be purists about this. Occasionally I'll use a Smalltalk term where I think it clarifies a point.

What's Missing from Our C++ Coverage?

Here are the main elements of C++ that I haven't covered, some of which I'll at least introduce later in the book. The others are left for your own postgraduate efforts. I've included many Help citations that should assist you.

- **Bit fields.** Check the Help index for *bit fields* and select the topic "C++ Bit Fields" in the Topics Found dialog box.

- **Exceptions.** Check the Help index for *exceptions* and select the topic "Exception Handling Topics (MFC)" in the Topics Found dialog box. Also see "MFC Diagnostic Facilities" in Chapter 13.

- **Multiple inheritance.** Check the Help index for *multiple inheritance.*

- **Namespaces.** Namespaces help you avoid collisions that might result from the same identifier being used in different parts of a complex program. Check the Help index for *namespaces.*

- **Operator overloading.** I have described this very briefly. Check the Help index for *operator overloading* and select the subtopic "general rules." I also advise you to consult a good C++ textbook. See Chapter 21 for suggestions.

- **Pointers to functions, including class member functions.** To learn about pointers to functions in general, consult a C or C++ textbook. (See Chapter 21.) For pointers to class members, check the Help index for *Pointers* and choose the subtopic "to members."

- **Recursion, the ability of a function to call itself.** Check the Help index for *recursive function calls.* The topic you get is for C, but it also applies to C++.

- **Run-time type information (RTTI).** Check the Help index for *RTTI.* (Note that MFC has its own run-time type system and doesn't use RTTI.)

- **Templates.** Check the Help index for *templates* and select the topic "Template Topics" from the Topic Found dialog box. One use for templates is in some of the MFC collection classes (lists, arrays, and maps), but I'll use only the nontemplate collection classes in this book. (See Chapter 14.)

- **Unions.** Check the Help index for *union* and choose the first two topics in the Topics Found dialog box.

- **User-defined conversions.** For example, MFC's *CString* class defines a conversion between *CStrings* and char∗ variables. Check the Help index for *conversion functions.* An example of converting from class *Money* to type *double* is given.

- **Virtual base classes.** Check the Help index for *virtual base classes* and choose the topic "Virtual Base Classes" in the Topics Found dialog box.

- **Volatile objects.** Check the Help index for *volatile* and choose the first topic in the Topics Found dialog box.

Try It Yourself

Here are this chapter's extra-credit exercises for the brave. The answers to exercises 2 and 3 are at the end of this section

1. Implement simple *CArray* and *CQueue* classes.

Use a *has-a* relationship to implement a *CQueue* class based on a *CArray* class. (See the discussion about *has-a* relationships earlier in this chapter.) A queue is like a line at the ice cream vendor: a new element can only join the queue at the back; an element can only receive ice cream at the front. You can call these operations *Add* and *Remove*, or *Put* and *Take,* for example. Include error checking in your *CQueue* member functions. Implement *CArray* with an array of *int*, 100 elements long, and include error checking. Typical array operations are *SetAt* (set the value of an element at a specified index), *GetAt* (return the value of an element at a specified index), and *GetCount* (return the number of elements actually assigned). I present one solution in program Ch5ex1 in the \learnvcn\Chap05 folder in the companion code.

2. Take this quiz on access specifiers.

Answer the questions that follow this code, which is also in the learnvcn\Chap05 folder in the companion code. You'll find the answers at the end of this chapter.

```
// ch5ex2.cpp : Defines the entry point for the console application.
// For Try It Yourself, exercise 2, Chapter 5

#include <stdafx.h>
#include <iostream.h>

// COne is a totally private class, inaccessible from outside.
class COne
{
// It's as if there's a private access specifier here.
//protected:
    COne() { m_one = 0; m_one_c = 'a'; };
    int m_one;
    char m_one_c;
    void DoOne() { cout << m_one << " " << m_one_c << endl; };
};

class CTwo : protected COne        // Note protected keyword here
{
public:
    // Constructor and DoTwo member function
    //  try to access COne members, but they're private.
    CTwo() { m_one = 1; m_one_c = 'b'; };
    int m_two;
    void DoTwo() { cout << m_one << " " << m_two << endl; };
};

int main(int argc, char* argv[])
{
    COne one;              // Can't call this constructor
                           //  because it's private.
    CTwo two;              // Tries to access COne members,
                           //  but they're private.
    two.DoTwo();           // Ditto

    return 0;
}
```

Question 1

What errors will you see when you try to build this code? If in doubt, try it.

Question 2

If you add a *protected* specifier before the first member of class *COne*, what errors do you get? Try it.

3. **Explain whether our *CShape* classes need a copy constructor, and why or why not?**

   Hint: Look at the data members. (But also see my remarks about class *CObject* in the section "Operator Overloading" in this chapter.)

Answers to Try It Yourself Exercises

Test yourself on exercises 2 and 3 before you peek!

Exercise 2, question 1

For a very simple reason, the compiler will reject this code with five errors. Recall that the members of a class declared with the *class* keyword are private by default. Since there is no *public* or *protected* specifier at the beginning of the class declaration for class *COne*, all of its members are private. The private members of a base class are inaccessible to members of a derived class, regardless of whether the overall derivation is public, protected, or private. Omitting the *public* keyword at the beginning of a class—when you mean for it to have public members, such as constructors—is a classic mistake. The first four errors occur in *CTwo*'s constructor and member function *DoTwo*. The fifth error occurs in *main*, when we try to construct a *COne* object. *COne*'s constructor isn't available because it's private.

Exercise 2, question 2

When you specify that *COne*'s members are protected, you get one error. As with Question 1, the *COne* constructor is unavailable in *main*. It would have to be public before we could construct a *COne* object there, outside class *COne*. *COne*'s members do become accessible in *CTwo*'s member functions. With *CTwo* declared a protected derived class in the class heading of *CTwo*, public members of *COne* (if there are any) are protected in *CTwo*; protected members of *COne* are protected in *CTwo*; and private members of *COne* are inaccessible to *Ctwo*. (Go back to Table 5-1 for a review of access specifiers in class headings.)

Exercise 3

In their current form, the *CShape* classes don't require a copy constructor because none of them has any data members that are pointers. Later, when we derive these classes from MFC class *CObject*, they'll require both a copy constructor and an overloaded assignment operator because of the way *CObject* is written. I'll discuss this further in Chapter 14.

What's Next?

With a good survey of C++ and object-oriented programming out of the way, let's move on to programming for Microsoft Windows, especially with MFC. Chapter 6 introduces the fundamental concepts of Windows programming. In Chapter 7 we'll dive into MFC and stay there through the rest of the book.

Windows and the Win32 API

Microsoft Visual C++ 6.0 lets you create many kinds of programs. But the principal kind, the one we'll focus on exclusively for the rest of this book, is the C++ application for Microsoft Windows, written with the Microsoft Foundation Class Library 6.0 (MFC).

In this chapter, we climb high for a bird's-eye view of what's involved in programming in any language for Windows 95, Windows 98, and Microsoft Windows NT. I'll take you through the fundamental concepts of the Windows operating system from the point of view of a programmer. In the next chapter, we'll circle back and see how MFC does Windows.

NOTE For a glimpse of the many kinds of programs you can create with Visual C++, select New from the Visual C++ File menu. The list includes at least three types of projects that use MFC in C++, and at least four kinds that use the Win32 API in C or C++. The type of project we'll work with in this book is called "MFC AppWizard (exe)" in the project list.

The Flavors of Windows

Windows 95, Windows 98, and Windows NT are all 32-bit variations of the Microsoft Windows operating system for personal computers. Windows 3.1 and its successor, Windows 3.11, are 16-bit versions of the operating system. Although many people still use these 16-bit versions, the rest of the world has moved on. This book is exclusively about the 32-bit world. (You can still use what you learn here to program for 16-bit Windows, but you'll need older software, including much older versions of Visual C++ and MFC—versions 2.5 and 1.5, respectively.)

Computer program data is fundamentally based on the size of a word of storage. The size of a word determines how much memory the system can address. Systems based on 32 bits have a 32-bit word size that is double that of the 16-bit word used in Windows 3.1. This means that the 32-bit systems can address a great deal more memory. In fact, in 32-bit systems, the amount of addressable memory grows exponentially to more than 4 GB. Furthermore, unlike 16-bit systems, in which memory addresses are divided into segments that result in complicated code, 32-bit memory is *flat*. There are no segments, just one big address space. This not only makes for easier programming, but also for more powerful programs.

The Windows API

Windows 95 and Windows 98 are quite different from Windows NT under the hood, but all of these 32-bit versions of Windows are written "in the same language," so to speak. All are based on the Windows Application Programming Interface (API), popularly known as the Win API. There's a 16-bit version of the Win API, but Windows 95, Windows 98, and Windows NT all use the 32-bit version, called the Win32 API, or, simply, Win32. (For clarity, the 16-bit version is now often called the Win16 API or just Win16.) This book focuses on the Win32 API.

Win32, the SDK, and Windows.h

What is the Win32 API? The API is a collection of several hundred functions, plus numerous constants, macros, *structs*, types, and other items. These programming elements are written in the C programming language, but nowadays you can call the functions and use the other items from C++, Microsoft Visual Basic, assembly language, Fortran, Pascal, and other programming languages.

Most of the API is defined in a file called Windows.h. This file comes with most programming environments for Windows, including Visual C++.

Although you can also get it with Microsoft's Windows Platform Software Development Kit (SDK), Windows.h is included with this book as part of Visual C++, so you don't need the separate SDK.

N OTE The Platform SDK was formerly known as the Win32 SDK.

Central Windows Concepts

The Win32 API functions are built around a set of underlying concepts, including a graphics environment, multiple overlapping windows, menus, icons, messages, files, resources, multitasking, and using a mouse. I'll introduce you to each of these concepts in this chapter.

The unifying concept, of course, is the idea of a window. Many functions in the API operate on windows—creating them, sizing them, moving them, and so on. Other API functions are for drawing in windows; opening, reading, writing, and closing files; communicating with the operating system or other programs; and much more.

Programming for Different Win32 Platforms

Basing the different 32-bit operating systems on a single API means that you can program all of the 32-bit Windows variants in much the same way. While it's true that the API contains some functions you can use only with Windows NT and others you can use only with Windows 95 and 98, the core of the API is identical across all of these platforms. So, if you can program for Windows 95, you can also program for Windows 98 and Windows NT, especially if you use MFC.

Multitasking and Multithreading

Windows—particularly in its 32-bit flavors—is a *multitasking* system. A multitasking operating system can run multiple programs at the same time. You already knew that, of course—no doubt, in your role as user, you routinely run several applications simultaneously. As of Windows 95, multitasking in Windows is *preemptive*. (Earlier versions of Windows used a simpler and less effective nonpreemptive approach in which programs had to cooperate explicitly to share the processor.) In a preemptive multitasking environment, the operating system doles out small slices of time to each running application (or *process*). Because the slices are small enough, it appears to the user that several programs are running simultaneously. In reality, each "sleeps" briefly until its turn comes around again. We human beings operate on a slower time scale, so the appearance of simultaneity is convincing.

The modern Windows systems also allow for *multithreading* within an application, a concept related to multitasking. Most programs have a single *thread of execution*. That is, there is one path through the code, and each statement along the way is executed in turn. But a program can split into two or more separate threads of execution that—as in multitasking—seem to run simultaneously. In this way, a program can spin off *worker threads* that take care of some independent tasks, like printing in the background, while the user continues to work in the main thread.

Multitasking and multithreading are topics too advanced for this book, so I won't say much more about them. However, if you reach a point where you want to try them, you'll find that the MFC library makes the process somewhat easier.

The Least You Need to Know About Windows

You've already sat at a computer that runs the Microsoft Windows operating system—Windows 95, Windows 98, or Windows NT—or you wouldn't be reading this book and thinking of programming for Windows yourself. You've seen the Windows desktop, the taskbar at the bottom of the screen, the Start menu, and so on. You know what a window looks like and how to work its controls with the mouse.

So picture yourself at your PC, perhaps using Microsoft Word, as I am to write this book. Sit for a minute without touching the mouse or the keyboard. Not much happens, right? The *caret*—the blinking cursor at the insertion point in your text—blinks. If you're using Word 97 or later and you have the assistant displayed, you might see a cartoon paper clip wiggle or move its eyes from time to time. But while you just sit there, not much else is going on.

Now start typing. The new text you type at the keyboard appears at the caret position. Next, select some text with the mouse. The text is highlighted. Click the Bold button on the toolbar. The selected text is redrawn in boldface print. With each of these actions, also called *events*, something happens while you, the user, control the pace and direction.

Events

Microsoft Windows is a *user-driven* system—meaning one that spends much of its running time waiting for the user to do something so it can respond. Such systems are also called *event-driven*. When the user presses a key, moves the mouse, or clicks a mouse button, the computer hardware lets Windows know that an event has occurred, what kind of event it was, when it happened, and where it happened in relation to the screen (at a particular set of coordinates inside a particular application's window, for example).

Events are generated in one of three ways. The first is through input devices, such as the keyboard and mouse. The second is through visual objects on the screen, such as menus, toolbar buttons, scroll bars, and the controls in dialog boxes. (True, you generate visual events with a mouse or keyboard too, but Windows ultimately sees them as coming from the objects you activate with your hardware.) The third avenue is from inside Windows itself, as, for example, when a window that was obscured by another window is suddenly uncovered.

How does Windows know where to display the typed character or how to interpret a mouse click-and-drag across an area of the screen as a text selection? In other words, how does Windows tell Word about these events, and how does Word translate events into visible manifestations in its window? Through messages.

Messages

When Windows learns of an event like the ones I just described, it composes a *message*, bundles relevant information (such as location and time) into a data structure to accompany the message, and sends the message to the appropriate program. Messages in Windows are constants defined with macros in the Windows.h file (or in one of the files that Windows.h includes). Message constant names have the form *WM_XXX*; for example, *WM_QUIT*, *WM_CHAR*, *WM_LBUTTONDOWN*, *WM_COMMAND*. The message gets routed to the right program based on the following information:

- Which application is currently active

- Which window in that application is currently active

- Where the cursor was at the time of the event

Windows puts the message into the target application's message queue, where it waits with any other pending messages until the application is ready to retrieve and process it. Under 32-bit Windows systems, every application has a message queue of its own.

The message loop

Inside the application, there's a *message loop*. In code, this loop looks something like the following:

```
while(GetMessage(&msg, NULL, 0, 0))
{
    TranslateMessage(&msg);
    DispatchMessage(&msg);
}
```

This little loop continues to operate as long as the message it retrieves from the application's message queue is not *WM_QUIT*. That message causes the loop to end because *GetMessage* returns *false* when it finds *WM_QUIT*, and the application terminates. But while the loop continues, it calls the Win32 API function *GetMessage* to retrieve the next message. If there are no messages in the queue, *GetMessage* sits there and waits for one. (This just means that the user isn't doing anything that the program needs to know about.)

When *GetMessage* does return a message, the loop hands it off to the *TranslateMessage* function to see whether it is a message from the keyboard that needs a little extra work. *TranslateMessage* converts raw keyboard messages into *WM_CHAR* messages designed to convey easy-to-use information about the character that was typed. *TranslateMessage* separates commands delivered by keyboard, such as combinations like Ctrl+X, from typed alphanumeric characters and printable symbols. *TranslateMessage* does nothing with nonkeyboard messages.

Finally, the *DispatchMessage* function determines which window in the application (if there's more than one) should get the message and sends the message on. Then the loop goes around again.

Message handlers

What happens to an incoming message inside the receiving application depends on what you, the application programmer, have done. There are two main possibilities:

■ You wrote a *handler*—some code that handles a particular message. If a handler for the message exists, the handler code executes to process the message.

■ You didn't write a handler for that message. Instead, you opted to pass that message back to Windows for whatever default processing Windows needs to do. In traditional Windows programming, you do this with a call to the *DefWindowProc* ("default window procedure") function.

Either way, somebody does something with the message—either your application, in the handler you provided, or Windows.

What happens in the handler for a message depends on what you need to accomplish. But there are many standard or typical things to do for particular messages. For example, a handler for the *WM_PAINT* message— sent when your window needs to repaint its contents—takes steps to reconstruct the image you're displaying in the window. You might need to redraw the visible lines of text, or the rectangles and ellipses the user has drawn, and so on. One message for which you'll frequently write handlers is *WM_COMMAND*, which is used to process commands from menus and buttons. *WM_COMMAND* handlers, often called simply *command handlers*, lie at the heart of your interactions with the user. A command handler might display a dialog box, perform a calculation, select an option, or initiate some other action.

Who calls whom?

You may have noticed that sometimes you seem to be in charge, and sometimes Windows does. Inside the code you write for your message handlers, you call various Win32 API functions (via MFC). But *you* don't call your handlers—Windows does. There's a back-and-forth here. Most of the time, your code just sits there waiting to be called, while Windows is off doing all the millions of mysterious things it does without any help from you.

Think of it this way. Windows is self-contained. If you don't write a handler for one of the several hundred Windows messages, does Windows crash? No. If you don't provide a handler, Windows provides one—called *DefWindowProc*. But if you do provide a handler, Windows calls yours first. You get the chance to intercept the message and deal with it your way instead of letting Windows use its default. (You might do something with the message and still pass it on to *DefWindowProc*, so that both your handler and Windows' handler are called, but that's another story. You still get the first chance.)

Inside your handler, you're in charge. Of course, you're mostly just taking advantage of the many services that the Win32 API provides. In practice, you'll seldom provide handlers for more than a few handfuls of the hundreds of possible Windows messages.

How does Windows know which functions to call? In Windows programs written in C (or in C++ without MFC), you specify the name of your *windproc* (window procedure) to the operating system at the beginning of the program. Then you write a function with that name. In Windows programming parlance, this function is known as a *callback function*, since it gives Windows a way to call you back in order to call your handlers. In the window procedure, you use a C/C++ *switch* statement to provide handler code for the Windows messages you expect to receive and process. When it has a message for your window, Windows calls your window procedure. In MFC programs, you don't write the window procedure. Instead, you write handler functions, which MFC calls via a message map every time it receives a message for your window for which you've supplied a handler function.

Drawing

Like the Apple Macintosh operating system and several similar systems, Microsoft Windows has a *graphical user interface* (GUI). Instead of interacting with a program solely by typing text in response to prompts—the old-fashioned approach, as in the console applications we've been writing, for instance—the Windows user interacts with the program through a visual display. The display includes elements such as menus, toolbars, scroll bars, and buttons in dialog boxes. While it's possible to operate most programs for Windows with the keyboard, most are designed to be operated by moving and clicking a mouse. For example, the user clicks a menu title, causing the menu to drop down. Then the user clicks a command or choice on the menu.

All of the menus, buttons, and other controls that the user sees on the screen are actually drawn there. A button in a dialog box, for instance, is just a bitmap—a collection of pixels in which some are turned on and some are turned off. It's just a picture, although it may look pretty three-dimensional. Hence it must be drawn, either by Windows or by code that you write.

Child windows and owned windows

In Windows, each of these controls and other user-interface objects is also itself a window. For example, a dialog box is a window, and each of the buttons, edit boxes, and other controls inside the dialog box is a window—a *child window* of some *parent window*. The parent of a dialog box control, for example, is the dialog box window. Child windows are contained by their parent windows—the child is entirely within the parent.

A window can also "own" other windows, even if the owned windows don't fall entirely within the owner's space. For example, a dialog box window is owned by some other window, such as the application's main frame window or a child of that window.

How and when drawing happens

How and when does drawing occur? That is, how does Windows know when to draw a child window? Through messages. Windows handles many of its own messages. And how does your code know when to draw the items it's responsible for, such as the text inside a word processor window? The drawing you do—also synonymously called *painting*—occurs at the following two points in relation to your program:

■ First, when your program initially displays a window, it needs to paint the window's interior, or *client area*, for the first time. The client area is the space surrounded by the window's borders, title bar, and other framing elements, as shown in Figure 6-1. The client area is almost always your responsibility, while the frame around it is Windows' responsibility.

■ Second, any time part of the window becomes "damaged," or *invalidated*, you need to repaint it. This can occur, for instance, when some other window covers your window, and then goes away so your window is fully visible again. Windows doesn't save an image of what was in the window, so it can't redraw the whole thing by itself. It therefore notifies you that you need to repaint the window's contents. (It's possible, that the data to be drawn might have changed while the window was obscured. So it needs to be redrawn, regardless.)

WM_PAINT messages

In either of the cases just described, Windows notifies you by sending you a *WM_PAINT* message. You nearly always have to write a handler for *WM_PAINT*. Sometimes Windows can pass along information that lets you redraw just a portion of the window's contents. Otherwise, you need to redraw the whole thing.

By the way, Windows prioritizes the messages that show up in your application's message queue. And it so happens that *WM_PAINT* is normally given a low priority. Thus, your window could go unpainted for a while. Think back to your own role as a user of Windows. Aren't there times when a window just hangs there with half its contents obliterated while some time-consuming, high-priority operation is going on? The high-priority operation temporarily hogs the processing time, and the repainting has to wait its turn. Of course, Windows does it this way because painting is less crucial than operations like recalculating a spreadsheet.

Such operations must be done first, and an unpainted window is just a minor inconvenience that clears up soon enough.

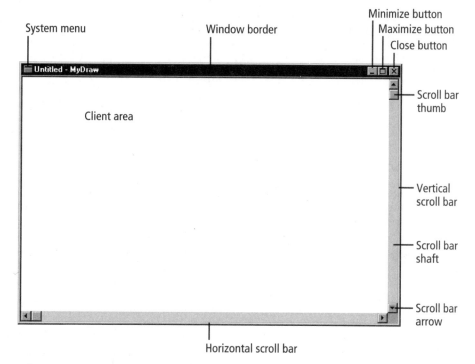

Figure 6-1.   *The parts of a frame window.*

The Device Context

Now then. When asked to paint, how do you do it? Well, there you are with a window. Windows is responsible for repainting the frame, while you're responsible for repainting the interior—the client area. (You're the client.) Corresponding to your client area, there's a Windows object known as a *device context* (often abbreviated as "DC"). A device context is really just a data structure maintained by Windows. It contains information about the area (window) it's for, the current background color or pattern of the area, what parts of the area are currently invalid (in need of repainting), and so on. In fact, the device context contains several smaller objects—a brush, a pen, and a font—that you use to draw in the client area. The most important object in the device context is its *bitmap*—this is a logical surface onto which you draw, and it's the bitmap that Windows displays on a screen, a printer, or some other output device.

It might be more helpful to think of the device context as your painting studio. It contains various painting and drawing tools as well as a canvas to paint on (the bitmap).

You can change these tools and the other attributes of the device context to suit your needs. For example, you can call a function that changes the text color from the default black to, say, red. Or you can substitute a different font for the default one. But you can't possibly draw without a device context. That's important. In any of your handlers that draw, you'll have to obtain a device context somehow. Sometimes you'll be handed a device context, and away you go. But sometimes you'll have to take steps yourself to obtain one. I'll show you how in Chapter 15.

> **NOTE** Every time you get a device context, Windows sets it to the default attributes. So you can't, say, change the text color to red in function *A*, and then get a new device context in function *B* and expect the color still to be red. You'll have to set any nondefault attributes each time you obtain a fresh device context. (Don't worry—there are ways around this.)

Handles

The way you get access to a device context is through a *handle* that Windows returns to you. The variable type for a handle to a device context is *HDC* (defined in Windef.h). The handle grants you certain rights and abilities inside your window. Providing a handle to some object or resource you need is a common Windows activity. In fact, Windows provides handles to many types of objects: windows, brushes, fonts, and so on. Each kind of object has an associated handle type: *HWND, HBRUSH,* and *HFONT*, for example. Table 6-1 shows the more common Windows objects for which handles can be retrieved.

Win32 API functions

With the *HDC* (handle for a device context) in your possession, you can call well over a hundred Win32 API functions for drawing in your window's client area. For example, Table 6-2 shows just a few of the most common drawing functions:

Windows Object	Associated Handle
Accelerator table	*HACCEL*
Bitmap	*HBITMAP*
Brush	*HBRUSH*
Cursor	*HCURSOR*
Device context	*HDC*
File	*HFILE*
Font	*HFONT*
Icon	*HICON*
Menu	*HMENU*
Palette	*HPALETTE*
Pen	*HPEN*
Region	*HRGN*
Window	HWND

Table 6-1. *Some common Windows objects and their handle types.*

Win32 Function	What It Does
TextOut	Draws a string of text at a specified location in the client area
Rectangle	Draws a rectangle at specified coordinates
Ellipse	Draws an ellipse at specified coordinates
GetBkColor	Gets the current background color
SetBkColor	Sets the background color
MoveToEx (*MoveTo* in MFC)	Moves the drawing position to a specified location
LineTo	Draws a line from the current position (see *MoveToEx*) to a specified position
Arc	Draws an elliptical arc—a segment of an elliptical curve
Polygon	Draws a polygon with two or more vertices
Pie	Draws a pie-shaped wedge, like the wedge in a pie chart

Table 6-2. *A small sampling of the many drawing functions associated with a device context.*

In MFC, the functions just named, and many more, are member functions of a class called *CDC*. *CDC* stands for "device context class." For more information, check the Help index for *CDC*. You can also check the Help index for *device contexts* and select the topic "Device Contexts" in the Topics Found dialog box.

The part of Windows responsible for device contexts and drawing functions is known as the *Graphics Device Interface* (GDI). GDI is a complete two-dimensional drawing system. It has the device context, drawing functions, and several coordinate systems for measuring and locating the images you draw with it.

Coordinates

Many of the drawing functions listed in Table 6-2 require you to specify location information when you call them: a point, a rectangle, two points, an array of points, and so on.

To specify locations for drawing and other tasks, you need a *coordinate system*. Figure 6-2 shows a couple of familiar coordinate systems that you'll probably recall from high school algebra and geometry. A coordinate system consists of an *origin* (or starting point) and in a plane (like the flat drawing surface in a window's client area) two *axes*, one horizontal and one vertical. Distances are measured along the *x* (or horizontal) axis, and the *y* (or vertical) axis, from the origin—the point where the *x* and *y* axes come together. The origin's coordinates are (0, 0)—that's (*x*, *y*). In some coordinate systems, the *x* and *y* values can be negative to one side of the origin and positive to the other side.

Windows is more than generous in supplying not one but eight coordinate systems, each for a different purpose. The default coordinate system, shown in Figure 6-3, is simple and will meet the majority of your needs. I'll describe other coordinate systems as the need for them comes up. The default coordinate system looks a little strange—its origin is at the top left corner of your window's client area. You might expect it at the bottom left, with *y* values increasing upwards and *x* values increasing to the right. But there's logic to this placement. You'll see why it makes sense to start there when we get to scrolling the window's contents, in Chapter 15. And think about this: on a page full of text (in most human languages), what corner of the paper does the text start closest to? (See Figure 6-4.) In the default coordinate system, positive *x* values do indeed increase to the right of the origin, but positive *y* values increase *downward* from the origin. There are no negative coordinates in this system, but some of the other systems do allow negative values. (On that page of text, is there anywhere to put text above or to the left of the origin?)

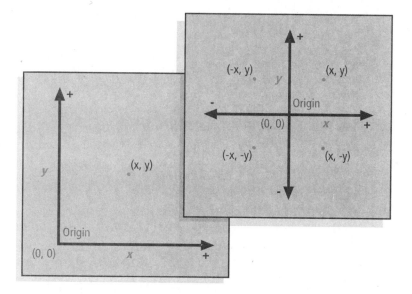

Figure 6-2. *Two typical coordinate systems.*

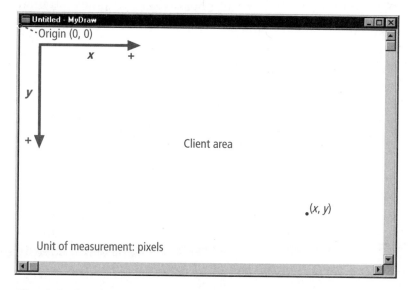

Figure 6-3. *The default coordinate system in Windows.*

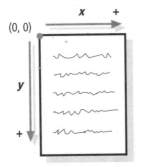

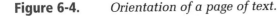

Figure 6-4. *Orientation of a page of text.*

Logical coordinates and device coordinates

Of course, having made coordinates look fairly simple, I'm about to complicate matters, but I won't take you too far down that road in this chapter. Remember that the coordinate system is part of the device context. And the device context you work with when you draw in your window is associated only with the client area of that window. This means the origin is at the top left corner of the client area portion of your window. There are no coordinates in this system for points outside the part of the window that belongs to you. Sometimes, however, Windows must pass you location information that is relative not to your window's coordinate system but to the entire screen. In cases such as mouse-related messages for a window's nonclient area (its title bar, scroll bars, borders, and so forth), Windows passes you a point in *screen coordinates*. (See Figure 6-5.) That means the coordinates are relative to an origin at the top left corner of the whole screen, not the top left corner of the client area.

A window can be viewed as a device as well—after all, it has a device context associated with it. One kind of coordinate system in your window, then, is called a *device coordinate system*. Device coordinates are *physical* locations on the screen, relative to a window's origin (or sometimes to the whole screen), measured in pixels. However, you usually want to draw in your window's *logical* coordinate system, so you have to translate the point passed to you into your own coordinates—see the sidebar "Physical vs. Logical Coordinates." Logical coordinates can be in pixels or other units, such as inches. Your window's device context defines the units used. Just keep in mind, for now, that there will be times when you must convert from one coordinate system to the other.

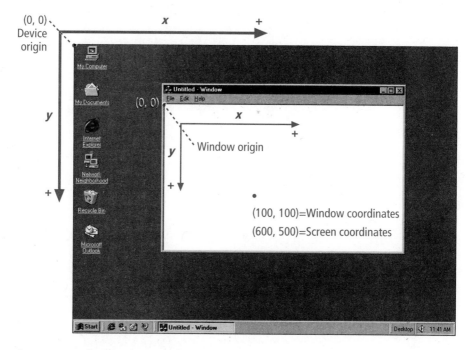

Figure 6-5.   *Screen coordinates vs. window coordinates.*

Physical vs. Logical Coordinates

Physical coordinates are measurements on a hardware device, while logical coordinates are measurements on a conceptual surface such as a text page or a drawing canvas.

In later chapters, we'll develop a drawing application that lets you draw on a surface. That surface is a logical construct unrelated to the layout of a monitor screen, a particular printer, or any other physical device (although we will size the surface for convenient printing on two pages).

(continued)

Physical vs. Logical Coordinates *continued*

In solving real-world problems, we tend to think in logical terms—locations and directions on a canvas, say—not in computer terms. Only when we implement the solution on a computer do we have to think in terms of physical computer devices, as when we convert mouse movements on the screen to coordinates on a logical drawing surface. The computer can tell us where the mouse was clicked, relative to the screen (or to a window on the screen). But we usually must translate that location into a location in our logical space.

Different logical spaces use different units of measurement. A *logical unit* in one scheme might be a pixel, while another scheme might use an inch or a millimeter.

Your window's default *logical coordinate system* is based on units that correspond to pixels on the screen. Thus a point is so many pixels down and so many pixels to the right of some other point, such as the origin. Luckily, the device coordinate system is also measured in pixels. So device coordinates and default logical coordinates are at least measured in the same units, even if their origins are in entirely different places.

Mapping modes

The part of a device context that determines which of the eight logical coordinate systems it uses is called the *mapping mode*. This is just a code that indicates which system the device context is using.

The default mapping mode is named *MM_TEXT*. That name doesn't mean "this is the mode to use when you're drawing text." All it means is that, like text on a page, its origin is at the top left corner and its *x* and *y* values increase to the right and downward, respectively. It happens that *MM_TEXT* is pretty convenient for drawing text in a window. But it may not be so convenient when it comes to printing that text through a device context that is associated not with a window but with a printer. You'll see what I mean and how to deal with it in Chapter 17.

Table 6-3 describes the other mapping modes in brief.

Mapping Mode	Distance Corresponding to One Logical Unit	Orientation of the x and y Axes
MM_TEXT	1 pixel	+x, +y
MM_LOMETRIC	0.1 mm	+x, -y
MM_HIMETRIC	0.01 mm	+x, -y
MM_LOENGLISH	0.01 in.	+x, -y
MM_HIENGLISH	0.001 in.	+x, -y
MM_TWIPS	$1/1440$ in. (0.0007 in.)	+x, -y
MM_ISOTROPIC	User-defined (x and y scale identically)	User-defined
MM_ANISOTROPIC	User-defined (x and y scale independently)	User-defined

Table 6-3. *An overview of the mapping modes (and logical coordinate systems) in Windows. This table is from* Programming Windows 95 with MFC, *by Jeff Proise, (Microsoft Press, 1996).*

NOTE Table 6-3 introduces several unusual terms, which I'll explain briefly here. One twip corresponds to $1/20$ of a point, which in turn is about $1/72$ of an inch. So a twip is ($1/20 * 1/72$), or $1/1440$ of an inch. Points are a traditional measuring system for typographical locations and sizes. The *MM_ISOTROPIC* and *MM_ANISOTROPIC* modes allow you, the programmer, to define your own coordinate system. The difference between the two (although not something we'll worry about in this book) is that the x and y axes scale identically in the *MM_ISOTROPIC* mode but can be independent in the *MM_ANISOTROPIC* mode.

Life Cycle of an Application for Windows

To wrap up the Windows fundamentals, let's take a look at the execution of an application from start to finish. I'll focus on the big picture, not every little detail.

1. The user starts the application, and Windows calls a function called *WinMain*.

2. *WinMain* registers a "window class"—information that identifies the type of window the application uses as its main window. (This "window class" is not the same as a C++ window class, such as *CWnd*. But you'll seldom need to think of the kind that *WinMain* registers. *Registering* a window class means defining its characteristics so that Windows can use the class to create windows according to your preferences.) It's at this point that you use *WinMain* to specify the name of your window procedure function, which Windows then calls each time it needs to deliver a message to your window.

3. *WinMain* calls the *CreateWindow* API function to create the application's main window (using the window class information).

4. *WinMain* then calls the *ShowWindow* API function to display the window.

5. *WinMain* calls the *UpdateWindow* API function to cause the application to draw the contents of its client area.

6. *WinMain* enters a message loop and stays in that loop until a *WM_QUIT* message appears. In the loop, it calls the *GetMessage* API function to get a message from the application's message queue, calls the *TranslateMessage* API function to do any translation needed for keyboard-related messages, and calls the *DispatchMessage* API function to dispatch the message to the appropriate window in the application (via its window procedure).

7. The appropriate window receives a Windows message by way of *DispatchMessage*, determines which message it is, and executes the appropriate message-handler code. If it has no handler for the message, it calls the *DefWindowProc* API function to provide default processing.

8. When the application's message loop encounters a *WM_QUIT* message, the message loop exits, *WinMain* exits, and Windows terminates the application.

That's a very high-level and fairly language-neutral description of the process. The description could be for an application written in C or one written with MFC. (That's why I haven't shown you any code here.) You'll soon see how some of the steps described "disappear into the woodwork" in MFC—and we'll look for the places they disappear to. This is one of the many ways that MFC takes over tedious chores that the programmer formerly had to do for every new program. Where C-language programmers for Windows have to write their own *WinMain* function and their own code to call the right message handler, MFC programmers mostly just write the handlers.

Try It Yourself

Start familiarizing yourself with the Win32 API. This won't be wasted time because MFC uses the same API. Here is a suggestion: Check the Help index for *Win32*, and select the topic "Win32 Topics" in the Topics Found box. Explore the items you find there.

> **TIP** You might want to add these topics to your Favorites list in Help so that you can easily find them again. In the left-hand window of Visual C++ Help, click the Favorites tab. To add the current topic to your Favorites list, click Add. To find the topic later, return to the Favorites tab and click the topic you want, and then click Display. The topic appears in the right-hand window.

What's Next?

In Chapter 7, you'll get to look at some real MFC code. I'll have you run the Visual C++ AppWizard to create a set of starter files for an MFC application. I'll show you what that starter application can already do. Then in Chapter 8, we'll tour the MFC code to see how it's divided into classes, and we'll look for the fundamental Windows elements I introduced in this chapter. You'll also write your first small MFC application and start on the book's main example application.

The MFC AppWizard: Code for Free

In this chapter, you'll begin to understand what Microsoft Foundation Class Library 6.0 (MFC) is, why it's so important to Microsoft Visual C++, and how it relates to programming for Microsoft's Windows 95, Windows 98, and Windows NT.

This chapter's focus is how to be productive with wizards. Visual C++ comes with a whole set of application wizards that help you get your project off the ground fast. I'll introduce you to the Visual C++ AppWizard, which gets you going with a set of starter files, and we'll write and build a very simple first MFC application. Then, in Chapter 8, I'll use those starter files to take you on a tour of MFC.

We'll also take the first step in developing the main application for the book, a drawing application called MyDraw.

MFC, the Win32 API, and the Learning Curve

Because the Microsoft Win32 API has hundreds of functions, it can be daunting to learn. If you're working in C, you can count on a steep learning curve over at least six months to a year. You can also count on establishing a deep, meaningful relationship with Charles Petzold, the guru of programming Windows in C, through his book *Programming Windows*, 5th edition (Microsoft Press, 1999).

The C language has been the standard for programming Windows for years, but more and more programmers are moving to C++, partly for the object-oriented benefits of the C++ language, and partly because of MFC. MFC simplifies programming for Windows and makes you a more powerful programmer, able to add features to your applications that you might not otherwise even consider. You may, however, still develop a relationship with Petzold, or perhaps with Jeff Prosise, whose book *Programming Windows 95 with MFC* (Microsoft Press, 1996) is the MFC equivalent of Petzold's bible. But even MFC isn't dead easy, and you still have to climb the learning curves for Windows programming and C++ to use it. (See Chapter 21 for more information about the Petzold and Prosise books and other sources of information about programming for Windows, especially in C++ with MFC.)

Although Windows itself is written in C, there's an undeniable object-orientation to it. The objects are things like windows, dialog boxes, device contexts, controls, brushes, pens, fonts—the objects whose handles we covered in Chapter 6. Each of these objects has some data associated with it. And each object also has a set of operations you can perform on it. Those are essential ingredients of object-oriented programming (although full-fledged OOP is much more than that).

Because Windows is object-oriented, it makes sense to program it with an object-oriented language. For this purpose, C++ is much better than C. C++ includes classes, which as we've seen, are powerful tools for representing objects, their attributes, and their behaviors.

The Class Library

You can program for Windows in straight C++. But a far more potent approach is to use a *class library*. A class library, such as the MFC library, supplies well-designed and thoroughly tested classes to represent the fundamental Windows objects. There's class *CWnd*, for example, to represent windows. And class *CFrameWnd* to represent windows with frames. And classes *CDialog* for dialog boxes, *CButton* for pushbutton controls, *CBrush* for paintbrushes, *CString* for strings—over 200 classes as of MFC version 6.0.

Figure 7-1 shows what the MFC class hierarchy looks like with only a few of the most important classes. You can check the Help index for *hierarchy chart* to see the whole thing. These classes contain thousands of lines of well-tested and time-tested code, written by some of the best programmers in the world.

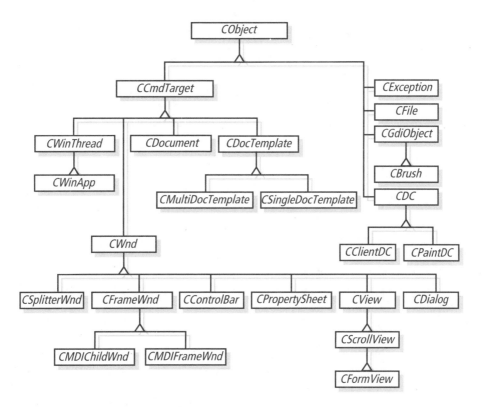

Figure 7-1.   *A portion of the MFC class hierarchy.*

The Application Framework

MFC is more than just classes, though. Taken together, the classes represent the *framework* of an application for Windows. What does that mean? Think back on your own programming in Basic, Pascal, C, or some other language. If you've had to write similar applications repeatedly, you probably had some sort of program *skeleton* to make the job easier and to make the resulting programs more alike. (We used a very simple program skeleton in the early chapters, one the wizard created for us.) MFC is something like that. But because MFC is written in C++, it's far easier to create a set of classes that contain well-designed, prefabricated solutions to many of the needs of programs for Windows.

MFC does just that. Its class *CWinApp*, for example, encapsulates the essence of an application for Windows. The class houses code for the following activities:

- Initializing the application

- Creating its main window

- Operating a message loop to obtain messages from the Windows operating system and dispatch them to the program's windows

- Quitting the application

- Cleaning up after the application

Class *CWinApp* also provides numerous *hooks*—places where you can insert your own code to affect what the application does. In fact, finding and using such hooks in all of the MFC classes is much of what MFC programming is all about. I'll say more about this along the way.

Other classes also contain plenty of code for things you'd otherwise need to do yourself. Class *CScrollView*, for instance, manages scrolling the contents of a window. Class *CDocument* contains code that greatly simplifies saving your data to a file, in conjunction with class *CArchive*, which abstracts the mechanics of writing and reading complex networks of objects to files or other data storage media. Class *CString* makes it extremely easy to work with string data—much easier than it is in C, or in C++ without MFC.

Throughout this book, I'll sometimes refer to MFC as the framework, the application framework, or the class library. The MFC documentation uses those terms as well.

By the end of the next chapter, you should understand the basics of using MFC to program for Windows. The rest of the book will fill in the details, at least those appropriate to an introductory book.

AppWizard: Code for Free

It's time to create some MFC code, and to do so we'll use the Visual C++ AppWizard for MFC executables. We used AppWizard earlier to create Win32 Console Applications. That AppWizard had one "page" to fill out. The MFC AppWizard has six pages.

Working Along with Me

As I've said several times already, the best way to really learn MFC and C++ is to work along with me as I show you example programs. At each stage, I'll tell you what you need to do. One important note about working along: I'll be introducing new versions of the example programs that continue where the previous version left off. For instance, we're about to create a simple example called MyDraw. This example is step 0 of a dozen or so steps throughout the book (counted from 0, as befits a C++ programmer). We'll be adding all sorts of features to this program.

When we get to step 1, I'll call my example MyDraw again, but it will be located in a folder named \learnvcn\Chap09\MyDraw1. The step 2 example will be in a folder named \learnvcn\Chap11\MyDraw2, and so on. This will distinguish the examples for the various steps of MyDraw.

TIP Instead of naming your programs MyDraw0, MyDraw1, and so forth, you should simply create one program named MyDraw. Then when we get to step 1, step 2, and so on, add the necessary code to your MyDraw files.

By the way, sometimes I'll have you remove old code in your version to replace it with something better. You can also find my step-by-step versions of MyDraw in the appropriate chapter folder in the companion code, listed there by step number. Use them for comparison if you have problems with the code you've entered for a step. Or use them if you want to jump in at step 2 or 3 instead of beginning with step 0.

Follow these procedures to start working along with me. (Some parts of this will look familiar from the programs we created earlier in the book.)

Try it now

To begin the new MyDraw project, follow these steps:

1. Select New on the Visual C++ File menu.

2. In the New dialog box, click the Projects tab. Figure 7-2 shows the New dialog box.

3. In the list of project types, click MFC AppWizard (exe). Up until now, I've always had you click the Win32 Console Application option, but with MFC we change gears.

4. In the Project Name box, type a project name. For this example, type *MyDraw*.

5. In the Location box, click the small browse button (**...**). In the Choose Directory dialog box that appears, choose a directory where you want the project created. Then click OK.

6. In the New dialog box, the following options should be set:

   ■ Create New Workspace should be selected.

   ■ The Platforms box should have Win32 selected.

7. Click OK.

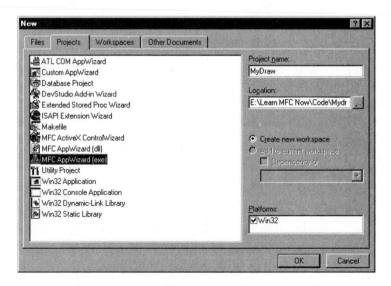

Figure 7-2.   *The New dialog box: an MFC application.*

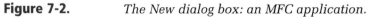

AppWizard proper—the MFC AppWizard for executables—appears as shown in Figure 7-3. This time the AppWizard guides us through a sequence of six numbered steps, or pages, each containing a group of related options. When you finish choosing options for a page, click the Next button to go to the next page. When you finish the last page, the Next button will be unavailable. Click Finish. (You can use the Back button to return to any page at any time before you finish.) For this exercise, fill out the pages as described in Table 7-1 and shown in Figures 7-4 and 7-5.

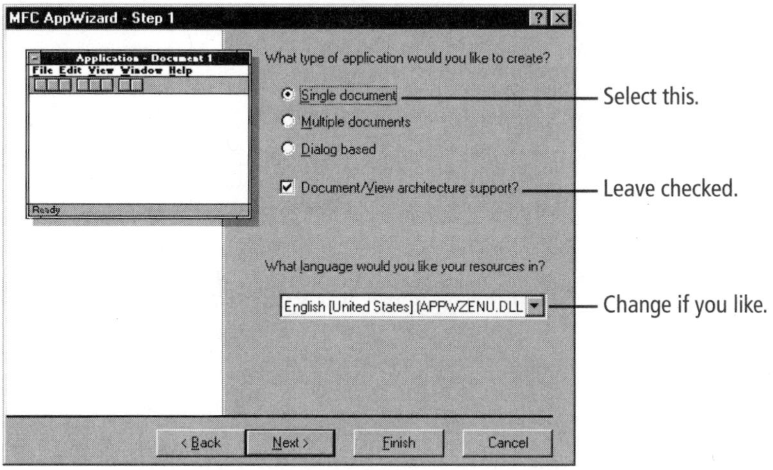

Figure 7-3. *AppWizard Step 1.*

Step in AppWizard	Action
Step 1	Select Single Document. (I'll discuss single document interface applications shortly.) Make sure Document/View Architecture Support is checked.
Step 2	Leave the page as it is. We won't be doing any database work.
Step 3	Clear the ActiveX Controls box. We won't implement any OLE functionality. Otherwise, leave page as it is.
Step 4	Click Advanced and, in the File Extension box, type *drw*. (See Figure 7-4 on the following page.) Otherwise, leave the page as is. Click Close. (Eventually, the MyDraw application will save files with a .drw extension.)

Table 7-1. *Options to choose as you create the MyDraw application* *(continued)* *with AppWizard.*

Table 7-1 *continued*

Step in AppWizard	Action
Step 5	Leave page as it is. I'll leave the Windows Explorer application style as an advanced exercise.
Step 6	Select class *CMyDrawDoc*. In the Header File box, change the name to DrawDoc.h. In the Implementation File box, change the name to DrawDoc.cpp. Select class *CMyDrawView*. In the Header File box, change the name to DrawVw.h. In the Implementation File box, change the name to DrawVw.cpp. (See Figure 7-5.) Click Finish.
New Project Information	Take a look at the New Project Information dialog box, then click OK.

IP The wizard's proposals for filenames are usually fine, but making the changes in Step 6 in Table 7-1 will make your filenames more closely resemble mine. That should keep things less confusing. (I use 8-character filenames for technical reasons relating to the book's CD-ROM disc.)

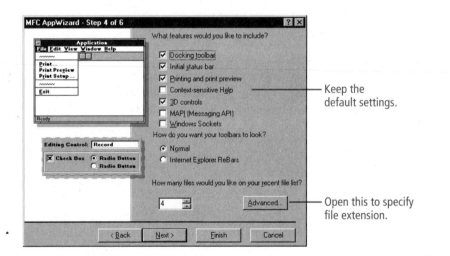

Figure 7-4. *AppWizard Step 4.*

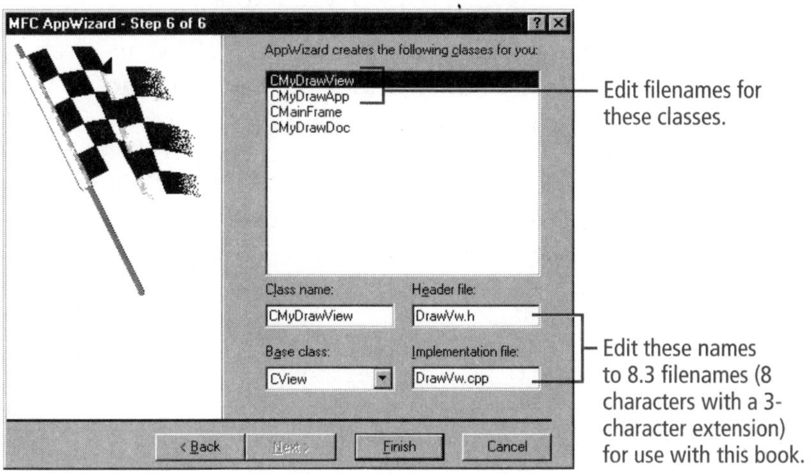

Edit filenames for these classes.

Edit these names to 8.3 filenames (8 characters with a 3-character extension) for use with this book.

Figure 7-5.   *AppWizard Step 6.*

For more information about AppWizard options, check the Help index for *MFC EXE program options in AppWizard*. Also see the "Try It Yourself" section at the end of this chapter.

We end up with a MyDraw directory—placed where we specified. It contains two subdirectories, one called Debug (which is empty) and one called Res (for resources, which initially contains four files), as well as 18 or so files at the root of the MyDraw directory (given the options we chose). The most important file extensions for you to recognize are summarized in the Help topic "File Types Created for Visual C++ Projects." To see that topic, check the Help index for *file types,* and select the subtopic "for C++ projects." Also see the file ReadMe.txt in your newly created MyDraw project directory. The wizard furnishes this file to explain some of the other files.

Following the Build Process

Consider this: So far, you've worked your way through one little wizard. It generated a huge number of files for you. To find out what this step has bought you, build your MyDraw project. Then run the finished application.

Try it now

As a reminder, here's how to build the application: On the Build menu, click Build MyDraw.exe. (Or just press F7.)

The Output window appears if it wasn't already visible. In it, you'll soon see text much like this:

```
------------------Configuration: MyDraw - Win32 Debug----------------
Compiling resources...
Compiling...
StdAfx.cpp
Compiling...
MyDraw.cpp
MainFrm.cpp
DrawDoc.cpp
DrawVw.cpp
Generating Code...
Linking...

MyDraw.exe - 0 error(s), 0 warning(s)
```

There. We just completed the build process. Here are some details about what Visual C++ does for us during a build:

1. Visual C++ runs the *resource compiler* to compile the resources in MyDraw.rc and MyDraw.rc2 as well as the icon and bitmap files. This results in a file called MyDraw.res, which contains the compiled resources. These and other output files are stored in the Debug sub-directory of the MyDraw directory. Check the Help index for *resource files,* and select the subtopic "working with."

2. Visual C++ runs the C++ preprocessor and the C++ compiler to compile all of the MFC header files. I covered the preprocessor in Chapter 2. Check the Help index for *preprocessor* and select the subtopic "overview." The compiler runs after the preprocessor. The first stage of compiling results in a *precompiled header* file called MyDraw.pch. Precompiling the headers saves time on subsequent builds. Headers

only need to be built once unless you make changes in them. Check the Help index for *precompiled header files compiler option* and *precompiling code.*

3. Visual C++ runs the compiler to compile all of the C++ source files (.cpp files) that constitute the heart of the MyDraw application. This results in several file types in the Debug subdirectory, especially .obj files, which are used as input to the linker. Check the Help index for *.OBJ files*, and select the subtopic "as linker input."

4. Visual C++ generates the program's code. However, at this stage, the code has lots of unresolved function references and other references in it. That's what the linker is for. Unresolved references are like blanks to fill in. The linker locates all the pieces and fills in the blanks.

5. Visual C++ runs the linker after the compiler and resolves those references, resulting in the finished MyDraw.exe file—the executable program file. Check the Help index for *linking*. If there were compiler or linker errors, you'd see instead a listing of errors, file by file. You need to correct those errors and build again before you can successfully complete the build process. I briefly explained how to correct build errors in Chapter 1. Also, check the Help index for *linker errors,* and select the subtopic "resolving."

TIP   In the build process, Visual C++ creates a lot of *intermediate files*: .obj files, .sbr files, .ilk files, .pdb files, the .pch file, an .idb file, and the .res file. These can fill up your hard disk pretty quickly. It's good to click the Clean command on the Build menu from time to time. Clean deletes all intermediate files except the .pch (precompiled header) file. To re-create them, just build the project again.

WARNING   Clean also deletes the .exe file, so in some cases you might want to copy it elsewhere before you use Clean. Of course, you can always build again to re-create it.

Running MyDraw.exe

Once you have a successful build for MyDraw, execute the program.

Try it now

Just click Execute MyDraw.exe on the Build menu (or press Ctrl+F5). Figure 7-6 shows the running MyDraw application.

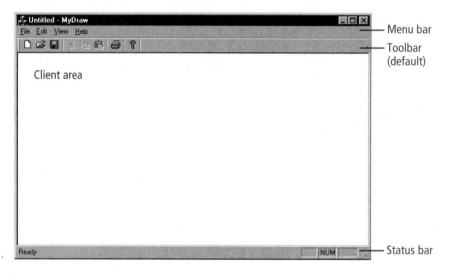

Figure 7-6. *MyDraw, version 1.0, step 0.*

What AppWizard Gives You for Free

At this point, you've added no code of your own to MyDraw. Everything is strictly AppWizard-generated code and resources. Yet when you run the application, it already has an amazing amount of working functionality.

Try it now

Go through the menus, toolbar buttons, and window controls. Be systematic. Try everything. The following sections describe what you'll see.

On the File menu

Nearly everything on the File menu works right out of the box. The New command on the File menu creates a new (empty) document although you won't see any visible change in the application. After you try out the Save command below, try the New command again. (You might not be able to tell that anything has happened, but it has.) In a single document interface (SDI) application like MyDraw, the new document replaces the one that was open. See the Notepad accessory in Windows for an example of this behavior. The Open command is even more impressive: it displays the standard Windows Open dialog box. Try the Save or Save As command next. The Save As dialog box opens, and you can actually save the empty .drw file. Choose the Save As command several times, with different filenames. Then you can use the Open command to open any of the existing (empty) files. Even the Print, Print Preview, and Print Setup commands work, displaying the correct dialog boxes and actually printing the (empty) file on your printer. Try it! Documents you've recently had open appear on the Recent Files list below the Print commands.

On the Edit menu

Nothing works on the Edit menu. We haven't implemented the Cut, Copy, Paste, and Undo commands. Those commands are highly application specific, and the only help MFC provides is several predefined commands such as *ID_EDIT_CUT*. Regretfully, time and space preclude my doing all I'd like. See Charles Petzold's book, described in Chapter 21.

On the View menu and the Standard toolbar

The View menu works, though. You can toggle its two commands to show or hide the application's toolbar and status bar. Speaking of the Standard toolbar, try its buttons—unless they're for unavailable commands, like the Edit menu commands, the buttons work. And try *dragging* the toolbar (click inside its boundary but outside all buttons). You can float it in the middle of the window, or you can dock it to any side of the window, like many windows in Visual C++. (I described floating and docking windows in Chapter 1.) Meanwhile, as you try the other commands, you see text strings on the left side of the status bar giving information about each command.

On the Help menu

The Help menu has only one command, About MyDraw. This command displays an About dialog box. We can edit the dialog box to customize it. (Wait until Chapter 19 for a tour of dialog box creation.)

The window controls

Even the window controls work. You can minimize the application, maximize it, restore it, and close it. You can also do those things from the system menu. To display the menu, click once on the small MFC icon at the left side of the title bar.

Why should you use AppWizard? That should now be obvious. How is all of that prefab functionality possible? In the next chapter, let's look at the code and see. But for now, let's run AppWizard again—only this time we'll write just a little bit of code to flesh out what the wizard gives us.

Let's Write Some Code

Let's write a very simple MFC application—the traditional "Hello, World!" application that everybody writes when they start learning a new language, as we did with the Hello program in Chapter 2. In this case, all we'll do is draw the string "Hi, MFC!" in the application's view. Let's call the application "MyHi." Don't worry too much when I mention classes and functions that we haven't covered before. I'll say considerably more about them in the next chapter, and by the end of the book they'll be old friends. (You can see my code for MyHi in the \learnvcn\Chap07\MyHi folder in the companion code.

Try it now

Here's the procedure:

1. Select New from the File menu. Click the Projects tab. Click MFC AppWizard (exe). Type *MyHi* for the Project name.

2. Fill out the steps of the AppWizard as shown in Table 7-2:

Step in AppWizard	Action
Step 1	Select Single Document. Make sure Document/View Architecture Support is checked.
Step 2	Leave the page as it is.
Step 3	Clear the ActiveX Controls box.
Step 4	Leave the page as it is, and don't bother with the Advanced options button.
Step 5	Leave the page as it is.
Step 6	Click Finish.

Table 7-2.   *Options to set in AppWizard for the MyHi application.*

3. Use ClassView to open the document class, *CMyHiDoc*, in the source code editor. Add the following boldface code under the public attributes section of class *CMyHiDoc* (file MyHiDoc.h):

```
⋮
class CMyHiDoc : public CDocument
{
protected: // create from serialization only
    CMyHiDoc();
    DECLARE_DYNCREATE(CMyHiDoc)

// Attributes
public:
    CString m_strText;
⋮
```

Recall that the ClassView window can be opened by clicking its downward-facing tab in the Workspace window (which you can toggle to show or hide with the Workspace command on the View menu). ClassView shows the class structure of your application. In ClassView, double-click the class whose class declaration you want to see. From there, you can use WizardBar to move to a specific member function definition in the source code editor. See Chapter 1 for a ClassView refresher.

4. Use WizardBar to select the document class, *CMyHiDoc*, and open its implementation file at the document class constructor, *CMyHiDoc:: CMyHiDoc*. Add the initialization—the boldface line—to the function on the following page.

```
CMyHiDoc::CMyHiDoc()
{
    // TODO: add one-time construction code here
    m_strText = "Hi, MFC!";
}
```

For a WizardBar refresher, see Chapter 1. You select the class in the leftmost drop-down list on WizardBar. You select a particular function definition in the class in the rightmost drop-down list.

5. Use WizardBar to select the view class, *CMyHiView*, and open its implementation file at the *OnDraw* function. Add the following boldface drawing code:

```
void CMyHiView::OnDraw(CDC* pDC)
{
    CMyHiDoc* pDoc = GetDocument();
    ASSERT_VALID(pDoc);
    // TODO: add draw code for native data here
    pDC->TextOut(100, 100, pDoc->m_strText);
}
```

6. Save all files and click Build MyHi.exe on the Build menu (or press F7).

7. Execute MyHi.exe (press CTRL+F5) and observe its behavior. (See Figure 7-7.)

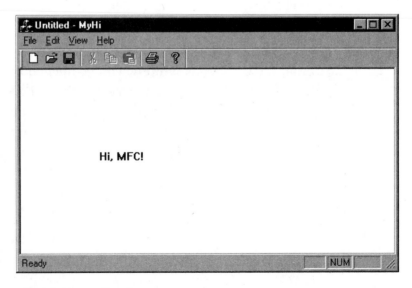

Figure 7-7. *The MyHi application.*

You'll observe that the *OnDraw* function calls the *TextOut* function to draw the string *m_strText* 100 pixels to the right (*x*-axis) and 100 pixels down (*y*-axis) from the origin of the view (which is, effectively, the window's client area). This will give you a feel for how large 100 pixels are. (We're using the default coordinate system with mapping mode *MM_TEXT*.) Before the string can be drawn, the string variable, declared as a member variable of class *CMyHiDoc*, has to be initialized. I've initialized the string's value in the document's constructor.

Try it now

Build and run the application. You're greeted by the message "Hi, MFC!"

Congratulations! If you're working along with me, you've just written your first MFC program. That should at least familiarize you with the mechanics. It should also *begin* to answer the question that nags new MFC programmers after they run AppWizard: *Now what?* For more on that story, see the last part of Chapter 8.

Try It Yourself

Try your hand at the following extra-credit exercises.

1. Create a multiple document interface application.

In this chapter, I had you create an SDI version of the MyDraw application—one that has only one document window. Run AppWizard again to create a multiple document interface (MDI) application—one that can have multiple open document windows. Call the project MyMDI. Then build and run the application. See what it can do. Try the New command on the File menu. And pay particular attention to the Window menu. That's something that MyDraw, as an SDI application, doesn't have. You can see my solution to this exercise in the \learnvcn\Chap07\MyMDI folder in the companion code.

2. Create a dialog-based application.

Run AppWizard again to create an application whose entire user interface is a dialog box. Call the application MyDlg. What do you see at the end of the creation process? Build and run the application. Does it have a menu?

What does the dialog box contain? How do you exit the application? See the program MyDlg in the \learnvcn\Chap07\MyDlg folder in the companion code.

3. **Create an application with a Windows Explorer–style user interface.**

   Run AppWizard to create a single-document application like MyDraw, called Explore. But on AppWizard step 5, select the Windows Explorer project type (at the top of the AppWizard page). What files and classes does this generate? Take a close look in particular at the two view classes, especially *CLeftView*, which is derived from MFC class *CTreeView*. Check the Help index for *CTreeView*. Notice the extra toolbar buttons in this application. Spend some time with Windows Explorer, examining its user interface and structure. See the Explore program in the \learnvcn\Chap07\Explore folder in the companion code.

What's Next?

This chapter gave you a little hands-on experience with MFC and AppWizard. In Chapter 8, we'll dig into MFC, looking at the AppWizard-generated classes in some detail to see what makes MFC tick, how it's implemented in C++, and how it works with Microsoft Windows.

Inside MFC

In Chapter 7, we ran AppWizard, the easiest way to begin an MFC application. In this chapter, we'll take a fairly detailed tour of the main classes that AppWizard writes for you up front. We'll figure out what the classes do, and we'll look for the fundamental Microsoft Windows concepts described in Chapter 6. The theme for this chapter is understanding how Microsoft Foundation Class Library 6.0 (MFC) *is* Windows.

Exploring MFC Through the AppWizard Files

We have three good reasons to take a close look at the AppWizard files:

■ First, to look for those key features of Windows that I went over in Chapter 6: the *WinMain* function, the message loop, the window creation code, and the message handlers, especially handlers for *WM_PAINT* and *WM_COMMAND*.

■ Second, to puzzle out how clicking a few choices in a few wizard steps enables all the features we can see in MyDraw.

■ And third, to get an introductory overview of MFC, its main classes, and the basic MFC techniques. We'll spend most of this chapter examining these classes to get that overview.

The text-file listings of the AppWizard-generated files are about 25 pages long, so I won't reproduce them here. Instead, you can easily see them yourself by following the directions for creating the MyDraw project in the previous chapter, under "Working Along with Me." Although they may appear daunting at first sight, it's well worth your while to become familiar with these files. They define classes derived from the five most frequently used MFC classes: *CWinApp*, *CFrameWnd*, *CDocument*, *CView*, and *CDialog*. That's only five out of the more than 200 MFC classes, so we're really starting gently. After generating the files, you might want to print them out. Select Print on the Microsoft Visual C++ File menu, specify the options you want, and click OK. You can first select Page Setup to specify any desired header and footer text, such as date, filename, time, page number, and so on. And you can specify page orientation and margins. Use ClassView or FileView, covered in Chapter 1, to open a different file. (You can also print Help topics by using the Print command in the Help window.)

Touring the Code

Let's tour this code, object by object, class by class, to see what's there. Then we can worry about what (apparently) is not there. Table 8-1 lists the main types of objects in a running MFC single document interface (SDI) application, along with the classes that the objects are *instantiated* (created) from and the files where you can find the classes. Figure 8-1 shows the same objects, illustrating how some of the objects create the others and then interact with them. Note that for the multiple document interface (MDI) case, the document template can point to more than one document.

Figure 8-2 on page 252 shows the general sequence of events as the MFC objects are created. The lower part of the figure shows how the objects exhange data and receive messages. This figure gives a bird's-eye view of the details we'll see in the next sections, which describe each major object in turn. During application initialization, the application object creates the other major objects. Then it starts the message loop and dispatches messages to the other objects for as long as the program runs. The document and view objects, in particular, shuttle data back and forth. All of the objects can respond to incoming messages.

Object	Class	MFC Base Class	Files
Application	*CMyDrawApp*	*CWinApp*	MyDraw.h and MyDraw.cpp
Document template	*CSingleDocTemplate*	*CDocTemplate*	Hidden in the MFC source files
Frame window	*CMainFrame*	*CFrameWnd*	MainFrm.h and MainFrm.cpp
Document	*CMyDrawDoc*	*CDocument*	DrawDoc.h and DrawDoc.cpp
View	*CMyDrawView*	*CView*	DrawVw.h and DrawVw.cpp
Dialog	*CAboutDlg*	*CDialog*	MyDraw.h and MyDraw.cpp

Table 8-1.   *The objects that AppWizard creates for MyDraw.*

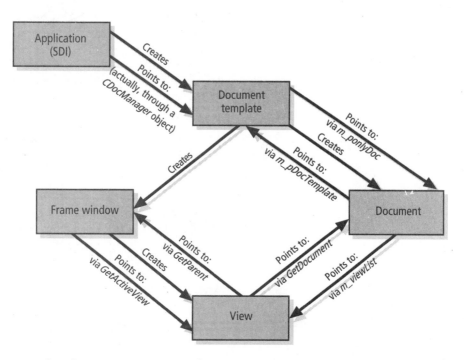

Figure 8-1.   *How the objects in an MFC application connect with each other.*

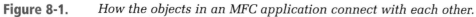

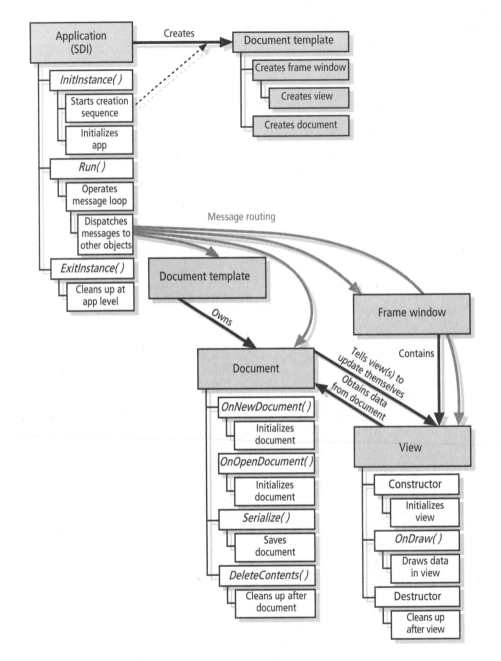

Figure 8-2. *Inside the application framework at run time.*

The Application Object

The application object represents the application as a whole. Class
CMyDrawApp defines the characteristics of the application object.
At first glance, the class in the file MyDraw.h doesn't look like much:

```
class CMyDrawApp : public CWinApp
{
public:
    CMyDrawApp();

// Overrides
    // ClassWizard generated virtual function overrides
    //{{AFX_VIRTUAL(CMyDrawApp)
    public:
    virtual BOOL InitInstance();
    //}}AFX_VIRTUAL

// Implementation
    //{{AFX_MSG(CMyDrawApp)
    afx_msg void OnAppAbout();
    //}}AFX_MSG
    DECLARE_MESSAGE_MAP()
};
```

The first thing you might notice is that the class declares only three member functions: *InitInstance*, *OnAppAbout*, and *CMyDrawApp*. We can begin to figure out the functions by their names: *InitInstance* initializes
something called an *instance*, *OnAppAbout* must have something to do
with an About dialog box. You might also recall that the function with the
same name as its class is the class constructor.

The one-and-only application object

So where is the application *object*? The *class* is declared in the file
MyDraw.h, so let's look in MyDraw.cpp, the implementation file. Here it is,
a little way into the file:

⋮
```
// The one and only CMyDrawApp object

CMyDrawApp theApp;
```

AppWizard has even labeled the object for us with a comment. The object
is a C++ variable, called *theApp*. The variable's type is *CMyDrawApp*, the

class name. And together, we have a perfectly normal C++ variable declaration. Note that it's a global variable—at file scope.

In a later section of this chapter, "Lifecycle of an MFC Application," I'll explain how and when *theApp* is created and how its member functions are called.

The *InitInstance* function

Now let's look inside the *InitInstance* member function, also in MyDraw.cpp:

```
BOOL CMyDrawApp::InitInstance()
{
#ifdef _AFXDLL
    Enable3dControls();
#else
    Enable3dControlsStatic();
#endif

    SetRegistryKey(_T("Local AppWizard-Generated Applications"));

    LoadStdProfileSettings();

    CSingleDocTemplate* pDocTemplate;
    pDocTemplate = new CSingleDocTemplate(
        IDR_MAINFRAME,
        RUNTIME_CLASS(CMyDrawDoc),
        RUNTIME_CLASS(CMainFrame),
        RUNTIME_CLASS(CMyDrawView));
    AddDocTemplate(pDocTemplate);

    EnableShellOpen();
    RegisterShellFileTypes(TRUE);

    CCommandLineInfo cmdInfo;
    ParseCommandLine(cmdInfo);

    if (!ProcessShellCommand(cmdInfo))
        return FALSE;

    m_pMainWnd->ShowWindow(SW_SHOW);
    m_pMainWnd->UpdateWindow();

    m_pMainWnd->DragAcceptFiles();

    return TRUE;
}
```

That's more like it—a function that appears to be doing a lot. Table 8-2 lists the calls in *InitInstance* and what they do.

Call in *InitInstance*	Description	Comments
Enable3dControls, or *Enable3dControlsStatic*	Give program windows and controls a 3D look. These calls are unnecessary except under Microsoft Windows NT 3.51. Under later Windows NT and Windows versions, you get 3D controls whether you call one one of these functions or not.	For information about the *#ifdef* construct that surrounds these calls, see the Appendix.
SetRegistryKey	Establishes a *key* for the application in the Windows Registry.	The application can store its options there between program runs. The "_T" prefix on the string parameter is a macro that makes the string portable for Unicode applications as well as for regular non-Unicode applications. Check the Help index for *Unicode*.
LoadStdProfileSettings	Loads any existing options from the Windows Registry.	This call retrieves things like the names of recently opened files.
new CSingleDocTemplate	Creates a document template on the heap.	Document templates create and manage windows, documents, and views. See the next section for more information about this call.
AddDocTemplate	Stores a pointer to the document template in the application object.	See the next section for more information about this call.

Table 8-2. *Summary of the actions taken in MyDraw's* InitInstance *function.*   *(continued)*

Table 8-2 *continued*

Call in *InitInstance*	Description	Comments
EnableShellOpen and *RegisterShellFileTypes*	Lets the user open the application's documents from Windows Explorer or File Manager. Also lets the user drag files to a printer icon to print them.	
ParseCommandLine	Analyzes command line for arguments (if program is run from an MS-DOS prompt).	Returns the command-line arguments in a *CCommandLineInfo* object.
ProcessShellCommand	Carries out any command actions that were on the command line.	These include things like Open, New, and Print on the File menu.
ShowWindow and *UpdateWindow*	Displays the application's main window and sends its first *WM_PAINT* message to cause drawing.	
DragAcceptFiles	Enables the window to open files dragged into it and dropped.	

For more detail about the functions called in *InitInstance*, check the Help index for the function names. I'll describe some of the most important function calls in *InitInstance* next.

Creating the document template, frame window, document, and view

At the heart of the *InitInstance* function is the section in which we create the application's window, as well as the *document template*, *document*, and *view* objects. (Window creation is one of the Windows elements we're looking for in the MFC code.) Here's that creation code again:

```
CSingleDocTemplate* pDocTemplate;
pDocTemplate = new CSingleDocTemplate(
    IDR_MAINFRAME,
    RUNTIME_CLASS(CMyDrawDoc),
    RUNTIME_CLASS(CMainFrame),
    RUNTIME_CLASS(CMyDrawView));
AddDocTemplate(pDocTemplate);
```

This code consists of a variable declaration (*pDocTemplate*, a pointer to a *CSingleDocTemplate* object) and two function calls. The first call, using the C++ *new* operator, creates a *document template* object. MFC uses document templates to create and manage the application's window, document, and view objects. The one we create here is a single document template, for our SDI application. This template manages one open document. If the user opens a new document, the new one replaces the old one, which is closed.

Notice that the document template creation call takes up five lines in the file, starting with the line that calls the *new* operator.

> **OTE** This could have been done on one line, but breaking it up this way makes the action more readable. C++ lets you break lines up any way you like without affecting how the code works. You can even split a quoted string, after a fashion:
>
> ```
> char str[100];
> strcpy(str, "this is a split"
> "string");
> ```
>
> The compiler will concatenate strings if it doesn't find an operator or parenthesis, so *"A" "B"* is the same as *"AB"*.

The first line in the document template creation code sets up the call to *new*, which allocates memory for a *CSingleDocTemplate* object. The second line specifies *IDR_MAINFRAME*, an ID for the application's resources. You'll see this ID again later. The third, fourth, and fifth lines use the *RUNTIME_CLASS* macro to specify the types of the application's document (*CMyDrawDoc*), frame window (*CMainFrame*), and view (*CMyDrawView*). *RUNTIME_CLASS* can take, as its parameter, the name of a class and return a pointer to a *CRuntimeClass* structure. The structure contains information—including the class name—that MFC can use to create the actual object specified as a parameter. Lines two through five of the call are the four parameters to the document template's constructor— the item right after the *new* operator,

```
CSingleDocTemplate(...)
```

is a call to the *CSingleDocTemplate* constructor. (I've omitted the constructor's four parameters here.)

The final line in this section of *InitInstance*, a call to the application object's *AddDocTemplate* member function, stores a pointer to the new document template object in the application object. Did you notice, though, that class *CMyDrawApp* doesn't list an *AddDocTemplate* function? For that matter, class *CMyDrawApp* doesn't explicitly list any of the functions listed in Table 8-2, either. Yet it does in fact have these functions—because it inherits the functions from its base class, *CWinApp*.

> **TIP** Whenever you look at the Visual C++ documentation for an MFC class, look for a link to that class's base class. You can use such links to work your way up the MFC hierarchy, through each class's base class. In that way, you can see what other members and behavior a class inherits from its ancestors.

After those lines of code have executed (and they set off a large sequence of actions when they do—check the Help index for *creation of documents and views* and read the two topics listed in the Topics Found dialog box), the application object contains a pointer to a document template object. The document template object, in turn, contains pointers to the application's main frame window object, its document object, and its view object. Those objects now exist and can be used.

> **NOTE** Technically, the application object actually contains a pointer to a *CDocManager* object, which in turn points to a *CDocTemplate* object. But *CDocManager* is undocumented, and it stays behind the scenes anyway. It's an implementation detail.

Displaying the window

So far, the application has worked behind the scenes. Its window has not yet been made visible. The next lines of interest in *InitInstance* call the *ShowWindow* function to make the application window visible and then the *UpdateWindow* function to cause the window's contents to be drawn for the first time.

Other possibilities for *InitInstance*

InitInstance does a lot—and we didn't have to write a line of it. Can we do anything else with this function? Yes, we can. This is the primary place for any application-wide initialization. Therefore, it's a good place to initialize global variables and generally set things up. We can also remove some of the function calls here if we don't want their functionality. The comments that AppWizard provides at the beginning of *InitInstance* tell you what you can do:

```
// Standard initialization
// If you are not using these features and wish to reduce the size
//  of your final executable, you should remove from the following
//  the specific initialization routines you do not need.
```

Some programmers also do one more thing with *InitInstance*. If they don't want MFC's default document/view architecture, they can replace the document template creation code with code that creates a window but not a document, view, or document template. From our point of view, that's advanced stuff, but I'll address this topic briefly in the box titled "Sidestepping Document/View" later in this chapter.

By the way, what is the "instance" that *InitInstance* initializes? It's an *instance* of the application. It's possible, in Windows, to run more than one copy, or instance, of a program simultaneously. So *InitInstance* is for initializing the current copy.

The *OnAppAbout* handler function

OnAppAbout is a handler for a menu command: the About MyDraw command on the Help menu in MyDraw. Since this is the first Windows message handler you've seen, let's dwell on it a bit.

First, here's the function:

```
void CMyDrawApp::OnAppAbout()
{
    CAboutDlg aboutDlg;
    aboutDlg.DoModal();
}
```

What does it do? It creates a dialog object—of class *CAboutDlg*—and calls the dialog object's *DoModal* function (inherited from *CDialog*, the base class). In English, *OnAppAbout* creates and displays MyDraw's About dialog box. The *DoModal* function actually displays the dialog and responds to user actions, such as clicking the dialog box's OK button to close it.

The *CAboutDlg* class is declared in file MyDraw.cpp, just after the application class. Here it is:

```
class CAboutDlg : public CDialog
{
public:
    CAboutDlg();

// Dialog Data
    //{{AFX_DATA(CAboutDlg)
    enum { IDD = IDD_ABOUTBOX };
    //}}AFX_DATA

    // ClassWizard generated virtual function overrides
    //{{AFX_VIRTUAL(CAboutDlg)
    protected:
    virtual void DoDataExchange(CDataExchange* pDX);    // DDX...
    //}}AFX_VIRTUAL

// Implementation
protected:
    //{{AFX_MSG(CAboutDlg)
        // No message handlers
    //}}AFX_MSG
    DECLARE_MESSAGE_MAP()
};
```

The most important elements of *CAboutDlg* are the *DoModal* function it inherits from *CDialog* and the *DoDataExchange* function that it overrides from the same source. We'll deal with those, especially *DoDataExchange*, in Chapter 19. *CDialog* derives from *CWnd*, *CCmdTarget*, and *CObject*.

For now, the interesting question is: how is *OnAppAbout* called? Who calls it, and from where?

The message map and command routing

MFC calls the *OnAppAbout* function when the user selects the About MyDraw command on the application's Help menu. That action causes Windows to send a *WM_COMMAND* message that indicates which command was selected, in this case the one with a command ID of *ID_APP_ABOUT*. The message loop inside our application object retrieves the message and dispatches it.

WM_COMMAND messages are special among all messages. They alone can be dispatched not only to windows but also to the application object or the document object. MFC routes these command messages to the application object, to any of its windows, to its view, and to its document.

These objects are all known as *command targets,* meaning they can accept *WM_COMMAND* messages. All command target objects are derived, ultimately, from class *CCmdTarget.* Thus, *CWinApp, CDocument, CWnd, CView,* and *CDialog* are all derived (sometimes with intermediate classes intervening) from *CCmdTarget.*

Figure 8-3 shows the ancestry of these classes in the MFC class hierarchy. Check the Help index for *command routing* and *command targets* for a fuller description of the routing process and of what the objects do with the command messages. Since command targets include all windows, they also include all objects that can have message maps.

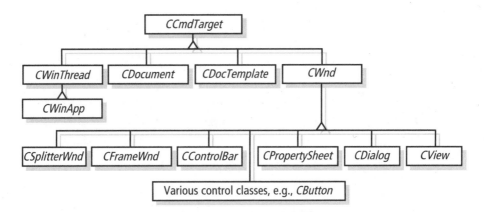

Figure 8-3. *Command target objects in the MFC class hierarchy.*

Here's how the actual routing works: A command target object, say MyDraw's window or its document, receives a command message through a call to its inherited *OnCmdMsg* handler. *OnCmdMsg* checks to see if its object can handle the particular message. If not, it calls the *OnCmdMsg* function of the next object in a chain of command targets to continue routing the message. Check the Help index for *command routing* and choose the topic "Command Routing."

How does *OnCmdMsg* check to see if its object can handle a command message? It checks the object's *message map*. Message maps are an MFC mechanism for routing Windows messages—all of them, including *WM_COMMAND*—to objects in the application. A message map specifies the connection between a message and its designated handler function. MFC then uses this information to call the handler. Under the hood, a message map is a lookup table associated with its class. MFC knows how to check a message map to see if it contains information about a handler for a particular message. The listing below is the MyDraw application object's message map. (The application and document objects, not being windows, can handle only *WM_COMMAND* messages.)

```
BEGIN_MESSAGE_MAP(CMyDrawApp, CWinApp)
    //{{AFX_MSG_MAP(CMyDrawApp)
    ON_COMMAND(ID_APP_ABOUT, OnAppAbout)
        // NOTE - the ClassWizard will add and remove mapping macros...
        //    DO NOT EDIT what you see in these blocks of generated...
    //}}AFX_MSG_MAP
    // Standard file based document commands
    ON_COMMAND(ID_FILE_NEW, CWinApp::OnFileNew)
    ON_COMMAND(ID_FILE_OPEN, CWinApp::OnFileOpen)
    // Standard print setup command
    ON_COMMAND(ID_FILE_PRINT_SETUP, CWinApp::OnFilePrintSetup)
END_MESSAGE_MAP()
```

This message map is one of the first items to appear in the file MyDraw.cpp. The first line, *BEGIN_MESSAGE_MAP*, begins the message map and identifies the class it's for as well as that class's base class. The message map ends with the *END_MESSAGE_MAP* statement.

In the middle of the message map are the *entries*. Each entry specifies a particular Windows message—here they're all *WM_COMMAND* messages, as represented by the *ON_COMMAND* macro. Then the entry specifies which handler in the class will process the message. For example, the line

```
ON_COMMAND(ID_APP_ABOUT, OnAppAbout)
```

makes an explicit connection between the command whose ID is *ID_APP_ABOUT* and the *OnAppAbout* handler function. So the message map entry provides all of the necessary pieces of information to get the message to its target, including the following elements:

- Which message it is: *WM_COMMAND*.

- The particular command: *ID_APP_ABOUT*. This ID is associated with the About MyDraw command on the Help menu and with the About toolbar button (the one with a question mark).

- The name of the handler function in the target object.

Notice that AppWizard does some "pre-wiring" in the message map, to hook up the New, Open, and Print Setup commands from the File menu— the menu commands that the application object handles. (Other objects handle the other menu commands.) That's why these commands already work. Class *CWinApp*, the base class of *CMyDrawApp*, already has handlers for these commands. Putting in the message map entries for them hooks them up so they work. You'll learn more about message maps later. Meanwhile, you can check the Help index for *mapping messages.*

Why does MFC use this apparently clunky approach to routing messages, involving all these C++ preprocessor macros? The alternative would be to have every class that can handle messages contain a virtual function for every message it might need to handle. Virtual functions require lots of space to store their v-tables, so the MFC developers came up with the message map scheme instead. It works very reliably and efficiently, and it has stood the test of time, since MFC 1.0 appeared in 1991.

This wraps up our discussion of the application object, *CMyDrawApp*. Notice one last thing. The file MyDraw.cpp has a group of *#include* statements at the top. These include the document, view, frame window, and other code so the application class can refer to those classes.

The Main Frame Window Object

The main frame window class, *CMainFrame*, is less exciting in MyDraw because we won't do much with the class in this book. But it's not without interest because of what it does with toolbars and status bars. This class defines an object derived from class *CFrameWnd*, MFC's base class for framed windows. Let's look at the class declaration.

```
class CMainFrame : public CFrameWnd
{
protected: // create from serialization only
    CMainFrame();
    DECLARE_DYNCREATE(CMainFrame)

// Attributes
public:

// Operations
public:

// Overrides
    // ClassWizard generated virtual function overrides
    //{{AFX_VIRTUAL(CMainFrame)
    virtual BOOL PreCreateWindow(CREATESTRUCT& cs);
    //}}AFX_VIRTUAL

// Implementation
public:
    virtual ~CMainFrame();
#ifdef _DEBUG
    virtual void AssertValid() const;
    virtual void Dump(CDumpContext& dc) const;
#endif

protected:  // control bar embedded members
    CStatusBar   m_wndStatusBar;
    CToolBar     m_wndToolBar;

// Generated message map functions
protected:
    //{{AFX_MSG(CMainFrame)
    afx_msg int OnCreate(LPCREATESTRUCT lpCreateStruct);
        // NOTE - the ClassWizard will add and remove member...
        //     DO NOT EDIT what you see in these blocks of...
    //}}AFX_MSG
    DECLARE_MESSAGE_MAP()
};
```

As you can see, the class is mostly air. Don't be fooled by that, though. Remember inheritance. *CMainFrame* is derived from *CFrameWnd*, which is derived from *CWnd* (and *CWnd* from *CCmdTarget*, and that from *CObject*), so the class inherits a great many members. Check the Help index for each of *CMainFrame's* base classes and scan the member lists.

(Try it. You'll be impressed.) All of those members can be called from *CMainFrame*.

SDI and MDI applications

CFrameWnd is used as a base class for the application window in SDI applications. SDI applications can open only one document at a time. The alternative to SDI applications is MDI applications. MDI applications can open multiple documents at the same time. Microsoft Word, Microsoft Excel, and Visual C++ are examples of MDI applications. MDI applications base their main frame windows on class *CMDIFrameWnd*.

MDI applications are more complicated, of course, than SDI applications. Figure 8-4 shows an MDI version of MyDraw with several documents open.

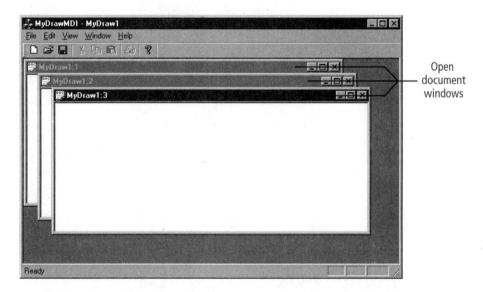

Open document windows

Figure 8-4. *MyDraw as an MDI application.*

The reason I've chosen to make MyDraw and most other examples in the book SDI applications stems from the direction that Microsoft is taking with its Windows operating systems. In the long run, Microsoft is aiming for a document-centered environment. In such an environment, users working with documents seldom think about which applications they're using to create and edit those documents. Ultimately, the applications will probably become increasingly generic, using standardized file formats—or so say the industry visionaries. You'll be able to use any word processor to edit text, any graphics editor to edit graphics, any spreadsheet program to edit spreadsheet data, and so on—possibly in a single document, if it contains those types of data. The document will be the centerpiece, and how it was created will be less important. Microsoft's OLE is a step in that direction. So is SDI.

In other words, in a document-centered environment, you open and work on documents. If you want two documents of the same kind to be open, you open them in two separate instances, or copies, of the appropriate program. As you move from editing a text portion of the document to editing a table or a graphic, different applications run, largely without your awareness. You focus on the document more than on the tools you use to work on it.

MDI puts the focus more on the application than on the document. For this reason, there are likely to be fewer and fewer MDI applications in the future.

With MFC, MDI applications aren't much harder to write than SDI applications. So even though we'll focus on SDI in this book, you'll be able to write MDI applications as well, if you choose to.

The frame window's message map

Class *CMainFrame* has a message map with one entry, for the *WM_CREATE* message. Windows sends *WM_CREATE* after a window has been created but before it becomes visible. The message map maps *WM_CREATE* to an *OnCreate* handler. Here's the message map, from the file MainFrm.cpp:

```
BEGIN_MESSAGE_MAP(CMainFrame, CFrameWnd)
    //{{AFX_MSG_MAP(CMainFrame)
        // NOTE - the ClassWizard will add and remove mapping...
        //     DO NOT EDIT what you see in these blocks of...
    ON_WM_CREATE()
    //}}AFX_MSG_MAP
END_MESSAGE_MAP()
```

Notice that the message map entry for *WM_CREATE* looks a bit different from the ones we've seen for *WM_COMMAND*. For all Windows messages other than *WM_COMMAND*, the message map macro name mirrors the message name more precisely. A macro like *ON_WM_CREATE* automatically maps to a handler of similar name: *OnCreate*.

The *OnCreate* handler

The *OnCreate* handler, though, actually does a lot of interesting work for *CMainFrame*. Here's the function:

```
int CMainFrame::OnCreate(LPCREATESTRUCT lpCreateStruct)
{
    if (CFrameWnd::OnCreate(lpCreateStruct) == -1)
        return -1;

    if (!m_wndToolBar.CreateEx(this, TBSTYLE_FLAT,
            WS_CHILD | WS_VISIBLE | CBRS_TOP | CBRS_GRIPPER
            | CBRS_TOOLTIPS | CBRS_FLYBY | CBRS_SIZE_DYNAMIC) ||
        !m_wndToolBar.LoadToolBar(IDR_MAINFRAME))
    {
        TRACE0("Failed to create toolbar\n");
        return -1;      // fail to create
    }

    if (!m_wndStatusBar.Create(this) ||
        !m_wndStatusBar.SetIndicators(indicators,
          sizeof(indicators)/sizeof(UINT)))
    {
        TRACE0("Failed to create status bar\n");
        return -1;      // fail to create
    }

    // TODO: Delete these three lines if you don't want the toolbar to
    //   be dockable
    m_wndToolBar.EnableDocking(CBRS_ALIGN_ANY);
    EnableDocking(CBRS_ALIGN_ANY);
    DockControlBar(&m_wndToolBar);

    return 0;
}
```

The next several sections discuss what's going on in *OnCreate*. The *TRACE0* calls are an MFC diagnostic mechanism. *TRACE0* is a special form of the more general *TRACE* macro; *TRACE0* takes no arguments other than a message string. Hereafter, when I talk about *TRACE*, I mean the general version as well as any of its specialized versions, *TRACE0*, *TRACE1*, and so on. *TRACE* statements are like print statements in a Microsoft Visual Basic program. They allow you to print useful diagnostic messages, which appear on the Debug tab of the Visual C++ Output window. For more information, check the Help index for *TRACE*.

The toolbar and status bar

Have you wondered where the nifty toolbar and status bar in MyDraw came from? Here they are. The toolbar and status bar objects are declared as members of class *CMainFrame* in the file MainFrm.h, like this:

```
protected:  // control bar embedded members
    CStatusBar  m_wndStatusBar;
    CToolBar    m_wndToolBar;
```

The code in *CMainFrame::OnCreate* creates the toolbar and status bar windows—yes, the toolbar and the status bar are windows, embedded in the frame window, as shown in Figure 8-5. They share space in the window with the view object, which I'll discuss shortly.

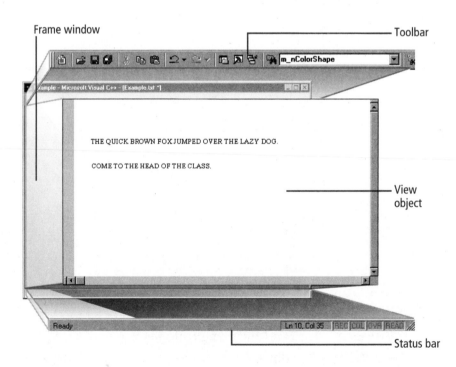

Figure 8-5. *How the toolbar, status bar, and view object fit into the frame window.*

First, *OnCreate* creates the toolbar with a call to *CToolBar::CreateEx*, and loads the toolbar's button images into memory by calling

CToolBar::LoadToolBar. You'll learn to create those button images later. The following code shows how the *CToolBar* object, *m_wndToolBar*, is used to call *CreateEx*:

```
m_wndToolBar.CreateEx(... ||
        !m_wndToolBar.LoadToolBar(IDR_MAINFRAME))
```

I've omitted most of the parameters to *CreateEx* to show how the *LoadToolBar* member function of the *m_wndToolBar* object is called within the *CreateEx* parameter list. The Boolean result of the *LoadToolBar* call is passed to the final parameter of *CreateEx*. If either function call fails, the *if* statement reports an error and the application terminates.

If the toolbar creation succeeds, *OnCreate* then creates the status bar window with a call to *CStatusBar::Create* and calls *CStatusBar::SetIndicators.* The *indicators* are the little boxes or panes that divide up the status bar. By default, AppWizard provides indicators that display the current status of the Caps Lock, Num Lock, and Scroll Lock keys. If any of these keys is pressed, the corresponding display reads CAP, NUM, or SCRL in the right-most panes. With some work, you can add other indicators—for example, one to contain the time of day. The leftmost pane is usually used to display messages, including prompts about what a particular menu or toolbar command is for. The indicators currently in effect are given in the following lines just below the window's message map (in the file MainFrm.cpp):

```
static UINT indicators[] =
{
    ID_SEPARATOR, // status line indicator
    ID_INDICATOR_CAPS,
    ID_INDICATOR_NUM,
    ID_INDICATOR_SCRL,
};
```

The *SetIndicators* function uses this array of *UINT* (unsigned 32-bit integer) values when it builds the status bar for display. MFC displays the correct information in each indicator based on the ID given in the array.

Tool tips for the toolbar

Try another experiment with MyDraw. Run the application and use the mouse to point to a toolbar button without clicking it. You may have noticed this behavior earlier, or maybe not. If you wait a second, a small light yellow window appears near the toolbar button. It contains a tip about what the button is for.

The *OnCreate* function sets up tool tips for MyDraw's toolbar during toolbar creation:

```
if (!m_wndToolBar.CreateEx(this, TBSTYLE_FLAT,
        WS_CHILD | WS_VISIBLE | CBRS_TOP | CBRS_GRIPPER
        | CBRS_TOOLTIPS | CBRS_FLYBY | CBRS_DYNAMIC) ||
    !m_wndToolBar.LoadToolBar(IDR_MAINFRAME))
```

These lines specify toolbar styles. The styles are added with the C++ bitwise OR operator, (|). Bitwise OR sets particular bits as "flags" in an integer. (The || character in the third line of this code is the logical OR operator, not the bitwise operator. It separates two Boolean conditions.) For information about the individual styles, search Help for *SetBarStyle* and for *Toolbar Button Styles*.

Docking and floating toolbars

Finally, *OnCreate* adds the code that lets the toolbar float or dock to any side of the window:

```
m_wndToolBar.EnableDocking(CBRS_ALIGN_ANY);
EnableDocking(CBRS_ALIGN_ANY);
DockControlBar(&m_wndToolBar);
```

These calls enable docking to any side of the window—that's what the *CBRS_ALIGN_ANY* style signifies in the *EnableDocking* calls—and then dock the window to its default spot at the top of the application's window. The first call is to *CToolBar::EnableDocking*—this enables the toolbar for docking. The next call, to *CFrameWnd::EnableDocking*, enables the window for docking.

Other *CMainFrame* functions

By the way, what are the rest of those functions you see in the file MainFrm.cpp? Table 8-3 describes them briefly. Although AppWizard writes these functions for you, you don't necessarily have to use them; in fact, you can delete them if you end up finding no use for them, as sometimes occurs. AppWizard provides them because programmers often do want them.

Function	Description
PreCreateWindow	Provided in case you want to modify the styles of MyDraw's frame window. For information on styles, check the Help index for *styles,* and choose the subtopic "frame window."
~CMainFrame	This is the class destructor. You might need this function for deleting any heap memory you allocate elsewhere in the class.
AssertValid	This is a diagnostic function you can use to help warn of problems when the window object is created. Check the Help index for *AssertValid member function*, and choose the subtopic "using."
Dump	This is another diagnostic function. You can implement this function to "dump" the objects you create. Output goes to the Debug tab in the Output window. *Dump* lists information about the objects in the program, including their sizes. Check the Help index for *Dump member function*, and choose the subtopic "overriding (procedure)." Also see Chapter 13.

Table 8-3.   *Remaining member functions of MyDraw's* CMainFrame *class.*

The Document Object

By default, AppWizard creates an application that uses MFC's *document/ view architecture*. That's a big name for a pretty simple concept, which I'll discuss in a moment. Meanwhile, here's what the document class contained in the file DrawDoc.h looks like:

```
class CMyDrawDoc : public CDocument
{
protected: // create from serialization only
    CMyDrawDoc();
    DECLARE_DYNCREATE(CMyDrawDoc)

// Attributes
public:

// Operations
public:
```

(continued)

```
// Overrides
    // ClassWizard generated virtual function overrides
    //{{AFX_VIRTUAL(CMyDrawDoc) public:
    virtual BOOL OnNewDocument();
    virtual void Serialize(CArchive& ar);
    //}}AFX_VIRTUAL

// Implementation
public:
    virtual ~CMyDrawDoc();
#ifdef _DEBUG
    virtual void AssertValid() const;
    virtual void Dump(CDumpContext& dc) const;
#endif

protected:

// Generated message map functions
protected:
    //{{AFX_MSG(CMyDrawDoc)
        // NOTE - the ClassWizard will add and remove member...
        //     DO NOT EDIT what you see in these blocks of...
    //}}AFX_MSG
    DECLARE_MESSAGE_MAP()
};
```

Like the main frame window class, *CMyDrawDoc* is pretty skeletal. But it also inherits considerable functionality from its base classes, *CDocument*, *CCmdTarget*, and *CObject*. We'll also be adding quite a bit to it later in the book.

Document/View Architecture

Other programming environments, such as Smalltalk, have used the concept of separating the data itself from how it's viewed or "rendered." MFC implements the same idea, separating data from view with two classes: *CDocument*, for data-holding objects, and *CView*, for viewing the data. The view is where your program draws the data. If the data is text, the view displays lines of text. If it's graphics, the view displays pictures. If it's spreadsheet data, the view displays a grid full of numbers and text. The text, graphics, or numbers are stored in the document's member variables. Alternatively, the document can serve as a conduit for data obtained elsewhere, such as a database or an instrument of some kind. Figure 8-6 shows the document/view relationship.

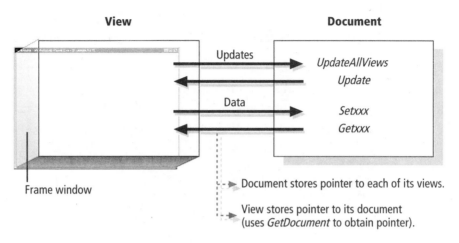

View   **Document**

Updates

UpdateAllViews
Update

Data

Setxxx
Getxxx

Frame window

Document stores pointer to each of its views.

View stores pointer to its document
(uses *GetDocument* to obtain pointer).

Figure 8-6.   *Document and view interactions.*

One of the chief things that this document/view split facilitates is easier implementation of applications with *more than one view* of the data. Microsoft Excel, for example, lets you view spreadsheet data in spreadsheet form, with columns and rows, or in chart form, as a bar chart, line chart, or pie chart. Either way, it's the same data.

In MFC, it's the job of a *document object* to contain the application's data. This works fine for applications with a clear notion of "document." Spreadsheets, for example, store each spreadsheet document in a disk file. You open a file to work with the spreadsheet document.

In the early days of MFC, the document/view architecture caused some unintended anguish among programmers whose applications didn't have that kind of document concept. Maybe they had an application that took a direct digital feed from some instrument and worked with the data that came in. Such programmers might not have seen the relevance of class *CDocument*. But in fact, *CDocument* does usually work for even unconventional applications such as this. You just need to think of "document" as "data repository" or "data stream"—a place where the application stores or obtains its data.

Having said that, let me also point out that it's not so hard to sidestep the document/view architecture in MFC applications if you really need to. See the following sidebar, "Sidestepping Document/View."

Sidestepping Document/View

You don't necessarily have to use MFC's document/view architecture. One approach to skipping it is to simply ignore the document and view classes that AppWizard creates. Their overhead isn't very large, so you can treat them as unused "vestigial appendages." You write any code that you might have written in those classes in class *CMainFrame* instead.

A better way to sidestep document/view is to replace the code in the application's *InitInstance* function that creates the document template, window, document, and view with something like this:

```
m_pMainWnd = new CMainFrame;
m_pMainWnd->ShowWindow(m_nCmdShow);
m_pMainWnd->UpdateWindow();
```

These lines create a main frame window with the *new* operator and store a pointer to the window in the application object's *m_pMainWnd* member variable. This variable always contains a pointer to the main window object. After the one-line creation, the code does what the AppWizard-generated code does. It calls *ShowWindow* to display the window and *UpdateWindow* to cause the window's contents to be repainted. (For an example of code that does it this way, see Jeff Prosise's book, *Programming Windows 95 with MFC*, Microsoft Press, 1996.) With no document or view objects, you write most of your code in the *CMainFrame* class.

A second approach is new in Visual C++ version 6. In AppWizard step 1—for an MFC AppWizard (.exe) application—you can simply clear the Document/View Support box. This generates an application with no document class, although it does have a rudimentary view class, called *CChildView*, whose role is similar to the view's role in a document/view application: it covers the main window's client area, and it's the view into which you draw, not the window. *CChildView* is derived from class *CWnd*, not *CView*, so it lacks all of the *CView* functionality that isn't generic to all windows. This includes no extra support for printing and print preview, no support for scrolling, and so on. You can still do those things, but you must write your own code for them. In some cases this might be just what you want. You can easily generate this kind of application with AppWizard to study its code and see what it can do. Try writing MyHi using this approach. (See the NoDV program in the \learnvcn\Chap08 folder in the companion code.)

One situation in which you might want to omit the document (and possibly the view) is in porting an application written in C to C++ and MFC. That task is simpler if you can map the C code to the frame window object instead of to a document and view. If you ever have to do such a port, see the *MFC Migration Guide*, available from Microsoft with the MFC Migration Kit.

The document's message map

Class *CMyDrawDoc* has a message map, but it's empty. Later, we might use the Visual C++ WizardBar or ClassWizard to add some command message handlers to the message map.

Document member functions

Table 8-4 summarizes the handful of member functions in class *CMyDrawDoc*. Keep in mind that *CMyDrawDoc* inherits members from its base class, *CDocument*, and from other ancestor classes on up the hierarchy.

Function	Description
CMyDrawDoc and *~CMyDrawDoc*	The constructor and destructor, currently empty.
OnNewDocument	A place to add reinitialization code for the SDI document. SDI applications reuse the document object rather than creating a new one. (See *DeleteContents*.) Also check the Help index for *OnOpenDocument*.

Table 8-4. *Document member functions that AppWizard creates for MyDraw.* *(continued)*

Table 8-4 *continued*

Function	Description
Serialize	MFC calls *Serialize* to write the document's data to a file, or to read the data from a file and re-create the document. We'll cover *Serialize* thoroughly in Chapter 16.
DeleteContents	AppWizard doesn't automatically supply an override of this function. I list it here because it's one you'll need often. In SDI applications, MFC reuses the *CDocument*-derived object when the user clicks New on the File menu. MFC calls *DeleteContents* to let you clean up—especially to delete heap memory—without deleting the document object.
Dump and *AssertValid*	See Table 8-3 for a discussion of these functions.

We haven't defined any data yet for the document in MyDraw to hold, or to serialize to a file, or to print. That will come in later chapters.

The View Object

Each document object in an MFC document/view application is associated with one or more objects derived from class *CView*—or from one of the other view classes that MFC provides.

A view is just a window, without a frame. It sits right over the top of the main frame window's client area. We won't draw into the frame window's client area at all. Instead, we'll draw into the view, which almost completely covers up that client area, leaving room only for the toolbar and status bar. (See Figure 8-6.)

It seems strange, of course, that we add an extra object and don't simply draw into the frame window's client area—almost like extra work that could easily be avoided just by drawing into the window as usual. But recall the discussion of MFC's document/view architecture. The view object exists to display the document's data. They're a team. More important, as you'll see in Chapter 20, there might be two *different* views of the same data. Figure 8-7 shows an application with two views set up as a *splitter window*. You can see both views at once, and you can drag the splitter bar between them to change their sizes relative to each other.

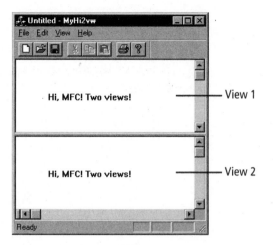

Figure 8-7.   *An application with two views of the same document.*

The ability to provide such multi-view applications is the biggest single reason to use the document/view architecture. When you do have multiple views of the same document, MFC provides a clean mechanism for updating the contents of other views when any single view changes. For example, suppose the user edits the data in an Excel spreadsheet view. Any other views, such as a chart created from the spreadsheet data, should reflect those edits immediately. The spreadsheet view can call the *CDocument::UpdateAllViews* member function to update all of its companion views at the same time.

Now let's look at some of the view class code for MyDraw. First, here's the class declaration (contained in the file DrawVw.h):

```
class CMyDrawView : public CView
{
protected: // create from serialization only
    CMyDrawView();
    DECLARE_DYNCREATE(CMyDrawView)

// Attributes
public:
    CMyDrawDoc* GetDocument();

// Operations
public:
```

(continued)

```
// Overrides
    // ClassWizard generated virtual function overrides
    //{{AFX_VIRTUAL(CMyDrawView)
    public:
    virtual void OnDraw(CDC* pDC);  // overridden to draw this view
    virtual BOOL PreCreateWindow(CREATESTRUCT& cs);
    protected:
    virtual BOOL OnPreparePrinting(CPrintInfo* pInfo);
    virtual void OnBeginPrinting(CDC* pDC, CPrintInfo* pInfo);
    virtual void OnEndPrinting(CDC* pDC, CPrintInfo* pInfo);
    //}}AFX_VIRTUAL

// Implementation
public:
    virtual ~CMyDrawView();
#ifdef _DEBUG
    virtual void AssertValid() const;
    virtual void Dump(CDumpContext& dc) const;
#endif

protected:

// Generated message map functions
protected:
    //{{AFX_MSG(CMyDrawView)
        // NOTE - the ClassWizard will add and remove member...
        //    DO NOT EDIT what you see in these blocks of...
    //}}AFX_MSG
    DECLARE_MESSAGE_MAP()
};

#ifndef _DEBUG  // debug version in DrawVw.cpp
inline CMyDrawDoc* CMyDrawView::GetDocument()
    { return (CMyDrawDoc*)m_pDocument; }
#endif
```

This class appears to contain a little more functionality than most of the MFC classes we've seen so far. It provides some printing support, a function to obtain a pointer to the document object, an override of the *PreCreateWindow* function, and a function called *OnDraw*. We'll look at all of that. *CMyDrawView* inherits members from *CView*, *CWnd*, *CCmdTarget*, and *CObject*.

The view class message map

Like the other objects discussed so far, the view class, *CMyDrawView*, has a message map. Initially, it has three items related to printing—these account for the printing ability we've seen in MyDraw. Here are the three entries, extracted from the message map in file DrawVw.cpp:

```
ON_COMMAND(ID_FILE_PRINT, CView::OnFilePrint)
ON_COMMAND(ID_FILE_PRINT_DIRECT, CView::OnFilePrint)
ON_COMMAND(ID_FILE_PRINT_PREVIEW, CView::OnFilePrintPreview)
```

Notice that the three print commands are mapped to member functions of *CMyDrawView*'s base class, *CView. CView* already has the handlers for them. You can actually see the code for these handlers in the MFC file ViewPrnt.cpp. See the Appendix for guidance on locating the file.

The *OnDraw* function

The single most interesting function in the *CMyDrawView* class is called *OnDraw. OnDraw* is an overridden virtual function. Despite its name, which resembles the names for message handlers, *OnDraw* doesn't directly handle a message and isn't mapped in the message map.

So what is *OnDraw* all about? It's where you do almost all drawing in an MFC document/view–based application, rather than in an *OnPaint* handler. Here's what the function looks like in class *CMyDrawView*:

```
void CMyDrawView::OnDraw(CDC* pDC)
{
    CMyDrawDoc* pDoc = GetDocument();
    ASSERT_VALID(pDoc);
     // TODO: add draw code for native data here
}
```

As shown here, *OnDraw* does only one thing. It obtains a pointer to the view's document by calling the *GetDocument* function. I'll discuss *GetDocument* next. The only remaining item in the function is an AppWizard-supplied comment reminding us that this is where to draw the document's data. In later versions of MyDraw, we'll draw geometric figures; we'll draw text in other examples. We already drew text in Chapter 7, with the MyHi application.

At this point you may be wondering—do we really do all of the drawing in this one function? That seems unusual, doesn't it? Well, maybe—but it's the Windows way to draw. With only a very few exceptions, all drawing in Windows is done in response to a *WM_PAINT* message. As I said in Chapter 6, you receive *WM_PAINT* messages in just two situations:

- The window has just been displayed, and it's time to paint its contents for the first time. A call to *UpdateWindow* sends the window its first *WM_PAINT* message.

- The window has become damaged—invalidated—perhaps by being obscured by another window that goes away, leaving the original window in an invalid state. This causes another *WM_PAINT* message to be sent.

But these two situations should cause MFC to call an *OnPaint* handler, right? Yes, and that's just what happens. The view object (a window) does have an *OnPaint* handler, but it is prewritten for any *CView*-derived class—so we don't usually write any code for it. The *OnPaint* handler performs two key tasks:

- It creates a *CPaintDC* object, which is one way to obtain a handle to the view's device context.

- It then calls *OnDraw*, passing along a pointer to the device context.

In *OnDraw*, you'll notice that there's a parameter, a pointer to an object of type *CDC*:

```
void CMyDrawView::OnDraw(CDC* pDC)
```

Inside *OnDraw*, you use this pointer—already prepared for you—to call drawing functions and set new attributes in the device context, such as a new text color or a new font or pen. You'll see plenty of examples of this later in the book.

NOTE Why does MFC need both *OnPaint* and *OnDraw*? *OnDraw* is called for printing as well as for drawing in a window. For printing, the device context is handled differently than for a window. *OnPaint* sets up the device context correctly for either case and then calls *OnDraw* for the drawing code. This lets us write one drawing function to handle screen drawing, printing, and even print preview.

By the way, this is a good time to point out some mechanics of the *CPaintDC* object. In *OnPaint*, the *CPaintDC* object is created as a local variable, on the stack:

```
CPaintDC dc(this);    // Note the use of this, by the way.
OnPrepareDC(&dc);
OnDraw(&dc);
```

So the device context is obtained as a local variable in *OnPaint*, called *dc*, and *dc's* memory allocation is destroyed when the variable goes out of scope. That happens when the *OnPaint* function returns, after *OnDraw* returns.

During that activity, something interesting occurs behind the scenes. The *CPaintDC* constructor and destructor actually do some useful work. The constructor calls the *::BeginPaint* Win32 API function, and the destructor calls *::EndPaint*. These functions are mandatory before and after drawing into the view. *BeginPaint* prepares a *PAINTSTRUCT* structure with information needed for drawing. *EndPaint* does some required cleanup. In *OnDraw*, we don't even notice this sleight of hand, but it makes painting in *OnDraw* that much simpler. There's no extra overhead code that we have to write, unlike the situation for a C-language programmer, who must declare a *PAINTSTRUCT* variable and call *BeginPaint* and *EndPaint*. I'll discuss the *OnPrepareDC* call in Chapter 15.

The *GetDocument* member function

Why does the view object need a pointer to the document object? Remember that it's the view's job to display the document data. So the view has to be able to obtain the data. One way to do that is through a pointer to the document, as shown earlier in Figure 8-6. Such a pointer allows the view to call document class member functions and directly access any public document member variables. The following code obtains the document pointer (in the *OnDraw* function) and tests it to ensure that it's valid:

```
CMyDrawDoc* pDoc = GetDocument();
ASSERT_VALID(pDoc);
```

Here's one use for the pointer: after the user edits data shown in one view, that view usually needs to call the document's *UpdateAllViews* member function to cause any other views to be updated to reflect the edits. (The following code isn't in MyDraw yet, but we'll be adding something similar to it later.)

```
pDoc->UpdateAllViews(this);
```

Here's what the *GetDocument* member function looks like:

```
CMyDrawDoc* CMyDrawView::GetDocument()
{
    ASSERT(m_pDocument->IsKindOf(RUNTIME_CLASS(CMyDrawDoc)));
    return (CMyDrawDoc*)m_pDocument;
}
```

The key here is that the view already contains a pointer to the document, obtained during document/view creation. It's stored in the view data member *m_pDocument*, which holds a pointer to a *CDocument*. *GetDocument* just tests the validity of the document pointer, then casts the pointer to the correct type and returns it as the *GetDocument* function result. Notice that *CMyDrawView*'s *GetDocument* function returns a pointer to a *CMyDrawDoc* object, not to a generic *CDocument* object. That simplifies our coding, so we don't have to do a cast ourselves. For information about the *ASSERT* macro and the *IsKindOf* function, check the Help index for *ASSERT* and *IsKindOf.*

OTE As always, use casting with great care. Consider the following code:

```
class A
{
public:
    int m_firstInt;
};

A* GlobalFunc();    // Returns a pointer to A

class B : public A
{
public:
    int m_secondInt;
}

void SomeFunction()
{
    B* pB = (B*)GlobalFunc();
    pB->m_secondInt = 7;              // Crash!
}
```

Inside *SomeFunction*, we call *GlobalFunc*, which returns a pointer to *A*. We cast this pointer to *B∗*. The pointer really points only to enough memory for an *A*, so we don't know what will happen when we assign a value to *m_secondInt*. That's a *B* member—but where is the space for that member in the object that *GlobalFunc* returns? We overwrite some memory that probably doesn't belong to us, with the result that sooner or later, something will crash.

The usual suspects

CMyDrawView has the usual *AssertValid* and *Dump* member functions as well as a constructor and a destructor. You'll typically use the constructor to initialize view class member variables. And you'll use the destructor to clean up—particularly to delete any pointer variables you may have created dynamically with the C++ *new* operator.

We also saw the *PreCreateWindow* member function for class *CMainFrame*. It works the same here in the view—giving you a place to modify the view's window styles if you need to.

The print handler functions

We'll look into the three printing-related view functions in Chapter 17. Those functions already enable printing, of a sort, but there will be much to do to make real printing work.

Where Is the Windows Stuff?

It's time now to see whether we've located the following important elements of an application for Windows in this MFC code:

- The *WinMain* function? No. There's no sign of it in the AppWizard-generated code. So where is it? It's actually buried deep inside MFC. Where a C-language programmer would have to write his own *WinMain* function, MFC does it for you. If you're curious, it's in the MFC WinMain.cpp file. See the Appendix for guidance on locating that file.

- The code that creates the application's window? Yes. It's in the application class's *InitInstance* function, somewhat hidden in the document template creation code.

- The message loop? It's not evident in the AppWizard-generated code, but in fact the message loop resides in another member function of the application class, called *PumpMessage*. *PumpMessage* is called from the application class's *Run* member function. You'll see how *Run* comes into play in the next section.

- Message handlers? Got those. They're the *OnXXX* functions in the various classes (where *OnXXX* represents functions such as *OnCreate*, *OnAppAbout*, etc.). MFC uses its message maps to map a Windows message to its *OnXXX* handler function, and there's a complicated routing mechanism to get messages, especially *WM_COMMAND* messages, to the right MFC object.

As you can see, all of Windows is actually here, either directly in the AppWizard-generated code or tucked away inside one of MFC's classes. I'll have just a bit more to say about the relationship between MFC and Windows before the chapter ends.

By the way—this is C++, right? So where's the mandatory *main* function that all C++ programs must have? It's hidden away too, somewhere inside Windows. Just as Windows hides *main* in favor of its own required *WinMain*, MFC hides *WinMain* in favor of its own *CWinApp::InitInstance* and *CWinApp::Run*. Think of it as an MFC layer on top of a Windows layer on top of C/C++.

Life Cycle of an MFC Application

Here's what happens to an MFC application from birth to death. You can compare this summary with "Life Cycle of an Application for Windows" in Chapter 6.

1. The user starts the application. The very first step is construction of the C++ application object, *theApp*. Because *theApp* is a global variable, the compiler allocates space for it immediately, before *WinMain* is called. The object's constructor is called at this time.

WARNING   This is about the only time it's safe to use a global MFC object—a class object (based on an MFC class) declared at global scope. MFC must be properly initialized before you use any of its objects. But globals are defined before MFC initialization, so some code may not behave correctly— such as code in the global object's constructor, called before MFC initialization. As a general rule, avoid using global MFC objects. (However, you can have a global pointer to an MFC object, as long as you initialize the pointer later, after MFC initialization.)

---

2. The application proper begins, and Windows calls *WinMain*, hidden away inside MFC.

3. *WinMain* calls other initialization functions. Somewhere, it registers not one but several *window classes* (not to be confused with C++ classes like *CWnd*) for general use. That's just another thing you don't have to do, although you can override the default window styles in *PreCreateWindow* if you wish.

4. *WinMain* calls the existing application object's *InitInstance* member function to initialize the application and create the main window (and the document and view). This *InitInstance* function is the one you write. You're required to override *InitInstance* in your application class, so AppWizard automatically does it for you. But you can add to or subtract from the contents of *InitInstance* as needed.

5. *WinMain* calls the application object's *Run* member function. Among other things, *Run* starts the message loop and begins dispatching messages to the application's objects, via their message maps.

6. When the message loop gets a *WM_QUIT* message, signifying that the user has done one of several things to exit the application, the message loop ends and the *Run* function calls the application object's *ExitInstance* member function. (When the user clicks Exit on the File menu, or clicks the window's close button, or clicks Close on the System menu, the application's main window receives a *WM_DESTROY* message. A handler inside MFC for *WM_DESTROY* calls the *PostQuitMessage* API function, which posts a *WM_QUIT* message to the application's message queue.)

7. *ExitInstance* does any cleanup work you need done for the application as a whole. It's up to you to override it in your application class if you need to use it.

8. When *ExitInstance* returns, the *Run* function returns, MFC does some cleanup of its own, and Windows terminates the application.

The process is actually more complex than this, but my description does capture the essence. You can follow the whole sequence yourself if you like. Begin by looking at MFC's *WinMain* function in the file WinMain.cpp. See the Appendix for guidance on locating the file. From there, find the functions that *WinMain* calls, then the functions they call, and so on. Try it.

For a quick simulation of an MFC application running, see the WinSim program in the \learnvcn\Chap08 folder in the companion code. The simulation is simplified but instructive—a straight C++ console application like those in earlier chapters.

I've Run AppWizard—Now What?

After running AppWizard, the answer to the question "Now what?" goes something like this:

- Plan your document's data. Design and implement any necessary data structures, such as data classes. Add the appropriate data variables to your document class. You'll learn more about each of these steps as we move ahead, so don't worry about unfamiliar terms at this point.

- Initialize member variables in all of your classes. For the document, determine which variables you can initialize in the document constructor and which you must initialize in *OnNewDocument*, *OnOpenDocument*, or both. If you use the *new* operator to create any data dynamically, be sure to delete that data. For most classes, you should do this in the class destructor. For SDI documents, you often need to override the *DeleteContents* member function and call *delete* on your pointers there. See the MyHi application in Chapter 7.

- Plan how the document's data will be viewed. Do you want one view, or more than one? Design the views, then add code to the *OnDraw* member function in your view classes to draw each view.

- Write code in the document's *Serialize* member function to save your data to a file and to read it back in. Or sidestep the serialization mechanism as described in the sidebar "Sidestepping Serialization" in Chapter 16.

- Use WizardBar or ClassWizard to create handler functions in your classes for any Windows messages or commands you want to handle. For example, you might need to handle the *WM_LBUTTONDOWN* message if you want to detect mouse clicks in your view.

- Add necessary menus and toolbar buttons (or whole new toolbars).

- Create any dialog boxes you need, along with the code to display them in response to a command.

- Add necessary scrolling code.

- Write code in your view classes to process the printing commands.

No doubt there will be other steps you must take in your real-world applications, and you won't always take them in the order I've shown. But these are fundamental to almost every MFC application. By the time you've practiced each of them, as you will with the MyDraw application through the rest of the book, you'll have a feeling for what to do.

MFC and Windows

Now that we've toured MFC and Windows, let's answer a fundamental question: what's the relationship between MFC and the Win32 API? Here it is in brief: MFC is the C++ API for Windows 95, Windows 98, and Windows NT. In other words, MFC is the C++ way to program Windows.

Did the MFC team at Microsoft rewrite the Win32 API in C++? Not at all. In fact, they realized early on that it was fruitless to "reinvent Windows" in C++. Instead, they saw that the way to provide access to the Win32 API for C++ programmers was to wrap the API in C++. (They also added some nice extras, such as documents and views, but the wrappers are the heart of it.)

A *wrapper* is like a capsule that holds the original software entity but bundles it up in new clothes. For example, a wrapper for a function is another function. Inside the wrapper function, you'll find a call to the original function that's being wrapped. Here's an example: an MFC function that wraps a Win32 API function of the exact same name. (I've omitted a few technical details that might obscure my point at this early stage.)

```
BOOL CDC::GetTextMetrics(LPTEXTMETRIC lpMetrics)
{
    return ::GetTextMetrics(m_hAttribDC, lpMetrics);
}
```

The wrapper function belongs to the MFC class *CDC*. You'll notice a few differences between the outer and inner functions. Those are due to MFC simplifications, so it's a little easier to call the MFC function than to call the underlying Win32 API function. Note, however, that you can indeed call either. MFC lets you call any of the Win32 API functions directly if you need to, but you'll seldom want to.

> **NOTE** If you call a Win32 API function directly from your MFC program, precede the function name with the *scope resolution operator* (::) as shown in the wrapper example.

You might be asking yourself, isn't this kind of thing inefficient? If you always have to go through an extra layer—two function calls, really, where one might do—doesn't that make it much more attractive to program in C than C++?

The situation is much better than you might think, though. For one thing, the vast majority of these wrapper functions are written using the C++ keyword *inline*. The keyword tells the C++ compiler to unwrap the wrapper, so to speak. When it's compiled, the wrapper turns into a straight call to the Win32 API function, so it's no less efficient. Yet the programmer can write the simplified MFC function call without worrying about these details. Overall, MFC loses no efficiency by calling the Win32 API in C. Besides, you'll gain a great deal in programming productivity through MFC, where, for example, it's a lot easier to create fancy, complex, user-interface features such as toolbars and print preview.

There's also more to the wrapper story. MFC groups those hundreds of wrapper functions using C++ classes. For example, most functions that require a *window handle* (called an *HWND*) in the Win32 API are grouped into the *CWnd* class—*CWnd* wraps the *HWND*. MFC uses the *CWnd* class to represent any window. The functions grouped into *CWnd* are *member functions* of the class. What's the advantage? This grouping conceptually simplifies the vast Win32 API. Instead of working with several hundred functions that might seem only vaguely related, you work with an object called a *window*. That object contains functions for manipulating its own position, size, styles, and so forth. It really does make your programming easier.

Another way MFC wraps the Win32 API is in its repackaging of Windows messages, such as *WM_LBUTTONDOWN*, into message-mapped handler functions like *OnLButtonDown*. MFC also repackages the information that comes with those messages—known to C-language Windows programmers as the message parameters *lParam* and *wParam*. You don't have to deal with those.

Here's one more way MFC wraps the Win32 API rather than rewriting it. Inside a class like *CWnd* that wraps a Windows handle, such as the *HWND*, MFC doesn't duplicate a lot of information that is already available through the *HWND*. Instead, MFC supplies a member variable in the class to store the *HWND* itself. In class *CWnd*, for example, there is a member called *m_hWnd*, of type *HWND*.

Finding and Using the Hooks in MFC

Early in the chapter, I claimed that much of MFC programming is finding the hooks in MFC—the places MFC provides for you to augment or override its default behaviors—and putting those hooks to good use.

A *hook* is a mechanism that MFC supplies that allows you to customize some object's behavior. For example, MFC lets you create your own handler functions for Windows messages and commands. You don't have to invent them; MFC provides them, and all you have to do is connect the message to the handler in the message map. Then you write the code in the handler to do what you need done for that message.

The many virtual functions in MFC classes are another example of hooks. Such virtual functions as *InitInstance* in class *CWinApp*; *OnUpdate*, *OnInitialUpdate*, *PreCreateWindow*, and *OnDraw* in class *CView*; and *OnNewDocument*, *OnOpenDocument*, *DeleteContents*, and *Serialize* in class *CDocument* provide places to intervene in MFC. These functions are there for you to override if you need to.

N OTE As with the message handlers, you'll often call the base class version of a virtual function to let the base class do what it needs. Sometimes you call the base class first, then add your own behavior. Other times you do your thing first, then call the base class. Usually the wizards will write the function definition for you, with the base class call already in place and a "TODO" comment to show you where to add your own code. When in doubt about whether to call the base class version, use this book's Appendix to track down the base class's definition of the function in the MFC source files. Sometimes the base class version of a function is empty; sometimes it does a lot.

Another kind of hook is the class itself. If an MFC class doesn't do what you want, you can almost always derive a new class from it and adjust the behavior as you see fit. That's essentially what you normally do with *CWinApp*, *CFrameWnd*, *CDocument*, *CView*, and *CDialog*.

If the hooks analogy doesn't work for you, try this one: MFC is like the human body, which has pressure points at various strategic locations. If you need to stop the bleeding, you press on the appropriate pressure point. MFC's pressure points are those same message handlers and virtual functions that you can override, and classes that you can subclass. The trick is to figure out how MFC does something you want to add to or alter, and then apply pressure to the right places.

Whether you think of them as hooks or pressure points, you'll see plenty of examples in this book.

Try It Yourself

See what you can do with the following extra-credit exercises.

1. Write an MDI version of MyHi.

In Chapter 7, I showed you how to create a small program called MyHi. That program was an SDI application like MyDraw. Now write the MDI equivalent of MyHi—a program with more than one window that says "Hi, MFC!" This will give you a sense of how the MDI version and the SDI version are similar and different. What might you need to do differently from the SDI version? Hint: one thing is the initialization we did in *OnNewDocument*. That's no longer necessary with MDI. Initialize in the document's constructor instead, because the document object isn't reused in MDI. See the MdiHi program in the \learnvcn\Chap08 folder in the companion code.

2. Study the MDI code.

In this chapter, you've seen the classes that AppWizard produces for an SDI application. Now take a comparative look at the classes you just created for exercise 1. How does each class differ from its counterpart in the SDI application MyHi?

3. **Study the code in the dialog-based application at the end of Chapter 7.**

   In Chapter 7, exercise 2, I suggested that you use AppWizard to create a dialog-based application. Now compare the classes created for that application with the SDI and MDI applications you've also created. Are there different classes? Where the class names are the same, how do the actual classes differ? See the MyDlg program in the \learnvcn\Chap07 folder in the companion code.

What's Next?

This chapter and Chapter 7 have given you a first look at MFC applications and shown you how to create them with AppWizard. You now have some idea of the architecture of an MFC application. This concludes Part 1, "Getting to Know Visual C++." In Chapter 9, we'll get to work on the MyDraw application in earnest, starting with menus and some simple but instructive drawing.

Fundamental MFC Skills

On the Menu

In Chapter 7, we used AppWizard to generate the skeleton of the book's primary example application, MyDraw. In this chapter, we'll take a look at what's in store for MyDraw—what features it will have and how we'll go about developing them.

We'll also cover Microsoft Windows resources, especially menus. Microsoft Visual C++ 6.0 makes it easy to create menu resources visually and then to hook them up to the code that carries out their commands. Thus we'll literally see what's on the menu for MyDraw. This chapter and Chapter 10 cover step 1 of MyDraw.

I'll round out the chapter by taking you through the process of using several Visual C++ tools in addition to the Source Code editor that you've been using all along. I'll introduce you to the Menu editor and the Accelerator editor.

Introducing MyDraw

MyDraw is an object-oriented or *vector* drawing application. There are two kinds of drawing applications: those that draw and save a bitmap, like the Windows Paint accessory, and those that draw discrete objects that you can move and modify easily without editing pixels. MyDraw is the second kind. It doesn't do very much, and it isn't fancy—it's limited to a few commands and a few kinds of drawing objects. But it does illustrate a lot about Microsoft Foundation Class Library 6.0 (MFC), programming for Windows, and C++.

TIP You can run the finished version of MyDraw now. Copy the project for MyDraw10 (found in the \learnvcn\Chap20 folder in the companion code) to your hard disk, then build and run it. There's also a bonus—a final version of MyDraw named MyDrawF (found in \learnvcn\Chap21), which adds extra features this book doesn't cover.

When you run MyDraw step 10 in Chapter 20, you'll see a menu bar, two toolbars, a status bar, and a blank canvas in the main window's client area. You'll draw rectangles and circles by first clicking a tool on one of the toolbars, and then dragging the mouse across the area you want the shape to occupy.

You'll be able to scroll in MyDraw so you can draw anywhere on a fairly large drawing surface. After drawing several shapes, you'll be able to select one, and it will give you visual feedback by displaying handles.

By default, shapes are drawn in black. But if you click the Color command on the Tools menu, the Color dialog box appears, and you can select a new color from it. From then on, until you change the color again, new shapes are drawn in the selected color.

In Chapter 20, you'll learn to split MyDraw's window into multiple panes and see different portions of the drawing surface in the panes. With MyDraw you'll find that among other things, you'll be able to print your drawing and save it to a file. You can create all the drawing files you like, and open and close them at will.

MyDraw will use object-oriented programming (OOP) techniques for its data, the shapes. Eventually, we'll resurrect class *CShape* and its subclasses, which we developed in Chapter 5.

Figure 9-1 shows the finished MyDraw application in action. Table 10-2, at the end of the next chapter, lays out the steps we'll take in developing all of MyDraw's features and functionality. After an introduction to menus in this chapter, Chapter 10 completes MyDraw step 1.

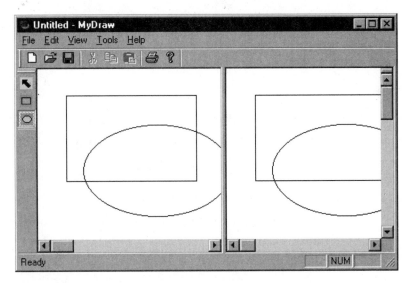

Figure 9-1. *The MyDraw application after step 10 has been completed.*

Menus

A distinguishing feature of graphical user interfaces (GUIs) like that of Windows is the use of menus as a way to present command choices to the user without taking up too much screen real estate. When the user clicks the mouse on a title in the *menu bar,* a menu of options drops down. The rectangle containing the menu temporarily obscures anything beneath it. (This is one of the few instances in which Windows itself saves the image of the obscured bits so that, when the menu closes, Windows can redraw what was there.) The menu closes when the user clicks a menu item—a command or option—or when the user clicks outside the menu or presses the Escape key. In some applications, menus are operable from the keyboard, as you will see later in this Chapter. In other applications, scroll bars can be controlled from the keyboard. (I'll get to that in one of the exercises at the end of Chapter 15.)

When the user clicks a menu item, a command is issued, resulting in the execution of some handler code. "Issuing a command" really means sending the Windows message *WM_COMMAND*, with accompanying information that identifies which menu item was involved—in the form of a *command ID,* such as *ID_FILE_PRINT.* In simplified form, that's how menus work. I'll say more about commands and writing command handlers after we add the new menus to MyDraw.

Menu Resources

How do you specify what menus you want? And how do you connect an item on a menu with a specific command ID? To specify your application's menus, you create a *menu resource* (or edit the one that AppWizard creates for you). When you edit the resource, you can add, delete, modify, or move menu items and whole menus. When you add a menu item, you specify an associated command ID as one of the menu item's properties. Other properties of a menu item include the item's *caption* (the text shown on the menu), a *prompt string* (shown in the status bar when the user passes the mouse pointer over the menu), and a set of *styles.* A menu item can be inactive, checked, bulleted, and so on, by default. You specify the defaults you want when you edit the menu.

> **N OTE** Command IDs play a prominent role in MFC. You'll see them used in other places too, including message maps and toolbars. We'll develop commands more fully in Chapter 10.

Menu mnemonics and accelerators

When you edit menus, you can also specify menu *mnemonics* and *accelerators.* Both are keystroke combinations with which a user can choose a command.

- A mnemonic is an Alt+*keystroke* combination, such as Alt+F+O for the Open command on the File menu. When a menu opens, the mnemonics are the underscored letters you see in the menu items' names.

- Accelerators are similar, but they simply carry out the associated command without involving the menu. Common accelerator key combinations include Ctrl+*keystroke* and Ctrl+Shift+*keystroke.* For example, the accelerator for the Open command on the File menu is customarily Ctrl+O.

When you click a menu in most applications, you'll often see both a mnemonic and an accelerator listed as part of the menu text for many of the menu items. Try it. The Open command on the File menu, for example, usually has the *O* in *Open* underscored (that's the mnemonic), with the text *Ctrl+O* listed after the command name (that's the accelerator name). The accelerator is listed beside its command in the menu as a convenient place for the user to look it up quickly. Not all menu commands have accelerators—they're optional—but all should have mnemonics. Accelerators need not correspond to a menu item at all, but they usually do.

Windows Resources

Resources in Windows are the text and graphics that define much of the user interface. They are stored with the application as part of its executable file. Resources include:

- **Accelerators.** MyDraw will include accelerators for some of the new commands it defines, as described in this chapter under "Add the Accelerators for MyDraw."

- **Bitmaps, icons, and cursors.** We'll eventually give MyDraw a distinctive application icon, and we'll edit the bitmaps displayed on toolbar buttons.

- **Dialog boxes and the controls they contain.** MyDraw will have three dialog boxes for setting application options.

- **Strings.** These include error messages, common text, and menu prompts. MyDraw will store some of its strings in string table resources.

- **Toolbars.** MyDraw will have two toolbars, one for ordinary file and edit operations, and one for drawing tools.

- **Version resources.** These contain information about the program, including its current version number. MyDraw will have a version resource, but I won't add it until the final, bonus version, called MyDrawF, located in the \learnvcn\Chap21 folder in the companion code.

- **Menus.** Stay tuned—we'll get to menu resources shortly.

Windows loads an application's resources as needed, at run time. When the application uses a resource for the first time, Windows reads it in. For example, if the user opens a dialog box, the resource for the dialog box is read into memory.

The virtues of resources

Resources go a long way toward standardizing the appearance and functionality of Windows applications. Although a dialog box or a menu contains application-specific items, the appearance and behavior of the items is standard. This makes Windows applications more consistent and thus easier to learn and to use. It also makes them easier to program. Imagine how hard it would be if you had to write code to produce all of the dialogs, buttons, and menus without resources.

Behind the scenes, as far as the user is concerned, there's often another reason for using resources. If an application will be translated for foreign markets (known as *localizing*), resources can help. If all of the visible elements of the program are stored in the application as resources, you can simply replace the program's resources with translated versions and rebuild. It's even possible to manage resource translation in a manner that doesn't require rebuilding the application's code, particularly if you use MFC. For more information, check the Help index for *localizing resources,* which leads you to MFC Technical Note 57.

You might also need to revise your C++ code, however, to handle languages that require multiple-byte characters, such as Unicode or Multibyte Character Systems (MBCS). Character strings in most European languages use single-byte characters, but some nonEuropean languages, such as Chinese and Japanese, require at least 2 bytes to represent all possible characters. For more information, check the Help index for *localizing code.*

N OTE The Visual C++ documentation includes a set of *technical notes* on topics that are often too specialized or technical to be covered in the general documentation. I won't say much about them in this introductory book, but you should know they are there. Check the Help index for *technical notes by category.*

Resource files

When you run the MFC AppWizard, the wizard creates a set of standard resources as well as the code files we toured in Chapter 8. Actually, it creates a file named *projectname*.rc, where *projectname* is something like MyDraw. This resource file contains items in a resource specification language—this is the raw source code that the Windows *resource compiler,* as part of the Visual C++ build process, turns into binary (compiled) resources that are added to the program's .exe file. You can look at an application's resource code by opening *projectname*.rc as text. (In the Open dialog box, choose Text in the Open As box.)

> **NOTE** AppWizard also creates two icon files (which have the .ico extension) and a bitmap file containing images for toolbar buttons (which has the .bmp extension). Some other AppWizard options generate additional resource-related files.

Resource editing

Originally, Windows programmers wrote much of the source code for their resources by hand, but programs like Visual C++ now commonly provide a set of resource editors that you can use to "draw" your resources—to lay them out with visual tools. Visual C++ supplies a resource editor for each resource type. We'll see many of those editors in this book, starting with the Menu editor and the Accelerator editor.

ResourceView

You manage your application's resources in Visual C++ by using the ResourceView pane in the Workspace window, shown in Figure 9-2 on the following page. I described the ResourceView pane briefly in Chapter 1.

In the ResourceView pane, each resource type has its own folder. If you double-click one of the folders (or click the plus sign in front of it), the folder opens, revealing one or more actual resources. For example, if you open your MyDraw project, click the ResourceView tab in the Workspace window, and open the Menu folder, you see one menu resource, identified as *IDR_MAINFRAME*. Try it. This resource ID is associated with the code in MyDraw.rc for the application's menu bar. There's nothing sacred about the name *IDR_MAINFRAME*. You can change it, but if you have no good reason to do so, I recommend that you just accept it.

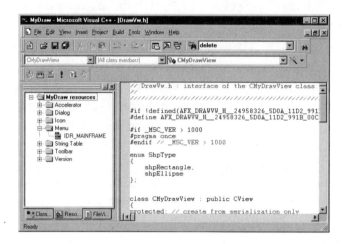

Figure 9-2.   *The ResourceView pane in MyDraw.*

By the way, the principal icon, accelerator, and toolbar resources in My-Draw have the same name as the menus: *IDR_MAINFRAME*. Resources of different types (for example, a menu resource and an accelerator resource) can conveniently share an ID, but you must use different IDs for multiple resources of the same type. Two menu resources, for example, must have different IDs. The *IDR_* prefix is an MFC naming convention for most resource IDs—you can use it or not, as you like. The "*MAIN-FRAME*" part of the ID name stands for the frame window with which the menu is associated.

The Resource.h file

AppWizard creates an additional resource-related file, called Resource.h. This header file contains *#define* directives for the resource IDs used in a project. The Visual C++ documentation calls the constants defined this way *symbols*. You can edit symbols or view them using the Resource Symbols command on the Visual C++ View menu. For information on editing resource symbols, check the Help index for *Resource Symbols*

Browser and choose the subtopic "managing." You may find that you seldom need to tinker with these symbols, but you can if you need to. (You can also edit Resource.h directly, in the Source Code editor. If you do, answer "yes" when asked if you want to reload resources. Then select Rebuild All on the Build menu. This gets everything back in sync.)

It's possible to use resources in multiple .rc files. The Resource Includes command on the Visual C++ View menu lets you manage such files. For more information, including reasons for putting resources in more than one file, check the Help index for *including resources from other files.* Besides an .rc file, AppWizard also supplies an .rc2 file. This file is intended for resources not created with the Visual C++ resource editors or wizards.

Adding a Tools Menu to MyDraw

In order to complete step 1 for MyDraw, we need to create a Tools menu. For now, this menu has two commands: Rectangle and Ellipse. These commands cause MyDraw to draw the corresponding shapes at random locations. (We'll add other ways to give drawing commands later, but for now we're limited to menus.) Since AppWizard has already given us a menu resource, *IDR_MAINFRAME*, that contains many standard commands, we don't need to create a new menu resource. Instead, we can edit the existing menu resource.

To edit the *IDR_MAINFRAME* menu resource, open it in the Visual C++ Menu editor. Just double-click the *IDR_MAINFRAME* menu resource in ResourceView. The Menu editor is shown in Figure 9-3 on the following page.

The *IDR_MAINFRAME* menu resource comes with File, Edit, View, and Help menus, most of them with commands that already work, as we saw in Chapter 7.

The Menu editor shows the new-item box—an empty box with a dotted outline—to the right of the Help menu. This box is where you create a new top-level menu, but you may need to move it from its default position.

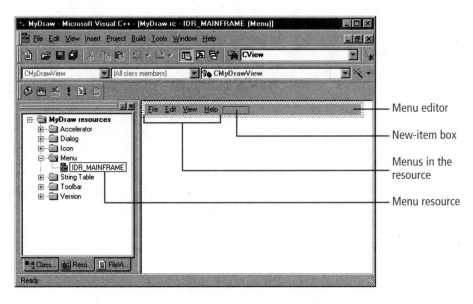

Figure 9-3. *The Visual C++ Menu editor, with the IDR_MAINFRAME resource open.*

Top-level menus occupy a position directly on the menu bar. They normally have *submenus* (also called *drop-down* menus) that appear when the top-level item is clicked. Items in a submenu can also have submenus, resulting in *hierarchical* or *cascading* menus. And you can create *pop-up,* or *context,* menus that pop up at the mouse location, usually in response to a click of the right mouse button. I'll say more about these kinds of menus in later chapters.

Adding the Top-Level Menu

Adding a new top-level menu is a matter of dragging the new-item box from the right of the Help menu to where you want it. Then you type a menu name, open the menu's Properties window, and specify desired options. Because this is our first resource editor, I'll be a bit more explicit here than I will for the other editors. Usually, I'll specify the characteristics of the resource you're editing and direct you to a Help topic about using the editor.

Try it now

Create the top-level menu for MyDraw as follows: Drag the new-item box and drop it between View and Help. It's conventional to make the Help menu the rightmost item on the menu bar, and it's typical that the first three menus are File, Edit, and View. Make sure the new-item box is selected (a fuzzy gray border surrounds it when selected). Then type *&Tools*.

As you type, the Menu Item Properties window opens and your text appears in the window's Caption box as well as on the menu bar. Top-level menus don't need command IDs unless there won't be any submenus under them, which is not a common thing to do, so the ID box is unavailable. Note that top-level menus have the style Pop-up checked.

> **TIP** The Properties window comes and goes. If you prefer, you can keep it in place while you work. Click the pushpin icon in the window to "pin" it in place. To unpin the window, click the pushpin again. The window's contents change as you select different items, such as different menus.

The ampersand (&) in the menu's caption identifies the character following the ampersand as the menu's mnemonic. Avoid duplicate mnemonics at the same level in your menus. For example, if you had File and Format as top-level menus, you'd need to give them different mnemonics, such as: &File (with *F* as the mnemonic) and F&ormat (with *o* as the mnemonic). If the user invokes a duplicated mnemonic, Windows uses the duplicate forms alternately, first executing one command, then executing the other, then the first again, each time the mnemonic is invoked. After creating the rest of the top-level Tools menu, you can check for duplicate mnemonics. Right-click in the Menu editor window and choose the Check Mnemonics command. If you find duplicates, use the Menu editor to make them unique.

> **NOTE** If you ever do use a top-level menu that invokes a command, it's conventional to put an exclamation point after the name, like this: Exit! Such one-item menus are seldom used any more.

Adding the Submenus

When you click a top-level menu item on the menu bar to select it, a second new-item box appears below it. Use that box for adding items to the drop-down menu under the top-level menu. Adding the menu's text and setting its properties is similar to what we did for the top-level menu.

Try it now

After you've added the Tools menu to MyDraw, add its submenu items. Select the Tools menu item. Click in the lower new-item box and type the string *&Rectangle\tCtrl+R*. The text *\tCtrl+R* specifies an accelerator key for the Rectangle command: Ctrl+R. The tab character, *\t*, neatly aligns this accelerator with any other accelerators in the Tools menu. As you type, the Menu Item Properties window opens. Submenu items don't usually need any styles checked, either on the General tab or the Extended Styles tab of the Properties window. But there are two new items to fill in—items we didn't have to add for the top-level menu:

- **ID.** Command IDs are usually named for the primary way to invoke them. For example, the Print command on the File menu is identified as *ID_FILE_PRINT* (the pattern is *ID_menu_command*). So, for the Rectangle command, specify *ID_TOOL_RECTANGLE*. This step is how we connect the menu item to the command it generates. (I've used the singular form "tool" here, but the plural, tools, would be fine too.)

- **Prompt.** The prompt is a string that appears in the status bar as the user moves the mouse across a menu item (or highlights the item with an arrow key). This string describes what the currently highlighted command does. This is an MFC feature that helps users understand the command by providing simple documentation right in the user interface. For the Rectangle command, type the string *Draw a rectangle.*

Try it now

After adding the Rectangle command, add the Ellipse command below it in the same manner. Type *ID_TOOL_ELLIPSE* for the command ID and *Draw an ellipse* for the prompt text. The full Caption string, with accelerator text, is *&Ellipse\tCtrl+E.*

TIP A command is often implemented by both a menu and a toolbar button. When you specify the command's Caption string, you can also specify the text to appear in a *tooltip*, the small yellow label that appears over toolbar buttons when you move the mouse over the button without clicking. I'll show you how to do this in Chapter 18, but here's a sample Caption string with tooltip: *&Ellipse\tCtrl+E\nEllipse.*

TIP Suppose that while you're editing menus, you want to briefly return to your C++ source code files, and then return to the Menu editor. The Menu editor window is a document window that shares space with the source files (so it may cover them up). You can switch among them by clicking the desired filename on the Visual C++ Window menu. The filename listed for the Menu editor is "MyDraw.rc – *IDR_MAINFRAME* (Menu)." Try it.

I've only covered the basics, so there's a good deal more to learn about menu editing. Check the Help index for *menu editor*. The topic that opens takes you to topics on menu editing, copying, and moving.

Adding the Accelerators for MyDraw

You might have thought that adding text like *\tCtrl+R* to a menu caption was enough to create an accelerator key. Unfortunately, that's not the case, although perhaps it should be. The added text just adds text to the menu so that users know what keys to press. We also need to add accelerator keys in the Accelerator editor.

Try it now

Let's add the accelerators for the Rectangle and Ellipse commands. The Accelerator resource window is shown in Figure 9-4. To open the accelerator resource, open the Accelerator folder in ResourceView and double-click the resource, *IDR_MAINFRAME*. Like the Menu editor, the Accelerator editor has a new-item box, located at the bottom of the table of accelerators. Complete the following procedures:

- For the Rectangle command, type *R* in the new-item box. In the Accel Properties window that opens (see Figure 9-5), verify that Ctrl is selected in the Modifiers group and that Virtkey is selected in the Type group. Type *ID_TOOL_RECTANGLE* in the ID box, press Enter, and save your work.

- Do the same for the Ellipse command, specifying *Ctrl+E* for the accelerator and *ID_TOOL_ELLIPSE* for the command ID.

For more information on the Accelerator editor, check the Help index for *accelerator editor*.

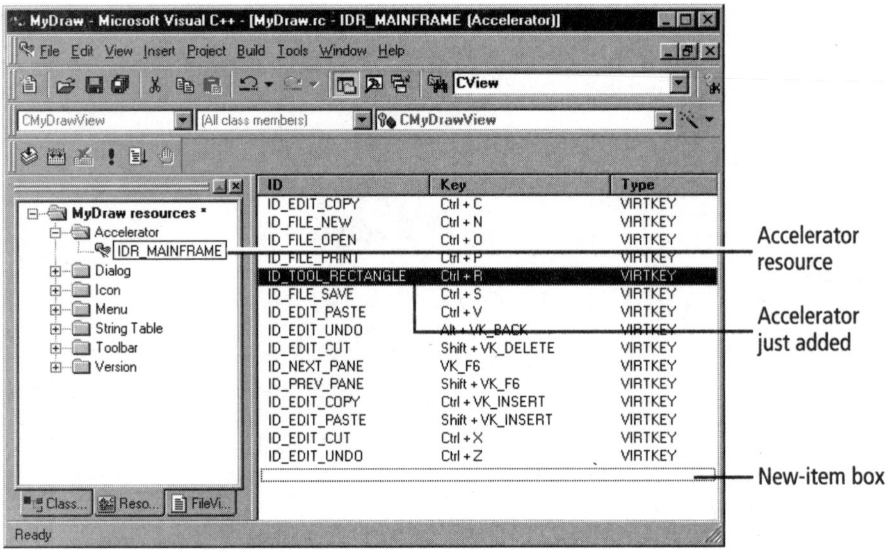

Figure 9-4. *The Visual C++ accelerator editor.*

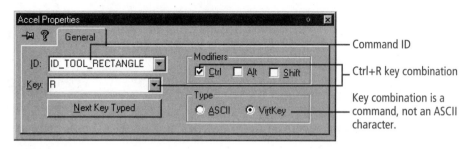

Figure 9-5.   *The Accel Properties window.*

Menus and Commands

Windows sends command messages in response to menu selections, clicks on toolbar buttons or other controls, and so on. In MFC, a command—including one issued by a menu item—is processed through a chain consisting of *command target* objects, including the frame window, document, and view objects, as well as the application object. Each command target object checks its message map to see if the object has a handler for the command ID. If so, it calls the handler, in some cases passing it parameters that come with the message.

So far, we've defined two commands by their command IDs: *ID_TOOL_RECTANGLE* and *ID_TOOL_ELLIPSE*. But we have yet to write the command handlers that carry out the user's wishes. That's coming in Chapter 10.

Try It Yourself

I've shown you the basic techniques for editing menu and accelerator resources, but there is more to learn.

1. Explore the Menu and Accelerator editors.

Explore the Menu and Accelerator editors more thoroughly. Try them out and read the Microsoft documentation on them. To read about the Menu editor, begin by checking the Help index for *menu editor*. To read about the Accelerator editor, check the Help index for *accelerator editor*. Take some of the other resource editors for a spin too—open them the same way you open the menu and accelerator resources, using ResourceView. Read more about ResourceView as well, by checking the Help index for *ResourceView*. One especially valuable ResourceView skill is copying resources from one resource file to another. Check the Help index for *Resources* and choose the subtopic "copying."

2. Get some background on Windows resources.

To begin learning about Windows resources in general, use the Contents tab in Help. Open the Platform SDK topic group, and then open User Interface Services, and then read the topics under Resources.

To learn about the standard resources in MFC, check the Help index for *resources,* choose the subtopic "MFC," and read the "TN023: Standard MFC Resources" topic. To learn about the common resources, or *clip-art* resources supplied with Visual C++, check the Help index for *Common.res*. The file Common.res contains numerous cursors, icons, and toolbar bitmaps that you can use.

What's Next?

This chapter added menus to MyDraw, but they don't work yet. In Chapter 10, we'll write command handler functions that implement the menu commands. We'll also start drawing real shapes.

Drawing Commands

Chapter 9 and this chapter cover MyDraw step 1. (We completed step 0 in Chapter 7). In Chapter 9, we added menu and accelerator resources to MyDraw. In this chapter, we'll wire up the menus with functions that handle the commands they generate, and introduce simple drawing with the Microsoft Windows Graphical Device Interface (GDI). The results are a bit crude in this step, but in subsequent steps we'll refine MyDraw considerably.

When I introduced the Windows drawing model in Chapter 6, I said that the bulk of an application's drawing occurs in the view class's *OnDraw* member function. This chapter begins a description of the drawing model that will span several chapters. You'll start to see why *OnDraw* is so important. Later you'll also see that you can do some drawing in other places as well. Just keep in mind that the drawing model will be an ongoing theme.

The MyDraw Application, Step 1, Continued

In step 1, the only files we alter are the header and implementation files for the view class, *CMyDrawView*, and the Windows resource file, MyDraw.rc. (We put the handlers for our drawing commands in the view class because they have to do with displaying the shapes. See the following Note.)

> **NOTE** How do you decide which class to put a handler or other function in? Base your decision on which object is most affected by the function. If it has something to do with maintaining the data, such as copying it, writing it to a file, refreshing it from a database, and so on, the document object is a good choice. If it has mostly to do with how data looks in the display, the view object is a good choice. Sometimes a function might belong to the application or frame window object instead. If you find yourself accessing other objects to make the function work, you might choose a better object to house the function.

In this step, the rest of the files remain as they were when AppWizard created them. All of the code I show you will be in the two view class files, DrawVw.h and DrawVw.cpp.

> **IMPORTANT** Keep in mind that I have developed this project in stages. Each chapter of this book contains the latest MyDraw project placed in a folder that contains the step number—for example, MyDraw1. You don't need to use the number when you name your projects. I'm going to lead you through this code to demonstrate points about Windows programming, especially the Windows drawing model, so it's an especially good idea to work along with me in your own MyDraw project. Keep in mind that we added some menu and accelerator resource items in Chapter 9. Review "Working Along with Me" in Chapter 7 for details on how to work through the example programs as I do.

Adding the Command Handlers

It's time to add the command handlers for the Rectangle and Ellipse menu commands, along with some associated code. We'll use both WizardBar and ClassWizard—close relatives—to add the two command handler functions to the view class. ClassWizard is a Swiss Army knife, with lots of capabilities. WizardBar puts a few of the handiest ClassWizard abilities on a toolbar. We'll also need to declare a couple of view class data members, add two helper functions for generating randomized shape locations, add a few *#include* directives, and do a bit of initializing.

Here's what we want to happen when a user clicks the Rectangle command on MyDraw's Tools menu. The *OnToolRectangle* handler function obtains a bounding rectangle, of type *CRect*, within which to draw its shape. Then it calls a member function of class *CDC* to do the drawing. (Figure 4-1 on page 127 illustrates the concept of drawing in a bounding rectangle.)

For MyDraw step 1, the shapes' bounding rectangles are randomly chosen, much as they were in program Shape3 in Chapter 5. We'll add two view class member functions, *RandomCoord* and *RandomRect*, to generate random bounding rectangles. *RandomCoord* is essentially the same as in program Shape3 in Chapter 5. *RandomRect* is new but very simple.

The next section describes what you need to do to work along with me.

Adding the *OnToolRectangle* and *OnToolEllipse* command handlers

Add two command handler functions in the view class, called *OnTool-Rectangle* and *OnToolEllipse*. You can add both by using WizardBar, as described in the first procedure below, but I suggest you add the second with ClassWizard to get a taste of working with both tools. The ClassWizard procedure follows the WizardBar procedure. See the sidebars "WizardBar: Fast Class Actions" and "ClassWizard: AppWizard's Partner, WizardBar's Big Brother."

Try it now

WizardBar is the easiest way to add a command handler. On WizardBar, verify that class *CMyDrawView* is listed in the class box (on the far left end of WizardBar). Change the class box listing if necessary.

1. On the WizardBar Action menu (the down arrow at the far right), click the Add Windows Message Handler command. Microsoft Visual C++ 6.0 displays the New Windows Message And Event Handlers dialog box. (See Figure 10-1 on the following page.) In the Class Or Object To Handle box, click *ID_TOOL_RECTANGLE*. That command is the "object" for which we need a handler.

2. In the New Windows Messages/Events box, click COMMAND. That's the type of handler we're adding.

3. Click the Add Handler button. In the Add Member Function dialog box (Figure 10-2), click OK to accept the suggested function name.

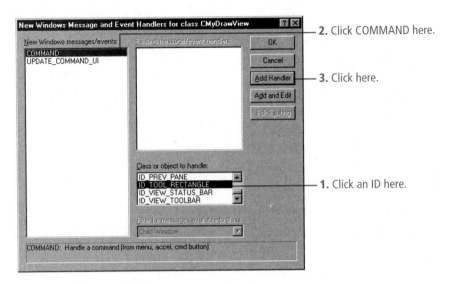

2. Click COMMAND here.

3. Click here.

1. Click an ID here.

Figure 10-1. *The New Windows Message And Event Handlers dialog box.*

Figure 10-2. *The Add Member Function dialog box.*

> **TIP** If the Add Windows Message Handler command and the Add Virtual Function commands ever disappear from the WizardBar Action menu, follow these steps to restore them: First make sure the Class box on the left displays a class name, not just "Globals." If that doesn't solve the problem, you may need to recreate a ClassWizard data file called, for MyDraw, MyDraw.clw. To do this, click ClassWizard on the Visual C++ View menu. A dialog box asks if you want to recreate the .clw file. Click Yes. In the Select Source Files dialog box, click Add All, then OK. In ClassWizard, click OK. The WizardBar commands should reappear.

WizardBar: Fast Class Actions

WizardBar is a Visual C++ toolbar with an interface for managing and modifying classes and their members. It's also an excellent navigational tool—you can use it to jump directly to the code for a particular class or function.

WizardBar contains three combo boxes and a button. The combo boxes show, from left to right, classes, filters, and class members. If you select a class in the Class box, the Members box is filled with the members of that class, assuming the Filters box reads "(All class members)." The Filters box lets you filter the items selected from the Members box. In some situations it lets you view command IDs as well as members.

The WizardBar Action button lists actions you can take on the currently selected class or member, such as adding a new class member, going to a class or function definition, or creating a new class. The Action button has two parts: a small control (a downward pointing arrow) that displays a menu of actions, and a magic wand icon that simply carries out the current default action (shown in bold text on the Action menu). As you work in your code, WizardBar tracks where you are, changing the contents of the Class and Members boxes accordingly. I'll have you use WizardBar many times in this book. For more information, check the Help index for *WizardBar*.

Try it now

Repeat the process above to create a handler for the *ID_TOOL_ELLIPSE* command. Or do it this way with ClassWizard instead of WizardBar:

1. On the Visual C++ View menu, click ClassWizard (or press Ctrl+W). Figure 10-3 shows ClassWizard. In the MFC ClassWizard window, make sure the Project box says MyDraw and the Class Name box says *CMyDrawView*. Change them if necessary.

2. In the Object IDs box, click *ID_TOOL_ELLIPSE*. That's the command we want to create a handler for.

3. In the Messages box, click COMMAND. That's the kind of handler we want to create. (I'll explain the other kind, UPDATE_COMMAND_UI, in Chapter 12.)

4. Click the Add Function button. In the Add Member Function dialog box (see Figure 10-2), click OK to accept the proposed function name. The names proposed are based on the command ID, so they're a good match.

For more information about the sequence of steps needed to create a message handler using ClassWizard, see the sidebar titled "ClassWizard: App-Wizard's Partner, WizardBar's Big Brother."

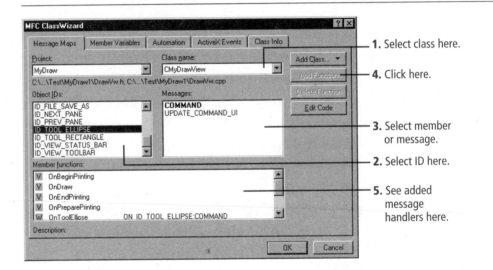

Figure 10-3.   *ClassWizard.*

After the WizardBar or ClassWizard steps, WizardBar leaves you at the new function's definition, ready to add code. You can click the Edit Code button in ClassWizard to arrive at the same place. Either way opens file DrawVw.cpp in the Source Code editor at the latest of the two new functions, which are called *OnToolRectangle* and *OnToolEllipse*.

The *On* prefix for Windows message handlers and command handlers is an MFC convention. Such handler names indicate what message or command they're handling. Adding the handlers with WizardBar actually adds two other things besides the function bodies in DrawVw.cpp:

- In DrawVw.h, WizardBar or ClassWizard adds two member function prototypes to the *CMyDrawView* class, in the area reserved for message handler functions, as follows:

```
// Generated message map functions
protected:
    //{{AFX_MSG(CMyDrawView)
    afx_msg void OnToolRectangle();
    afx_msg void OnToolEllipse();
    //}}AFX_MSG
    DECLARE_MESSAGE_MAP()
```

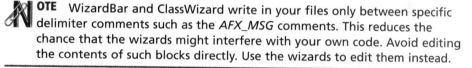

NOTE WizardBar and ClassWizard write in your files only between specific delimiter comments such as the *AFX_MSG* comments. This reduces the chance that the wizards might interfere with your own code. Avoid editing the contents of such blocks directly. Use the wizards to edit them instead.

- In DrawVw.cpp, WizardBar adds two message map entries near the top of the file. Here's the whole message map—the new entries are in boldface:

```
BEGIN_MESSAGE_MAP(CMyDrawView, CView)
    //{{AFX_MSG_MAP(CMyDrawView)
    ON_COMMAND(ID_TOOL_RECTANGLE, OnToolRectangle)
    ON_COMMAND(ID_TOOL_ELLIPSE, OnToolEllipse)
    //}}AFX_MSG_MAP
    // Standard printing commands
    ON_COMMAND(ID_FILE_PRINT, CView::OnFilePrint)
    ON_COMMAND(ID_FILE_PRINT_DIRECT, CView::OnFilePrint)
    ON_COMMAND(ID_FILE_PRINT_PREVIEW, CView::OnFilePrintPreview)
END_MESSAGE_MAP()
```

When you add a member function of any kind with WizardBar, or its sibling, ClassWizard, you always get these three ingredients: function prototype in the class declaration, message map entry, and function definition. WizardBar is the quick way to work on a class. ClassWizard is the more comprehensive way.

I'll show you the handler function definitions later in this chapter when you're ready to add code to them.

ClassWizard: AppWizard's Partner, WizardBar's Big Brother

AppWizard is a run-it-once tool, but ClassWizard is available any time you need to add members to a class, or create a class, or do quite a variety of things. Take a look at the tabs in the ClassWizard window. (See Figure 10-3.) Most of ClassWizard's most common functionality is available through WizardBar. Use ClassWizard for heavy lifting, WizardBar for quick work.

ClassWizard's main purpose is to manipulate message maps. With it, you can add or delete handler functions for standard Windows messages like *WM_CREATE*, and override virtual functions like *OnInitialUpdate*. You can also use the Add Class button in ClassWizard to add a class derived from an MFC class or a generic class of your own design. (You can instead use WizardBar or the New Class command on the Visual C++ Insert menu for this purpose.) ClassWizard can also delete class member functions, and can be used as a navigational tool. To do either, simply select the class and class member you want, and then click the appropriate button.

One of ClassWizard's (and WizardBar's) chief advantages is that it never lets you forget to add one of the essential ingredients. If you add a member function to a class by hand, you might forget the message map entry or the function prototype in the class declaration.

I'll use WizardBar more than ClassWizard in this book, but some things are best done in ClassWizard, so you'll meet the wizard again. For more information, check the Help index for *ClassWizard*.

TIP If WizardBar is not visible, open it as you would any toolbar. Right-click in the toolbar area of the screen. On the Toolbars context menu, click WizardBar.

Adding the *m_boxShape* data member to the view class

Now we need to store some information in the view, namely the bounding rectangle in which to draw the current shape—in effect, the shape's location on the drawing surface.

Try it now

In the file DrawVw.h, add the *m_boxShape* data member in the public attributes section:

```
⋮
// Attributes
public:
    CMyDrawDoc* GetDocument();

    CRect m_boxShape;       // Bounding box for drawing current
                            //  shape
```

The data member is of type *CRect*, an MFC class designed to represent rectangles. Rectangles are one of the most commonly used data types in Windows.

> **OTE** The *CRect* and *CPoint* classes you see mentioned in the MyDraw code are the MFC classes, not the simple approximations for them that I created in Chapter 4, before we were working with MFC. But they serve the same purpose and function much the same.

Adding the two helper functions, *RandomCoord* and *RandomRect*

RandomCoord is borrowed from the Shape3 program in Chapter 5. It uses the *rand* run-time function to generate a random number in the range 0 to *COORD_MAX*, which at the moment equals 1000. *RandomRect* calls *RandomCoord* four times to generate the coordinates for the upper-left and lower-right points of a randomly located rectangle.

In order to use the *rand* function, we need some supporting items in the files:

- Two #*include* directives to include run-time files Stdlib.h and Time.h

- A call to the companion *srand* function to seed the random number generator

Try it now

1. Near the top of file DrawVw.cpp, add the following *#include* directives (anywhere in relation to the other *#include* directives there):

```
#include <stdlib.h>    // For rand and srand and abs
#include <time.h>      // For time function
```

2. In file DrawVw.cpp, add code to the view class constructor to make it look like this:

```
CMyDrawView::CMyDrawView()
{
    // TODO: add construction code here
    // Initialize random number generator for random bounding rects
    srand((unsigned)time(NULL));
}
```

This call gets the current time, then uses that value to seed the random number generator. Next we'll add the two randomizing helper functions.

Try it now

Add two ordinary member functions to the view class. (They aren't Windows message handlers, and they aren't virtual function overrides.)

1. On the WizardBar Action menu, click the Add Member Function command.

2. In the Add Member Function dialog box, add the information listed in Table 10-1 for the *RandomCoord* member function. Figure 10-4 shows the sequence of steps needed to fill in the dialog box.

3. Then use Add Member Function again to add the information listed in Table 10-1 for the *RandomRect* member function.

Item in the Dialog Box	For *RandomCoord*	For *RandomRect*
Function Type	*int*	*void*
Function Declaration	*RandomCoord();*	*RandomRect(CRect* pRect);*
Access	Public	Public

Table 10-1. *Data to enter in the Add Member Function dialog box.*

4. Finally, add code to the two functions so they look like this:

For *RandomCoord*,

```
const int COORD_MAX = 1000;

// Generate a random positive coordinate within a COORD_MAX-
//   by COORD_MAX-unit drawing area.
int CMyDrawView::RandomCoord()
{
    static int nLastCoord;

    int nNextCoord = rand();
    int nFudge = rand() % 100;
    nLastCoord = (nNextCoord > nLastCoord ? nNextCoord : nLastCoord);
    nLastCoord = (nLastCoord + nFudge) % COORD_MAX;

    return nLastCoord;
}
```

For *RandomRect*,

```
// Generate a random CRect.
void CMyDrawView::RandomRect(CRect* pRect)
{
    ASSERT(pRect != NULL);  // Error if user passes a bad rect
    pRect->top = RandomCoord();
    pRect->left = RandomCoord();
    pRect->bottom = RandomCoord();
    pRect->right = RandomCoord();
}
```

Notice the constant declaration for *COORD_MAX* above the *RandomCoord* function. You'll need to add that by hand while you're filling in the functions.

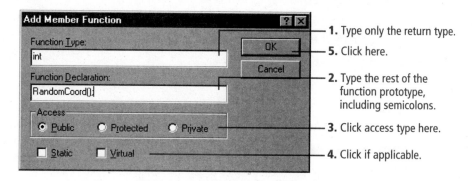

Figure 10-4.   *The Add Member Function dialog box for a plain member function.*

Writing code in the two command handlers

With all of the supporting code now in place, fill in the bodies of the two command handler functions in the file DrawVw.cpp.

 Try it now

Add code to the *OnToolRectangle* and *OnToolEllipse* handlers so they look like this:

```
void CMyDrawView::OnToolRectangle()
{
    // TODO: Add your command handler code here
    CClientDC dc(this);
    RandomRect(&m_boxShape);
    dc.Rectangle(m_boxShape);
}

void CMyDrawView::OnToolEllipse()
{
    // TODO: Add your command handler code here
    CClientDC dc(this);
    RandomRect(&m_boxShape);
    dc.Ellipse(m_boxShape);
}
```

That completes our preliminary round of coding. We'll add a bit more after some testing and experimenting.

Testing OnDraw's Menus and Shape Drawing

Try an experiment. Build and run MyDraw with the additions we made in the previous section. Use the menus to draw random shapes. Try it. (To build, click the Build MyDraw.exe command on the Build menu, or press F7. To run the program, click Execute MyDraw.exe on the Build menu, or press Ctrl+F5.)

The shapes will vary considerably in size and location. In some cases, only part of a shape may be visible. In other cases, you may think nothing has happened in response to your command at all. That's because MyDraw uses a large drawing surface, much bigger than the MyDraw window usually is. A particular random bounding rectangle might not lie within the area visible through the view, or it might lie only partially inside the view. You can see more by maximizing the MyDraw window, but the problem persists: not all of the shapes are visible. Try it. We'll deal with this problem in Chapter 15, when we cover scrolling.

> **NOTE** Each shape also appears to have an opaque (white) center area, so that you can't see any part of a shape that another shape partially or completely covers. We'll tackle the problem of seeing shapes behind other shapes in Chapter 11.

Disappearing Shapes

What happens when you maximize the MyDraw window, and then restore it? What happens if you click outside MyDraw's window, say in the Visual C++ window, and then make MyDraw visible again, perhaps by pressing Alt+Tab? Try it.

Any shapes you've drawn disappear. That's because the view has become invalid, due to resizing or covering and reexposing the window, and must be drawn again. The only way we can draw at the moment is by calling *OnToolRectangle* or *OnToolEllipse* again, but we're at the mercy of the user to call them, and they draw randomly anyway. We'll rectify this problem partly here in Chapter 10 and completely in Chapter 14.

Redrawing Shapes on Update

The biggest problem we face is called the *update problem*. When the view is invalidated, we have to redraw it—Windows sends us a *WM_PAINT* message, and MFC calls *OnDraw*. This happens often in the Windows environment, with its multitasking and multiple overlapped windows. But redrawing requires information. At the moment, the only piece of information we store is the location of the last shape drawn—its bounding rectangle, in *m_boxShape*. But we can't even redraw the last shape without knowing the shape type as well—do we redraw a rectangle or an ellipse? And, of course, we can't redraw any shapes at all, other than the last one.

Later in this chapter, we'll solve the problem of redrawing the last shape on update. It won't be a great solution, but it will do for now.

> **MPORTANT** Pay attention to what this update problem says about the Windows drawing model. It seems that if we do any drawing outside *OnDraw*, we must also do it a second time inside *OnDraw*. This may seem inefficient, but the nature of the Windows environment requires some such approach. Many applications do all of their drawing in *OnDraw* to avoid the double drawing penalty.

Keeping Track of Shape Types

So far, MyDraw is hardwired to draw each shape type, in the *OnToolRectangle* and *OnToolEllipse* member functions. To redraw on update, we need to write some code in *OnDraw*. MFC calls *OnDraw* in response to each *WM_PAINT* message.

Try it now

One thing is certain. *OnDraw* has to know which type of shape to redraw. Then it can use a *switch* statement, like the one shown here, to do the drawing. Add the boldface lines:

```
void CMyDrawView::OnDraw(CDC* pDC)
{
    CMyDrawDoc* pDoc = GetDocument();
    ASSERT_VALID(pDoc);

    // TODO: add draw code for native data here
    switch(m_typeShape)
    {
    case shpRectangle: pDC->Rectangle(m_boxShape);
        break;
    case shpEllipse: pDC->Ellipse(m_boxShape);
        break;
    }
}
```

To make this switch statement possible, the view class has to store not only the last shape's bounding rectangle but also its type. For that, we need a shape type and a view class data member of that type. We're back to our shape type from program Shape3 in Chapter 5.

Try it now

Let's add a new data member to class *CMyDrawView* (file DrawVw.h), called *m_typeShape*, of type *ShpType*:

```
// Attributes
public:
    CMyDrawDoc* GetDocument();

    CRect m_boxShape;       // Bounding box for drawing current
                            //  shape
    ShpType m_typeShape;    // Currently: rectangle or ellipse
```

We add the new data member as a public attribute.

Try it now

Just above the view class declaration in file DrawVw.h, we add another old friend, the *ShpType* enumeration from Chapter 5. Add these lines:

```
enum ShpType
{
    shpRectangle,
    shpEllipse
};

class CMyDrawView : public CView
    :
```

Try it now

Just one more change. In the *OnToolRectangle* and *OnToolEllipse* member functions, we now need to store the shape type in the *CShape* object's *m_typeShape* data member. Here's *OnToolRectangle* (*OnToolEllipse* is similar):

```
void CMyDrawView::OnToolRectangle()
{
    // TODO: Add your command handler code here
    CClientDC dc(this);
    m_boxShape = RandomRect();
    dc.Rectangle(m_boxShape);
    m_typeShape = shpRectangle;
}
```

Now go add the following line to *OnToolEllipse:*

```
m_typeShape = shpEllipse;
```

The final line of the function assigns an enumeration value to *m_typeShape*. Now the *switch* statement in *OnDraw* works to determine which kind of shape to draw. Then it calls the same *CDC* functions to do the drawing.

Try it now

Test the results by building and running the application. Draw a few shapes. Maximize the MyDraw window, then restore it. Draw more shapes. Do something to cover all or part of the window, then reexpose it. In each case, you should see the last shape redrawn (unless it happens to lie outside the view), but not the others.

How Good Is It?

This update to MyDraw is hardly an elegant solution. But it does emphasize what's needed to solve the update problem in general: stored data, often called state data. MyDraw can't redraw any shapes without the necessary information—the shape's type and its bounding rectangle. After this partial solution, we store that data, but only for the last shape. Each new shape's data overwrites that of the previous shape. Stay tuned for a limited improvement in Chapter 11 and a complete, and much more elegant, solution in Chapter 14.

Future Versions of MyDraw

At the beginning of Chapter 9, I took you through the features of the final MyDraw program, as it will be by the time we finish Chapter 20. Table 10-2 summarizes the steps we'll take in developing MyDraw.

MyDraw Step	Chapter	Description
Step 0	7	Step 0 is just the output of AppWizard, given a few specific options. We explored that output in Chapter 8.
Step 1	9 and 10	In Chapters 9 and 10, we've covered menus, accelerators, and basic command handlers, along with editing menus, accelerators, and source code. We also used WizardBar and ClassWizard.
Step 2	11	Step 2 introduces drawing with the mouse and handling Windows messages other than *WM_COMMAND*. Step 2 also covers string resources.

Table 10-2.   *The steps to come in MyDraw.*

MyDraw Step	Chapter	Description
Step 3	12	Step 3 covers adding color to the drawings via a hierarchical Color menu.
Step 4	14	In step 4, we'll revise class *CShape* and its subclasses from Chapter 5 and put them to work in MyDraw as we discuss MFC documents and views. This will solve most of our redrawing problems.
Step 5	15	Step 5 solves another of the issues raised in Chapter 10—viewing shapes on the whole drawing surface. In Chapter 15, we'll add scrolling to MyDraw, with a short side trip through some text-handling topics.
Step 6	16	Once we're able to draw nice shapes, it's time to save them to a file. Step 6 adds MFC *serialization* code to do just that.
Step 7	17	It would also be good if we could print a drawing. That's what we'll do in step 7.
Step 8	18	Through step 7, we've been choosing a drawing tool from the Tools menu. In step 8, we'll put the tools on a second toolbar and cover toolbar lore, including the Toolbar editor. We'll also let the user select a shape, and we'll show the selection with a set of selection handles on the shape's bounding rectangle.
Step 9	19	We aren't communicating with our users much so far, so step 9 adds dialog boxes and introduces the Dialog editor. One of our dialog boxes will augment MyDraw's Color menu—a Windows common dialog box that lets users pick colors.
Step 10	20	The last step that we cover in MyDraw adds the ability to split the drawing into multiple panes so users can view several parts of the drawing surface at once.

What Have You Learned?

This chapter made an important point about the Windows drawing model. By illustrating the update problem, I showed you why you need to draw in *OnDraw* even if you've already drawn in some other function.

We'll continue that discussion through Chapter 15, as we pursue several loose ends. At this point the shape display is faulty in several ways:

- The drawing surface is bigger than the viewport, so we can't reach all of it to see all possible random shapes.

- So far we're only redrawing the last shape in *OnDraw*. The others disappear if the view is invalidated.

- The shapes currently have opaque centers, which might be fine in some cases. But suppose we want transparent centers so we can see through to any shapes behind?

Try It Yourself

Here's your extra credit for this chapter.

1. Learn more about MFC commands and command handlers.

Check the Help index for *commands and messages* and choose the sub-topic "managing with ClassWizard." Also check the index for *Commands* and choose the subtopic "connecting to handler functions." And check the Help index for *command routing* and *command IDs*.

2. Learn more about the Windows Graphical Device Interface.

We've touched on a few GDI drawing commands in this chapter, but take a look at GDI overall. Check the Help index for *device contexts*. (Choose the first listing of "device contexts" in the Index.) From that overview topic, you can access both MFC and Microsoft Win32 API topics on device contexts and related GDI topics. (In the Win32 API topics, you may need to use the Up and Down arrows on the Help window's toolbar to move to the next or previous topic.)

What's Next?

Chapters 11 and 12 take up the theme of empowering users, who'll get to draw directly with the mouse (in color) instead of relying on menu commands. We'll fix most, but not all, of our drawing problems, create a hierarchical menu, and add color to the shape drawing.

Power to the User

Chapters 9 and 10 got us started on the MyDraw application with step 1, but we have a long way to go. MyDraw does draw shapes, and it does use menu commands to determine which shape to draw. But in step 1, other than choosing a tool from the menu, the user has no further control over the process. This deviates from the convention that, typically, in Microsoft Windows applications, the user, not the program, is in control. User control is our theme for this chapter.

In this chapter and the next, we'll give the user more control in two ways:

- We'll still let the user choose which type of shape to draw—using our menu commands. But in this chapter, in MyDraw step 2, we'll also let the user draw directly with the mouse. The user will be able to click anywhere in the view and drag the mouse to outline the shape. As the user drags with the mouse button still down, we'll show where the shape would go by drawing it each time the mouse moves. We'll continually erase the old shape outline and draw a new one until the mouse button is released, and then we'll draw the shape's final form. You've no doubt seen this done in some of the Windows programs you use.

■ In the next chapter, we'll also let the user choose the color of the shape's outline. The user can select Color on the Tools menu and then select a color on a hierarchical menu.

While we're at it, we'll solve two of the viewing issues raised in the last chapter—at least partially. We'll allow the user to make the interior of a shape transparent, so that any shapes "behind" the current shape (that is, shapes we drew earlier and that we're now drawing "on top of") can be seen. And we'll store all of the shapes drawn so we can redraw not only the most recently drawn shape, but all of them. These solutions are still not the last word on the subject—we'll improve them further in Chapter 14, after a brief pause in Chapter 13 to look at the Microsoft Visual C++ 6.0 debugger.

TIP Be on the lookout for a logic bug intentionally planted in the code in this chapter. We'll debug it in Chapter 13.

Drawing with the Mouse

How do we go about letting the user draw with the mouse? The technique is to *track* the mouse, using handlers for several Windows messages that the mouse generates. Think about the act of drawing with the mouse. You press the left mouse button where you want to start the shape. With the mouse button still pressed, you drag out a box that will contain the shape you want to draw. The box is the shape's bounding rectangle. When you're finished, you release the mouse button and the shape is drawn within that bounding rectangle.

Mouse-Related Messages

During the drawing sequence, Windows generates the following messages, which we'll be working with in MyDraw throughout this book.

■ *WM_LBUTTONDOWN*, when the user presses the left mouse button

■ *WM_MOUSEMOVE*, as the user drags the mouse across the screen

■ *WM_LBUTTONUP*, when the user releases the left mouse button

Windows sends fewer *WM_MOUSEMOVE* messages than you might expect. It could send one every time the mouse moves at all, but that would overwhelm an application trying to process the messages. Instead, Windows generates an initial *WM_MOUSEMOVE* message, then sets a flag so further messages of that type are generated only periodically, as long as the mouse continues to move. The application receives a stream of *WM_MOUSEMOVE* messages, but not the flood it might. It can reasonably process the messages, as we'll see.

After a brief discussion of other aspects of mouse messages, we'll develop the mouse message handlers that mouse drawing requires.

Windows can generate other mouse-related messages besides the three I've mentioned. The two most important kinds are double-click messages and nonclient mouse messages. We won't be working much with these messages in the MyDraw application in this book, but they're still important for you to know about.

Double-click messages

Double-click messages tell you when the user has clicked the mouse twice in rapid succession—a double-click. Double-clicking is used to quickly initiate an action, such as opening a folder in Windows Explorer. That application interprets the first click as selecting the folder. On the second click, the application then carries out the most logical operation—in this case, opening the folder. When the user double-clicks, Windows sends the application a *WM_LBUTTONDBLCLK* message. If the user double-clicks the right mouse button instead of the left, the message is *WM_RBUTTONDBLCLK*. (There are also messages for a middle mouse button. Nowadays, those are used primarily for the "wheel" on the Microsoft IntelliMouse, which makes long scrolls much easier. You can enable the wheel by creating handlers for these messages.)

Two other factors affect double-click handling. First, the user can specify how far apart the clicks must come, using the Mouse Properties dialog box available in the Windows Control Panel. Windows uses that value to determine when to send double-click messages. Mostly, this doesn't affect your code. The second factor affecting double-clicks is that the window in which the double-click occurs must be able to accept double-clicks. A window can accept double-clicks if the style *CS_DBLCLKS* is included in its window styles. Windows created with most of the Microsoft Foundation Class Library 6.0 (MFC) window and view classes include this style, so you'll seldom need to be concerned with this requirement. But if you ever derive a window class directly from class *CWnd* and you want it to accept double-clicks, you must specify the style.

> **NOTE** Users of multibutton mouse devices can change which button is the primary button (usually the left button) and which is secondary (usually the right button). In this book, I use "left" when I mean the primary mouse button and "right" when I mean the secondary button.

Nonclient mouse messages

Windows sends out mouse-related messages not only for clicks and mouse movements inside a window's client area but also for mouse actions on the window's nonclient parts: the title bar; the Close, Minimize, and Maximize buttons; the scroll bars; the system menu icon; and the window borders. In most cases, you won't need to worry about nonclient mouse messages, but you should know that you can use them if you need them. For example, you might want to take some special action if the user double-clicks the title bar of your application. You can create a handler for a nonclient mouse message with WizardBar or ClassWizard, just as you would for any other message. Nonclient versions of the mouse messages listed earlier have the form WM_NC*XXX*. Examples are *WM_NCLBUTTONDOWN* and *WM_NCRBUTTONDBLCLK*.

Mouse Message Handlers

Windows keeps your application apprised of mouse actions, but you need to take advantage of those messages. To do so, you write handlers for the messages. The following sections summarize the process.

Starting the drawing

When the mouse button goes down, you want to start drawing. So you write an *OnLButtonDown* handler mapped to the *WM_LBUTTONDOWN* message. In the handler, you note where the mouse was when the button went down. (Windows gives you that information.) In MyDraw, we store that point as the coordinates of one corner of our shape's bounding rectangle. We won't be able to complete the shape, though, until the *WM_LBUTTONUP* message arrives, which lets us define a second corner.

Ending the drawing

On receiving a *WM_LBUTTONUP* message, handled with an *OnLButtonUp* handler, we note where the mouse is and store that point as the opposite corner of the shape's bounding rectangle. Now, if we know what type of shape to draw, we have enough information. At that point, we draw the final rectangle or ellipse.

Supplying visual feedback during drawing

There's one further complication, which we'll explore more as we develop the handler functions for the three key mouse messages. As the user drags the mouse while drawing, we want to display some visual feedback to guide the drawing. Without it, the user is just guessing what the shape will look like. So each time we receive a *WM_MOUSEMOVE* message, our *OnMouseMove* handler draws the outline of the shape—showing where the shape would be, and how big, if the user were to release the mouse button at that moment. On the next *WM_MOUSEMOVE* message, we erase the shape drawn for the previous message, note where the mouse is now, and draw a new outline there. As the user moves the mouse, the shape outline appears to stretch like a rubberband, hence the technique is called *rubberbanding*.

Adding the Mouse Message Handlers

Now let's add the handlers to MyDraw. We'll test them in a simple way, then add the code that does the drawing and rubberbanding.

Try it now

With your MyDraw project open, add handlers for the three main mouse-related messages: *WM_LBUTTONDOWN*, *WM_MOUSEMOVE*, and *WM_LBUTTONUP*. These handlers belong to the view class, so make sure class *CMyDrawView* is selected in WizardBar's (or ClassWizard's) Class box. These handlers are a little different from the command handlers we've added before, so read on for some guidance.

In Chapter 10, you created handlers for the *WM_COMMAND* message. To do that in WizardBar, you clicked a command ID in the Class Or Object To Handle box. To do the same thing in ClassWizard, you clicked a command ID in the Object IDs box. Adding a handler for any other Windows message besides *WM_COMMAND* is slightly different. Instead of clicking a command ID in WizardBar or ClassWizard, you click a Windows message name. In WizardBar, the messages are listed in the New Windows Messages/Events box. In ClassWizard, the messages are listed in the Messages box. Otherwise, the procedure for adding a message handler is similar to that for *WM_COMMAND*—see "Add the *OnToolRectangle* and *OnToolEllipse* command handlers" in Chapter 10. (For a Windows message other than *WM_COMMAND*, select the class name in the Class Or Object To Handle box, and then the message name in the New Windows Messages/Events box.) Rather than repeating the instructions for *WM_COMMAND* in detail, I'll just remind you that you're creating handlers for the following three Windows messages:

- *WM_LBUTTONDOWN*

- *WM_MOUSEMOVE*

- *WM_LBUTTONUP*

When you finish, you'll have three function bodies in the file DrawVw.cpp, three member function prototypes in the *CMyDrawView* class declaration in the file DrawVw.h, and three messagemap entries near the top of the file DrawVw.cpp. Remember that the message map entries for *WM_COM-MANDs* will look different from those for other Windows messages. I'll say more about this later.

Here's what one of the three handlers looks like without any code added:

```
void CMyDrawView::OnLButtonDown(UINT nFlags, CPoint point)
{
    // TODO: Add your message handler code here and/or call default

    CView::OnLButtonDown(nFlags, point);
}
```

Calling the base class

So far, the handlers are just stubs—almost-empty function bodies. They do nothing except call their base class counterparts in class *CView*, thus passing the message up the class hierarchy in search of a handler that will do more. Recall that class *CView* is the base class of our class *CMyDraw-View*. *CView* or its base class, *CWnd*, has its own versions of these three handlers, which do default processing when they're called. Why does the wizard lead us to call them in our overriding versions in *CMyDrawView*? Because in most circumstances, we need to let MFC and Windows do certain default actions either before or after we perform our own actions. The Visual C++ wizards are helpful enough to add these base class calls when we create the handlers, and the TODO comment helps you see where to place your code in relation to the base class call—before it or after it.

There are cases in which you can omit the base class call, but you should carefully examine the base class functions (and any functions they call) in the MFC source code before you make that decision. Be sure you don't cut off some action that's essential to your program's functioning. (See the Appendix for guidance on finding what you're looking for in the MFC source code.)

New message map macros

Besides the three mouse message handler bodies, we get corresponding message map entries. Here's our view class message map, slightly abbreviated, containing three new entries for the mouse message handlers:

```
BEGIN_MESSAGE_MAP(CMyDrawView, CView)
    //{{AFX_MSG_MAP(CMyDrawView)
    ON_COMMAND(ID_TOOL_RECTANGLE, OnToolRectangle)
    ON_COMMAND(ID_TOOL_ELLIPSE, OnToolEllipse)
```

(continued)

335

```
        ON_WM_LBUTTONDOWN( )
        ON_WM_MOUSEMOVE( )
        ON_WM_LBUTTONUP( )
        //}}AFX_MSG_MAP
        // Standard printing commands
          ⋮
END_MESSAGE_MAP( )
```

We've gotten used to the *ON_COMMAND* macro in message map entries for our menu command handlers. Now, though, three new MFC macros are used instead:

- *ON_WM_LBUTTONDOWN*

- *ON_WM_MOUSEMOVE*

- *ON_WM_LBUTTONUP*

ON_COMMAND is a special case. It manages the *WM_COMMAND* message, which Windows sends for a variety of different commands. Each menu item issues a different command, with a unique command ID. The *ON_COMMAND* macro is set up to accept those command IDs.

Nearly all other Windows messages, however, are processed in the message map with unique MFC macros, one per message. The macro name takes the form of the message name with *ON_* attached to the front: *ON_WM_MOUSEMOVE*. For a complete reference listing all of the macros with all of their corresponding handler prototypes, check the Help index for *message maps* and double-click the third topic listed in the Topics Found dialog box, titled "Message Maps."

Testing the Handlers with *AfxMessageBox*

Let's examine the behavior of the three mouse message handlers.

Try it now

Test the three mouse message handlers, one at a time:

1. In the *OnMouseMove* handler, add a call to the *AfxMessageBox* global function, as this example shows:

```
void CMouseView::OnMouseMove(UINT nFlags, CPoint point)
{
    // TODO: Add your message handler code here...
    AfxMessageBox("In OnMouseMove");
    CView::OnMouseMove(nFlags, point);
}
```

AfxMessageBox is a handy substitute for *CWnd::MessageBox*.
Unlike *MessageBox*, you can call *AfxMessageBox* anywhere in
your program. For more information, check the Help index for
AfxMessageBox.

2. To test the handler, build and run MyDraw. As soon as you move
   the mouse, the message box appears—and won't go away. To get out
   of this situation, press Ctrl+Alt+Delete. This displays the Close Program dialog box. Select "Untitled – MyDraw" and click End Task.
   When prompted, click End Task again to shut down MyDraw and
   return to Visual C++. I'll explain why the message box wouldn't go
   away in a moment.

3. Test the other two handlers as follows: Remove the *AfxMessageBox*
   call from *OnMouseMove* and add *AfxMessageBox* calls to both
   OnLButtonDown and *OnLButtonUp*. In your *AfxMessageBox* calls,
   use the strings "In OnLButtonDown" and "In OnLButtonUp," respectively. Build and run MyDraw. Click in the client area. What
   happens? Comment out the *AfxMessageBox* call in *OnLButton-
   Down*, build, run, and click again. What happens this time?

What have we learned about mouse message handlers?

You can see that MFC calls *OnMouseMove* over and over as the mouse
moves. The way we've written the *OnMouseMove* handler, MyDraw never
gets a chance to process mouse click messages, because as it processes the
first mouse move message, it displays a modal message box. We must respond to the message box before anything else can happen. Any other
mouse move messages are lost. (Note that the mouse button doesn't need
to be pressed for Windows to send mouse move messages as the mouse
pointer moves around. They're sent whether the button is down or not.)

When we move the *AfxMessageBox* calls to the other two mouse message handlers, MyDraw can only handle the *WM_LBUTTONDOWN* message—the first mouse button message that is sent. Again, a modal message box prevents processing the *WM_LBUTTONUP* message. It's displayed in *OnLButtonDown*, and because we have to respond to it, the button-up message is lost.

Once we remove the message box call from *OnLButtonDown*, we see the message box from *OnLButtonUp* when we release the mouse button.

While you're trying out *OnLButtonUp*, drag the mouse out of the window altogether and release it there. What happens? That's just a hint of another issue we'll have to deal with in our mouse message handling code. When the mouse is released outside the window, there's no *WM_LBUTTONUP* message to match the previous *WM_LBUTTONDOWN* message.

IP Instead of passing hard-coded strings to *AfxMessageBox*, or using them elsewhere in your program, consider using string resources. Check the Help index for *string editor*. In *AfxMessageBox* calls, pass the string resource ID instead of a hard-coded string: *AfxMessageBox(IDS_MYSTRING)*. Using string resources is good coding practice, and it makes applications easier to localize.

The MyDraw Application

By now you should be getting a feeling for how to work in Visual C++. You understand the layout of C++ classes, and MFC classes in particular. You know how to use WizardBar to locate a function's definition or its prototype, or to add new member functions to a class. You know how to use the Source Code editor. You can use at least two resource editors. And you know how to build and run your program. As we go along, I'll be giving you less guidance on the details of these familiar activities. Instead, I'll present the code and explain the elements you need to add to your version of MyDraw to catch up with my latest version.

Bringing MyDraw Up-To-Date

The following sections describe what you need to do to your MyDraw files to bring them up to date for step 2. Add the boldface code lines, and remove the items listed in "Removing old code" on page 346.

Creating the *Shape* data type

Because we're now going to store individual shapes so we can redraw all shapes, not just the latest one, we need a data type to contain shape data. We'll use an array for the next couple of chapters, but there are better choices, such as one of MFC's collection classes. We'll use one of those classes starting in Chapter 14.

Try it now

Add the following *Shape struct* and the constant *SHPS_MAX* to the file DrawVw.h, just below the *ShpType* enumeration.

```
    ⋮
enum ShpType
{
    shpRectangle,
    shpEllipse
};

// A simple shape class
struct Shape
{
    CRect m_boxShape;        // Bounding rectangle
    ShpType m_typeShape;     // Rectangle, ellipse, etc.
};

// Number of shapes to store at a time
const int SHPS_MAX = 1000;

class CMyDrawView : public Cview
    ⋮
```

Replacing view class data members

We'll also need a completely new group of view class data members to allow us to store the individual shapes.

 Try it now

Add and initialize the new view class data members:

1. Add the following data members to the public attributes section of the view class declaration in DrawVw.h (replacing the old data members *m_boxShape* and *m_typeShape*):

```
    ⋮
// Attributes
public:
    CMyDrawDoc* GetDocument();
    ShpType m_typeNext;        // Type of shape to draw next
    Shape m_shpTemp;           // The current shape being drawn
    Shape m_arShps[SHPS_MAX];  // Array of drawn shapes
    int m_countShapes;         // Number of shapes drawn so far
    bool m_bCaptured;          // True if mouse has been captured
    CBrush* m_pBrushOld;       // Store brush for interior of shapes
```

We'll use *m_shpTemp* to build up the attributes of a shape as it's being drawn. When the shape is finished, we'll add it to the *m_arShps* array and increment the count of shapes created, *m_countShapes*. You'll see how the other data members are used as we go along.

2. Initialize the data members in the view class constructor, *CMyDraw-View::CMyDrawView*, in the file DrawVw.cpp (replacing any previous code):

```
CMyDrawView::CMyDrawView()
{
    // TODO: add construction code here
    m_typeNext = shpRectangle;
    m_bCaptured = false;
    m_pBrushOld = NULL;
    m_countShapes = 0;
}
```

One thing we have replaced here is the call to the *srand* run-time function, which we added in Chapter 10. We don't need any of the randomizing code anymore.

Rewriting the *OnDraw* function

The view's *OnDraw* function looks a bit different. Instead of drawing one shape, it now draws all shapes in the document's *m_arShps* array, using a *for* loop.

Try it now

Replace the old *OnDraw* with this one:

```
void CMyDrawView::OnDraw(CDC* pDC)
{
    CMyDrawDoc* pDoc = GetDocument();
    ASSERT_VALID(pDoc);

    // TODO: add draw code for native data here
    SetPenBrush(pDC);
    for(int nShp = 0; nShp < m_countShapes; nShp++)
    {
        // Draw
        ASSERT(m_arShps[nShp].m_typeShape == shpRectangle ||
                m_arShps[nShp].m_typeShape == shpEllipse);

        switch(m_arShps[nShp].m_typeShape)
        {
        case shpRectangle:
            pDC->Rectangle(m_arShps[nShp].m_boxShape);
            break;
        case shpEllipse:
            pDC->Ellipse(m_arShps[nShp].m_boxShape);
            break;
        // Add other shape tools here.
        default: ;
        }
    }
    // Restore DC's old attributes.
    ResetPenBrush(pDC);
}
```

First we call a helper function, *SetPenBrush*, to make some changes in *OnDraw's* device context. At the end, we call a companion function, *ResetPenBrush*, to restore the old device context attributes. Notice that in each case, we pass a pointer to the device context. I'll introduce the helper functions shortly.

To draw all of the shapes in the array, we loop from 0 through *m_count Shapes − 1*. Each time through the loop, we use the following array-access expression in the switch statement to determine the type of the shape stored in the current array element (at index *nShp*):

```
m_arShps[nShp].m_typeShape
```

Then we switch on that *ShpType* value. Inside the *switch* statement, we draw either a rectangle or an ellipse. (Note that using pointer arithmetic in *OnDraw* would be more efficient. See Chapter 3 for a review of using pointer arithmetic to walk through an array.)

To draw individual shapes, we call one of two class *CDC* member functions, *Rectangle* or *Ellipse,* both familiar from Chapter 10. We pass to this function the bounding rectangle of the shape to draw, obtained with this array-access expression:

```
m_arShps[nShp].m_boxShape.
```

Keep in mind that *OnDraw* is drawing all the shapes in response to a *WM_PAINT* message. You get this message when something has happened that could damage the shapes drawn previously with the mouse. We'll get to mouse drawing shortly.

You'll notice that we're using lots of *switch* statements in MyDraw. That's something we worked hard to eliminate in Chapters 4 and 5 by designing successive versions of the *CShape* class. We'll return to *CShape* in Chapter 14 and streamline this code considerably.

Adding handlers for mouse commands

If you've been working along with me, you've already created the three mouse message handlers, but all you did in them was make calls to the *AfxMessageBox* function.

Try it now

Now it's time to add the real mouse drawing code.

1. Add code to make your *OnLButtonDown* handler look like this:

```
void CMyDrawView::OnLButtonDown(UINT nFlags, CPoint point)
{
    // TODO: Add your message handler code here...
    SetCapture();
    m_bCaptured = true;

    ASSERT(m_typeNext == shpRectangle || m_typeNext ==
        shpEllipse);
    m_shpTemp.m_typeShape = m_typeNext;

    // Store starting point - literally a point, initially
    //   (topLeft == botRight).
    m_shpTemp.m_boxShape.left =
        m_shpTemp.m_boxShape.right = point.x;
    m_shpTemp.m_boxShape.top =
        m_shpTemp.m_boxShape.bottom = point.y;

    CView::OnLButtonDown(nFlags, point);
}
```

2. Add code to make your *OnMouseMove* handler look like this:

```
void CMyDrawView::OnMouseMove(UINT nFlags, CPoint point)
{
    // TODO: Add your message handler code here...
    if(m_bCaptured)
    {
        CClientDC dc(this);

        // Erase previous rectangle first.
        InvertShape(&dc, m_shpTemp);

        // Store new temporary corner as bottom right.
        m_shpTemp.m_boxShape.bottom = point.y;
        m_shpTemp.m_boxShape.right = point.x;

        // Draw new rectangle (latest rubberbanded rectangle).
        InvertShape(&dc, m_shpTemp);
    }
    CView::OnMouseMove(nFlags, point);
}
```

3. Add code to make your *OnLButtonUp* handler look like this:

```
void CMyDrawView::OnLButtonUp(UINT nFlags, CPoint point)
{
    // TODO: Add your message handler code here...
    if(m_bCaptured)
    {
        ::ReleaseCapture();
        m_bCaptured = false;

        CClientDC dc(this);

        // Erase previous rubberband rectangle.
        InvertShape(&dc, m_shpTemp);

        // Set the botRight corner's final values.
        m_shpTemp.m_boxShape.right = point.x;
        m_shpTemp.m_boxShape.bottom = point.y;

        // Draw final rectangle.
        InvertShape(&dc, m_shpTemp, false);  // Draw

        // Put current Shape in array.
        m_arShps[m_countShapes] = m_shpTemp;
        m_countShapes++;
    }
    CView::OnLButtonUp(nFlags, point);
}
```

We'll look at what's going on in these handlers in a moment.

Adding drawing helper functions

We need to alter the device contexts that *OnDraw* and other drawing functions (including two of the mouse message handlers) use. We'll change the device context's default brush, and later the default pen. Add the following functions with the Add Member Function command on the WizardBar Action menu. (If you need a reminder for this procedure, see "Adding the *OnToolRectangle* and *OnToolEllipse* Command Handlers" in Chapter 10.)

Try it now

Since we need to make the same, or similar, device context alterations from several functions, we'll encapsulate the alterations in three helper functions:

1. Add the *SetPenBrush* helper function to the DrawVw.cpp file:

```
void CMyDrawView::SetPenBrush(CDC * pDC)
{
    ASSERT(pDC != NULL);
    // Make shape's interior empty (transparent).
    m_pBrushOld = (CBrush*)pDC->SelectStockObject(NULL_BRUSH);

    // Device context restored in companion function
    //   ResetPenBrush
}
```

2. Add the *ResetPenBrush* helper function:

```
void CMyDrawView::ResetPenBrush(CDC * pDC)
{
    ASSERT(pDC != NULL);
    // Restore previous pen and brush to device context after use.
    ASSERT(m_pBrushOld != NULL);
    pDC->SelectObject(m_pBrushOld);
    m_pBrushOld = NULL;
}
```

These functions will grow as we go along. I'll show you the third helper, *InvertShape*, a little later.

Don't forget to add the function prototype as well—which you'll get automatically if you use the Add Member Function command on the Wizard-Bar Action menu. These aren't message handlers, so there are no message map entries.

Rewriting the tool command handlers

In Chapter 10, the handlers for the *ID_TOOL_RECTANGLE* and *ID_TOOL_ELLIPSE* commands actually drew the shapes. Now all they do is specify what type of shape is to be drawn the next time the user draws with the mouse.

Try it now

Replace the code in your *OnToolRectangle* and *OnToolEllipse* handlers so they match the following code:

```
void CMyDrawView::OnToolRectangle()
{
    // TODO: Add your command handler code here
    m_typeNext = shpRectangle;
}

void CMyDrawView::OnToolEllipse()
{
    // TODO: Add your command handler code here
    m_typeNext = shpEllipse;
}
```

The handlers just set a viewclass data member to the selected shape type. We'll consult that data member any time we draw a new shape.

Adding update handlers for the tool commands

We also want to give the user a way to remember which shape type is in force (after having been selected on the menu). I'll soon explain how MFC applications do things like adding a check mark to a menu item.

Removing old code

Several items need to be removed from your MyDraw code, in addition to those items we've already replaced. Recall that MyDraw now lets the user draw with the mouse instead of drawing shapes at random locations.

Try it now

Remove the following items:

■ The two helper functions for generating random numbers: *Random-Coord* and *RandomRect*. Be sure to delete the function prototypes in file DrawVw.h as well as the function definitions in file Draw-Vw.cpp. There are no message map entries.

■ The *COORD_MAX* constant, from just above the random functions' definitions in DrawVw.cpp.

■ The two #*include* statements at the top of the DrawVw.cpp file for StdLib.h and Time.h.

Drawing in the Mouse Message Handlers

Let's look in greater detail at what's happening in all three phases of mouse drawing: starting to draw (*OnLButtonDown*), tracking mouse movements (*OnMouseMove*), and finishing a shape (*OnLButtonUp*).

Mouse button down: we start to draw

In MyDraw, we interpret a *WM_LBUTTONDOWN* message as the beginning of drawing. (Later, we'll discriminate between drawing a new shape and selecting an existing shape for editing.) At this point, when we receive the message that the mouse button is down, we take these steps:

■ *Capture* the mouse (discussed below).

■ Set the starting corner of the new shape, and the shape's type, based on the currently selected tool on the Tools menu.

■ See if our view's base class wants to do anything more with the message.

Capturing the mouse

Earlier in this chapter, in "Testing the Handlers with *AfxMessageBox*," we experimented with releasing the mouse button outside the window after pressing it inside. Here's what happened: When we pressed the mouse button inside the window, Windows sent the window a *WM_LBUTTONDOWN* message and MFC called our *OnLButtonDown* handler. As the mouse moved from that initial point, Windows sent us a stream of *WM_MOUSE-MOVE* messages and, for each, MFC called our *OnMouseMove* handler. But then an odd thing happened. Although our window received a button down message, it never received a matching *WM_LBUTTONUP* message. That's because when we released the button, the mouse was no longer over our window. The message went to some other window, if it went anywhere.

How can we deal with this problem? The solution is to *capture* the mouse with a call to the *CWnd::SetCapture* member function. This means that our window lays claim to a future *WM_LBUTTONUP* message, even if the mouse is no longer over our window. The mouse temporarily belongs to our window, until we release the capture with a call of the *ReleaseCapture* function. After that, another window can claim the mouse if it wants to. Of course, we don't want to keep the mouse captured for too long, and we can only capture it while the mouse button is being pressed anyway, so we maintain the capture only long enough to draw one shape. Then we recapture it the next time a new shape begins.

So that we can tell in other functions that we own the mouse, we set a flag variable, a view class data member called *m_bCaptured*, to *true*. Each of the other mouse handlers can then check that variable to see if drawing is still in progress.

Setting the starting corner of a shape

The following code (in *OnLButtonDown*) stores the shape type. Then it takes note of where the mouse was at the time the button was pressed (information that's available in the *point* parameter of *OnLButtonDown*), and stores that location.

```
m_shpTemp.m_typeShape = m_typeNext;

m_shpTemp.m_boxShape.left =
    m_shpTemp.m_boxShape.right = point.x;
m_shpTemp.m_boxShape.top =
    m_shpTemp.m_boxShape.bottom = point.y;
```

To build up the information needed for the current shape, we use *m_shp-Temp*, a *Shape* object whose data members store the shape's bounding rectangle and type.

At the outset, before the user has dragged the mouse at all, the shape is literally a single point. So we store that point as both the top left and bottom right corners of the bounding rectangle for *m_shpTemp*. (By the way, notice the chained assignments in the second and third lines of code. C++ allows this kind of assignment statement, which is more compact than listing each separate assignment on its own line.)

Mouse drag: tracking the mouse during drawing

As explained earlier in "Supplying Visual Feedback During Drawing," we draw—or rubberband—a temporary outline of the shape for each *WM_MOUSEMOVE* message, to provide visual feedback as the user drags the mouse. We've already set the upper left corner of the shape in *OnLButtonDown*, so in *OnMouseMove* we note the new mouse location and use that point as our new bottom right corner:

```
m_shpTemp.m_boxShape.bottom = point.y;
m_shpTemp.m_boxShape.right = point.x;
```

> **NOTE** If the user drags the mouse up and to the left, for example, the point we're storing as the "bottom right" corner is technically the top left corner. However, this discrepancy makes no difference in MyDraw, so we'll ignore it. MyDraw simply uses the two points stored in the *CRect* object to draw a rectangle, regardless of what we've named the points. The alternative would be to check our final rectangle for corners with oddball coordinates and swap them so they're correct.

The tricky part of *OnMouseMove* is that we must first erase the old shape, drawn for the previous *WM_MOUSEMOVE* message, and then draw the new shape in its place. It's time to learn how to erase something in Windows.

Erasing lines: the *R2_NOT* drawing mode

Normally, when we draw a line, rectangle, or other shape, we're setting the pixels of the shape from white to black (or sometimes to some other color). But Windows provides a variety of *drawing modes* that let you control exactly what drawing means. These modes specify a relationship between the *destination pixels* on the drawing surface and the *source pixels* of a pen or brush. Some modes concentrate on the destination, others on the source, and still others on both at once, blending or adjusting them in some way.

I'll give just one example of a drawing mode here—the one we'll use for erasing in MyDraw. For more information, check the Help index for *SetROP2*. That's the name of the class *CDC* member function that we'll use to set the drawing mode for erasing. The documentation for *SetROP2* lists the mode constants you can pass as parameters to *SetROP2*. "ROP" stands for *raster operation* and has to do with your computer's video hardware and display capabilities.

The drawing mode we'll use is *R2_NOT*. As you might guess, this applies the logical NOT operation to our drawing's destination pixels. That is, if we draw a rectangle where there was none before, *R2_NOT* causes white pixels to turn black (or colored, if some other color is in effect)—just as in ordinary drawing. But if we then redraw the same rectangle, where now there are black pixels on the drawing surface, *R2_NOT* causes those black (or colored) pixels to flip to white (or to any other color being used for the background). That is, it erases the lines of our previous rectangle. *R2_NOT* flips pixels.

The *InvertShape* helper function

Since MyDraw needs to draw and erase in both the mouse message handlers and the *OnDraw* member function, we encapsulate the actual erasing and drawing actions in our third helper function, *InvertShape*, a private member function of class *CMyDrawView*.

Try it now

Use the Add Member Function command to add the *InvertShape* member function. You're adding its prototype as well, since you are using WizardBar.

```
void CMyDrawView::InvertShape(CDC *pDC, Shape &s, bool bInvert)
{
    ASSERT(pDC != NULL);
    // Drawing mode is R2_NOT: black -> white, white -> black,
    //   colors -> inverse color.
    // If shape already drawn, this erases; else draws it.
    int nModeOld;
    if(bInvert)
    {
        nModeOld = pDC->SetROP2(R2_NOT);
    }
```

```
// Draw the shape (or erase it).
SetPenBrush(pDC);
switch(s.m_typeShape)
{
case shpRectangle: pDC->Rectangle(s.m_boxShape);
    break;
case shpEllipse: pDC->Ellipse(s.m_boxShape);
    break;
}
// Restore old values in DC.
if(bInvert)
{
    pDC->SetROP2(nModeOld);
}
ResetPenBrush(pDC);
}
```

> **IMPORTANT** When you add *InvertShape* with the Add Member Function
> command, specify its function prototype this way:
>
> InvertShape(CDC* pDC, Shape& s, bool bInvert = true);
>
> The = *true* expression specifies a default value for the *bInvert* parameter.
> The default value shows up in the function's prototype, but not in the
> heading of its function definition. Take a look at your results in the file
> DrawVw.h.

InvertShape sets the *R2_NOT* drawing mode with this line:

```
nModeOld = pDC->SetROP2(R2_NOT);
```

As usual when setting a new device context characteristic, we store the
old characteristic, then restore it at the end of the function. With *R2_NOT*
in effect, *InvertShape* uses a *switch* statement to draw the shape, or to
erase it if it already exists.

Successive calls to *InvertShape* for the same shape cause it to be drawn,
erased, drawn, and so on. For rubberbanding, we use two calls to *Invert-
Shape* in *OnMouseMove* to erase a previously drawn rubberband shape
and then draw a new one.

Notice that the *bInvert* parameter lets us call *InvertShape* either with inversion or without (normal drawing). Passing *false* in *bInvert* causes *InvertShape* not to set the *R2_ROP* drawing mode for that call. Because *bInvert* has a default value of *true*, we'll usually call it without specifying a third parameter at all, thus using the default.

Mouse button up: we finish drawing

OnLButtonUp is more complicated than the other two mouse message handlers. It must perform the following functions:

- Do nothing if the mouse is not currently captured.

- Release the capture if the mouse is captured.

- Erase the previous rubberbanded shape.

- Set the final corner of the shape's bounding rectangle.

- Draw the final shape.

- Add the new shape to an array of shapes and increment the shape count.

- Call the base class version of *OnLButtonUp* in case MFC needs to do some default processing.

Releasing the capture

If we captured the mouse earlier—as indicated by our Boolean flag variable, *m_bCaptured*—we need to release the capture after drawing a shape. Since MFC wraps the *SetCapture* function in class *CWnd* but doesn't wrap its counterpart, *ReleaseCapture*, we call the Win32 API version of the function, using the global scope resolution operator. (It's really only a convention to use ::, because there is no possible ambiguity between the Win32 version and an MFC version in this case. Try taking the operator out to see what happens.)

Drawing the final shape and adjusting its coordinates

After releasing the capture, we call *InvertShape* to erase the previous shape outline—the last rubberbanded shape. Then we set the final shape corner to the mouse location that *OnLButtonUp* receives in its *point* parameter and draw the final shape, again with *InvertShape*. In this case, we pass *false* in *InvertShape's* final parameter, *bInvert*, so the shape is not drawn with *R2_NOT*:

```
InvertShape(&dc, m_shpTemp, false);
```

Storing the shape in an array

The *m_arShps* array is an array of *Shape* objects, where *Shape* is our simple struct with a couple of data members and no member functions.

```
struct Shape
{
    CRect m_boxShape;        // Bounding rectangle
    ShpType m_typeShape;     // Rectangle, ellipse, etc.
};
```

The array declaration looks like this:

```
Shape m_arShps[SHPS_MAX]; // Array of drawn shapes
```

where *SHPS_MAX* is initially set to 1,000. The array can thus store up to 1,000 *Shape* objects.

Using the array

In declaring the array as I did in MyDraw, I've set the constant *SHPS_MAX* to 1,000. Each time the user draws a shape, we add it to the next array element and increment *m_countShapes*. I'll have more to say about the limitations of the array in Chapter 13, and in Chapter 14 we'll replace it with a better data structure. We'll also start using pointers to shapes there.

Checkmarking the Selected Drawing Tool: Updating Menus

Clicking an item on the Tools menu now determines not only what the next shape will be, but also what all future shapes will be until the user changes tools again. Because of that, it would be helpful to put a check mark next to the current tool on the menu. That would let users open the Tools menu to see which tool is selected.

Putting a check mark beside a particular menu item (and removing one from another item) turns out to be a specific example of a more general operation: keeping MyDraw's menus synchronized with program conditions.

Take a look at the menus in Visual C++, for instance. Some menu items are dimmed (disabled and unavailable) at any given time. As program conditions change, Visual C++ updates the menus accordingly. Some commands might be disabled or enabled. Menu items might be checked or unchecked, bulleted or unbulleted. Sometimes the text of a menu item will change. For example, the Undo command in Visual C++ changes its caption from "Undo *x*" to "Redo *x*," where *x* describes the command last done or undone.

Update handlers

MFC makes it ridiculously easy to update menu items in all of the ways I just described. Simply create an *ON_UPDATE_COMMAND_UI* handler for the menu item's command ID—just as you created the original command handler itself. Here's an example from MyDraw: an update handler that checkmarks the Rectangle command on the Tools menu if the current tool has been set to *shpRectangle*. I'll show you how to add the two update handlers in a moment, in "Adding an update handler."

```
void CMyDrawView::OnUpdateToolRectangle(CCmdUI* pCmdUI)
{
    // TODO: Add your command update UI handler code here
    pCmdUI->SetCheck(m_typeNext == shpRectangle);
}
```

This function uses a pointer to an object of class *CCmdUI* to call its *SetCheck* member function. *SetCheck* puts a check mark beside the Rectangle command on the Tools menu if a Boolean condition evaluates to true. The condition in this case tests whether the view class data member *m_typeNext* is equal to the enumeration constant *shpRectangle*. If the condition is not true, the call removes a check mark if one was already there.

But when is *OnUpdateToolRectangle* called? Every time the user clicks the Tools menu, MFC calls the update handlers for any commands on the menu that have handlers. This occurs between the time the user clicks the Tools menu and the time the menu drops down. So by the time the menu opens, its items have been appropriately updated—provided we've supplied the update handlers.

Notice too that *OnUpdateToolRectangle* and *OnUpdateToolEllipse* work together. The data member *m_typeNext* can have only one value at a time, so the condition for *SetCheck* is going to be true in one of the update handlers and false in the other. Thus we checkmark one menu command and uncheckmark the other.

Class *CCmdUI*

When MFC calls your update handler, it passes a pointer to an object of MFC class *CCmdUI*. This object is associated with a particular user interface object, such as one of these items:

- A menu command
- A toolbar button
- A status bar pane
- A control on an MFC dialog bar (a toolbar that can contain any control that a dialog box can contain, not just buttons)

Class *CCmdUI* provides an abstraction that stands in for all of these different types of user interface (UI) objects. In fact, the same update handler can handle updating several user interface objects, provided they all have the same command ID. This means, for example, that you can write one update handler for a menu command and its counterpart button on a toolbar. Both will be updated properly. (MFC updates toolbars during idle time, when nothing else is happening in the program, but it calls the same update handlers as those used for a corresponding menu command.)

The *CCmdUI* class has several useful members, including *SetCheck*, *Enable*, *SetRadio*, and *SetText*. It also contains a pointer to the user interface object it represents, in case you need to access the object through the *CCmdUI* object. For more information, check the Help index for *CCmdUI*, and examine the class data members.

Adding an update handler

You can use WizardBar or ClassWizard to add an update handler for a user interface object, such as one of the items in the bulleted list above. I'll give the WizardBar procedure here.

1. On the WizardBar Action menu, click Add Windows Message Handler. This opens the New Windows Message And Event Handlers dialog box.

2. In the Class Or Object To Handle box, click the command ID for which you want an update handler—in this case either ON_TOOL_RECTANGLE or ON_TOOL_ELLIPSE.

3. In the New Windows Messages/Events box, click UPDATE_COMMAND_UI.

4. Click Add And Edit. Add And Edit takes you to the handler so you can write code immediately.

5. In the Add Member Function dialog box, click OK to accept the suggested handler function name.

Try it now

Use WizardBar to Add the update handlers *OnUpdateToolRectangle* and *OnUpdateToolEllipse* to MyDraw. Your code should look like this:

```
void CMyDrawView::OnUpdateToolRectangle(CCmdUI* pCmdUI)
{
    // TODO: Add your command update UI handler code here
    pCmdUI->SetCheck(m_typeNext == shpRectangle);
}

void CMyDrawView::OnUpdateToolEllipse(CCmdUI* pCmdUI)
{
    // TODO: Add your command update UI handler code here
    pCmdUI->SetCheck(m_typeNext == shpEllipse);
}
```

Making the Shapes Transparent

Earlier we noted that by default our shapes have an opaque interior. Thus, if you draw a new shape over an old one, the old one is hidden. Try it. That might actually be your preference, but if you'd rather have shapes with transparent interiors, this section describes how to make them so. And in keeping with this chapter's theme, we'll let the user decide whether a given shape is transparent or not.

We haven't discussed the *SetPenBrush* helper function yet. That's where we'll take care of specifying whether the shape is transparent or opaque. We'll also use a companion function, *ResetPenBrush*, to restore the device context when we finish drawing the shape. You added *SetPenBrush* earlier in this chapter in the section "Adding drawing helper functions." Here it is again, and we'll add more to it in the next chapter.

Try it now

Now add the boldface lines shown here:

```
void CMyDrawView::SetPenBrush(CDC * pDC)
{
    ASSERT(pDC != NULL);
    // Make shape's interior empty (transparent)
    if(m_bTransparent)
    {
        m_pBrushOld = (CBrush*)pDC->SelectStockObject(NULL_BRUSH);
    }
    else
    {
        m_pBrushOld = (CBrush*)pDC->SelectStockObject(WHITE_BRUSH);
    }
    ASSERT(m_pBrushOld != NULL);

    // Device context restored in companion function
    //   ResetPenBrush
}
```

SetPenBrush uses the *CDC* member function *SelectStockObject* to select a special brush into the device context, either *NULL_BRUSH* or *WHITE_BRUSH*. These brushes are among the "stock objects" that Windows keeps on hand for quick selection—objects that programmers use again and again. *NULL_BRUSH* specifies a brush that paints nothing—it paints a transparent background, in other words. *SelectStockObject* returns a pointer to an object of the *CGdiObject* class, the base class of *CBrush*, so we have to cast the returned pointer to the correct type. We store that pointer in a view class data member, *m_pBrushOld*, because we'll be restoring the device context in a separate helper function, *Reset-PenBrush*. (As with *SetPenBrush*, you added this code earlier in this chapter in the section titled "Adding drawing helper functions.")

Of course, we only select the null brush if the user has chosen to make shape interiors transparent, hence the *if* statement. I'll explain the Boolean data member *m_bTransparent* in a moment.

We call *SetPenBrush* and *ResetPenBrush* from *OnDraw* as well as from *InvertShape*. That's why I've made them helper functions.

We'll need a few more things to complete our transparency feature.

Try it now

Make the following changes:

1. Add the *m_bTransparent* data member to the view class in the public attributes.

   ```
   bool m_bTransparent;      // True if Transparent selected
   ```

2. Initialize *m_bTransparent* in the view class constructor.

   ```
   m_bTransparent = true;
   ```

3. Add a Transparent command to the Tools menu. Use the letter *T* for the menu's mnemonic and *ID_TOOL_TRANSPARENT* for the command ID. Also add a separator line to separate the Transparent command from the two shape tool commands. Then double-click the new-item box at the bottom of the Tools menu, click the Separator box in the Properties window that appears, and press Return. Add an accelerator for the Transparent command if you like.

4. Add a command handler, *OnToolTransparent*, using the Add Windows Message Handler command. The function should look like this:

   ```
   void CMyDrawView::OnToolTransparent()
   {
       // TODO: Add your command handler code here
       m_bTransparent = !m_bTransparent;
   }
   ```

   The command handler toggles *m_bTransparent* between *true* and *false*. If it was *true*, it's set to *false* (turned off). If it was *false*, it's set to *true* (turned on).

5. Add a command update handler, *OnUpdateToolTransparent*. The function should look like this:

```
void CMyDrawView::OnUpdateToolTransparent(CCmdUI* pCmdUI)
{
    // TODO: Add your command update UI handler code here
    pCmdUI->SetCheck(m_bTransparent);
}
```

The Transparent menu item gets a check mark if *m_bTransparent* is *true*. Otherwise, the check mark is removed.

Fixing a final transparency problem

There's still a problem with our transparency code. If you hide MyDraw's window and then redisplay it, the *OnDraw* function redraws the shapes using the current value of *m_bTransparent* in the view. That value might be the appropriate value for drawing some shapes but not others. Some transparent shapes could become opaque, or some opaque shapes could become transparent. The solution is to give each shape a data member, *m_bTransparent*, that stores the transparency state of that shape. Then we use each shape's transparency information when we redraw the shape.

Try it now

Add individual transparency to the shapes.

1. In the declaration of class *Shape*, in the file DrawVw.h, add a transparency data member as follows:

```
    ⋮
struct Shape
{
    CRect m_boxShape;        // Bounding rectangle
    ShpType m_typeShape;     // Rectangle, ellipse, etc.
    bool m_bTransparent;
};
    ⋮
```

2. Add a transparency parameter to the *SetPenBrush* function. Be sure to add it in both the function prototype (in DrawVw.h) and the heading of the function definition (in DrawVw.cpp).

```
void SetPenBrush(CDC* pDC, bool bTransparent);
```

3. Inside *SetPenBrush*, in the *if* statement, change *m_bTransparent* to *bTransparent*.

```
if(bTransparent) ...
```

4. In the *OnDraw* function, move the calls to *SetPenBrush* and *Reset-PenBrush* inside the *for* loop. (Be sure to move the function, rather than simply adding another call.)

```
   ⋮
for(int nShp = 0; nShp < m_countShapes; nShp++)
{
    // Draw
    ASSERT(m_arShps[nShp].m_typeShape == shpRectangle ||
           m_arShps[nShp].m_typeShape == shpEllipse);
    SetPenBrush(pDC);

    switch(m_arShps[nShp].m_typeShape)
    ⋮
    default: ;
    }
    // Restore DC's old attributes.
    ResetPenBrush(pDC);
}
```

5. Find all calls to *SetPenBrush* in DrawVw.cpp and add the appropriate transparency parameter.

In *OnDraw*,

```
SetPenBrush(pDC, m_arShps[nShp].m_bTransparent);
```

In *InvertShape*,

```
SetPenBrush(pDC, s.m_bTransparent);
```

In *OnDraw*, you pass the transparency of the shape at the current array index, *nShp*. In *InvertShape*, you pass the transparency of the shape in the *s* parameter to *InvertShape*. The idea is to pass the transparency of an individual shape.

6. In *OnLButtonDown*, add a line that initializes the newly created shape with its transparency.

```
    ⋮
    ASSERT(m_typeNext == shpRectangle || m_typeNext == shpEllipse);
    m_shpTemp.m_typeShape = m_typeNext;
    m_shpTemp.m_bTransparent = m_bTransparent;
    ⋮
```

Figure 11-1 shows MyDraw with several shapes drawn. Notice the mixture of transparent and opaque interiors. Remember that opaque interiors are painted with the default white background brush. With some extra work, we could allow users to fill shapes with any color they like.

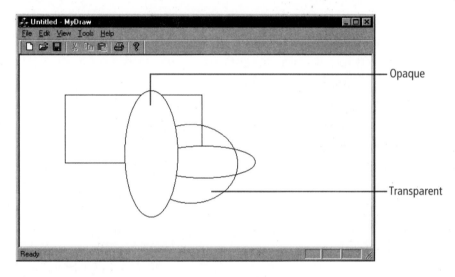

Figure 11-1.   *MyDraw with a transparent shape and several opaque shapes.*

Try It Yourself

Try your hand at the following extra-credit exercises. My solutions are part of MyDrawF in the /learnvcn/Chap21 folder in the companion code.

1. Erase the most recent shape.

Add an Erase command to the Edit menu, with *ID_EDIT_ERASE* as its command ID. Write a handler for the command that erases the most recently drawn shape. For now, a simple way to erase the shape is to decrement *m_countShapes*. The next time the user adds a shape, its data will overwrite the deleted shape in the array. Don't forget to force the view to repaint itself—call *CWnd::Invalidate* in your handler.

Don't forget an update handler.

2. **Erase all shapes with a double-click.**

Add a double-click handler to let the user delete all shapes previously drawn in the view. For now, one way to delete the shapes is to reset *m_countShapes* to 0. Whatever was previously stored in the array won't matter then. Don't forget to force the view to redraw itself.

Since it's considered bad form to have commands that the user can access only through some sleight-of-hand trick like a double-click, add an Erase All command to the Edit menu.

TIP Implement the menu command first. Then you can call the *OnEdit-EraseAll* handler from your double-click handler to do the dirty work. Don't forget an update handler for the menu command. When should the command be enabled, and when not?

What's Next?

We'll add another feature to MyDraw in Chapter 12—the ability to draw shapes in a user-specified color. We'll add a Color menu with a choice of ten colors, and we'll select a pen of the current color into the device context.

Shapes in Color

Now that the user can draw rectangles and ellipses at will with the mouse, let's add color. This chapter covers MyDraw step 3. The ability to draw colored shapes requires two main elements: a way for the user to select a color, and code that selects a pen of the proper color into the device context. When we finish step 3, a user will be able to select a color that will remain in effect for all future shapes until the user selects a different color. The color is applied to the shape's outline, not its interior. We won't add a fill color for the shape's interior. To allow users to select an outline color, we'll add a hierarchical Color menu to the Tools menu. A hierarchical menu cascades out of a higher-level menu, like the submenus on the Microsoft Windows 95 and Windows 98 Start menu. You'll also see how to handle a whole range of commands with a single command handler.

In Chapter 19, we'll augment our simple Color menu with a more sophisticated way for users to select colors: the Windows Color common dialog box, represented in Microsoft Foundation Class Library 6.0 (MFC) by class *CColorDialog*.

The RGB Color System

We'll specify the colors of our shapes with the *COLORREF* data type. *COLORREF* uses the RGB color system, which requires three values to specify each color: the intensity (meaning the amount) of red, the intensity of green, and the intensity of blue.

Creating a Color with the *RGB* Macro

To build up a *COLORREF* value, you use the *RGB* macro, a C++ macro that the preprocessor evaluates and replaces with the equivalent value when you build your application. The *RGB* macro takes three parameters: the intensities of red, green, and blue. You express these values as numbers (unsigned byte values) from 0 through 255. Table 12-1 shows the RGB values for a selection of common colors. Other colors can be generated by varying the intensities of the three RGB colors.

Color	Red Value	Green Value	Blue Value
Black	0	0	0
Blue	0	0	255
Green	0	255	0
Cyan	0	255	255
Red	255	0	0
Magenta	255	0	255
Yellow	255	255	0
White	255	255	255
Dark gray	128	128	128
Light gray	192	192	192

Table 12-1.   *RGB color values for some common colors.*

Working with Color

Besides setting the color of the device context's pen or brush, you can set the background color that the device context uses behind the things you draw, and you can set the color in which text is drawn. You use the class *CDC* member functions *GetBkColor*, *SetBkColor*, *GetTextColor*, and *SetTextColor*.

You can also use predefined constants with these functions to tell Windows to use the current system colors—whatever the user has set them to—as shown here for the text color and the window's background color. This is really the preferred approach, as it puts the user in control:

```
CDC dc;
dc.SetTextColor(COLOR_WINDOWTEXT);
dc.SetBkColor(COLOR_WINDOW);
```

You won't often need to dissect a *COLORREF* value into its red, green, and blue components. More likely, you'll obtain it and use it as is for some other purpose. If you do need to dissect the color, check the Help index for *GetRValue*, *GetGValue*, and *GetBValue*. These are other macros that return the red, green, or blue component of a *COLORREF*.

Adding the Hierarchical Color Menu

Figure 12-1 shows what our hierarchical Color menu will look like in the menu editor. (Go back to "Adding a Tools Menu to MyDraw" in Chapter 9 if you need a menu editing refresher.)

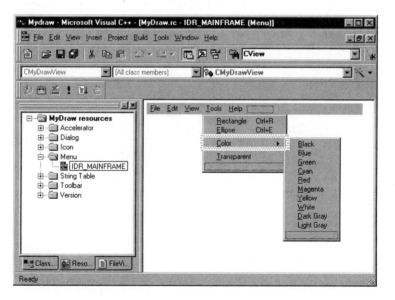

Figure 12-1. *The hierarchical color menu in MyDraw.*

 Try it now

Add a top-level Color menu in MyDraw's *IDR_MAINFRAME* menu resource, and then drag the menu onto the Tools menu.

1. With your MyDraw project open, use ResourceView to open the *IDR_MAINFRAME* menu resource.

2. Add a top-level menu named Color. Set the *C* in Color as the menu mnemonic.

3. To the Color menu, add the submenus listed in Table 12-2, along with their mnemonics, IDs, and status bar prompt strings. Everything that appears in Table 12-2 is user input that you type in the Properties window.

 ARNING   It's easy to make mistakes while creating the Color menu items, so here are some tips for your menu editing: Pin the Properties window by clicking the pushpin icon in the window's upper left corner. Create the menu items in one pass. As you create each item, type its Caption in the menu and it will appear in the Properties window. Then use Shift+Tab to tab backward from the Caption box to the ID box and type the ID. Tabbing forward to the ID box automatically creates an ID based on the menu names, but we want IDs of the form ID_COLOR_BLACK, not of the form ID_TOOLS_COLOR_BLACK. It also helps to use the mouse to click the next box in the Properties window that you want to work in rather than tabbing. If you get messages afterward about unknown IDs, see the file MenuEdit.doc in the \learnvcn\Chap12 folder in the companion code for guidance in fixing the problems.

Menu Text	Command ID	Status Bar Prompt
&Black	ID_COLOR_BLACK	Future shapes drawn in black (default)
B&lue	ID_COLOR_BLUE	Future shapes drawn in blue
&Green	ID_COLOR_GREEN	Future shapes drawn in green
&Cyan	ID_COLOR_CYAN	Future shapes drawn in cyan (blue-green)
&Red	ID_COLOR_RED	Future shapes drawn in red
&Magenta	ID_COLOR_MAGENTA	Future shapes drawn in magenta (purple)
&Yellow	ID_COLOR_YELLOW	Future shapes drawn in yellow
&White	ID_COLOR_WHITE	Future shapes drawn in white (may not show)
&Dark Gray	ID_COLOR_DKGRAY	Future shapes drawn in dark gray
L&ight Gray	ID_COLOR_LTGRAY	Future shapes drawn in light gray

Table 12-2.   *Values to enter in the Properties window for the Color menu items.*

4. Drag the finished Color menu onto the Tools menu. Place it below the separator under the Ellipse command and above the Transparent command.

For additional information about menu editing, check the Help index for *menu editor*.

Writing an Efficient Handler for the Color Menu Commands

Now that a Color menu exists, must we create ten separate command handlers for the ten colors on the menu? No, there's a more efficient way that uses a single handler for a *range* of commands. This works because the color command IDs form an unbroken sequence from *ID_COLOR_BLACK* (value 32795 on my machine) to *ID_COLOR_LTGRAY* (32804). (Remember that command IDs are simply constants that have assigned values. In this case, the values are assigned by the Microsoft Visual C++ Menu editor, and are contained in the file Resource.h.) The command ID is a way to capture the user's color choice, which we then translate into a color by using the ID to index an array of *COLORREF* values. Then we use the color from the array to create our pen. We'll get to all of that in "Translating color command IDs to RGB colors."

Neither ClassWizard nor WizardBar supports adding command range handlers, so you'll have to add the necessary code by hand. MFC supplies the *ON_COMMAND_RANGE* macro for the message map and specifies the form the function prototype needs to take. I'll show you where and how to add the code.

Try it now

Take the following steps to add a command range handler for the Color menu:

1. Add the function prototype to the view class declaration in the file DrawVw.h. The prototype belongs in the "Generated message map functions" section of the view class declaration. Make sure you place the prototype outside the *AFX_MSG* comments that bracket

the message handlers you add with the wizards, and remember to place them that way anytime you edit the message handlers by hand rather than with a wizard. Here's the prototype to add, shown in relation to the bracketing comments:

```
 ⋮
// Generated message map functions
protected:
//{{AFX_MSG...
 ⋮
//}}AFX_MSG...
afx_msg void OnToolColor(UINT nID);  // ON_COMMAND_RANGE handler
DECLARE_MESSAGE_MAP()
 ⋮
```

IMPORTANT If you create a handler with a wizard, always use the wizard to edit or delete it. Don't directly edit the handler elements between the *AFX_MSG* comments.

---

2. Add the message map entry near the beginning of file DrawVw.cpp, again outside the *AFX_MSG_MAP* comments that bracket entries made with the wizards. Here's the message map entry:

```
     ⋮
BEGIN_MESSAGE_MAP(CMyDrawView, CView)
    //{{AFX_MSG_MAP(CMyDrawView)
     ⋮
    //}}AFX_MSG_MAP
    ON_COMMAND_RANGE(ID_COLOR_BLACK, ID_COLOR_LTGRAY, OnToolColor)
    // Standard printing commands
    ON_COMMAND(ID_FILE_PRINT, CView::OnFilePrint)
    ON_COMMAND(ID_FILE_PRINT_DIRECT, CView::OnFilePrint)
    ON_COMMAND(ID_FILE_PRINT_PREVIEW, CView::OnFilePrintPreview)
END_MESSAGE_MAP()
     ⋮
```

3. Still working by hand, add the command range handler definition, with other message handlers in file DrawVw.cpp:

```
void CMyDrawView::OnToolColor(UINT nID)
{
    // Set the color for future shape drawing.
    m_nColorNext = nID;
}
```

The *OnToolColor* handler is easy to understand. The *nID* parameter contains the command ID of the menu command that caused the handler to be called. That's an ID from the range *ID_COLOR_BLACK* through *ID_COLOR_LTGRAY* that we specified in the *ON_COMMAND_RANGE* message map entry. We assign the value to a view class data member, *m_nColorNext*, which stores the color to use in drawing the next shape. We'll add *m_nColorNext* to the code a bit later.

Using the command range mechanism saves us writing ten separate handlers for the ten colors. That's efficiency, and we can do the same thing with the Color menu's update handler, as described in the next section.

Putting a Check Mark on the Color Menu

We checkmark the currently selected color on the Color menu just as we checkmarked the currently selected shape on the Tools menu, using an update handler.

In this case, because we're dealing with a range of ten colors, we need the update handler equivalent of our *ON_COMMAND_RANGE* handler *OnToolColor*. MFC supplies the *ON_COMMAND_UI_RANGE* macro for the message map.

Try it now

Add the handler function prototype, the message map entry, and the update handler function for updating the Color menu. As with the *ON_COMMAND_RANGE* handler, you'll have to add this code by hand. Be sure to add the prototype and message map entry outside the *AFX_MSG* comment brackets.

Here's the handler's prototype:

```
afx_msg void OnUpdateToolColor(CCmdUI* pCmdUI);
```

Here's the message map entry:

```
ON_UPDATE_COMMAND_UI_RANGE(ID_COLOR_BLACK, ID_COLOR_LTGRAY,
                                    OnUpdateToolColor)
```

And here's the handler's function definition:

```
void CMyDrawView::OnUpdateToolColor(CCmdUI* pCmdUI)
{
    // Check or uncheck all color menu items.
    // Check item if it's the currently selected color.
    // Uncheck all other colors.
    pCmdUI->SetCheck(pCmdUI->m_nID == m_nColorNext);
}
```

The update handler for the Color menu works much like the update handler for the Tools menu. It calls the *SetCheck* member function, and *SetCheck* either checkmarks or uncheckmarks the appropriate items based on the Boolean expression passed as its parameter. In this case, we obtain the command ID for the selected color and compare it to the current color stored in *m_nColorNext*. Since the update handler passes a pointer to a *CCmdUI* object, we have to learn the command ID indirectly, via *pCmdUI*'s *m_nID* member. The result is that the newly selected color is checkmarked on the menu, and the check mark is removed from the old color.

Drawing Shapes in Color

Now that we have the Color menu set up, it's time to add a little drawing code to use the current color. The following sections discuss the changes and show you what to do in your own MyDraw project.

Managing the Currently Selected Color

You should track the currently selected color, so that new shapes will be drawn in that color. The Color menu handler, *OnToolColor*, sets a new *m_nColorNext* data member to the ID of the color the user selects on the menu. Later in this chapter we'll be using that color to create a pen before drawing each shape.

Try it now

Add and initialize three new data members.

1. In the file DrawVw.h, add the following three new data members to the public Attributes section:

```
        ⋮
bool m_bTransparent;        // True if Transparent selected
UINT m_nColorNext;          // Store ID for color to simplify
                            //  updating menus
CPen* m_pPenOld;            // Pen for drawing shape outlines
CPen* m_pPenNew;            // Store pens we create
```

2. In the view constructor, *CMyDrawView::CMyDrawView* (in the file
   DrawVw.cpp), initialize the new data members:

```
m_nColorNext = ID_COLOR_BLACK;
m_pPenOld = NULL;
m_pPenNew = NULL;
```

Translating Color Command IDs to RGB Colors

Create a color table for translating color IDs like *ID_COLOR_BLACK* into
the corresponding RGB color. We need to specify an RGB color value (of
type *COLORREF*) when we create a pen for drawing, so we have to
translate our color command ID into an RGB value.

Try it now

Add the following array code just above the declaration of class
CMyDrawView in the file DrawVw.h:

```
// Array of actual colors, indexed
//   by CMyDrawView::m_nColorNext
static COLORREF arColors[10] =
{
    RGB(0,0,0),           // Black
    RGB(0,0,255),         // Blue
    RGB(0,255,0),         // Green
    RGB(0,255,255),       // Cyan
    RGB(255,0,0),         // Red
    RGB(255,0,255),       // Magenta
    RGB(255,255,0),       // Yellow
    RGB(255,255,255),     // White
    RGB(128,128,128),     // Dark gray
    RGB(192,192,192)      // Light gray
};
```

To specify a color for the pen, we index the *arColors* array with the
color command ID. Remembering that command IDs are really constants,

suppose we have the color *ID_COLOR_GREEN*. The following expression evaluates to the third element of the array:

```
arColors[ID_COLOR_GREEN - ID_COLOR_BLACK];   // RGB(0,255,0), green
```

This trick often beats the alternative of having to insert several identical *switch* statements in various parts of the program. It's called a table-driven solution.

Selecting a Pen of the Current Color

Select a pen of the current color into the device context, and reselect the old pen after drawing.

Try it now

You'll need to revise both *SetPenBrush* and *ResetPenBrush*, along with all calls to *SetPenBrush*.

1. Change the *SetPenBrush* member function to look like the following (don't forget to add the new *nColor* parameter):

```
void CMyDrawView::SetPenBrush(CDC *pDC, bool bTransparent,
                              UINT nColor)
{
    ASSERT(pDC != NULL);
    // Make shape's interior empty (transparent)
      if(bTransparent)
    {
        m_pBrushOld = (CBrush*)pDC->SelectStockObject(NULL_BRUSH);
    }
    else
    {
        m_pBrushOld = (CBrush*)pDC->SelectStockObject(WHITE_BRUSH);
    }
    ASSERT(m_pBrushOld != NULL);

    // Set up the pen.
    ASSERT(nColor - ID_COLOR_BLACK >= 0 &&
           nColor - ID_COLOR_BLACK <=
           (sizeof(arColors) / sizeof(arColors[0])));
    // Construct pen object on heap so we can clean it up after use
    m_pPenNew = new CPen();
```

```
    // Create the GDI pen & select it into the device context.
    m_pPenNew->CreatePen(PS_INSIDEFRAME, 0,
                            arColors[nColor - ID_COLOR_BLACK]);
    m_pPenOld = (CPen*)pDC->SelectObject(m_pPenNew);

    // Device context restored in companion function
    //   ResetPenBrush
}
```

We create an MFC *CPen* object on the heap (storing a pointer to it so we can later clean up the GDI pen resource), and then call its member function *CreatePen* to create a pen with the color specified by indexing our color array:

```
arColors[nColor - ID_COLOR_BLACK]
```

Note that we have to add the *nColor* parameter to the function, both in the *SetPenBrush* function definition (file DrawVw.cpp) and in the function prototype (file DrawVw.h).

We subtract *ID_COLOR_BLACK* from *nColor* to obtain a value within the index range of our color array: 0–9. When we created the Color menu, the menu editor assigned arbitrary numeric values to our color command IDs—in my case, they began with *ID_COLOR_BLACK* = 32795 and ran through *ID_COLOR_LTGRAY* = 32804. The numbers might be different on your machine. Just using the color ID to index the array won't work because the values aren't in the right range. But the subtraction corrects for that.

The *createPen* function takes three parameters: a style (such as *PS_INSIDEFRAME*), a pen width (such as 0), and a *COLORREF* value. The *PS_INSIDEFRAME* style causes our shape to be drawn completely inside the specified bounding rectangle. The often-used style *PS_SOLID*, if used with pens wider than one pixel, can cause a shape to protrude slightly outside the bounding rectangle because the bounding rectangle corresponds to the center of the pen, not the outer edge. For more information about pen styles, check the Help index for *CreatePen*. We specify a width of 0, resulting in a pen width of 1 pixel regardless of the device context's mapping mode.

2. Add the *nColor* parameter to the *SetPenBrush* prototype (file DrawVw.h). Change the prototype to look like this:

```
void SetPenBrush(CDC * pDC, bool bTransparent, UINT nColor);
```

3. Insert the boldface lines into the *ResetPenBrush* member function so that it looks like this:

```
void CMyDrawView::ResetPenBrush(CDC *pDC)
{
    ASSERT(pDC != NULL);
    // Restore previous pen and brush to device context after use
    ASSERT(m_pBrushOld != NULL);
    pDC->SelectObject(m_pBrushOld);
    pDC->SelectObject(m_pPenOld);
    // Our responsibility to delete the heap object
    delete m_pPenNew;
    m_pPenNew = NULL;
    m_pPenOld = NULL;
    m_pBrushOld = NULL;
}
```

In this step, we use the *m_pPenOld* data member to restore the old pen to the device context after drawing with a new one. We also have to call *delete* on the *m_pPenNew* data member. This destroys the C++ *CPen* object on the heap and releases the GDI pen object associated with it. Without this step, we'd keep using pens without returning them to GDI, and eventually we'd run out of pens. Color drawing would stop at that point, and eventually the program would probably crash. Try commenting out the *delete* call and see what happens.

4. In *OnDraw*, add the color parameter to the *SetPenBrush* call, as shown here:

```
void CMyDrawView::OnDraw(CDC* pDC)
{
    CMyDrawDoc* pDoc = GetDocument();
    ASSERT_VALID(pDoc);
    // TODO: add draw code for native data here
    for(int nShp = 0; nShp < m_countShapes; nShp++)
    {
        // Draw
        ASSERT(m_arShps[nShp].m_typeShape == shpRectangle ||
```

```
                m_arShps[nShp].m_typeShape == shpEllipse);
        SetPenBrush(pDC, m_arShps[nShp].m_bTransparent,
            m_arShps[nShp].m_nColorShape);
            ⋮
```

5. Add the new color parameter to the other call to *SetPenBrush* in *InvertShape*. Change the call to *SetPenBrush* to look like the following:

```
SetPenBrush(pDC, s.m_bTransparent, s.m_nColorShape);
```

Setting the Color of a New Shape

Each *Shape* object needs to store a new piece of information—the shape color—along with its bounding rectangle and shape type. We set the shape's color when we create it.

Try it now

Add a color data member to the *Shape* class and set the color of *m_shpTemp*, our *Shape*-in-progress, in *OnLButtonDown*.

1. Make the change to class *Shape* so that it looks like this:

```
// A simple Shape class
struct Shape
{
    CRect m_boxShape;
    ShpType m_typeShape;
    bool m_bTransparent;
    UINT m_nColorShape;
};
```

2. Then add the following line to *OnLButtonDown*:

```
void CMyDrawView::OnLButtonDown(UINT nFlags, CPoint point)
{
    // TODO: Add your message handler code here and/or...
    SetCapture();
    m_bCaptured = true;

    ASSERT(m_typeNext == shpRectangle || m_typeNext ==
        shpEllipse);
    m_shpTemp.m_typeShape = m_typeNext;
    m_shpTemp.m_bTransparent = m_bTransparent;
```

(continued)

```
    m_shpTemp.m_nColorShape = m_nColorNext;

    // Store starting point - literally a point, initially
    // (topLeft == botRight)
    m_shpTemp.m_boxShape.left =
        m_shpTemp.m_boxShape.right = point.x;
    m_shpTemp.m_boxShape.top =
        m_shpTemp.m_boxShape.bottom = point.y;

    CView::OnLButtonDown(nFlags, point);
}
```

The *m_nColorShape* data member of *m_shpTemp* is set to the current color—the color most recently selected on the Color menu.

Build and test the program. There you have it. You've successfully added color to MyDraw. You've also completed another step toward letting the user control the program through mouse drawing.

Try It Yourself

I'll give some exercises at the end of Chapter 13 that are also pertinent to this chapter. MyDraw needs to stay in its current state until we finish the debugging discussion in the next chapter.

What's Next?

MyDraw is beginning to look pretty good. But somewhere in that code there's an ugly bug. In Chapter 13, we'll explore the Visual C++ debugger and the techniques used to find, analyze, and fix the bug.

Debugging Your Mistakes

In this chapter, we'll chase down and fix a bug that I left in the code in Chapter 11. Then, in Chapter 14, we'll return to the main discussion of MyDraw. (This chapter doesn't count as a MyDraw step, because we aren't adding new functionality.)

This chapter includes the following broad subject areas:

- The Microsoft Visual C++ 6.0 debugger

- Debug vs. Release builds

- Finding a bug by using the debugger

- Analyzing a bug by using the debugger

- Fixing a bug

Besides the debugger, Visual C++ offers additional diagnostic facilities as part of the Microsoft Foundation Class Library 6.0 (MFC). These facilities help you track down problems, handle errors and exceptional conditions, and deal with memory leaks. I'll give you some pointers to information about these facilities at the end of the chapter.

The Visual C++ debugger is versatile and easy to use, but you have to learn a bit before it becomes easy. I'll assume that you haven't used a visual debugger like the one in Visual C++. Although my approach might seem like overkill, and you might understand the bug well before I finish describing it, this chapter is a debugger tutorial intended to cover as many key debugger features and techniques as possible. If debugging is familiar ground for you, skim the chapter.

Visual C++ Debugger Overview

When you run the Visual C++ debugger, the Build menu becomes the Debug menu, the Debug toolbar appears, and a list of debugger windows is enabled on the View menu (and on the Debug toolbar). One or more of the debugger's windows might be open already. Figure 13-1 shows the Debug menu and Figure 13-2 shows the toolbar.

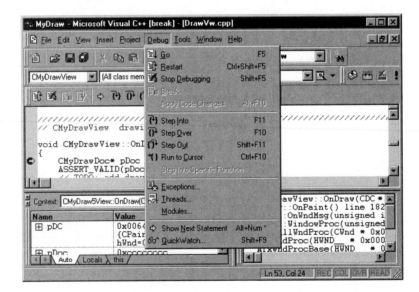

Figure 13-1. *The Debug menu.*

If you set any breakpoints in your source code files before running the debugger, your program runs to the first breakpoint it encounters and then suspends execution. (I'll describe breakpoints soon.) If you don't set any breakpoints, the program runs as usual, but you can suspend it at any time by choosing Break from the Debug menu. Then you can switch windows to view debugger information. You set breakpoints to control where the debugger pauses. Once the debugger pauses, you can do the following:

■ Examine variable values using the QuickWatch dialog box or the Watch or Variables windows. You can also use DataTips to examine variable values directly in the source code.

■ Trace the sequence of function calls in the Call Stack window.

■ Examine the contents of a particular memory address in the Memory window.

■ Examine machine register contents in the Registers window.

■ See your code translated to assembly language in the Disassembly window.

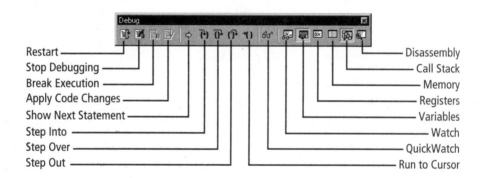

Figure 13-2.   *Buttons on the Debug toolbar.*

I won't describe the Registers window or the Disassembly window, but Help can teach you more about them. Check the Help index for *registers window* and select the topic "using during debugging." Check also for *disassembly window* and select the topic "using." The Visual C++ documentation covers special debugging situations, such as debugging MFC *ASSERT* statements and exceptions. Check the Help index for *debugging* and choose the subtopics "assertions" and "exceptions." From there, you can use the Locate button on the Help toolbar to see what else Help covers in adjacent topics.

Debug Builds vs. Release Builds

Before you run the debugger, you need to build a Debug version of your program. This adds symbolic debugging information to your compiled object files. You can run the debugger on a Release build, but you won't find that very useful.

A Release build omits the debugging information (and can also optimize the code for greater speed or smaller size, at least in the Professional and Enterprise editions of Visual C++). You perform a Release build once the program has been debugged. It's also useful to do a Release build from time to time during development, and it's important to test the Release build as well as the Debug build. Some bugs don't show up until a Release build is run.

Debug builds are the default in Visual C++, but if you have previously performed a Release build (without the symbolic debugging information), you'll need to select the "debug target." To do so, choose Set Active Configuration from the Build menu. In the Set Active Project Configuration dialog box, double-click the line containing "Win32 Debug." (If "Win32 Debug" is already selected in the dialog box, you're OK.) Use the Set Active Configuration menu option to switch between Debug and Release builds. You can also set the configuration using the Build toolbar, as shown in Figure 13-3.

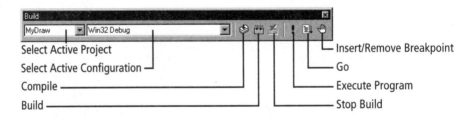

Figure 13-3.   *The Build toolbar. You set the active configuration in the second drop-down list box from the left.*

Visual C++ puts the intermediate files and the final executable file for Debug builds in a Debug subdirectory under your project directory. It puts similar files for Release builds in a Release subdirectory. There are a few other files that store option settings, ClassWizard information, and the like, but we won't discuss those files here. The source code files remain in the root project directory. (Advanced programmers can use the Settings dialog box to change the names of these subdirectories if they wish.)

For Debug builds, program optimization should be turned off. Optimizations make debugging more complicated. Setting the Win32 Debug target disables optimizations. (You can see this in the Optimizations box on the C/C++ tab of the Settings dialog box.) It also enables generation of debug information. (You can see this in the Link tab in the Settings dialog box.) Setting Win32 Release reverses those settings. (Optimization is not available in the version of Visual C++ supplied with this book.)

You might sometimes find that your application runs fine in a Debug build but crashes when you run a Release build. For useful information about debugging such problems, check the Help index for *release builds* and select the topic "difference from debug builds."

Example: Using the Debugger

Let's look at an extended example to see some of these features in action. In Chapter 11, I left a bug in MyDraw. You won't have encountered the bug unless you drew more than 1000 shapes in one sitting. We'll use the debugger to observe the behavior of this bug and then to fix it. First, we need to set things up.

Try it now

Open your MyDraw project and, in the file DrawVw.h, locate the declaration of the *SHPS_MAX* constant above the *arColors* array definition. Change the value of *SHPS_MAX* from 1000 to 10. (Earlier, I set *SHPS_MAX* to 1000 so that you'd be unlikely to encounter the bug until now. But with the constant set to 10, the bug shows its ugly face very quickly.) Then build MyDraw and run it. Don't forget that you must build a debug version in order to use the debugger. Draw shapes, counting them as you go. When you get to 10, draw one more shape and observe what happens. The 11th shape seems sticky, and instead of simply releasing the mouse button, you have to click the mouse to end the shape. The first thing you see (after the mouse click) is a dialog box containing the message "Debug Assertion Failed!" This dialog box contains three buttons: Abort, Retry, and Ignore. Click Retry to debug the program. A second dialog box appears, containing the message "This program has performed an illegal operation and will be shut down." This dialog box contains three buttons: Close, Debug, and Details.

If you click Debug, the Visual C++ debugger runs and you see a third dialog box containing a message something like this: "User breakpoint called from code at 0x403e94." (The address listed might be different on your machine.) Click OK in the dialog box. The debugger opens the source code file DrawVw.cpp and puts the cursor in the *CMyDrawView::SetPenBrush* function. Depending on what you did in your last debugging session (if there was one), some of the debugger windows might also be open.

Let's use some Visual C++ debugger tools to find the bug and figure out what caused it.

Finding the Bug

To debug MyDraw, let's first determine where the error occurred. The best way to find out is to use the Call Stack window, which shows the sequence of function calls that led up to the error. The most recent call is at the top of the window, which shows, as we'll see, that the error occurred in the *CMyDrawView::SetPenBrush* function. Here's how to use the Call Stack window.

 ### Try it now

From the Visual C++ View menu, choose Debug Windows and then Call Stack. If the Call Stack window, shown in Figure 13-4, wasn't already open, it will appear now. You will see a small yellow arrow in the window's left margin that points to *CMyDrawView::SetPenBrush*, which is the function name where the error occurred. The line below the function name lists *CMyDrawView::InvertShape*, which MyDraw uses to draw rubberband images of the current shape. *InvertShape* called *SetPenBrush* just before the failure.

Double-click the line containing the function *InvertShape* in the Call Stack window. (This switches the Source Code editor window to that function's "context.") In the code window's left margin, the triangular arrowhead is just past the offending line:

```
SetPenBrush(pDC, s.m_bTransparent, s.m_nColorShape);
```

The arrow points to the left brace immediately following the start of the *switch* statement. However, the last statement executed was the call to *SetPenBrush*.

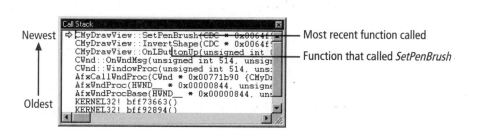

Newest → Most recent function called

Function that called *SetPenBrush*

Oldest

Figure 13-4. *The sequence of function calls in the Call Stack window.*

The Call Stack window is useful for backtracking through all function calls that have not yet returned. You can see which function called which function, and that helps you see how your program arrived at a particular place. It's a bit like watching a car hit a tree, and then tracing back through time to see where the tie rod broke.

Most bugs won't lead us neatly back to the moment of truth, of course. Some bugs don't result in immediate crashes. In such cases, you might need to halt the program in the debugger and step through it line by line to look for problems. The debugger supplies a versatile set of tools for analyzing a buggy program.

Analyzing the Bug

Now that we know that the problem occurred in the *SetPenBrush* function, make sure you're looking at that function in the Source Code window. (If necessary, double-click the line of code containing *SetPenBrush* in the Call Stack window to select that function's context.) The Source Code window contains the DrawVw.cpp file with a portion of *SetPenBrush* on display. Notice that a small yellow arrow in the left margin points to the *ASSERT* statement just before we set up the pen (actually to the last line of the *ASSERT* statement). That statement is the source of our error dialog boxes. A debug assertion failed (causing the first dialog box to appear), and then the buttons we clicked led to the other dialogs.

> **NOTE** The *ASSERT* macro is MFC's version of the *assert* macro we used in Chapters 4 and 5. If its Boolean condition is false, *ASSERT* halts the program with a message, as we've seen. *ASSERT* is used for detecting logic errors during development, so it works only in Debug builds; it's not compiled in Release builds. Check the Help index for *ASSERT*.

But why did our assertion fail? Let's examine the Boolean conditions inside the *ASSERT* statement. Both conditions must be true (because they're connected by the logical AND operator, &&) or the assertion will fail. The first condition,

```
nColor - ID_COLOR_BLACK >= 0
```

checks whether the color of the shape currently being drawn is within an acceptable range. (When we subtract *ID_COLOR_BLACK* from the color, the result must be greater than or equal to 0, the lower bound value for the *arColors* array.) The second condition,

```
nColor - ID_COLOR_BLACK <=
                (sizeof(arColors) / sizeof(arColors[0]))
```

checks whether the color is less than or equal to the upper bound value of the *arColors* array. (We use the C++ *sizeof* operator to get the correct upper bound value regardless of how many elements the array might have. To get the size of the array, I divide the total storage for the array by the storage required by one element.) Apparently, we have a color value that is not within the acceptable range—hence the assertion failure. We'll use the debugger to find out what's going on. We'll start by examining the color value, *nColor*, which is associated with the current shape. We can hypothesize that there's something wrong with the data contained in that shape.

IP You can make the next steps easier by selecting the Hexadecimal Display option. Choose Options from the Tools menu to display the Options dialog box, select the Debug tab, select the Hexadecimal Display option, and then click OK.

Try it now

Examine the *nColor* value in *SetPenBrush*. In the Source Code window, rest the cursor on *nColor*, where it first occurs inside the *ASSERT* statement. A small light yellow window appears beside the variable, containing the value 0x00000000, hexadecimal notation for the decimal value 0. (You might see simply 0 if you don't have the Hexadecimal Display option set on the Debug tab in the Options dialog box.) The small window is a DataTips window. Visual C++ lets you examine variable values right in the Source Code window when the program is halted in the debugger.

So what's wrong with a value of 0 for *nColor*? Let's try subtracting *ID_COLOR_BLACK* from 0, as in the *ASSERT* statement. To find the value of *ID_COLOR_BLACK*, select the Resource Symbols command on the Visual C++ View menu. Next to the name *ID_COLOR_BLACK* is a numeric value (32774 in my project—it could be different in yours). Close the Resource Symbols dialog box. Subtracting 32774 from 0 yields a large negative number, which fails the first Boolean test in the *ASSERT* statement.

What range should *nColor* – *ID_COLOR_BLACK* be in? The *arColors* array has 10 elements, so our value after the subtraction must fall between 0 and 9 inclusive in order to index the array. Let's go on to backtrack how *nColor* might have gone wrong. We'll check how it gets its value.

Try it now

The *nColor* variable is a parameter to *SetPenBrush*, which is called by *InvertShape*. In the Call Stack window, double-click the line of code containing *InvertShape*. Let's see what *InvertShape* passes for the color parameter. In *InvertShape*, the *SetPenBrush* call passes the value *s.m_nColorShape*.

The object *s* is a reference to a *CShape* object passed to *InvertShape*. What function called *InvertShape*? The Call Stack window shows it to be *OnLButtonUp*.

IMPORTANT   The Call Stack window could instead show *OnMouseMove* as the function that called *InvertShape*—that could happen if you moved the mouse as you clicked to complete the sticky 11th shape. Both *OnMouse-Move* and *OnLButtonUp* call *InvertShape*, so either could be implicated in the bug. You can substitute *OnMouseMove* for *OnLButtonUp* in the rest of this section.

Double-click the line of code containing *OnLButtonUp* (or *OnMouseMove*) in the Call Stack window. In the Source Code window, a green arrowhead points to the line just past the first *InvertShape* call in *OnLButtonUp*. That first *InvertShape* call passes the object *m_shpTemp*, so inside *InvertShape*, *s* refers to *m_shpTemp*.

What is the color value now stored in the current shape, *m_shpTemp*? I'll show you how to determine that in the next section.

Examining Variables

At this point, there are several ways to see the value of a variable such as *m_shpTemp*. I'll describe each briefly.

Try it now

Try examining variables in the following ways—you'll probably develop your own favorites:

- Use QuickWatch to see the variable's value. Right-click *m_shpTemp* in *OnLButtonUp* (or *OnMouseMove*) and choose the QuickWatch command. This opens the QuickWatch dialog box, which shows the value of each of *m_shpTemp*'s members. The *m_nColorShape* member has the value 0x00000000. Try it. For more information, check the Help index for *QuickWatch*. Figure 13-5 shows Quick-Watch. Note that your values for the *m_typeShape* and *m_bTrans-parent* expressions might differ because of the type of drawing you were doing in MyDraw when the failure occurred.

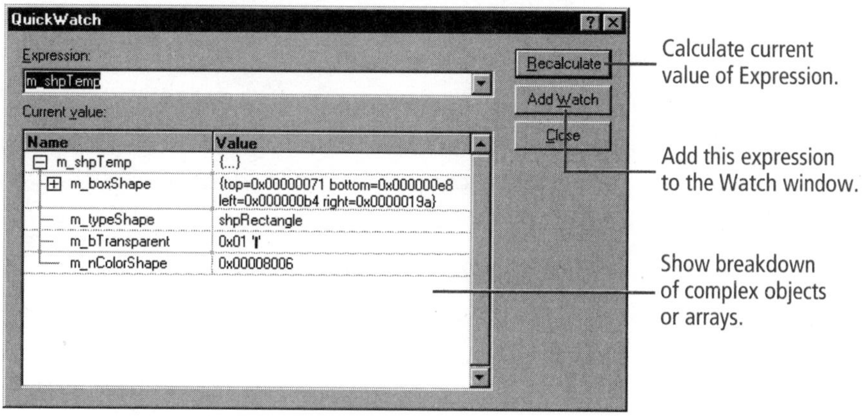

Calculate current
value of Expression.

Add this expression
to the Watch window.

Show breakdown
of complex objects
or arrays.

Figure 13-5.   *The QuickWatch dialog box.*

■ From QuickWatch, add *m_shpTemp* to the Watch window, one of
the main debugger windows. With *m_shpTemp* in the Expression
box in QuickWatch, click Add Watch. The Watch window opens (if
it wasn't already open) and displays the variable name *m_shpTemp*.
Click the plus sign before the variable name to see the value of
m_shpTemp. Try it. Where QuickWatch gives you a temporary
glance, Watch can remain available. Position the Watch window as
you like. (For guidelines on positioning windows, see Chapter 1.)
For more information about the Watch window, check the Help index for *watch window*. Figure 13-6 shows the Watch window.

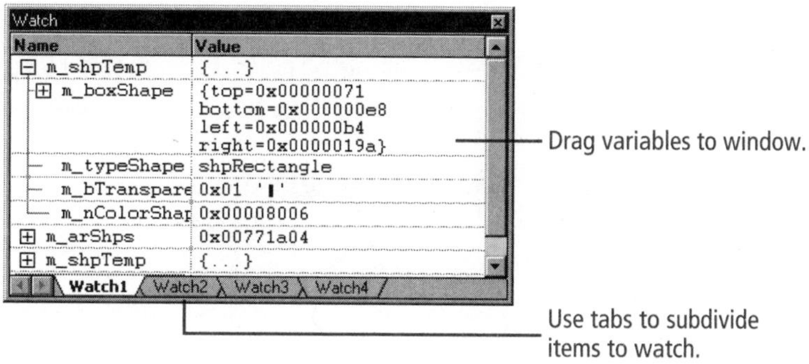

Drag variables to window.

Use tabs to subdivide
items to watch.

Figure 13-6.   *The Watch window.*

■ From any window, including the Source Code editor window, locate and select a variable, such as *m_arShps*, and drag it into the open Watch window. Be sure to select the variable by double-clicking it before you attempt to drag it. The debugger supports many drag-and-drop operations from one of its components to another. Try some.

■ Open the Variables window. From the Visual C++ View menu, choose Variables on the Debug Windows submenu (or click the Variables button on the Debug toolbar). The Variables window automatically adjusts its contents to show items from the present context—usually items visible within a function. It has three tabs: Auto, Locals, and This. The Auto tab displays variables used in the current statement and the previous statement or two. It also displays return values when you step over or out of a function (techniques we'll explore soon). The Locals tab displays just the local variables declared in the current function context. The This tab displays the value of the *this* pointer for the current object (the view object in our case). You can't add variables to the Variables window (use Watch instead), but you can examine in considerable detail the variables that are displayed by clicking the + and − buttons to expand or collapse variable displays. When the latest instruction changes the value of a variable, the Variables window (and other debugger windows) shows the variable in red. You can also change variable values in the Variables window and then continue running with the new values in effect. Try it. Check the Help index for *variables window*. Figure 13-7 shows the Variables window.

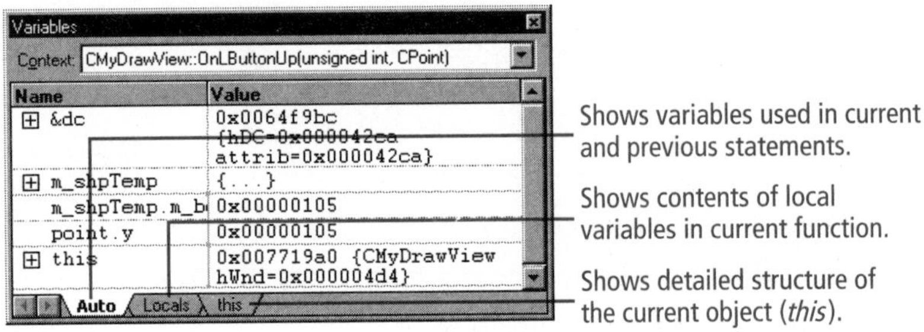

Shows variables used in current and previous statements.

Shows contents of local variables in current function.

Shows detailed structure of the current object (*this*).

Figure 13-7.   *The Variables window.*

- When a variable is in scope, as *nColor* is in the *SetPenBrush* function, you can display a ToolTip-style window containing the variable's value, as we've seen. You'll need to have executed the line containing the variable before you can see its value. To see the DataTip, simply rest the mouse pointer on the variable name in the Source Code editor window. (If the variable is a member of a structure or member of a class, select the qualifying class name and the member-access operator as well.) A DataTip window appears near the variable name, containing the variable's value if it has a value in the current context. Check the Help index for *datatips pop-up information*. Figure 13-8 shows a DataTips display.

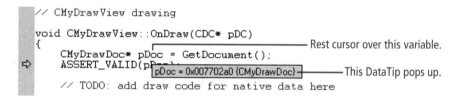

Figure 13-8. *A DataTips display.*

Now that you've explored ways to examine variables, exit the debugger. On the Debug menu, select Stop Debugging.

TIP To see the type of a variable in one of the debugger windows such as the Watch or Variables windows, right-click the variable and choose Properties from the shortcut menu that appears.

TIP You can adjust the width of a column in a debugger window by dragging the column divider line one way or the other.

Breakpoints

The next question is how the shape in *m_shpTemp* got its faulty color value. The color is assigned to the shape in *OnLButtonDown*, and we know that MyDraw blows up while drawing the 11th shape. So let's watch that assignment in action.

We begin our observation in *OnLButtonDown* just as we're drawing the eleventh shape. To do that, we'll set a *breakpoint* at the beginning of *OnLButtonDown*. A breakpoint tells the debugger to execute the program up to that point and then stop so we can examine what's going on. It's like taking a snapshot. And to keep from breaking on every shape, we'll arrange to skip the first 10 shapes, breaking only on the 11th. Visual C++ lets you set quite a variety of *breakpoint conditions*.

Visual C++ lets you set a variety of breakpoint types too. The simplest type, which is set as described in the next section, is a *location breakpoint*. A location breakpoint breaks at a specified location in the code. You can modify a location breakpoint by supplying an additional condition that you require to be true.

You can also set various kinds of *data breakpoints*. Data breakpoints break at an appropriate place based on the value of a variable or on some other condition that you specify. (Data breakpoints can affect program execution speed; be prepared to wait.)

Among the conditional breakpoints you can set is a *message breakpoint*. A message breakpoint breaks on receiving a given Windows message. However, don't use message breakpoints in MFC unless you need to break on a message for which you have no handler. (The debugger will stop inside MFC source code.) Instead, you should usually set a location breakpoint on the message handler associated with the desired message. For example, to break on the *WM_LBUTTONDOWN* message, you set a location breakpoint on your *OnLButtonDown* handler.

 IP If you specify a data breakpoint by typing the name of a pointer, you must dereference the pointer: for example, specify *m_arShps[0]*, not just *m_arShps*; or **ptr*, not just *ptr*. You can also specify how many array elements or string characters you want to watch. If you specify only a pointer or an array name, the debugger will break when the pointer changes, not when the object pointed to changes.

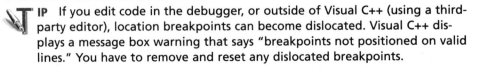 **IP** If you edit code in the debugger, or outside of Visual C++ (using a third-party editor), location breakpoints can become dislocated. Visual C++ displays a message box warning that says "breakpoints not positioned on valid lines." You have to remove and reset any dislocated breakpoints.

Setting the breakpoint in MyDraw

Here are several ways to set the breakpoint we need in *OnLButtonDown*. First, click in the source code at the line where you want to break. Then set the breakpoint using one of these methods:

- Press F9 to set or remove a location breakpoint at the line containing the blinking cursor. A red dot appears in the left margin before the line, or the whole line appears in a red-shaded box if you haven't selected the Selection Margin option on the Editor tab of the Options dialog box in the Visual C++ Tools menu. (This method and the next don't allow us to set conditions for our breakpoints, so we'll end up using the final method below for the real thing.)

- Right-click a line in the source code. On the shortcut menu that pops up, choose Insert/Remove Breakpoint.

- Choose the Breakpoints command from the Edit menu. In the Breakpoints dialog box, click the small, right-facing arrow beside the Break At box. Choose an option from the menu that pops up— for now, you want the option that lists a line number or a function prototype. You can also specify conditions for when the debugger should break at this breakpoint. That's what we'll do next. Figure 13-9 shows the Breakpoints dialog box.

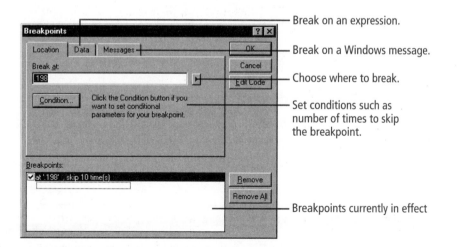

Figure 13-9.   *The Breakpoints dialog box.*

Try it now

Now let's set a conditional breakpoint at the opening curly brace of the *OnLButtonDown* function:

1. Make sure you've exited the debugger. (Choose Stop Debugging from the Debug menu, or press Shift+F5.)

2. In the Source Code editor, click the line where you want to insert a break. (Remember that when run in the debugger, the program execution will break just before this line.)

3. Choose Breakpoints from the Edit menu to open the Breakpoints dialog box. Select the Location tab.

4. Click the small arrow beside the Break At box and select the line number option from the menu that pops up.

5. Click Condition.

6. In the Breakpoint Condition dialog box, type *10* in the box labeled Enter The Number Of Times To Skip Before Stopping.

7. Click OK twice to close both dialog boxes.

TIP You can also set location breakpoints by typing a function name or label in the Break At box. For a function name, the breakpoint is at the beginning of the function. For C++ class member functions, include the class name and the scope resolution operator, as in *CMyDrawView::OnLButtonUp*. Note that such a breakpoint is not marked in red in the source code because the Source Code editor lacks a line number.

Stepping Through Code

Let's stop at our breakpoint, step through some code lines to execute them, and then examine some variable values.

Try it now

Run MyDraw—but do so in the debugger this time. From the Visual C++ Build menu, choose Start Debug, and then Go (or press F5). The My-Draw window appears. Draw 10 shapes, and then start drawing the 11th shape. The debugger stops the program at the opening curly brace of the *OnLButtonDown* function body.

From there, follow these directions to step through the statements in *OnLButtonDown*:

1. Start by choosing the Step Over command from the Debug menu (or press F10, or click the Step Over button on the Debug toolbar), stopping when the yellow arrow in the source code window points to the line

    ```
    SetCapture();
    ```

    The Step Over command causes function calls to execute, but the debugger doesn't step inside those functions.

2. Next, choose the Step Into command from the Debug menu or press F11 to step into the *SetCapture* call. This opens the Afxwin2.inl file, a part of MFC's source code. Stepping further inside the *Set-Capture* function would execute its code statement by statement. If you were to step over or into each of the statements in *SetCapture* and then step past the closing curly brace, stepping would continue in the calling function at the first line past the function you stepped into. (Note that the debugger can only step into code for which the source files are available. For example, it won't step into Win32 API calls such as the call to *ReleaseCapture* in *OnLButtonUp*, but it will step into the MFC wrappers for those calls.)

3. Instead of stepping on through *SetCapture*, let's use the Step Out command (Shift+F11) to jump back out of *SetCapture* and down to the next line of *OnLButtonDown*. Step Out is handy when you inadvertently step into a function.

4. Now scroll down in the source code file and click the following line, and then choose the Run To Cursor command (Ctrl+F10) to execute up to that line:

    ```
    m_shpTemp.m_nColorShape = m_nColorNext;
    ```

5. Use Step Into one more time to execute the current line. We'll stop there to examine some variables.

6. Use any of the techniques described earlier in this chapter in the section on "Examining Variables" to observe the value of the view's *m_nColorNext* data member. The current value is 0x00008006 (in my project). You can use the Calculator accessory to convert that to decimal; the value is 32774, which is the value of *ID_COLOR_BLACK*. (If you selected a different color before drawing, the numbers will differ but should still translate to a valid color value as determined from the Resource.h file.)

As a result of this search, we know the current shape, *m_shpTemp*, has a valid value initially, when *OnLButtonDown* assigns it the current color value for a new shape. Yet we know this value has gone bad by the time we stop rubberbanding the shape in *OnLButtonUp*. That's when we call *InvertShape*, passing the current shape, and *InvertShape* calls *SetPenBrush* with a bad color value, tripping our *ASSERT*. Sometime during the shape's creation sequence in the three mouse message handlers, something changes the shape's color value. We're going to have to follow that creation sequence.

IP   If you go hunting through source files and lose track of the next statement to execute, click Show Next Statement on the Debug menu (or on the Debug toolbar).

Try it now

Let's start spying on the creation of the 11th *m_shpTemp* by looking at the end of the process, in *OnLButtonUp*.

1. Stop debugging (press Shift+F5) and use the Breakpoints dialog box to remove all existing breakpoints. (In the dialog box, click Remove All.)

2. Set a new breakpoint at the opening curly brace of *OnLButtonUp*, just as you set the breakpoint in *OnLButtonDown* in "Setting the Breakpoint in MyDraw." Skip the first 10 times *OnLButtonUp* is called—the first 10 shapes.

3. Run MyDraw in the debugger (press F5), draw 10 shapes, and then start drawing shape 11. The program stops at the breakpoint.

4. Step over statements until the yellow arrow points to the first *InvertShape* call. At this point, use any technique you like (such as the Variables window) to examine the color value in *m_shpTemp*. You'll see that before the call to *InvertShape,* the color value, black (0x00008006), is valid.

5. Step into *InvertShape,* and then step over statements in *InvertShape* until the yellow arrow points to *SetPenBrush.* Examine the color value, *m_nColorShape,* in the shape variable *s.* You'll see that it hasn't changed.

6. Step into the *SetPenBrush* call and step over its statements. The *ASSERT* doesn't fail on this call, and we step all the way through. Examine the value of *nColor*—it's still valid.

7. Step on out of *SetPenBrush,* and then step out of *InvertShape* and back into *OnLButtonUp.* Then step over statements until the yellow arrow points to the following line:

```
m_arShps[m_countShapes] = m_shpTemp;
```

8. Examine the values stored in the members of the *m_arShps* array. Use either the Locals tab or the This tab in the Variables window. Expand the array by clicking the plus sign in front of *m_arShps.* Scroll down to see the 10th shape (*m_arShps[0x9]*). You can expand that shape to see that its color is valid. But where is the 11th shape?

9. Step over the current line and take a look around. Examine the values of other variables, such as the view data member *m_count-Shapes.* Our shape counter, *m_countShapes,* should contain the value 0x0000000a (10 decimal) now that we've supposedly drawn an 11th shape and stored it in the array (although we haven't yet incremented the counter for that shape). But note that its value is actually something else—in my project, it's 0x00000081 (129 decimal). We certainly haven't drawn 129 shapes!

Looking for Shape Eleven

So far, we've tried out several debugger features, but we still don't know what's going wrong with our shape color. Let's look a little further, keeping in mind the phony *m_countShapes* value of 129 (or possibly something equally bogus on your machine).

Our strongest clue so far is in the number of shapes we can draw before things blow up. Recall that we set *SHPS_MAX* to 10, and that on our attempt to draw an 11th shape the program derails. What's *SHPS_MAX* used for? For dimensioning our array, of course. We declare the array *m_arShps* this way:

```
Shape m_arShps[SHPS_MAX];
```

Bells should be going off in our heads by now. Could this be a problem with array bounds? That seems likely—but how exactly does the blowup happen?

Two problems have the potential to damage the color value in shape 11—either a bad pointer that somehow overwrites good data, or an array that overshoots its bounds and writes its contents over good data. The array problem is our most likely suspect.

Looking for the array problem

It's time to examine our data. The view stores the array as an embedded object. (It could instead have stored a pointer to an array allocated on the heap.) Here are the pertinent data member declarations in class *CMyDrawView* again:

```
ShpType m_typeNext;
Shape m_shpTemp;
Shape m_arShps[SHPS_MAX];    // The array
int m_countShapes;
bool m_bCaptured;
CBrush* m_pBrushOld;
bool m_bTransparent;
UINT m_nColorNext;           // Current color
CPen* m_pPenOld;
CPen* m_pPenNew;
```

Given these declarations, the layout in memory from the beginning of the class follows the same order. Picture these variables laid out end to end, as in Figure 13-10. A *Shape* object contains a bounding rectangle (*m_boxShape*) and three data members, so for each *Shape* object, we're storing the following items:

- Four *ints* for the coordinates of the shape's bounding rectangle, *m_boxShape*

- One *int* for its *ShpType*, *m_typeShape*

- One *bool* (same size as an *int*) for its transparency setting, *m_bTransparent*

- One *unsigned int*, a *UINT*, for its color, *m_nColorShape*

The total storage for one *Shape* object is 28 bytes, at 4 bytes per integer. (Note that a *ShpType*, a *COLORREF*, and a pointer are all the same size as an *int*.)

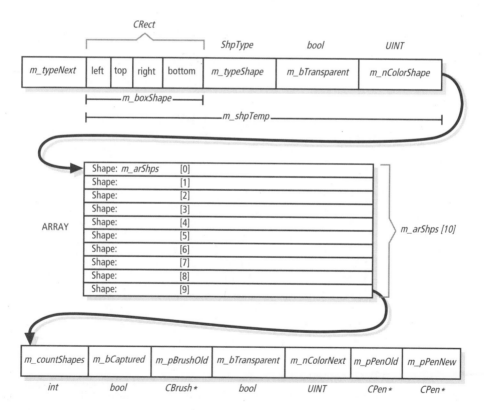

Figure 13-10. *Layout of data members in a CMyDrawView object.*

Within our view object, then, we have the following:

- An *int*-sized object (*m_typeNext*, a *ShpType* enumeration value)
- A *Shape* object (*m_shpTemp*, 28 bytes)—our temporary shape-in-progress
- An array dimensioned to hold 10 *Shapes* (*m_arShps*, 280 bytes)
- Another *int* (*m_countShapes*, 4 bytes)
- Another *int*-sized object (*m_bCaptured*, a *bool*)
- Another *int*-sized object (*m_pBrushOld*, a pointer)
- Another *int*-sized object (*m_bTransparent*, a *bool*)
- An *unsigned int* (*m_nColorNext*, a *UINT*)
- Another *int*-sized object (*m_pPenOld*, another pointer)
- A final *int*-sized object (*m_pPenNew*, another pointer)

Up to the end of the array, we have 312 bytes, adding up 4 bytes for *m_typeNext*, 28 bytes for *m_shpTemp*, and 280 bytes (28 bytes per shape ×10 shapes) for *m_arShps*. If we then add the 4 bytes for *m_countShapes*, 4 bytes for *m_bCaptured*, 4 bytes for *m_pBrushOld*, 4 bytes for *m_bTransparent*, and 4 bytes for *m_nColorNext* (stopping there), we're up to 332 bytes. Figure 13-11 shows this arrangement.

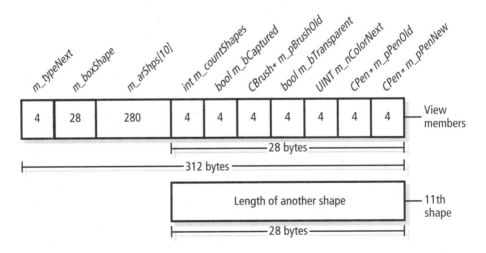

Figure 13-11. *The array of shapes and what follows it.*

Now for the crucial question: If we add an 11th *Shape* object beyond the end of *m_arShps*, will it overwrite something—such as our color value, *m_nColorNext*—thereby causing our error? That's most likely what's happening. Recall that one *Shape* object is 28 bytes long. The end of the array is at 312 bytes (from the start of the data members), and 312 + 28 = 340 bytes—well past the beginning of *m_nColorNext* at 332. Bingo again. The 11th shape has "clobbered" the color we use to set all new shapes—along with other view class data members. Almost any of these overwritten data members might have caused a similar crash. But the program ran into the color problem first.

Using the Memory window

Let's use the debugger's Memory window to look in on this state of affairs. We'll position the Memory window at the last *Shape* object in the array, then see what lies beyond.

Try it now

The first stage of this operation is to bring the program to a point in the middle of drawing the 11th shape by following these steps:

1. If MyDraw is running in the debugger, stop debugging. (Choose Stop Debugging on the Debug menu.)

2. Start debugging (press F5) and draw 11 shapes. As you complete the 11th shape, the debugger breaks in, stopping at the beginning of *OnLButtonUp*, as before.

3. Step through *OnLButtonUp* until the yellow arrow points to the line that increments *m_countShapes*:

```
m_countShapes++;
```

Exploring memory

With everything correctly positioned, let's look at what's in memory using the Memory window.

Try it now

Set up the Memory and Variables windows to look at the 10th and 11th shapes.

1. Open the Memory window. Choose Debug Windows and then Memory from the Visual C++ View menu. Position the Memory window so you can see the Source Code editor stopped in *OnLButtonUp*. (You might want to close other debugger windows, such as the Watch and Call Stack windows.)

2. Open the Variables window as well. Choose Debug Windows and then Variables from the Visual C++ View menu. Position the Variables window so you can see a reasonable amount of its contents in addition to the Memory window and the Source Code editor.

Interpreting what's in memory

Examine the code as described below. If you're unfamiliar with the Memory window's display (most memory displays use a similar format), see the sidebar "Reading the Memory Window" on page 405. The first 4 bytes of the memory display are highlighted in Figure 13-12.

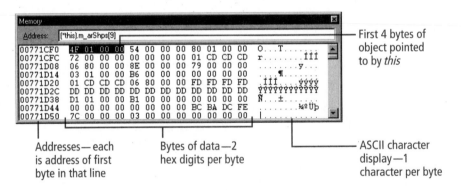

Figure 13-12. *The Memory window.*

We'll start by looking at the beginning of the 10th array element. At this point, element 10 contains the 10th shape's data, so the first 28 bytes we see should be that *Shape* object.

Try it now

In the Variables window, on the This tab, locate the following expression:

m_arShps

Click the plus sign in front of it. The array's 10 elements (0–9) appear below *m_arShps*. Click the line that says *0x9*—that's the 10th element, the last shape we drew. Click the plus sign in front of that line. Drag the *0x9* line to the upper left corner of the Memory window—the window's client area, not the Address box. The cursor might become a circle with a diagonal line through it, suggesting that this operation isn't allowed, but persist. After you drop the item in the window, you see the following expression in the Address box: *(*this).m_arShps[0x9]*. That's the 10th element of the array *m_arShps*, a member of the object that *this* points to (the view). (Note that we're currently looking at valid data, not at the bug. The bug doesn't come until shape 11.)

In the Variables window, the 10th shape's *m_boxShape* data member appears on the line below *0x9*. We don't particularly care what the bounding rectangle's coordinates are, but we'll move through them in the Memory window to get to what's past them. Let's look at the first four *ints* in memory (the first 16 bytes, at 2 digits per byte in the display—see the sidebar "Reading the Memory Window" for tips on interpreting the display). The values you see will be different on your system, but you can follow the same verification procedure that I use. On my system, the first *int* in the Memory window (the first 2-digit column in the display, on the top line, plus the next three columns following it) has the hexadecimal value 4F 01 00 00 = 0x01 4F, which is 335 decimal. That's the *left* data member of the shape's bounding rectangle. Figure 13-12 shows the Memory window with the first *int* highlighted. You can compare our figure for the *left* data member with the display in the Variables window to check that this really is the *left* data member. Click the plus sign in front of *m_arShps[0x9]* in the Variables window (if you haven't already) to expand its display. You can see the values for the shape's *m_boxShape* data member, including the *left* data member of the *CRect* value stored in *m_boxShape*. This value should match what you read in the Memory window for that data member. The following are the next three *ints*:

- 54 00 00 00 = 0x54 = 84 decimal: the *top* data member of the rectangle

- 80 01 00 00 = 0x0180 = 384 decimal: the *right* data member

- 72 00 00 00 = 0x72 = 114 decimal: the *bottom* data member

> **TIP** Recall that you can use the Windows Calculator accessory to convert between hexadecimal and decimal numbers. See "Numerical Notation in C++" in Chapter 3 to review hex numbers and the calculator technique.

The values on your machine might be different, but you get the idea. The first three variables in Table 13-1 show the remaining 12 bytes of the 10th *Shape* object, followed by the 11th object's variables *m_countShapes*, *m_bCaptured*, *m_pBrushOld*, *m_bTransparent*, and *m_nColorNext*. (There's no reason to go beyond *m_nColorNext*.)

Variable	Contents in Memory	Remarks
m_typeShape	00 00 00 00 = 0x00	*shpRectangle* has the value 0 in the *ShpType* enumeration. If you drew an ellipse, the value would be 01 00 00 00.
m_bTransparent	01 CD CD CD = 0xCDCDCD01	Only the least significant byte is used for a *bool*. The rest of the *int*-sized value is filled with a recognizable filler value, CD. The variable's value is 1 (*true*) because the Transparent menu is checked.
m_ncolorShape	06 80 00 00 = 0x8006 (To see why we read the number in memory in this backward way, see the sidebar "Reading the Memory Window.")	0x8006 (32,774 decimal on my machine) represents the color black: the value of *ID_COLOR_BLACK* in the file Resource.h. This would be different if you drew with a different color.

Table 13-1. *Values in memory for the class data members we're interested in.*

Variable	Contents in Memory	Remarks
m_countShapes	8E 00 00 00 = 0x8E (142 decimal)	We're on the 10th shape, counting from 0, so this should be 0x00000009 = 9 decimal. We're seeing instead the *left* coordinate in the 11th shape's *m_boxShape*: 142. It overwrites *m_countShapes*. I'll show you after the table how to verify that we're really looking at the *left* coordinate.
m_bCaptured	79 00 00 00 = 0x79 (121 decimal)	The variable's value should be 0 (*false*) because we've released the capture already, but we're seeing the 11th shape's *top* coordinate, 121.
m_pBrushOld	03 01 00 00 = 0x0103 (259 decimal)	This should be a pointer address, but instead we're seeing the *right* coordinate, 259.
m_bTransparent	B6 00 00 00 = 0xB6 (182 decimal)	This should be 0x01CDCDCD, *true*, but we're seeing the *bottom* coordinate, 182.
m_nColorNext	00 00 00 00 = 0x0 (0 decimal)	This should be a value between *ID_COLOR_BLACK* (32,774) and *ID_COLOR_LTGRAY* (32,783). We're seeing the 11th shape's type, *shpRectangle*.

In the fourth row of Table 13-1, I said that we're looking at the *left* coordinate of the 11th shape's *m_boxShape* data member, which has overwritten *m_countShapes*. You can verify that. In the Variables window, click the plus sign in front of *m_shpTemp* to expand its values. Recall that *m_shpTemp* contains shape 11. In the Variables window, you can see that the *left* coordinate for that shape is the same as the value you see in your Memory window at the location of *m_countShapes* (after you convert that value to decimal).

If you examine the contents of the view class data members following the array, a number of the values stand out as glaringly wrong. For example, as shown in Table 13-1, *m_countShapes* should be 0x0000000a (we haven't incremented for shape 11 yet), but with the *left* coordinate of the 11th shape's bounding rectangle overlaying *m_countShapes*, we see instead something like 0x0000008E (142). Similarly, *m_nColorNext* has been obliterated, so its value now appears to be 0x0, an out-of-range value for colors. All of this provides the smoking gun that tells us the array is really overwriting other class data members.

Damage Report

When does the color bug catch up to us? The car is damaged long before it hits a tree: the color bug's effects show up well before the *ASSERT* statement in *InvertShape* finally notices them. As you start drawing the 11th shape in *OnLButtonDown*, the value of *m_nColorNext* is still valid when you assign it to the new shape's color member. You're still fine while rubberbanding the shape, but recall how the 11th shape gets "sticky" during rubberbanding. You can't just let the mouse button up to stop drawing the shape. Instead, you have to click the mouse button again. That starts a 12th shape (which you can verify by setting a breakpoint in *OnLButtonDown*, skipping 11 shapes). The subsequent call to *OnLButtonUp* (for the 12th shape) trips the *ASSERT* because the 12th shape's color value is 0. *OnLButtonDown* sets it to that value during the creation of shape 12. So shape 11 clobbers *m_nColorShape* and shape 12 sounds the alarm.

Fixing the Bug

We've found the bug, now, so it's time to fix it. The problem is that our array can hold 10 shapes at a time but the user is perfectly free to go on drawing more shapes until things blow up. A quick fix is to display a message box when the user has drawn the maximum number of shapes allowed and then allow no more shapes.

That's not a good real-world solution, of course, but it will patch up the bug for now. In Chapter 14, we'll use a much more robust data structure and solve the problem for good.

 Try it now

To fix the problem, add the following boldface lines near the end of *OnLButtonUp*, just before adding the new shape to the array:

```
⋮
// Put current shape in array
if(m_countShapes >= SHPS_MAX)
```

```
{
    // Maximum number of shapes exceeded
    // Must erase some shapes or start a new drawing
    AfxMessageBox("Too many shapes");
    return;
}
m_arShps[m_countShapes] = m_shpTemp;
m_countShapes++;
⋮
```

Rebuild and test this solution. You'll now see a message box when you try to draw an 11th shape. The *AfxMessageBox* call passes a hard-coded string literal to display in the message box, but you could instead pass the ID of a string resource that you create with the String editor. Check the Help index for *string editor*. So how does this avoid the error? The *return* statement at the end of the *if* statement we just added ends the *OnLButtonUp* function before the current shape can be added to the shape list.

Reading the Memory Window

The Memory window displays chunks of memory in rows (whose size depends on the width of the window), beginning with a particular starting address that you can set. You can see an Address box at the top, with columns of numbers below it—look again at Figure 13-12. The leftmost column, 8 digits wide, lists addresses of successive memory chunks. The address in the upper left corner of the window is the *lowest* memory address on view in the window. If the window is sized so that each line currently displays 20 bytes, each of the other addresses in the leftmost column is 20 bytes (0x14) *higher* in memory. You set the first address by typing an 8-digit hex address in the Address box or by dragging a pointer (or array) name into the Memory window.

To the right of the address column are a number of 2-digit columns. (The number depends on the window width.) Each pair of hex digits (each column) represents 1 byte of memory. Each single hex digit represents 4 bits (a "nybble"), so 2 digits represent an 8-bit byte.

(continued)

Reading the Memory Window *continued*

On the far right is an ASCII display. In each row of that display, one character matches each byte in the row of byte columns to the left. A character in the ASCII display usually has nothing to do with the actual kind of data stored in that stretch of memory. It's just a way to display a bit pattern that probably represents an *int* or a *bool* in your program, something the debugger doesn't know. However, sometimes the ASCII display is useful because you can use it to look for strings of actual characters.

There's an additional complication. On Intel machines, a *word* of storage is stored in what's called *Little-Endian* order. This means the most significant byte of a 32-bit word is on the right end of the word, and the least significant byte is on the left. (The "little end" comes first in the normal left-to-right reading order of the English language.) That's the opposite of the ordering of storage words on the Macintosh computer and on many network machines. Figure 13-13 illustrates this situation.

The Little-Endian byte ordering explains why we interpret 10 01 in memory as 0110 hex rather than as 1001 hex, and why we read out pointer values backward.

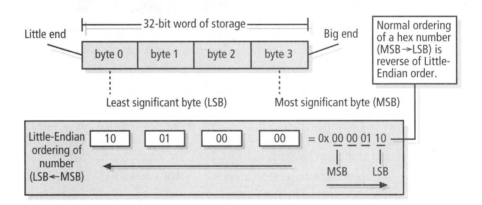

Figure 13-13. *Little-Endian byte ordering.*

Display Bugs

Debugging display bugs—bugs that involve drawing in the view—can be especially difficult. You can get locked into endless cycles of *WM_PAINT* or *WM_MOUSEMOVE* messages. Debugging in such a situation calls for ingenuity in setting breakpoints—that's one reason I set a condition on the breakpoint in *OnLButtonUp* so that it would only break after 10 calls to the function. To break out of a cycle like this, or out of an infinite loop, choose Break from the Debug menu (or the Debug toolbar).

MFC Diagnostic Facilities

To supplement the debugger, you can use some of the diagnostic facilities built into MFC. These include the following:

- The *TRACE* macro, which is used to print debug output in the Output window when your program runs in the debugger. Check the Help index for *TRACE* and double-click the *TRACE* keyword. You want the all-upper-case name.

MPORTANT To use *TRACE*, you must first run the MFC Tracer tool from the Tools menu. In the MFC Trace Options dialog box, make sure Enable Tracing is selected, and then click OK. Then run your program in the debugger to see *TRACE* output in the Output window.

- A set of macros to help you test the validity of objects (for example, *ASSERT_VALID*) and test your assumptions about the validity of function returns, object constructions, parameters, results of calculations, and the like (for example, *ASSERT* and *VERIFY*). Check the Help index for these macros and see the file Diagnost.doc in the \learnvcn\Chap13 folder in the companion code.

- A mechanism to help you detect memory leaks. Check the Help index for *memory leaks,* and see the file Diagnost.doc in the \learnvcn\Chap13 folder in the companion code.

- A way to obtain a diagnostic dump of the contents of your objects. Check the Help index for *diagnostic dump* and select the topic "object contents." Check also for *diagnostic dump* and select the topic "all objects." Also see the file Diagnost.doc in the \learnvcn\Chap13 folder in the companion code.

■ A method for handling exceptional conditions, or "exceptions," such as a File Not Found or an I/O error. Check the Help index for *exceptions* and see the file Diagnost.doc in the \learnvcn\Chap13 folder in the companion code.

Try It Yourself

You should be starting to feel more at ease with Visual C++ by now. Use the following homework to reinforce and expand on what you just learned about debugging.

1. Study the debugger documentation.

In Visual C++ Help, click the Contents tab, click Visual Studio 6.0 Introductory Edition. Then click Welcome To The Visual Studio 6.0 Introductory Edition. Click Using Visual C++. The debugger documentation is in the Visual C++ User's Guide. Start with the topic "Home Page: Debugger," (under the topic Debugger) which focuses on the debugger and its user interface. Some of the material will be familiar from this chapter, but the topics will also fill in some details I haven't mentioned.

2. Study debugging techniques.

The documentation on debugging techniques is in the Visual C++ Programmer's Guide. On the Contents tab, click Visual Studio 6.0 Introductory Edition, and then click Welcome To The Visual Studio 6.0 Introductory Edition. Click Using Visual C++. Then Click Visual C++ Programmer's Guide, and then click Debugging. Start with the topic "Debugging Your Program." This and adjacent topics focus on debugging techniques. They tend to amplify and go beyond my discussion in this chapter.

What's Next?

In Chapter 14, we'll adopt our final data structure for storing shapes, and thereby really fix this chapter's bug and solve our drawing problems once and for all. Well, most of them. The lions won't quite lie down with the lambs yet, but things are looking up.

Data, Documents, and Views

We've dealt with a good many design problems so far, most of them related to how MyDraw's data is displayed. It's time now to change our focus to the document and the data itself. We've been getting by with a loose definition of what a shape is. Now that you understand some of the user interface issues in Microsoft Windows programming, it's time to design a good shape data type and choose a good data structure to house the shapes. This chapter covers step 4 of MyDraw. We'll look at

- Designing data classes derived from the Microsoft Foundation Class Library 6.0 (MFC) *CObject* class—in this case, *CShape* and two classes derived from it

- MFC data structures: the "collection classes" used to store our shape data

- How the data fits into MFC's document/view architecture

We'll proceed from the top down. First we'll look at the document/view relationship and the document object's role in handling data. Then we'll select the right data structure from among the many offered by MFC. Finally, we'll discuss designing the *CShape* class and its subclasses—following up on the work we did in Chapter 5. And we'll explore some issues that arise when we roll up our sleeves and try to fit our data classes into MFC.

Designing the Document

Because we've decided to use the MFC document/view architecture, we'll move our list of shape objects into class *CMyDrawDoc*, the document class. In the document class, we'll build a user interface for our data around one of MFC's collection classes. In the view class, therefore, we'll work with the data strictly using that interface.

The Document/View Architecture Again

We discussed the MFC document/view architecture briefly in Chapter 8, but it will probably make more sense as we put it into practice in this chapter. Putting the shape data into the document object separates the program's data from how we draw the data on the screen:

- The view class focuses on drawing the data, which it obtains as needed from the document. In later chapters, we'll also look at the view object as an interface for editing the data.

- The document class focuses on maintaining the data and does the work of adding and manipulating shapes.

See Figure 8-6 for an illustration of the document/view relationship.

The document object also manages storing shape drawings in a file (covered in Chapter 16); the view object not only draws the shapes on the screen but also draws them on a printer or on a special *Print Preview* screen. (It's also through the view object that users manipulate the document's data by editing it.) This is a useful division of labor, especially when we later split the display into multiple views of the data (in Chapter 20). This division of labor is the essence of the document/view architecture. It simplifies file saving, printing, print preview, and displaying multiple views of data, and a considerable amount of it comes for free. You might want to quickly review the document/view discussion in "Document/View Architecture" in Chapter 8.

How a view communicates with the document

Let's look for a moment at document/view collaboration. How do the two classes communicate? The view object maintains a pointer to its associated document object. You can obtain that pointer in any view member function with these lines of code:

```
CMyDrawDoc* pDoc = GetDocument();
ASSERT_VALID(pDoc);
```

AppWizard makes these lines part of the *OnDraw* function. But you can copy the lines and paste them into any other view function. A call to the view object's *GetDocument* member function returns a pointer to the document object. The *ASSERT_VALID* macro causes the document object to run a validity test on itself—a little insurance. For more information, check the Help index for *ASSERT_VALID*, and see the file Diagnost.doc in the \learnvcn\Chap14 folder in the companion code.

Through the *pDoc* pointer, you can call any public document member function or directly access any public document data member. You'll normally use the pointer to add new data items, such as when the user draws a new shape, and to get data items for display. *OnDraw* uses the *pDoc* pointer extensively.

How the document communicates with a view

Meanwhile, over in the document object, you can always obtain a pointer to any particular view object associated with the document object—not that you'll need to very often. Keep in mind that some applications provide multiple views of the same document—a feature we will add to MyDraw later—so the document object stores a list of all views associated with the document. You can use document-class member functions such as *GetFirstViewPosition* and *GetNextView* to walk (meaning walk through) the list of views until you find the one you need. It might be useful to check the Help index for *CDocument* and review the class's member list. Here's sample code to walk the view list:

```
POSITION pos = pDoc->GetFirstViewPosition();
while(pos != NULL)
{
    CMyDrawView* pView = (CMyDrawView*)GetNextView(pos);
    // Do something with the view
}
```

The other major communication mechanism between the document object and its view objects is the document's *UpdateAllViews* member function. Typically, if the user changes some data by editing it through view A, view A uses the *pDoc* pointer to call *UpdateAllViews*. This causes the document object to call each view object's *OnUpdate* member function, which is equivalent to sending a *WM_PAINT* message to each view. (The default version of *OnInitialUpdate* also calls *OnUpdate*.) Each view's *OnUpdate* function invalidates all or part of the view, so each view updates its drawn image of the document object's data. An *UpdateAllViews* call thus synchronizes all views of the document so each displays the latest data.

Choosing an Appropriate Data Structure

We need a data structure that can store a large but indeterminate number of shape objects. It also needs to be more robust and flexible than a C++ array. We saw in Chapter 13 how error-prone our shape array was. Fortunately, MFC supplies approximately 20 *collection classes,* some of which will surely do the job. A collection class is designed to contain multiple objects of some type or types—the simplest collection class resembles a C++ array except that it can grow to accommodate more data. For detailed information about MFC's collection classes, a subject well worth investigating, check the Help index for *collection classes* and select the "Collections Topics" article in the Topics Found dialog box.

To choose a good data structure, we'll use the following decision process:

1. Choose between classes based on C++ templates and classes not based on templates. Template-based classes are preferable in some ways, especially in terms of type safety. A type-safe collection can hold only one kind of data. But since we aren't covering C++ templates in this book, we'll go with a nontemplate solution. MFC has 17 nontemplate collection classes designed to hold various kinds of data.

2. Choose among three collection class *shapes*—broad categories based on the semantics of arrays, linked lists, and maps. *Maps,* also known as dictionaries, map a lookup key to an element stored in the map. Think of a dictionary, in which a word is the lookup key and its definition is the stored data. There's no particular kind of key for our shape data, so that leaves either an array or a linked list. Either should work, and each has its strengths and weaknesses.

3. **Narrow the field of possibilities.** For a variety of reasons, we're going to derive class *CShape* from the MFC class *CObject*. Given that requirement, two MFC classes will hold the appropriate kind of data—pointers to *CShape* objects—*CObArray* and *CObList*. Class *CObArray* encapsulates an array of pointers to *CObject*, so if we derive *CShape* from *CObject*, we can store pointers to *CShape* in such an array. Likewise, class *CObList* stores pointers to *CObject* in a doubly linked list, one that allows traversal in both directions along the list.

4. **Choose between *CObArray* and *CObList*.** Different data structure types have different performance characteristics and offer different capabilities. We want a data structure that *OnDraw* can iterate quickly in order to draw all shapes. And eventually we'll want to move shape objects around in the data structure to support commands such as Bring To Front, Send To Back, Bring Forward, and Send Behind. Most object-oriented drawing applications support such commands. Linked lists such as *CObList* make inserting, deleting, and moving elements easier than arrays do. But arrays are faster and easier to iterate. Figure 14-1 illustrates the structure of *CObList*.

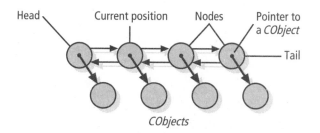

Figure 14-1. *The abstract structure of a* CObList.

I've chosen to implement the shape data structure with *CObList*, partly because this class presents a more interesting interface and illustrates more about the collection classes. If we find later that iteration is too slow for *OnDraw*—which is likely only if users commonly draw very large numbers of shapes in one drawing—it won't be hard to replace the

CObList implementation with a CObArray implementation. In any case, I'll provide some tips about using CObArray in the Try It Yourself exercise at the end of the chapter.

Try it now

In the file DrawDoc.h, add the following boldface data members (note that this is a private attributes section) below the // Attributes comment:

```
// Attributes
public:
private:
    CObList m_listShapes;  // Linked list of all shapes drawn so far
    POSITION m_pos;        // Latest position accessed
```

I'll discuss m_pos in a moment—think of it as similar to a pointer variable that is used to walk the list using pointer arithmetic.

MyDraw's Document Interface

I've chosen to hide MyDraw's data in a private section of the document class because I want the view classes to access the data only through a controlled interface. This lets me insert some error checking in the process and simplify somewhat the CObList interface. My data interface consists of the following document member functions.

- CreateShape creates a new CShape object and stores a pointer to it in our CObList. We return the same pointer so the mouse handlers that build up a new CShape object can use the pointer to work on the latest shape, in place in the list.

- DeleteLatestShape deletes the shape last drawn. We can use this in the future to implement an Erase command.

- DeleteAllShapes deletes all shapes in the drawing, presumably to start over. We'll use this later to clean up the document object for reuse.

- *SetToOldestShape* starts a traversal of the list by pointing to its tail end, where the oldest shape is located. The list holds objects in the reverse of the order in which we added them. So the latest shape is at the head of the list, and the oldest shape is at the tail. We add new shapes at the head. Calling *SetToOldestShape* is like setting a pointer to the last element of an array so you can walk the array backward (although we aren't really using pointer arithmetic). When *OnDraw* iterates the list, we want it to draw the oldest shapes first so the newer ones come out "on top of" the older ones. By calling *GetPrevShape* repeatedly, we'll walk the list from oldest to newest shape. We'll also add a *SetToLatestShape* function for walking the list from latest to oldest shape. We'll use this function in Chapter 18.

- *GetPrevShape*, moving along the list from tail to head, returns a pointer to the "previous" shape—the next one closer to the head. The pointer is a *CShape**. To match *SetToLatestShape*, we'll also add a *GetNextShape* function, which we'll use in Chapter 18.

- *GetPos* gets the "position" of our conceptual pointer, *m_pos*, as it marks successive elements in the list.

- *GetCount* returns the number of objects stored in the list.

For now, we only need to iterate the list in one direction, but I've added corresponding functions to iterate it in the other direction as well. They'll be there when we need them.

Initializing the list

By declaring the *m_listShapes* data member, we arranged for the *CObList* to be constructed as part of the document object—it's constructed just before the document object is constructed. It's initially an empty list, and we don't need to initialize it further except to set the *m_pos* data member to *NULL* in the document constructor. At this point, we aren't yet pointing into the list.

Try it now

Add the boldface line to the document constructor:

```
CMyDrawDoc::CMyDrawDoc()
{
    // TODO: add one-time construction code here
    m_pos = NULL;
}
```

Creating a new shape and adding it to the list

As before, we create a new shape object in the view's *OnLButtonDown* mouse message handler. At that point, instead of calling *new*, we call the document's *CreateShape* member function (which we'll add in a moment). *CreateShape* constructs a new *CShpRectangle* or *CShpEllipse* on the heap, depending on which shape type is currently selected on the Tools menu. *CreateShape* is one case where we need a *switch* statement, so we create the right type of object. *CreateShape* stores the new object in the list by calling *CObList's AddHead* member function. Then *CreateShape* passes a pointer to the object back to *OnLButtonDown*, and we use that pointer through the rest of the mouse drawing process. This lets us eliminate the *m_shpTemp* data member in the view class. We no longer need a dummy shape object to build up with data and then stash in our data structure. Instead, we work on the new shape object in place, through a pointer, after we've added it to the list.

Try it now

We'll take this in stages. As described below, create a new shape in *OnLButtonDown*. Remove the old array data implementation that we're replacing with a *CObList* implementation. Add the *CreateShape* member function to the document class.

First, in the file DrawVw.cpp, change *OnLButtonDown* so it looks like the following. (Note the boldface lines.)

```
void CMyDrawView::OnLButtonDown(UINT nFlags, CPoint point)
{
    // TODO: Add your message handler code here and/or call default
```

```
        SetCapture();
        m_bCaptured = true;

        ASSERT(m_typeNext == shpRectangle || m_typeNext ==
            shpEllipse);
        CMyDrawDoc* pDoc = GetDocument();
        ASSERT_VALID(pDoc);
        // Create shape and add it to our list; return a ptr to it.
        m_pShpTemp = pDoc->CreateShape(m_typeNext);
        // Mark the document as changed.
        pDoc->SetModifiedFlag();

        // Start setting properties of the new shape.
        m_pShpTemp->m_bTransparent = m_bTransparent;
        m_pShpTemp->m_nColorShape = m_nColorNext;

        // Store starting point - literally a point, initially
        //   (topLeft == botRight).
        m_pShpTemp->m_boxShape.left =
            m_pShpTemp->m_boxShape.right = point.x;
        m_pShpTemp->m_boxShape.top =
            m_pShpTemp->m_boxShape.bottom = point.y;

        CView::OnLButtonDown(nFlags, point);
}
```

The document's *CreateShape* member function stores the new shape object in its list and then returns a pointer to the shape, which we store in *m_pShpTemp*. (The former *m_shpTemp* variable is now a pointer instead of an object.) Then we tell the document that its data has changed. When the user closes the document or exits the program, the document checks its "modified flag." If the flag is *true*, the document displays a dialog box asking if the user wants to save the changes. The modified flag mechanism is part of class *CDocument*—we don't have to code it; we just activate it by calling *SetModifiedFlag*. *SetModifiedFlag* takes a Boolean parameter. If the parameter is *true*, the document is marked as "dirty" (modified)—this is the default. If the parameter is *false*, the document is marked as no longer dirty. You might use the *false* parameter, for example, if you applied an Undo command for an operation that had changed some data.

Now get rid of the old array implementation.

1. In the file DrawVw.cpp, delete the following lines from the *OnLButtonUp* member function:

```
// Put current shape in array
m_arShps[m_countShapes] = m_shpTemp;
m_countShapes++;
```

Also remove the initialization of the *m_countShapes* data member from the *CMyDrawView* constructor.

2. In the file DrawVw.h, delete the *m_arShps[]* and *m_countShapes* data members and the *SHPS_MAX* constant.

Those lines are part of the old array implementation that we've now replaced with a *CObList* implementation.

3. In the files DrawVw.h and DrawVw.cpp, use Find/Replace to replace *m_shpTemp* everywhere with *m_pShpTemp*. In all calls to the *InvertShape* member function, change the second parameter to *∗m_pShpTemp*. The function expects an object, not a pointer. (It's a reference to *CShape*, so you pass it an existing object.) Thus we dereference *m_pShpTemp*.

4. In DrawVw.h and DrawVw.cpp, replace *Shape* everywhere with *CShape*. Make sure you use the Match Whole Word option in the Replace dialog box. Then you can use the Replace All button.

5. Change the type of the *m_pShpTemp* declaration from *Shape* to *CShape∗* (in the file DrawVw.h). You must also use the -> notation when accessing members using the new pointer. In *OnMouseMove*, change the following two lines:

```
m_pShpTemp.m_boxShape.bottom = point.y;
m_pShpTemp.m_boxShape.right = point.x;
```

to look like the following:

```
m_pShpTemp->m_boxShape.bottom = point.y;
m_pShpTemp->m_boxShape.right = point.x;
```

6. In *OnLButtonUp*, change the following two lines:

```
m_pShpTemp.m_boxShape.right = point.x;
m_pShpTemp.m_boxShape.bottom = point.y;
```

to look like the following:

```
m_pShpTemp->m_boxShape.right = point.x;
m_pShpTemp->m_boxShape.bottom = point.y
```

Finally, use WizardBar's Add Member Function command to add a new member function, *CreateShape*, to the file DrawDoc.cpp:

```
CShape* CMyDrawDoc::CreateShape(ShpType st)
{
    ASSERT(st >= shpRectangle && st <= shpEllipse);
    switch(st)
    {
    case shpRectangle:
        {
            CShpRectangle* pRectangle = new CShpRectangle;
            ASSERT(pRectangle != NULL);
            m_listShapes.AddHead(pRectangle);
        }
        break;
    case shpEllipse:
        {
            CShpEllipse* pEllipse = new CShpEllipse;
            ASSERT(pEllipse != NULL);
            m_listShapes.AddHead(pEllipse);
        }
        break;
    default: ;  // Nothing
    }

    // Return the object just created.
    if(m_listShapes.GetCount() > 0)
        return (CShape*)m_listShapes.GetHead();
    else
        return NULL;
}
```

In Chapter 3, we discussed the dangers of returning a pointer as a function result. However, the *CShape* pointer returned by *CreateShape* is perfectly safe. The object to which it points is stored in the list data structure, and we already have a mechanism for deleting those objects once we finish with them. It's not up to us to remember to call *delete* on this pointer.

Redrawing all shapes in *OnDraw*

Our new version of *OnDraw* uses the document's *SetToOldestShape* member function to position its conceptual pointer to the end of the list. Then *OnDraw* repeatedly calls *GetPrevShape* to move backward along the list, drawing each shape as it goes. This draws the shapes in the same order in which the user originally drew them.

Try it now

Replace the old *OnDraw*, in the file DrawVw.cpp, with the following. (Note the boldface lines.)

```
void CMyDrawView::OnDraw(CDC* pDC)
{
    CMyDrawDoc* pDoc = GetDocument();
    ASSERT_VALID(pDoc);
    // TODO: add draw code for native data here

    // Iterate the shapes from oldest to newest.
    // (Draw them in the same order as originally drawn.)
    CShape* pShape;
    pDoc->SetToOldestShape();
    while(pDoc->GetPos() != NULL)
    {
        // Get the shape and use it to set the pen and brush.
        // Last shape sets position to NULL.
        pShape = pDoc->GetPrevShape();
        SetPenBrush(pDC, pShape->m_bTransparent,
            pShape->m_nColorShape);
        // Ask the shape to draw itself.
        pShape->Draw(pDC);
        // Clean up.
        ResetPenBrush(pDC);
    }
}
```

To control the *while* loop, we call the document's *GetPos* member function. If *GetPos* returns *NULL*, the *m_pos* data member has been set to *NULL*, either by *SetToOldestShape* or by *GetPrevShape*. This tells us we've walked past the final element in the list—actually the first element, since we're walking the list backward—so it's time to stop iterating. On each pass through the loop, we obtain a pointer to the next shape, *pShape*. We pass *pShape*'s color and transparency data members as parameters in a call to *SetPenBrush*. This sets the brush to a *NULL_BRUSH* if the shape is transparent and sets the pen to *pShape*'s *m_nColorShape* value. With the pen and brush set, we call *pShape*'s *Draw* member function to do the drawing and then we reset the pen and brush. The call to *Draw* invokes *Draw* for the correct data class, *CShpRectangle* or *CShpEllipse*, depending on which class was used to create the current shape object.

Redrawing shapes in *InvertShape*

Changing our shape representation to a class hierarchy also requires drawing differently in the view's *InvertShape* function.

 Try it now

In the file DrawVw.cpp, change the *InvertShape* implementation to remove the *switch* statement, replacing it as shown here.

```
void CMyDrawView::InvertShape(CDC *pDC, CShape &s, bool bInvert)
{
    ASSERT(pDC != NULL);
    // Drawing mode is R2_NOT: black -> white, white -> black,
    //   colors -> inverse color.
    // If shape already drawn, this erases; else draws it.
    int nModeOld;
    if(bInvert)
    {
        nModeOld = pDC->SetROP2(R2_NOT);
    }

    // Draw the shape (or erase it).
    SetPenBrush(pDC, s.m_bTransparent, s.m_nColorShape);
    s.Draw(pDC);

    // Restore old values in DC.
    if(bInvert)
    {
        pDC->SetROP2(nModeOld);
    }
    ResetPenBrush(pDC);
}
```

We simply replace the *switch* statement with a call to the current shape's *Draw* member function—exactly the kind of benefit we wanted from the new implementation.

Inside the document's data interface

Let's add and examine *SetToOldestShape*, *GetPrevShape*, and the other new document member functions. We'll implement these functions as inline functions; we'll put the entire implementation for an inline function in the header file, not the implementation file. This suggests to the compiler that, everywhere it encounters the function name, it should replace the function call with the body of the function, "in line," right on the spot. It's a suggestion only; the compiler can ignore it. But in most cases the compiler will make the function inline and improve MyDraw's efficiency a bit. I introduced inline functions in "Defining member functions inline" in Chapter 4.

Try it now

In this section and the next, you'll add the *SetToOldestShape*, *SetToLatestShape*, *GetPrevShape*, *GetNextShape*, *GetPos*, *GetCount*, *DeleteLatestShape*, and *DeleteAllShapes* functions to the document class.

First, add the *SetToOldestShape* and *SetToLatestShape* inline member functions to the document class, in the public attributes section of the file DrawDoc.h. You don't need the Add Member Function command for inline functions, since all of the code is in the header file. Here's the code. (Don't forget the semicolon at the end of the function body or the semicolon following the line of code inside the function body.)

```
void SetToOldestShape() { m_pos = m_listShapes.GetTailPosition(); };
void SetToLatestShape() { m_pos = m_listShapes.GetHeadPosition(); };
```

Here you begin to see some of the interface to *CObList* itself. *CObList* has *GetHeadPosition* and *GetTailPosition* member functions. These set an internal position marker to the head or tail of the list, respectively, and return that marker as an object of type *POSITION*. Most of the MFC collection classes use the *POSITION* type. Check the Help index for *POSITION* and *CObList*. We store the returned position in the document's *m_pos* data member so we can then pass it when we call *GetPrevShape* (in conjunction with *SetToOldestShape*) or *GetNextShape* (in conjunction with *SetToLatestShape*).

Next, add the inline member functions *GetPrevShape* and *GetNextShape* to the document class, in the file DrawDoc.h:

```
CShape* GetPrevShape()
    {
        // Sets m_pos to NULL if no shapes or if
        //   latest shape is last in list.
        return (CShape*)m_listShapes.GetPrev(m_pos);
    };

CShape* GetNextShape()
    {
        // Sets m_pos to NULL if no shapes or if
        //   latest shape is last in list.
        return (CShape*)m_listShapes.GetNext(m_pos);
    };
```

GetPrevShape just calls the list object's *GetPrev* member function, passing *m_pos* as a parameter. *GetPrev* returns a pointer to the next object toward the head of the list. Notice that we have to cast the returned pointer from *CObject** to *CShape**. This is because *CObList* is a linked list of *CObject* pointers. Since *CShape* will be derived from *CObject*, the list can store pointers to *CShape* (because it's derived from *CObject*), but inside the list we can't readily tell what types the pointers point to because they all look like nothing but pointers to *CObject* there—see Figure 14-2 on the following page. Actually, they're pointers to *CShpRectangle* or *CShpEllipse* objects, but we pretend they're all *CShape* pointers inside the list elements. That works because *CShape* defines the full interface for accessing objects of classes *CShpRectangle* and *CShpEllipse*: all of the data members plus the *Draw* member function. *GetNextShape* works like *GetPrevShape* except that it calls the list object's *GetNext* member function.

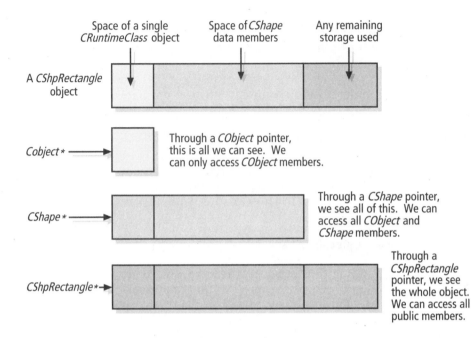

Figure 14-2. *How a* CObject *pointer conceals its actual content.*

You'll notice that the document's data interface parallels *CObList's* interface pretty closely. *SetToOldestShape* calls *GetTailPosition*, *GetPrevShape* calls *GetPrev*, and so on. This wrapper interface hides details such as the *CShape** cast and error checking (which you'll see in some of the member functions in the companion code). Iterating the list in *OnDraw* is therefore pretty clean.

Try it now

Now add the inline member function *GetPos* to the document class (file DrawDoc.h):

```
POSITION GetPos() const
    {
        // m_pos tells you where you are in a list of the shapes.
        // Use GetPos with either iteration direction to test for end.
        return m_pos;   // Can be NULL
    };
```

GetPos is a simple access function that returns the value of the private *m_pos* data member. We use that value to control the *while* loop in *OnDraw*.

Next, add the inline member function *GetCount* to the document class (file DrawDoc.h):

```
int GetCount() const
    {
        // Return the number of stored shapes.
        return m_listShapes.GetCount();
    };
```

GetCount calls the list's *GetCount* member function. We use *GetCount* in *CreateShape* to make sure there's a shape we can return a pointer to.

Finally, use the WizardBar Add Member Function command to add the *DeleteLatestShape* and *DeleteAllShapes* member functions to the document class. (These functions are a bit larger, so we won't make them inline.) Here's what you need in the file DrawDoc.cpp, in addition to function prototypes in file DrawDoc.h. (Remember that WizardBar adds the prototypes for you.)

```
void CMyDrawDoc::DeleteLatestShape()
{
    ASSERT(!m_listShapes.IsEmpty());
    CShape* pShape = (CShape*)m_listShapes.RemoveHead();
    delete pShape;
}

void CMyDrawDoc::DeleteAllShapes()
{
    POSITION pos = m_listShapes.GetHeadPosition(); // NULL if empty
    while(pos != NULL)
    {
        delete m_listShapes.GetNext(pos);
    }
    m_listShapes.RemoveAll();
    SetModifiedFlag(false); // Nothing to save now
}
```

DeleteLatestShape uses an *ASSERT* statement to test that the list isn't empty, using the list's *IsEmpty* member function. In debug builds only, the *ASSERT* statement halts the program with a message if we try to remove an object that doesn't exist. When we have the program functioning correctly, a release build removes the *ASSERT* (by not compiling it). After the test for empty, *DeleteLatestShape* calls the list's *RemoveHead* member function to extract the last shape drawn from the list. *RemoveHead* returns a pointer to the removed object, and we call *delete* on that pointer. Note the combination of steps we have to take to delete a list member: we remove it from the list, like lifting it out of a basket, and then delete it.

DeleteAllShapes must iterate through the list, deleting all of the pointers stored in it. Notice how similar this iteration loop is to the loop in *OnDraw*. First, we position to one end of the list with *GetHeadPosition*. Then we repeatedly call *GetNext*, deleting the returned pointers until *GetNext* returns *NULL*. At the end of the loop, we finish by calling the list's *RemoveAll* member function. As shown in Figure 14-3, *RemoveAll* gets rid of the linked list nodes the list was using, thus cleaning up the space used by *CObList* itself, as opposed to the space used by the shape pointers we had stored there. For more information, check the Help index for *deleting all objects in CObject collections*.

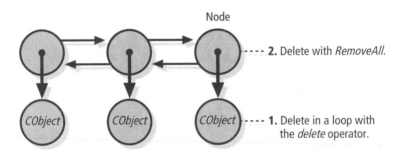

Figure 14-3.   *Deleting objects in a* CObList *and deleting the list itself.*

Cleaning Up the Document

Recall that MyDraw is a single document interface (SDI) application. SDI applications reuse the document object when the user chooses New or Open from the File menu. But before it reuses the object, MFC gives you a chance to clean up after the previous document and then reinitialize the document for reuse. For the cleanup, MFC calls the document's *DeleteContents* member function, a virtual function that you can override using WizardBar. In MyDraw, we use *DeleteContents* to deallocate all memory associated with the shape objects and with the *CObList*. That's exactly the kind of task that *DeleteContents* was designed for. (For reinitializing the document, MFC calls *OnNewDocument* for the New command and *OnOpenDocument* for the Open command.)

Try it now

Use WizardBar to override the *DeleteContents* virtual function in the document class. Select Add Virtual Function from the WizardBar Action menu, select *DeleteContents* from the New Virtual Function list, and then click Add And Edit. Add the boldface lines shown here:

```
void CMyDrawDoc::DeleteContents()
{
    // TODO: Add your specialized code here and/or call the base class
    DeleteAllShapes();
    UpdateAllViews(NULL);

    CDocument::DeleteContents();
}
```

We've already solved the problem of deleting all the shape and *CObList* heap allocations, so we simply call our own *DeleteAllShapes* member function to clean up the document. A call to *CDocument::UpdateAllViews* removes drawn objects from the client area. We don't need to reinitialize anything, so we don't do anything to *OnNewDocument*, even though App-Wizard has kindly provided an override. Now let's develop our real data type, class *CShape*, and two subclasses to represent rectangles and ellipses.

The *CShape* Class

Class *CShape* contains basically the same data as our simpler *Shape* struct. But it also has member functions, including a virtual *Draw* function so that each shape object "knows" how to draw itself. *CShape* is also now derived from an MFC class, *CObject*, thus gaining some impressive and useful abilities.

I'll present the three classes—*CShape* and two subclasses, *CShpRectangle* and *CShpEllipse*—but discuss only the base class and *CShpRectangle*. Because *CShpEllipse* is very similar to *CShpRectangle*, I'll just present its code for you to add to your project.

Why change our shape data type? Two reasons. First, we want the shape object do more of the work, especially drawing. That will also simplify some of the code in the view class. Second, in order to store the shapes in a *CObList*, the shape classes must be derived from class *CObject*.

Defining Class *CShape*

Let's define *CShape*. We'll add *CShpRectangle* and *CShpEllipse* shortly. First, we need to do some housecleaning.

Try it now

In the file DrawVw.h, remove the *Shape* declaration above the view class declaration. Remember that we renamed *Shape* to *CShape*, and it is moving to files of its own.

Next, create the *CShape* class:

1. Choose New Class from the WizardBar Action menu. This opens the New Class dialog box.

2. In the Class Type box, select Generic Class.

3. In the Name box, type *CShape*.

4. In the Base Class(es) box, click the highlighted area under Derived From and type *CObject*. Press Enter and click OK.

5. Ignore the message box that appears by clicking OK.

6. Add code to the file Shape.h so your new class looks like the following:

```
// Shape.h: interface for the CShape class.
//
////////////////////////////////////////////////////////////

#if !defined(AFX_SHAPE...
#define AFX_SHAPE...

#if _MSC_VER > 1000
#pragma once
#endif // _MSC_VER > 1000

class CShape : public CObject
{
public:
    DECLARE_SERIAL(CShape)
```

```
    // Constructors and operators
    // Default constructor
    CShape();

    // Copy constructor
    CShape(const CShape& s)
    {
        m_boxShape = s.m_boxShape;
        m_bTransparent = s.m_bTransparent;
        m_nColorShape = s.m_nColorShape;
    }

    // Overloaded assignment operator
    CShape& operator=(const CShape& s)
    {
        m_boxShape = s.m_boxShape;
        m_bTransparent = s.m_bTransparent;
        m_nColorShape = s.m_nColorShape;
        return *this;
    }

    // Attributes - deliberately left public for easy access
    // Note: no longer need an m_typeShape member.
    CRect m_boxShape;
    bool m_bTransparent;
    UINT m_nColorShape;

    // Overridables and operations
    virtual void Draw(CDC* pDC)
                    { TRACE("My Error: In CShape::Draw.\n");
                      ASSERT(FALSE); };

// Implementation
public:
    virtual ~CShape();

};

#endif
// !defined(AFX_SHAPE...
```

Move the *ShpType* enumeration declaration from file DrawVw.h to file Shape.h, just above class *CShape*.

```
    ⋮
#endif // _MSC_VER > 1000
```

(continued)

```
enum ShpType
{
    shpRectangle,
    shpEllipse
};

class CShape : public CObject
    ⋮
```

Deriving from *CObject*

The vast majority of MFC library classes derive ultimately from *CObject*, the root class of the MFC hierarchy. I discussed root classes in Chapter 5. To see the whole MFC hierarchy tree and *CObject*'s place in it, check the Help index for *hierarchy chart*.

Benefits of deriving from *CObject*

CObject provides a number of useful services, including:

- **Diagnostic support to aid debugging.** This includes the *Dump* and *AssertValid* member functions and the *ASSERT_VALID* mechanism for testing the validity of objects. I covered these topics in the file Diagnost.doc in the \learnvcn\Chap13 folder in the companion code. You can also check the Help index for the function names.

- **Run-time type information for determining an object's class.** *CObject* provides the *IsKindOf* member function as well as the *RUNTIME_CLASS* macro.

- **Dynamic object creation and other support for serialization, MFC's primary technique for writing and reading files.** We will add serialization support to *CShape* by including the *DECLARE_SERIAL* macro in its class declaration and the *IMPLEMENT_SERIAL* macro in its implementation file, Shape.cpp. The preprocessor expands these macros to add serialization support code to the class.

Taken together, these services often make it worthwhile to derive a new class from *CObject* (unless it should instead derive from some other MFC class—an important decision you should make in each case).

Quirks of deriving from *CObject*

Along with the benefits come a few costs, although the overhead involved is not high. Deriving a class from *CObject* entails the overhead of only four virtual functions and one *CRuntimeClass* object. In other words, each object of a class derived from *CObject* inherits those items, making the object somewhat larger so that creating many such objects uses more run-time memory. The amount involved in this case is minimal and not enough to worry about in most programs.

Here are some of the limitations and quirks you'll face, illustrated by *CShape* and its subclasses:

■ We will at times want to assign a pointer to a *CShape*, *CShpRectangle*, or *CShpEllipse* object to a variable of type *CShape∗* as shown in the code below. We do just that when we create a new shape and store it in the shape list. The second and fourth lines below illustrate such assignments. Because we expect to make such assignments, we have to add two public items to *CShape*: a copy constructor and an overloaded assignment operator. (I covered these C++ elements in Chapter 5.)

```
CShpRectangle* pRectangle = new CShpRectangle;
CShape* pShape = pRectangle;    // Initialize pShape
CShpRectangle* pRectangle2;
pRectangle2 = pRectangle;       // Assign to pRectangle2
```

This is because *CObject*'s copy constructor and assignment operator overload are declared private, for MFC implementation reasons. We can't use those functions because they're private, but at the same time their presence prevents the compiler from generating a public default copy constructor and assignment operator for us, as it normally would when we don't supply them ourselves. So each of our *CObject*-derived classes must provide these items if we want to be able to assign objects of the class. That's why *CShape* has the default constructor (with no parameters), the copy constructor, and the overloaded assignment operator. Here are their prototypes, as specified in the *CShape* declaration.

```
CShape();                           // Default constructor
CShape(const CShape& s);            // Copy constructor
CShape& operator=(const CShape& s); // Assignment operator
```

For more information about the need for these functions, check the Help index for *compiler errors with CObject-derived classes.*

■ Classes that provide MFC serialization support (for reading and writing files)—by containing the *DECLARE_SERIAL* and *IMPLE-MENT_SERIAL* macros—can't be abstract classes. Recall from Chapter 5 that an abstract class is intended to be used only as a base class. You'll never create an actual object from the class. The normal way to ensure that a class is abstract is to declare at least one pure virtual member function in the class, like this:

```
virtual void Draw() = 0;
```

However, as much as we'd like to, we can't make *CShape's Draw* member function pure virtual because, as it turns out, MFC's implementation of the *IMPLEMENT_SERIAL* macro creates a *CShape* object as part of its functioning. This means we must be able to construct objects of class *CShape*, but that precludes making the class abstract as we'd like to do. Thus we're forced to compromise in this case and pretend that *CShape* is really abstract when technically it's not. That's why *CShape::Draw* is not pure virtual, even though it was in our original design, back in Chapter 5. I'll say a bit more about the serialization macros shortly. By the way, notice the *TRACE* and *ASSERT* calls I've added to the definition of *CShape::Draw* for this chapter:

```
virtual void Draw(CDC* pDC)
            { TRACE("My Error: In CShape::Draw.\n");
              ASSERT(FALSE);  };
```

Because we're pretending that *CShape* is abstract, we're never meant to call this version of *Draw*, but if we somehow do, an error message and an assertion failure—*ASSERT(FALSE)* always halts the program—should alert us to the fact so we can see that we've somehow made a function call that should never be made. That's one way to make up—a bit—for our inability to use a pure virtual function.

Other considerations in deriving from *CObject*

Because *CShape* contains a virtual function (*Draw* is virtual even if not pure virtual), it also needs to have a virtual destructor (and so would its subclasses if they needed destructors, which they don't, as we'll see). *CShape*'s virtual destructor declaration looks like this:

```
virtual ~CShape();
```

The destructors, if any, in all subclasses of a class with a virtual destructor are also virtual, automatically—even though we don't customarily include the *virtual* keyword in their declarations. (I discussed destructors and virtual functions in Chapter 5.)

Why virtual destructors? In a polymorphic situation, we might not know which kind of shape object is stored in a *CShape* variable. When that object is destroyed, we want the proper destructor invoked—the destructor of the actual object in the variable (if it has one), not *CShape's* destructor. This is an application of the virtual function mechanism I described in Chapter 5. And it works even though virtual destructors, unlike other virtual functions, have different names—each class's constructor and destructor are named after the class.

So far, the destructor isn't doing anything, but that might not always be the case.

CShape as a Base Class

Besides deriving from *CObject*, *CShape* is designed to be a base class for further derivation. That's why we would have preferred to make it a true abstract class.

CShape also defines the interface—the data members and the *Draw* member function—through which all shape operations occur. That's why *CShape* itself includes all of the key data members that its subclasses need and why we declare the *Draw* member function at that level of the hierarchy. We'll store actual *CShpRectangle* and *CShpEllipse* objects in *CShape* variables—actually, in elements of a data structure that store pointers to *CShape*. Those rectangle and ellipse objects will be anonymous inside a *CShape*: we won't know at run time whether a particular *CShape* pointer points to a *CShpRectangle* or a *CShpEllipse*. We can't use a *CShape* pointer to access any members of the actual object pointed to that aren't also members of *CShape* itself. Thus we have to rely on two facts about *CShape*:

- It contains any public data members we might want to access directly (and anonymously, through a *CShape* pointer), as in these examples:

```
CShpRectangle* pRectangle = new CShpRectangle;
CShape* pShape = pRectangle;
pShape->m_boxShape = ...        // Access a data member
```

- It allows us to call the correct *Draw* member function polymorphically through a *CShape* pointer. Thus, if we have these assignments:

```
CShpRectangle* pRectangle = new CShpRectangle;
CShape* pShape = pRectangle;
    ⋮
pShape->Draw(pDC);
```

we can call *Draw* through the pointer and expect the *CShpRectangle* version of *Draw* (overridden from *CShape*) to be called.

With those design features—plus the virtual destructor—*CShape* provides everything its subclasses are likely to need.

A Derived Class: *CShpRectangle*

The *CShpRectangle* class and its sibling, the *CShpEllipse* class, are derived from *CShape* (and indirectly from *CObject*). *CShpRectangle* has the following features:

- Like *CShape*, it adds serialization support by including the *DECLARE_SERIAL* and *IMPLEMENT_SERIAL* macros. I'll cover serialization (writing and reading a shape data file) in detail in Chapter 16.

- Unlike *CShape*, *CShpRectangle* doesn't declare any data members. It inherits three data members from *CShape*. Note that we no longer need the *m_typeShape* data member in any of these classes. A *CShpRectangle* can't be anything other than a *shpRectangle*-type object, so it's redundant (and costly) to store that information in a data member. If we need to extract type information from a *CShape** pointer, we can use the *RUNTIME_CLASS* macro, like this:

```
if(pShape->IsKindOf(RUNTIME_CLASS(CShpRectangle)))...
```

The *CObject::IsKindOf* function returns *true* if *pShape*'s run-time class type is *CShpRectangle*.

■ *CShpRectangle* can simply inherit *CShape*'s copy constructor and overloaded assignment operator. With no new data members in *CShpRectangle*, the *CShape* versions can do what's needed.

■ *CShpRectangle* overrides the virtual *Draw* member function— which, like the *CShpRectangle* destructor, is virtual because it was so in *CShape*. If we had been able to declare *CShape::Draw* as a pure virtual function, we would be forced to override *Draw* in *CShpRectangle*. We did it anyway, requirement or not, since that was the whole idea all along: we wanted each type of shape object to be responsible for its own drawing. No outside object should "know" how to draw a rectangle. It should only know that it can tell a *CShpRectangle* object to draw itself and that it will do so.

Try it now

Add the *CShpRectangle* and *CShpEllipse* class declarations to the file Shape.h below the *CShape* declaration:

```
⋮
// Implementation
public:

    virtual ~CShape();

};

// Concrete subclass of abstract base class CShape
class CShpRectangle : public CShape
{
public:
```

(continued)

```
    DECLARE_SERIAL(CShpRectangle)

    // Constructors are inherited from CShape.
    // Attributes inherited include:
    //   m_boxShape, m_bTransparent, m_nColorShape

    // Operations
    void Draw(CDC* pDC);      // Overrides CShape::Draw

// Implementation
public:
};

// Concrete subclass of abstract base class CShape
class CShpEllipse : public CShape
{
public:
    DECLARE_SERIAL(CShpEllipse)

    // Constructors are inherited from CShape.
    // Attributes inherited include:
    //   m_boxShape, m_bTransparent, m_nColorShape

    // Operations
    void Draw(CDC* pDC);      // Overrides CShape::Draw

// Implementation
public:
};

#endif // defined(AFX_SHAPE...
```

CShape Implementation

It's time to finish class *CShape* by writing its definitions.

Try it now

In the file Shape.cpp, we provide the following definitions for *CShape*:

1. Include the Resource.h file at the top of Shape.cpp:

```
#include "StdAfx.h"
#include "MyDraw.h"
#include "Shape.h"
#include "Resource.h"
```

The unusual step of including Resource.h is necessary because we need to mention the *ID_COLOR_BLACK* symbol as part of *CShape's* default constructor (step 3, below). Most AppWizard-created files already include Resource.h indirectly, but the files Shape.h and Shape.cpp don't have access to the symbol without this special #*include*. We define the default constructor in Shape.cpp rather than inline in Shape.h because we don't want the inclusion of Resource.h to propagate throughout the project. (Many files ultimately include Shape.h, but most of those files already include Resource.h indirectly.) That's why we define the default constructor here rather than inline, like the other constructors.

2. Add the *IMPLEMENT_SERIAL* macro for *CShape* (to the bottom of Shape.cpp):

```
/////////////////////////////////////
// Class CShape implementation

IMPLEMENT_SERIAL(CShape, CObject, 1)
```

As parameters, the macro names the class it's for (*CShape*), the base class (*CObject*), and a number called a *schema number*. I'll explain the schema number when we add serialization to MyDraw in Chapter 16.

3. Add the default constructor for *CShape*—the constructor was actually added by WizardBar when you created the class, so just add the boldface contents:

```
CShape::CShape()
{
    m_boxShape.SetRect(0, 0, 0, 0);
    m_bTransparent = true;
    m_nColorShape = ID_COLOR_BLACK;
}
```

CShpRectangle and *CShpEllipse* Implementations

In the file Shape.cpp, we provide the following definitions for class *CShpRectangle*, following those for class *CShape*. We'll add definitions for class *CShpEllipse* in a moment.

Try it now

Add *CShpRectangle*'s serialization support and its *Draw* function override (in the file Shape.cpp).

1. Add the *IMPLEMENT_SERIAL* macro for this class:

```
/////////////////////////////////////
// Class CShpRectangle implementation

IMPLEMENT_SERIAL(CShpRectangle, CShape, 1)
```

Like the *IMPLEMENT_SERIAL* call for *CShape*, this one names the class, the base class, and the schema number.

2. Override the *Draw* member function from *CShape*.

```
void CShpRectangle::Draw(CDC* pDC)  // Virtual override
{
    pDC->Rectangle(m_boxShape);
}
```

Since this code is strictly for a *CShpRectangle* object, *Draw* can call the class *CDC* member function *Rectangle* without needing a *switch* statement to determine the shape's type. The shape's type is a given. Note that we pass *Draw* a pointer to a device context object, already prepared with the proper brush and pen by an earlier call to the view class member function *SetPenBrush*.

Now take the following steps to add definitions for class *CShpEllipse* (in the Shape.cpp file):

1. Add the *IMPLEMENT_SERIAL* macro for this class:

```
/////////////////////////////////////
// Class CShpEllipse implementation

IMPLEMENT_SERIAL(CShpEllipse, CShape, 1)
```

2. Override the *Draw* member function from *CShape*.

```
void CShpEllipse::Draw(CDC* pDC)  // Virtual override
{
    pDC->Ellipse(m_boxShape);
}
```

This parallels the *CShpRectangle* version of *Draw*.

Fixing Up MyDraw's Header Structure

With the addition of the files Shape.h and Shape.cpp to the project, the header structure needs to change a bit. You already added an include statement for Resource.h at the top of the file Shape.cpp. Now we need to make a few more changes. Figure 14-4 illustrates the new header structure.

Try it now

Make the following header changes:

■ In the file DrawDoc.h, include Shape.h.

⋮
```
#endif // _MSC_VER > 1000

#include "Shape.h"
```
⋮

■ In the file DrawVw.h, include DrawDoc.h (but not Shape.h—the view gets *CShape* by including the document header file).

⋮
```
#endif // _MSC_VER > 1000

#include "DrawDoc.h"
```
⋮

■ In the files MyDraw.cpp (the application class) and DrawVw.cpp (the view class), remove the #*include* directives for DrawDoc.h. The view and application now include the document and *CShape* by including DrawVw.h.

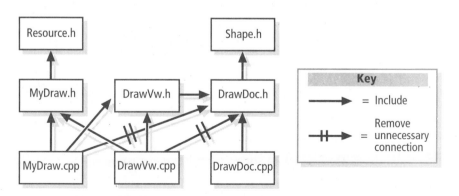

Figure 14-4. *The new header structure for the program MyDraw4.*

Having made all of those changes, you can build and run MyDraw. Its outward behavior doesn't change much, since the alterations we've made are primarily infrastructure changes rather than user interface changes. The one new thing you'll notice is that when you exit MyDraw after drawing some shapes, the document displays a dialog box asking if you want to save the drawing. This occurs because we called *SetModifiedFlag* in *OnLButtonDown*. Click No for now, since we haven't implemented file saving. (Actually, clicking Yes does display the Save As dialog box and then saves a zero-length file with the name you specify. By default, the filename is Untitled.drw.)

Summary of Data Class Design Considerations

The design of our *CShape* class hierarchy illustrates several points to keep in mind. We can distinguish between classes that represent values—*value classes*—and classes that are real extensions to the MFC framework—*framework classes*. *CShape* and its subclasses are basically value classes, somewhat like *ints* and *chars*. We expect to pass them as parameters, assign them to variables, and otherwise treat them as values.

Typically, value classes such as *CString* or *CRect* don't have virtual functions, aren't used as base classes, aren't designed to be derived from, and do have an overloaded assignment operator and a copy constructor. Typically, two objects of a value class can be compared. The *CShape* classes follow some of these guidelines but not others: the shape classes do have an assignment operator and a copy constructor. But they also do have virtual functions, and *CShape* is designed as a base class, from which we intended to derive other classes. (The derived classes are the real value classes for us.) I also haven't implemented the ability to compare two shapes; I haven't seen the need for that so far. (If we did need it, I'd write an overloaded equals operator (==) and possibly overloaded !=, <, and other comparison operators. I discussed overloaded C++ operators in Chapter 5.)

If it weren't for some special needs, though, I would have tried to adhere to those typical principles. *CShape* used to be a true value class in most respects, since it could represent any type of shape. I chose to create a class hierarchy from it, though, to take advantage of polymorphism. I wanted shape objects to be able to draw themselves, and I needed to have the proper shape drawn even if I didn't know what shape it was at run time. The class hierarchy gave me those abilities.

The *CShape* classes also:

- **Define virtual destructors.** Well, *CShape* itself does, and the sub-classes would if they had any data members of their own. A virtual destructor lets you destroy an object without knowing its type.

- **Declare most of their members as public.** Where we're changing the data in a shape object frequently, it's more convenient to access most shape data members directly than to use access functions.

- **Use *const* where possible.** The *const* keyword is a guarantee to users of the class that a particular function or parameter doesn't alter the object declared *const*. It's good public relations.

At rock bottom, a key consideration is my own convenience in using these classes (and showing you some of the C++ possibilities). These are really one-off classes, not written to be reused widely by many programmers in their own programs. Your code might not fit that description, though, so your design constraints might be stricter.

Try It Yourself

Here's the latest batch of do-it-yourself projects for extra credit. (By the way, you *have* been getting your extra credit, haven't you?)

1. Experiment with class *CObArray*.

Copy all of the files from MyDraw into a new directory and reimplement the document's data structure using class *CObArray* rather than class *CObList*. You might want to rewrite the *OnDraw* member function first, using *CObArray* member functions (and assuming that *m_listShapes* is now a *CObArray*). With an array, you'll want to store new shapes in array fashion, starting with the oldest shape in element 0 and adding new shapes beyond that. Adding each new shape at the "head" of the array would be very costly because array insertions are time consuming.

To access array elements, you can use *CObArray*'s overloaded array access operator [] or its *GetAt* member function. Thus, you can write code like this as if *m_listShapes* were an ordinary C++ array—but you don't have to worry as much about overshooting the bounds:

```
m_listShapes[0] = m_pShape;
m_pShape = m_listShapes[nIndex];
```

Make sure you understand the difference between *CObArray::GetSize* and *CObArray::GetUpperBound*. *GetSize* tells you how many elements there are (including element 0). *GetUpperBound* tells you, in a zero-based array, what the highest used array index is. This should be one greater than the value from *GetSize*. You'll also need to call *SetSize*, perhaps in the document constructor, to specify how the array can grow. Parameters of 30 and, say, 10 might be a good place to start. You can use *Add* to add new shapes in *CreateShape*. Don't forget to clean up the array as we did the list. Check the Help index for *CObArray* and see Figure 14-5. Also see the program Ch14Ex1 and the program BBall in the \learnvcn\Chap14 folder in the companion code. Ch14ex1 is a version of MyDraw that uses *CObArray* as described here. BBall illustrates using a *CStringArray*, which is very similar to a *CObArray*.

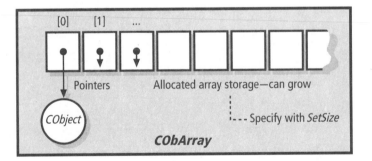

Figure 14-5. *The abstract structure of a* CObArray.

2. **Experiment with AppWizard's option to eliminate document/view support.**

Run AppWizard and select MFC AppWizard (exe) in the Projects tab. In step 1, clear the Document/View Architecture Support box. Set the remaining AppWizard options however you like, though I recommend sticking with a single document application (SDI). Examine the resulting files. In particular, note that there's no document class, and that there is a view class, called *CChildView*, which is derived from class *CWnd*, the root class of all window classes, not from *CView*. The view class works like the ordinary *CView*-derived class except that there are lots of things it can't do, such as help you with scrolling, printing, and print preview. The view overlies the frame window's client area, and you draw in an *OnPaint* handler, not in *OnDraw*. Also note that the view's *PreCreateWindow* member function actually does some work. It calls the MFC global function *AfxRegisterWndClass* to register a window class with certain styles. This is how you would use *PreCreateWindow*—if you needed to register window styles—in any MFC application.

Write a simple Hello program using this model. It might help to review our MyHi program in "Let's Write Some Code" in Chapter 7. Program Ch14ex2 in the \learnvcn\Chap14 folder in the companion code demonstrates how to write such a non-document/view application. Why wouldn't the non-document/view option be the best option to choose for MyDraw?

What's Next?

In Chapter 15, we'll deal with one of our main viewing problems by adding scrolling to MyDraw. We'll also briefly look at drawing text instead of geometric shapes.

Rounding Out
Your MFC Skills

Scrolling

Recall that MyDraw step 4 doesn't let you see the entire drawing surface. MyDraw step 5 does. Step 4 has no scroll bars, so although you can draw shapes that lie partially outside MyDraw's window, you can't adjust the window to see those shapes entirely. In this chapter, we'll solve that final viewing problem for good. Along the way, I'll also explain a few things about drawing text.

Why We Need Scroll Bars

If why we need scroll bars in MyDraw is not completely apparent to you, try the experiments in this section.

Try it now

Run MyDraw again and draw some shapes—including some for which you release the mouse button outside the window. As shown in Figure 15-1 on the following page, only part of such a shape is visible. With the default window size, you can't see all of the shapes you drew. Where are they? The program tried to draw all of the shapes, but any whose y coordinates placed them below the bottom of the window or whose x coordinates placed them to the right of the window's right border got *clipped*. That is, Microsoft Windows limited the drawing to the client area rectangle.

Windows clips the drawing to keep programs from drawing over windows belonging to other programs, and possibly even across window borders and title bars. The device context tracks which regions of the client area need repainting, and it can constrain drawing to just those regions. This feature can limit the amount of repainting that Windows does. You can get the rectangle that *OnDraw* updates (the painting area) using the *GetUpdateRect* function in class *CWnd*. You can then use this function in your *OnDraw* or *OnUpdate* function. *GetUpdateRect* can boost your program's efficiency if there's a lot of data to redraw. Restricting drawing to part of the client area can also give you some drawing advantages.

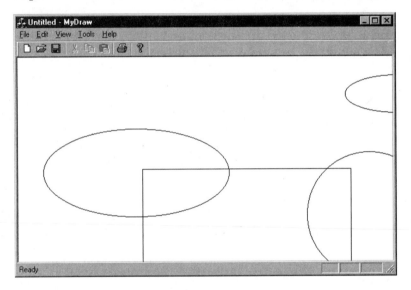

Figure 15-1.   *MyDraw with shapes that don't fit in the window.*

How can you see the rest of those shapes—the parts that lie outside the client area? Try the following experiment.

Try it now

With the shapes you drew for the last experiment still showing, click MyDraw's Maximize button (located on the right side of the window's title bar). This might reveal all of your shapes—as the client area enlarges with the window—if you have a large monitor and use a high display resolution. But on my laptop, for example, I can't enlarge the window very much. If I were in VGA mode rather than 800 by 600, it would be even worse. Furthermore, after maximizing the window, I can continue drawing shapes that lie partially outside the window. Clearly, relying on the ability to resize the window won't solve this problem.

The solution is to add *scroll bars* to the window so that MyDraw users can scroll through all of the drawn shapes. Doing so is pretty easy with Microsoft Foundation Class Library 6.0 (MFC).

> **NOTE** Even with scroll bars, you can still drag the mouse and release it outside the window to draw shapes only partially visible in the window.

Some Scrolling Theory

The concept of scrolling is based on the idea of a drawing surface that is larger than the window that you use to look at the surface. Visualize a window moving over a larger surface or, alternatively, a long parchment scroll being rolled and unrolled to reveal certain sections. The window is a *viewport* or peephole through which you can see the graphical objects drawn on the surface "below." (See Figure 15-2 on the following page.)

To move the viewport around, you drag or click its scroll bars. A horizontal scroll bar moves you from side to side, and a vertical scroll bar moves you up and down. To see the end of a vertically oriented document such as a text file, for instance, you drag the vertical scroll bar's *thumb* (the small box or indicator that moves between the sides of the scroll bar shaft) as far down as it goes. Figure 15-3 on the following page shows the parts of a scroll bar.

Inside the program, scrolling is accomplished by translating scroll bar movements into adjustments of the view's *origin* with respect to the drawing area's origin. The view's origin is initially the (0, 0) point in the device context's device coordinate system. It's normally located at the upper left corner of the view's window. Scrolling down and to the right by 100 units each actually moves the view origin to that point—called the *scroll position*—on the drawing area. For example, when you scroll to (100, 100), the upper left corner of the view appears to move to that coordinate on the drawing area. It's as if the upper left window corner jumps to the scroll position. MFC moves the origin by calling the *CDC::SetViewportOrg* function or the *CDC::SetWindowOrg* function. You can call them too, but if you let MFC handle scrolling, you won't normally need to think much about the origin, let alone moving it. See the sidebar "*SetViewportOrg* and *SetWindowOrg*" for a bit of information about these functions.

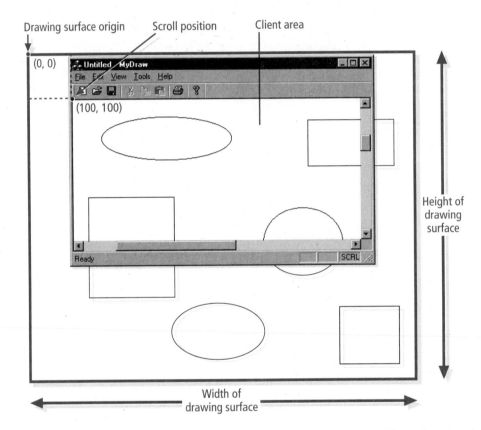

Figure 15-2.   *Scroll position after scrolling the window 100 units horizontally and 100 units vertically.*

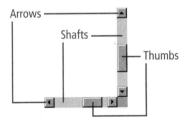

Figure 15-3.   *Scroll bar parts.*

Managing scrolling on your own is complex and somewhat counterintuitive. It's much simpler with MFC's *CScrollView* class, though, and that's what I'll show you here. However, be aware that *CScrollView* is not suitable for files larger than about 32,000 characters—it slows down and can't always accommodate them. Figure 15-4 on the following page shows *CScrollView*'s place in the MFC class hierarchy.

SetViewportOrg and *SetWindowOrg*

Using *SetViewportOrg* and *SetWindowOrg* is a bit advanced, but here's a brief discussion of them. Device coordinate systems have their origins (0, 0) at the upper left corner of the device context's display area. The *x* and *y* axes increase to the right and down, respectively, and the unit of measurement is the pixel. In logical coordinate systems, the orientation of the *x* and *y* axes and the units of measurement are determined by the current mapping mode—but the origin can be moved. By default, it's at the upper left corner, but you can adjust its location with either *SetViewportOrg* or *SetWindowOrg*.

SetViewportOrg works with device coordinates. You feed it a device coordinate, and it resets the origin of the view window to that point. It maps the logical point (0, 0) to the point you specify in device coordinates.

SetWindowOrg works with logical coordinates. You feed it a logical coordinate, and it moves the origin of the view window to that point. It maps the supplied logical point to the device point (0, 0). Which function you use depends on the coordinates of the location you choose for your view's origin.

Why would you move the origin? You might, for example, wish to represent mathematical curves in a Cartesian coordinate system that allows negative coordinates. You could achieve that by moving the origin to the center of your view. I won't illustrate this, but some of the books listed in Chapter 21 do.

A *CScrollView* is derived from a *CView*, which is derived from a *CWnd*, which is derived from a *CObject*. *CCtrlView* is a sibling of *CScrollView*, so it and its descendants lack scrolling ability. But *CFormView* and its descendants, the record-view classes for working with databases, are scrollable.

If your view class is derived from *CScrollView* instead of *CView*, you can easily hook up its scrolling functionality to fit your needs. When Windows sends your view window a *WM_VSCROLL* (or *WM_HSCROLL*) message, *CScrollView*'s *OnVScroll* (or *OnHScroll*) member function handles the message. *OnVScroll* determines from the message what part of the scroll bar was clicked (up arrow, down arrow, scroll bar shaft, or scroll bar thumb). It translates these into line up or down, page up or down, or thumb-dragging actions. Then it adjusts the scroll position and uses *CWnd::ScrollWindow* to do the scrolling (by adjusting the origin). The user sees the text or graphics inside the window move up, down, right, or left.

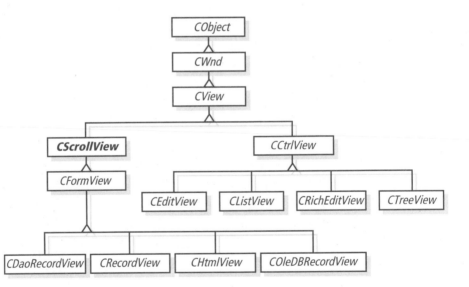

Figure 15-4.   *MFC view class hierarchy, including* CScrollView.

Scrolling: The Basic Technique

The main thing you have to do to implement scrolling with class *CScrollView* is supply information about the size of the drawing surface you want to scroll over and specify how much the view should scroll in response to clicks in a scroll bar arrow or the scroll bar shaft. *CScrollView* also takes care of tracking the scroll bar thumb as the user drags it with the mouse, sending appropriate *WM_VSCROLL* or *WM_HSCROLL* messages. Here's a summary of how to implement scrolling in your MFC program:

1. Change the derivation of your view class from *CView* to *CScrollView*. If you know you'll need scrolling at the time you run AppWizard, you can change it in the wizard. If you decide on it later, you can simply search the .h and .cpp files for the view class for all occurrences of "*CView*" and replace them with "*CScrollView*." You can also base your view class on any MFC view classes that derive from *CScrollView*. See the view hierarchy in Figure 15-4.

2. Set up any variables you'll need to keep as view class members, in the view's .h file. A good place to initialize them is in an override of the *OnInitialUpdate* member function or the *OnUpdate* member function. You'll need to add the override for that virtual function.

3. Plan the dimensions of your drawing surface, and define how the view should respond to clicks in the up, down, right, or left scroll arrows or in the scroll bar shafts. I'll give guidelines and examples.

4. In *OnInitialUpdate*, or possibly in *OnUpdate*, initialize variables and call the *CScrollView::SetScrollSizes* member function. Pass the information you worked out in step 3 just above.

The following MFC sample programs use *CScrollView* or one of its subclasses: Scribble, DrawCli, ChkBook, and ViewEx. Check the Help index for the sample names if you want a closer look.

Scrolling Lines of Text

Regardless of what you're drawing in your view, you want the scroll bars to scroll the contents by appropriate amounts depending on which part of which scroll bar is clicked. Before we tackle scrolling the graphics in MyDraw, let's look at a simple text-drawing example. Remember that everything that appears in your window, including text, is *drawn*.

Try it now

Create a new MFC AppWizard (.exe) project called MyText, with settings the same as those in MyDraw (single document interface, no database or ActiveX Controls, and so on).

1. Add the boldface code shown below to the application's *OnDraw* member function:

```
///////////////////////////////////////////...
// CMyTextView drawing
const int MARGIN_LEFT = 5;
const int LINES = 30;

void CMyTextView::OnDraw(CDC* pDC)
{
    CMyTextDoc* pDoc = GetDocument();
    ASSERT_VALID(pDoc);
    // TODO: add draw code for native data here
    ASSERT(m_nHeightLine > 0);
    CString strLines;
    for(int nLines = 0; nLines < LINES; nLines++)
    {
        strLines.Format("%d: ", nLines);
        if(nLines < 10)
            strLines += "   ";
        pDC->TextOut(MARGIN_LEFT, nLines * m_nHeightLine,
                                    strLines + m_strTextDraw);
    }
}
```

Notice the two constant declarations just above *OnDraw*'s definition.

2. In the view class declaration, add the following data members as public attributes:

```
int m_nHeightLine;
CString m_strTextDraw;
```

3. Use WizardBar to create the *OnInitialUpdate* virtual function override shown here:

```
void CMyTextView::OnInitialUpdate()
{
    CView::OnInitialUpdate();

    // TODO: Add your specialized code here...
    CClientDC dc(this);
```

```
    // Declare a TEXTMETRIC variable.
    TEXTMETRIC tm;

    // Fill up the variable with information.
    dc.GetTextMetrics(&tm);

    // Compute various sizes needed for drawing.
    //int m_cxChar = tm.tmAveCharWidth;      // Other useful values
    //int m_cyChar = tm.tmHeight;
    m_nHeightLine = tm.tmHeight + tm.tmExternalLeading;

    m_strTextDraw = "No matter where you go, there you are.";
    m_strTextDraw += "  -- Buckaroo Banzai, ";
    m_strTextDraw += "The Adventures of Buckaroo Banzai Across ";
    m_strTextDraw += "the Eighth Dimension";
}
```

Now build and run the application. You see a number of lines of text, but you almost certainly don't see all 30 lines that the program draws.

Before we continue the scrolling discussion, let's briefly look at text drawing in Windows with MFC. We focus on drawing graphical shapes in this book, so consider this a short introduction to the other side.

Drawing Text

When you draw text, you specify where it starts in the view, and you specify the text itself. Most of the rest of what you need comes from the device context. The device context stores a current font—by default, it's a font called *SYSTEM_FONT*, but you can select a different font into the device context using class *CFont*. The font determines most of the visual characteristics of your drawn text, including all of its typographical characteristics—its typographical style. Thus, the Times New Roman font looks different from the Arial font. Besides the font, the device context stores a current text color and a current text background color. Both colors are part of the device context, not part of the font, and you can change them with *CDC::SetTextColor* and *CDC::SetBkColor*. You can also determine their current values with *CDC::GetTextColor* and *CDC::GetBkColor*. Check the Help index for these function names and for class *CFont*. The color values are of type *COLORREF*, the type used in the RGB color system we looked at in Chapter 12.

The text drawing in MyText consists of two phases:

1. We determine the important sizes associated with text drawn in the device context's current font. This helps us position and space lines correctly.

2. We draw the text in a loop, using *CDC::TextOut*, which you've seen before. I'll briefly introduce several other text drawing functions later in this chapter.

Obtaining text metrics

We'll want to query the device context for text measurements before MFC calls *OnDraw*. The *OnInitialUpdate* member function is called once, just before *OnDraw* is called the first time, so it's a logical place for these queries. (Another place often used for this purpose is an overridden *OnCreate* member function.)

The important size value for us is the overall line height based on the height of the actual text (including risers like the upper line of the letter *h* and descenders like the lower line in *y*), plus the amount of external leading (vertical blank space) between two lines of text. For completeness, the *OnInitialUpdate* function shows two other values often used in handling text: the height of a character in the current font (*m_cyChar*) and the average width of a character in the current font (*m_cxChar*). We use average width because most fonts are *proportional*—different characters have different widths (so *m* is wider than *i*). Figure 15-5 shows the parts of a font, with the font terminology used here. All of the descriptions of fonts in this book refer to TrueType fonts, the most recent of the font technologies for Windows.

To determine the text sizes, we call *CDC::GetTextMetrics* to obtain a *TEXTMETRIC* object. *TEXTMETRIC* is a Windows data structure that contains a great deal of information about how the current font draws text. Here's an abbreviated version of the structure. (You can check the Help index for *TEXTMETRIC* to learn more.)

```
typedef struct tagTEXTMETRIC {
    LONG tmHeight;
    LONG tmAscent;
    LONG tmDescent;
    LONG tmInternalLeading;
```

```
  LONG tmExternalLeading;
  LONG tmAveCharWidth;
  LONG tmMaxCharWidth;
  LONG tmWeight;
    ⋮
} TEXTMETRIC;
```

We use the text metrics information returned by *GetTextMetrics* to set the view class member variable *m_nHeightLine,* as in this code from the *OnInitialUpdate* function:

```
// Declare a TEXTMETRIC variable
TEXTMETRIC tm;

// Fill up the variable with information
dc.GetTextMetrics(&tm);

// Compute various sizes needed for drawing
//int m_cxChar = tm.tmAveCharWidth;        // Other useful values
//int m_cyChar = tm.tmHeight;
m_nHeightLine = tm.tmHeight + tm.tmExternalLeading;
```

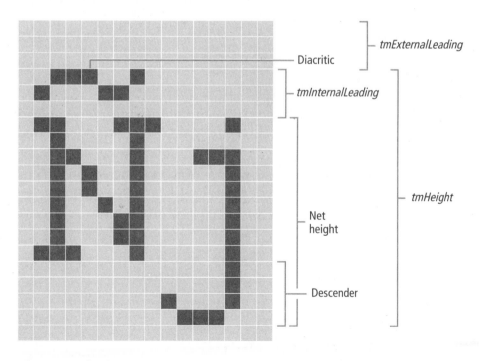

Figure 15-5. *The parts of a font.*
(From *Programming Visual C++,* 5th edition, by David J. Kruglinski, Microsoft Press, 1998.)

You can set other variables as well, such as *m_cxChar* and *m_cyChar*, as shown in the commented-out lines in *OnInitialUpdate*.

Drawing the text

To draw the text, we use a *for* loop in *OnDraw*:

```
⋮
const int MARGIN_LEFT = 5;
const int LINES = 30;
⋮
for(int nLines = 0; nLines < LINES; nLines++)
{
    ⋮
    pDC->TextOut(MARGIN_LEFT, nLines * m_nHeightLine,
                                        m_strTextDraw);
}
```

The *TextOut* call takes three parameters: a horizontal starting coordinate, *x*; a vertical starting coordinate, *y*; and the text to draw. These specify where the upper left corner of the text will be placed. We specify the *x* value as a left margin, five logical units to the right of the view's left edge. We recalculate the *y* value each time through the loop to obtain the correct line spacing so that lines are drawn successively down the page. If *nlines* is the current line number, the current line begins at this *y* coordinate:

```
nLines * m_nHeightLine
```

The text is from the American film *The Adventures of Buckaroo Banzai Across the Eighth Dimension* (Twentieth Century Fox, 1984)—a cult classic directed by W.D. Richter. I've set this as the value of *m_strTextDraw* in *OnInitialUpdate*. Note the use of the += operator, which is overloaded for class *CString* to mean "concatenate the string following this operator to the *CString* variable on the left side of the operator." Here's the code from *OnInitialUpdate*:

```
m_strTextDraw = "No matter where you go, there you are.";
m_strTextDraw += "  -- Buckaroo Banzai, ";
m_strTextDraw += "The Adventures of Buckaroo Banzai Across ";
m_strTextDraw += "the Eighth Dimension";
```

Other text drawing member functions of class *CDC* include:

- **DrawText.** You specify a rectangle in which you want the text drawn. You can also specify alignment: centered, right justified, or left justified. Check the Help index for *DrawText*.

- **ExtTextOut.** This is a close relative of *TextOut*, which, like *DrawText*, draws the text in a bounding rectangle that you supply. Check the Help index for *ExtTextOut*.

- **TabbedTextOut.** This function draws text that contains tab characters, replacing the tabs with the amount of space you specify. Check the Help index for *TabbedTextOut*.

Some of these text-drawing functions are illustrated in Program Tabs in the \learnvcn\Chap15 folder in the companion code.

> **NOTE** If you ever need to write code with strings that work under Unicode, pass your literal strings to the _T macro, like this: _T("This is my string"). This creates strings whose characters are 2 bytes wide if Unicode is in effect, or 1 byte wide if not. Unicode uses 2-byte characters. I haven't used _T in this book, but for more information, check the Help index for *Strings* and select the subtopic "Unicode support in MFC." Also check the index for *Unicode* and take some time to study class *CString*.

A little extra

To dramatize the need for scroll bars, I've added code to MyText to prefix each line of text with a line number, as shown here in the boldface lines from the *OnDraw* function:

```
⋮
CString strLines;
for(int nLines = 0; nLines < LINES; nLines++)
{
    strLines.Format("%d: ", nLines);
    if(nLines < 10)
        strLines += "   ";
    pDC->TextOut(MARGIN_LEFT, nLines * m_nHeightLine,
                                    strLines + m_strTextDraw);
}
```

I use the *strLines* variable to store the current line number converted to a string. Inside the loop, I convert the line number *nLines* to a string using the *CString::Format* member function, which works a lot like the now familiar *printf* run-time function. If the line number is less than 10, I pad it with extra space for better vertical alignment of the printed line numbers. To attach the line number to the text to draw, I use class *CString*'s concatenation operator +, directly in the output statement.

Now let's figure out how to scroll the text.

Setting Scroll Sizes

The *scroll area* is the *extent* of the text—the width and height through which you can scroll, meaning the width of a line and the height of all lines of text combined.

Clicks in the *scroll bar arrows* are interpreted, for text drawing, as line up or line down commands, so you need to specify a suitable value, such as the height of a line of your text (including external leading). You can get the text width by calling *CDC::GetTextExtent*, which returns both the width and the height of a string of text. For the text height, it's safer to use our *m_nHeightLine* variable rather than the *y* value returned by the function *GetTextExtent*. (If there's a horizontal scroll bar as well as a vertical one, you also need to specify how much to move from side to side in response to a horizontal scroll bar arrow click. That's usually some fraction of the scroll area's width, such as 1/10 or 1/8, but you may need to experiment to see what looks right. I use 1/10 in MyText.)

Clicks in the shaft of the scroll bar—not the arrows and not the thumb—are interpreted, for text drawing, as Page Up or Page Down commands, like those often produced by the Page Up and Page Down keys. So you need to specify a suitable page height. (This is an amount to scroll, not the same thing as the height of a printable page of your document.) Values commonly used for page height include a few multiples of the line height (for text), or often the current height of the client area. If you're drawing text instead of graphical shapes, you can get the line height as part of the text metrics. You can get the client area height from *CWnd::GetClientRect*. (If there's a horizontal scroll bar, you need to specify how much to move from side to side in response to a click in a horizontal scroll bar shaft. For text, this might be half or one-third of the overall text width, obtainable from *GetTextExtent*.)

Adding Scrolling to MyText

Now it's a pretty simple matter to add scrolling to MyText.

Try it now

Make the following changes to MyText:

1. Use the Find/Replace command to replace all instances of the string *CView* with *CScrollView* throughout the two view class files. In other words, rederive your view class from *CScrollView*.

2. Add the boldface lines shown here to the *OnInitialUpdate* member function:

```
    ⋮
m_strTextDraw = "No matter where you go, there you are.";
m_strTextDraw += "  -- Buckaroo Banzai, ";
m_strTextDraw += "The Adventures of Buckaroo Banzai Across ";
m_strTextDraw += "the Eighth Dimension";
CString str = "999: " + m_strTextDraw;   // Allow for line
                                          //  numbering.
CSize size = dc.GetTextExtent(str);

const int FUDGE_H = 60;
const int FUDGE_V = 30;

int nWidth = size.cx + FUDGE_H;
int nHeight = m_nHeightLine * LINES + FUDGE_V;

CSize sizeTotal = CSize(nWidth, nHeight);
CSize sizePage = CSize(nWidth / 3, nHeight / 3);
CSize sizeLine = CSize(nWidth / 10, m_nHeightLine);

SetScrollSizes(MM_TEXT, sizeTotal, sizePage, sizeLine);
```

That's all it takes to add scrolling.

Rederiving the view class

We could have rederived the view class from *CScrollView* instead of from *CView* in AppWizard, but it's easy to make the change after the fact (and it shows that you can usually add AppWizard features later, even if you fail to select them when you run the wizard).

> **TIP** To add an AppWizard feature after the fact, run the wizard again with that feature selected (and most other features not selected), then again without the desired feature, and compare the two sets of files. You can use a program like WinDiff to perform this comparison. (WinDiff is available with the Microsoft Visual C++ 6.0 Introductory Edition. Click the Windows Start button, look under Programs, Microsoft Visual C++, and then under Microsoft Visual C++ Tools. WinDiff is second from the bottom on the menu that pops up.) Then, to your ongoing project, add the lines of code that show up as extras in the comparison, and test the updated project.

Computing scroll sizes

The code we wrote in *OnInitialUpdate* computes some scroll size information and passes it to the *CScrollView::SetScrollSizes* member function. Then *CScrollView* does the rest.

The code in *OnInitialUpdate* uses several function calls to perform its computations. These functions warrant further description.

Call *CDC::GetTextExtent* to measure the width of the text to draw based on the current font. This returns a *CSize* object. Class *CSize* contains *cx* and *cy* members: *cx* contains a horizontal size value (the width of our line of text in logical units), and *cy* contains a vertical size value (the height of a line of text in logical units). For line height, we'll use the safer value *m_nHeightLine* instead of the *cy* value from *GetTextExtent*.

Next I compute the total width and height of 30 lines of text—the document sizes. Note that I've added some small fudge factors to these computations:

```
const int FUDGE_H = 60;    // Logical units
const int FUDGE_V = 30;

int nWidth = size.cx + FUDGE_H;
int nHeight = m_nHeightLine * LINES + FUDGE_V;
```

These fudge factors allow for a little white space at the end of a line of text and below the last line. Seeing a little space there reassures users that they're really seeing all of the text when they scroll.

Then I create more *CSize* objects to represent the following items:

■ The total size: the width and height of our "document" or drawing. These are computed in the two lines below the fudge factors, as shown in the last code snippet, and are placed into a *CSize* object:

```
CSize sizeTotal = CSize(nWidth, nHeight);
```

See Figure 15-6, which illustrates the meanings of the terms width and height, as they pertain to a page of text.

■ The widths and heights to scroll in response to clicks in a scroll bar shaft ("page") or arrow ("line"), respectively. They are computed this way:

```
CSize sizePage = CSize(nWidth / 3, nHeight / 3);
CSize sizeLine = CSize(nWidth / 10, m_nHeightLine);
```

■ The function *SetScrollSizes*, which specifies the mapping mode to use (*MM_TEXT*) and the three size values we computed:

```
SetScrollSizes(MM_TEXT, sizeTotal, sizePage, sizeLine);
```

When you build and run MyText with these changes, you see both horizontal and vertical scroll bars. Windows adds these automatically when the size information passed to *SetScrollSizes* exceeds the width and height of the client area. If a scroll bar isn't needed, it isn't added.

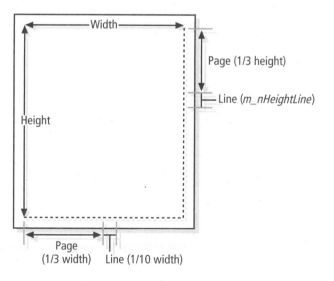

Figure 15-6. *Meanings of text page terms.*

Back to MyDraw

The task of implementing scrolling in MyDraw is just a bit different from implementing it in MyText. In MyText, I had a fixed amount of text: 30 lines using the same text, which was a certain number of logical units wide and high. If I had been writing a text editor program instead, of course, the height of a document would vary as more text was added or deleted.

But in MyDraw, a document is conceived as a drawing surface with a certain width and a certain height, and these dimensions never vary. So, the question is how wide and how high to make that surface. Thinking ahead to printing, I visualize a drawing surface that will print on two 8.5-by-11-inch sheets of paper (standard business size in the United States). I want to allow for a small margin all around, so that leaves an actual drawing area of a little under 10 by 16 inches. See Figure 15-7.

For now, ignore the fact that those dimensions are in inches. I'll describe how to manage such measurements—a matter important for printing too—in Chapter 17.

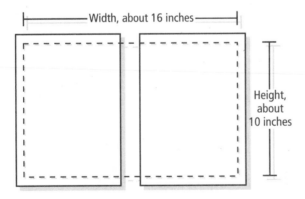

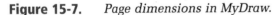

Figure 15-7. *Page dimensions in MyDraw.*

Where to Call *SetScrollSizes*

Where should you call *CScrollView::SetScrollSizes* with these values? This depends on whether your drawing area has a fixed size, as in MyDraw, or adjusts in size as the data grows, as in a program such as Microsoft Word.

If your document tends to get longer, or wider, you'll need to adjust the scroll sizes periodically to fit its new dimensions. The width of a word processing document, for example, might be constant except for adjustments to margins, while its length will change. If you set the sizes only once, at the beginning of such a program, your scrolling logic will begin to degrade as the document grows. You might even lose the ability to see all of the document. You could reset the scroll sizes each time you draw, in *OnDraw*, or in an *OnUpdate* function. Or you could reset them each time the document grows. The document might recalculate scroll sizes each time a line of text is added, storing the values where the view's *OnDraw* function could get them when it's time to draw.

Having the Document Compute Its Own Sizes

Typically, you'll store (or compute) size information about your document in your *CDocument*-derived class itself, as I do in MyDraw, rather than in the view class (though for simplicity I have placed it in the view class in MyText). It's easy to adjust the size figures in the document as it changes. Here are a couple of approaches.

- When the view needs to call *SetScrollSizes*, it can obtain the scroll information by calling a document member function, perhaps named *GetDocSizes*. Then it can call *SetScrollSizes* itself, using the information returned from *GetDocSizes*. MyDraw step 5 illustrates this approach. (You will add this functionality in a moment.)

- Alternatively, the view can call a document member function (perhaps named *SetDocSizes*), passing a pointer to the view class with *this*. The *SetDocSizes* function would calculate the sizes, using information it has access to in the document. Then *SetDocSizes* could call *SetScrollSizes*, back in the view, through the pointer you passed.

TIP You may sometimes have to tinker with your scroll sizes. If your text is absolutely regular—one font, one size, one style—you can calculate precise measurements. But if your text mixes any fonts, sizes, and styles, you might have to use averages and estimates. You might even need to add a fudge factor as you try out the scrolling code and see how it behaves on your target text data. See the MyText sample program in the \learnvcn\Chap15 folder in the companion code. (Note that this example also includes the solutions to the extra credit exercises at the end of this chapter.)

Adding Scrolling to MyDraw

Step 5 for MyDraw applies what I've covered on scrolling to the MyDraw application we've been developing all along.

Try it now

As you did with MyText, use the Visual C++ Find/Replace command to change all instances of *CView* to *CScrollView* in the files DrawVw.h and DrawVw.cpp. We are rederiving class *CMyDrawView* from *CScrollView*. We could have derived *CMyDrawView* from *CScrollView* at the outset with AppWizard, but I wanted to save scrolling details until now.

Teaching the document to report its size

What part of your program should be better suited to providing information about document size than the document itself? That's what we'll do next for MyDraw.

Try it now

Use WizardBar's Add Member Function command to create a document class member function called *GetDocSizes*. The view can call this function when it needs the document size information for setting scroll sizes.

```
void CMyDrawDoc::GetDocSizes(int nMapMode, CSize& sizeTotal,
                            CSize& sizePage, CSize& sizeLine)
{
    // Pass it 3 CSizes and get back sizeTotal, sizePage, sizeLine.
    // (Could perform some sort of check of the mapping mode here.)

    // For now, the size figures are in pixels
    // This will change to inches (in 0.01" units) in Step 7.
    sizeTotal = CSize(1000, 1600);

    // sizePage and sizeLine are same as CScrollView defaults.
    sizePage = CSize(sizeTotal.cx / 10, sizeTotal.cy / 10);
    sizeLine = CSize(sizePage.cx / 10, sizePage.cy / 10);
}
```

The most important line is the definition of *sizeTotal*. It's a *CSize* object whose *cx* member variable will hold the width of the document and whose *cy* variable will hold the height of the document. For now, we specify those in pixels. In Chapter 17, we'll revisit them and specify them in inches instead, as part of setting up printing.

For convenience, we also have the document specify the following as fractions of the total document width and height:

- The number of units to scroll for a click in a scroll bar shaft, *sizePage*.

- The number of units to scroll for a click in a scroll bar arrow, *sizeLine*.

These values aren't very important here, because all we did was specify the same values that *CScrollView* would use by default. But if those values don't look quite right in practice, we can always use this function as a convenient way to tinker with them.

Setting the scroll sizes for MyDraw

For MyDraw, we override the virtual function *OnInitialUpdate*. MFC calls this function after the view has been created, but just before it calls *OnDraw* for the first time. After that, a call to *OnUpdate* precedes each call to *OnDraw*. If we needed to get the latest document size for a growing document, we'd probably do that from *OnUpdate*. But since the MyDraw document never changes size, we can get the information just once, in *OnInitialUpdate* (file DrawVw.cpp).

Try it now

Add the following virtual function override to the view class:

```
void CMyDrawView::OnInitialUpdate()
{
    CScrollView::OnInitialUpdate();

    // TODO: Add your specialized code here and/or call the base class
    CClientDC dc(this);

    m_nMapMode = MM_TEXT;
    CSize sizeTotal, sizePage, sizeLine;
    sizeTotal = sizePage = sizeLine = CSize(0,0);
```

(continued)

```
        CMyDrawDoc* pDoc = GetDocument();
        ASSERT_VALID(pDoc);

        pDoc->GetDocSizes(m_nMapMode, sizeTotal, sizePage, sizeLine);
        SetScrollSizes(m_nMapMode, sizeTotal, sizePage, sizeLine);
}
```

At the moment, we're still using the default mapping mode, *MM_TEXT*, as shown by the following line of code that you just added to *OnInitialUpdate*:

```
m_nMapMode = MM_TEXT;
```

The next two lines in *OnIntialUpdate* construct three *CSize* objects and initialize them to zero. That way, we can pass empty *CSize* objects to *GetDocSizes* to fill them up:

```
CSize sizeTotal, sizePage, sizeLine;
sizeTotal = sizePage = sizeLine = CSize(0,0);
```

After declaring *pDoc*, a pointer to the document, and asserting that it is valid, we finally get to the meat of the matter:

```
pDoc->GetDocSizes(m_nMapMode, sizeTotal, sizePage, sizeLine);
SetScrollSizes(m_nMapMode, sizeTotal, sizePage, sizeLine);
```

The first line uses the document pointer to call the document's *GetDocSizes* member function. We pass the mapping mode we want (*MM_TEXT*) and the three empty *CSize* objects. When *GetDocSizes* returns, the three *CSize* objects have been filled up with the document's size information. The last line is a call to *CScrollView::SetScrollSizes* with that same information.

Coordinate Conversion Rears Its Ugly Head

Back in Chapter 6, when I first introduced GDI coordinate systems, I said we'd sometimes have to convert between device and logical coordinates. So far, we haven't had to worry about that—but the time has come. Why is conversion necessary? Try the following experiment.

Try it now

Build and run MyDraw as it is now. Scroll all the way to the right and all the way down, which leaves the window viewing the farthest lower right corner of the drawing surface. Draw a shape there, close to the lower right corner of the window. Scroll all the way back to the left and top. *OnDraw* is called, and what do you know? It redraws the shape in the lower right corner of the window—but we know it's supposed to be far to the right and down from that location and not even visible with the window in its current scroll position. What's happened? Figure 15-8 illustrates the situation.

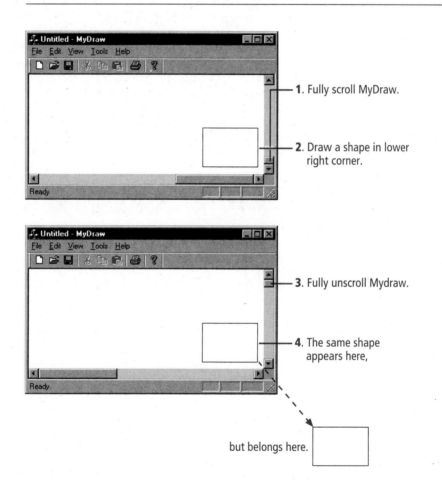

1. Fully scroll MyDraw.

2. Draw a shape in lower right corner.

3. Fully unscroll Mydraw.

4. The same shape appears here,

but belongs here.

Figure 15-8. *Why we have to convert coordinates.*

Adding the conversions

Now let's add code to the functions *OnLButtonDown*, *OnMouseMove*, and *OnLButtonUp* to convert the mouse location received in those functions—in device coordinates—into logical coordinates.

Try it now

Convert device coordinates to logical coordinates in three places:

1. In MyDraw's *OnLButtonDown* handler, add the boldface lines shown here:

    ```
    ⋮
    // Start setting properties of the new shape.
    m_pShpTemp->m_bTransparent = m_bTransparent;
    m_pShpTemp->m_nColorShape = m_nColorNext;

    // Convert point to logical coordinates.
    CClientDC dc(this);
    OnPrepareDC(&dc);
    dc.DPtoLP(&point);

    // Store starting point - literally a point, initially
    //   (topLeft == botRight).
    ⋮
    ```

2. In both *OnMouseMove* and *OnLButtonUp*, add the boldface lines shown here:

    ```
    ⋮
    CClientDC dc(this);
    OnPrepareDC(&dc);
    dc.DPtoLP(&point);

    // Erase previous...
    ⋮
    ```

OnMouseMove and *OnLButtonUp* already create a device context. We simply add code to adjust the device context for scrolling.

What coordinate conversion is all about

I've never yet seen an explanation of coordinate conversion that satisfied me, so I'll try to be really clear here. The present situation in MyDraw illustrates the problem dramatically.

We have a problem of shifting frames of reference. Until we added scrolling, the drawing surface was limited to the visible client area within MyDraw's window. Now we can draw on a much bigger canvas, and when we scroll the window to view distant parts of the canvas, the view's origin shifts to the right and down, as illustrated in Figure 15-8. As this happens, the view's origin (the upper left corner of the client area) and the "document's" origin (the upper left corner of the drawing surface) move apart. That's exactly how scrolling is accomplished, remember?

The problem is this: When you click the mouse in the view (as when you draw a shape in the MyDraw window), Windows reports the click location in coordinates relative to the view window's upper left corner, not relative to the logical origin of our drawing surface. MyDraw's device context is associated with its view window—we obtain a device context into which we draw, and that device context comes with its own device coordinate system, always relative to the view window's upper left corner. Windows reports mouse coordinates to us in device coordinates, relative to the device's origin. So far, we've stored those coordinates just as we received them, to define the upper left and lower right corners of a shape's bounding rectangle.

But if the user has scrolled the view window, we're storing coordinates relative to the wrong origin. Think of our drawing surface as fixed, and the view window as a movable viewport onto the surface. A shape drawn on the drawing surface should be at a fixed location on that surface, regardless of the view window's location over the surface. So when a user presses a mouse button or scrolls the window, we want to store coordinates relative to the origin of the drawing surface—logical coordinates—not slippery device coordinates that change all the time as we scroll the view window.

NOTE Remember that the logical origin is the origin of the drawing surface, which doesn't move when you scroll. The moving origin is the device origin, which is the origin of the view.

Since Windows hands us mouse locations in device coordinates, we have to convert those coordinates to logical coordinates to compensate for scrolling (or for different mapping modes, which use different logical units). Compensating for scrolling is a two-step process:

1. We pass our device context to the *CScrollView::OnPrepareDC* function. *OnPrepareDC* adjusts the device context to compensate for movement of the view's origin relative to the document's origin.

2. Then we pass our mouse location to the *CDC::DPtoLP* function, which replaces the *x* and *y* coordinates stored in a *CPoint* with values adjusted for the shift due to scrolling.

After these two steps, everything is in sync, all in the same kind of coordinates, and we can store logical points in our shape objects rather than device points that shift at the whim of a scroll bar.

When is conversion necessary?

Note that we did our device-to-logical coordinate conversion in the three mouse handlers but not in *OnDraw*. We did it this way for a number of reasons. First, *OnDraw* doesn't deal with a mouse location, so there's no need to call *DPtoLP*. Second, *OnDraw* receives a pointer to a device context as its parameter. *OnDraw* is called by *OnPaint*, and before the call, *OnPaint* calls *OnPrepareDC* to prepare the device context before passing it. Thus *OnDraw* doesn't need to call *OnPrepareDC* either. But, other functions in which we create our own device context with the *CClientDC* constructor do need to call *OnPrepareDC* if there's any possibility of a shift in the view's origin, as with scrolling. I'll say more about *OnPrepareDC* in a moment. (Check the Help index for *CClientDC*.)

Here are some basic rules of thumb for when you must convert coordinates and when you can let them be.

■ Most member functions of class *CDC* take logical coordinates, while most *CWnd* member functions take device coordinates. This makes sense—*CWnd* functions have nothing to do with device contexts, so they don't know anything about the device context's logical coordinate system. It's at the interface between *CDC* and *CWnd* that you'll most often have to perform a conversion, as when the *CWnd* function *OnLButtonDown* receives mouse coordinates relative to the view's origin (device coordinates) but you need to store and work with logical coordinates.

■ Generally, you'll perform operations such as testing for a mouse hit on *CRects* and regions using device coordinates. (*Regions*, nonrectangular areas, are beyond this book's scope. See the list of suggested follow-up books in Chapter 21 for more information.)

The underlying Windows data structures take device coordinates, and if you change mapping modes, the top of a rectangle can be greater than the bottom due to the reorientation of the axes, which isn't the case in the *MM_TEXT* mapping mode. You might need to convert logical coordinates to device coordinates to adjust for this reorientation. You can use *CDC::LPtoDP* for this.

■ As in MyDraw, values you *store* need to be in logical coordinates because, as we've seen, device coordinates don't remain valid during scrolling. That's why we convert the mouse locations in the three mouse handlers.

You'll need to take the additional step of preparing the device context with *OnPrepareDC* when scrolling or similar transformations are involved. *CView::OnPrepareDC* does nothing when called for screen display. *CScrollView* overrides *CView::OnPrepareDC*, adding a call to *CDC::SetViewportOrg*. That call adjusts the view's origin to account for scrolling. When the view's *OnPaint* function calls *OnDraw*, the origin has thus already been adjusted before you draw. Also, wherever you obtain your own device context with *CClientDC* in your *CScrollView*-based view class, you need to make the same origin adjustment to that device context. This keeps the drawing synchronized with any scrolling that occurs.

Parting Thoughts

MyDraw now scrolls the width and height of its document. You can scroll over or down, draw figures, and then scroll back. The new figures may be partially or completely outside the client area, but they are still there and you can get to them by scrolling. That's exactly what we wanted.

> **NOTE** By the way, if you start a figure toward one side of the client area and drag the mouse outside the window before letting go, MyDraw draws the figure, although you can't see all of it. But you can scroll to see it as long as you have not drawn over the edge of the drawing surface. (Remember that the drawing surface has a finite size—we set it.) Try it.

I offer a couple of last comments about scrolling:

■ Some applications are set up to scroll automatically if the user drags the mouse below the bottom or to the right of the window. This is often called *autoscrolling*. I haven't added such functionality to MyText or MyDraw.

■ Class *CScrollView* has its limits. With a large enough drawing surface, a *CScrollView* becomes slow if you take the default course and simply redraw everything each time, as we've done in MyText and MyDraw. There are ways to constrain drawing to just the visible area in the window, but rest assured they complicate your *OnDraw* code. Check the Help index for *Scribble tutorial,* and then choose the subtopic "enhancing view." In that topic, click the link to "Updating Multiple Views" and, on the Help toolbar, click Locate. In the Contents pane, click the next topic below "Updating multiple views." In that topic, click the link to "Define a Hint for Scribble."

Here are a few additional pointers about text. MFC richly supports text handling by providing classes for each of the following operations:

■ **Using two of the Windows text-oriented dialog controls,** *CEdit* and *CRichEditCtrl.* Use these controls in your dialog boxes for text entry, in plain or formatted text.

■ **Basing views on those controls.** Use *CEditView* and *CRichEditView.* These views provide simple text editing. For example, you might allow users to enter substantial amounts of text through a *CEdit* control or, better, through a *CEditView. CEditView* has a large *CEdit* control covering its client area. *CEditView* handles scrolling, cutting and pasting, saving to a text file, and other handy features. In fact, using a *CEditView*, it's easy to write a simple text editor like the Windows Notepad accessory. (For one example of such code, see the CtlDemo1 program in Jeff Prosise's book, *Programming Windows 95 with MFC.* See Chapter 21 for more information about the book.) *CRichEditViews* are even more powerful. They support displaying text in multiple fonts, colors, and styles within the same text document. Of course, using a *CRichEditView* is more work, because you have to provide font-selection menus and other supporting code. For an example of *CRichEditView* in action, check the Help index for *WordPad*. This MFC sample program gives you the source code for the Windows 95 WordPad accessory. Try WordPad to see what's possible; with the WordPad sample, you can even tinker with a copy of the code.

> **TIP** This is a popular learning style for MFC programmers. Find an MFC sample that does something you're interested in. Copy the files to your hard disk. Then use them to experiment. In Microsoft Visual C++ 6.0 Help, you can browse the MFC samples under Samples in the Welcome to the Visual C++ 6.0 Introductory Edition section on the Contents tab. You can use the same approach with the examples in this book.

- **Handling list-like data.** Such data might be lists of database records or the lists of filenames and other information you see in programs like the Windows Explorer. Use *CListView*. *CListView* even gives you the "header controls" for name, size, type, and so on that you see in Windows Explorer and other programs. For database records, MFC also supplies classes *CRecordView*, *CDaoRecordView*, and *COleDBRecordView*.

- **Allowing users to select from lists of text strings in a dialog box.** Use *CListBox* and *CComboBox*.

I'll revisit some of the controls I've mentioned here in Chapter 19.

Try It Yourself

There's not a lot more to say about scrolling, so here are some extra-credit projects based on working with text. Program MyText in the \learnvcn\Chap15 folder in the companion code contains commented solutions.

1. Change the text color.

In MyText, add code to *OnDraw* to change the color of the text or the background behind the text or both. You'll want to make this change just before you draw. Try a variety of settings for both the text color and the text background color. This will show you the range of possibilities.

2. **Change the font used to draw the text.**

   See the file Fonts.doc in the \learnvcn\Chap15 folder in the companion code. If you're moving to a larger size, you might need to take the size into account when calculating text dimensions. This means that you might need to recalculate text dimensions after you change the font.

3. **Add a keyboard interface to MyText.**

   See the file Keyboard.doc in the companion code. That file shows you how to write an *OnKeyDown* handler function that translates keystrokes such as the arrow keys into scrolling commands.

What's Next?

This chapter begins a sequence of chapters focused on user-interface features that MFC makes vastly simpler to program. In the rest of Part 3, we'll write shape data to a file, print it, add a second toolbar for working with shapes, add dialog boxes for specifying user options, and add multiple views of the shape data. We'll also add the ability to select drawn shapes with the mouse. Chapter 16 takes up MFC's serialization mechanism for storing data in a file and reading it back in.

Storing Data in a File

Now that we can draw shapes all over the drawing surface, it's time we gained the ability to store a drawing in a file. When we ran AppWizard to create the first version of MyDraw, we specified that MyDraw document files have the extension .drw. All we have to do now is implement our part of the Microsoft Foundation Class Library 6.0 (MFC) serialization mechanism to write our shape objects to a file. The same mechanism allows MyDraw to open and read an existing .drw file and display its contents.

This chapter covers MyDraw step 6. We'll examine the following topics:

- An overview of MFC serialization.

- Serialization requirements in data classes such as *CShape*. We'll review the small amount of serialization code we wrote in Chapter 14.

- The *DECLARE_SERIAL* and *IMPLEMENT_SERIAL* macros.

- *CShape*'s *Serialize* member function—serializing the data for one shape.

- Class *CArchive*'s role in serialization.

- Using class *CArchive*'s serialization operators (<< and >>) vs. calling a data object's *Serialize* member function directly.

- Writing to a file (storing), which serializes the data for all the shapes.

- Reading from a file (loading).

- Dynamic object creation. When we read a file, its data objects don't exist yet, so we have to arrange for their creation based on data stored in the file.

- How MFC responds to the Save, Save As, and Open commands on MyDraw's File menu.

- Class *CFile* and its derived classes. These play a role in serialization but can also be used independently to support other file input/output models, sidestepping serialization.

- Managing changing versions of MyDraw's files with MFC schemas.

Serialization and Deserialization

To *serialize* means to write out the data members of one *CShape* object after another, serially—usually to a disk file. Classes derived from *CDocument* can serialize their data, and the process is quite easy. Data classes derived from *CObject*—such as *CShape*—can also serialize their data members. Also, collection classes such as *CObList* know how to serialize the objects they contain.

To *deserialize* means to read the previously serialized objects from a file and reconstitute the actual *CShape* objects whose data you've read in. To make deserialization possible, MFC stores class information with the serialized data objects. When MFC deserializes a file, it uses that information to create the *CShape* objects dynamically, automatically loading them into the shape list data structure.

Serialization lets you make the objects in your program *persistent*. That is, they persist, or continue to exist, between runs of the program. You can serialize them, quit the program, run it again, and then deserialize the same objects (that is, load the file) and continue working with them. Hence serialization is one way to implement object persistence. Persistent data is crucial to many applications.

We've already added some of the necessary code to class *CShape* to allow a newly created object derived from *CShape* to read its own data from a file. That's one of the hallmarks of object-oriented programming—the class object does its own work. Class *CObList*, which we're using to store the drawn shapes in a MyDraw document, can tell each *CShape* object that it stores to serialize itself. So when the user chooses a Save, Save As, or Open command in MyDraw, MFC calls the document's *Serialize* member function. For Save and Save As, the *Serialize* function serializes the document's data. For Open, *Serialize* deserializes the data, reconstituting it in the document. Inside the document's *Serialize* function, we tell the shape list to serialize or deserialize itself, and in turn the shape list's *Serialize* function calls the *Serialize* function of each stored *CShape* object, telling it to serialize or deserialize itself.

To devise a file format for storing *CShape* objects on disk, you'd probably write out each shape's data in turn, as a sequence of records. That's essentially what MFC serialization does, except that the serialization mechanism can deal with special situations that arise from using C++ class objects. For example, suppose we're going to write out objects *A* and *B*, both of which point to the same object *C*. If we were to write out *A*, then *C* via *A*, then *B*, and finally *C* via *B*, what would happen when the objects are read back in from the file? Would we create an *A*, then a *C*, then a *B*, and finally another *C*? That's not what we want—originally there was only one *C* object. Figure 16-1 on the next page illustrates this situation. MFC serialization is smart about such problems. It knows which objects exist and it's able to write and read complex webs of objects that point to other objects without committing the "extra *C*" error just described.

Note that MFC serialized files are not compatible with other programs that don't use MFC serialization. If your program needs to write or read a commonly used file format, you'll need to use something besides serialization. I'll take up ways to sidestep MFC serialization later in the chapter. Another alternative to serialization is storing your data in a database, such as a Microsoft Access database. This book doesn't get into database programming, but check the Help index for *database topics*. MFC and Visual C++ provide extensive database programming support.

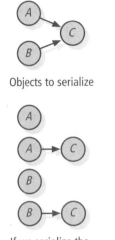

Objects to serialize

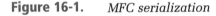

If we serialize the
objects like this,

we get an extra C object
upon deserialization,

but MFC is smart enough to
give us this, which is correct.

Figure 16-1. *MFC serialization*

Implementing Serialization in MyDraw

We already did some of the serialization work for MyDraw in Chapter 14 when we wrote the *CShape* classes. Those classes are already partially outfitted for MFC serialization. All that's left to do is make one small change in our document class and a few changes to class *CShape*.

Serialization Requirements in Data Classes

To serialize a *CShape*-derived object, you need to prepare classes *CShape*, *CShpRectangle*, and *CShpEllipse* for the job.

IMPORTANT We already took the three steps below, in Chapter 14, when we created the *CShape* classes.

In any data classes whose objects you plan to store in a file via MFC serialization, take the following steps:

1. Derive your data class from *CObject* (or from a suitable *CObject* subclass). We already did this with class *CShape* and its two subclasses. Here's the heading of the *CShape* class declaration:

```
class CShape : public CObject
```

2. Use the *DECLARE_SERIAL* macro in the class declaration. If you look back at the *CShape* classes, you'll see that inside each class declaration (in Shape.h) the macro looks like the one shown here. Note that the macro takes one parameter—the name of the class to be serialized—and is not followed by a semicolon.

```
class CShape : public CObject
{
public:
    // Enable MFC serialization (file storage for class objects)
    DECLARE_SERIAL(CShape)
    ⋮
```

3. Use the *IMPLEMENT_SERIAL* macro in the class implementation file. We also did this for each of the shape classes, in the file Shape.cpp. For *CShape* itself, the macro comes just above the *CShape* constructor:

```
///////////////////////////////////
// Class CShape implementation

IMPLEMENT_SERIAL(CShape, CObject, 1)

CShape::CShape()
{
    m_boxShape.SetRect(0, 0, 0, 0);
    m_bTransparent = true;
    m_nColorShape = ID_COLOR_BLACK;
}
```

The macro takes three parameters: the name of the class it's for, the name of that class's base class, and an integer, called the schema number. I'll explain the schema number later in this chapter.

For the shape subclasses, the macro also comes at the beginning of the class implementation. Here's the macro for class *CShpRectangle*, just above that class's default constructor:

```
///////////////////////////////////
// Class CShpRectangle implementation

IMPLEMENT_SERIAL(CShpRectangle, CShape, 1)
```

(continued)

```
void CShpRectangle::Draw(CDC* pDC)   // Virtual override
{
    pDC->Rectangle(m_boxShape);
}
```

For a derived data class such as *CShpRectangle* to be serializable, its base class must also be serializable. That's why we'll make *CShape* serializable when in reality we'll be serializing only *CShpRectangle* and *CShpEllipse* objects.

If the constructor for your data class does some work, such as initializing data members or allocating memory, a final step in serialization is to define a default constructor for the class—one that takes no arguments. For classes *CShpRectangle* and *CShpEllipse*, there's nothing to initialize (they have no data members other than the ones they inherit from *CShape*) or allocate, so we don't need default constructors for these classes. These classes inherit constructors from *CShape*, and those constructors, including a default constructor, do the necessary initialization.

For more details about carrying out these steps, check the Help index for *serialization*. Choose the topic "Serialization (Object Persistence)" from the Topics Found dialog box.

Serializing One Shape

Class *CShape* needs one more thing in order to be serializable: an override of the *Serialize* member function from its base class, *CObject*. First, though, we need to decide what pieces of data to save for each shape. Each *CShape*-derived object contains three data members. Which ones we write to a file depends on which ones are needed to reconstitute the shape object when we read it back in from the file later and draw it again on the screen. It turns out that we need to write all three *CShape* data members: *m_boxShape*, the bounding rectangle; *m_bTransparent*, the transparency or opaqueness of the shape; and *m_nColorShape*, the shape's outline color.

Try it now

Add an override of the virtual function *Serialize* in class *CShape*. You'll have to do this by hand because the Add Virtual Function command isn't available on the WizardBar Action menu for classes such as *CShape* that weren't created by MFC.

1. In the file Shape.h, add the following function prototype in the *CShape* class declaration:

```
    ⋮
// Overridables and operations
virtual void Draw(CDC* pDC)
                { TRACE("My Error: In CShape::Draw.\n");
                    ASSERT(FALSE); };
virtual void Serialize(CArchive& ar);
```

2. In the file Shape.cpp, add the function's definition:

```
void CShape::Serialize(CArchive& ar)
{
    BYTE byTransparent;

    CObject::Serialize(ar);

    if (ar.IsStoring())
    {
        // TODO: add storing code here.
        byTransparent = (BYTE)m_bTransparent;
        ar << m_boxShape << byTransparent << m_nColorShape;
    }
    else
    {
        // TODO: add loading code here.
        ar >> m_boxShape >> byTransparent >> m_nColorShape;
        m_bTransparent = (bool)byTransparent;
    }
}
```

We'll look at the function in detail shortly.

What about *Serialize* in the *CShape* subclasses?

Since a *CShpRectangle* or a *CShpEllipse* doesn't add any new data members beyond those that both classes inherit from *CShape*, the derived shape classes can simply inherit *Serialize* from *CShape*. They don't need to override the function themselves. If the subclasses did add new data members that we wanted to serialize, we'd need to override *Serialize* in them.

Serializing All Shapes in the Document

MyDraw's document class houses the *m_listShapes* data member, which contains the shapes that we need to serialize.

Try it now

In class *CMyDrawDoc* (in the file DrawDoc.cpp), locate the *Serialize* member function. AppWizard assumes that we'll want to add serialization to the program, so it writes a skeleton override of the *Serialize* member function. Add the boldface line to your *Serialize* function:

```
void CMyDrawDoc::Serialize(CArchive& ar)
{
    m_listShapes.Serialize(ar);
    if (ar.IsStoring())
    {
        // TODO: add storing code here
    }
    else
    {
        // TODO: add loading code here
    }
}
```

Try it now

After adding the one line of code to *CMyDrawDoc::Serialize*, build MyDraw and run it. (For now, ignore the warning that the compiler issues during the build.) Draw some shapes. Choose Save As from the File menu. In the Save As dialog box, specify a directory and a filename, and then click Save. Exit MyDraw, and then run it again. Choose Open from the File menu. In the Open dialog box, specify the file you saved earlier and open it. You should see the same shapes you drew earlier.

That finishes the serialization code for MyDraw, but let's explore the mechanism a bit.

CShape's *Serialize* Member Function

Let's take a detailed look at *CShape::Serialize*. Here's the function again. (You've already added it to MyDraw.)

```
void CShape::Serialize(CArchive& ar)
{
    BYTE byTransparent;

    CObject::Serialize(ar);

    if (ar.IsStoring())
```

```
    {
        // TODO: add storing code here.
        byTransparent = (BYTE)m_bTransparent;
        ar << m_boxShape << byTransparent << m_nColorShape;
    }
    else
    {
        // TODO: add loading code here.
        ar >> m_boxShape >> byTransparent >> m_nColorShape;
        m_bTransparent = (bool)byTransparent;
    }
}
```

IP Remember to deserialize data members in the same order that you serialize them.

Calling the base class version of *Serialize* in *CShape*

The first thing *CShape::Serialize* does is call *CObject*'s version of *Serialize*. It turns out that *CObject::Serialize* does nothing, but it's conventional to call the base class version of overridden member functions (unless you're explicitly replacing the entire base class implementation). Calling the base class version of a member function lets MFC perform any necessary backstage work. If you know the base class version does nothing, you can omit the call.

Try it now

You can confirm what *CObject::Serialize* does. Set a breakpoint at the beginning of *CShape::Serialize*, and then run the debugger (press F5). Draw a couple of shapes and save the document. The debugger stops at your breakpoint, and you can step into the *CObject::Serialize* call. (You can do the same thing for *CMyDrawDoc::Serialize*—but first you'll need to add a call to *CDocument::Serialize*.)

Storing or loading

After the base class call, *CShape::Serialize* enters an *if* statement:

```
if(ar.IsStoring())
{
    // TODO: add storing code here.
    ⋮
}
```

(continued)

```
else
{
    // TODO: add loading code here.
    ⋮
}
```

The condition for the *if* statement is the Boolean result of a call to something called *ar.IsStoring*. The *ar* parameter to *Serialize* is a reference to a *CArchive* object. I'll discuss archives later in the section "*CArchive* and *CFile.*" If the archive *ar* is *storing* (we're writing to disk instead of reading), the first branch of the *if* executes. Otherwise, if we're *loading* (reading), the second branch executes. Thus the *Serialize* function handles both writing to a file and reading from a file. Of course, one call to *Serialize* does only one of these things. It's either storing or loading, but not both in one call.

Writing to a file (storing)

In the *CShape* version of *Serialize*, here's how we write out the data for one shape. (You've already added this code.)

```
// TODO: add storing code here.
byTransparent = (BYTE)m_bTransparent;
ar << m_boxShape << byTransparent << m_nColorShape;
```

The *CArchive* variable, *ar*, resembles the *iostream* objects we met back in Chapter 2. We use an *insertion operator* (<<), to send each piece of data to the archive, which in turn writes the data to a file. (*CArchive* writes binary data to a file rather than writing formatted text to a display, so *CArchive* doesn't have the fancy formatting features of the *iostream* objects.) Note that because the operator returns a reference to a *CArchive*, we can chain these insertions to put them all compactly on one line of code. (You've already added this code.)

```
ar << m_boxShape << byTransparent << m_nColorShape;
```

There's some sleight of hand going on here that I should mention. Class *CArchive's* insertion and extraction operators (<< and >>) are overloaded for a sizable number of data types, but *bool* is not one of them (although I believe it will be added to a future version of MFC). Thus I have to convert the *bool* data in *m_bTransparent* to something that *CArchive* understands, such as *BYTE* (a data type that represents any byte value). I declare a local variable called *byTransparent*, of type *BYTE*, and then use it in a type cast. I pass the type cast *BYTE* value to the archive. I have to do something like that when I read the data back in as well. You can find out about the data types supported by *CArchive* by checking the Help index for *serialization*. In the Topics Found dialog box, choose the topic "Serialization (Object Persistence)," follow the link to "Serialization: Serializing an Object," and scroll down to the heading "Using the CArchive << and >> Operators."

By the way, if you do use a type cast between *bool* and *BYTE*, as I did in the version of *Serialize* above, you'll get a compiler warning (not an error): "warning C4800: 'unsigned char': forcing value to *bool* 'true' or 'false' (performance warning)." In other words, we're doing something inefficient here, namely trying to convert between a Boolean value, which isn't technically a number in C++, and a *BYTE* value, which is. C++ compilers have grown stricter in enforcing type rules—C compilers and even early C++ compilers might not have complained about this small bending of the rules.

Try it now

The following code shows a safer way to accomplish our aims without invoking the warning. Make your version of *CShape::Serialize* look like this (removing code as necessary):

```
void CShape::Serialize(CArchive& ar)
{
    BYTE byTransparent;

    CObject::Serialize(ar);

    if (ar.IsStoring())
    {
        // TODO: add storing code here.
        byTransparent = (m_bTransparent ? 1 : 0);
        ar << m_boxShape << byTransparent << m_nColorShape;
    }
    else
    {
        // TODO: add loading code here.
        ar >> m_boxShape >> byTransparent >> m_nColorShape;
        m_bTransparent = (byTransparent != 0);
    }
}
```

The following line uses the C++ arithmetic if operator (?:) to assign the numeric value 1 or 0 depending on the Boolean value of *m_bTransparent*. If the Boolean value is *true*, assign 1; if *false*, assign 0.

```
byTransparent = (m_bTransparent ? 1 : 0);
```

The following line uses the not equal operator (!=) to convert a numeric value to a Boolean value.

```
m_bTransparent = (byTransparent != 0);
```

If *byTransparent* equals 1, the expression *byTransparent != 0* is true, and we set *m_bTransparent* to *true*. If *byTransparent* equals 0, the expression is false, and we set *m_bTransparent* to *false*. These tricks avoid type casting and thus avoid the warning by not violating any type rules.

Note that I'm not telling you never to cast. Using casts in *Serialize* between legitimate numeric types is fine, and the compiler won't complain. For example, suppose I use the following *typedef* statement:

```
typedef double salary;    // Define a salary data type
salary mySalary;          // Declare a salary variable
```

CArchive knows nothing about the *salary* type, so we'd need to cast *mySalary* back to double:

```
ar << (double)mySalary;
```

Reading from a file (loading)

The loading code in *CShape::Serialize* is similar to the storing code, but it works in the other direction.

```
// TODO: add loading code here.
ar >> m_boxShape >> byTransparent >> m_nColorShape;
m_bTransparent = (byTransparent != 0);
```

This code uses *CArchive's* extraction operator (>>). *CArchive* can read a *BYTE* value but not a *bool*, so we do the tricky conversion again.

CMyDrawDoc's Serialize Member Function

Let's turn now to what the *CMyDrawDoc::Serialize* function does. Here's the function again:

```
void CMyDrawDoc::Serialize(CArchive& ar)
{
```

```
m_listShapes.Serialize(ar);
if (ar.IsStoring())
{
    // TODO: add storing code here
}
else
{
    // TODO: add loading code here
}
}
```

Serializing the shape list

This time something is radically different in the main part of *Serialize* for *CMyDrawDoc*. There's no code at all in the body of the *if* statement. Instead, there's one line of new code, just above the *if* statement, and it doesn't use the archive operators:

```
m_listShapes.Serialize(ar);
```

Recall that we stored our shapes in the document's *m_listShapes* data member, a *CObList* object. When you examine the document's remaining data member, *m_pos*, you realize that the only data we need to store in a file is the contents of the shape list. The *m_pos* data member is just a working variable that we use only while manipulating the shape list.

Why did we bypass the *if* statement? Because we'd do the same thing in both branches—directly call *CObList's Serialize* function, which loads or stores, depending on which direction the *CArchive* parameter specifies. We can even delete the *if* statement this time.

To serialize the shapes, we could walk through the shape list, extracting a pointer to each shape in turn, and pass that pointer to the archive via the << operator. However, there are good reasons not to do it that way. Doing so would be complex and troublesome—and just not necessary. The *CObList* class happens to have its own *Serialize* member function. Since *m_listShapes* is a *CObList* object, all we have to do is call *CObList::Serialize*, passing it an archive object, and let it do the work. *CObList::Serialize* knows how to walk the list and call each object's *Serialize* member function. That's exactly what we need.

Calling *Serialize* vs. Using *CArchive* Operators

When should you use the << and >> operators of class *CArchive*? And when should you instead call an object's *Serialize* member function directly? Here are some guidelines.

First, let's establish exactly what it is that we're serializing—and what we aren't. While I might speak loosely about "serializing the document," we aren't actually writing the document object itself to a file. We're just writing its contents, and not necessarily all of them. For instance, we won't actually write the *CObList* data member, *m_listShapes*, to the file—just its contents, the *CShape* objects.

When we write a *CShape* object, MFC writes some administrative information that will be needed later for deserializing the object. Then MFC turns things over to each *CShape* object in turn, by calling the shape object's *Serialize* function. The shape itself writes the values of its three data members. Then MFC takes over again, writes a tag for its own use, and calls *Serialize* for the next shape. What the data file ultimately contains is some header information about the number of shapes to be written, and then shape, shape, shape, and so on. When we later read the file, the *CObList* data member in the document already exists. We just have to fill the list up from the file, and *CObList::Serialize* takes care of that for us. We do recreate each shape object—we don't recreate the document or *CObList* objects.

Therefore most of what I'm about to say applies primarily to data classes, such as *CShape*, and their internal data members. The examples that follow discuss hypothetical *CThing* data members and how to serialize them. You can see how *CThing* is declared just after the next Note. We'll look at four cases—summarized in Table 16-1 on page 493 and described below.

■ **Case 1: Primitive data type.** For primitive data types, such as *int*, *char*, *double*, and other types for which *CArchive* has overloaded << and >> operators, use the operators. Cast or convert types if you must, as I did in *CShape::Serialize*.

OTE   MFC also overloads the *CArchive* operators for quite a few of its own classes. Check the Help index for *CArchive operators* and double-click the index keyword "using." Then scroll down several screens, where you'll see a table listing the types and classes for which the operators work.

- **Case 2: Embedded class object derived from *CObject*.** Suppose class *CThing* has a data member that is an embedded class object, something like this:

```
class CThing : public CObject
{
public:
    CSomeClass m_Obj;     // Embedded class object
    ⋮
```

Also suppose *CSomeClass* is derived from *CObject*, directly or indirectly. In such a case, call the embedded object's *Serialize* member function from *CThing::Serialize*. When we read the *CThing* in question, MFC creates the *CThing* object and in the process creates the *CSomeClass* object as well. We just need to fill up the object from serialization. Inside *CThing::Serialize*, we call *m_Obj.Serialize(ar)* to serialize *m_Obj's* contents, not *ar << m_Obj*. *CSomeClass* must override *Serialize* for this to work, of course. (For related information, see "Sequence of Constructor and Destructor Calls" in Chapter 5.) What if *CSomeClass* isn't derived from *CObject*? See case 4.

- **Case 3: Pointer to object derived from *CObject*.** Now suppose *CThing* contains a data member that is a pointer to a *CSomeClass* object (not an embedded *CSomeClass object*) and that *CSomeClass* is derived from *CObject*, directly or indirectly:

```
class CThing : public CObject
{
public:
    CSomeClass* m_pObj;     // Pointer to a CSomeClass
⋮
```

In this case, ask yourself: Am I constructing the object pointed to by *m_pObj* in the *CThing* constructor? If so, the *CSomeClass* object will already exist when *Serialize* is called. Thus, inside the function

CThing::Serialize, call *m_pObj's Serialize* member function, if it has one:

```
m_pObj->Serialize(ar);
```

Because *m_pObj* is constructed when the *CThing* is constructed, you don't otherwise need to construct the object that *m_pObj* points to as part of serialization. If you don't construct the object in *CThing's* constructor, you can use << and >>, as long as *CMyClass* is ultimately derived from *CObject*.

■ **Case 4: Embedded object or pointer to object not derived from CObject.** What if an object such as the ones discussed in case 2 or case 3 doesn't have a *Serialize* member function? Or what if the object containing the embedded object or pointer isn't derived from *CObject*? In such a situation, use << and >> to serialize from and to the object's data members. You'll need to work indirectly, using member access operators, as shown below. (The *m_Obj* or *m_pObj* object itself will be constructed along with its containing class, if it is embedded, or it should be constructed in the containing class's constructor, if it is a pointer. In either case, the *m_Obj* or *m_pObj* object will exist prior to serializing its contents.) Suppose the object is declared like this:

```
class CSomeClass
{
public:
    int m_int;
    CString m_str;
};
```

and an object of this class is embedded in class *CThing* as follows:

```
class CThing : public CObject
{
public:
    CSomeClass m_Obj;
    :
```

In the function *CThing::Serialize*, you could handle the embedded object this way:

```
if(ar.IsStoring())
{
    ar << m_Obj.m_int << m_Obj.m_str;
}
else
{
    ar >> m_Obj.m_int >> m_Obj.m_str;
}
```

If instead you have a pointer to *CSomeClass*, replace the dot operator (.) in the code just above with the arrow operator (->). In general, though, if you mean to serialize a class, derive the class from *CObject* (assuming you have control over the class).

Table 16-1 summarizes the four cases.

Data Type	How to Serialize
Primitive data type, such as *int*, *char*, or *double* (case 1)	Use << and >>.
Class object derived from *CObject*—either embedded or pointed to (cases 2 and 3)	Use the object's *Serialize* function, if it has one.
Class object not derived from *CObject* (case 4)	Use << and >> on the object's members if the object is pointed to, construct it in *CThing*'s constructor.

Table 16-1.   *Serialization techniques for various data types.*

For more information, check the Help index for *serialization* and double-click the index keyword "details." From the topic "Serialization Topics" that appears, follow the links to other topics on serialization.

> **NOTE**   When serializing data, keep in mind that file operations sometimes fail—perhaps a disk is full, for example. Thus it's wise to use MFC's exception handling mechanism to deal with exceptional conditions such as a full disk. For an introduction to exception handling, see the file Diagnost.doc in the \learnvcn\Chap16 folder in the companion code. Also check the Help index for *exception classes*. The BBall program in the \learnvcn\Chap16 folder in the companion code illustrates handling exceptions in file input/output (I/O) code. By the way, if saving to a file fails, MFC ensures that the previous version of the file you're saving to isn't corrupted. It keeps a mirror file to preserve that data. It's just one of the many ways MFC takes care of you.

Application Version Control with MFC Schemas

One problem you face while developing an application is successive versions of the application that differ from one another. Suppose in version 1 you serialize three data members. Then, in version 2, you add another data member and serialize it as well. At this point, neither version can read files produced by the other. To obtain "backward compatibility" between the versions, you need to endow version 2 with the ability to read version 1 files as well as its own. MFC can help.

Recall the parameters to the *IMPLEMENT_SERIAL* macro: the name of the class you want to serialize, the name of that class's base class, and an integer called the *schema number*:

```
IMPLEMENT_SERIAL(CShape, CObject, 1)
```

For purposes of serialization, the schema number functions as a version number, so MFC can tell version 1 files from version 2 files. When you write version 2 of an object such as *CShape*, change the schema number to 2. For version 3, change it to 3, and so on. The schema number must be an integer greater than or equal to 0. If the schema number of the object on disk doesn't match the schema number of the class in memory, MFC throws a *CArchiveException*, which you can catch if you like. (For information about MFC exception handling, check the Help index for *exception classes*.) If you don't catch the exception, MFC displays a dialog box describing the version mismatch.

To make version 2 backward compatible with version 1, you can use the *VERSIONABLE_SCHEMA* macro as part of the schema number itself, as shown below. (Use the C++ bitwise OR operator (|) to combine the macro and the schema number.)

```
IMPLEMENT_SERIAL(CShape, CObject, 1 | VERSIONABLE_SCHEMA)
```

This creates a *versionable object*—an object whose *Serialize* member function can read multiple versions. The Help topic for the *GetObjectSchema* function shows how to set up a *switch* statement in your *Serialize* function to read the various versions. Check the Help index for *GetObjectSchema*.

How Serialization Works

Now that serialization is working in MyDraw, let's discuss how it works. I'll explain the serialization macros, dynamic object creation, how the *Serialize* function in the document is called, and the roles of the *CArchive* and *CFile* classes. I'll also briefly address how you can sidestep the serialization mechanism if it doesn't meet your needs.

The *DECLARE_SERIAL* and *IMPLEMENT_SERIAL* Macros

What do these macros do? A macro is an item that the C++ preprocessor expands at compile time into whatever the macro is defined to stand for. For example, you've seen this #*define* directive before in MFC files:

```
#define new DEBUG_NEW
```

Everywhere in the file that the preprocessor finds the symbol *new*, it replaces it with the symbol *DEBUG_NEW* (to facilitate checking for memory leaks and other memory problems). But instead of replacing a symbol with another single symbol, you can replace a symbol or something that looks like a function call, such as the following, with rather complex code.

```
IMPLEMENT_SERIAL(CShape, CObject, 1)
```

You can even pass parameters to be used in expanding the macro. That's what the two macros do. *DECLARE_SERIAL* adds some new members to the class in which you invoke it—members involved in serializing objects of the class. *IMPLEMENT_SERIAL* adds the implementations for those members. For more information about macros, check the Help index for *preprocessor* and double-click the index keyword "macros." (Preprocessor macros are not the same as VBScript macros, which I discussed briefly in Chapter 1.)

Try it now

You can see for yourself how the two macros are defined in the MFC source code files. See the Appendix for guidance in using the Find In Files command to search the MFC source code files for each of the macros. The macros are defined in the file Afx.h. It's worth looking at the two #*define* directives.

Creating Objects from Thin Air

Reading from the file is actually more interesting than writing to it. When you have an object write its data, the object is there already. You just have to ask it to serialize itself. But when you read data for an object, the object doesn't exist yet—somehow MFC has to turn that data into an object of the appropriate type. In other words, MFC has to conjure a *CShpRectangle* or *CShpEllipse* object out of nowhere.

How? When it writes the file in the first place, MFC includes information in the file that later helps it recreate the objects when they're read. Under the hood, MFC writes some identifying information to the file just before it writes the *CShape* data. First, it writes the number of such objects that will be written out—the number of consecutive *CShape* objects to be stored. Then there's a flag value, *0xffff*, which signals that a new class is about to be written out. Next, there's the class's schema number, then the length, in bytes, of the class's name (*CShpRectangle* has 13 characters), and finally the text of the class name (*CShpRectangle*). Then the object itself writes out its data members, after which MFC writes a tag for the start of the next *CShape* object. (There's no need to repeat the class name or schema number for each one.)

When *Serialize* deserializes from the file in the loading branch of the *if* statement, it reads the tag information first. This gives it enough information to create an object of the correct type on the fly. (It uses the class name to look up the appropriate *RUNTIME_CLASS* information in a table, and it can compare the newly created object's schema number with the one in the file.) Then it tells the new object to read its own data, which follows the tag information.

If you step through the *Serialize* calls, as I suggested in the "Try it now" exercise in "Calling the Base Class Version of *Serialize* in *CShape*" earlier in this chapter, you'll probably wonder where MFC's part of this action occurs. Recall the two serialization macros, *DECLARE_SERIAL* and *IMPLEMENT_SERIAL*. The code that these two macros expand to is used to manage most of the serialization mechanism. One thing that the code does is create a linked list of *CRuntimeClass* objects—the table I mentioned in the previous paragraph. MFC searches the list for the class name and can thus obtain a *CRuntimeClass* object that contains everything needed to synthesize an appropriate object on the spot. *CRuntimeClass* has a *CreateObject* member function, which MFC calls to conjure the new object. This process is called *dynamic object creation*. I won't delve into the arcane depths of dynamic object creation in this book, but you can begin learning about it by checking the Help index for *dynamic creation support* and studying the MFC source code for serialization.

How *Serialize* Is Called

So far, there's still something mysterious about *Serialize*. How and when does MFC call the document's *Serialize* member function? Since serialization is about writing and reading data, let's look at the Save, Save As, and Open commands on MyDraw's File menu.

Saving a document

When the user chooses the Save or Save As command from MyDraw's File menu, MFC calls the document object's *OnFileSave* or *OnFileSaveAs* member function. This initiates a complex sequence of events in which the following occurs:

1. With Save As, MFC calls *CWinApp::DoPromptFileName*, a member function of the application object, to prompt the user to supply a filename. MFC displays the Save As dialog box, one of the Microsoft Windows common dialog boxes.

2. The document object obtains a *CFile* pointer to the currently open file. Then the document creates a *CArchive* object attached to the file.

3. The document object calls its own *Serialize* member function, passing the new *CArchive* as the parameter to *Serialize*.

4. *Serialize* determines that the archive's *IsStoring* member function returns *true* and executes the first branch of its *if* statement. This uses the archive, which uses the *CFile*, to write out the document's data.

Try it now

I've left out a good many details, but that is the essence of saving a document. You can follow the sequence of calls yourself using the Find In Files command. Start by searching the MFC source code files for the string *::OnFileSave* or *::OnFileSaveAs*. Choose the first topic listed in the Output window. Then search for the functions called by *OnFileSave*, the functions called by those functions, and so on. It might help to make a diagram of the calls as you go—I suggest a tree-like structure, something like this:

```
CDocument::OnFileSave
    CDocument::DoFileSave
        CDocument::DoSave
            CDocument::GetDocTemplate
                CWinApp::DoPromptFileName
                    ⋮
```

For information on using Find In Files this way, see the Appendix.

Opening a document

When the user chooses Open from MyDraw's File menu, MFC again initiates a complex sequence of events:

1. MFC calls *CWinApp::OnFileOpen*. The document object is responsible for opening, saving, and closing its own file, and the application object is in charge of opening a new file. No document object exists yet to manage and display the file.

2. *CWinApp::OnFileOpen* calls *CDocManager::OnFileOpen*. *CWinApp* delegates opening files to a subordinate *CDocManager* object. *CDocManager::OnFileOpen* calls *CDocManager::DoPromptFileName* to prompt the user for the name of the file to open, and then *DoPromptFileName* displays the Open dialog box (another common dialog box).

3. *CDocManager::OnFileOpen* next calls *CWinApp::OpenDocumentFile*, which calls *CDocManager::OpenDocumentFile*. That function locates the appropriate document template object and calls the template's *OpenDocumentFile* member function. That function—in this case belonging to class *CSingleDocTemplate*—goes through the

very complex process of creating the document object and its associated view object and frame window object. During this process, for an SDI application, MFC calls the new document object's *DeleteContents* member function to let you clean up the document object and calls its *OnOpenDocument* member function to let you initialize the document's data members (at least those that aren't serialized).

 OTE   We discussed document templates briefly in Chapter 8. A document template is an object that creates and manages one or more *CDocument*-derived objects (one object if the application is SDI, or potentially a whole list of them if it's MDI). The document template object is associated, in the application's *InitInstance* member function, with the document, view, and frame window classes it will use to create new documents. *InitInstance* is where we create the document templates the application needs and add them to the application object's list of document templates. (See "Creating the document template, frame window, document, and view" in Chapter 8.)

---

4. The document template's *OpenDocumentFile* function then creates a *CFile* object and a *CArchive* object attached to the *CFile*, and it calls the new document object's *Serialize* function, passing the archive.

5. *Serialize* determines that the archive is for loading and executes the second branch of its *if* statement. This code reads the data.

6. For MyDraw, deserialization repopulates the *CObList* in which we store the shapes and forces the shapes to be drawn. This results in a call to the view's *OnDraw* member function. The shapes appear on the screen.

Try it now

Follow the sequence of calls with the Find In Files command. (See the Appendix for information on using this command to search the MFC source code.) Start with *CWinApp::OnOpenFile*.

CArchive and *CFile*

At the heart of the MFC serialization mechanism is class *CArchive*. An archive object abstracts serializing data to any place that can hold the data in a serial form. An archive might be used to serialize to a file, to an in-memory data structure, or even to the Windows Clipboard.

When a *CArchive* is used to serialize to a file, you attach the archive to an object of class *CFile* to represent the actual file on disk. *CFile* wraps an operating system file handle, through which you can perform general-purpose file I/O operations. *CFile* directly supports *unbuffered binary disk I/O*. The term *unbuffered* indicates that you must read groups of bytes yourself, by making direct calls to *CFile* member functions such as *Read* and *Write*. Buffered file I/O is more efficient, because reading a disk is a slow operation. The idea is to read lots of data at once into a buffer—a chunk of heap storage to which you have a pointer. One big read operation is less costly than lots of small ones, and you can then do lots of small reads from the buffer much more quickly. The term *binary* indicates that the data stored is binary bytes rather than text characters; to store and load text, you can use the *CFile*-derived class *CStdioFile*. (See the Note below.)

NOTE The companion code includes a sample program called BBall, which uses *CStdioFile* to read lines of text from a .txt file and to write lines of text to such a file. BBall also illustrates the *CStringArray* collection class, which is similar to *CObArray*. I'll say more about BBall later in the chapter.

Combining *CArchive* with *CFile* is one way to get buffered file I/O. *CArchive* contains an internal buffer whose size you can set when you construct the archive. (Its default size is 4096 bytes.) It works like this: Via serialization, you read *x* bytes from the archive (say, 4 bytes to fill an integer data member). The archive has previously read a large number of bytes from the file into its buffer. You keep reading from the archive, not worrying at all about where those bytes are really coming from. If the buffer runs out of data, the archive reads from the file again, and you can keep on reading as long as there is data in the archive.

To create a *CArchive*, you must first create a file object derived from class *CFile*. The *CFile* subclasses are shown in Figure 16-2. We've so far let MFC create all of the *CArchive* and *CFile* objects we've needed, but you can create these objects yourself, as you might need to do if you bypass serialization and do your own file I/O. I'll discuss that option in the next section.

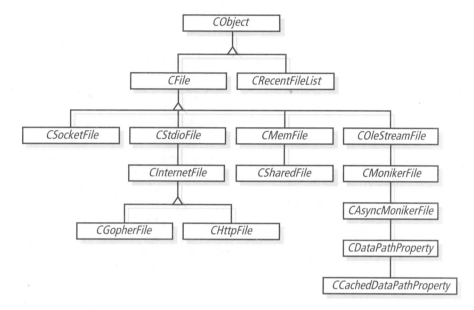

Figure 16-2. *The file-related classes in MFC.*

For more about archives and files, check the Help index for *CArchive*, *CFile*, and *files*. For *files*, choose the first topic in the Topics Found dialog box, "Files Topics."

Sidestepping Serialization

Serialization is ideal for some applications, but not for others. The main situation in which you might want to sidestep serialization is when you need to write to or read from a particular file format. For example, you might need to write rich text (.rtf) files, plain text files, or some graphics format, such as .bmp or .gif. In such cases, you'll need to write your own file I/O (and understand the file format).

You can still use the *CFile* classes—there are subclasses for text files, Internet files, in-memory files, shared files (such as a file used to write to the Windows Clipboard), OLE-based files, and Windows Sockets files for sending or receiving data across a network. See Figure 16-2 and check the Help index for *hierarchy chart*. Class *CDocument* has a handy member function for obtaining information about the file associated with the document: *CDocument::GetFile*.

Where should you put your I/O code? The key is to find the right "hook" in the sequences of function calls I outlined earlier in this chapter in "How *Serialize* Is Called."

File I/O with Document/View

For example, suppose you want to use the document/view architecture but not serialization. The BBall program in the \learnvcn\Chap16 folder of the companion code illustrates one approach to file I/O with document/view but without serialization. BBall has three View menu commands that accomplish the following tasks:

- Display a list of all present-day Major League Baseball teams

- Display a list of all World Series winners

- Display a list of all present-day teams that have never won a World Series (at least in their modern form—for example, the San Francisco Giants haven't won, but they did when they were in New York)

BBall's I/O is limited to reading and writing preset files—the user can't select files to open. All reading and writing occurs in two places:

- In the document's *OnNewDocument* member function, which MFC calls as the document is being created and initialized. This reads data from two text files that list, respectively, the modern teams and the teams that have won the series.

- In the view's *WriteNonWinners* function, which is called by the *ListNeverWinners* function, which in turn is called by the *OnViewNeverwon* menu command handler. *ListNeverWinners* compares the team list with the World Series winners list and builds a list of nonwinners. *WriteNonWinners* writes the results to a third text file.

Serialize isn't used at all, yet the document/view architecture still plays its normal role. The file I/O code shows you how to use a *CFile* object by itself.

File I/O Without Document/View

Here's one more example. Suppose you're writing an application that doesn't use document/view. In this case, there's no document class, so there's no *Serialize*. The application might use the AppWizard project that creates a rudimentary view class, derived from *CWnd* rather than *CView*, or it might use just the application and frame window objects. Here's the scheme:

1. To open a file, override *CWinApp::OnFileOpen*. Place your file opening and loading code in the override. You can display a *CFileDialog* yourself to obtain the filename. And you can open the file and read it using class *CFile* or one of its subclasses.

2. To save a file, add your own *OnFileSave* and *OnFileSaveAs* handlers to the application class. (Normally, these handlers are in the document, not the application object, so you can't do them as overrides.) In *OnFileSaveAs*, display a *CFileDialog* yourself to obtain a filename. From both *OnFileSave* and *OnFileSaveAs*, call a helper function, say, *SaveFile*. Put your file saving code in that function. I'll discuss classes such as *CFileDialog* in Chapter 19.

Try It Yourself

It's time to test yourself with these extra-credit offerings.

1. Use this chapter to learn how to spelunk in MFC.

I presented a number of tasks for you to try out. It's worth following through on those tasks to get used to going underground in MFC. A serious Windows application is a complex warren of interconnecting parts, and an MFC application is no less complex. The more you understand how to explore its hidden depths, the more readily you'll be able to override and specialize its behavior.

2. Write an application to play with *Serialize*, <<, and >>.

Write a small application with a variety of data types among its document class data members. Include the four cases discussed in the section "Calling *Serialize* vs. Using *CArchive* Operators."

- Several different primitive types
- Embedded objects derived from *CObject*
- Pointers to objects derived from *CObject*
- Embedded objects or pointers to objects not derived from *CObject*

Serialize and deserialize these objects. This will get you used to writing serialization code for the range of data objects. See the Ch16ex2 program for one solution, and the file Ch16ex2.doc for an explanation of that solution. Both are located in the \learnvcn\Chap16 folder in the companion code.

What's Next?

No drawing application is complete if it can't print out drawings. In Chapter 17, we'll add printing support. Not only that, but we'll give MyDraw the ability to allow users a print preview—a view of what the drawing would look like if printed (but without printing it). Printing is traditionally hard, but MFC makes it much easier.

Printing the Document

Printing is traditionally one of the harder parts of writing a program. It's so hard in fact that developers of many smaller programs don't add printing capability. But some applications, such as MyDraw, really require the ability to print what the user has created. The Microsoft Foundation Class Library 6.0 (MFC) helps us out by making printing much easier than it would otherwise be.

MyDraw can already print, in a simple way, and it can even give the user a *print preview*—a window showing what the document's pages will look like when printed. In this chapter we're going to fine-tune the printing process so that MyDraw can print attractive, useful documents. This won't be a thorough tour of all that you can do in the printing code for a Microsoft Windows application. But I'll cover the essential issues, giving you a conceptual framework for later explorations.

This chapter constitutes step 7 of MyDraw. It covers the following fundamentals of document printing:

- Planning the document's layout and appearance with printing in mind

- Making the printing in MyDraw device-independent by changing the mapping mode

- Printing a multipage document
- Dealing with portrait and landscape printing modes
- Adding extras such as headers or footers
- Taking advantage of MFC's implementation of Print Preview

Planning for Printing

Before we write a line of printing code, let's look at some of the issues we need to plan for as we add printing to MyDraw.

The chief issue deals with correctly setting the size of the document (MyDraw's drawing surface) to allow for clean printing. We'll examine three areas here: calculating how much of a sheet of paper is available to us given the default printer established on a computer, matching that printable area to the size of MyDraw's drawing surface, and allowing room for things like headers and margins.

It's possible to obtain pretty reliable information about the printable area of a sheet of paper. MFC provides the *CDC::GetDeviceCaps* function for this purpose. *GetDeviceCaps* stands for "get device capabilities." Depending on what parameter we pass to *GetDeviceCaps*, we can obtain a wide variety of information about the computer that MyDraw is running on and about the peripherals attached to it or connected to it on a network.

With the printable area worked out, we'll make one more adjustment to the drawing surface, to allow for things like headers, footers, or margins. In MyDraw, I'll implement a header and a footer on each page. We'll get down to details later in this chapter, in "Paginating the Document."

The MFC Printing Architecture

In programs written for MS-DOS, writing an application's printing code was an arduous and thankless job. You had to write code designed to deal with the vagaries of hundreds of printers and print drivers. It wasn't uncommon to ship a whole disk full of printer drivers with an MS-DOS application. And the code had to reach down to a very low level, close to the hardware.

Printing in Windows

Printing in Windows applications written in C is much more device-independent than printing in MS-DOS applications. But it's still pretty demanding. Here's a short synopsis of Windows printing without benefit of MFC:

1. The application obtains a device context for the printer. A printer device context is set up to deal with a particular printer rather than a display device such as a monitor. (There are various ways to specify which printer: it might be the current default printer, or you might supply a user interface to let the user select a printer from those available.)

2. The application calls the *StartDoc* Win32 API function to begin the print job.

3. The application calls the *StartPage* function to begin the first page of the document.

4. The application calls whatever Graphical Device Interface (GDI) functions it takes to draw the page. For example, MyDraw uses the *Rectangle* and *Ellipse* functions.

5. The application calls the *EndPage* function. Then it loops back, for a multipage document, and calls *StartPage* again to print page 2. You call *StartPage* and *EndPage* even if there's only one page to print. It helps considerably if you can specify up front the maximum number of pages to print, but it's possible to do "print-time pagination," keeping the print loop going as long as there are pages to print.

6. When all pages have been printed, the application calls *EndDoc* to finish up the print job. One catch is that *EndDoc* must be called only if the print job was successful. Otherwise, you must call *AbortDoc*. It's typical to manage this with a Boolean variable that you set to *true* if the printing has been successful or *false* if the printing has not been successful.

The main complication is that for a long print job you need to supply a way for the user to interrupt the printing and cancel the job. In a Windows program written in C, you can supply an abort procedure and display an abort dialog box.

There are, of course, additional complications to the above printing scheme. However, because this is an MFC book, and MFC manages them for you, I won't dwell on them.

Printing with MFC

MFC takes care of most of the details of printing for you. It creates a printer device context and later destroys it; it calls the *StartDoc*, *EndDoc*, *StartPage*, and *EndPage* functions for you; it handles the abort procedure; and it supplies the necessary dialog boxes for the Print and Print Setup commands. MFC also supplies an implementation of the nifty Print Preview functionality that users enjoy in many commercial applications. Print Preview lets the user display, on screen, how the printed document would look. MFC implements the Print Preview window and simulates printing in it.

IP Having Print Preview available is also a great help while you're working on your printing code. You can use it to work out positioning and alignment details.

MFC printing, like drawing on the screen, is managed by *CView*-derived class—another good reason to use the document/view architecture. The view object obtains data to print just as it does for display, via the *GetDocument* function and the pointer to the document object returned by that function. Most MFC applications also draw on the printer just as they draw on the screen—in the *OnDraw* member function. You use the same code to draw in both places. (Yes, you draw on the printer just as you do on the screen. Actually, you print in the background by drawing into a file, which Windows *spools* to the hard disk, from which it's sent to the printer when time permits.) Printing via *OnDraw* is not a requirement, but it's a very useful default, one that we'll be sure to use in MyDraw. The alternative is to draw in two separate places, *OnDraw* and *OnPrint*. Sometimes the printed output is so different from the display output that separating the two makes the best sense.

The essence of MFC printing and Print Preview lies in customizing the general print process for your particular documents. MFC provides several overridable member functions of the view class for this purpose, listed in Table 17-1. These overridable functions let you intervene in the printing process to tailor it. You can put almost all of your printing code in these functions.

Function	Description
OnPreparePrinting	MFC calls this function at the beginning of the print job. You can use it to insert values into the print dialog box before the user sees the dialog. By default, *OnPreparePrinting* calls *DoPreparePrinting* to do the real work, including the dialog. Override *OnPreparePrinting* primarily to specify the page count. Customize the *CPrintInfo* object to provide information about the print job. The printer device context doesn't exist yet.
OnBeginPrinting	MFC calls this function just before printing starts. This is the place to allocate fonts and other resources needed for the print job. The printer device context now exists.
OnPrepareDC	MFC calls this function both for printing and for screen drawing. For printing, it's called before each page begins. MyDraw overrides it to adjust which part of the drawing surface to draw for the next page. This adjustment lets us first print the left side of the drawing as page 1, and then print the right side as page 2. A text document would use it to mark the next set of lines to print as a new page.
OnPrint	MFC calls this function to print (or preview) one page. Normally, you actually draw the printed page by calling *OnDraw* from *OnPrint*. Override to print headers and other page elements not drawn by *OnDraw* or to do all printing here instead of in *OnDraw*.
OnEndPrinting	MFC calls this function when printing ends. Override it to deallocate fonts or other resources you allocated in *OnBeginPrinting*.

Table 17-1. *The view class functions you can override to customize printing.*

In MyDraw, we override four of these functions to accomplish printing tasks as follows:

- We override *OnPreparePrinting* to specify the page count for the print job and to customize Print Preview.

- We override *OnBeginPrinting* to calculate the printable area.

- We override *OnPrepareDC* to adjust which part of the drawing surface is to be drawn for the current page.

- We override *OnPrint* to print or preview the page header, call *OnDraw* to draw the page, and print the footer. We print the header and footer with our own helper functions, *PrintHeader* and *PrintFooter*.

Note that we did not override *OnEndPrinting*. We override only those functions we need to change. Thus our total printing code amounts to four function overrides in the view class plus a couple of helper functions. That's miniscule compared to what's required in a Windows program written in C. Note that Print Preview calls the same functions as Print does.

Changing the Mapping Mode: The Size Problem

One problem we need to solve has to do with the mapping mode. Recall from Chapter 6 that the mapping mode is a characteristic of the device context. It specifies which coordinate system and which units of measurement to use.

The problem is that so far we're using the default mapping mode, *MM_TEXT*, whose unit of measurement is the pixel. That has worked fine for us so far, where all drawing has been to the screen. But printer resolutions vary so much that a rectangle drawn with *MM_TEXT* appears much smaller on many printers than it does on the screen. I call this the size problem.

Try it now

If it's possible for you to print to more than one printer, try this exercise on each of them. Even with only one printer, or none, you can do the following experiment: Run MyDraw and draw several shapes. If you're connected to a printer, select Print on the File menu and then click OK in the Print dialog box. Or if you're not connected to a printer, select Print Preview on the File menu. Either way, compare the results to the drawing on the screen. The shapes seem tiny. On some printers they may seem infinitesimal.

By the way, you can also print by clicking the Printer icon on MyDraw's toolbar. This displays the Print dialog box set to print to the default printer. Try it.

IP MyDraw's printing works best in portrait mode. (I'll discuss what happens in landscape mode later.) If your printer doesn't default to portrait mode, you can change the mode each time you print from MyDraw. (Choose Print Setup on MyDraw's File menu, and then click Properties in the Print Setup dialog box and click Portrait in the Orientation box.) Or you can change the default for your printer. In Windows 98 Help (not Microsoft Visual C++ Help), check the Index for *printers,* select the subtopic "settings" and select the topic "To change the paper size or layout for printing" in the Topics Found dialog box. In Windows 95 Help, check the Help index for *printers* and select the topic "Changing the paper size or layout for printing."

Try it now

Now let's change the mapping mode. In *CMyDrawView::OnInitialUpdate,* change the mapping mode from *MM_TEXT* to *MM_LOENGLISH* by replacing the existing line that specifies the mapping mode:

```
void CMyDrawView::OnInitialUpdate()
{
    CScrollView::OnInitialUpdate();

    // TODO: Add your specialized code here and/or call the base class
    CClientDC dc(this);

    m_nMapMode = MM_LOENGLISH;
    ⋮
```

Consequences of Changing the Mapping Mode

Changing to the *MM_LOENGLISH* mapping mode has two major consequences, which may need to be reflected throughout MyDraw:

- The logical unit of measurement changes from a pixel to a hundredth of an inch.

■ The coordinate system changes so that the y axis now increases upward rather than downward. Positive y values are above the origin rather than below it, and the y values within our client area are all negative. This is important, as you saw in Chapter 15.

The change in units is what we want for MyDraw—pixel sizes vary from one device to another, especially from a monitor to a printer, so measuring in inches instead of pixels makes our shapes appear the same size on both the screen and the printer. But to get that benefit, we have to reckon with the altered coordinate system.

Think of the coordinate change in these terms. Suppose we have a rectangle with coordinates (10, 10, 50, 50). The second and fourth coordinates are y coordinates, so they're the ones affected by the new coordinate system. Figure 17-1 shows what happens to this rectangle with the mapping mode change.

 NOTE The mapping mode is called "LOENGLISH" because it uses English units (inches) and the units are lower resolution than "HIENGLISH": 0.01 inch per logical unit vs. 0.001 inch per unit with the *MM_HIENGLISH* mapping mode.

➤ Try it now

Follow these steps to create a quick demo application:

1. Use AppWizard to create a new MFC AppWizard (.exe) application called YCoord.

2. Click the Next button in the wizard until you reach page 6 of 6. On that page, select the view class name in the upper box (*CYCoordView*). This results in a multiple document interface (MDI) application, which is fine for our purposes.

3. In the Base Class box, select *CScrollView*. This derives the view class *CYCoordView* from *CScrollView* instead of from *CView*. (This is how you make your view a scrolling view from the start, rather than change the class derivation after the fact, as we did in Chapter 15.)

4. Click Finish, and then click OK.

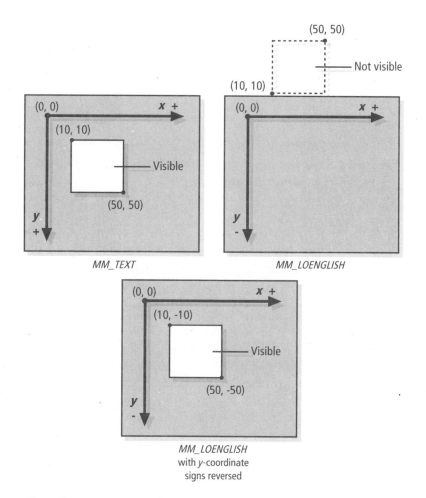

Figure 17-1. *The effect on a rectangle of changing mapping modes.*

 Try it now

Now add some code to YCoord, as follows:

1. Add the highlighted code to YCoord's *OnDraw* function:

```
void CYCoordView::OnDraw(CDC* pDC)
{
    CYCoordDoc* pDoc = GetDocument();
    ASSERT_VALID(pDoc);
    // TODO: add draw code for native data here
    CRect rect = CRect(10, 10, 110, 110);
    pDC->Rectangle(rect);
}
```

2. Build and run YCoord. You should see a rectangle, slightly offset down and to the right of the origin—remember that we're still using *MM_TEXT*, the default mapping mode. Choose Print Preview on the File menu to see how the rectangle would look if it were printed. Notice how tiny the rectangle will look in print vs. onscreen.

3. In *CYCoordView::OnInitialUpdate*, which AppWizard adds for you when you derive the view class from *CScrollView*, change the mapping mode passed to *SetScrollSizes* from the default *MM_TEXT* to *MM_LOENGLISH*. Build, run, and observe the results. Where did the rectangle go? See Figure 17-1.

4. Back in *OnDraw*, change the signs of the second and fourth coordinates in the *CRect* constructor call—these are the *y* coordinates of the rectangle's upper left and lower right corners:

```
CRect rect = CRect(10, -10, 110, -110);
```

Build and run. The rectangle reappears. Choose Print Preview on the File menu. The rectangle appears larger than it did in the *MM_TEXT* mapping mode. If printed, it would appear on the paper to be about 1-inch square, much closer to the size of the rectangle on the screen.

Changing the mapping mode to *MM_LOENGLISH* reversed the *y* axis, so *y* coordinates in our drawing area inside the client area are all negative. Negating the *y* coordinates in the rectangle put the rectangle back into the visible region. This corrected the drawing problem in YCoord. But what about MyDraw?

To fix MyDraw after changing to *MM_LOENGLISH*, we have to reverse the signs of *y* coordinates anywhere that we use *y* coordinates for drawing or printing. Table 17-2 summarizes where we might have to make sign changes in *y* coordinates.

Function	Negate *y* coordinates?
OnDraw	No. No coordinates are directly expressed here in MyDraw. They might be in another application, as they were in YCoord.
OnInitialUpdate	No.
Printing functions	Yes. We'll deal with *OnPrint*, *PrintHeader*, and *PrintFooter* when we get there.
OnPrepareDC	Yes. We'll specify a *y* coordinate when we tell MFC how to break up the drawing surface into pages.
OnLButtonDown, *OnMouseMove*, *OnLButtonUp*	No, but see the discussion following this table.
Other functions in the class	No.

Table 17-2. *Do we need to change y-coordinate signs in view class member functions?*

We only need to reverse some signs when we write the printing code. Otherwise, there are no sign changes in MyDraw, although there might be in other applications. We use *y* coordinates when we draw shapes in *OnLButtonDown*, *OnMouseMove*, and *OnLButtonUp*, but we have another way to correct the *y* coordinates in these functions. These functions receive a *CPoint* parameter that we convert from device coordinates to logical coordinates with the *CDC::DPtoLP* function before the point is used— and that correction also corrects its *y*-coordinate sign. We use the corrected points to construct the current shape's bounding rectangle, so the rectangle is OK.

I'll bring up this topic again when we write the printing functions. For a second example of dealing with the coordinate change, check the Help index for *Scribble tutorial* and double-click the index keyword "printing." In the topic "Enhancing Printing," scroll down and select the link to "Enhance Scribble's printing." Follow the first and second links from that topic.

Paginating the Document

Paginating means dividing into pages. MyDraw's drawing surface is larger than what can be printed on a single standard sheet of paper. We have to divide that drawing surface into page-sized chunks. And then we have to convey the pagination information to MFC's printing code.

We've already taken printing into account in designing the drawing surface—the drawing surface is to be whatever size we can print on two standard pages. (Once we've done it this way, it wouldn't be hard to increase the surface to four pages or more using the same basic logic.) To settle on that size, I calculated the printable area of a standard sheet on my Hewlett Packard 600c inkjet printer. Then I specified a value close to that in setting the scroll sizes for MyDraw's document. Figure 17-2 shows how MyDraw's drawing surface maps to two printed pages side by side. For a second example of pagination, check the Help index for *Scribble tutorial* and double-click the index keyword "printing." Then follow the links "Enhance Scribble's printing" and then "Paginates a Scribble document."

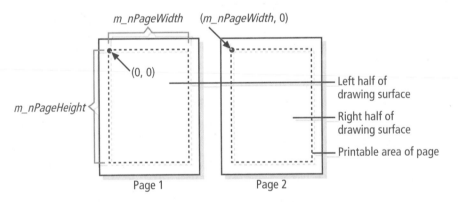

Figure 17-2. *MyDraw's drawing surface mapped to two printed pages.*

Calculating the Printable Area

The printable area is obtained via the *GetDeviceCaps* function. The exact area available for printing on an 8.5-by-11-inch sheet of paper (the standard size in the United States) depends on the printer and on the printer driver being used. To determine that, MyDraw queries *GetDeviceCaps* for each print job to learn the *resolution* of the printer—the printable area expressed as a width and a height.

Passing *HORZSIZE* or *VERTSIZE* to *GetDeviceCaps* returns the width or height of the printable area in millimeters. We can convert millimeters to inches with the following formula:

$$\frac{\text{dimension in millimeters}}{25.4 \text{ millimeters/inch}} = \text{dimension in inches}$$

Then we multiply the new dimension in inches by 100 to get the number of logical units. (A logical unit is 0.01 inch.) If the width dimension, say, is 7 inches, we use 700 logical units. For more information, check the Help index for *GetDeviceCaps*. Where should we call *GetDeviceCaps*?

Calculating the printable area in *OnBeginPrinting*

Our first opportunity to use *GetDeviceCaps* to calculate the printable area for the selected printer comes in the view's *OnBeginPrinting* member function. By this point, the user has seen the Print dialog box and chosen a printer, and the device context has been set up. Figure 17-2 shows the printable area of a page. Figure 17-3 shows how the printable area is divided into header, footer, and drawing areas.

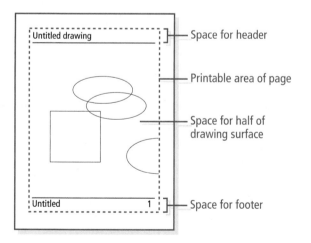

Figure 17-3. *Sections of the printable area of a page.*

Try it now

AppWizard has anticipated that we might want to override the *OnBeginPrinting* function, so it has added the override to our view class (in the file DrawVw.cpp). Let's flesh it out.

1. Fill in the boldface code. (Note the changes to the *OnBeginPrinting* parameters—they are no longer comments.)

```
void CMyDrawView::OnBeginPrinting(CDC* pDC, CPrintInfo* pInfo)
{
    // TODO: add extra initialization before printing
    // Get the printer's resolution in millimeters
    int nHorzSize = pDC->GetDeviceCaps(HORZSIZE);  // Millimeters
    int nVertSize = pDC->GetDeviceCaps(VERTSIZE);

    // Compute page width and height in logical units (0.01 in).
    // Accept double to int truncation (cuts off fractional units).
    // TRACE statements let us see values for planning purposes.
    m_nPageWidth = (double)nHorzSize / 25.4 * 100.0;
    TRACE("m_nPageWidth = %d\n", m_nPageWidth);

    m_nPageHeight = (double)nVertSize / 25.4 * 100.0;
    TRACE("m_nPageHeight = %d\n", m_nPageHeight);
}
```

We calculate using *double* values for better accuracy. However, we ultimately want *int* values, so we assign the *double* result of the calculation to an *int* variable. This truncates the *double* value, losing any fractional units. (Fractional parts of pixels or of hundredths of an inch aren't worth bothering over.) The truncation causes the compiler to report two warnings, but we'll ignore those—they're just warnings, not errors. I've added MFC *TRACE* statements so I can visually capture the width and height (on my HP printer). I'll use those numbers to validate my choice of dimensions for the drawing surface, ensuring that the printer's printable area for the chosen paper size is enough.

T IP AppWizard generates *OnBeginPrinting* with the parameter names commented out. You'll need to remove the comment notations around those names, *pDC* and *pInfo*, so you can refer to them in the function.

---

2. Declare *m_nMapMode*, *m_nPageWidth*, and *m_nPageHeight* as data members of the view class. (See the file DrawVw.h.)

```
// Attributes
public:
    CMyDrawDoc* GetDocument();
    ShpType m_typeNext;
    ⋮
    Cpen* m_pPenOld          // Pen for drawing shape outlines
    Cpen* m_pPenNew          // Store pens we create
    int m_nMapMode;          // Current mapping mode in use
    int m_nPageWidth;        // The width of a printed page
    int m_nPageHeight;       // The height of a printed page
```

Although we've done our calculations using *doubles*, we need *int* values when we later use the data members in *OnPrepareDC*.

Specifying the drawing surface dimensions

Up until now, we've been using rough guesswork to set the size of our drawing surface. In *OnInitialUpdate*, we calculate scroll sizes, and it's there that we set the drawing surface dimensions by specifying a horizontal and a vertical scrolling range. Now we can use better figures for this.

Try it now

Change the document's *GetDocSizes* function to reflect a drawing surface size of 16 inches wide by 9.25 inches high.

Change the following line:

```
sizeTotal = CSize(1000, 1600);
```

to

```
sizeTotal = CSize(1600, 925);
```

Recall that the drawing surface covers the printable area of two 8.5-by-11-inch sheets. We double the width of 850 logical units (8.5 x 100 units/inch) to get a total paper width of 1700 logical units (17 inches). Then we subtract half an inch (50 units) on each side for margins, to get 1600 logical units. Vertically, we'll use 925 units. After deducting an inch (100 units) for top and bottom margins (1100 − 100 = 1000), I've shortened the vertical dimension of 1000 units (by deducting 75 units or 0.75 inches—a rough choice) to allow plenty of space on the printed page for the header and footer as well as the drawing surface. We'll come back to this later. Meanwhile, you can confirm that these dimensions will work in the printable area of an 8.5-by-11-inch sheet.

Try it now

Having added the code to calculate dimensions, choose MFC Tracer on the Visual C++ Tools menu, and then click OK in the MFC Tracer dialog box. Run MyDraw in the debugger. (Press F5.) Draw a shape or two, either print the document or ask for a print preview, and then exit the program. In the Output window, scroll until you can see the effect of our two *TRACE* statements in the *OnBeginPrinting* function. For my printer, the following figures appear:

```
m_nPageWidth = 799
m_nPageHeight = 1035
```

That's pretty close to the figures we arrived at above, taking into account the extra deduction of 0.75 inches vertically, and should be ample room for our printing.

Telling MFC Where to Break the Pages

Now we can impart precise information to MFC about how to print the document. There will be exactly two pages to print. The first page begins at logical coordinates (0, 0) relative to the drawing surface. On my printer, the second page begins 800 units to the right of that, at coordinates (*m_nPageWidth*, 0). Refer to Figure 17-2 on page 516 to see the layout with these dimensions.

We have to do two things:

- Tell MFC how many pages there are to print.
- Specify where the second page begins.

Specifying the maximum number of pages

The best place to tell MFC the maximum number of pages is in the *OnPreparePrinting* function. This function calls *DoPreparePrinting* to display the Print dialog box. We can intervene to specify the pages before that dialog displays so that the user will see the default page range.

Try it now

Add the following boldface line to *CMyDrawView::OnPreparePrinting*:

```
BOOL CMyDrawView::OnPreparePrinting(CPrintInfo* pInfo)
{
    pInfo->SetMaxPage(2);
    // default preparation
    return DoPreparePrinting(pInfo);
}
```

MFC has already prepared a *CPrintInfo* object with information about the default printer. By calling its *SetMaxPage* member function, we can put a 2 into the To box in the Print Range section of the Print dialog box. Try it by building and running MyDraw and selecting Print on the File menu.

Class *CPrintInfo*'s data members include a pointer to the *CPrintDialog* object that displays the Print dialog box, a flag indicating whether we're in Print Preview mode, a flag indicating whether we're still looping through the pages, the current page number, the number of pages (one or two) to display in Print Preview mode, and a rectangle representing the printable area. It also has a number of member functions. Check the Help index for *CPrintInfo*.

MFC passes a *CPrintInfo* pointer to nearly all of the view class printing member functions. Consider it your medium of exchange with MFC for printing information. It contains the values the user sees in the Print dialog box, the values retrieved when the user closes the Print dialog box, and other values you can change along the way, such as the maximum number of pages to print.

Setting coordinates for the next page to print

We tell MFC how to print the second page (and subsequent pages in applications that print more than two pages) in the *OnPrepareDC* member function. We've met *OnPrepareDC* before, in Chapter 15 on scrolling. The view class's *OnPaint* member function calls *OnPrepareDC* to set up the device context it hands to *OnDraw*, taking scrolling into account. We also called *OnPrepareDC* in the mouse message handlers, *OnLButtonDown*, *OnMouseMove*, and *OnLButtonUp*, when we converted points from device coordinates to logical coordinates with *DPtoLP*.

Now we're going to override *OnPrepareDC* for its role in printing. The *OnPrepareDC* override that AppWizard has created for us calls the base class function *CScrollView::OnPrepareDC*. We'll add some printing code.

Try it now

Let's override the *OnPrepareDC* member function in the view class. (Note that the *y* coordinate has been negated to adjust for *MM_LOENGLISH*.)

1. Use the Add virtual function command in WizardBar to add an override of the *OnPrepareDC* virtual function.

2. In *CMyDrawView::OnPrepareDC*, add the boldface lines:

```
void CMyDrawView::OnPrepareDC(CDC* pDC, CPrintInfo* pInfo)
{
    // TODO: Add your specialized code here and/or call...

    CScrollView::OnPrepareDC(pDC, pInfo);
    if(pDC->IsPrinting())
    {
        int nPages = pInfo->m_nCurPage - 1;
        int x = (nPages & 1) * m_nPageWidth;
        int y = (nPages / 2) * -m_nPageHeight;

        pDC->SetWindowOrg(x, y);
    }
}
```

We use the *IsPrinting* member function of class *CDC* to determine whether *OnPrepareDC* has been called for printing or for screen drawing. This keeps us from executing printing code when we're drawing on the screen. Inside the *if* statement, we calculate the *x* coordinate for the upper left corner of the current page, relative to the origin of the drawing surface and the printable area. Notice the use of the bitwise AND operator (&) to calculate the *x* coordinate and division by 2 to calculate the *y* coordinate, and notice the negated *y* coordinate. Table 17-3 shows the *x* and *y* coordinates thus calculated for several different page numbers.

Page # (*m_nCurPage*)	*nPages*	*nPages & 1*	*nPages / 2*	*x*	*y*
1	0	0	0	0	0
2	1	1	0	page width	0
3	2	0	1	0	-page height
4	3	1	1	page width	-page height

Table 17-3. x *and* y *coordinates for up to four pages.*

Notice how the third column (nPages & 1) in Table 17-3 alternates between 0 and 1—that's the effect of using bitwise &. As the table shows, if *m_nCurPage* is 1, *x* and *y* are both 0. The point (0, 0) specifies the upper left corner of page 1. If *m_nCurPage* is 2, *x* is one times the page width, or *m_nPageWidth* (800 units), and *y* is 0. The point (*m_nPageWidth*, 0) specifies the upper left corner of page 2. If *m_nCurPage* is 3, the point (0, -*m_nPageHeight*) specifies the upper left corner of page 3, and so on. This code will continue to work for an indefinite number of pages if you choose to increase the number of pages possible. (That would require additional changes in other parts of the program.) Figure 17-4 on the next page shows how these coordinates map to the drawing surface.

The call to *CDC::SetWindowOrg* sets a new window origin at the specified point. Thus for page 1, the window origin is at (0, 0). For page 2, it's at (*m_nPageWidth*, 0)—halfway across the drawing surface horizontally. When we draw in *OnDraw*, the drawing begins at the specified point, drawing down and to the right from there. This is how a particular page gets printed. Check the Help index for *SetWindowOrg*. For printing purposes, page numbers begin at 1, not 0.

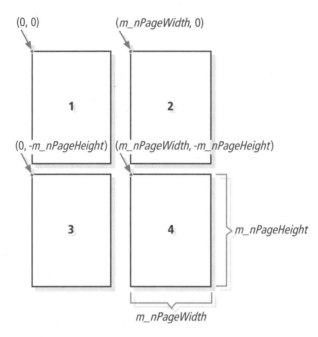

Figure 17-4. *Mapping printed pages to parts of the drawing surface.*

> **NOTE** The printable area, or rectangle, isn't the same on all printers. For example, a dot matrix printer might have a different print rectangle than a laser printer. We've simplified the discussion in this chapter by assuming that printers are the same, but in the real world, if you're likely to be printing on a variety of printers, you should make your code more flexible. When MFC calls *OnPrint*, the *CPrintInfo* object holds information about the printing rectangle in *pInfo->m_rectDraw*. The dimensions of *m_rectDraw* might be different from our *m_nPageWidth* value, so you should really base calculations on *m_rectDraw*, obtained for the current printer. I won't try to deal with this issue here, but be warned.

If we were printing a linear text document, we'd want to set a new *y* coordinate for each page instead of a new *x* coordinate. That's because text document pages are laid out vertically, but MyDraw's two pages are side by side, as shown in Figure 17-5. A spreadsheet application—or MyDraw with more than two pages—might define its pages as blocks of columns and rows, and it might print them either as horizontal first, and then vertical, or as vertical first, and then horizontal.

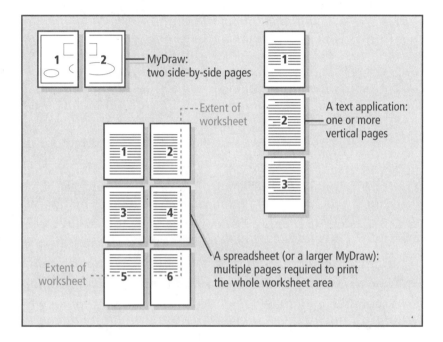

Figure 17-5. *Different ways to lay out printed pages.*

Adjusting the device context before drawing

We have one more change to make in relation to pagination. Just before we call *OnDraw* to draw our shapes, we need to set the window origin again, this time specifying coordinates derived from the *CPrintInfo* object we've been passing around. (Note that the *y* coordinate has been negated to adjust for *MM_LOENGLISH*.)

Try it now

Override the *OnPrint* member function in the view class.

1. Use WizardBar to override the virtual function *OnPrint*.

2. In the *OnPrint* override, add the boldface lines shown on the next page.

```
void CMyDrawView::OnPrint(CDC* pDC, CPrintInfo* pInfo)
{
    // TODO: Add your specialized code here and/or...
    ASSERT_VALID(pDC);
    pDC->SetWindowOrg(pInfo->m_rectDraw.left,
                      -pInfo->m_rectDraw.top);

    CScrollView::OnPrint(pDC, pInfo);
}
```

The call to *SetWindowOrg* gets the upper left corner of the printable area,

`pInfo->m_rectDraw`

and passes its coordinates as the new window origin for drawing. We've already set this rectangle to correspond to the current page. The call to *SetWindowOrg* makes sure we take account of the space needed for a page header, which will already have been printed at that point. Our function *PrintHeader* will adjust the page rectangle to make room for the header, so this call to *SetWindowOrg* reflects that change. It prepares the way for printing the shapes and then the footer. We'll set up the header shortly. Try commenting out the *SetWindowOrg* call after adding the header code in the upcoming "Add the header" section to see what happens without the call.

IMPORTANT The *SetWindowOrg* call is one of those places where we have to reverse the sign of the *y* coordinate, because of the *MM_LOENGLISH* mapping mode. Note the minus sign before the second parameter:

```
pDC->SetWindowOrg(pInfo->m_rectDraw.left,
                  -pInfo->m_rectDraw.top);
```

The Portrait vs. Landscape Problem

One problem not addressed by MyDraw occurs if the user chooses to print in landscape mode rather than in portrait mode. Figure 17-6 shows the MyDraw Print Preview window for a document in both portrait and landscape modes. Create your own document and try it.

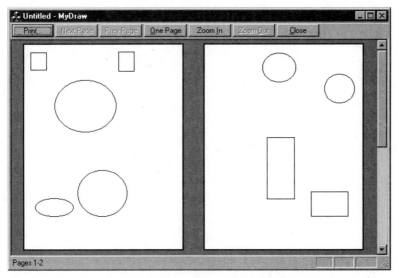

MyDraw Print Preview in portrait mode

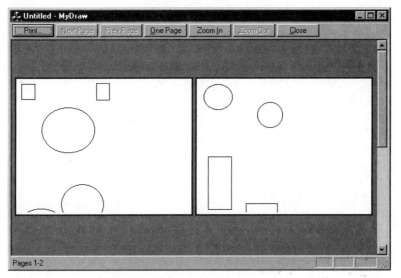

MyDraw Print Preview in landscape mode

Figure 17-6. *MyDraw Print Preview in both portrait and landscape modes.*

MyDraw currently assumes that the user will choose to print in portrait mode, so all the calculations are based on that mode. If the user chooses landscape, either intentionally or inadvertently, the results are not pretty.

The drawing is printed in landscape orientation, but the drawing itself is not adjusted to fit on landscape-oriented pages. Much of the drawing surface is cut off at the bottom of the printed page, and the right side of the drawing surface is nowhere near the right edge of the paper.

A really serious version of MyDraw would need logic that's capable of the following tasks:

- Detecting when landscape mode has been selected

- Performing its page calculations differently if landscape orientation is in effect

Unfortunately, both of these tasks are beyond the scope of this book.

For a discussion and a code sample that sets the orientation mode, see Microsoft Knowledge Base article number *Q126897*. The article is titled "How to Change Default Printer Settings in an MFC Application."

IP The Knowledge Base (KB) is a part of the Visual C++ documentation we haven't discussed yet. KB articles are written by Microsoft support engineers as they deal with customer questions. If you have a problem, someone else has often already discussed the same problem with the support team. For information on using the KB, use the MSDN website to access the KB. (Select Knowledge Base in the Contents list on the MSDN Online Library page.) One of the options on the KB website is to search by specific article ID number. Help for the Visual C++ Introductory Edition doesn't include the KB, but you can access it on Microsoft's website. The website address is *http://support.microsoft.com*. See "Microsoft on the Web and MSDN Online" in Chapter 1 for an easy way to get to the site.

Adding a Header and a Footer

Before we wrap up printing, let's go for a classier look by adding a header and a footer. A header is a string of text across the top of each page in a printed document. A footer is a string across the bottom of each page.

The header will contain the user's own title for the document or, if the document hasn't been titled yet, the string "Untitled drawing." For now, we'll default to "Untitled drawing." (We'll give the user the ability to supply a drawing title in Chapter 19.)

The footer will contain the file location of the drawing if it has been saved, plus the current page number. If the document has been saved, the footer contains the full path to the file unless the path is too long, in which case we'll use just the filename returned by *CDocument::GetTitle*. If the document hasn't been saved yet, we use the string *Untitled* in the footer.

One horizontal line crosses the page below the header and another sits above the footer. Both are drawn with the default pen in the device context. Figure 17-7 shows MyDraw's header and footer.

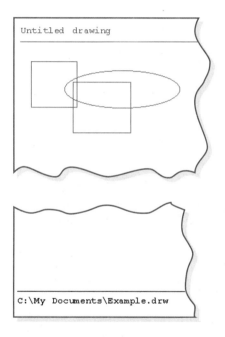

Figure 17-7. *MyDraw's header and footer.*

Positioning the header and footer requires some calculations or some trial and error. The biggest issue we face is positioning these elements so they don't interfere with the shapes the user has drawn. The header, for example, must be below the top of the printable area but above the top of the drawing area. The footer must be above the bottom of the printable area but below the bottom of the drawing area.

Let's look at the header and footer code. I'll discuss the calculations as we go. For a second example of printing a header, check the Help index for *Scribble tutorial* and double-click the index keyword "printing." Follow the links to "Enhance Scribble's printing" and then to "Adds a page header."

Adding Calls to *PrintHeader* and *PrintFooter* Functions

We'll call these functions from *OnPrint*. We call *PrintHeader* just before we call *OnDraw* to draw the current page, and we call *PrintFooter* just after.

Try it now

Add calls to the header and footer functions in *OnPrint*.

```
void CMyDrawView::OnPrint(CDC* pDC, CPrintInfo* pInfo)
{
    // TODO: Add your specialized code here and/or call the base class
    ASSERT_VALID(pDC);
    PrintHeader(pDC, pInfo);
    pDC->SetWindowOrg(pInfo->m_rectDraw.left,
                      -pInfo->m_rectDraw.top);

    CScrollView::OnPrint(pDC, pInfo);  // Calls OnDraw to draw shapes
    PrintFooter(pDC, pInfo);
}
```

It's a good idea to validate the device context here. Then we print the header, position the page so that drawing won't overlap the header or footer, call *OnDraw* through *OnPrint* to draw the shapes, and print the footer.

Adding the Header

A call to the helper function *PrintHeader* prints the header on each page.

Try it now

Add the *PrintHeader* function and a new view class data member.

1. Use the Add Member Function command in WizardBar to add the following function to the view class:

```
void CMyDrawView::PrintHeader(CDC* pDC, CPrintInfo* pInfo)
{
    // Start header at left margin.
    pDC->SetTextAlign(TA_LEFT);

    // Print the header string.
    pDC->TextOut(pInfo->m_rectDraw.left, -25, m_strDrawing);

    // Draw a line under the header and across the page.
    TEXTMETRIC tm;
    pDC->GetTextMetrics(&tm);
    int y = -35 - tm.tmHeight;

    pDC->MoveTo(0, y);
    pDC->LineTo(pInfo->m_rectDraw.right, y);

    // Compensate for the header with the rest of the drawing.
    // Subtract space used by header from drawing rectangle.
    y -= 25;
    pInfo->m_rectDraw.top += y;
}
```

2. In the file DrawVw.h, add the following new data member to class *CMyDrawView*:

```
// Attributes
public:
    CMyDrawDoc* GetDocument();
    ⋮
    int m_nPageHeight;        // The height of a printed page
    CString m_strDrawing;     // User's title for the drawing
```

3. Initialize the *m_strDrawing* data member in the view class constructor, *CMyDrawView::CMyDrawView* (file DrawVw.h).

```
CMyDrawView::CMyDrawView()
{
    // TODO: add construction code here
    ⋮
    m_pPenNew = NULL;
    m_strDrawing = "Untitled drawing";
}
```

We'll store the drawing title in *m_strDrawing*. In Chapter 19, we'll provide a Drawing Title dialog box so users can specify the value of *m_strDrawing*.

Positioning the header involves two steps in the *PrintHeader* function. First, we left-align the header text on the page by calling *CDC::SetTextAlign*. Then we position the text in the *x* and *y* parameters to *CDC::TextOut*. We start the text at the left edge of the printable area, given by

```
pInfo->m_rectDraw.left
```

and place it 25 logical units below the origin—that's the negative *y* coordinate in the *TextOut* call. It's negative, remember, because of the coordinate system imposed by the *MM_LOENGLISH* mapping mode.

To underscore the header, we use *CDC::GetTextMetrics* to get the height of a character in the device context's default font. (We could create a new font and select it into the device context first.) We place the underscore 35 logical units down from the origin, and also move down the character height—this puts the line 10 units below the header text. Then we use *CDC::MoveTo* to position the pen and *CDC::LineTo* to draw the underscore. We specify that it stops at the right edge of the printable area with

```
pInfo->m_rectDraw.right
```

Then comes the interesting step—adjusting the area we can print to by adjusting *pInfo*'s *m_rectDraw* data member. We first come down an additional 25 units below the underscore, and then we alter the drawing rectangle in the *CPrintInfo* object. We've just limited drawing MyDraw's shapes to a slightly smaller area.

Adding the Footer

The footer is a bit trickier than the header. It was easy to know where to start the header. My footer strategy is two-fold:

- Allow for the footer by subtracting some of the drawing area. Shrink the drawing area in the vertical dimension by about 75 logical units—I know the printable area of a standard sheet of paper, on my printer, is about 1000 units, but I use a figure of 925 units. That leaves a sizable area below the drawing surface for the footer.

- Use the freed up space as a basis for calculating the footer's location. This is a matter of determining where to put the *y* coordinates for the footer text and for the separator line above the footer in relation to our free space.

Let's add the footer, test both header and footer, and then discuss the footer code.

Try it now

Use Add Member Function to add the *PrintFooter* function to the view class.

```
void CMyDrawView::PrintFooter(CDC *pDC, CPrintInfo *pInfo)
{
 CMyDrawDoc* pDoc = GetDocument();
    ASSERT_VALID(pDoc);

    // Construct a footer string with document's pathname or title
    //  and current page number.
    // If document's pathname is too long or doc hasn't been saved,
    //  use its title in footer instead of pathname.
    const int LINE_WIDTH = 75;
    CString strFooter = pDoc->GetPathName();
    CString strTitle = pDoc->GetTitle();
    int nLength = strFooter.GetLength();
    if(nLength > LINE_WIDTH || strTitle == "Untitled")
        strFooter = strTitle;

    // Add the page number to the footer.
    CString strPage;
    strPage.Format("%d", pInfo->m_nCurPage);
    strFooter = strFooter + "     " + strPage;

    pDC->SetTextAlign(TA_LEFT);
    pDC->TextOut(pInfo->m_rectDraw.left,
                 pInfo->m_rectDraw.bottom + 100, strFooter);

    // Draw a line over the footer and across the page.
    TEXTMETRIC tm;
    pDC->GetTextMetrics(&tm);
    int y = pInfo->m_rectDraw.bottom + 90 + tm.tmHeight;

    pDC->MoveTo(0, y);
    pDC->LineTo(pInfo->m_rectDraw.right, y);
}
```

Try it now

Test the header and footer code. Build and run MyDraw. Draw a few shapes. Click Print Preview on the File menu. You should see a header and a footer on each page of the printout. Close Print Preview and click Print on the File menu to see the actual printed results. Save the drawing and print again. The footer should now reflect the path to the file in which you stored the drawing. Exit MyDraw.

Most of the code in *PrintFooter* is used to construct the string to print. First, we obtain a document pointer and use it to gather information from the document. If the document has been saved, calling *CDocument::GetPathName* returns the path to the file and calling *CDocument::GetTitle* returns the filename (usually the name without the extension). If the document hasn't been saved, *GetPathName* returns an empty string and *GetTitle* returns the string *Untitled*. We take the length of the path using *CString::GetLength*. If the length exceeds 75 characters (an approximate line length that I found by printing the footer a few times, adjusting the value as I went), or if the document has not yet been saved, we use the title instead of the path.

Next, we obtain the page number from our *CPrintInfo* parameter and format it as a string using *CString::Format*. Then we append a few spaces to *strFooter* and append the page number. The *strFooter* variable now contains something like this: *Title 1*.

With all the calculation finished, we align the text on the left as we did with the header and output the footer string with *CDC::TextOut*. The coordinates at which we begin printing the footer text are determined by the printable area—but take into account our need for a little extra space for the footer. The *y* coordinate is the interesting one. By adding 100 logical units (one inch) to *m_rectDraw.bottom*, we really subtract that inch from the space available for drawing shapes. It subtracts because we're dealing with negative-signed coordinates due to the mapping mode. (I settled on 100 units through a little trial and error.)

Drawing a line across the page just above the footer is similar to what we did for the header. We draw the line one character-height plus 10 units above the footer text.

Wrapping Up

We'll add one last touch to our printing code. Print Preview can display either one or two pages at a time. Since we always have two pages, we'll tell MFC to show both by default.

Try it now

Change the view's *OnPreparePrinting* function so that it looks like the following code. Note that I've introduced an *int* variable to capture the return value of the call to *DoPreparePrinting*—that's the value I want to return from *OnPreparePrinting*, but I can't return it until I set the number of preview pages.

```
BOOL CMyDrawView::OnPreparePrinting(CPrintInfo* pInfo)
{
    pInfo->SetMaxPage(2);
    int nResult = DoPreparePrinting(pInfo);
    pInfo->m_nNumPreviewPages = 2;
    return nResult;
}
```

In this case, we've already shown the Print dialog to the user. On returning from that, we use *pInfo* to set the number of pages to show in Print Preview.

> **W**ARNING One last word of caution about code for printing. Printers and printer drivers vary so widely that you should always test your printing code as thoroughly as possible on as wide a variety of printers as possible.

Printing Topics Not Covered

Among the printing topics I haven't covered are the following:

- Allowing the user to print just the current selection or a range of pages rather than the whole document.

- Allowing the user to print multiple copies in collated or uncollated order.

- Allowing the user to adjust margins and otherwise edit pages while in Print Preview mode. This is advanced stuff.

Some of these topics are covered in Jeff Prosise's *Programming Windows 95 with MFC* (Microsoft Press, 1996) or in Charles Petzold's *Programming Windows*, 5th edition (Microsoft Press, 1999). Chapter 21 gives more information about these books.

Try It Yourself

Here's a little extra credit.

1. Tinker with my code.

Try changing some of the coordinate values in *PrintHeader* and *PrintFooter* to see what happens. You'll get a more concrete sense of how the elements of the printed page fit together.

2. Check out the Microsoft Knowledge Base online.

On the Visual C++ Help menu, select Microsoft On The Web and then select the MSDN Online command. Once your browser connects to the website, follow the link in the left-hand pane to MSDN Online Library. Take a look at the MSDN page, and then scroll down and click Knowledge Base in the Contents listing on the left side. This takes you to the Microsoft Support Online site, where you can search the Knowledge Base. This service is free, but you will have to register for it.

What's Next?

In Chapter 18, we'll make the drawing tools—rectangle and ellipse—more visible and easier to use by putting them on a new drawing toolbar. We'll also add a new Selection tool to the toolbar and use it to implement a selection mode that enables the user to select a shape and thereby display selection handles. Selection handles are the nifty little black knobs you see on selected graphics in commercial drawing programs.

Toolbars and Selections

So far, the only way I've shown you to choose a drawing tool in MyDraw is by way of the Tools menu. But most commercial drawing applications place tools such as our Rectangle and Ellipse commands on a toolbar for easier access. Step 8 of MyDraw adds a second toolbar that offers three tools: the Rectangle and Ellipse commands and a Selection command.

Clicking the Rectangle or Ellipse toolbar button sets the type of shape to draw next. Clicking the Selection button puts MyDraw into selection mode instead of drawing mode.

Adding a Toolbar

MyDraw already has one toolbar, which AppWizard provided back in step 0 in Chapter 7. Adding a second toolbar requires three steps: creating a new toolbar resource, drawing its buttons, and then adding the code to support the toolbar.

The Toolbar Classes

Classes *CToolBar*, *CStatusBar*, and *CDialogBar* all derive from class *CControlBar* in the Microsoft Foundation Class Library 6.0 (MFC). In addition, there's a new kind of toolbar, *CReBar*. Like the toolbars in Microsoft Internet Explorer, *CReBar* is a *rebar control*—a container for a child window, usually a common control. Rebars can consist of multiple *bands*. Each band can have a *gripper bar* that the user grabs to drag the band to a different position on the rebar, plus a bitmap, a text label, and a child window. AppWizard supplies an option for using rebar-style toolbars. (You can see what this looks like by running AppWizard and selecting the Internet Explorer ReBars option in step 4 of 6. Try it.)

Except for *CDialogBar*, all of the MFC control bar classes are really wrappers for underlying Microsoft Windows common controls. For example, *CToolBar* wraps class *CToolBarCtrl*, which wraps the Windows toolbar common control. You can manage your toolbar with *CToolBar* members, or you can use *CToolBar::GetToolBarCtrl* to get a pointer to a *CToolBarCtrl* and take additional actions through its members. (A *CDialogBar* is an MFC concoction that provides a toolbar that can contain any control you can put in a dialog box.)

For information about MFC's control bar support, check the Help index for the individual classes named above. Also check the Help index for *control bar* and follow the various links in the topic "Control Bar Topics."

Creating the New Toolbar Resource

A toolbar resource is similar to other resources. It has an ID, which is used to load the resource at run time, and it has an appearance, which is a bitmap for each button. We'll first create the new resource and define its ID. Then we'll draw the button images using the Toolbar editor.

Try it now

Use the Insert menu to create a new toolbar resource.

1. Choose Resource from the Insert menu.

2. In the Insert Resource dialog box, double-click Toolbar. The Toolbar editor opens, showing one blank button image, as shown in Figure 18-1.

3. On the ResourceView tab in the Workspace window, right-click the IDR_TOOLBAR1 resource ID in the Toolbar folder, and then choose Properties from the context menu that pops up. (Alternatively, you

can select the resource ID using the left mouse button and choose Properties from the View menu.)

4. In the Properties window for the toolbar, change the ID to *IDR_DRAWING*. Press Enter to close the Properties window.

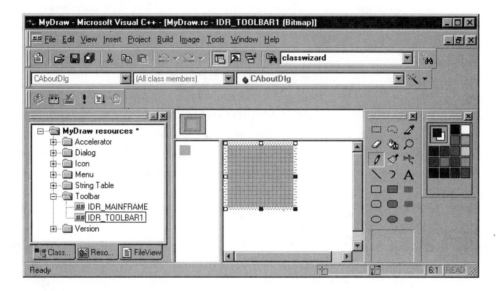

Figure 18-1. *The Toolbar editor.*

Try it now

Draw the button images in the Toolbar editor. The first button is already selected, and the Pencil tool is selected on the Toolbar editor's Graphics toolbar. Black is selected as the foreground drawing color on the Color Indicator of the editor's Color Palette. The button's initial background is light gray. For information about using the Toolbar editor, check the Help index for *toolbar editor*. Double-click the index entry "Toolbar editor" (Note the capital *T*) to open the topic "Overview: Toolbar Editor."

1. To draw the first button, for our Selection command, use the pencil tool to draw an arrow pointing up and to the left, as shown in Figure 18-2 on the next page. Then choose Properties from the View menu. In the ID box, type *ID_TOOL_SELECTION*. In the Prompt box, type *Select a shape\nSelect*.

2. To draw the second button, for our Rectangle command, click the new second button that appears to the right of the first button in the Toolbar editor. Use the Rectangle tool on the Graphics toolbar to draw a rectangle on the button. Choose Properties from the View menu. In the ID box, select the existing ID for the Rectangle command, *ID_TOOL_RECTANGLE*. The Prompt box might already say "Draw a rectangle" because we associated that prompt text with the ID when we created the ID. If it doesn't, type in the prompt text. At the end of the prompt, type *nRectangle*. The final prompt string is "Draw a rectangle\nRectangle."

3. To draw the third button, which we will use for our Ellipse command, click the new third button to the right of the second button. Use the Ellipse tool on the Graphics toolbar to draw an ellipse on the button. Choose Properties from the View menu. In the ID box, select *ID_TOOL_ELLIPSE*. The Prompt box might already say, "Draw an ellipse." If not, type the following prompt text: *Draw an ellipse\nEllipse*.

4. For a little fun, use the Paint Bucket tool on the Graphics toolbar to fill areas of the new buttons with different colors. I've colored the background of the Selection button yellow and the backgrounds of the other buttons cyan (light blue).

5. Save your work and close the Toolbar editor by choosing Close from the File menu.

Figure 18-2.   *The new toolbar in the Toolbar editor.*

Toolbar command IDs

Notice that we gave our Rectangle and Ellipse buttons the same command IDs that we gave to the menu items for those commands. The command is its ID. We can associate that ID with any number of user interface elements—menu items, toolbar buttons, or accelerators—to cause the interface element to issue the command. As a result, the Rectangle and

Ellipse toolbar buttons now duplicate the Rectangle and Ellipse commands on the Tools menu.

Tooltips

Adding \n*Text* to the prompt string for each command supplies a tooltip for the button. While MyDraw is running, when we rest the mouse pointer on the toolbar button, it displays a tooltip—a small yellow box containing the text we supplied. In this case, the Selection button will say "Select," the Rectangle button will say "Rectangle," and the Ellipse button will say "Ellipse." Adding tooltips for your toolbar buttons is that easy. You can also add tooltip text at other points in the development process—when you create the ID in the first place (for a menu item) and any time after that (using the String editor).

Editing an existing toolbar

You can also edit the buttons on an existing toolbar. The Scribble tutorial provided by Visual C++ describes how to add a button and draw the button's bitmap. Check the Help index for *Scribble tutorial* and double-click the subtopic "binding visual objects to code." Scroll down in the topic "Binding Visual Objects to Code Using WizardBar" and follow the link to "Edit Scribble's Toolbar."

Writing the Toolbar Code

The code to support our new toolbar consists of the following elements:

- Additions and changes to the *OnCreate* member function of class *CMainFrame*, our frame window class. Because a toolbar is just a child window of the application's main frame window, we put the toolbar-related code there. (For a brief discussion of child windows, see the sidebar on the next page, "Parent and Child Windows vs. Owner and Owned Windows.")

- Slight modifications to the existing *OnToolRectangle* and *OnToolEllipse* handlers, which are in the view class.

Adding the second toolbar's code is mostly a matter of copying and then modifying what AppWizard supplied for the first toolbar.

Parent and Child Windows vs. Owner and Owned Windows

Except for "top-level windows" such as the main window of an application, every window is either the *child* of a *parent* window or a window *owned* by an *owner* window. Windows such as our toolbars and our view are children of the main application frame window. Dialog box windows, on the other hand, are owned windows. Owned windows can themselves be top-level windows, on a par with the window that owns them. The owner is usually the window that creates an owned window, such as when our view window creates a dialog box. (We'll do this in Chapter 19.)

The view and the toolbars in an MFC application are child windows. Child windows are embedded directly in a parent window and have the style *WS_CHILD*. No part of a child window lies beyond the parent's bounds. But a dialog box can lie partly or completely outside its owner window. Dialog boxes and other owned windows usually have the style *WS_POPUP* instead of *WS_CHILD*. You can use the *CWnd::GetParent* function to obtain any child window's parent or any owned window's owner.

Try the following experiment: Make the main window in Visual C++ less than maximized (but not minimized). Open a dialog box in the program, and drag it completely outside the program's window. Now let's try to drag a child window outside the program window. Restore a maximized document window, such as the Source Code editor window (not a dockable window) in Visual C++. (You'll find the Restore button between the Close button and the Minimize button.) Then try to drag the window outside the main program window. You can't because it's a child window. (You can, however, drag Visual C++'s dockable windows out, which suggests that they're implemented as pop-up, or owned, windows.) I discussed Visual C++ dockable and document windows in Chapter 1.

Check the Help index for *parent window* and *child window*. Also check the Help index for *owner window* and *owned window*.

Naming the Standard and Drawing toolbars

To distinguish the toolbars, we'll call the toolbar created by AppWizard the Standard toolbar and the new toolbar the Drawing toolbar. We need to name data members of class *CMainFrame* accordingly.

Try it now

In the class declaration for class *CMainFrame* (in the file MainFrm.h), there's a protected section below the implementation comment where the first toolbar, *m_wndToolBar*, is declared. Change the name *m_wndToolBar* to *m_wndToolBarStd*. Also, add the second toolbar as *m_wndToolBarDraw*:

```
      ⋮
protected:  // control bar embedded members
    CStatusBar   m_wndStatusBar;
    CToolBar     m_wndToolBarStd;
    CToolBar     m_wndToolBarDraw;

// Generated message map functions
      ⋮
```

Notice the variable *m_wndStatusBar*, a *CStatusBar* object that defines the program's status bar. The two toolbars are *CToolBar* objects.

Creating the toolbars at run time

CMainFrame::OnCreate is called when the main frame window for MyDraw is created. At that time, we create the toolbars from our toolbar resources, set the styles of the toolbar buttons, and specify docking information if the toolbars are to be dockable to a side of MyDraw's window. I discussed the code for the default toolbar in "The *OnCreate* Handler" in Chapter 8. The frame window manages displaying the toolbars, which share space in the window with the view.

Try it now

Let's start by cloning the creation code for the Standard toolbar to use for the Drawing toolbar:

1. In *CMainFrame::OnCreate* (in the file MainFrm.cpp), change the name *m_wndToolBar* to *m_wndToolBarStd* in two places: the *CreateEx* call and the *LoadToolBar* call, as shown by the boldfaced items.

```
    ⋮
// Changed window name when adding new toolbar
// Create the Standard toolbar
if (!m_wndToolBarStd.CreateEx(this, TBSTYLE_FLAT, WS_CHILD
        | WS_VISIBLE | CBRS_TOP | CBRS_GRIPPER | CBRS_TOOLTIPS
        | CBRS_FLYBY | CBRS_SIZE_DYNAMIC) ||
        !m_wndToolBarStd.LoadToolBar(IDR_MAINFRAME))
{
    TRACE0("Failed to create toolbar\n");
    return -1;        // fail to create
}
    ⋮
```

2. Copy all of the code shown above—the *CreateEx* call, which includes a call to *LoadToolBar*, plus the body of the *if* statement—and paste it just below where you copied it. You end up with two copies of the same code fragment.

3. In the second copy of the toolbar creation code, change the toolbar name from *m_wndToolBarStd* to *m_wndToolBarDraw* in two places and change the ID passed to *LoadToolBar* from *IDR_MAINFRAME* to *IDR_DRAWING*. Make the second copy look like this:

```
// Added for new toolbar
// Create the Drawing toolbar
if (!m_wndToolBarDraw.CreateEx(this, TBSTYLE_FLAT, WS_CHILD
            | WS_VISIBLE | CBRS_TOP | CBRS_GRIPPER | CBRS_TOOLTIPS
            | CBRS_FLYBY | CBRS_SIZE_DYNAMIC) ||
        !m_wndToolBarDraw.LoadToolBar(IDR_DRAWING))
{
    TRACE0("Failed to create toolbar\n");
    return -1;        // fail to create
}
```

You might also want to customize the error message in each *if* statement to indicate which toolbar couldn't be created.

Setting styles for the Drawing toolbar

One thing that the *CToolBar::CreateEx* call does is specify a set of styles for the toolbar. Styles are flags that tell Windows how to display and operate the toolbar. Some of the styles have the prefix *WS_*, for "window style." These styles can be applied to any window. (Check the Help index for *window styles*.) Others have the prefix *CBRS_*, for "control bar style." These styles apply only to control bars (the generic name for toolbars, status bars, and dialog bars in MFC).

For information about the control bar styles, check the Help index for *cbrs* and then find the specific style you want. Also check the Help index for *CreateEx* and choose the "*CToolBar::CreateEx*" topic. *CreateEx* is an extended version of the original *Create* function. Extending a function is a typical way in which Microsoft adds new functionality to Windows without breaking older code. *Create* is still supported; it just can't do as much as *CreateEx* can.

Try it now

Change the Drawing toolbar's style so that it docks by default on the left edge of MyDraw's main window rather than on the top. In the long list of toolbar styles for *m_wndToolBarDraw*, change *CBRS_TOP* to *CBRS_LEFT*:

```
⋮
if (!m_wndToolBarDraw.CreateEx(this, TBSTYLE_FLAT, WS_CHILD
        | WS_VISIBLE | CBRS_LEFT | CBRS_GRIPPER | CBRS_TOOLTIPS
        | CBRS_FLYBY | CBRS_SIZE_DYNAMIC) ||...
⋮
```

Setting the behavior of the Drawing toolbar buttons

On the Standard toolbar in MyDraw, all of the buttons are independent pushbuttons. When the user clicks a button, it appears to depress briefly, then springs back to its original position. On the Drawing toolbar, we want a different behavior because the buttons put the application into mutually exclusive modes. The buttons should behave like a group of radio buttons in a dialog box—clicking a button "turns it on" (causing it to appear depressed) and clicking another button "turns off" the previous button. Only one button can be "on" at a time. By default, toolbar buttons have the style *TBBS_PUSHBUTTON*, which provides the behavior we see on the Standard toolbar. We want to set the buttons on the Drawing toolbar to *TBBS_CHECKGROUP*, to switch to radio-button-like behavior.

Try it now

Specify styles for the buttons on the Drawing toolbar. Just below the *CreateEx* call for *m_wndToolBarDraw*, add the boldface code on the following page to walk through the buttons on the toolbar and set the style for each.

```
    ⋮
    return -1;        // fail to create
}

// Set the style of Drawing toolbar buttons
const int NUM_DRAW_BUTTONS = 3;
for(int i = 0; i < NUM_DRAW_BUTTONS; i++)
{
    m_wndToolBarDraw.SetButtonStyle(i,
        m_wndToolBarDraw.GetButtonStyle(i) | TBBS_CHECKGROUP);
}

if (!m_wndStatusBar.Create(this) ||
    ⋮
```

The trick here is to call *CToolBar::SetButtonStyle* with the index of a button as its first parameter. The second parameter is the result of a call to *GetButtonStyle* combined with the *TBBS_CHECKGROUP* style using the bitwise OR operator (|). This keeps the button's existing (default) styles but adds the new style to them.

Assigning titles for floating toolbars

Both of MyDraw's toolbars can either dock or float. Right now, when they float they have no window title. We'd like them to be better identified. (Try floating a toolbar in Visual C++—it has a title.) We simply call the *CWnd::SetWindowText* member function that class *CToolBar* inherits. A toolbar is a window, so it has all of *CWnd's* capabilities as well as those added by *CControlBar* and *CToolBar*.

 Try it now

Add the following boldface code to *CMainFrame::OnCreate* to specify window titles for the toolbars when they float. (Put it just below the code that sets the toolbar button styles.)

```
    ⋮
for(int i = 0; i < NUM_DRAW_BUTTONS; i++)
{
    m_wndToolBarDraw.SetButtonStyle(i,
        m_wndToolBarDraw.GetButtonStyle(i) | TBBS_CHECKGROUP);
}
```

```
// Set window captions for when toolbars are floating.
m_wndToolBarStd.SetWindowText("Standard");
m_wndToolBarDraw.SetWindowText("Drawing");

if (!m_wndStatusBar.Create(this) ||
⋮
```

Making the toolbars dockable

The last thing we need to do in *CMainFrame::OnCreate* is make the Drawing toolbar dockable. This requires three steps:

1. Enabling docking for the toolbar object.

2. Enabling docking for the frame window to which the toolbar will dock.

3. Docking the toolbar in its initial docking position.

We need to take one additional step for the Standard toolbar. It's already set up for docking, but we need to change the toolbar name in that code.

Try it now

Make the boldfaced changes in *CMainFrame::OnCreate*:

```
⋮
// TODO: Delete these lines if you don't want the toolbars to
//   be dockable
// Changed window name while adding new toolbar
m_wndToolBarStd.EnableDocking(CBRS_ALIGN_ANY);
m_wndToolBarDraw.EnableDocking(CBRS_ALIGN_ANY);
EnableDocking(CBRS_ALIGN_ANY);
// Changed name while adding new toolbar
DockControlBar(&m_wndToolBarStd);
DockControlBar(&m_wndToolBarDraw);

Return 0;
⋮
```

The flag *CBRS_ALIGN_ANY* allows the toolbars to dock at any edge of the main frame window. Calling *CFrameWnd::DockControlBar* docks a toolbar to the initial edge we specified when creating it: the top edge for the Standard toolbar and the left edge for the Drawing toolbar.

You can build MyDraw at this point and run it to see the new toolbar. The Rectangle and Ellipse buttons already work because they're already wired up to the appropriate command handlers. We have to write some code to implement the Selection button. You can see at this point, though, that MyDraw is starting to look more impressive.

Implementing Selection Mode

The Selection button turns on selection mode. In this mode, the user can click inside the bounding rectangle of a shape to select it. The shape takes on a special appearance to indicate that it is selected: *selection handles* appear around its bounding rectangle, as shown in Figure 18-3. We'll allow the selection of only one shape at a time. Selecting a new shape will turn off the selection handles on any previously selected shape. A more sophisticated program might allow selecting multiple shapes at the same time so that the user can apply a command to all of the selected shapes, such as dragging them together to a new location.

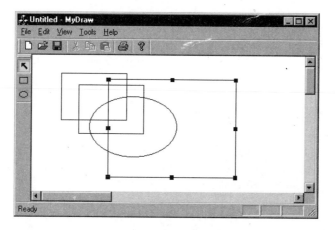

Figure 18-3.   *A shape with selection handles.*

These things also occur in selection mode:

■ The *OnLButtonDown* handler behaves differently. It distinguishes between selection mode and drawing mode.

■ Clicking the drawing surface cancels any previous selection and removes the selection handles—unless the click occurred inside the bounding rectangle of an existing shape, in which case that shape becomes the new selection. It also cancels selection mode (and restores the selected shape's state to what it was before selection mode was invoked).

- The user can click shape after shape, moving the selection handles from one shape to another. Selecting a drawing tool instead cancels selection mode and any existing selection.

We should ultimately go further than just selection, of course, and allow the user to edit the selected shape. Unfortunately, in this book we don't have space to add code for (and discuss at length) such features as these:

- Dragging the selected shape to a new location

- Dragging the selection handles to resize the shape

- Choosing commands such as Bring Forward, Send Behind, Bring To Front, and Send To Back, which reorder the list of shapes so that a shape can be moved "in front of" or "behind" another shape

How Selection Mode Works

Selection begins when the user clicks the Selection button on the Drawing toolbar. This sets a variable that defines the current mode: selecting or drawing. The next step occurs in *OnLButtonDown*, when the user clicks the drawing surface with selection mode on. In selection mode, *OnLButtonDown* skips its usual shape creation code and calls a function to do *hit testing*—detecting where the mouse was clicked and relating that to some object that might have been clicked. Our hit testing routine walks the shape list, testing to see if the mouse location is inside the bounding rectangle of any shape. The key to our hit testing is that we walk the list from the most recently added shape back toward the shape that was first added.

Picture the shapes as if each were drawn on its own layer of transparent plastic. (See Figure 18-4 on the next page.) The bottom layer contains the first shape. The top layer contains the most recently drawn shape. Looking down through the layers of plastic, we see all of the shapes. Some might appear to overlap. The layers give us a way to determine which shape is intended when the user clicks on an area where two shapes overlap. We walk the list of shapes in a consistent way—from newest to oldest (top layer of plastic to bottom layer). When the mouse location falls within a shape's bounding rectangle we stop walking. A "hit" occurs on the shape in the layer closest to the top. Windows uses a similar top-to-bottom mechanism for its overlapping windows, called *Z order* (named for the third axis in a three-dimensional coordinate system).

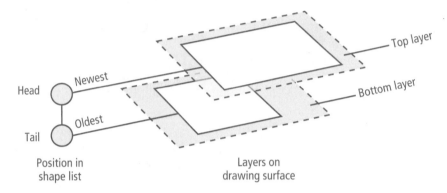

Figure 18-4.   *Shapes drawn in layers.*

To track which shape, if any, has been selected, we add an *m_bSelected* data member to each shape. This member is set to *true* when the shape is selected and to *false* when it isn't.

We'll look at the code for selection in four parts:

- The code that sets or cancels selection mode
- The code that makes class *CShape* and its derived classes selectable
- The code that does the hit testing to see whether a shape has been selected
- The code that draws the selection handles

The Selection Button

First, we need a convenient way to turn selection on and drawing off, and vice versa. To keep the toolbar buttons in sync, we'll treat selection mode as an extra shape type. When that type is active, selection mode is on and drawing is off. We'll also set a Boolean variable when selection mode is on and use that in our hit-testing code.

Try it now

To synchronize the toolbar buttons, we'll revise the *ShpType* enumeration above class *CShape*, adding a new shape type. We'll set *ShpType* to *ShpSelecting* in the *OnToolSelection* handler that responds to a click on the Selection button. We'll cancel selection mode in the *OnToolRectangle* and *OnToolEllipse* handlers when other shape types are selected.

1. In the file Shape.h, change the *ShpType* enumeration to add the new shape type:

```
enum ShpType
{
    shpSelecting,    // With selection tool in effect
    shpRectangle,
    shpEllipse
};
```

2. Use the Add Windows Message Handler command to add an *OnToolSelection* handler in the view class, associated with command *ID_TOOL_SELECTION* (the ID we assigned to the Selection button). Add the boldface code to the code that WizardBar provides:

```
void CMyDrawView::OnToolSelection()
{
    // TODO: Add your command handler code here
    m_typeFormer = m_typeNext;  // Save old tool for restoration
    m_typeNext = shpSelecting;  // For toolbar management
    m_bSelectionMode = true;
}
```

The *m_typeFormer* data member remembers which shape tool was in effect when we entered selection mode so we can return to that tool when the mode ends. The *m_bSelectionMode* data member is set to *true* if selection mode is on, and set to *false* if not.

3. Use the Add Windows Message Handler command to add an update handler for *OnToolSelection*:

```
void CMyDrawView::OnUpdateToolSelection(CCmdUI* pCmdUI)
{
    // TODO: Add your command update UI handler code here
    pCmdUI->SetCheck(m_typeNext == shpSelecting);
}
```

4. Add two new data members to the view class declaration in the DrawVw.h file:

```
CString m_strDrawing;      // User's title for the drawing
bool m_bSelectionMode;     // True if selection mode in effect
ShpType m_typeFormer;      // Save current tool while selecting
  ⋮
```

5. Initialize the new data members in the view class constructor:

```
m_strDrawing = "Untitled drawing";
m_bSelectionMode = false;   // Added for selection
m_typeFormer = m_typeNext;  // Added for selection
  ⋮
```

6. Cancel selection mode in the existing *OnToolRectangle* and *OnToolEllipse* handlers (in the view class). Here are the two handlers with the revision:

```
void CMyDrawView::OnToolRectangle()
{
    // TODO: Add your command handler code here
    m_typeNext = CShape::shpRectangle;
    CancelSelection();
}

void CMyDrawView::OnToolEllipse()
{
    // TODO: Add your command handler code here
    m_typeNext = CShape::shpEllipse;
    CancelSelection();
}
```

7. Use the Add Member Function command to add the following helper function, which is called from the tool command handlers:

```
void CMyDrawView::CancelSelection()
{
    // End selection mode because another tool was chosen
    // Other tool sets m_typeNext to other than shpSelecting
    CMyDrawDoc* pDoc = GetDocument();
    ASSERT_VALID(pDoc);
    m_bSelectionMode = false;
    pDoc->UpdateAllViews(NULL);
}
```

Canceling the selection has two effects: *m_bSelectionMode* is set to *false*, and we force redrawing by calling *UpdateAllViews*.

OTE The Rectangle and Ellipse commands are represented both on the toolbar and on the menu. Should the Selection command also be on the menu? Hint: the toolbar can be hidden.

Selection Code in the Shapes

Each shape has an *m_bSelected* data member that is set to *true* if the shape is selected and set to *false* if not. We'll set a shape's selection value when we create the shape and again during hit testing. When shapes are redrawn, they can draw themselves with or without selection handles.

Try it now

Add selection code to the shape classes. We'll fill in the details of handle drawing later in the chapter.

1. In class *CShape* (in the file Shape.h), add the *m_bSelected* data member:

   ```
   ⋮
   // Attributes - deliberately left public for easy access
   // Note: no longer need an m_typeShape member
   CRect m_boxShape;
   bool m_bTransparent;
   UINT m_nColorShape;
   bool m_bSelected;

   // Overridables and operations
   ⋮
   ```

2. Initialize *m_bSelected* in the *CShape* copy constructor and the overloaded assignment operator function in Shape.h:

   ```
   ⋮
   // Copy constructor
   CShape(const CShape& s)
   {
       m_boxShape = s.m_boxShape;
       m_bTransparent = s.m_bTransparent;
       m_nColorShape = s.m_nColorShape;
       m_bSelected = s.m_bSelected;
   }

   // Overloaded assignment operator
   CShape& operator=(const CShape& s)
   ```

(continued)

```
{
    m_boxShape = s.m_boxShape;
    m_bTransparent = s.m_bTransparent;
    m_nColorShape = s.m_nColorShape;
    m_bSelected = s.m_bSelected;
    return *this;
}
    ⋮
```

3. Initialize *m_bSelected* in the *CShape* default constructor in the file Shape.cpp:

```
CShape::CShape()
{
    m_boxShape.SetRect(0, 0, 0, 0);
    m_bTransparent = true;
    m_nColorShape = ID_COLOR_BLACK;
    m_bSelected = false;
}
```

4. Add a parameter to the *Draw* function declarations (in the file Shape.h), classes *CShape*, *CShpRectangle*, and *CShpEllipse*—note that the modifier *virtual* will only appear in class *CShape*:

```
virtual void Draw(CDC* pDC, bool bSelectionModeOn)...
```

5. In classes *CShpRectangle* and *CShpEllipse* (but not *CShape*, because it is virtual), revise the *Draw* function so it looks like this (in the file Shape.cpp):

```
void CShpRectangle::Draw(CDC* pDC, bool bSelectionModeOn)...
{
    pDC->Rectangle(m_boxShape);
    if(m_bSelected && bSelectionModeOn)
        DrawHandles(pDC);
}
    ⋮
void CShpEllipse::Draw(CDC* pDC, bool bSelectionModeOn)...
{
    pDC->Ellipse(m_boxShape);
    if(m_bSelected && bSelectionModeOn)
        DrawHandles(pDC);
}
```

After drawing the shape, *Draw* adds selection handles to it if the shape is marked as selected in *m_bSelected* and if the *bSelection-ModeOn* parameter indicates that selection mode is on. We don't want to draw the handles if we aren't in selection mode.

6. Add an array of *CRect* objects just above the *CShape* declaration (in the file Shape.h):

```
    ⋮
enum ShpType
{
    shpSelecting,    // With selection tool in effect
    shpRectangle,
    shpEllipse
};

static CRect arHandles[8];

class CShape : public CObject
    ⋮
```

We'll use the array later when we calculate sizes and positions for a shape's selection handles.

7. Use the Add Member Function command to add two helper member functions in class *CShape* (in the file Shape.cpp). Here are the prototypes for the two functions:

```
// Helper functions for shape selection
void CreateHandleRects();
void DrawHandles(CDC *pDC);
```

We'll add code to the two functions in "Drawing the Selection Handles" later in the chapter.

8. Update serialization code in the *Serialize* member function of class *CShape*:

```
    ⋮
else
{
    // TODO: add loading code here
    ar >> m_boxShape >> byTransparent >> m_nColorShape;
    m_bTransparent = (byTransparent != 0);
    m_bSelected = false; // We don't store selection state
}
```

When writing shapes to a drawing file, we won't store their selection state because when opening a file and reading its shapes in, we don't care if any of them have been selected in the past. However, when reading shapes in, we must initialize the new *m_bSelected* member so the shapes are complete. Since this doesn't change our file structure, we don't need to increment the schema number for the shape classes.

9. We also need to initialize a shape's *m_bSelected* member when the shape is first created. Add the following boldfaced line of code to *OnLButtonDown* in DrawVw.cpp:

```
    ⋮
// Start setting properties of the new shape.
m_pShpTemp->m_bTransparent = m_bTransparent;
m_pShpTemp->m_nColorShape = m_nColorNext;
m_pShpTemp->m_bSelected = false;

// Convert point to logical coordinates.
    ⋮
```

10. One last change: we need to call *CShape::Draw* in two places in the view, *OnDraw* and *InvertShape*. Add the second parameter to each of those calls, first in *OnDraw*:

```
    ⋮
// Get the shape and use it to set the pen and brush.
//   Last shape sets position to NULL.
pShape = pDoc->GetPrevShape();
SetPenBrush(pDC, pShape->m_bTransparent,
    pShape->m_nColorShape);
// Ask the shape to draw itself.
pShape->Draw(pDC, m_bSelectionMode);
// Clean up.
ResetPenBrush(pDC);
    ⋮
```

and then in *InvertShape*:

```
    ⋮
int nModeOld;
if(bInvert)
{
    nModeOld = pDC->SetROP2(R2_NOT);
}

// Draw the shape (or erase it).
SetPenBrush(pDC, s.m_bTransparent, s.m_nColorShape);
s.Draw(pDC, m_bSelectionMode);
    ⋮
```

Hit Testing

When the user clicks on the drawing surface in selection mode, we don't want to capture the mouse and create a new shape. Instead, we want to observe that *m_bSelectionMode* is *true* and use the *CPoint* passed to the *OnLButtonDown* handler to detect where the click occurred. Hit testing determines whether that point is within one of our shapes. If it is, we mark the shape as selected. Subsequent redrawing draws that shape with selection handles. While we're at it, we mark all unselected shapes as well.

Try it now

Make the following changes in the view class to manage hit testing in selection mode:

1. Detect selection mode in *OnLButtonDown* and call a helper function to do hit testing. Add and delete code to make *CMyDraw-View::OnLButtonDown* (in the file DrawVw.cpp) look like the following code, including the closing right brace just before the call to *CScrollView::OnLButtonDown*:

```
void CMyDrawView::OnLButtonDown(UINT nFlags, CPoint point)
{
    // TODO: Add your message handler code here...
    CMyDrawDoc* pDoc = GetDocument();
    ASSERT_VALID(pDoc);

    if(m_bSelectionMode)      // Selecting
    {
        // Find which shape was clicked, if any.
        // Sets the selected shape, if there is one.
        DoHitTesting(point);
    }
    else                      // Drawing
    {
        SetCapture();
        m_bCaptured = true;
        ASSERT(m_typeNext == shpRectangle || m_typeNext ==
            shpEllipse);
        // Create CShape and add it to our list...
        m_pShpTemp = pDoc->CreateShape(m_typeNext);
```

(continued)

```
                    ⋮
      m_pShpTemp->m_boxShape.left =
          m_pShpTemp->m_boxShape.right = point.x;
      m_pShpTemp->m_boxShape.top =
          m_pShpTemp->m_boxShape.bottom = point.y;
  } // Add this brace
  CScrollView::OnLButtonDown(nFlags, point);
}
```

Because of the way *OnMouseMove* and *OnLButtonUp* already work, we don't need any code in those functions for selection. The code in both is bypassed if the mouse hasn't been captured, and we skip capturing it in *OnLButtonDown* if selection mode is on.

2. Use the Add Member Function command to add the *DoHitTesting* function to the view class:

```
void CMyDrawView::DoHitTesting(CPoint point)
{
    CMyDrawDoc* pDoc = GetDocument();
    ASSERT_VALID(pDoc);

    // Convert point to logical coordinates.
    // Corrects y coordinate for mapping mode
    CClientDC dc(this);
    OnPrepareDC(&dc);
    dc.DPtoLP(&point);

    // Walk the shape list from newest to oldest
    bool bSelectionMade = false;
    CRect rect;
    CShape* pShape;
    pDoc->SetToLatestShape();
    while(pDoc->GetPos() != NULL /*&& !bSelectionMade */)
    {
        // Start with last shape in list.
        pShape = pDoc->GetNextShape();
        // Normalize the shape's bounding rectangle
        //   to correct for mapping mode.
        rect = pShape->m_boxShape;
        rect.NormalizeRect();
        // See if shape has been hit.
        // But ignore a hit if there has already been one in a
        //   higher layer (higher shape overlaps current).
```

```
                    if(!bSelectionMade && rect.PtInRect(point))
                    {
                        // m_pSelectedShape = pShape;
                        // Tell shape it has been selected.
                        pShape->m_bSelected = true;
                        // Once a selection has been made, no other
                        //   is possible (but we still need to turn off
                        //   selection in rest of shapes).
                        bSelectionMade = true;
                    }
                    else
                    {
                        // Only one selected shape at a time,
                        //   so turn off selection in any other shapes.
                        pShape->m_bSelected = false;
                    }
                }
                // Click was outside any shape: cancel selection.
                if(!bSelectionMade)
                {
                    m_typeNext = m_typeFormer;   // Restore previous tool.
                    CancelSelection();
                }
                else     // Update any other views to show new selection.
                {
                    pDoc->UpdateAllViews(NULL);   // Moved out of while
                                                  //   for selection
                }

        }
```

The function *DoHitTesting* first converts the mouse location in the *point* parameter to logical coordinates. This is important because it corrects for the *y*-axis reversal in *MM_LOENGLISH* mapping mode. Then it uses another document function to locate the most recent shape (the one in the topmost drawing layer). From there, the function walks through the shape list from newest to oldest. For each shape, *DoHitTesting* first calls *CRect::NormalizeRect* to normalize the shape's bounding rectangle, which also corrects for the mapping mode. *NormalizeRect* puts the rectangle into the same coordinate framework as our hit point.

Actual hit testing works as follows: As we come to each shape in the list, we test it for a hit, but only if we haven't already found the selected shape.

If we've detected a hit in a higher layer of the drawing, there can't be a hit in a subsequent lower layer. (We're walking from highest to lowest layer.) However, we still keep walking the shape list, because we need to set *m_bSelected* to *false* for all shapes except the one selected shape. Eventually, all unselected shapes will contain *false* in *m_bSelected*.

DoHitTesting uses the *CRect::PtInRect* function to test whether the mouse point (contained in the *Cpoint* object) falls within the shape's bounding rectangle. If so, it sets the shape's *m_bSelected* member to *true* and sets the Boolean variable *bSelectionMade* to indicate that the hit shape has been found. This causes *DoHitTesting* to skip further hit testing and to execute the *else* branch of the *if* statement for each subsequent shape (setting the shape's *m_bSelected* to *false*).

When the *while* loop ends, we see if a selection was made. If not, we cancel selection mode—there was a click, but it was outside of all shapes—and set the drawing tool back to what it was before selection mode was turned on. If the user did select a shape, the document updates all of its views. (There's only one for now, but we'll split the view into multiple views in Chapter 20.) Check the Help index for *NormalizeRect* and *PtInRect*.

Updating the views leads to redrawing, which is what we want, so the selected shape is redrawn with selection handles. Canceling selection mode also causes redrawing, so the old selected shape, if any, is redrawn without handles.

Drawing the Selection Handles

Clicking the mouse in a shape to set a new selection causes the shape to be redrawn with selection handles. Clicking outside all shapes to cancel the current selection also causes redrawing.

Try it now

When shapes are redrawn, we want the selected shape to draw itself with selection handles (if selection mode is on) and any previously selected shape to draw itself without handles.

1. Fill in the following boldfaced code in the *DrawHandles* helper function that we created earlier in class *CShape* (in the file Shape.cpp):

```
void CShape::DrawHandles(CDC *pDC)
{
    // Put selection handles on a selected shape.

    // Set up brush for painting selection handles.
    CBrush* pBrush = new CBrush(COLOR_HIGHLIGHT);
    CBrush* pBrushOld = (CBrush*)pDC->SelectObject(pBrush);
    // Calculate areas to paint for handles.
    CreateHandleRects();
    // Draw the handle rects with black interior brush.
    for(int i = 0; i < 8; i++)
    {
        pDC->Rectangle(arHandles[i]);
    }
    pDC->SelectObject(pBrushOld);
    // We created this brush, so we must dispose of it.
    // We only borrowed pBrushOld, so Windows disposes of it.
    delete pBrush;
}
```

Recall that we call *DrawHandles* from the *Draw* member function of the selected shape. Most of the work is done by another helper function, *CreateHandleRects*. It fills an array called *arHandles*—which we added to the file Shape.h earlier—with the rectangles bounding the eight selection handles we plan to draw. With those rectangles calculated, we loop through the *arHandles* array, drawing a rectangle for each element in the array. The rectangles are filled with the system color for highlighted selections, *COLOR_HIGHLIGHT*. (Check the Help index for *GetSysColor*.)

2. Fill in the following boldfaced code in the *CreateHandleRects* function that we created earlier in class *CShape*:

```
void CShape::CreateHandleRects()
{
    // Calculate the rectangles for a set of selection
    //   handles and store them in array of handle rects.

    int nHandSize = GetSystemMetrics(SM_CXBORDER) * 7;
```

(continued)

```
// Create an inflated rect around the shape's bounding
//   rect, m_boxShape.
CRect ri = m_boxShape;
ri.InflateRect(nHandSize, -nHandSize);

// Calculate rects for corner handles.

// Left top corner selection handle
CRect rectLeftTop(ri.left, ri.top,
                            m_boxShape.left, m_boxShape.top);
rectLeftTop.OffsetRect(4, -4);
arHandles[0] = rectLeftTop;

// Right top corner selection handle
CRect rectRightTop(m_boxShape.right, ri.top,
                              ri.right, m_boxShape.top);
rectRightTop.OffsetRect(-4, -4);
arHandles[1] = rectRightTop;

// Right bottom corner selection handle
CRect rectRightBottom(m_boxShape.right, m_boxShape.bottom,
                                ri.right, ri.bottom);
rectRightBottom.OffsetRect(-4, 4);
arHandles[2] = rectRightBottom;

// Left bottom corner selection handle
CRect rectLeftBottom(ri.left, m_boxShape.bottom,
                          m_boxShape.left, ri.bottom);
rectLeftBottom.OffsetRect(4, 4);
arHandles[3] = rectLeftBottom;

// Calculate rects for handles in centers of sides.

// Calculate x values for top and bottom center
//   selection handles.
int centerVert = ri.left + (ri.right - ri.left) / 2;
int leftVert = centerVert - (nHandSize / 2);
int rightVert = centerVert + (nHandSize / 2);

// Bottom center selection handle
CRect rectBottomCenter(leftVert, ri.top, rightVert,
                          m_boxShape.top);
rectBottomCenter.OffsetRect(0, -4);
arHandles[4] = rectBottomCenter;

// Top center selection handle
CRect rectTopCenter(leftVert, m_boxShape.bottom,
                        rightVert, ri.bottom);
rectTopCenter.OffsetRect(0, 4);
```

```
    arHandles[6] = rectTopCenter;

    // Calculate y values for left and right center
    //   selection handles.
    int centerHorz = ri.top + (ri.bottom - ri.top) / 2;
    int topHorz = centerHorz - (nHandSize / 2);
    int bottomHorz = centerHorz + (nHandSize / 2);

    // Right center selection handle
    CRect rectRightCenter(m_boxShape.right, topHorz,
                          ri.right, bottomHorz);
    rectRightCenter.OffsetRect(-4, 0);
    arHandles[5] = rectRightCenter;

    // Left center selection handle
    CRect rectLeftCenter(ri.left, topHorz, m_boxShape.left,
                         bottomHorz);
    rectLeftCenter.OffsetRect(4, 0);
    arHandles[7] = rectLeftCenter;
}
```

CreateHandleRects is our workhorse. A lot of the work involved in graphics programming goes into such calculations. Following Microsoft's interface guidelines for Windows, we'll set the dimensions of each of the eight selection handles based on a multiple of the size of a window border, obtained with a call to *GetSystemMetrics*. We use *GetSystemMetrics* to set a variable, *nHandSize*. *GetSystemMetrics* is a handy Win32 API function that returns all sorts of official system measurements. (Check the Help index for *GetSystemMetrics*.)

Since the selection handles protrude slightly beyond the shape's bounding rectangle, we'll first use the *CRect::InflateRect* function to create a new bounding rectangle slightly larger than the original one—*nHandSize* units larger in each dimension. This rectangle will be the outer boundary for calculating the locations of our handles.

TIP To comply with Microsoft's standards for designing user interfaces in Windows applications, we'll inset the handles slightly, straddling the shape's bounding rectangle. Technically, our handles should be hollow when they indicate selection but aren't available for such things as dragging, and they should be filled when they can be used to manipulate a shape. I've drawn the handles filled, on the assumption that once a shape is selected, the user might start dragging it. In Chapter 13 of the *Windows Interface Guidelines for Software Design* (Microsoft Press, 1995), see the topic "Handles" under

"Selection Appearance." You should develop an intimate acquaintance with the *Interface Guidelines*, which you can find in the MSDN Online Library at http://msdn.microsoft.com. (See Chapter 21 for details about the library.)

Let's look at the calculation for one handle—the one at the shape's right top corner, shown in Figure 18-5. For starters, we set the handle's top to the top of the inflated rectangle, *ri*. The handle's left side is defined by the right side of the original bounding rectangle, the shape's *m_boxShape* data member. The handle's right side is defined by the right side of the inflated rectangle, *ri*. And the handle's bottom is defined by the top of the original bounding rectangle, *m_boxShape*. But once we set these initial values, we use a call to *CRect::OffsetRect* to slide the whole handle rectangle inward by a rough four logical units. This insets the handle across the bounding rectangle for the desired look. The code for that calculation looks like this in *CreateHandleRects*:

```
// Right top corner selection handle
CRect rectRightTop(m_boxShape.right, ri.top,
                                  ri.right, m_boxShape.top);
rectRightTop.OffsetRect(-4, -4);
arHandles[1] = rectRightTop;
```

We store each handle's rectangle in *arHandles*. From the left top handle clockwise around the shape (corner handles only), we store each rectangle in the next element of *arHandles*. Then we calculate and store the four handles at the centers of the shape's sides. Calculating the rectangles for the center handles is a bit more work—it requires locating the center of each side and basing calculations on that. Again, after setting initial dimensions, we inset the handle by calling *OffsetRect*, eyeballing a rough four logical units. Here's the code for one center handle:

```
// Calculate x values for top and bottom center
//   selection handles
int centerVert = ri.left + (ri.right - ri.left) / 2;
int leftVert = centerVert - (nHandSize / 2);
int rightVert = centerVert + (nHandSize / 2);

// Bottom center selection handle
CRect rectBottomCenter(leftVert, ri.top, rightVert,
                      m_boxShape.top);
rectBottomCenter.OffsetRect(0, -4);
arHandles[4] = rectBottomCenter;
```

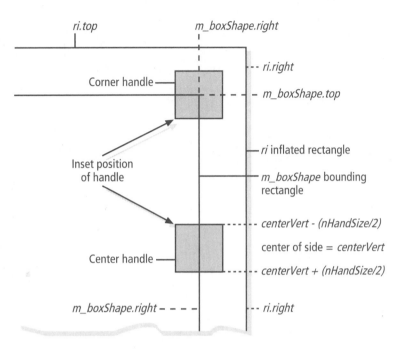

Figure 18-5. *Calculating a handle's rectangle.*

This completes our implementation of the Selection button on the new toolbar. You can build and test MyDraw with these additions. Run the program, draw a few shapes, and click the Selection button. Then click a shape, click outside all shapes, click another shape, and finally click the Rectangle button or Ellipse button. Draw a new shape.

Try It Yourself

I promised some things for you to try, so here's your extra credit. Solutions are provided in the final version of MyDraw, called MyDrawF, in the \learnvcn\Chap21 folder in the companion code.

1. Add commands to the View menu to hide or show the toolbars.

AppWizard supplies toggle commands on the View menu for the initial toolbar and status bar. Change the command for the toolbar to work as our Standard toolbar, and add a new command for the Drawing toolbar. Also add update handlers to checkmark the commands on the View menu when the toolbars are visible. Since the toolbars share space with the view in the frame window, the frame window class (*CMainFrame*) is the place to implement these commands. In the command handlers, you can call the *CFrameWnd::ShowControlBar* member function.

2. Implement commands to reorder the shapes.

Create the following menu commands:

- **Bring Forward.** This command moves the selected shape "up" one drawing layer (one place closer to the beginning of the list). The newest shape is at the head of the shapelist.

- **Send Behind.** This command moves the selected shape "down" one drawing layer.

- **Bring To Front.** This command moves the selected shape to the head of the shape list.

- **Send To Back.** This command moves the selected shape to the tail of the shape list.

Class *CObList* has members you can use to implement these operations. Which MFC object should contain the handlers? Hint: Which are we manipulating more, the data or its representation on the screen?

What's Next?

In Chapter 19, we'll explore dialog boxes, including common dialog boxes such as the Color dialog box, which lets users select colors by double-clicking on colored boxes rather than from a list of color names, as we've done in our Color menu. We'll look at modal dialog boxes, property sheets (dialog boxes that contain tabs), and common dialog boxes. Along the way, we'll also look at a selection of the Windows common controls and learn how to work with them.

Dialog Boxes and Controls

As input methods, toolbars and menus can take you only so far. Often you need specific information from the user—data for a calculation, say, or preferences so you can do a task the user's way. At such times, you turn to dialog boxes. This chapter adds code for MyDraw step 9, showing how to create and use a variety of dialog boxes. We'll look at dialog editing, dialog classes, and the following specific types of dialog boxes:

- **A simple *modal* dialog box,** one the user must respond to before the program can continue. I won't cover the opposite, the *modeless* dialog box, which can stay open while the user works in other windows.

- **A Microsoft Windows *common dialog box*,** one of several "canned" dialog boxes supplied by Windows that you can invoke from your programs. We'll use the Color dialog box to let users pick a color for shapes, greatly extending our Color menu.

- **A more complex *property sheet dialog box*,** containing several tabs, each tab in turn containing several Windows controls.

While we're at it, we'll examine the following three aspects of working with controls in a dialog box:

- How to initialize the controls just before the user sees them. This includes tasks such as filling up a combo box control with strings.

- How to extract information that the user entered in the controls.

- How to respond to notification messages from a control and treat controls as windows and as Microsoft Foundation Class Library 6.0 (MFC) class objects.

This chapter illustrates using static text controls, edit box controls, group box controls, radio button controls, check box controls, combo box controls, and spin button controls.

About Dialog Boxes and Controls

A *dialog box* is a pop-up window, with the style *WS_POPUP*, whose purpose is to give information to the user, obtain information from the user, or both. You can display a dialog box at any point in your program, with or without user input. The typical approach is to provide a menu command or toolbar button that opens the dialog box at the user's behest. The handler for that command creates a dialog object, initializes it, and displays it. When the user closes the dialog box, the command handler retrieves any information that the user entered in the dialog box.

A *control* is a small window embedded in a dialog box or other parent window, designed to display or obtain some kind of information. Edit box controls collect text or numeric data. Check boxes collect Boolean data—yes/no or true/false options. Radio buttons let the user select one of several mutually exclusive options. List boxes and combo boxes let the user select one or more of several options presented as text strings or graphics. Pushbuttons let the user open a secondary dialog box or perform a command action. Scroll bar controls let the user specify a selection along a continuous range.

There are several historical groups of controls in Microsoft Windows (not considering new kinds of controls such as Microsoft ActiveX controls): the original six controls just described, which are stored in the file User.exe, a part of the Windows operating system; 15 additional "common" controls introduced with Windows 95, stored in the file ComCtl32.dll; and several controls added to support Microsoft Internet

Explorer 4.0 and later, which can be used in other Windows applications as well. Figure 19-1 shows a dialog box containing a selection of controls (not quite all of them). The term *common controls* is often used to describe the Windows controls collectively.

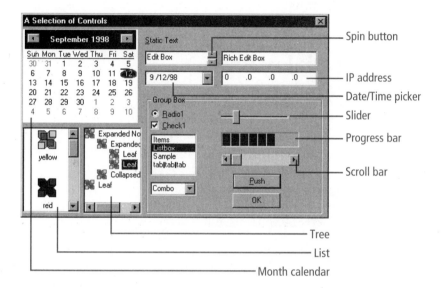

Figure 19-1.   *Some of the Windows controls available.*

Both dialog boxes and controls are windows (even a pushbutton is a window). As windows, they can do all the things that we've seen other windows do. You can write code to move them, display them, hide them, change their attributes, access their device contexts, and so on. I'll say more about this near the end of the chapter. The MFC library wraps dialog boxes in class *CDialog* and each control in its own class: *CButton*, *CComboBox*, *CToolBarCtrl*, *CSliderCtrl*, *CTreeCtrl*, and so on. (Class *CButton* represents check boxes and radio buttons as well as pushbuttons.) All of the classes mentioned in this paragraph are derived from class *CWnd* (and from the ancestors of *CWnd*, such as *CCmdTarget*), so they inherit the members and capabilities of those classes. For example, dialog boxes and controls can have message maps and contain message handler functions. Some of the controls, such as the toolbar control or the tree control, are also used as the basis for other MFC classes, such as *CToolBar* or *CTreeView*.

All of this means that you can exercise considerable control over the appearance and behavior of dialog boxes and controls. I won't cover every type of dialog box or control, or say everything there is to say about the ones I do cover. But you should come away with a good introductory grasp of how to work with dialog boxes and controls and a sense of what's possible with them.

A Simple Modal Dialog Box

To start by presenting dialog boxes in the simplest way, we'll give MyDraw a modal dialog box with just four controls. The dialog box shown in Figure 19-2 lets the user type a title for the drawing. The title shows up when we print the document or examine it with print preview.

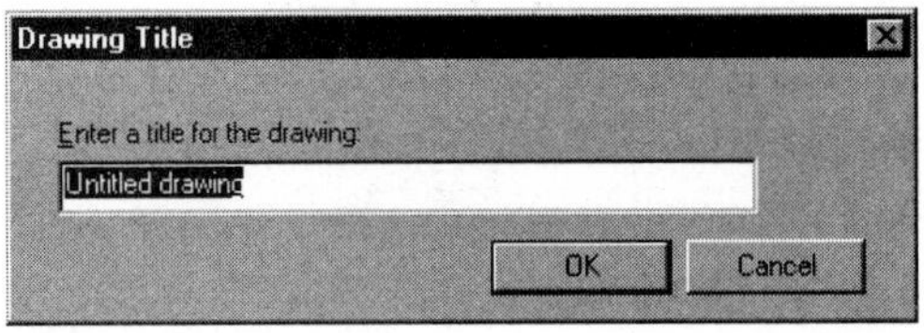

Figure 19-2. *A simple modal dialog box that obtains a title for the drawing.*

You'll see how to create the dialog resource used to display the dialog box, edit the resource in the Microsoft Visual C++ Dialog editor, and create a dialog class with the New Class command. Then I'll show you how to *wire up* the dialog box so users can display it with a command. You'll also learn how to initialize the dialog box's controls before the user sees them and how to extract the information the user enters in the controls.

Creating and Editing the Dialog Resource

Windows uses a *dialog template* to create and display a dialog box and its controls. It's possible to write code that creates the template in memory, using a data structure, but the normal approach is to create a *dialog template resource* using the Visual C++ Dialog editor. At run time, Windows reads in the resource and displays the dialog box as you laid it out in the Dialog editor.

IP Become familiar with Chapter 8, "Secondary Windows," in the *Windows Interface Guidelines for Software Design*, listed under Books in the left-hand pane at the MSDN Online website. You can reach this website through the MSDN Online command on the Visual C++ Help menu. (Or go to *http:// msdn.microsoft.com/developer*.) At the website, click the link in the left-hand pane to MSDN Library Online. You will have to register, but it's free. Then search the left-hand pane for the information you want. The chapter on secondary windows offers design guidelines that apply to dialog boxes.

The next section shows Dialog editor basics, but for more information, check the Help index for *Dialog editor* (capitalized as shown) to open the topic "Overview: Dialog Editor." You can follow links from that topic to learn more about using the Dialog editor. Save the topic as a favorite.

Try it now

Create a dialog template resource in MyDraw, assign it a meaningful ID and a caption, and use the Dialog editor to add controls and set their properties by following these steps:

1. Create a new dialog template resource (dialog resource, for short). Select the Resource command on the Insert menu and, in the Insert Resource dialog box, double-click Dialog. The new resource opens in a Dialog editor window, appearing almost as it will when we display it for the user in MyDraw. You see a dialog box with OK and Cancel buttons, a Controls toolbar floating nearby, and a Dialog toolbar docked at the bottom of the Visual C++ window. See Figure 19-3, which shows the Dialog editor open with the dialog resource we are creating in this section.

IP If the Controls and Dialog toolbars aren't visible, you can display them by right-clicking the toolbar area. On the context menu, select the toolbar you want to display.

2. Right-click the dialog box in the Dialog editor, then click Properties on the menu that pops up. In the Properties window, replace *IDD_DIALOG1* with *IDD_DRAWING_TITLE*. The IDD prefix for a

dialog resource is an MFC convention. Also change the Caption box to read "Drawing Title." This is the text that will appear in the title bar of the dialog window when displayed.

3. In the Dialog editor, make your dialog box look like the one in Figure 19-3 by dragging controls from the Controls toolbar. See the Note below for detailed instructrions on how to drag Controls into a dialog box. Add the following Controls to your dialog box:

   ■ A *static text* control with the caption *&Enter a title for the drawing:* (Notice the mnemonic ampersand—any captions in a dialog box can have mnemonics, which let the user operate the controls from the keyboard. You can also add mnemonics to the text on the OK and Cancel buttons, for example, &OK, or &Cancel.)

   ■ An *edit box* control for entering the drawing title.

OTE To add a control to the dialog box, click the control's icon on the Controls toolbar, also shown in Figure 19-3, and drag it to where you want the control. Tooltips identify each control type on the toolbar—we want a static text control and an edit box control. Reposition and resize the controls using the selection handles that appear when you click a control in the dialog box. Use commands on the Layout menu (or on the corresponding Dialog toolbar) to align, space, size, and otherwise adjust your controls. Press Shift and click multiple controls to apply the same command, such as alignment, to all of them. (Figure 19-3 shows the Controls toolbar reshaped from its normal default appearance.)

---

4. Set the properties for the new controls. Right-click to select a control, then click Properties on the menu that pops up.

   For the static text control, simply accept the default properties. For the edit box control, change the ID from *IDC_EDIT1* to *IDC_DRAWING_TITLE*. IDC is the conventional MFC prefix for control IDs.

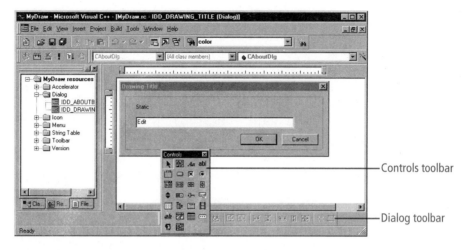

Controls toolbar

Dialog toolbar

Figure 19-3. *The Dialog editor with two added controls.*

> **TIP** You can open the Properties window for a selected control or for the dialog box, by clicking the item and selecting Properties on the View menu or by right-clicking the item and selecting Properties on the context menu. Click the Pushpin icon in the Properties window if you want the window to stay in place—though its contents will change as you select different controls in the dialog box.

5. To finish up the new dialog resource, click Save on the File menu. Don't close the Dialog editor window yet. (To close it, you can click Close on the File menu, just as for any other Visual C++ document window.)

> **TIP** Try out your dialog box's appearance and general behavior with the Test command on the Layout menu. This displays your dialog box as it will appear at run time in your program. The controls may not work exactly as you intend in Test mode, but the dialog box is otherwise accurate.

Creating the Dialog Class

After creating the dialog resource, we need to associate it with a class derived from *CDialog*. We can then use an object of that class to display and manipulate the dialog box. The new class also needs one data member.

Try it now

Create an associated dialog class for our dialog resource by following these steps:

1. With the new dialog resource still open in the Dialog editor, press Ctrl while double-clicking in the dialog box (not on a control).

2. In the Adding A Class dialog box, click OK to create a new class.

3. In the New Class dialog box, type a name for the class: *CTitleDialog*.

4. Click the Change button and type these new names for the files the dialog class will be stored in: *Dialogs.h* and *Dialogs.cpp*. Click OK. In MyDraw, we'll put all of our dialogs, except for the About dialog box, in one pair of files, although that's not the only way to do it.

5. Click OK in both the New Class dialog box, and the ClassWizard dialog box to create the new class. You're accepting *CDialog* as the base class for the new class and *IDD_DRAWING_TITLE* as the associated dialog resource ID. This is where the class and the resource become associated.

Try it now

The new dialog class needs one more thing: a data member to hold the data for the edit box control.

1. Back in the dialog editor, press Ctrl and double-click the edit box control. (This only works if you have already added a class for the dialog box.)

2. In the Add Member Variable dialog box, complete the data member name as *m_strDrawing*. The dialog box conveniently begins the name for you with the conventional *m_* used to name data members in MFC.

   Note that the new member is in the Value category, meaning that we're interested in the edit box's value, not in the box itself as an object. You'll see a case shortly where we want the Control category instead. The data type of the new data member is *CString*.

3. Click OK to add the data member to the new dialog class.

You'll see in a moment how the new data member is used.

Try it now

Add the following include directive at the top of the file DrawVw.h:

```
#include "dialogs.h"
```

Displaying the Dialog Box and Retrieving Its Contents

With a dialog class available, we can now write a menu command handler that creates a *CTitleDialog* object and displays the dialog box.

Try it now

Create a new Drawing Title menu command at the bottom of MyDraw's Edit menu, then create a handler for the command in the *view* class.

1. Use the Menu editor to add the new menu item. Type *&Drawing Title...* (with the ellipsis) as the caption; *ID_EDIT_DRAWING_TITLE* as the command ID; and *Supply a title for the drawing (up to 70 characters)* as the prompt string. The ellipsis in the caption is a Windows convention meaning that the command displays a dialog box instead of executing a direct command.

2. Create a new handler in the view class called *OnEditDrawingTitle* for the *ID_EDIT_DRAWING_TITLE* command ID. The ID is in the Class Or Object To Handle box.

3. In the new *OnEditDrawingTitle* function, add the boldface code:

```
void CMyDrawView::OnEditDrawingTitle()
{
    // TODO: Add your command handler code here
    CTitleDialog dlg;
    // Put current drawing title in dialog.
    dlg.m_strDrawing = m_strDrawing;
    if(dlg.DoModal() == IDOK)
    {
        // Retrieve value entered by user.
        m_strDrawing = dlg.m_strDrawing;
    }
}
```

The first highlighted line of code creates a dialog object of class *CTitleDialog*. The *DoModal* statement creates the dialog window, displays it, and manages the dialog box until the user dismisses it by clicking either OK or Cancel.

The most interesting feature of this function actually occurs in the two assignment statements. The first one, before the *DoModal* call, assigns the current value of *m_strDrawing*, a view class data member, to the dialog object's *m_strDrawing* data member—the one we just added. MFC then transfers the contents of the dialog object's data member to the edit box control. This is how MFC initializes the contents of the edit box control when it appears on the screen. By default, this value will be "Untitled drawing," a value set in the view class constructor (added in Chapter 17).

The second assignment, following the *DoModal* call, does just the opposite. When the user clicks OK, MFC extracts the data from the edit box control and stores it in the dialog object's data member. Then, after the *DoModal* call, we assign the value stored in the dialog object's *m_strDrawing* data member to our view class data member, *m_strDrawing*. The mechanism we've just seen is called dialog data exchange (DDX). See the sidebar "DDX and DDV" for details.

4. Limit the amount of text entered in the edit box to 70 characters, a generous allowance that still ensures the drawing title will always fit across a printed page. Open ClassWizard and click its Member Variables tab. In the Class Name box, select class *CTitleDialog*. In the Control IDs box, select *IDC_DRAWING_TITLE*. In the Maximum Characters box that appears at the bottom, type *70*. See the sidebar "DDX and DDV" for details.

That finishes up our simple modal dialog box. Remember that *modal* means the user can't do anything else in the program without first responding to the dialog box. You can build MyDraw and test the dialog box now.

DDX and DDV

MFC simplifies initializing and retrieving information in dialog box controls. The dialog data exchange (DDX) work is performed by function *CTitleDialog::DoDataExchange* (in the file Dialogs.cpp), which the Wizards write when you create the dialog class. You complete the function by adding DDX and dialog data validation (DDV) function calls in the function's data map section. For MyDraw, that code looks like this:

```
void CTitleDialog::DoDataExchange(CDataExchange* pDX)
{
    CDialog::DoDataExchange(pDX);
    //{{AFX_DATA_MAP(CTitleDialog)
    DDX_Text(pDX, IDC_DRAWING_TITLE, m_strDrawing);
    DDV_MaxChars(pDX, m_strDrawing, 70);
    //}}AFX_DATA_MAP
}
```

DoDataExchange calls functions such as *DDX_Text* to transfer data between the dialog box's controls and the dialog class object's data members. This transfer mechanism is called DDX. The *pDX* parameter, a pointer to a *CDataExchange* object, contains information about which way we're transferring the data: from dialog class data members to controls (initialization) or from controls to dialog class data members (retrieval). The *DDX_Text* function call works in both directions. It passes the contents of *CTitleDialog::m_strDrawing* to the control identified as *IDC_DRAWING_TITLE* for initialization, or from the control to the *m_strDrawing* data member for retrieval.

DoDataExchange also manages DDV. The *DDV_MaxChars* function call limits the amount of text the user can enter into the data member *CTitleDialog::m_strDrawing* to 70 characters. You can also set DDV limits on the range of values a numeric data member can accept. If the user enters data outside the specified limits, MFC displays a message box and waits for the user to try again. It's possible, as well, to write your own custom DDX and DDV

(continued)

DDX and DDV *continued*

---

routines like *DDX_Text* and *DDV_MaxChars* for special kinds of data, but that's an advanced topic. Check the Help index for *DDX* and select the subtopic "custom."

How is *CTitleDialog::DoDataExchange* called? When the dialog box is about to display, MFC calls its *CDialog::OnInitDialog* function. The default *OnInitDialog* calls *CWnd::UpdateData*, with a parameter of *false*, signaling a DDX transfer from the dialog object to the controls. *UpdateData* calls *DoDataExchange*. When the user clicks OK to dismiss the dialog box, the default *OnOK* handler calls *UpdateData* again, this time with a parameter of *true*, signaling a DDX transfer from the controls back to the dialog object.

Note that most of the work of DDX and DDV is done for you by MFC and ClassWizard , although you can certainly hand edit the *DoDataExchange* code for any special needs. For more information about DDX and DDV, check the Help index for *DDX* (look at any of the first three topics in the Topics Found dialog box) and for *DDV* (see any of the topics in the Topics Found dialog box). Also check the Help index for the classes and functions mentioned here.

A Windows Common Dialog Box

Now that you know how to create and display a simple dialog box, we'll borrow one of Windows' common dialog boxes, the Color dialog box (shown in Figure 19-4, but not in color). This dialog box lets users pick any color they wish instead of being limited to the ten colors on our Color menu. This time we don't have to create the dialog resource—Windows provides it. We just need to create a menu item and a handler to display the dialog box and extract the color the user selects.

We'll actually end up displaying the Color dialog box from two places, but one of them is in the third dialog box we'll add to MyDraw later in the chapter. For now, we'll display the dialog box from the Color submenu of the Tools menu.

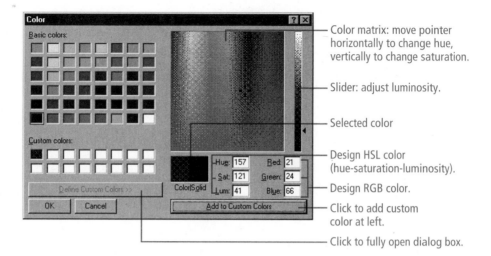

Color matrix: move pointer horizontally to change hue, vertically to change saturation.

Slider: adjust luminosity.

Selected color

Design HSL color (hue-saturation-luminosity).

Design RGB color.

Click to add custom color at left.

Click to fully open dialog box.

Figure 19-4. *The Windows Color common dialog box.*

About the Common Dialog Boxes

To use any of the six Windows common dialog boxes in MFC, just create an object of the appropriate MFC wrapper class for the dialog box you want. Table 19-1 lists and describes the dialog boxes, which help standardize common activities such as obtaining a filename from the user. They're easy to use, yet you can also customize them in a variety of ways. For more information, check the Help index for *common dialog classes* and, in the Topics Found dialog box, select the topic "Common dialog classes." Customizing the common dialog boxes is beyond the scope of this book, but see any of the more advanced books described in Chapter 21 for more information.

MFC Common Dialog Class	Description
CColorDialog	Provides a standard Color dialog box that lets the user select a color, including custom colors
CFileDialog	Provides standard Open and Save As dialog boxes
CFindReplaceDialog	Provides a standard Find/Replace dialog box; you still have to do the searching

Table 19-1. *The Windows common dialog boxes.* (continued)

Table 19-1 *continued*

MFC Common Dialog Class	Description
CFontDialog	Provides a standard Font selection dialog box (Try adding one of these to program MyText, from Chapter 15.)
CPageSetupDialog	Provides a standard Page Setup dialog box for adjusting margins, paper size, header and footer layout, and the like
CPrintDialog	Provides a standard Print dialog box, with printer selection, page ranges, number of copies, and so on

Adding the Color Dialog Box to MyDraw

We'll need a Custom Color item at the bottom of our Color menu, plus a handler for the menu item, and an update handler to checkmark the item when it's the most recently chosen color.

Try it now

Add the Custom Color menu command and several pieces of supporting code, as follows:

1. Add a separator and the menu item at the bottom of the Color menu. Use *C&ustom Color...* with the ellipsis and the mnemonic ampersand as shown. Use *ID_TOOL_CUSTOM_COLOR* as the command ID and *Display a dialog box that lets you pick any color* as the prompt.

2. Add a new last item to the *arColors* array in the file DrawVw.h. (Don't forget to change the array dimension from 10 to 11, and to add a comma after the RGB macro for Light Gray.)

```
// Array of actual colors, indexed
//   by CMyDrawView::m_nColorNext
static COLORREF arColors[11] = by
{
    RGB(0,0,0),          // Black
    ⋮
    RGB(192,192,192),    // Light gray
    RGB(0,0,0)           // Custom color
};
```

3. Add the following highlighted definitions just under the *arColors* array in the file DrawVw.h:

```
RGB(0,0,0)              // Custom color
};

const UINT CUSTOM_COLOR_INDEX = 10;
const UINT CUSTOM_COLOR = ID_COLOR_BLACK + CUSTOM_COLOR_INDEX;

class CMyDrawView : public CScrollView
    ⋮
```

We'll use these to index the array.

Try it now

Now we can add the custom color handler and its corresponding update handler.

1. Add a Windows message handler named *OnToolCustomColor* to the view class for the object *ID_TOOL_CUSTOM_COLOR*, and add the highlighted code to the handler (in the file DrawVw.cpp):

```
void CMyDrawView::OnToolCustomColor()
{
    // TODO: Add your command handler code here
    CColorDialog dlg;
    // Put current color in dialog.
    COLORREF color = arColors[m_nColorNext - ID_COLOR_BLACK];
    dlg.m_cc.rgbResult = color;
    if(dlg.DoModal() == IDOK)
    {
        m_nColorNext = CUSTOM_COLOR;
        arColors[CUSTOM_COLOR - ID_COLOR_BLACK] =
            dlg.GetColor();
    }
}
```

This handler manages the Custom Color command, while the *OnToolColor* handler manages the ten standard colors on our Color menu. I've kept those old color items as a handy shortcut for when you don't want some exotic color.

In the code above, we construct a *CColorDialog* object, initialize the dialog box with the current color (obtained from the view), display the dialog box with *DoModal*, and finally retrieve the selected color if *DoModal* returns *IDOK*. Most of this is much like what we did for the Drawing Title dialog box.

To initialize the dialog box, we access a field in the dialog object's *m_cc* data member, which is a *CHOOSECOLOR* structure. We assign our current color to the *rgbResult* member of that structure. To retrieve the dialog box's data, we call the *CColorDialog::GetColor* function, assigning the result to index 10 in our *arColors* array. Note that until now we've used this array in a read-only fashion. Now we're writing to the last element of it as a convenient place to store the actual *COLORREF* value most recently selected with the Custom Color command. The two lines within the *if* statement update the view's data members with the latest color index and the latest actual color.

2. Add the *OnUpdateToolCustomColor* update handler for *ID_TOOL_CUSTOM_COLOR* and fill in the boldface code shown here:

```
void CMyDrawView::OnUpdateToolCustomColor(CCmdUI* pCmdUI)
{
    // TODO: Add your command update UI handler code here
    pCmdUI->SetCheck(m_nColorNext == CUSTOM_COLOR);
}
```

Checkmarking the value of the view's *m_nColorNext* data member in this handler parallels the way we updated the 10 standard color items on the Color menu. Now if the Custom Color command is checkmarked on the menu, none of the other colors will be, and vice versa.

That's it for the Color dialog box—for now. We'll provide another way to access it from our next dialog box. You can build and test MyDraw now.

A More Complex Property Sheet Dialog Box

To illustrate a greater variety of controls and some valuable dialog box techniques, we'll give MyDraw a Settings dialog box. Like the Options dialog box in Visual C++, the Settings dialog box contains several tabs that resemble the tabs on file folders. Clicking a tab displays the associated page of controls. It's as if the dialog box contained several nested dialog boxes.

Property Sheets and Property Pages

A property sheet dialog box consists of the containing *property sheet* and the contained *property pages*. It's called a *property sheet* dialog box because this "tabbed" dialog box style is frequently used in Windows 95, Windows 98, and Microsoft Windows NT, and in applications written for these operating systems, to present an object's properties to the user for editing. For example, right-clicking a filename in the Visual C++ Workspace window pops up a shortcut menu (also known to programmers as a context menu) on which you can click a Properties command. This displays a property sheet dialog box with one or more tabs. (Take a look—the property sheet displays some useful information for programmers.) We'll use an ordinary menu command to display our Settings dialog box, but the principle is the same. (For fun, I've added a context menu containing the Settings command to the final version of MyDraw, named MyDrawF in the companion code. See *CMyDrawView::OnContextMenu* in that version for the code, and see the *IDR_CONTEXTMENU* resource it uses. I won't discuss the menu here.)

Property sheets are most valuable when you have a large number of controls to display, and when those controls can be factored into several logical groups. In MyDraw, we'll present six functional controls on two pages. The first page, the Line page, contains controls for setting attributes of the lines used to draw future shapes: line thickness and color. Figure 19-5 shows the Line page with an edit box, a spin button control, a combo box, and two static text controls (also referred to as *labels*). An edit box accepts typed text , or numbers. A spin button control lets the user click a small arrow to increase or decrease the value shown in its *buddy* control, an adjacent edit box. Figure 19-5 shows both an edit box and a spin button control.

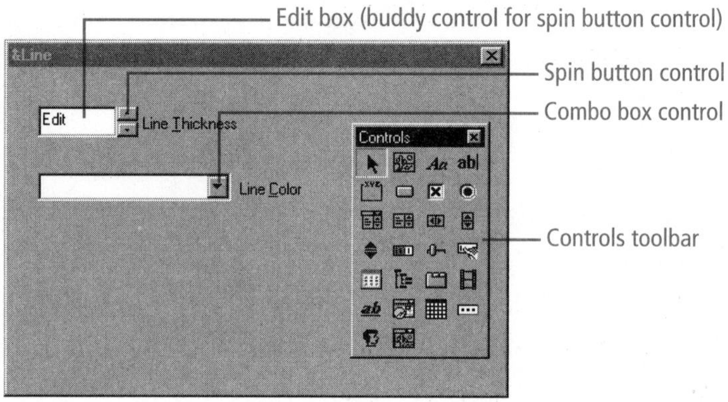

Figure 19-5.   *The Line page in MyDraw's Settings dialog box.*

The second page of the Settings dialog box, the Shape page shown in Figure 19-6, displays two radio buttons inside a group box, and a single check box. The radio buttons duplicate MyDraw's Rectangle and Ellipse commands on the Tools menu and the Drawing toolbar. The check box duplicates the Transparent command—checked if the next shape will be transparent, cleared if the next shape will be opaque. Radio buttons are small circular buttons with labels; they usually occur as groups of mutually exclusive buttons. Only one button in the group can be set (meaning activated) at a time. The other buttons are cleared. Check boxes are small boxes with labels; they usually represent options that can be checked (turned on) or unchecked (turned off). Groups of related controls are often contained within a group control—a box with a label. The group control is not functional; it simply groups related items visually. Figure 19-6 shows a check box as well as a group box with two radio buttons in it.

The property sheet is an object of class *CPropertySheet*, or of a class derived from *CPropertySheet*. We'll use *CPropertySheet* itself because we don't need to modify it in any way. We might write a derived class instead if we were, for example, going to implement the Apply button that MFC places on a property sheet in addition to OK and Cancel buttons. The Apply button puts current settings in the dialog box into effect without closing the dialog box. Because our property sheet isn't modeless, there's little incentive to implement Apply, although it can sometimes be useful in a modal dialog box as well. A modeless property sheet would allow the user to work in other windows while it remained open. In that case, it would be handy to be able to set some properties on one of the pages and press Apply to apply the new settings immediately. For more information about Apply, check the Help index for *Property Sheets* (capitalized) and select the subtopic "handling Apply button."

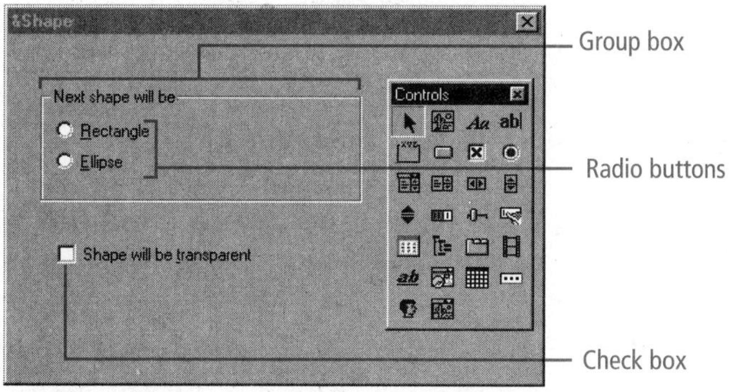

Figure 19-6.   *The Shape page in MyDraw's Settings dialog box.*

Unlike the property sheet, the contained property pages have no OK or Cancel buttons. Each property page is derived from class *CPropertyPage*, which is itself derived from *CDialog*. Where the property sheet knows how to contain property pages (and a few standard controls), a property page knows how to contain controls and is based on a dialog template. The property sheet needs no dialog resource.

Preparing our property sheet and property pages involves these steps:

1. Using the dialog editor to create a dialog resource for each of the property pages and lay out its controls.

2. Invoking ClassWizard to create a dialog class associated with each property page.

3. Adding dialog class data members used for DDX and DDV and for manipulating complex controls like the combo box as C++ objects.

4. Writing code to implement the controls. For example, the combo box works by itself, but we have to load it up with strings, and then detect when the user makes a new selection and extract the selection so we can report the new color to the view.

Let's get an overview of the whole property sheet by looking at how to display it.

Displaying the Settings Dialog Box

We'll display the Settings dialog box just as we did our other dialog boxes—with a menu command on the Tools menu. We need to add the menu command and a handler for it. The handler contains the code that creates the property sheet and its pages, adds the pages to the property sheet, initializes their controls, displays the dialog box, and retrieves any new settings.

Try it now

Add a Settings menu command and an *OnToolSettings* handler for it.

1. Add a separator and a Settings command to the bottom of MyDraw's Tools menu. Use *ID_TOOL_SETTINGS* as the ID, *&Settings...* as the caption (with the trailing ellipsis), and *Change settings that control how shapes are drawn* as the prompt string.

2. Add an *OnToolSettings* command handler to the view class, associated with *ID_TOOL_SETTINGS*. Add the boldface code shown below:

```
void CMyDrawView::OnToolSettings()
{
    // TODO: Add your command handler code here
    // Create property sheet and the 3 contained pages.
    CPropertySheet settings("MyDraw Settings");
    CLinePage dlgLine;
    CShapePage dlgShape;

    // Add the pages to the sheet, in desired order.
    settings.AddPage(&dlgLine);
    settings.AddPage(&dlgShape);

    // Initialize members associated with controls.
    dlgLine.m_nThickness = 1;
    dlgLine.m_nColorIndex = m_nColorNext - ID_COLOR_BLACK;
    dlgLine.m_colorRGB = arColors[m_nColorNext -
        ID_COLOR_BLACK];
    // Radio buttons: 0 = Rectangle, 1 = Ellipse
    dlgShape.m_nShpRectangle =
                    (m_typeNext == shpRectangle ? 0 : 1);
    // Check box
```

```
dlgShape.m_bTransparent = m_bTransparent;

if(settings.DoModal() == IDOK)
{
    // Retrieve values set by user: radio buttons.
    m_typeNext = (dlgShape.m_nShpRectangle ?
                        shpEllipse : shpRectangle);
    // Check box
    m_bTransparent = (dlgShape.m_bTransparent == 1 ?
                        true : false);
    // Get selected color.
    m_nColorNext = dlgLine.m_nColorIndex + ID_COLOR_BLACK;
    // Store selected color in color array.
    if(m_nColorNext == CUSTOM_COLOR)
    {
        arColors[CUSTOM_COLOR_INDEX] = dlgLine.m_colorRGB;
    }
    // Other values in view updated
        during dialog operation
}
}
```

We'll discuss details of the code as we implement each control in the property sheet. Generally, though, here's what we do in the handler:

1. Construct an object called *settings*, of class *CPropertySheet*, passing "MyDraw Settings" as the caption that will appear in the title bar.

2. Construct two *CPropertyPage*-derived objects, *dlgLine* and *dlgShape*, of classes *CLinePage* and *CShapePage*. We'll write those classes in the next section.

3. Call the *settings* object's *CPropertySheet::AddPage* member function to add each page to the sheet.

4. Initialize data members of the two property page objects before *DoModal* and retrieve data after *DoModal*.

Creating Dialog Resources for the Settings Dialog Box

Creating these dialog resources is like creating the dialog resource for the Drawing Title dialog box. Note that a considerable part of implementing the Settings dialog box can be accomplished with the Dialog editor.

Try it now

We'll create a dialog resource for the Line page of our property sheet, set its properties, and add controls to it. Then we'll adjust the tab order of the controls so they behave as we want when the user presses the Tab key.

1. Create a new dialog resource by selecting Resource on the Insert menu and double-clicking Dialog in the Insert Resource dialog box. To allow ample room in the dialog box for the controls we'll be adding, drag the sides or corners of the dialog box to adjust the size to 250 by 150 units. (To assure easy sizing, select Guide Settings on the Layout menu and, in the Guide Settings dialog box, make sure Layout Guides is set to None or to Rulers And Guides, not to Grid.) The dialog box's dimensions appear near the right end of the Visual C++ status bar during dialog editing. For a review of dialog editing, see "Creating and Editing the Dialog Resource" earlier in the chapter.

2. In the Properties window for the new dialog resource, set the ID to *IDD_PS_LINE* and the caption to *&Line* (use *L* as the mnemonic). The caption is the label that appears on the tab; it has a mnemonic like a menu command so users can select the tab from the keyboard. (Note that the ampersand character appears on the title bar in the Dialog editor, but when the property sheet is displayed, the caption and mnemonic appear on the tab portion of the Line page). To set properties for the property page as a whole, right-click the dialog box and click Properties on the context menu.

> **IMPORTANT** For property page dialog resources, delete the OK and Cancel buttons. Simply select the buttons and press the Delete key. Property pages on a property sheet don't have these buttons.

3. Add the controls listed in the following bullets to the dialog resource, in the order shown, moving down and to the right in the dialog box you're editing—see Figure 19-5 for placement. Then set the properties for those controls. To set properties for the controls, right-click the first control and select Properties from the context

menu. In the Properties window, click the pushpin control to pin the Properties window in place. (Selecting a new control puts its properties in the window.) Then drag controls from the Controls toolbar to the dialog box and edit their properties. For all of our controls, use a default control ID; it's fine for different controls to have the same ID, such as *ID_STATIC*, unless you need to distinguish one control from others of the same type. If you plan to directly access the controls from your code, make the IDs unique. Add controls with the following properties:

- **An edit box control.** In the Properties dialog box, set the ID to *IDC_EDIT1*. This box will display the width for drawn lines, in pixels. We'll be setting a range of 0–5 for it later. The box will also become the buddy control of the spin control next to it. That is, the two will be linked so that clicking the spin control changes the value in the edit box.

- **A spin button control.** Set the ID to *IDC_SPIN1*, and use the following styles: set the Visible and Tab Stop styles on the General tab; and on the Styles tab, set Vertical Orientation, Right Alignment, Auto Buddy, Set Buddy Integer, Wrap, and Arrow Keys. The Right Alignment style puts the spin button control just inside the right edge of its buddy, the edit box. The Auto Buddy style causes the spin button control to associate with the edit box just before it in the tab order. The Set Buddy Integer style causes clicks on the spin button control to increase or decrease the integer in the buddy control. The Wrap style causes the values in the buddy control to wrap around to the minimum value when the maximum value is passed and vice versa. The Arrow Keys style enables operating the spin button control from the keyboard. Most of our controls' functionality is already taken care of through these styles, but we still must set the ranges for both the edit box and the spin control.

- **A static text control.** Set the ID to *IDC_STATIC* and type the caption *Line &Thickness*. This labels the combined edit box and spin button control below.

- **A combo box.** Set the ID to *IDC_COMBO1*, and on the Styles tab, set the Type box to Drop List and clear the Sort box. This combo box will display the name of one of our 10 standard colors or the string "Custom Color." One more thing: in the Dialog editor, point to the downward arrow portion of the combo box, and handles will appear. You can drag the handles down to enlarge the box. This sets how far the list portion of the combo box opens and thus how many strings it can display without scrolling. (Windows adds a scroll bar if needed.) Drag the handles far enough to display three or four strings. You can adjust the box later.

- **A static text control.** Set the ID to *IDC_STATIC*, and type the caption *Line &Color*. This labels the combo box.

> **NOTE** I'll discuss each control type in more detail when we implement the controls' behavior. For more information on each type, check the Help index for *controls*. In the Topics Found dialog box, choose the topic "Control Topics" and in that topic scroll down to the table under "Finding Information About Windows Common Controls." Links in the table take you to more information.

4. Adjust the *tab order* for the controls just added to the Line page. To see the current tab order, click Tab Order on the Layout menu. A small numbered box appears near each control to show the order used when the user presses the Tab key to move from control to control. (Only controls with the Tab Stop style are really in the tab order.)

   Since only three of our Line page controls really do any work, we want them first in the tab order for the user's convenience. To change the tab order, click Tab Order on the Layout menu, then click each control in sequence: first the edit box at the top, then the spin button control, then the combo box control at the bottom, and finally the two static text controls from top to bottom. For more information, check the Help index for *Dialog Boxes* (capitalized) and select the subtopic "changing tab order."

Try it now

1. Create another new dialog resource (select Resource on the Insert menu, and double-click Dialog). As with the Line dialog resource, adjust the size to 250 by 150 units.

2. In the Properties dialog box for the new resource, set the ID to *IDD_PS_SHAPE* and type the caption *&Shape.* Delete the OK and Cancel buttons.

3. Add the controls in the list below to the Shape dialog resource, in the order shown, moving down and to the right—see Figure 19-6 for placement.

   ■ **A group box.** Set the ID to *IDC_STATIC*, and type the caption *&Next shape will be.* Group boxes visually group the controls inside them. Otherwise, they have no effect on the controls and don't, for instance, cause the radio buttons we'll put inside our group box to be mutually exclusive just because they're visually grouped. We have to code that behavior by setting the styles of the buttons. Tip: To select the group box so you can edit its properties, click on the box's outline or its caption.

   ■ **Two radio buttons.** Place them inside the group box, and set the IDs to *IDC_RADIO1* and *IDC_RADIO2*, with captions *&Rectangle* and *&Ellipse*, respectively. Make sure the Rectangle radio button has the styles Visible, Group, and Tab Stop set on the General tab. The Ellipse radio button should have only Visible and Tab Stop set—not Group. I'll explain why shortly. (The Group style has nothing to do with the group box control.) On the Styles tab, check Auto for both controls. These controls are mutually exclusive. They act just like our Rectangle and Ellipse commands, allowing the user to change the next shape type here as well as on the Tools menu or the Drawing toolbar.

- ■ **A check box control.** Set the ID to *IDC_CHECK1*, and type the caption *Shape will be &transparent.* (Note placement of the mnemonic ampersand.) Set the Visible, Group, and Tab Stop styles on the General tab and the Auto style on the Styles tab. This box is equivalent to the Transparent command on the Tools menu. If checkmarked, the next shape will be transparent; otherwise, it will be opaque. Notice that check boxes and radio buttons come with attached text labels (their captions).

  The check box control has the Group style to tell Windows that all subsequent controls, in tab order, are grouped together. The group runs from the first control with the Group style (the first radio button) up to, but not including, the present control (the check box). Thus the group includes only the two radio buttons.

4. Set the tab order for the Shape page in the following sequence: the Rectangle radio button, the Ellipse radio button, the check box, and finally the group box.

5. Save your work in both dialog resources. Keep both dialog resources open in the Dialog editor for the next step.

Creating Dialog Classes for the Settings Dialog Box

With both of the new dialog resources still open in the Dialog editor, create corresponding classes. The classes will allow us to create the pages in the property sheet and manipulate them through class members.

 Try it now

First, to create class *CLinePage* for the Line tab, display the dialog resource for the Line tab in the Dialog editor. Then follow these instructions:

1. Press the Ctrl key as you double-click the Line dialog box. This opens ClassWizard's machinery for adding classes.

2. In the Adding A Class dialog box, click OK to create a new class.

3. In the New Class dialog box, type the class name *CLinePage*. Click Change and type *Dialogs.h* and *Dialogs.cpp* as the filenames in which to store the class declaration and implementation. Click OK.

Then, back in the New Class dialog box, change the Base Class box to *CPropertyPage*. The Dialog ID should be *IDD_PS_LINE*. This connects the class to the dialog resource.

4. Click OK, and then click OK again to finish creating the class.

5. Add the following boldface line to the top of Dialogs.h so that *CLinePage* and *CShapePage* will have access to the view class functions:

```
      ⋮
// Dialogs.h : header file
//
#include "DrawVw.h"
      ⋮
```

6. Now create the *CShapePage* class in the same way you created the *CLinePage* class (steps 1-4). Display the dialog resource, press Ctrl while you double-click the dialog box, and specify information for the new class. Put the new class in the same files: Dialogs.h and Dialogs.cpp. Be sure to derive the class from *CPropertyPage*. The Dialog ID should be *IDD_PS_SHAPE*.

You can examine the classes in files Dialogs.h and Dialogs.cpp, and we'll be adding members to some of them.

Adding Class Data Members Mapped to the Controls

To finish up the dialog classes for the Settings dialog box, we need to create class data members mapped to several of the controls for DDX purposes.

Try it now

Open ClassWizard from the View menu, click its Member Variables tab, and take the following steps—we'll add two data members for class *CShapePage* and three for *CLinePage*, all for use with DDX and DDV.

1. Select *CShapePage* in the Class box. In the Control IDs box, select *IDC_CHECK1*, for the check box, and click Add Variable. In the Add Member Variable dialog box, type the name *m_bTransparent*, and specify the category Value and variable type *BOOL*. Click OK. This data member will hold the value of the check box for DDX purposes.

2. In ClassWizard, select *IDC_RADIO1* and click Add Variable. Type the name *m_nShpRectangle*, and specify the category Value and variable type *int*. For DDX purposes, this data member will hold the value 0 if the Rectangle radio button is set or 1 if the Ellipse button is set. The numbers are the zero-based indexes of the controls in the radio button group. We don't need a data member for each radio button, just the group. Click OK.

3. Back in ClassWizard, select *CLinePage* in the Class box. (Click Yes to save *CShapePage* if prompted.) In the Control IDs box, select *IDC_EDIT1*, and click Add Variable. Type the name *m_nThickness*, and specify the category Value and variable type *UINT*. Click OK. At the bottom of ClassWizard, set a range of values that can appear in the edit box: type *0* in the Minimum Value box and type *5* in the Maximum Value box.

4. In ClassWizard, select *IDC_SPIN1* and click Add Variable. Type the name *m_spinThickness*, and specify the category Control and variable type *CSpinButtonCtrl*. Notice that we're using the Control category this time and our data member is a *CSpinButtonCtrl* object. We'll use that object to manipulate the spin button control. We'll have to specify a range for this control in code, to match the range we set for the edit box that serves as the spin button control's buddy. Click OK.

5. In ClassWizard, select *IDC_COMBO1* and click Add Variable. Type the name *m_comboColor*, and specify the category Control and variable type *CComboBox*. Click OK twice to close ClassWizard.

6. Add two public data members to class *CLinePage* (in the file Dialogs.h):

```
    ⋮
CLinePage();
~CLinePage();
UINT m_nColorIndex;
COLORREF m_colorRGB;
    ⋮
```

Implementing the Shape Page

Although the Line page will appear first in the property sheet, we'll implement the controls on the Shape page first. All of the implementation for the radio buttons and the check box is in the following three places:

- The data members we just added to the *CShapePage* class.

- The styles we set for the controls in the Dialog editor.

- A few lines in the *OnToolSettings* handler we already presented in "Displaying the Settings Dialog Box." Let's take a quick look at those lines.

The radio buttons

The following code fragment from *CMyDrawView::OnToolSettings*, which you've already added, initializes the radio buttons and the check box and retrieves their values after the dialog box closes:

```
   ⋮
// Radio buttons: 0 = Rectangle, 1 = Ellipse
dlgShape.m_nShpRectangle =
                (m_typeNext == shpRectangle ? 0 : 1);
// Check box
dlgShape.m_bTransparent = m_bTransparent;

if(settings.DoModal() == IDOK)
{
    // Retrieve values set by user: radio buttons.
    m_typeNext = (dlgShape.m_nShpRectangle ?
                        shpEllipse : shpRectangle);
    // Check box
    m_bTransparent = (dlgShape.m_bTransparent == 1 ?
                        true : false);
   ⋮
```

The first two lines assign an initial value to the Shape page's *m_nShp-Rectangle* data member. We assign 0 if the view's *m_typeNext* data member equals *shpRectangle*, or 1 if it's *shpEllipse*. The values 0 and 1 are the zero-based indexes of the two radio button controls. From there, DDX transfers the data into the corresponding controls. The first two lines of code after the *DoModal* call retrieve the current value of the Shape page's *m_nShpRectangle* member. If it's 1, we set the view's *m_typeNext* member to *shpEllipse*; otherwise, we set it to *shpRectangle*. (This is the same sort of conversion between types that we used in the serialization code in Chapter 16.) DDX transfers data from the controls to these Shape page data members when the user closes the dialog box by clicking OK.

The check box

In the same code fragment above, the third line of code assigns the view's *m_bTransparent* data member to the Shape page's *m_bTransparent* data member. DDX puts that into the check box on the Shape page. The box is checkmarked if the data member is set to *true*, or cleared if set to *false*. The last two lines after the *DoModal* call set the view's *m_bTransparent* member to *true* if the Shape page's *m_bTransparent* member equals 1, or to *false* if *CShapePage::m_bTransparent* is 0. After *DoModal*, DDX transfers data from the check box back to the Shape page data member, where we can pass it on to the view.

For a review of DDX and DDV, see the sidebar "DDX and DDV" earlier in the chapter.

Implementing the Line Page

To get the Line page completely up and running, we need to take two steps:

1. Initialize and manage the combo box for setting colors. This will be the most complex code for the Settings dialog box.

2. Initialize and manage the spin button control and its buddy control.

NOTE Although I'm setting up a way for the user to enter a line thickness value, I haven't written any line thickness code in the view class for this step of MyDraw because I want to focus on the controls here.

The combo box

The Line page's combo box duplicates MyDraw's color menu in a convenient way. Clicking the downward-facing arrow beside the combo box drops down a list of colors. Clicking a color puts its name into the edit box portion of the combo box. We then pass the selected color back to the view.

To implement the combo box, we need to complete these tasks:

■ Initialize the combo box by adding the color names to it and setting it to the current color, which is passed to the Line page from the view in *CMyDrawView::OnToolSettings*.

■ Handle a *CBN_SELCHANGE* notification message sent to the Line page when the user selects a new color.

■ Display the Color common dialog box if the user selects Custom Color in the combo box.

Try it now

If the combo box were in an ordinary dialog box, we'd initialize it in the dialog object's *OnInitDialog* handler. Called just before the dialog box is displayed, *OnInitDialog* is the perfect place to initialize controls that can't be initialized using DDX. But the combo box is in a property page embedded in a property sheet dialog box, so there's an extra level of indirection. We need to initialize the combo box not when the containing property sheet opens but when the contained Line page displays.

1. To do that, use the Add Virtual Function command to add an override of the *OnSetActive* handler in class *CLinePage*. The handler processes the *WM_SETACTIVE* message. Click Edit Existing and add the boldface lines:

```
BOOL CLinePage::OnSetActive()
{

    // TODO: Add your specialized code here and/or...

    // Initialize combo box just before
    //   Line tab becomes active.
    // Load color names into combo box.
    for(int i = 0; i < 11; i++)
    {
        m_comboColor.AddString(arColorNames[i]);
    }
    // Set the combo box to the current color.
    m_comboColor.SetCurSel(m_nColorIndex);

    return CPropertyPage::OnSetActive();
}
```

In the *for* loop, we load the names of our 10 standard colors, plus the string "Custom Color." To add a string, we use the *CComboBox* object we created earlier as the *CLinePage::m_comboColor* data member and call its *CComboBox::AddString* function. We get the strings from an array called *arColorNames*, which we need to add. To set the combo box's initial value, we set its current selection with the *CComboBox::SetCurSel* member, which uses the value of *CLinePage::m_nColorIndex* (set in *OnToolSettings*) as a zero-based index into the combo box's list of strings.

2. Next, add the *arColorNames* array at the top of the file Shape.h, just above class *CShape* (that's a convenient location for other uses I plan to make of the array later):

```
⋮
static CRect arHandles[8];

static CString arColorNames[11] =
{
    "Black",
    "Blue",
    "Green",
    "Cyan",
    "Red",
    "Magenta",
    "Yellow",
    "White",
    "Dark Gray",
    "Light Gray",
    "Custom Color"
};

class CShape : public CObject
⋮
```

This static array, declared at global scope, is visible to the dialog classes.

Try it now

To respond when the user makes a new selection in the combo box, we need a handler for the *CBN_SELCHANGE* notification message. When some interesting event occurs in a control, the control sends a notification message (sometimes called, simply, a "notification") to its parent window. In the case of a control in a dialog box, the dialog window is the parent window.

1. Add an *OnSelchangeComboColor* handler for the *CBN_SELCHANGE* notification message associated with *IDC_COMBO1*. Using Wizard-bar, select Add Windows Message Handler. In the New Windows Message And Event Handlers dialog box, select *IDC_COMBO* in the Class Or Object To Handle box, click *CBN_SELCHANGE* in the New Windows Messages/Events box, click Add Handler, and modify the name to *OnSelChangeComboColor*. Then add the boldface code:

```
void CLinePage::OnSelchangeComboColor()
{
    // TODO: Add your control notification handler code here
    m_nColorIndex = m_comboColor.GetCurSel();
    m_colorRGB = arColors[m_nColorIndex];
    // Respond if user chose "Custom Color" in the combo box.
    if(m_nColorIndex == CUSTOM_COLOR_INDEX)
    {
        GetCustomColor(); // Display the Color dialog.
    }
}
```

When the user invokes this handler by selecting a new color, we first retrieve the selection (an index into the combo box) by calling the combo box's *GetCurSel* function. We assign that to *CLinePage::m_nColorIndex*, so DDX can pass it back to the view eventually. We also use it to index the *arColors* array in DrawVw.h, returning a *COLORREF* value in *m_colorRGB*.

Recall that in the section "A Windows Common Dialog Box" we added an extra element to the *arColors* array to hold the most recent custom color. We also added two constants below the array to the view class: *CUSTOM_COLOR_INDEX* (which equals 10) and *CUSTOM_COLOR*. The first constant is an index into the *arColors* array with a value between 0 and 10. The second constant is equal to *ID_COLOR_BLACK + CUSTOM_COLOR_INDEX*, or, in my version of MyDraw, 32,774 + 10. Each has its uses in the view class and Line page class code.

Next, we compare *m_nColorIndex*, the index of the combo box item selected, with the ID for the Custom Color selection, in the form of

CUSTOM_COLOR_INDEX. In other words, if *m_nColorIndex* equals 10, the user has selected Custom Color in the combo box. In that case, we want to display the Color dialog box so that the user can pick a custom color. To do that, we call *GetCustomColor*, which we'll add in a moment.

2. Using WizardBar's Add Member Function option, add the *GetCustomColor* helper function called from *OnSelchange-CustomColor*:

```
void CLinePage::GetCustomColor()
{
    // Display the Color dialog box.
    CColorDialog dlg;
    dlg.m_cc.rgbResult = m_colorRGB;
    if(dlg.DoModal() == IDOK)
    {
        m_colorRGB = dlg.GetColor();
        m_nColorIndex = CUSTOM_COLOR_INDEX;
    }
}
```

This code is a near duplicate of the code we wrote earlier in the chapter to display the Windows common Color dialog box. (Fortunately, it's brief, or we'd want to find a way for the view class and the *CLinePage* class to share the code—but that's a bit advanced for this book.) After retrieving the selected color, we set *m_nColorIndex* to CUSTOM_COLOR_INDEX, indicating that the user has selected some custom color. The color itself is in *m_colorRGB*. Keep in mind that we call this function when the user has selected Custom Color in the combo box.

The spin button control

Given the styles we set for it, and the buddy we arranged for it, the spin button control takes care of itself completely—except that we need to initialize its range to 0–5. If the spin control were in an ordinary dialog box, we'd use an *OnInitDialog* handler, called just before the dialog box was displayed. In our property pages, however, we'll need to initialize our spin button control in the *CLinePage::OnSetActive* handler we used to initialize the combo box.

Try it now

Add the boldface lines to *CLinePage::OnSetActive*:

```
BOOL CLinePage::OnSetActive()
{
    // TODO: Add your specialized code here and/or call the base class

    // Initialize combo box just before Line tab becomes active
    // Initialize spin button control.
    m_spinThickness.SetRange(0, 5);

    // Load color names into combo box
    for(int i = 0; i < 11; i++)
    :
```

Recall that we created a data member in class *CLinePage*, of type *CSpin-ButtonCtrl*, called *m_spinThickness*. Since it's a C++ class object, we can call any of its member functions. We only need to call *CSpinButton-Ctrl::SetRange*, passing the minimum and maximum values for the range. We pass 0 and 5 to match the range we set for line thickness values in the buddy control.

TIP Using a pushbutton in your dialog box, you can display a secondary dialog box. To do so, write a handler for the *BN_CLICKED* notification message associated with the pushbutton's control ID. For an example, check the Help index for *message handling* and select the subtopic "in dialog boxes." Then select the second topic in the Topics Found dialog box.

Controls as Windows

Recall that I pointed out early in the chapter that dialog boxes and controls are windows. I want to remind you of that fact, because the implication is that you can treat them as window objects. Which means that you can perform the following manipulations, among others:

■ Obtain a *CWnd** pointer to a control, using *CWnd::GetDlgItem* in one of your dialog class member functions, like this:

```
CWnd* pWnd = (CWnd*)GetDlgItem(IDC_MY_STATIC);
```

- Use that pointer to obtain a *CDC** pointer to the control window's device context, like this:

```
CDC* pDC = pWnd->GetDC();
```

- Use those pointers to call any *CWnd* or *CDC* member function. For example, to change the color of the text in a static text control, you could call *CDC::SetTextColor*:

```
pDC->SetTextColor(m_nColorNext);
```

As another example, to change the text itself in a static text control, you could call *CWnd::SetWindowText*:

```
pWnd->SetWindowText("Now the control says this");
```

- Redraw the containing dialog box to reflect the updated text color, like this:

```
Invalidate();      // From within a dialog-class member function
```

These kinds of manipulations are something that MFC makes pretty easy, and they're quite powerful. Using similar approaches, you have a great deal of control over the attributes and actions of your dialog boxes and controls.

IP Here's something handy about control notification messages: Normally they're sent to the control's parent window, but in MFC you can *reflect* control notifications from the parent so they come back to the control. This lets you write self-contained controls, a neat bit of object-oriented modularization. You need a class derived from the control's class so you can add a handler for the reflected message. Check the Help index for *message reflection*.

What's Missing?

Even with the addition of the dialog boxes, MyDraw is still lacking a few things:

- A way to let the user know which custom color is currently selected. (See the discussion in "Controls as Windows" for some ideas.)

- Code to implement the line thickness option.

I won't cover those topics here, but MyDrawF, the final version of MyDraw, provides a solution to the first one. And see the exercise that follows.

Try It Yourself

Want more extra credit? Try this exercise.

Show the user which custom color is currently selected.

One approach to this problem is to add a static text control to the Line page, perhaps with the caption *This is the color the next shape will use.* Then you could use the fact that a control is a window to access its device context and call *CDC::SetTextColor*, setting the color to our current color. You'll need to update the color on demand, so I recommend an *UpdateStaticColor* function in *CLinePage*. Have that function obtain *CWnd** and *CDC** pointers for the static text control, then directly call a *CLinePage::OnCtlColor* handler (you'll need to add one), passing those pointers. Change the text color in that handler. *OnCtlColor* handles the *WM_CTLCOLOR* message, and handling it as I've described changes the text color either in response to an actual *WM_CTLCOLOR* message or by calling *OnCtlColor* directly. Here's a tip: after the change, invalidate the dialog window in *UpdateStaticColor*. For one solution, see the final version of MyDraw, called MyDrawF, in the \learnvcn\Chap21 folder in the companion code.

What's Next?

In Chapter 20, we wrap up development of MyDraw by adding multiple views of MyDraw's document. Users will be able to split the drawing surface to see different parts of it at the same time. The views will be set up using an MFC splitter window.

Multiple Views

As with many programs, MyDraw's drawing area is too large to fit on a computer screen. We've added scrolling to let users access all of the drawing area. But suppose a user wants to see and possibly work in two different parts of the drawing area simultaneously. To meet this need we supply an additional aid: a *splitter window*. A splitter window can be divided into two or more *panes*, horizontally, vertically, or both. Splitter windows are derived from class *CSplitterWnd* in the Microsoft Foundation Class Library 6.0 (MFC). In this chapter, in MyDraw step 10, we'll add a splitter window to MyDraw and expand our discussion of MFC views. (We'll complete MyDraw step 10 in Chapter 21 by giving the program its own application icon.)

NOTE If MyDraw were a multiple document interface (MDI) application, another way to let users work in distant parts of the document would be through the New Window command. New Window is a standard command already implemented in MFC for MDI applications (such as Microsoft Word, for example). When you choose this command, MFC creates a new document frame window within the MDI frame window. The new window contains the same kind of view object as the active document window, so the user sees two windows containing the same document. You can scroll to a remote location in one window while leaving the other window in place. The new window has the same caption as the old one, but with *:2* appended. The NWnd program in the \learnvcn\Chap20 folder in the companion code illustrates this behavior. Take a look.

Splitter Windows

MFC provides two kinds of splitter windows: *dynamic* and *static*. Figure 20-1 shows MyDraw with a dynamic splitter window dividing the view into four panes. We'll add the code for this feature in a moment. A dynamic splitter window lets the user control how many rows and columns of panes to use, while a static splitter window requires these values to be set at the outset, when the splitter window is created.

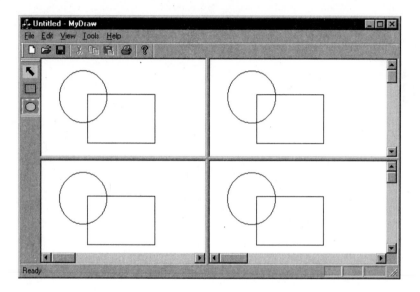

Figure 20-1.   *MyDraw's window split into two rows and two columns of panes.*

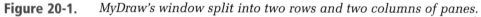

Try it now

Let's examine the behavior of splitter windows. In Microsoft Visual C++ 6.0, with a source code document open, choose the Split command on the Window menu. Move the mouse around in the document window without clicking it. The intersection of two *split bars* follows the mouse. When you click in the window, the split bars lock into place. Try double-clicking a split bar to make it disappear. Try dragging a split bar all the way to a window edge and letting it go. With both split bars gone, click on the small *split box* above the document window's vertical scroll bar (see Figure 20-2) and drag it down. A horizontal split bar again divides the window. Try the same thing with the split box to the left of the horizontal scroll bar. Try scrolling the exposed panes to different parts of the document.

In both dynamic and static splitter windows, the user can drag the split bars that divide up the window to resize the panes with respect to each other. For example, in a static splitter window with two panes, the user can drag the split bar all the way to the right or left so one view disappears (except for the split bar). In a dynamic splitter window, the user can also remove the split bars, as you saw in the last "Try it now." Removing split bars reduces the number of rows or columns of panes. Double-clicking a split bar or dragging it all the way to a window edge removes it from the window. However, a small split box remains, tucked in above the vertical scroll bar (as in Figure 20-2) or to the left of the horizontal scroll bar.

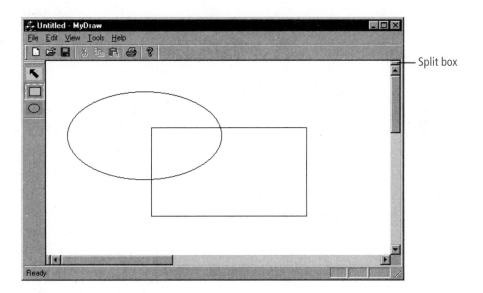

Figure 20-2.   *MyDraw with split boxes.*

When to Use Dynamic and Static Splitter Windows

Use a dynamic splitter window to display multiple panes based on the same view class. This enables the ability we discussed earlier—it lets the user view different parts of the same document in multiple panes.

Use a static splitter window when you want to display different view classes in the panes. For example, the left pane might hold a form view—a dialog-like view with controls—while the right pane might hold a drawing surface as in MyDraw. The Stat program in the \learnvcn\Chap20 folder in the companion code illustrates a static splitter window with two panes: a form view in the left pane and a graphics view in the right pane.

Static splitter windows are useful for creating complex windows whose panes contain highly diverse work areas. For example, suppose you need a main window with a control panel on one side and another control panel along the bottom. You could partly accomplish this with toolbars, but as an alternative, a static splitter window might offer exactly what you need.

Combining Static and Dynamic Splitter Windows

Dynamic splitter windows are limited to a maximum of 2 rows and 2 columns, but the user can dynamically add or remove panes by manipulating the split bars. You can design static splitter windows with up to 16 rows and 16 columns. It's even possible to combine static and dynamic splitter window panes. For example, the left pane of a static splitter window could contain a form view, while the right pane contained several embedded dynamic splitter window panes. Another possibility is to derive your own class from *CSplitterWnd* and override member functions so you can embed different view types in the panes of a dynamic splitter window. I won't illustrate these more advanced techniques, but Jeff Prosise explains them in his book *Programming Windows 95 with MFC* (Microsoft Press, 1996). (See Chapter 21 for information about this and other more advanced Visual C++ and MFC books.)

Adding a Dynamic Splitter Window to MyDraw

Let's add the few lines of code needed to give MyDraw a dynamic splitter window. Each pane of the splitter window will be based on MyDraw's one view class, *CMyDrawView*.

Try it now

Adding a dynamic splitter window requires one data member and one single-line function. Take these three steps:

1. In class *CMainFrame* (in the file MainFrm.h), add a data member of type *CSplitterWnd*. Put it in the first *protected* section under the *// Implementation* comment:

```
// Implementation
public:
    ⋮
protected:  // control bar embedded members
    CStatusBar   m_wndStatusBar;
    CToolBar     m_wndToolBarStd;
    CToolBar     m_wndToolBarDraw;
    CSplitterWnd     m_wndSplitter;
```

2. Use the Add Virtual Function command to add an override of the *OnCreateClient* virtual function to class *CMainFrame* and fill in the boldface line of code below (replacing the existing *return* statement):

```
BOOL CMainFrame::OnCreateClient(LPCREATESTRUCT lpcs,
                               CCreateContext* pContext)
{
    // TODO: Add your specialized code here and/or...
    return m_wndSplitter.Create(this, 2, 2, CSize(1,1),
        pContext);
}
```

3. In the *OnLButtonUp* member function (in the file DrawVw.cpp), add the following boldface lines just before the closing brace of the *if* statement:

```
if(m_bCaptured)
{
    ⋮
    // Draw final rectangle.
    InvertShape(&dc, *m_pShpTemp, false);  // Draw

    // Update extra views with the new shape.
    CMyDrawDoc* pDoc = GetDocument();
    ASSERT_VALID(pDoc);
    pDoc->UpdateAllViews(NULL);
}
```

Now that the user can split the window, we need to make sure all views are updated with anything drawn in one of them.

The data member embeds a splitter window within the application's main frame window, just as the *m_wndToolBarX* and *m_wndStatusBar* data members embed toolbars in the window. The visible manifestation of embedding the splitter window is the two split boxes nestled next to the scroll bars.

MFC calls the *CMainFrame::OnCreateClient* member function when the frame window is being created, thereby allowing us to embed our toolbars and splitter windows. Our highlighted code calls *CSplitterWnd::Create* to create and initialize the splitter window. *Create* takes five parameters. The first, *this*, identifies the splitter window's parent window. The next two parameters specify the maximum number of rows and columns (in that order)—these values must not exceed 2. The fourth parameter sets the minimum size of a pane to 1 pixel. The final parameter passes along the *CCreateContext* pointer received as a parameter to *OnCreateClient*. This object contains information that MFC uses to create the view objects to display in the panes. For additional parameters with acceptable default values, check the Help index for *Create* and choose the "*CSplitterWnd::Create*" topic in the Topics Found dialog box.

That's all it takes to create a dynamic splitter window. Build and run MyDraw to try it out. (But first see the Warning below.)

TIP If you want to allow dynamic splitting into two side-by-side panes only, pass 1 and 2 for the row and column values. For one pane above the other, pass 2 and 1. Note that passing 1 and 1 results in an error. Either the number of rows or the number of columns (or both) must be 2. You can test these variations in MyDraw.

WARNING Introducing the splitter window is simple, but it creates some side effects. I won't follow up on those here in the text, but see the final version of MyDraw, MyDrawF, for a solution. If you split MyDraw's view now, you find that the panes are not synchronized. The problem is that splitting creates multiple copies of the view object, each containing its own data members for color, transparency, selection, and so forth. If you click in one pane to make it active and then change color, transparency, or selection mode, the data members in the other views don't change to match these selections. Experiment with MyDraw to see the problems. How would you solve them? The document MyDrawF.doc in the \learnvcn\Chap21 folder in the companion code describes my strategy for coordinating the panes.

Creating a Static Splitter Window

We won't use a static splitter window in MyDraw, but the Stat program in the companion code shows how to set one up. That example displays two side-by-side panes. The left pane is a form view with some (unimplemented) controls, and the right pane is a view that draws an ellipse near its upper left corner. Figure 20-3 shows the Stat program.

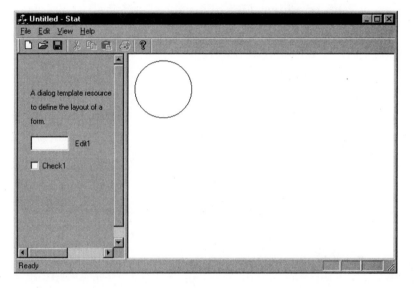

Figure 20-3. *A program whose static splitter window contains a form view and a drawing surface.*

To create a static splitter window in some hypothetical application, such as Stat, follow these steps:

1. As with the dynamic splitter window, embed a *CSplitterWnd* object in the main frame window class, *CMainFrame*, by adding a *CSplitterWnd* data member.

2. Add an override of the *OnCreateClient* member function to the main frame window class. In it, write code something like the following:

```
BOOL CMainFrame::OnCreateClient(LPCREATESTRUCT lpcs,
                                CCreateContext* pContext)
{
    // TODO: Add your specialized code here...
```

(continued)

```
        if(!m_wndSplitter.CreateStatic(this, 1, 2) ||
           !m_wndSplitter.CreateView(0,0,
               RUNTIME_CLASS(CStatForm),
               CSize(165, 0), pContext) ||
           !m_wndSplitter.CreateView(0,1,
               RUNTIME_CLASS(CStatView),
               CSize(0, 0), pContext))
        {
               return false;
        }
        return true;
}
```

We make three function calls here, one to *CSplitterWnd::CreateStatic*, then two to *CSplitterWnd::CreateView*, one call per static pane. If any of the calls fail, we return *false*, and the application terminates.

The *CreateStatic* member function is the static counterpart to the *Create* function that is used for dynamic splitter windows. *CreateStatic* takes a parameter identifying the parent window and two parameters specifying the number of rows and columns (one row, two columns in the example above). This creates and initializes the static splitter window, but for a static splitter window we still must specify the view classes to use in the panes. That's what the two calls to *CreateView* do. The first two parameters to *CreateView* specify the zero-based row and column number of the pane the call is for: passing 0, 0 for our splitter window with one row and two columns (two panes, side by side) specifies the left pane. In the second *CreateView* call, we pass 0, 1 for the right pane. Each *CreateView* call then passes a *CRuntimeClass* object, obtained with the *RUNTIME_CLASS* macro. Passing this object identifies the view class in a way that lets MFC create the view object as needed. In the example, we specify view classes *CStatForm* and *CStatView* for the right and left panes, respectively.

The two *CreateView* calls also pass a *CSize* value to specify the widths of the two panes. In our example, passing *CSize(165, 0)* in the first *Create-View* call specifies that the left pane is initially to be 165 pixels wide, a value I determined by experiment—wide enough to expose all of the text and controls in the form view used in the Stat example on the CD. Passing *CSize(0, 0)* in the second *CreateView* call specifies that the right pane is to use all the horizontal space left after its companion pane is placed.

Finally, the *CreateView* calls pass along the *CCreateContext* pointer that *OnCreateClient* receives from MFC.

> **TIP** To create a form view like the one in the Stat program, create a dialog template resource containing the controls you want. Give the dialog resource the following styles: do not enter a caption on the General tab in the Properties window. On the Styles tab, select *Child* style and *None* for Border, and on the More Styles tab, make sure the *Visible* box is not checked. Next, hold down the Ctrl key and double-click the dialog resource to create a class. In the New Class dialog box, name the class, specify the files it's to be stored in, derive the class from the base class *CFormView*, and confirm that the dialog resource ID supplied in the Dialog ID box is correct. Write code in your resulting form view class to manage the controls. Form views are described further below.

What Can You Do With Views?

In Chapter 14, we looked at the notion of an MFC document as a data repository or a data manager. A document is just a receptacle that you can tailor to manage some particular kind of data. (The document doesn't necessarily have to correspond to a disk file.) Class *CMyDrawDoc*, for example, has an interface designed for containing and manipulating shapes. Now it's time to pay more attention to views, the other half of MFC's document/view architecture.

Views for User Interaction

Views have a twofold nature. On one hand, they display data, with each view specialized for some particular kind of data. In this aspect, they're the visual side of a related document. On the other hand, views often not only display data but also provide ways for users to interact with the data and edit it. For instance, in MyDraw we designed class *CMyDrawView*, which allows direct drawing with the mouse and even begins to add the rudiments of direct editing with the mouse: actions such as selecting, dragging, and resizing the shapes drawn in drawing mode.

Views as Windows

Views are windows, so they inherit a huge amount of functionality, not only from *CView* but also from *CWnd* and all of its base classes. Here's a partial list of what views can do:

■ Handle Windows messages, including *WM_COMMAND* messages.

- Communicate with their parent window. They can also obtain a pointer to the parent with the *CWnd::GetParent* member function.

- Communicate with a document object, via *CView::GetDocument*, *CDocument::UpdateAllViews*, and *CDocument::SetModifiedFlag*, among other functions.

- Contain child windows of their own, which can include controls and custom-designed child windows derived from *CWnd*.

Both documents and views can have message maps. Both, therefore, can handle *WM_COMMAND* messages from menus, toolbars, and controls. It's common to map some commands to the document, some to the view, some to the frame window, and some to the application object. For example, you typically map the Open and New commands on the File menu to the application object, while you map the Save, Save As, and Close commands to the document, and you map commands related to drawing to the view.

Unlike documents, views are windows, so they can also handle a great many Windows messages besides *WM_COMMAND*. As we've seen, views often handle mouse and keyboard messages, messages related to window creation and destruction, scrolling messages, messages related to window visibility and activation, and so on.

Finally, both *CDocument* and *CView* supply sets of virtual member functions that you can override, such as *OnBeginPrinting* and *OnPrepareDC* for the view and *OnNewDocument* and *DeleteContents* for the document.

MFC Views as Bases for Your Own Views

With all of the functionality I just described, the MFC view classes are versatile design templates—starters for any sort of view you might need. All view classes are based on *CView*, of course. Classes based on *CScrollView*, such as our *CMyDrawView*, build in scrolling ability. Classes based on *CFormView* present a dialog-like interface that can also be scrolled (because *CFormView* is derived from *CScrollView*). Classes based on *CCtrlView* build a view around a single Windows control, such as an edit box, a tree control, or a list control. Class *CEditView*, for example, supplies fairly sophisticated display and editing of plain text. The view is completely covered by a *CEdit* control. You can easily use a *CEditView* to write a simple text editor like the Windows Notepad accessory. Other view classes are specialized for displaying and manipulating database data.

The point is that you can design any sort of view you need, either starting with one of the more specialized MFC view classes or starting from scratch, more or less, by deriving from class *CView*. The possibilities are limitless.

Combining Views

Not only can you base your view on one of the MFC view classes, but you can combine views in various ways. You can, for example, install views in a dynamic or static splitter window, as we've seen. One promising approach for many applications is a Windows Explorer–style interface, with a *CTreeView* in one pane and some other view, typically a *CListView*, in a second pane. AppWizard even supports generating an Explorer-style interface instead of a standard document/view interface. (Look at AppWizard steps 5 and 6 in Chapter 7, and also see Exercise 3 at the end of Chapter 7.)

With a bit more work, you can design switchable views, so that the view changes to suit a change of mode. For example, in Microsoft Excel, you can examine the same set of data either in spreadsheet view or in chart view.

It's also possible to design applications with multiple views (and even multiple document types) based on different document templates. For example, your application might provide two commands, each of which opens a window using a different view (and perhaps a different kind of document). You'd create two different document templates in your application class's *InitInstance* member function and use the appropriate document template to create a document/view pair and their enclosing frame window. Visual C++ works this way: different commands create source code documents, resource script documents, bitmap documents, icon documents, and so on. All of these possibilities allow you to design very complex user interfaces for your programs.

For more information, check the Help index for *samples* and choose the "Views Samples" topic in the Topics Found dialog box. That topic describes several MFC sample applications that use views in interesting ways. You can access the samples from there, and Help lets you copy the sample files to your hard drive. Don't forget that examining, running, and modifying the samples is a popular and effective way to learn new MFC techniques.

Communicating Among MFC Objects

Back in Chapter 8 I discussed the objects that make up a running MFC application. In that discussion, I stressed treating the objects as individual entities. At this point, I'd like to stress the objects' cooperation and point you toward useful information about how they communicate among themselves. The Help topic "Relationships Among MFC Objects" details interobject communication. Check the Help index for *accessing*. Double-click the subtopic "MFC objects." The table in that topic describes the functions you can use to access one kind of object from another—for example, how to use the global function *AfxGetApp* to obtain a pointer to the application object. Many of the MFC sample applications use the functions described in that table.

Congratulations!

Think back for a moment about what you've accomplished. Besides learning to find your way around in the Visual C++ environment, you've not only covered the essentials of the C++ language but also gone on to apply many of them in a pretty good practice application. You have by now mastered the fundamentals of MFC programming, which is to say Windows programming in C++. Think also of the specific techniques you've learned: working with Windows resources; using the document/view architecture; drawing in a window; working with the mouse; using color; deriving your own classes from MFC classes; handling Windows messages and overriding virtual functions; scrolling; writing and reading files; printing; and adding sophisticated features like toolbars, property sheets, and splitter windows; and last but not least, debugging.

More important than those accomplishments, you've also learned to think as an MFC programmer. You can select the right class to handle a message. You can find the hooks in MFC that let you accomplish your goals.

You can work with objects such as dialog boxes and Windows controls in MFC terms. And you can apply object-oriented programming to practical projects.

Is there more to learn? You bet. But you deserve my hearty congratulations for climbing three difficult learning curves at once: C++, Windows, and MFC. That's quite an accomplishment.

Try It Yourself

Here are your final exercises. I hope you've found these small projects worthwhile. Remember that answers and sample solutions are provided in the text in some chapters, or in small sample applications or the final version of MyDraw, MyDrawF, in the companion code.

1. Try your hand at a static splitter window.

Study the Stat program in the companion code and develop your own similar application. You might try more panes or different kinds of views. In particular, try creating your own form view.

2. Create an MDI application and experiment with its New Window command.

Test the New Window command and study the code to see how it's implemented. You can find the implementation in the *CMDIFrame-Wnd::OnWindowNew* function in the file WinMdi.cpp. See the Appendix for guidance on finding the file.

3. Study the MFC view samples.

Check the Help index for *samples* and choose the "Views Samples" topic in the Topics Found dialog box. That topic takes you to a variety of MFC sample applications that do interesting things with views. Copy those samples to your hard disk, build them, and start learning what makes them tick.

What's Next?

Chapter 21 directs your attention to books and World Wide Web sites that can help you go on from here. And to round out our MFC tour, we'll also finish MyDraw step 10 by adding one last feature to MyDraw. Think of it as a graduation gift.

Stepping Out from Here

In the Introduction, I described this book as an on-ramp, a way to get up to speed with Microsoft Visual C++. You've accomplished quite a bit in the last 20 chapters, but you've also gotten a glimpse of how much more there is to Visual C++ than an introductory book like this can cover. I'll use this chapter to suggest where you might go from here. And, as a parting gift, I'll show you how to give MyDraw its own custom application icon.

Books on C++, Visual C++, and MFC

The following books are the ones I consulted most frequently while writing *Learn Microsoft Visual C++ 6.0 Now*, in the order of probable usefulness to introductory readers:

- Jeff Prosise, *Programming Windows 95 with MFC* (Microsoft Press, 1996). Excellent Microsoft Foundation Class Library 6.0 (MFC) programming information and examples. Jeff Prosise is the Charles Petzold of MFC.

- Beck Zaratian, *Microsoft Visual C++ 6.0 Programmer's Guide*, 2nd edition (Microsoft Press, 1998). Zaratian focuses on using the Visual C++ product, with special emphasis on the Visual C++ environment.

- Stanley B. Lippman and Josèe Lajoie, *C++ Primer*, 3rd edition (Addison-Wesley, 1998). This one's a favorite of many members of the MFC development team.

- Mike Blaszczak, *Professional MFC with Visual C++ 5* (Wrox Press, 1997). This book is more advanced than Prosise and quite comprehensive at over 1,000 pages. It was written by the current MFC development team leader. It's fun, too, especially if you like hockey.

- David J. Kruglinski, George Shepherd, and Scot Wingo, *Programming Microsoft Visual C++*, 5th edition (Microsoft Press, 1998). This one's more advanced than Prosise, and more oriented to the Visual C++ product than Blaszczak, who focuses on MFC.

- Charles Petzold, *Programming Windows*, 5th edition (Microsoft Press, 1999). This is the bible for thousands of C-language Microsoft Windows programmers, which, in its newest incarnation, adds Windows 98 to its comprehensive coverage.

- Frank Crockett with Jocelyn Garner, *MFC Developer's Workshop* (Microsoft Press, 1997). This collection of often-requested MFC techniques and tasks that are somewhat advanced or off the beaten track includes database programming.

- *The Windows Interface Guidelines for Software Design* (Microsoft Press, 1995) and its online version, updated through 1998. Here you'll find Microsoft's guidelines for the design of your program's user interface. Later in this chapter, I'll tell you how to find this book on the Web.

- Jeffrey Richter, *Advanced Windows*, 3rd edition (Microsoft Press, 1997). Richter's advanced Windows programming topics include many not covered in Petzold.

- Scott Meyers, *Effective C++: 50 Specific Ways to Improve Your Programs and Designs*, 2nd edition (Addison-Wesley, 1997). Meyers' books dwell on C++ pitfalls and ways to avoid them.

- Scott Meyers, *More Effective C++: 35 New Ways to Improve Your Programs and Designs* (Addison-Wesley, 1996). This book extends Meyers' previous offering.

- Margaret A. Ellis and Bjarne Stroustrup, *The Annotated C++ Reference Manual* (Addison-Wesley, 1990). Stroustrup was the original designer of C++, and this is his definitive guide for implementers of C++ compilers and for C++ programmers.

- Steve McConnell, *Code Complete* (Microsoft Press, 1993). This book contains lots of indispensable programming lore and techniques.

One of the best places to look for books on Visual C++ and MFC is the Microsoft Press website: *http://mspress.microsoft.com.* Other publishers of technical books also offer many such titles.

What I Haven't Covered

Here are some of the topics that I'll leave to your postgraduate training. Most of them are fairly advanced. Each bullet includes pointers to good sources to get you started.

- **Programming with certain new or advanced features of C++, including templates, namespaces, and multiple inheritance.** At the end of Chapter 5 there's a list of C++ features that are beyond the scope of this book. To learn about these items, consult a comprehensive text on the C++ language, such as Lippman and Lajoie. See the book list in the previous section.

- **Programming with Microsoft's Active Template Library (ATL).** Using ATL requires that you understand the Component Object Model (COM) and C++ templates, both of which are too advanced for this book. Get started on ATL and COM with Kruglinski, Shepherd, and Wingo.

- **Using certain more advanced graphics techniques, including bitmaps, regions, and paths.** It would take a book twice this size, at least, to cover everything there is to know about Windows graphics. Aside from Petzold, a good place to start is Prosise, who is your best bet for MFC. For more advanced MFC information, try Blaszczak. Also see Kruglinski, Shepherd, and Wingo.

- **Writing multithreaded applications and using a host of other advanced Windows programming techniques.** Multithreaded applications spread processing among multiple concurrently running threads of execution. For example, you might use a thread to perform lengthy operations such as printing in the background. See Prosise. You might also consult Richter.

- **Writing forms of Windows-based code besides the kind of graphical .exe programs we've done through most of this book.** These might include dynamic-link libraries (DLLs), device drivers, Microsoft ActiveX controls, Automation clients, OLE-enabled applications (OLE stands for object linking and embedding), Web servers and clients for the Internet, ActiveX Document servers, and programs for the Microsoft Windows CE operating system. All of these are too advanced if you don't already know C++ and at least intermediate-level Windows programming. A good place to start is Richter, and several specialist books are also available, such as Adam Denning, *ActiveX Controls Inside Out*, 2nd edition (Microsoft Press, 1997). Kruglinski, Shepherd, and Wingo cover many of these topics in an introductory way, and see also Crockett and Garner.

- **Writing database programs, especially using the Microsoft Transaction Server (MTS).** Unfortunately, I lack the space to do justice to any of the database programming environments available with Visual C++: Open Database Connectivity (ODBC), Data Access Objects (DAO), or OLE DB. Kruglinski offers a good start, and you can also consult specialist books such as the *Microsoft ODBC 3.0 Software Development Kit and Programmer's Reference* (Microsoft Press, 1997) and Dan Haught and Jim Ferguson's book, *Microsoft Jet Database Engine Programmer's Guide*, 2nd edition (Microsoft Press, 1997). Kruglinski, Shepherd, and Wingo introduce database programming. Also see Crockett and Garner.

- **Programming in the C language instead of in C++.** This represents a different direction from postgraduate training, but if you want to program in C, you can do so with Visual C++.

Microsoft on the Web and MSDN Online

If you can connect to the Internet on your computer, you can access Microsoft on the Web, via the Microsoft On The Web command on the Help menu in Visual C++. You can also click any of the other commands, wait while your machine connects, and explore the various Web sites. All of this is free except for any online charges imposed by your Internet service provider. Microsoft's web site is at *http://www.microsoft.com*.

For more information, help, and tools, join the Microsoft Developer Network (MSDN) at the MSDN Web site at *http://msdn.microsoft.com*. Sign up for a free program called MSDN Online Membership, which offers the MSDN Library online, free downloads, and other benefits. Beyond that are three levels of paid subscriptions, each offering additional tools, information, and assistance. (You can also visit the MSDN Web page by clicking MSDN Online on the Visual C++ Help menu.) One especially valuable feature of MSDN Online is access to all of Microsoft's documentation, including articles and books, such as *The Windows Interface Guidelines for Software Design*, mentioned earlier in the book list. On the MSDN Online page, follow the link to MSDN Library Online. The library's contents are listed in the left-hand pane.

A growing number of sites on the World Wide Web offer information, guidance, and example programs for the C++ language, Visual C++, and MFC. Categorized Web search engines such as Yahoo and HotBot are a good way to locate such sites.

One Last MyDraw Feature

Every Windows application should have its own icon. This is the icon that will appear in Windows Explorer. We'll finish off our work on MyDraw step 10 by changing the default icon used for the application. It's easy to do.

 Try it now

Use ResourceView in the Workspace window to view MyDraw's resources. We'll design a new icon and use it to replace the default application icon.

1. Create a new icon resource. On the Insert menu, click Resource, and in the New Resource dialog box, double-click Icon.

2. Edit the icon using the Graphics toolbar and the Color Palette. Figure 21-1 shows the icon I designed (colors aren't shown). You can either imitate it or just have fun. Save your work. For information about icon editing, check the Help index for *Graphics editor* and select the subtopic "icons and cursors."

3. In ResourceView, open the Icon folder and locate the icon resource *IDR_MAINFRAME*. That's the default icon used for the application. You can open it first to see that it's an MFC logo. Delete that icon resource.

4. In ResourceView, right-click the *IDI_ICON1* resource. On the context menu, select Properties.

5. In the Properties window, change the ID name *IDI_ICON1* to *IDR_MAINFRAME*. Save and build MyDraw.

To see the icon, use Windows Explorer to open the project folder for MyDraw. Open the Debug subfolder and locate the file MyDraw.exe. Its icon should be the one you designed. The icon should also appear in the title bar when you run MyDraw.

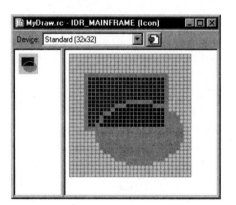

Figure 21-1.   *My design for MyDraw's application icon.*

While you're at it, try out the Visual C++ components and controls gallery, which lets you add sophisticated features to your programs with prefabricated C++ components and ActiveX controls. The file Gallery.doc in the \learnvcn\Chap21 folder in the companion code shows how to add system information (available memory and disk space) to your program's About dialog box. The final version of MyDraw, described below, includes the system information component.

The Final Version of MyDraw

Because this book could not possibly cover everything about Visual C++ or MFC, I've written one final version of MyDraw, called MyDrawF, in the companion code. MyDrawF implements additional features, including many of those I suggested that you add in the book's "Try It Yourself" sections. As my farewell to you, I urge you to examine the code in MyDrawF. I've commented it thoroughly, and there are documentation files for some features that you can read with the WordPad accessory. The file MyDrawF.doc, located in the \learnvcn\Chap21 folder in the companion code, describes what I've done with MyDrawF. Enjoy!

The MFC Source Code Files

One potential problem with using Microsoft Foundation Class Library 6.0 (MFC) is that you can easily treat MFC's classes as black boxes. In many cases, you can get by without knowing a lot about what they're doing behind the scenes—in fact that's the idea. But viewing the classes as black boxes can be frustrating when your code does something out of step with the MFC code and you get an error, assertion failure, or exception. Then the more you know about the insides of those black boxes, the easier it is to deal with your problem. There's also a lot of potential in those classes that you might never discover through the documentation alone.

It's no accident that the MFC development team ships the source code files for MFC with the product. Those files are there to be used, for several reasons:

- You sometimes need to delve inside MFC to find out how your code is out of step with MFC's code.

- You can learn a lot about C++ and object-oriented programming from browsing in the files.

- You can see those things, like the *WinMain* function, that MFC hides away.

- You can find the "hooks" for customizing MFC's behavior: the functions to override or the classes to subclass.

This appendix is here to introduce you to the MFC source files. I'll be showing you these tricks of the trade:

■ Where to find the files and how to track down a particular file.

■ What tools can help you find a particular function, variable, or class in the source files.

■ How to read the source files—that is, how to understand the coding and commenting conventions that the MFC developers use in the files.

■ How to understand the cryptic extras that AppWizard and ClassWizard add to your starter files.

> **WARNING** I strongly advise you not to make any changes in the MFC source code files. You can accomplish what you need without such a drastic step. Only MFC gurus ever even contemplate such a thing, and they know it's risky. Besides, in order for your changes to take effect, you have to rebuild the appropriate MFC libraries, a task that itself is not for the faint of heart. The great virtue of C++ classes and of MFC is that if something doesn't work the way you want it to, you can usually derive a class of your own to change the behavior. Often you can bypass or override MFC features that you feel are in your way.

Where to Find the MFC Source Code Files

When you install Microsoft Visual C++ 6.0, Introductory Edition, the installation directory is: [*Drive*]:\Program Files\Microsoft Visual Studio\Vc98 unless you have specified otherwise during installation. (Visual Studio includes Microsoft Visual Basic, Microsoft Visual J++, and other programming products as well as Visual C++.) The drive depends on where you installed Visual C++. The Mfc directory under Vc98 contains three subdirectories: Include, Lib, and Src.

The Include Subdirectory

The three most important file types in MFC's Include subdirectory are the following:

■ **Headers (.h files).** These files contain declarations for the MFC classes, global variables and functions, macros, and constants. Of particular interest are the files Afx.h and Afxwin.h. Afx.h contains declarations for the parts of MFC that don't relate directly to Microsoft Windows. Afxwin.h contains declarations for the Windows-related classes.

- **Inline files (.inl files).** These files contain inline function definitions, primarily of the MFC wrapper functions for the Win32 API. If you can't find what you're looking for in the header files (.h files) or the implementation files (.cpp files), look in the .inl files, especially if what you're looking for is part of the Win32 API. See Chapter 4 for information about inline functions in C++.

- **Resource files (.rc files).** The .rc files contain resources that MFC uses for the features it implements for you: icons, bitmaps, string tables, and the like.

TIP Visual C++ comes with some *clipart* files. Among them is a file called Common.res (also available in uncompiled form as Common.rc), which contains many icons, bitmaps, and cursors. The path to these files in the Visual C++ 6.0, Introductory Edition CD is VCIntEd\Disk1\Msdn_vcb\Samples \Vc98\Mfc\General\Clipart\Common.res. Copy this file to your hard disk.

The Lib Subdirectory

MFC's Lib subdirectory contains the MFC library files (.lib files). These are object-code libraries for various flavors of applications. There are Release and Debug versions for ANSI compliance, Unicode, and so on. For a description of these files and their naming conventions, check the Help index for *MFC libraries*.

The Src Subdirectory

MFC's Src subdirectory contains the .cpp files that implement the MFC classes and global functions. This is where to look for the actual function bodies for most functions—except the Win32 API wrappers, which are usually in the .inl files in the Include subdirectory.

Table A-1 on the next page gives a few examples of how the .cpp files are related to the .h files. Afx.h and AfxWin.h are large files full of declarations.

These two header files (along with some others) map to a large number of categorized .cpp files whose names usually reveal their content. The filenames are usually prefixed with an abbreviated class name.

Windows-Related Classes that AfxWin.h Declares	Sampling of Files that Implement the Class
Class *CWinApp*	App3d.cpp (3D aspects of user interface) AppCore.cpp (core functions) AppDlg.cpp (dialog-related functions) AppHelp.cpp (help-related functions) AppHelpX.cpp (more help functions) AppInit.cpp (application initialization) …
Class *CDocument*	DocCore.cpp (core functions) DocMulti.cpp (MDI document) DocSingl.cpp (SDI document)

Table A-1. *The many-to-one relationship between .cpp files and a .h file.*

Finding What You Need in the MFC Source Code Files

I recommend two kinds of tools for locating files and their contents easily:

- The Visual C++ Find In Files command, which is quite powerful, much like the familiar Grep tool. With Find In Files you can search the source code in files on disk as well as in open files, including whole directories and their subdirectories. It's the perfect way to search the MFC source code files.

- The Visual C++ Source Browser command, which uses the Browse Information file for searching by class and function rather than by file. The difference between using Source Browser and using Find In Files is like the distinction between ClassView and FileView. The class browser shows class derivation relationships and members rather than raw source code. You can prepare a file containing code browsing information for just your project, and you can also obtain a pre-built browse information file that contains information about all of the classes and functions in MFC.

Using the Visual C++ Find In Files Command

Among the most useful features of Find In Files are the following:

- **Support for *regular expressions*, as in the UNIX command Grep, in addition to ordinary searching.** A regular expression is a search string that uses special characters to match a text pattern in a file—much like using wildcard characters with MS-DOS files. The Find In Files dialog box even has a button (the small right-facing arrow next to the Find What box) that helps you construct regular expressions. Be sure also to select the Regular Expression box in the dialog box if you are using regular expressions.

- **Two output panes in the Visual C++ Output window.** You can conduct one search in the Find In Files 1 pane. When you open Find In Files again, click the Output To Pane 2 box and conduct your second search. The output from the second search appears in the Find In Files 2 pane.

- **The Advanced button in the Find In Files dialog box.** This opens a Look In Additional Folders pane in which you can list additional directories to search. These paths remain listed in the Find In Files dialog box for future invocations of the dialog. I find this a handy place to list the two most important MFC subdirectories, Include and Src, which contain the MFC source files.

A sample search using Find In Files

Here's a sample search. Suppose I want to locate the source code for the constructor in class *CView*. That's an MFC class, and I know it's not in the files in my project, so I want to look at the MFC source files.

1. On the Visual C++ Edit menu, select Find In Files. (Or click the Find In Files button on the Standard toolbar. The icon shows a folder with a pair of binoculars.)

2. In the Find In Files dialog box, click the Advanced button (if the advanced Find options are not visible already). Then specify the information shown in table A-2 on the following page.

3. Click the dotted rectangle under Look In Additional Folders, click the browse button next to that row (its icon is an ellipsis (...)), and locate the folder you want to list in the pane. In this case, locate the MFC Src subdirectory, since you're looking for a function definition. These paths are relative to where you installed Visual C++.

4. Click Find. After a pause, the search results appear in the Find In Files 1 pane of the Visual C++ Output window. Here's sample output based on the sample search data listed in Table A-2:

```
Searching for '::CView'...
D:\Program Files\VC98\MFC\SRC\VIEWCORE.CPP(49):CView::CView()
1 occurrence(s) have been found.
```

5. Double-click on the output line that lists the path to the function *CView::CView*. This opens the file ViewCore.cpp at that function. Try it.

For more information about Find In Files, check the Help index for *Find In Files command*.

Box in Find In Files	Contents to Fill In	Remarks
Find What	*::CView*	Typing the scope resolution operator (::) as well as the text narrows the search from just "*CView.*"
In Files/File Types	*.c; .*.cpp; *.cxx; *.tli*	We want *.cpp.
In Folder	Doesn't matter	We know we're looking for an MFC file.
Look In Subfolders	Checked	
Look In Folders For Project Source Files	Unchecked	We know it's not in our project.
Look In Folders For Project Include Files	Unchecked	We know it's not in our project.

Table A-2.   *Data to enter for the Find In Files search example above.*

Using the Visual C++ Source Browser Command for MFC

Here's an even better solution than Grep or Find In Files for most searching. Visual C++ lets you browse your C++ classes, functions, and variables. You can use this ability to answer questions and find your way around either just in your own current project or in your project files plus all of MFC. For example, given a class name, what's the base class? Or what classes are derived from the class? The *Source Browser* lets you locate the symbol you need and open the MFC source files at the appropriate place so you can look directly at the code. You must enable source browsing before you can use it—I'll explain this below.

Source browsing helps you easily find the following information in the MFC source files:

- Information about all the symbols in any source file

- The source code line in which a symbol is defined

- Each source code line where there is a reference to a symbol

- The relationships between base classes and derived classes

- The relationships between calling functions and called functions

To learn about source browsing, check the Help index for *browse information* and for *browsing symbols from ClassView*.

To enable source browsing for your current project, create a browse information file (extension .bsc). Check the Help index for *browse information*. If you choose the Source Browser command without already having enabled source browsing, Visual C++ asks if you want to enable it. If you say yes, Visual C++ rebuilds your project with source browsing on.

Once you have built your project with browse information turned on, the easiest way to browse for a particular symbol—such as a class name—is to select the name in a file you have open and click the Source Browser command on the Tools menu (or press Alt-F12). A dialog box lets you select the kind of browsing you want: Definitions And References, File Outline, Base Classes And Members, Derived Classes And Members, Call Graph, or Callers Graph. Select what you want and click OK. A browse dialog box opens. You can click the pushpin icon on the dialog to make it stay on screen if you like.

The File Outline browse dialog box is particularly interesting. It lets you see just the data members, just the functions, just the classes, just the macros, just the types, or any combination by pressing the appropriate buttons on the toolbar. From any of the browse dialog boxes, you can double-click an item to go to that item in the source files. The appropriate source code file opens in the Visual C++ Source Code editor and scrolls to the symbol.

Here's a way to make your work even easier: you can also use a pre-built browse file for all of MFC. The file Mfc.bsc is available on the Visual C++ installation disc at \VCIntEd\Disk1\Vc98\Mfc\Src. It isn't installed automatically when you install Visual C++, so you must manually copy this file to \Vc98\Bin on your hard drive. Then follow the directions in the previous paragraph to enable source browsing for your project. This includes building your project with source browsing turned on. You can then browse through MFC's code as well as your own.

Take advantage of source browsing. Besides answering questions about a symbol, it's a very handy way to navigate through your code (and MFC's). You can use source browsing for navigation in much the same way you can navigate using the Visual C++ WizardBar or ClassView. (The difference between source browsing and ClassView is that ClassView shows only the classes in your project, while source browsing can potentially show you all of MFC as well.)

Keep in mind that you must explicitly turn on source browsing as described above. Visual C++ doesn't build a browse file by default, so you must turn on source browsing and then rebuild your program, even if you only want to use the MFC browse information file. You don't get a browse file by default because building it adds noticeably to the overall build time for your program. It's best to build with browsing on, and then turn it off until you've made a substantial number of changes and turn it back on just long enough to build again. That way you get a refreshed browse file periodically.

For more information, check the Help index for *browse information,* double-click it, and choose the first topic in the Topics Found dialog box. One useful link in that topic is "Class Browsing Tasks."

Source Files Other than MFC

In addition to the MFC source files, you can also use the source code for the C/C++ run-time library. You'll find the run-time library's functions used liberally in MFC code (and in this book), and it can be useful to step into a run-time function during debugging. Check the Help index for *source code*, then double-click the subtopic "C run-time library functions." You have the option to install these source files on your hard disk during Setup, using the Custom installation option. Select Custom, and then VC++ Runtime Libraries. Click Change Option, select the CRT Source Code check box, click OK, and then click Continue to go on with the installation. You can also install the source code later. (The MFC source files are installed by default.) If you don't do that, you can still step into the source files as long as the Visual C++ installation disc is in your CD-ROM drive. You can also do a Custom reinstallation of Visual C++ and add the run-time sources.

Unlike the C/C++ run-time library functions, the Win32 API functions are not available in source code. You'll need to rely on the documentation and on third-party books like this one for information about the API.

Don't forget about Help for the MFC classes, the C/C++ run-time functions, and the Win32 API, either. You can always put the cursor on a symbol and press F1 for help. Sometimes a combination of looking at the function or class code and reading its documentation will clear things up for you.

MFC Coding and Commenting Conventions

One key to understanding the MFC source code files is understanding how they're coded and commented. MFC code uses some special conventions for the few comments that are left in its sparsely commented files. In particular, class declarations are divided into categories of member functions and variables, such as *attributes*, *operations*, and *overridables*. The most interesting and valuable comment is the *implementation* comment. Check the Help index for *commenting conventions for MFC classes*, double-click it, and follow the link to the topic "MFC: Using the MFC Source Files." Reading that topic will clarify a lot about the source code. I also briefly discussed these conventions in Chapter 4.

As a general rule, I try to follow the same coding and commenting conventions as the MFC team (except that I comment more liberally). This makes my code consistent with theirs and, I think, improves understanding. You can do as you like, but I recommend you do the same.

Reading the AppWizard Files

The files that AppWizard generates have some pretty cryptic lines in them. When you start adding handlers with ClassWizard or WizardBar, you'll see more weird-looking stuff. Among the oddities you'll see are the following:

- **Conditional compilation directives: *#if...#endif*.** These directives cause the code lines that they bracket to be compiled or not, depending on the *if* statement's condition. One use for conditionals is to prevent us from inadvertently including the same header file multiple times. As an example, here is some AppWizard generated code from a view class header file (I've omitted portions to make the lines fit these pages):

  ```
  #if !defined(AFX_TEXTVW_H__8DEF9A50_0858_11D2_...)
  #define AFX_TEXTVW_H__8DEF9A50_0858_11D2_...

  #if _MSC_VER >= 1000
  #pragma once
  #endif // _MSC_VER >= 1000

  // Code in the header file is here, and then ...
  #endif // !defined(AFX_TEXTVW_H__8DEF9A50_0858_11D2_...)
  ```

  In effect, this says, "If this long, ugly symbol hasn't yet been defined in the program, define it now. Then compile the rest of the file; otherwise, skip it." The directive ends with the second *#endif* statement at the end of the file. The *#pragma once* directive requires the compiler to compile this code only once if the MFC version number in use is 1.0 or later.

- **MFC macros such as *DECLARE_DYNCREATE*, *IMPLEMENT_DYNCREATE*, *DECLARE_MESSAGE_MAP*, and *DECLARE_SERIAL*.** The preprocessor expands these to code that implements MFC features such as dynamic object creation, message maps, and serialization. This is MFC's way of adding implementation code to your files only if you want it added. I discussed many of these macros in the book. See the index at the back of the book and look up the names in the Help index.

■ **Special bracket comments—such as *AFX_VIRTUAL* and *AFX_MSG*—that tell AppWizard, ClassWizard, and WizardBar where to put declarations for overridden virtual functions and for message handler functions.** The wizards write only between these brackets, which provides assurance that the wizards won't damage your files. Look up these items in the Help index for more information.

NOTE The *afx_msg* qualifier on message handler function declarations is an MFC convention that identifies them as message handler functions. When the code is built, the qualifier is replaced by white space.

■ **The StdAfx.h file include.** By including the file StdAfx.h in your AppWizard-generated files, the wizard sets up inclusion of the necessary MFC components in your program. You don't usually need to do anything else. StdAfx.h lists the header files that are to be used to build a precompiled header file (*projectname*.pch) and a standard types file (StdAfx.obj). *Search* Help for "stdafx.h" (with the quotes, and with none of the checkboxes at the bottom of the search tab checked) and read article number 9 in the Rank column of the results list. That article illustrates using StdAfx.h to add header files to the list of files for precompilation. You can do the same in Win32 Console Applications, too. Also check the Help index for *precompiled header files* and double-click the subtopic "creating."

With these things in mind, you can begin to master the art of reading MFC source code. If you find a mysterious item in your wizard-generated code or in the MFC code, you can often look it up in Help.

Page numbers in italics refer to figures or tables.

Special Characters

A

Y

Z

About the Author

Chuck Sphar spent six years at Microsoft as a senior technical writer on the MFC documentation team, starting with MFC version 1.0. His work there included writing the original Scribble tutorial, designing the MFC encyclopedia format, helping redesign Visual C++ documentation to be more task oriented, and engaging in some colossal water fights.

In his previous lives, Chuck taught technical writing and composition at the college level, worked in information systems shops for NASA's Apollo and Shuttle programs, and wrote a Macintosh programming book, published in 1991 by Microsoft Press. These days, Chuck does technical writing on his own from a mountainside in Colorado with his wife, Pam, four cats—Buji-San, Striper, Sydney, and Tippy—and assorted bears, cougars, foxes, and deer.

The manuscript for this book was prepared and submitted to Microsoft Press in electronic form. Text files were prepared using Microsoft Word 97 for Windows 95. Pages were composed by Microsoft Press using Adobe PageMaker 6.52 for Windows, with text in Melior and display type in Frutiger Condensed. Composed pages were delivered to the printer as electronic prepress files.

Cover Designer
The Leonhardt Group

Interior Graphic Artist
Rob Nance

Principal Compositor
Elizabeth Hansford

Principal Proofreader/Copy Editor
Cheryl Penner

Indexer
Julie Kawabata

The Industry bible
for
Visual C++
development

PROGRAMMING MICROSOFT VISUAL C++,® FIFTH EDITION is the newest edition of the book that has become the industry's most trusted text (previously published as *Inside Visual C++*). Newly expanded and updated for Microsoft Visual C++ 6.0, it offers even more of the detailed, comprehensive coverage that's consistently made this title the best overall explanation of the capabilities of this powerful and complex development tool. You'll find a full discussion of control development with ATL, the latest database programming enhancements, recent COM improvements, C++ programming for the Internet, and loads more.

U.S.A.	**$49.99**
U.K.	£42.99 [V.A.T. included]
Canada	$71.99
ISBN 1-57231-857-0	

Microsoft Press

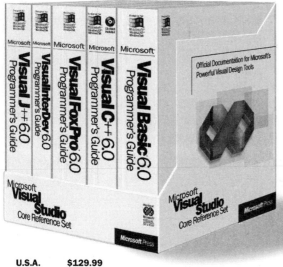

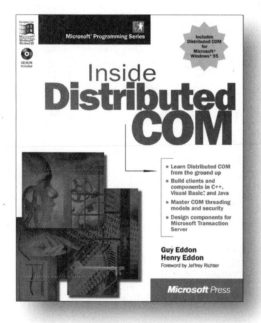

MICROSOFT LICENSE AGREEMENT

(Book Companion CD)

IMPORTANT—READ CAREFULLY: This Microsoft End-User License Agreement ("EULA") is a legal agreement between you (either an individual or an entity) and Microsoft Corporation for the Microsoft product identified above, which includes computer software and may include associated media, printed materials, and "online" or electronic documentation ("SOFTWARE PRODUCT"). Any component included within the SOFTWARE PRODUCT that is accompanied by a separate End-User License Agreement shall be governed by such agreement and not the terms set forth below. By installing, copying or otherwise using the SOFTWARE PRODUCT, you agree to be bound by the terms of this EULA. If you do not agree to the terms of this EULA, you are not authorized to install, copy or otherwise use the SOFTWARE PRODUCT; you may, however, return the SOFTWARE PRODUCT, along with all printed materials and other items that form a part of the Microsoft product that includes the SOFTWARE PRODUCT, to the place you obtained them for a full refund.

SOFTWARE PRODUCT LICENSE

The SOFTWARE PRODUCT is protected by United States copyright laws and international copyright treaties, as well as other intellectual property laws and treaties. The SOFTWARE PRODUCT is licensed, not sold.

1. **GRANT OF LICENSE.** This EULA grants you the following rights:

   a. **Software Product.** You may install and use one copy of the SOFTWARE PRODUCT on a single computer. The primary user of the computer on which the SOFTWARE PRODUCT is installed may make a second copy for his or her exclusive use on a portable computer.

   b. **Storage/Network Use.** You may also store or install a copy of the SOFTWARE PRODUCT on a storage device, such as a network server, used only to install or run the SOFTWARE PRODUCT on your other computers over an internal network; however, you must acquire and dedicate a license for each separate computer on which the SOFTWARE PRODUCT is installed or run from the storage device. A license for the SOFTWARE PRODUCT may not be shared or used concurrently on different computers.

   c. **License Pak.** If you have acquired this EULA in a Microsoft License Pak, you may make the number of additional copies of the computer software portion of the SOFTWARE PRODUCT authorized on the printed copy of this EULA, and you may use each copy in the manner specified above. You are also entitled to make a corresponding number of secondary copies for portable computer use as specified above.

   d. **Sample Code.** Solely with respect to portions, if any, of the SOFTWARE PRODUCT that are identified within the SOFTWARE PRODUCT as sample code (the "SAMPLE CODE"):

      i. **Use and Modification.** Microsoft grants you the right to use and modify the source code version of the SAMPLE CODE, *provided* you comply with subsection (d)(iii) below. You may not distribute the SAMPLE CODE, or any modified version of the SAMPLE CODE, in source code form.

      ii. **Redistributable Files.** Provided you comply with subsection (d)(iii) below, Microsoft grants you a nonexclusive, royalty-free right to reproduce and distribute the object code version of the SAMPLE CODE and of any modified SAMPLE CODE, other than SAMPLE CODE, or any modified version thereof, designated as not redistributable in the Readme file that forms a part of the SOFTWARE PRODUCT (the "Non-Redistributable Sample Code"). All SAMPLE CODE other than the Non-Redistributable Sample Code is collectively referred to as the "REDISTRIBUTABLES."

      iii. **Redistribution Requirements.** If you redistribute the REDISTRIBUTABLES, you agree to: (i) distribute the REDISTRIBUTABLES in object code form only in conjunction with and as a part of your software application product; (ii) not use Microsoft's name, logo, or trademarks to market your software application product; (iii) include a valid copyright notice on your software application product; (iv) indemnify, hold harmless, and defend Microsoft from and against any claims or lawsuits, including attorney's fees, that arise or result from the use or distribution of your software application product; and (v) not permit further distribution of the REDISTRIBUTABLES by your end user. Contact Microsoft for the applicable royalties due and other licensing terms for all other uses and/or distribution of the REDISTRIBUTABLES.

2. **DESCRIPTION OF OTHER RIGHTS AND LIMITATIONS.**

   - **Limitations on Reverse Engineering, Decompilation, and Disassembly.** You may not reverse engineer, decompile, or disassemble the SOFTWARE PRODUCT, except and only to the extent that such activity is expressly permitted by applicable law notwithstanding this limitation.

   - **Separation of Components.** The SOFTWARE PRODUCT is licensed as a single product. Its component parts may not be separated for use on more than one computer.

   - **Rental.** You may not rent, lease, or lend the SOFTWARE PRODUCT.

   - **Support Services.** Microsoft may, but is not obligated to, provide you with support services related to the SOFTWARE PRODUCT ("Support Services"). Use of Support Services is governed by the Microsoft policies and programs described in the user manual, in "online" documentation and/or other Microsoft-provided materials. Any supplemental software code provided to you as part of the Support Services shall be considered part of the SOFTWARE PRODUCT and subject to the terms and conditions of this EULA. With respect to technical information you provide to Microsoft as part of the Support Services, Microsoft may use such information for its business purposes, including for product support and development. Microsoft will not utilize such technical information in a form that personally identifies you.

- **Software Transfer.** You may permanently transfer all of your rights under this EULA, provided you retain no copies, you transfer all of the SOFTWARE PRODUCT (including all component parts, the media and printed materials, any upgrades, this EULA, and, if applicable, the Certificate of Authenticity), **and** the recipient agrees to the terms of this EULA.

- **Termination.** Without prejudice to any other rights, Microsoft may terminate this EULA if you fail to comply with the terms and conditions of this EULA. In such event, you must destroy all copies of the SOFTWARE PRODUCT and all of its component parts.

3. **COPYRIGHT.** All title and copyrights in and to the SOFTWARE PRODUCT (including but not limited to any images, photographs, animations, video, audio, music, text, SAMPLE CODE, REDISTRIBUTABLES, and "applets" incorporated into the SOFTWARE PRODUCT), and any copies of the SOFTWARE PRODUCT are owned by Microsoft or its suppliers. The SOFTWARE PRODUCT is protected by copyright laws and international treaty provisions. Therefore, you must treat the SOFTWARE PRODUCT like any other copyrighted material **except** that you may install the SOFTWARE PRODUCT on a single computer provided you keep the original solely for backup or archival purposes. You may not copy the printed materials accompanying the SOFTWARE PRODUCT.

4. **U.S. GOVERNMENT RESTRICTED RIGHTS.** The SOFTWARE PRODUCT and documentation are provided with RESTRICTED RIGHTS. Use, duplication, or disclosure by the Government is subject to restrictions as set forth in subparagraph (c)(1)(ii) of the Rights in Technical Data and Computer Software clause at DFARS 252.227-7013 or subparagraphs (c)(1) and (2) of the Commercial Computer Software—Restricted Rights at 48 CFR 52.227-19, as applicable. Manufacturer is Microsoft Corporation/One Microsoft Way/Redmond, WA 98052-6399.

5. **EXPORT RESTRICTIONS.** You agree that you will not export or re-export the SOFTWARE PRODUCT, any part thereof, or any process or service that is the direct product of the SOFTWARE PRODUCT (the foregoing collectively referred to as the "Restricted Components"), to any country, person, entity or end user subject to U.S. export restrictions. You specifically agree not to export or re-export any of the Restricted Components (i) to any country to which the U.S. has embargoed or restricted the export of goods or services, which currently include, but are not necessarily limited to Cuba, Iran, Iraq, Libya, North Korea, Sudan and Syria, or to any national of any such country, wherever located, who intends to transmit or transport the Restricted Components back to such country; (ii) to any end-user who you know or have reason to know will utilize the Restricted Components in the design, development or production of nuclear, chemical, or biological weapons; or (iii) to any end-user who has been prohibited from participating in U.S. export transactions by any federal agency of the U.S. government. You warrant and represent that neither the BXA nor any other U.S. federal agency has suspended, revoked, or denied your export privileges.

DISCLAIMER OF WARRANTY

NO WARRANTIES OR CONDITIONS. MICROSOFT EXPRESSLY DISCLAIMS ANY WARRANTY OR CONDITION FOR THE SOFTWARE PRODUCT. THE SOFTWARE PRODUCT AND ANY RELATED DOCUMENTATION IS PROVIDED "AS IS" WITHOUT WARRANTY OR CONDITION OF ANY KIND, EITHER EXPRESS OR IMPLIED, INCLUDING, WITHOUT LIMITATION, THE IMPLIED WARRANTIES OF MERCHANTABILITY, FITNESS FOR A PARTICULAR PURPOSE, OR NONINFRINGEMENT. THE ENTIRE RISK ARISING OUT OF USE OR PERFORMANCE OF THE SOFTWARE PRODUCT REMAINS WITH YOU.

LIMITATION OF LIABILITY. TO THE MAXIMUM EXTENT PERMITTED BY APPLICABLE LAW, IN NO EVENT SHALL MICROSOFT OR ITS SUPPLIERS BE LIABLE FOR ANY SPECIAL, INCIDENTAL, INDIRECT, OR CONSEQUENTIAL DAMAGES WHATSOEVER (INCLUDING, WITHOUT LIMITATION, DAMAGES FOR LOSS OF BUSINESS PROFITS, BUSINESS INTERRUPTION, LOSS OF BUSINESS INFORMATION, OR ANY OTHER PECUNIARY LOSS) ARISING OUT OF THE USE OF OR INABILITY TO USE THE SOFTWARE PRODUCT OR THE PROVISION OF OR FAILURE TO PROVIDE SUPPORT SERVICES, EVEN IF MICROSOFT HAS BEEN ADVISED OF THE POSSIBILITY OF SUCH DAMAGES. IN ANY CASE, MICROSOFT'S ENTIRE LIABILITY UNDER ANY PROVISION OF THIS EULA SHALL BE LIMITED TO THE GREATER OF THE AMOUNT ACTUALLY PAID BY YOU FOR THE SOFTWARE PRODUCT OR US$5.00; PROVIDED HOWEVER, IF YOU HAVE ENTERED INTO A MICROSOFT SUPPORT SERVICES AGREEMENT, MICROSOFT'S ENTIRE LIABILITY REGARDING SUPPORT SERVICES SHALL BE GOVERNED BY THE TERMS OF THAT AGREEMENT. BECAUSE SOME STATES AND JURISDICTIONS DO NOT ALLOW THE EXCLUSION OR LIMITATION OF LIABILITY, THE ABOVE LIMITATION MAY NOT APPLY TO YOU.

MISCELLANEOUS

This EULA is governed by the laws of the State of Washington USA, except and only to the extent that applicable law mandates governing law of a different jurisdiction.

Should you have any questions concerning this EULA, or if you desire to contact Microsoft for any reason, please contact the Microsoft subsidiary serving your country, or write: Microsoft Sales Information Center/One Microsoft Way/Redmond, WA 98052-6399.